Containing abundant new source material, Tim Jeal's comprehensive biography is the first to separate the man from the deeply ingrained legend and to present a new argument: that it was Livingstone's ideals and influence which, years after his death, played a major part in establishing British imperial power in Africa.

KT-371-707

To my parents

Tim Jeal

Livingstone

Futura Publications Limited

An Omega Book

First published in Great Britain in 1973
by William Heinemann Limited

First Omega edition published in 1975
by Futura Publications Limited
Warner Road, London SE5

ISBN 0 8600 77217

Printed in Great Britain by
Hazell Watson & Viney Ltd
Aylesbury, Bucks

Futura Publications Limited
Warner Road, London SE5

CONTENTS

PREFACE 9

NOTE ON SPELLING 13

INTRODUCTION: *A Contradictory Hero* 15

PART ONE: ASPIRATION

 1. *Factory Boy, 1813–1836* 23
 2. *Medical Studies and Missionary Training, 1836–1840* 33
 3. *Africa and South Africa in 1841* 45
 4. *Early Disappointment: Kuruman, 1841–1843* 54
 5. *A False Start: Mabotsa, 1844–1845* 71
 6. *Livingstone and the Boers: Chonuane, 1845–1847* 92
 7. *The Only Convert: Kolobeng, 1847–1849* 101

PART TWO: ACHIEVEMENT

 8. *North to the Zambesi, 1849–1851* 117
 9. *Return to Linyanti, 1852–1853* 142
 10. *From Coast to Coast, 1853–1856* 152

PART THREE: FAME

 11. *National Hero: the First Visit Home, 1856–1858* 205
 12. *The Price of Optimism: the Makololo Mission, 1857–1860* 219
 13. *Her Majesty's Consul* 231

PART FOUR: REVERSAL

14. The Zambesi Expedition Sets Sail   245
15. The Rocks in God's Highway, 1858   251
16. Colonial Dreams: the Shire and
    Lake Nyassa, 1859–1860   265
17. Death of a Fighting Bishop   289
18. Disaster and Collapse: the End of the
    Zambesi Expedition, 1862–1864   315

PART FIVE: REJECTION

19. The Last Visit Home, 1864–1865   339

PART SIX: ATONEMENT

20. Nyassa to Tanganyika, 1866–1869   359
21. Fantasy in Manyuema, 1869–1871   392
22. Stanley and the Livingstone Myth   410
23. The Last Journey, 1872–1873   430
24. Livingstone and the British Empire   449

APPENDIX A: The Date of the Stanley–
Livingstone Meeting   469

APPENDIX B: 'Dr. Livingstone, I Presume?'   470

SOURCES   472

NOTES   477

INDEX   497

LINE ILLUSTRATIONS

1. Encounter with a lion   *83*
2. Livingstone's reception at Shinte's   *168*
3. Loanda, from a sketch by Captain Henry Need   *179*
4. 'Boat capsized by an hippopotamus'   *200*
5. Missionaries buying food at Magomero   *297*
6. Zanzibar   *364*
7. Slaves abandoned   *372*
8. The massacre at Nyangwe   *406*
9. 'Dr. Livingstone, I presume?'   *409*
10. 'The main stream came up to Susi's mouth'   *439*
11. The last entries in Livingstone's Journal   *444*

Line illustrations nos. 1, 2, 3 and 4 are reproduced from D. Livingstone, *Missionary Travels and Researches in South Africa* (London, John Murray, 1857); no. 5 from H. Rowley, *The Story of the Universities' Mission to Central Africa* (London, Saunders, Otley and Co., 1866); nos. 6 and 9 from H. M. Stanley, *How I Found Livingstone* (London 1872); and nos. 7, 8, 10 and 11 from H. Waller (ed.), *The Last Journals of David Livingstone in Central Africa* (London, John Murray, 1874).

MAPS

1. Livingstone's journeys 1841 to 1852   *58*
2. Livingstone's trans-continental
   journey 1853 to 1856   *153*
3. The Zambesi Expedition 1858 to 1863   *253*
4. Livingstone's last journeys   *369*
5. The central African watershed as it is   *395*
6. The watershed as Livingstone believed it to be   *395*

PREFACE

I have two main reasons, or excuses, for writing a new biography of David Livingstone. The first is provided by the unsatisfactory nature of previous published works about him, and the second by the large quantity of primary and published source material that has come to light during the last ten years:

There have been three major biographies in the hundred years since Livingstone's death, all of them written by clergymen, and all primarily concerned with Livingstone's religious experience. As studies they were too confined and too uncritical. In contrast are the late Sir Reginald Coupland's *Kirk on the Zambesi* (1928) and George Martelli's *Livingstone's River* (1970). However, as the title implies, the first of these was more concerned with John Kirk than with Livingstone, and the second does not significantly alter Coupland's picture; also, by its confinement to six years of Livingstone's life, *Livingstone's River* is inevitably a limited study. Previous works have, it seems to me, failed to depict Livingstone in the context of his times. Professor Simmons's *Livingstone and Africa* (1955) partially remedied this, but was far too short to provide a complete picture. Professor Debenham's *The Way to Ilala* (1955) confined itself to a study of Livingstone as a geographer. The only realistic analysis of Livingstone's motivation to date is to be found in the introductions to Professor Schapera's editions of *Family Letters 1841–1856* (1959) and *Livingstone's Missionary Correspondence 1841–1856* (1961); this examination however does not extend beyond 1856. Apart from a few brief but illuminating passages in H. A. C. Cairns's *Prelude to Imperialism* (1965), there has been no thorough analysis of Livingstone's colonial thinking.

The two principal manuscript collections, previously unavailable to all but Livingstone's first and extremely

circumspect biographer, Dr Blaikie, are the eighty-five letters presented in 1963 to the British Museum (Ad. MS.
50184) by Miss Diana Livingstone Bruce (now Mrs Harryhausen); and the Wilson Collection, recently deposited
by Dr Hubert Wilson, Livingstone's grandson, in the
National Library of Scotland. The first of these collections
is particularly important, since it includes a series of letters
from Livingstone to his daughter Agnes, and these provide
a far fuller and more personal account of Livingstone's
later years than has hitherto been available.

Large collections which have, to date, received little
attention are those in the National Archives of Rhodesia,
and, of less importance, the Charles Livingstone Papers in
the Livingstone Museum, Zambia. The first of these collections adds significantly to our knowledge of Livingstone's colonial ambitions. The London Missionary Society Archives have been far more exhaustively examined,
but the Moir and Helmore Papers and the Watt Correspondence have not been thoroughly assessed. The same
applies to much of Livingstone's government correspondence in the Public Record Office. Minor collections that
have been hitherto neglected are those in the Wellcome
Medical Library, Mrs Harryhausen's private collection and
a small group of letters in the possession of Mr A. B.
Pyne. Further additions include the recent discovery, at
the Livingstone Memorial, Blantyre, of an important journal for the crucial years 1861–3.

The last few years have not just seen the addition of
new manuscript sources, for there have been significant
moves in the field of published research material. The
work of Professor Schapera has been of the greatest possible value, and his published volumes of *Family Letters*
(1841–56), his three volumes of Livingstone's journals
between 1851 and 1856, and his edition of his *Missionary
Correspondence* to 1856, have all made my task easier.
Professor Schapera's work has finally replaced David
Chamberlin's *Some Letters from Livingstone* (1940),
which hampered previous biographers who relied on its
heavily edited contents. The recent publication of the journals of two members of the Zambesi Expedition and one
member of the Universities Mission has added substantially to knowledge of the years between 1858 and 1864.

These new sources, both published and manuscript,
have, I hope, provided the basis for a fuller and more

truthful account of Livingstone's life than has hitherto been possible.

I should like to thank Dr Hubert Wilson who has made available new information by depositing his valuable collection of Livingstone letters in the National Library of Scotland. I am also most grateful to Mr W. Cunningham on the Livingstone Memorial, Blantyre, for general assistance; Mrs Harryhausen for letting me see her private collection of Livingstone letters; Mr A. B. Pyne for doing the same; Miss I. Fletcher of the London Missionary Society for help on points of detail relating to Livingstone's missionary years; Mr R. A. G. Dupuis for copious information about the Scottish religious background; Mr Quentin Keynes for letting me see his collection of Livingstone's letters; Mrs Venetia Pollock for many invaluable suggestions and ideas; and Mr Peter Lavery for assistance with the final preparation of this book. Mr G. L. Guy of Dullstroom, South Africa, kindly let me read two unpublished articles on Mary and Robert Livingstone. My thanks also to Mr P. Emmerson and Dr L. Holy for sending me microfilm and photocopies of letters in the National Archives of Rhodesia and the Livingstone Museum, Zambia, respectively.

T. J.

NOTE ON SPELLING

As a rule I have followed Livingstone's own spelling of African names. Only where clarity demands it, have I used modern spellings. I thought it right, when quoting direct, not to alter Livingstone's spelling of names; and since modern versions are very different, to avoid confusion I decided to use the same spellings in my text as in the quotations. To prove my point about these confusing differences, here is a list of some of Livingstone's spellings, followed by their modern equivalents:

Ajawa: Yao   Bechuanaland: Botswana
Bakhatla: BaKgatla   Bechuana people: BaTswana
Bakwains: BaKwena   Mosilikatse: Mzilikazi
Bamangwato: BaNgwato   Sebitoane: Sebetwane

With tribal names I have made one exception. Since Livingstone wrote Matebele and Matibele in almost equal proportion, I have used the more familiar spelling: Matabele. With place-names, Livingstone's versions are usually immediately recognizable. There is little difference between Livingstone's Loanda and Luanda, and the same can be said of his Quilimane and the more usual Quelimane. Two exceptions should be mentioned. Livingstone's Kebrabasa is the modern Cabora Bassa, and his Lake Moero is Lake Mweru. While I have stuck to Livingstone's Lake Nyassa, in line with my general policy, I have spelled Nyasaland with a single 's'. This is because Livingstone never wrote the word Nyasaland or Nyassaland; it was coined later and spelled from the beginning with a single 's'. It should perhaps be added that there is no overall consensus of agreement by many African scholars on the correct spellings of a wide range of names and places.

Livingstone spelled his own name without a final 'e' until the latter part of 1855. I have used the later form throughout the book. Livingstone was the usual spelling in

Scotland, but Livingstone's father Neil had dropped the
'e' because, according to his daughter Janet, 'he thought
his name long enough without it'.* For reasons best known
to himself, he resumed it in the mid-fifties. Shortly after
using the final 'e' in spelling his name on the title deeds
of a new cottage in Hamilton, he wrote to his children
asking them to revert to the old spelling. David Livingstone did so from September 1855.

* Note written by Janet Livingstone *c.* 1880 for Dr Blaikie, National
Library of Scotland.

INTRODUCTION

A Contradictory Hero

On 18 April 1874 Dr Livingstone's body was buried in Westminster Abbey. The Prime Minister and the Prince of Wales attended, thick crowds lined Pall Mall and Whitehall, and many people wept, inside and outside the Abbey. The press agreed that there had been nothing like it since Lord Palmerston's funeral.

During his last wanderings in Africa no fewer than four search parties had been sent out in as many years, and the most expensive journalistic venture of all time had been instigated by the *New York Herald* when the proprietor sent Stanley to find him. Three years after their much publicized meeting, Livingstone's body, disguised as a bale of cloth, had been carried by his native followers from the heart of Africa to the coast: a journey of fifteen hundred miles which took over eight months. This feat of devotion seemed the poignant but fitting finale to a saintly life. When Florence Nightingale had called him 'the greatest man of his generation',[1] there would have been few discordant voices; to have questioned his greatness in 1874 would have seemed sheer perversity.

Yet today such excessive adulation and reverence are hard to understand, for Livingstone appears to have failed in all he most wished to achieve. He failed as a conventional missionary, making but one convert, who subsequently lapsed. He failed as the promoter of other men's missionary efforts (the two missions that went to Africa at his behest ended in fiasco and heavy loss of life). His first great journey across Africa from coast to coast was an outstanding achievement, but even this was partially marred by his discovery that Portuguese and Arab traders had already reached the centre of the continent. His subsequent return to the Zambesi, as the leader of a government-sponsored expedition, was disastrous. The abrupt ending of his optimistic dream that the Zambesi would

prove a navigable river was not offset by the discovery of
Lake Nyassa—a lake which, in all probability, had been
reached by the Portuguese some years before. Other
explorers, such as Burton, Speke and Baker, had travelled
fewer miles but had made discoveries of equal importance.
None of them enjoyed such fame or received such praise.
Livingstone was considered by many to be the greatest
geographer of his age, yet a series of miscalculations
deceived him into believing that he had found the source
of the Nile when he was in fact on the upper Congo.
There were other failures too: failure as a husband and a
father, failure to persuade the British Government to
advance into Africa—yet, almost unbelievably, failures
that did nothing to impair his influence, for Livingstone's
ideas, both original and inherited, were to change the
way Europeans viewed Africans and Africa itself.

His thinking would lead to a reassessment of the role of
missions; his elevation of trade to the position of an equal
and indispensable partner of the gospel would prove the
pattern for future advances. And within thirty years of his
death these theories, coupled with his desire to undermine
tribal institutions by introducing Western economics, and
his ardent propagation of a new form of colonization,
would have played a crucial part in precipitating the British Government into annexing vast areas of a previously
ignored continent. By then the thoughts and actions of
those who had gone to Africa, in direct response to his
lead, would have altered the whole basis of Empire.

He was a failure in the aims he set himself, yet famous;
successful only after his death through those who came
after; a man remembered primarily as a missionary but
completely neglected for his greater significance as a colonial theoretician and prophet. These are not the only contradictions that surround Livingstone. His thinking sprang
from a bewildering range of paradoxical views: many of
them contradictory, some naïve, others prescient beyond
his times.

Livingstone believed that the rising industrial society
(which he knew at first hand through a childhood spent
in the cotton mills) was pernicious and cruel, but he also
maintained that it would bring great benefits to the African. He recognized that Scotland's cities were over-
crowded and 'starved their inhabitants', so he begged his
parents to emigrate; yet he thought this same industrialism

would bring a golden age to the African. He considered that the inhabitants of workhouses enjoyed more numerous material benefits than did poor African chiefs. His glorification of trade, and his insistence that without commerce Christianity could make no headway, was in direct opposition to his feeling that individual traders were exploiting Africans scandalously. He felt that Africans were usually made worse by contact with Europeans, yet he wished to increase that contact. Unlike most of his contemporaries he made considerable efforts to understand tribal customs and was annoyed by those who condemned polygamy as adultery and thought initiation rites a barbarous form of black magic; yet, while seeing many benefits in tribal life, he was also aware that no missionaries could make any progress till that life style had been disorganized and destroyed. Failing to convert even a few people, he advocated new methods to bring Christianity to whole tribes. His actions were often at variance with cherished personal beliefs.

Yet Livingstone's fame was not due so much to what he had done, nor even to what he had been; the crucial factor was what he had come to represent. For he, more than any of his contemporaries, had become a myth in his own lifetime. It was not simply that he could be admired as exemplifying bravery, endurance, modesty and self-sacrifice—all the virtues Victorians wished to possess—nor even that he had been a humanitarian and a Christian. It was more subtle. By praising him, the British public could feel pride without guilt, reconciling seemingly contradictory elements in a soothingly self-righteous combination of patriotism and Christianity, recalling for many the sense of moral superiority and national virtue experienced when Britain led the fight against slavery. The parallel was certainly there, since Livingstone had devoted the latter part of his life to the extermination of the east African slave-trade. But, more than that, he had told his countrymen that they were the most philanthropic and freedom-loving in the world, and had emphasized this by saying that on them, above all others, was laid the sacred trust of bringing progress and liberty to the benighted.

Sources made available in the last ten years show Livingstone to have been far more extraordinary than any of the Victorian stereotypes of him. Today it is particularly interesting to look at Livingstone afresh, for now we can do so without either the fulsome praise lavished by his contemporaries or the self-denigrating collective guilt that later, during the dying days of Empire, marred so many examinations of colonial history. The incorporation of Nyasaland, Uganda and Kenya into the British Empire owed much to Livingstone's posthumous influence. Now, with most of British Africa independent for a decade, we can view that influence with greater detachment. British statesmen at the end of the nineteenth and the beginning of the twentieth centuries were convinced that European colonial expansion in Africa was exclusively beneficial: a means of bringing peace, stability and progress. After the First World War the pendulum began to swing the other way. Nineteenth-century missionaries and traders in Africa were characterized as arrogant interferers wantonly enforcing alien and unsuitable values on innocent and ideal societies. Expansion was seen as exploitation and greed, thinly disguised as philanthropy. There were those who felt that if Africans had been left in peace they would have found their own way into the modern world with far less pain. Yet it is clear now that both approaches were inadequate. The motives were as mixed as the men themselves who went to Africa at the end of the last century.

Today we can acknowledge the full complexity of the situation, and, while granting that Livingstone and others like him were culturally arrogant, admit that Africa by the middle of the Victorian age had ceased to be an earthly paradise. By 1860 the slave-trade and the search for ivory had already brought disintegration and death to the heart of the continent. The alien influence of the Portuguese and the Arabs had ended Africa's isolation long before Livingstone made his discoveries. By the time he died, an expanding gun frontier, and the willingness of many Africans to sell their own people into slavery, gave a strong basis to the case for European intervention on humanitarian grounds.

As with Africa, so too with Livingstone: there were many facets to his whole character. He was neither saint nor cultural wrecker, philanthropist nor advocate of trade. He was more than all these.

In this book I hope to resolve some of the contradictions inherent in this most strange and unusual of men, to explain how apparent failure was claimed as success, and to show, within the context of his time and against the background of nineteenth-century Africa, how his character and thinking altered as his personal circumstances changed and his knowledge of the African hinterland grew. To demonstrate how, even when forced into illogical action and contradictory aims, failure only reinforced his determination.

Ultimately I hope to prove that Livingstone's direct influence on the next generation of nineteenth-century missionaries and politicians changed not only the way in which they viewed Africa and its peoples but also their vision of the Empire. Livingstone, with his missionary aims and his almost messianic passion for exporting British values and culture, seemed to his successors to have provided the moral basis for massive imperial expansion. The coupling of moral fervour with the right to power had been implicit in much of what he wrote and said. Twenty years after his death, his notion of Britain as a country with a unique mission was recognized, with many consequences that he had never envisaged.

PART ONE

Aspiration

I

Factory Boy, 1813–1836

The harsh conditions which David Livingstone endured
during his childhood wore down and destroyed all but a
handful of those who experienced similar early hardships.
Survivors won through by a strength of determination that
marked their characters for life. With Livingstone the
effect was to be a lasting sense of personal isolation and
an incapacity to live with or tolerate less exceptional
people.

Scotland, at the end of the eighteenth and the beginning
of the nineteenth century, was going through a period of
intense and drastic social change. At a time when landowners discovered that they could make more money from
their estates by expelling their tenants and devoting the
land to sheep-grazing, the dispossessed crofters poured in
thousands into the already crowded and insanitary industrial cities. David Livingstone's grandfather, Neil, was one
of these men. Formerly a tenant farmer on the small
island of Ulva, off the west coast of Mull, he was evicted
in 1792. Coming to Glasgow, he found work in a newly
established cotton mill at Blantyre, eight miles south-east
of the city. He was lucky; for the many thousands who
did not find work, starvation or emigration were the only
other choices.

Livingstone's father, also called Neil, was four when the
family came to Blantyre. One of five sons in a poor family, he was put to work in the mills as a child, but his
father, after several promotions, felt secure enough to
apprentice him to a local tailor. Young Neil was not grateful for this new opportunity and disliked tailoring from
the beginning, but he stuck the job long enough to meet
and subsequently marry the tailor's daughter, Mary
Hunter. The couple moved to Glasgow itself for a while
and Neil gave tailoring a last chance, but the wages were
low, the rents in the city high, and he grew disgusted

with the language and behaviour of his workmates.[1] So
the Livingstones returned to Blantyre where Neil became
a travelling tea-salesman, a job which paid little but gave
his religious interests greater scope, enabling him to dis-
tribute tracts to his customers. It was in Blantyre on 19
March 1813 that David Livingstone was born, the second
of seven children, two of whom died in infancy.

The tenement in which Livingstone was born and spent
his childhood was owned by the company which ran
Blantyre Mills. Built in 1775, it housed twenty-four families, eight on each of its three floors. Every family had a
'single kitchen apartment house' which consisted of a single room fourteen feet by ten, with two bed recesses: one
for the parents and one for the children. Truckle beds
were pulled out at night to cover the whole floorspace.
Cooking, eating, reading, washing and mending all went
on in the one room. There was no piped water, and slops
and garbage were sloshed down crude sluice-holes cut into
the sides of the communal circular staircases. The earth
closets at the back of the building stank, and while regu-
lations for refuse collection and a tenants' rota for clean-
ing stairs and passages were observed, recently dispossessed
crofters found it hard to break rural habits and ignored
the company's orders forbidding the keeping of poultry
and other animals in their rooms. Shuttle Row, Blantyre,
was not as bad as many tenement blocks in Glasgow, but
that did not make it any more adequate for satisfactorily
housing over a hundred people. Having suffered fourteen
years of overcrowding, David and his brother John were
eventually boarded out with their grandparents, who lived
in a neighbouring cottage. The only wonder is how five
children and two adults penned into a single room could
have endured each other so long.

Although Neil Livingstone had a great admiration for
learning and had devoted considerable energy to his own
self-education, the size of his family and the small financial
rewards of tea-selling forced him to put his three sons to
work in the mills while still children. David started at the
age of ten. Previous biographers have glossed over the
conditions in which he worked and represented them as a
suitably rigorous upbringing for a future explorer. The
reality was very different. All employees at Blantyre Mills,
both adults and children, worked from six in the morning
till eight at night, with half an hour for breakfast and an

hour for lunch: a working day of twelve and a half hours, six days a week. The management claimed that times were too hard to shorten working hours, and constantly referred to cotton shortages to back up their case; but James Monteith, the owner of the mills, in five bad years made a personal fortune of £80,000,[2] and his employees only had to gaze across the park adjoining the works and see the manager's large house to know just how hard times were.

Three-quarters of the work force at Blantyre were children, and most of these, like Livingstone, were employed as 'piecers', their job being to piece together threads on the spinning frames if they looked like breaking. Contemporary manuals on cotton-spinning stress how important this job was, for unless flaws were detected early on they were incorporated into the finished yarn. Piecers needed sharp eyes and the power of constant attention if they were to avoid frequent beatings. They also had to be unusually agile since their work often involved climbing under the machinery or balancing over it. Piecers walked anything up to twenty miles a day in the mills and much of this distance was covered crawling or stooping. Long hours on their feet often gave them bow legs and varicose veins.

Each adult spinner had three piecers attending to his machines and, since he was paid in proportion to what he produced, it was in his interests to force the children on. Often towards evening they started to fall asleep on their feet, but a beating with a leather strap or a dousing with a bucket of water generally renewed their energies. Evidence given to contemporary government commissions enquiring into factory conditions confirmed that many of these children ended up with 'limbs deformed and growth stunted'.[3] The mills were steam-heated to temperatures of between 80° and 90° Fahrenheit since this was thought ideal for the production of fine thread. So the workers inevitably caught colds on leaving work. Also these conditions encouraged promiscuity, for to make the heat and humidity more endurable, most employees, male and female, would shed their clothes.

By the end of the working day most piecers were too tired to play, and certainly in no frame of mind to learn. David Livingstone and a handful of other children were made of sterner stuff. Defying aching limbs and tired minds, they made their way to the company school to spend two hours, from 8 to 10 p.m., learning to read and write. Less than ten per cent of the child workers ever achieved any degree of literacy. Against this background, Livingstone's scholastic perseverance and success astounded his schoolmaster. Already taught to read and write by his father, Livingstone started Latin during his first year of evening school. During the next few years he spent what little money he did not give to his mother on classical textbooks. At night he often read till midnight, his mother frequently having to take his book away before he would go to sleep. Six hours later he would be in the mills again. There was no time for playing. David Livingstone had no childhood in any normally accepted sense of the word.

It would be surprising if the events of Livingstone's boyhood and adolescence had been minutely chronicled either by himself or by any other member of his family. They were busy enough trying to survive, and none of them had the slightest reason to feel that their daily lives might interest their contemporaries of posterity. There was small reason to expect anything except continued drudgery in the mills. Many of the stories about Livingstone's boyhood were therefore related after he became famous, and tend to be apocryphal rather than authentic, intended to illustrate the early development of saintliness and honesty. The picture that emerges from the few existing letters written by his father, and from his sister Janet's reminiscences,[4] is of an overearnest boy, exceptional not for his intelligence but for his obsessive determination to learn. This got him a reputation for unsociability and remoteness, and did not gain him any sympathy or admiration. A man who had worked with him as a child, when interviewed in old age in the late 1880s, said that Livingstone 'was no thocht to be a by-ordinar [out of the ordinary] laddie; just a sulky, quiet, feckless sort o' boy'.[5] The charge of fecklessness was solely due to his constant reading; it got him into trouble with a local farmer who complained that he paid him to watch his cattle on Sundays and not to be 'aye lyin' on his belly readin' a book', and at work it made him a laughing stock. When he tried to balance textbooks on the frame of the spinning-jenny, the other children pitched bobbins to knock them off. His relationship with his fellow-workers was never easy, as he told his brother-in-law, J. S. Moffat, many years later.

'When I was a piecer,' he wrote, 'the fellows used to try to turn me off from the path I had chosen, and always began with "I think you ought etc.", till I snapped them up with a mild "You think! I can think and act for myself; don't need anybody to think for me." '[6]

And nothing did turn him from his chosen path. From the age of thirteen he attended an extra class in Latin given by the village schoolmaster; when all the others gave up, he was the only one to stay on. Only the abandonment of the class by the master forced him to stop.

On Sundays, in the time that was left to him after lengthy religious observance and occasional extra tasks like cattle-watching, he rarely indulged in ordinary childhood playing; Livingstone's reactions were usually more practical. In his early teens he would leave Blantyre, when he could, and roam the neighbouring countryside, studying rocks and trees, and bringing home plants and herbs to identify with the help of William Patrick's *The Indigenous Plants of Lanarkshire* and *Culpeper's Herbal*. He was an unusually hardy boy, and his sister, Janet recalled only one instance when she had seen him in tears. That was when as a child of nine he had dropped his piece of oatcake into the burn at Hamilton Muir. Janet's only lighthearted story was of the occasion when he and his brother Charles had poached a salmon; to disguise it, David stuck it down Charles's trouser leg and got the boy to limp painfully to persuade anybody they might meet that the concealed fish was a monstrous swelling. Later Livingstone enthusiasts, unable to accept that their hero could have been a poacher, insisted that the fish was dead when he found it.

At home Mrs Livingstone had a hard job making ends meet, even with the children's earnings, but in spite of this she was a fastidious woman—as fastidious as was possible with seven people living in one small room. On Sunday all her boys were dressed with frills and ribbons round their necks, which must have caused them considerable embarrassment with other local children. The wife of the manager of the works was most put out with their smart appearance and considered it altogether above their station. Mrs Livingstone could not afford to be generous with luxuries, but on special occasions she treated the children to barley sugar and indulged her own pleasure in tobacco by smoking a clay 'cutty' pipe.

The dominant figure in David's early life was his father Neil, a man who rarely did things by halves. His disapproval of alcohol was expressed by total abstinence, while he labelled all literature not of a religious nature as 'trashy novels'. About the use of bad language he was fanatical. No word could be spoken if there was any chance of it having a religious connotation that could be sullied by casual use. David preferred reading travel books and scientific manuals to the religious tracts which his father pushed at him, and once he was thrashed for refusing to read Wilberforce's *Practical Christianity*, an experience that increased his dislike of what he was to call 'dry doctrinal reading'. But while he was ready to laugh at his sister for being afraid of divine punishment, he was still terrified by the possibility of his personal damnation. A child could have few defences to pit against a determined father's reiteration of impending doom. Worse still, all Calvinists believed that deeds and conscious effort were irrelevant and could not guarantee a man's salvation or place him with the Elect. Salvation or damnation were God's affair and his only. The Elect generally knew their good fortune for they felt that the holy spirit had touched them; Livingstone however had no such conviction, and from the age of twelve this began to distress him. He reproached himself for his sinfulness and prayed for peace of mind, but this was useless since the Holy Spirit could not be cajoled. Eventually he acknowledged that his only resort was 'to wait for the good pleasure of God'. During this time, as he later admitted: 'I found neither peace nor happiness, which caused me (never having revealed my state of mind to anyone) often to bewail my sad estate with tears in secret.'[7]

This religious fear was to last throughout Livingstone's boyhood and was only to be resolved when he was almost twenty. His distress increased with his father's frequent denunciations of his interest in science as ungodly. Relief from this worry only came in his nineteenth year when by chance he purchased a book by a Scottish nonconformist minister and amateur astronomer, Dr Thomas Dick. Dick's style is maddeningly profuse and his sentences often a page long, but they did not stop Livingstone reading the contents of *The Philosophy of a Future State* with avid enjoyment. Science, the elderly astronomer assured his readers, was in no way opposed to Christian beliefs and did not in any sense render God obsolete. Far from it; a greater awareness of the complexity and variety of creation only confirmed Christians in the necessity of there being a Maker. At last convinced that his botanical excursions had been innocent, Livingstone wrote to Dr Dick expressing his gratitude. Some months later he went to see Dick at his home in Broughty Ferry, near Dundee, eighty miles from Glasgow. Dick was an eccentric old man who had built his house on an enormous mound which was the result of eight thousand barrowfuls of earth that had taken him the best part of a year to heap up. The idea was to provide him with a suitable site for an observatory.[8] Whatever Livingstone made of him, it did nothing to weaken his new sense of well-being.

Once influenced away from orthodox Calvinism, he became increasingly aware of the religious revival which was taking place in Scotland during these crucial years of his life. After 1830 there was increasing agitation for reform of abuses within the Scottish Church. The Established Kirk was felt by growing numbers to be conservative, restrictive and moribund. The link between Church and State was attacked as unscriptural, and the central authority of the Presbytery was challenged by local churches wanting more autonomy in matters of church government. There was indignation about the system of church government. There was indignation about the system of church patronage, whereby a minister could be forced on a congregation whether they wanted him or not. A significant cause for dissatisfaction was the feeling that insufficient attention was given to foreign missions. Although most of the protests were about the autocratic discipline that the central Presbytery continued to enforce on distant churches, complaints about the form of church government also led to attacks on orthodox theology.

It may seem superfluous to record Livingstone's religious influences in detail, but since strong Christian beliefs dominated his life and much of his thinking, it is vital to understand the nature of his religious ideas at the time they crystallized in his mind; otherwise his later attitudes and behaviour might often seem incomprehensible. In 1832, the same year that Livingstone read Dick for the first time, his father was unexpectedly persuaded by some friends to go and listen to Henry Wilkes, a young Canadian preacher well known for his liberal theological views. Wilkes's with-

ering attack on the Established Kirk and on orthodox
Calvinist theology proved a turning-point in Neil Livingstone's life. He had heard this sermon in the independent
church at Hamilton, near Blantyre, and shortly afterwards
he applied for membership of that church. The independent churches had no unified approach to theology but
reserved the right to govern their own affairs on the Congregational principle—the congregation electing their own
elders and making their own decisions about church discipline. At this date the Congregational Union was only a
voluntary fellowship of churches sharing the same auto-
nomous form of church government; it implied no common theology although, in practice, beliefs were usually
less rigid than orthodox Calvinism.

Neil Livingstone's change of heart brought him closer
to David than he had ever been before and the old rifts
were completely healed when at this time they went to
hear the famous Glaswegian congregationalist, Dr Wardlaw, lecturing on the atonement. They were not the sort
of lectures that would attract many today, but then, in the
atmosphere of growing religious revival, they came in
thousands. For people in fear of eternal damnation, anybody who suggested that salvation might be universal was
worth coming a great many miles to listen to. Strict Calvinists believed that atonement was limited to the Elect,
and its benefits secured to them alone by the special influence of the Spirit over which the individual had no control;
now Wardlaw allowed that the atonement was available to
all if they were able to receive the Holy Spirit. The distinction may sound trivial now, but to Livingstone it was a
real release from fear.

His father's membership of the Hamilton Church was
important to Livingstone in another way too. It brought
him in touch with a far wider social circle. Several members of the congregation were relatively wealthy and well-
educated men, like Henry Drummond, a lace-manufac-
turer, and Fergus Ferguson, a draper. These two corresponded with theologians in America, where a simultaneous religious revival was taking place. The new American
theology was more liberal than anything Wardlaw had
formulated. Livingstone read much of this literature and
was greatly influenced by one particular American theolo-
gian, Charles Finney. The impact on the rest of the family
was just as great. David's younger brother, Charles, would

shortly leave Scotland to attend Oberlin College where
Finney taught. This was Drummond's help. Livingstone
himself completely accepted Finney's proposition that
'the Holy Spirit is promised to all who ask it'.[9]

Previous biographers have described his religious beliefs
as simple Calvinism, but this is far from the truth. He
imbibed the new liberalism from both sides of the Atlantic
and his beliefs were founded on this knowledge.

Today, with religion so often pronounced dying, if not
entirely dead, it is hard to describe the intense pride that
Livingstone and likeminded men felt in their more liberal
faith. They believed themselves to be in the vanguard of
contemporary thought, modern pioneers of a new and
stronger truth. Moreover, to reject the tenets of the established Presbyterian Church seemed a more significant protest than any political defiance, for their passions were
concerned not with mere worldly institutions but with the
eternal state of man. There was nothing archaic about
ardent belief at a time when Protestantism saw itself
marching towards the conquest of the world. This great
revival was closely linked with the anti-slavery movement,
which in 1833 recorded its greatest triumph; in that year
slavery was abolished throughout the British Empire by
Act of Parliament. This victory against massive vested
interests had been achieved by the concerted action of
Protestants, both Anglican and nonconformist. Success also
spurred on the missionary societies, whose members considered freeing the slaves to be the first step towards
spiritual freedom; the heathen must next be given the gospel. And 1832 was the year of the Reform Bill, which
stimulated rather than abated demands for social and edu-
cational reform. The Temperance, Bible and Tract Societies joined with the purely secular and humanitarian
reformers in demanding better conditions for the urban
poor. It would not be enough to stamp out drunkenness
and vice by moral preaching; the conditions that bred
them would also have to be destroyed. The confident
optimism of the 1830s was to stay with Livingstone long
after he had left Britain. Within ten years many hopes of
the glorious approaching dawn would have been blighted,
but Livingstone would not be at home to see it. His
optimism remained.

Optimist or not, at twenty-one Livingstone was still
working in the mills. Two years earlier he had been pro-

moted to spinner, but the increase in wages brought no real
hope of freedom. He had expressed interest in medicine,
but his father had made it clear that he would oppose any
medical training unless his son was to put it to a specifically religious end. And so the matter rested for a while,
and might have rested for ever had the same luck that
once led him to read Dick not saved him again. This
time, in the middle of 1834, he happened to read a pam-
phlet his father brought home from the Hamilton Church;
it had been issued in the previous year from Canton by
Karl Gutzlaff of the Netherlands Missionary Society and
was an appeal for missionaries to be sent from Britain and
America to China. There was nothing very special about
that, certainly nothing dramatic enough to change Livingstone's situation. It was the sort of missionary Gutzlaff
wanted that convinced David that a turning-point had
been reached. Medical missionaries were a comparatively
new phenomenon and it is probable that Livingstone had
heard little or nothing about them before. Gutzlaff argued
that a medical training made the missionary far more
effective in converting, for gratitude inevitably followed
the relief of physical suffering. This argument was not
crucial for Livingstone, but he saw at once that if his
father could be made to see how medicine could serve a
religious purpose, he himself could leave the mills and
train as a doctor. Fortunately Gutzlaff was highly
respected in the missionary world and in the same year his
account of *Three Journeys along the Coast of China* had
been published with an introduction by the Foreign Secretary of the well-known London Missionary Society. Neil
Livingstone was duly convinced and his son seemed at last
to have found a way in which science and religion could
be combined in a practical manner. The idea of missionary
work would have been impossible before his recent renewal
of faith, but coming at the time it did, it seemed a real
possibility, and revived his childhood interest in travel. He
read more about Gutzlaff, who was represented in current
missionary literature as a romantic figure, but practical
with it, speaking Chinese and dressing in Chinese clothes.
China, too, was a field hardly touched by Protestant missionaries, and the people themselves presented the greatest
of all missionary challenges, comprising as they did the
largest non-Christian population in the world. The idea of

a missionary life in China soon became much more than an excuse to leave the mills.

A medical education still remained the first requirement and there were severe problems to be overcome before he could obtain it. For the vast majority of boys at the mills the idea would have been unthinkable. But Livingstone knew enough Latin to be able to understand most medical terms and had read remarkably widely for a boy from his background. University entrance requirements at this time were hardly stringent and the main obstacle to becoming a student was financial. The fees for each session came to £ 12 and, since Livingstone for much of his working life had been earning less than four shillings a week, this was an enormous sum to find. But, with his father's encouragement and his own determination, he saved most of the money during the next year and a half, and with a little help from his brother John the goal appeared attainable. He would, of course, have to work at the mills during his vacations to make a further year's study possible.

When Livingstone began his first session at Anderson's College, Glasgow, in the autumn of 1836, he had already achieved something that statistics alone made grotesquely improbable. Of all the children put to work in mills during the first three decades of the nineteenth century, less than ten per cent learnt to read or write with any proficiency. Those who managed to do this and devote time to Latin, botany, theology and simple mathematics were virtually unheard of. The working stint from six in the morning to eight at night was alone enough to make any effort in the evening a severe trial, quite apart from the exhausting nature of the work, the heated work-places, the noise of machines and the mockery of work-fellows. At the age of twenty-three Livingstone had already shown himself a rarity.

2

*Medical Studies and Missionary
Training, 1836–1840*

On a day in the late autumn of 1836, David Livingstone and his father trudged the eight miles to Glasgow through thick snow to try to find a room. They took with them a

list of likely lodgings provided by a friend from Hamilton,
but this was not as useful as they had hoped, and as they
grew colder and more tired, still no place was to be found
at a rent they could afford. In the evening they at last
came upon a room costing only two shillings a week. The
name of the street was Rotten Row.

Although he came home at weekends Livingstone confessed to his sister Janet how lonely he was during these
early days in Glasgow; his solitary digs could hardly have
been less like the crowded single room at Blantyre. He
was horrified to find that his landlady sneaked into her
tenants' rooms when they were out, and helped herself to
their tea and sugar. He decided to move, and after a few
weeks found rooms in the High Street that were sixpence
more a week but where his food was left alone. Loneliness
was not his only hardship. During his first session at
Anderson's College, he suffered badly from inflammation
of the bowels that became bad enough for his father to
have to hire a conveyance to get him back to Blantyre.
But he recovered, and allowed nothing to interfere with
his studies. He went home to Blantyre each weekend, and
although Fergus Ferguson offered to take him to Glasgow
each Monday morning in his gig, Livingstone refused, preferring a long walk through the snow to missing part of
one of the morning's lectures. His refusal of the offer also
meant that he had to get up before five in order to reach
Glasgow by eight.[1]

The medical training Livingstone received so eagerly,
between 1836 and 1838, was primitive. Surgical operations
were performed at hazardous speed because of the lack of
anaesthetics. Chloroform and ether were not introduced
till seven years later and the discovery of antisepsis lay
twenty-five years ahead. The study of chemistry was growing, but that of physics had hardly started and biochemis-
try and bacteriology were unknown. Knowledge of the
origins of diseases was extremely limited and largely inaccurate. Opposing views were held, most of them entirely
mistaken. External stimuli, such as excessive heat, were
believed by some medical men to cause chemical changes
that affected the normal functions of the body; others put
every disease down to inflammation of the veins or impuri-
ties in the gastro-intestinal tract. Livingstone himself later
used leeches applied to the abdomen to try to cure intesti-
nal complaints. During Livingstone's training he would

have learnt little about clinical heart disease or lung complaints.[2] Nothing at all was known about the tropical diseases he was to encounter; like malaria and blackwater fever, and the role played by insects in their transmission was unguessed at till almost the end of the century. The sale of bodies for dissection had only been legalized four years before Livingstone began his training, and so knowledge of anatomy was not extensive. Before that only the body-snatchers had provided the medical profession with corpses to dissect. The benefits of Livingstone's medical education should not be exaggerated. He was to be as incapable of dealing with serious illness as were the native witch-doctors he would soon be meeting. Nevertheless he would manage to cure some skin diseases and he could also treat scurvy: a complaint common in countries with a largely cereal diet. He also read about later innovations and whenever possible had *The Lancet* sent to him. Thus he learned about chloroform and helped his wife through several pregnancies with it. Wide reading also drew his attention to the benefits of quinine in the treatment and prevention of malaria. He did not, however, forsake bleeding for many years, and near the end of his own life was to remain convinced that inducing heavy loss of his own blood relieved his headaches and acted as a 'safety valve'.

During the next two years, as well as studying medicine, he went to Greek classes at Glasgow University and attended more theology lectures given by Dr Wardlaw. He also made a range of new contacts which would have been inconceivable at Blantyre. The most important of these was James Young, a chemist who was soon to invent a process for distilling oil from shale and was, as a result, appropriately dubbed 'Sir Paraffin' by Livingstone. Young was to remain a lifelong friend and correspondent, and thirty years later his generosity offset the Government's stinginess and enabled Livingstone to depart on his final journey.

During his second year at Anderson's College, Livingstone began to think seriously about which missionary society he ought to apply to, and on his visits home he discussed the matter with his father. In the end he chose the London Missionary Society, largely because of its sympathies for congregational church government and its acceptance of candidates from all Protestant denominations: Methodists, Baptists, Presbyterians were all able to

apply. The Society, founded in 1795, had been the second
of the score of missionary societies set up in Britain,
Europe and America between 1790 and 1840. By the time
Livingstone applied, towards the end of 1837, the Society's
operations were worldwide and included missions in China,
the South Seas, the West Indies, India, Sierra Leone and
South Africa. In January 1838, after a delay of three
months, Livingstone was sent a small booklet by the
Directors of the Society. He was supposed to write in it
his answers to seventeen questions, mainly concerned with
his background and reasons for wishing to be a missionary.
Livingstone's replies were decisive to the point of brusque-
ness. His answer to a question relating to marriage is a
good example: 'Unmarried; under no engagement relating
to marriage, never made proposals of marriage, nor con-
ducted myself so to any woman as to cause her to suspect
that I intended anything relating to marriage . . .'[3]

But, decisive or not, he was kept waiting so long for a
reply that his father felt impelled to write to the Directors,
telling them a few facts about his son, which the young
man in his modesty might not have divulged. David's
refusal of Fergus Ferguson's lift into Glasgow was made
much of, as was young Livingstone's early aptitude for
Latin. The Directors were told that David had recently
turned down a teaching job worth £150 a year because
acceptance would have meant returning to the tyrannical
Established Church. Neil Livingstone went on to point out
why refusal of such an offer was even more praiseworthy:
'The manager of the factory who is frequently under the
influence of whisky, told him yesterday that if he went
to Glasgow any more, following after education, he must
lose his work as he would not keep it for him.'[4]

Neil concluded by assuring the Directors that he had not
told his son that he was writing and would rather he never
knew, since he would certainly disapprove. This touching
letter must have taken him a long time to plan and write
and is an impressive achievement for a man who had had
little or no formal education. Whether it tilted the balance
in favour of his son is impossible to say, but David was
eventually invited to appear in London for an interview
with the Directors set for 13 August 1838. No decision
was made at once and a further interview took place on
the 20th, and after this second scrutiny the Directors
decided to accept Livingstone on probation. He might

never have got to London had Fergus Ferguson not given him the money for his fare.

The plan worked out was that Livingstone's probation should be spent under the tuition of the Rev. Richard Cecil at the small market town of Chipping Ongar in Essex. Then, if he proved competent in Latin, Greek and theology, he would go on to a theological college, such as Cheshunt, and after that complete his medical training in London. He must have impressed at his interviews, for this treatment was reserved only for the pick of London Missionary Society recruits. Many went out to their respective mission fields as artisan missionaries, trained only in basic theology and a craft such as carpentry or bricklaying—both extremely necessary in places where missionaries often had to build their own houses.

In Chipping Ongar, Livingstone lodged with six other students in a long, low building where they lived by themselves, doing their own cooking, washing and so on. His room was over a central arch that led to the Congregational Chapel. The teaching took place in Richard Cecil's large house a couple of hundred yards down the road. It would be hard to think up a worse training for aspiring missionaries than the rigid diet of Greek, Latin, Hebrew and theology meted out to the young men at Ongar with Livingstone. Their new knowledge would have been excellent if they were destined for work as ministers in British university towns or in affluent areas of major cities, but for practical assistance in converting Indians, Africans or Chinese it was worse than useless. But Richard Cecil, an elderly and pedantic man, took his job seriously and judged his charges by exacting standards. By January 1839 he had already formed a far from favourable opinion of Livingstone: 'His heaviness of manner, united as it is with a rusticity, not likely to be removed, still strikes me as having importance, but he has sense and quiet vigour; his temper is good and his character substantial, so that I do not like the thought of his being rejected.'[5]

But rejection was still a distinct possibility, in spite of quiet sense and vigour. Livingstone's twelve years in the mills had not made him refined, and his pronounced Scots accent jarred on southern ears. But Cecil was also disappointed with his academic progress. In February he wrote again to the Directors and regretfully told them that Livingstone was 'hardly ready in point of knowledge' to go

to a theological college, whatever plans had been entertained for him. Cecil's judgment was more than a little
harsh considering that Livingstone was almost entirely self-
taught. The other students at Ongar, while none of them
coming from privileged homes, had almost all enjoyed several years of continuous formal education in the past. Cecil
considered Livingstone plodding, 'worthy but remote from
brilliant', and described his progress as 'steady but not
rapid'. He ended his report wearily with the hope that his
stodgy Scottish student 'might kindle a little'.[6]

Since Livingstone's primary interest was in medicine and
not in the classics, there was little sign of 'kindling' in the
next few months. Livingstone's attempts at preaching were
equally unimpressive and on one occasion, when, as part
of his training, he had to stand in for the minister of the
chapel at a neighbouring village, he forgot everything he
had intended to say and, having admitted as much, hurried
out of the pulpit. Later, when he had managed to complete a sermon, he himself confessed that his delivery had
been so bad that many members of the congregation had
told him that if they 'knew he was to preach again they
would not enter the chapel'.[7]

Livingstone's awkward manner was not his only problem as a preacher. His uvula, at the back of his throat,
was too large and made his speaking voice rather thick
and indistinct. Eventually it troubled him so much that he
had it cut out.

Walter Inglis, one of his contemporaries, later wrote a
description of Livingstone which confirms the picture of
him at twenty-six as an awkward, sullen young man.

> I have to admit he was 'no bonny'. His face wore at
> all times the strongly marked lines of potent will. I
> never recollect of him relaxing into the abandon of
> youthful frolic or play . . . . I only recollect of him
> playing one practical joke. A man came with a ripe
> boil that only required to be lanced. He gave the
> boil an honest skelp with a book. He had a grin for
> dry Scottish humour . . .[8]

What was so humorous about biffing a ripe boil is hard to
say, but another fellow-student, Joseph Moore, liked him
in spite of 'all his rather ungainly ways and by no means
winning face'. Moore confessed himself at a loss to know

why he liked the young Scot but claimed that he possessed an 'indescribable charm'.[9] It was evidently an elusive quality for it did not help him in his courtship of a girl he knew at Ongar.

Catherine Ridley was the first middle-class girl he had ever met and his background made him feel gauche and inept in her company. In a letter to her he confessed sadly that he was 'not very well acquainted with the feelings of those who have been ladies all their lives'.[10] But although they met quite often and exchanged little gifts, she preferred Thomas Prentice, another student at Ongar. Before that, Livingstone had sent her some sentimental religious verses by an elderly Scottish spinster called Miss Sigourney. The poems were full of clichés and stock images of 'parting bosoms bleeding' and 'native shores receding' and were so sickly that it would be comforting to feel that they reflected Miss Ridley's taste rather than Livingstone's. But he evidently liked Miss Sigourney's work since he later sent his sister Janet a copy of *Lays from the West* with a covering note assuring her that the book contained 'some very good pieces & all religious'.[11] After his rejection, Livingstone derided religious verse and wrote poor Janet a stern reprimand for sending him the work of a pair 'of poetastresses who would have been far more usefully employed darning their grannies' stockings than clinking words together, cruelly murdering the English language in the attempt'.[12] Although there was undoubted humour in the reproof, Catherine's decision to marry Prentice hurt Livingstone more than he cared to admit, and in a letter written to his son Thomas, thirty years later, he told him that he had broken with Catherine and not the other way round. Livingstone's claim was that she had been too much of a lady to make a good missionary's wife.[13] Long before that he told a friend that Prentice had got her on false pretences since he had never intended to be a missionary. In fact Prentice was prevented from going abroad by ill health, but that did not stop Livingstone's bitter remark, made some five years later, that Catherine 'did not enjoy the married state' and was miserably unhappy. She consoled herself by joining the strict Plymouth Brotherhood, which, Livingstone argued, showed that it was lucky he had never married her.

In 1839 world events altered Livingstone's subsequent career in a manner far more decisive than Catherine Ridley's rejection. In September of that year Britain and China drifted into the inglorious Opium War that was to last till August 1842. The British claimed that the Chinese Emperor was trying to exclude all British trade from Canton; the Emperor, with more justification, argued that he had been forced into counter-measures to stem the vast illicit opium trade carried on openly with Chinese smugglers by members of the British East India Company. Right was on the Chinese side, might on the British, and the war finally ended with Britain wresting massive trading concessions and taking Hong Kong. The opium trade went on.

At the outset nobody knew how long the war would last and the Directors of the London Missionary Society were not prepared to speculate. They decided that no more missionaries ought to be risked in China till the war was over. Livingstone therefore had to think of somewhere else to begin his missionary life. The Society in fact made the first suggestion in July, when it was proposed that he should go to the West Indies. Although the British West Indies were then facing horrifying social and economic problems posed by the decay of many sugar plantations struggling with the after-effects of the abolition of slavery, Livingstone objected on the grounds that the islands had been settled so long that a post there would be too 'like the ministry at home'. Apart from that, as he pointed out, there were numerous medical men already there and the addition of another would only cause resentment. He wanted a more taxing field of labour and suggested South Africa.[14]

The Directors accepted his arguments later that month and told him that after Christmas he would continue his medical studies in London 'to fit himself for some station in South Africa or the South Seas'.

His move to London took place on 2 January 1840 and he stayed in a boarding-house for young missionaries in Aldersgate. It was there that he met the famous South African missionary, Robert Moffat, whose tales of 'the smoke of a thousand villages where no missionary had ever been' have previously been said to have made Livingstone decide to go to South Africa. In fact he had made his mind up six months before. Mr and Mrs Moffat did, however, worry him about his unmarried condition and distressed him considerably by suggesting a Miss Collier, a lady fully ten years his senior, as a suitable future wife.[15] Their warnings that he would be lonely and wretched in South Africa without a partner did nothing to help him find one and only left him feeling confused and, as he put it to a friend, 'as deep in the mud as any man was'.[16]

The pressure of work in London left him no time to make friends with likely ladies and within a few months the strain had made him take to his bed. His complaint he believed was congestion of liver and lungs, caused by 'too much effluvia of sick chambers, dissecting rooms etc.'.[17] He had been attending numerous lectures at the British and Foreign Medical School, Charing Cross Hospital and Moorfields. The subjects ranged from Medical Practice, to midwifery and botany. He also managed to fit in a course in comparative anatomy at the Hunterian Museum. After his illness, he returned to Scotland, and in November, after sitting the relevant exams, qualified as a doctor, having gained the licence of the Faculty of Physicians and Surgeons, Glasgow. The costs for sitting similar exams set by the Royal College of Surgeons in London were more than the Directors of the London Missionary Society were prepared to pay.

Unrelated to his medical studies, but of far greater importance for his subsequent thinking, was his attendance, on 1 June 1840, of the vast public meeting in Exeter Hall, in the Strand, mounted by the Society for the Extinction of the Slave Trade and for the Civilization of Africa. The Prince Consort was there, and Livingstone heard for the first time Thomas Fowell Buxton, Wilberforce's successor, propound his panacea for the remedy of every African evil. Africans would only be saved from the slave-trade if they were woken up to the possibilities of selling their own produce; otherwise chiefs would continue to sell their own people to pay for the European beads, cloth, guns and trinkets they coveted. Commerce and Christianity could achieve the miracle, not Christianity alone. Free trade, legitimate commerce, the end of protectionism would all help usher in the new era. These were ideas which Livingstone would one day publicize on a massive scale. With this meeting, Buxton set in motion the Niger Expedition that was to end with heavy loss of life and little or no achievement. Even when Livingstone later learned about the failure, it did not make him doubt that

Buxton's ideas had been right. This meeting meant that before Livingstone even arrived in Africa he held views shared by very few missionaries. Most of those he would meet in South Africa considered trading a distinctly immoral business quite unsuitable for missionaries to have anything to do with.

On 20 November 1840 Dr Livingstone had returned from Scotland and was ready for the culmination of his missionary training. On that day he went to Albion Chapel, Finsbury, to be ordained a minister. His exact standing after the ceremony needs further explanation. He had become a nonconformist minister, not affiliated to any Church or Establishment, but within the voluntary Congregational Union of England and Wales, of which the Albion Chapel was a member. Congregationalism, as will be recalled, was not an institutionalized Church, nor a body of theology; it was merely a word describing the system of church government shared by the members of the voluntary Union. Livingstone's purely academic preparation for ordination had not been very different from that of a contemporary Anglican, with the exception of some crucial points of theology, and the major difference of church organization and the relationship of Church and State. Livingstone's ordination would have been recognized by all nonconformists, but not by Anglicans or Catholics who would not have allowed him to preach in their churches. His full designation would have been 'a minister within the Congregational Union serving overseas under the London Missionary Society, with its fundamental principle of non-alliance'.[18]

Livingstone's date of sailing was now set for 8 December. Shortly before leaving, he sat down to compose a farewell letter to his mother. Previously unpublished, this cold and priggish letter deals with none of the topics a young man leaving his own country for a very long time might have been expected to mention: moments of shared happiness, memories of mutual suffering, personal love. Livingstone's tone was moral and admonitory. He began by reminding his mother that he had normally written to both parents and then went on:

> Now, however, as I am sorry to learn your health and strength are declining, and as we are separated for some time, who knows but it is forever . . . I now

take this opportunity to draw your mind and direct
my own to that subject which of all others, concerns
us most, viz that of eternity . . . You have had many
trials in passing through life, I believe it has been to
you one continual long struggle with poverty for
many years, perhaps this may still be your lot, this
may have been temptation, you may have felt it was
impossible you could bestow much attention on the
concerns of the soul, but this just exactly is what you
should certainly have felt . . .[19]

Later he would be able to show the same concern for his
mother's soul with more humour and with precisely the
personal touch that is here lacking. In fact in a letter to
her, dated October 1859, he laughs to recall the story of a
young minister in Aberdeen who 'visited an old woman in
affliction and began to talk very fine to her on the duty of
resignation, trusting—hoping and the rest of it—when the
old woman looked up and said "Teer thing, ye ken naeth-
ing aboot it." '[20]

But at twenty-seven, on the eve of his departure for
South Africa, David Livingstone did not easily entertain
thoughts that were not closely related to his calling. He
was very conscious of what he had achieved, and at what
cost: no real childhood or adolescence, little or no play or
recreation, day after day in the mills, evening after evening working. At nine he had managed to repeat the 119th
Psalm—the longest, with 176 verses—with only five errors
on two successive evenings. At thirteen he had been the
only boy at the mills prepared to go on with Latin. At
twenty-one he had been ready to walk through a snow-
storm rather than miss a single lecture. To achieve this
demanded qualities that left little room for any but serious
sentiments. Sometimes it is hard not to be chilled by his
resilience and almost inhuman perseverance. Yet he had
been homesick in Glasgow and had cried when he dropped
his oatcake in the burn at Hamilton. He was soon to begin
writing numerous letters to friends, many of them affectionate and many spiced with a caustic wit. And yet the
obstacles he had overcome and the suffering he had
endured had made lasting marks. He was never to be able
to judge others except by the standards he had set himself,
and, as time passed, these standards became less flexible;

nor did he have much patience with views that ran counter
to his own.

When Livingstone sailed from London on 8 December
1840, on the *George*, he would have known that many
humanitarians disapproved of missionary work abroad,
believing like Charles Dickens that 'the work at home must
be completed thoroughly or there is no hope abroad',[21]
but Livingstone would have brushed aside such arguments
with scorn. All men had the right to hear God's word. No
nation ought to hoard the gospel like a miser. The social
problems of Britain might take a generation to sort out
and in the meantime the African could hardly be expected
to wait for the boundless blessing of true religion. Christianity was for all men at all times in all places. Besides,
the needs of the heathen were great, the labourers few
and the potential harvest immeasurably greater than any
that could ever be imagined in a small island like Britain.
Men like Livingstone were firmly convinced that interest
in work abroad would stimulate religious life at home.
Besides there was the sin of the former British involvement in the slave-trade to expiate. No anti-missionary arguments nor any fears of the discomforts ahead would have
troubled Livingstone as he watched the London docks fall
astern.

The wide use of steamships by shipping companies did
not get under way till the late 1850s, and before that the
voyages in small, cramped and often rotting wooden vessels were not pleasant experiences for the steerage passen-
gers. Whole families were invariably crammed together,
with all their luggage and possessions, in less than ten
square feet. In this area they sometimes cooked their own
food, vomited when the weather was rough and the
hatches closed, and on occasions even died when cholera
broke out aboard. Irritations included cockroaches and
screaming children, and every storm brought a pandemonium of crashing packing cases and falling people.

In mid-voyage the *George* nearly foundered in a severe
gale and one of the masts split, obliging the Captain to
make a detour to Rio de Janeiro to refit. Livingstone
remembered Rio for the prevalence of drunkenness, particularly among British and American sailors. One evening,
with more daring than good sense, he went to a notorious
waterfront bar and started handing out temperance tracts.
At one time, surrounded by twenty drunk and angry sail-

ors, he was lucky to get out unscathed.[22] The incident proved his courage but underlined his priggishness. Ten years later he had learned a lot and was to say of drinking: 'We ought perhaps to judge acts more leniently to which we have no temptation ourselves.'[23] But at twenty-eight Livingstone was intolerant, narrow and self-opinionated. He was also determined, courageous and resilient. Taken together these characteristics did not make him likeable, but considering his early life it would have been strange if he had emerged a polished, kindly and open-minded young man. Without his absolute self-confidence and belief in his own rectitude, he would never have left the mill, trained to be a doctor or voyaged to Africa.

On 15 March 1841, after a voyage of over three months, the *George* anchored in Simon's Bay, and Livingstone went ashore. A few days later he was in Cape Town.

3

*Africa and South Africa in 1841**

When Livingstone landed at the Cape in 1841, the geography of central Africa was still as much of a mystery to Europeans as it had been to the Greeks and Romans two thousand years before. The existence of the great lakes was not suspected, and the positions of the sources of major rivers such as the Nile and Congo were matters only for wild and unproductive speculation.

At first sight it seems unlikely, even improbable, that in the fourth decade of the nineteenth century so little was known of a continent which, over a thousand years before, had seen the establishment of Arab settlements along its eastern seaboard from Mombasa in the north to Sofala, opposite Madagascar, in the south. But the Arabs, south of the Sahara at least, had been happy merely to pursue a coastal trade, leaving the native tribes to fetch to their settlements slaves, ivory and gold dust from the interior. When the first European invaders tried to push inland six hundred years later their efforts were hampered and largely nullified by problems not to be overcome for another four centuries.

* See note on page 479 for sources.

These first European efforts had been made in the early sixteenth century by the Portuguese. By 1450 Portuguese ships had sailed south down the west coast of Africa past Sierra Leone, and just before 1500 Vasco da Gama had reached Moçambique and finally India via the Cape of Good Hope. During the first decade of the sixteenth century Portuguese forts were built along the east African coast from Mombasa to Sofala and the Arabs were crushed or overawed. Still confident, and driven on by rumours of inexhaustible silver and gold mines in the interior, the Portuguese thrust their way inland into east Africa up the Zambesi. By the middle of the century forts had been established at Tete and Sena, but the dreams of swift progress and easily accessible wealth had ended; the problems of tropical Africa were not understood.

The Zambesi had been hard enough to sail into at all, and it was soon to be found that the river's surf-beaten sand bars and complete lack of natural harbours at the estuary were defects to most African waterways. Then there were the cataracts, the intense heat and the inexplicable and sudden deaths. Malaria might carry off entire expeditions of three or four hundred men with such effectiveness and speed that at first the Portuguese believed that they had been poisoned by Africans or coastal Arabs. The climate brought more than disease: periodic rains could turn flat, dry, easily traversable country into impassable swamp within a matter of weeks. All supplies had to be brought from the coast, and, in a country where tropical forests obstructed wheeled transport and the tsetse fly killed horses and oxen, human porterage provided the only means of conveyance. Worst of all, the black inhabitants of the country clearly possessed neither wealth nor an easily exploitable terrain. A few Portuguese stayed on the lower Zambesi, but did not prosper. All interest in Africa might have died away in the sixteenth century had not events elsewhere suggested a use for one African commodity: the African himself.

Six years before da Gama rounded the Cape, Christopher Columbus had landed in the West Indies. By the time the Portuguese were struggling up the Zambesi, their fellow-countrymen were settling in Brazil, and the Spanish in the Caribbean, Mexico and Peru. The European discoverers of the western New World soon found that its sparse population was insufficient for its development.

More labourers would be needed for the mines, sugar plantations and later for the cotton fields. At that very moment thousands of strong, hardy black men were known to be living lives of apparent idleness on the other side of the Atlantic. The transatlantic slave-trade was the inevitable result. Taken up at first by the Portuguese and Spanish, the French, Dutch, English and Danes were not slow to join in. The European settlement of North America during the seventeenth century greatly increased the demand for slaves. By that time the Portuguese had founded their colony of Angola on the west African coast, and most of the other European nations had established coastal slaving forts further north. The first English fort was set up at the mouth of the Gambia river in 1618. Within a hundred years this commerce had become so essential a part of the British system of trade, and apparently so vital to the economy of the Caribbean and Americas, that it would take the humanitarians some fifty years of struggle to end British participation in 1833. For another thirty years after the triumphs of Wilberforce and Buxton, the British naval blockade on the west African coast would not be able to stop completely the flow of slaves to Brazil, Cuba and the southern states of America. Meanwhile in east Africa the Arabs had reasserted themselves, after their earlier humiliation by the Portuguese, and continued supplying Arabia, the Gulf States and Persia with thousands of African slaves. The extent and volume of this other slave-trade was to remain largely unknown in Britain till the late 1850s.

The anti-slavery movement of the late eighteenth and early nineteenth centuries had implications for Africa that went beyond curbing the trade itself. The humanitarians demanded a more positive policy in the dark continent. In 1791 a British philanthropic association received a charter for the purpose of settling freed Negro slaves from the New World in their continent of origin. The result was the British colony of Sierra Leone. Liberia had similar beginnings. Running parallel with this new humanitarian interest came a new fascination with African geographical problems. In 1788 the African Association was founded to promote exploration. Between 1795 and 1831, British explorers like Park, Clapperton, Lander and Laing had together traced the Niger from source to sea, and in east Africa, Bruce had reached the source of the Blue Nile.

These journeys were not followed up, largely because the
problems known to the Portuguese for centuries now confronted the unsuspecting British. Africa was still a continent of fringe coastal settlement in 1841.

Only in Africa south of the Zambesi had events been
different; there, with a clement climate, no malaria and,
in the Cape Colony at least, no tsetse fly, there was a real
opening for a European colony to rival any in north America or Australia. But the British did not get there first;
in 1652 the Dutch made their first small settlement at the
Cape. The Directors of the Dutch East India Company
had had no intention of founding a colony, let alone a
nation; all they wanted was a victualling port for their
vessels en route for the spice markets of the east. But the
port could only be supported by a permanent farming
community, so Europeans received grants of land so that
they might produce grain, meat and wine to sell to the
garrison and to passing Dutch East Indiamen. At first all
went well, but since the Company would not sanction emigration from the Netherlands on any scale, the new settlement had to depend for labour on the services of the sparse
aboriginal population: the Hottentots and Bushmen. The
Bushmen were hunters, the Hottentots cattle farmers, and
the habits of the former did not endear them to the latter.
The Bushmen were diminutive and by most African standards extremely primitive, while the Hottentots, although
more advanced, were insufficiently numerous and too dispersed to supply the labour needs of the new settlement.
The decision was made to import slaves. These did not
come from a single source but were drawn from places as
far apart as west Africa and Malaya. Slaves and Hottentots intermarried and a sizable half-caste population
brought worse social problems, which interbreeding with
Europeans complicated still further.

Although the settlement at the Cape grew, and Cape
Town itself came to comprise over a thousand houses by
the end of the eighteenth century, the little colony was not
a happy or a prosperous one. The economic history of an
isolated European community, based on slave labour and
oppressed by a now failing monopolistic company, was
inevitably dismal. The company did not allow the colonists
sufficient freedom in trade to dispose of their surplus produce and it cut the farmers' profits by buying their grain
at a fixed price. The introduction of sheep failed, tobacco

would not grow, olives likewise, and bad harvests and cattle disease, striking simultaneously, could bring the entire population to the brink of starvation. The decline of the Dutch East India Company through bad management and increasing French and British competition added to the colonists' miseries. In 1750 only sixty-eight ships called at the Cape; the same number had anchored in Table Bay fifty years before.

However, world events were shaping a new future for the Cape Colony. The 1750s and 1760s saw an intensification of Franco-British rivalry in India and this in turn led both powers to see the Cape as a useful strategic base for future acquisition. But neither nation was prepared to fight the Dutch for it. Only with the advent of the war waged by Revolutionary France against Britain in the 1790s did the situation change, for the Netherlands were dragged in on the French side. Britain, to protect her shipping routes to India and the Far East, occupied the Cape in 1795. This first occupation did not last long and the Dutch were handed back their colony when peace came. But when war again broke out between Britain and Napoleonic France, the British returned to the Cape in 1806 and this time they stayed.

From the beginning the British Government saw the Cape Colony as a strategic gain and were not interested in its development as a territory. They wished to maintain the existing situation with as little extra expenditure as possible. The realities of the situation decreed otherwise.

Early on in the colony's history, the entirely Dutch society had been a divided one: there were the townsmen at the Cape, predominantly European in dress, manners and habits; and the farmers or Boers, who as early as the 1720s had started to trek east from the Cape beyond the Drakenstein Mountains into the plains of the Karoo. The further the Boers went, the more remote the Company's administration became for them, and the more these frontiersmen liked it. They relished their new independence and made a virtue of their simple nomadic life. Their visits to Cape Town were infrequent and endured only because they had to sell their cattle and buy supplies such as gunpowder, tea and sugar. The Company tried to contain their dispersal but failed.

In 1776 the Boers made their first contact with a new African people, the Xhosa, at the Great Fish river, five

hundred miles east of Cape Town. Soon it was realized
that while the Boers were moving east and north-west, a
vast Bantu tribal migration was sweeping towards them
from the north. Confrontation was inevitable. The British
Government inherited a border problem which they had
no idea how to solve. They could not control the Boers
and they could not control the Xhosa. In the land and
cattle squabbles that took place between white and black
during the following years it was impossible for the British
to determine the guilty party. The Boers wanted the British to expand the borders of the colony and sweep back
the Bantu, and the British administrators, seeing that this
would create a wider and less accessible border, opted for
a policy of containment. To implement the policy, troops
had to be sent. To create a white buffer between the Cape
Colony proper and the advancing Bantu, the administrators,
acting with the British Government, launched a state-aided
immigration scheme for British settlers to come out and
farm just west of the Great Fish river. The Boers, checked
in their eastward expansion, viewed these new aliens as
rivals and interlopers. The British got on well enough with
the Dutch in and around Cape Town, but with the more
distant Boers their relations steadily worsened. An important additional cause for this deterioration came with the
arrival of foreign missionaries.

In the late 1730s a German missionary, George Schmidt,
had enraged the Boers by baptizing slaves and was
impelled to leave by the ensuing outcry. Seventy years
passed before the London Missionary Society sent their
first member to the Cape to work among the slaves and
Hottentots. By 1816 there were twenty men from the
same Society working in the colony. By this time the anti-
slavery movement was at its strongest in England and abolition of slavery throughout the British Empire seemed a
real possibility. While the missionaries looked forward to
the day of liberation with delight and did everything they
could to hasten its advent, the slave-owning colonists
viewed the future with apprehension and the missionaries
with dislike. The missionaries, however, were men not
easily intimidated, and in 1811 two London Missionary
Society men, Vanderkemp and Read, working near the
eastern border, informed the Governor of the Cape of
crimes committed by various farmers against Hottentots
and slaves. As a result a number of Boers were charged

with brutal crimes and some were convicted. From that time the Boers considered the members of the London Missionary Society to be dangerous enemies.

In 1819 the London Missionary Society sent out John Philip to supervise their work within the colony. Philip quickly realized that the Government wished to restrict missionary activities in the borderlands both to the north and to the east: nor was he slow to see why. The pressure of the advancing colonists in search of cheap labour and fresh land had led to an official policy of expediency. This enabled the farmers to use forced labour and take land from natives without government intervention, so long as no major border incident was provoked. Philip sent evidence home to England which was examined by Wilberforce and Buxton and led within months to the appointment of Crown Commissioners to come to South Africa 'to inquire into the state not only of the civil government and legal administration of the Cape, but into the general condition of the slave and Hottentot populations'. This was a slap in the face for the Cape Government and from now on the missionaries could add the colonial administrators to the list of those who mistrusted them. In 1828 Westminster, acting on the recommendations of the Crown Commissioners, passed a resolution desiring that 'directions be given for effectually securing to all the natives of South Africa the same freedom and protection as are enjoyed by other free persons residing at the Cape, whether they be English or Dutch'.

With the abolition of slavery throughout the British Empire in 1833, the colonists could see that these were not merely words. The abolition of slavery did not bring equality or anything remotely resembling it, but the decision made by some seven thousand Boers, during the late 1830s and early to mid 1840s, to trek north-east beyond the borders of the colony owed a lot to what they considered a real and significant change in the direction of government native policy. The Boers objected not so much to the emancipation but to the idea bred by the missionaries that natives should be considered the equals of white Christians. Their trek was also inspired by land hunger and the Government's refusal to remove the Xhosa barrier to the east. The Boers, used to moving their cattle on when a given acreage was exhausted, were further incensed when the Government informed them that in future land would not be granted freely but would be sold at auction. This combination of circumstances increased the numbers of those leaving the colony for the lands north of the Orange and Vaal rivers. The massive Boer exodus was welcome neither to the Government nor to the missionaries. The Government was now left with a depopulated eastern frontier at a time when Xhosa pressure was increasing, and the missionaries saw that, away from the powers of British officials, the Boers would be able to do what they wanted with the natives in the areas they had removed to. From now on, the same missionaries who had once been so strongly opposed to colonial expansion tried to persuade the Government to extend the colony to include the new Boer Republics. The missionaries would fail, for in 1852 the Government was to recognize the independence of the Orange Free State and the Transvaal.

The Government's new policy of *laissez-faire* towards the trekkers was to have serious repercussions for the missionaries long before the formal recognitions of the Republics' independence. As early as 1805 the first London Missionary Society station had been established north of the Orange river in Namaqualand, outside the borders of the colony. Since then, Kuruman and Griqua Town had become not only the London Missionary Society's remotest missions* but also their most cherished ones. With the arrival of the Boers just to the east in the adjacent Transvaal, the missionaries in Kuruman and Griqua Town were convinced that they would attempt to stop the expansion of all missionary activity to the north and the east of their present situation. The Boers' known hostility towards missionaries made these fears realistic rather than alarmist. Trouble in Bechuanaland between missionary and Boer could not be far off. If and when that trouble did come, the missionaries knew that they could expect little help from the Cape Government, which had originally tried to discourage missionary activities beyond the colonial borders.

Kuruman was used by the Directors of the London Missionary Society in all their propaganda at home to show what a mission station ought to be: neat, well laid out, well watered, houses made of stone with little gardens and orchards of fruit trees. To fit in with the ideal, the native

---

* Both were between 500 and 600 miles N.E. of Cape Town.

Christians should also be neat and tidy; they should wash with European soap, and, so as not to offend European ideas about physical modesty, they should cover their bodies with European clothes. Tribal values and patterns of behaviour should be condemned and rooted out. There was an ideal missionary too, and he was also to be found at Kuruman. Robert Moffat had started his work there in 1821 as a young man in his early twenties. Through his labours the watercourses were dug, the houses built and the orchards planted. Through his patient and inflexible persuasion the first converts had been made, not after weeks, nor even months, but after eight years of disappointment and frustration. The Directors of the London Missionary Society did not, however, dwell on the length of time that had passed before conversions had been made. Moffat had spent decades translating the Bible into Sichuana, the language of the Bechuanas. He had set up a printing press to disseminate the newly translated gospel and had run a school to teach the natives to read and write in their own language. His devotion to a single tribe and a single place for a lifetime exemplified the Directors' considered opinion of the best type of missionary life: that led by the settled, patient missionary who did not aim at converting a whole nation but contented himself with the gradual 'civilization and Christianization' of a small tribal community. Of course the diligent efforts of thousands of Moffats working in this way would never have made much of an impression on Africa as a whole, not even on Africa south of the Zambesi. But the Directors were happy, and pointed to Kuruman with its small population as the jewel in the south African missionary crown. Besides, they could remind the sceptic that there had been no foreign missionaries in southern Africa in 1800, but that, following their lead, several hundred had come out by 1841 and were at work on a total of eighty mission stations scattered throughout the colony, with a handful outside it. These men came from Europe as well as Britain, and missionaries from the Moravian, Rhenish and Paris Societies worked alongside members of the London, Glasgow and Wesleyan Societies. In 1835 six American missionaries had come out. In the year that Livingstone came to Africa, the Directors of the London Missionary Society might have admitted privately that the speed and number of conversions had disappointed them, but they would have denied emphatically that any new missionary policy was needed or that the future would not see a massive acceleration in the number of conversions.

4

Early Disappointment: Kuruman, 1841–1843

The plan was that Livingstone should spend a short period at the Cape, recovering from his sea voyage, before going on to Bechuanaland and Kuruman to begin his life work. There was nothing specifically African that Livingstone could see in Cape Town as he wandered through the streets, looking around. The place was still very much the small Dutch port it had been fifty years before. The streets were largely unpaved and the vehicles most in evidence were not smart carriages but the lumbering ox waggons of the farmers. The buildings were pleasant ga-bled houses, mostly stuccoed, and either whitewashed or painted green. Avenues of oaks had been planted along many streets and most houses had gardens in front. It had been arranged for Livingstone to stay with the veteran campaigner John Philip. The young missionary ought to have enjoyed his time in Cape Town staying with such a famous man as Dr Philip, but from the beginning Living-stone felt uneasy.

When Livingstone had met Robert Moffat in London early the previous year, the venerable founder of Kuru-man had launched into a scathing attack on Philip, whom Livingstone had previously felt bound to consider the champion of the Hottentots and slaves. Moffat claimed that Philip had started to use his position as the London Missionary Society's financial agent at the Cape to exer-cise authority over the missions north of the Orange river. Furthermore, Moffat went on, Philip had become senile, autocratic and more interested in politics than in the con-version of the heathen. Livingstone had listened to all this and had believed it implicitly; it was hardly for him to doubt what the ideal missionary had to say.

At Cape Town, however, everything seemed rather dif-ferent. Philip appeared to be a calm, reasonable and unambitious man with no desire to exercise authority over

Moffat or anybody else. Livingstone wrote to a friend rather shamefacedly, acknowledging that he had come out expecting to find a monster and had instead discovered 'an amiable man . . . who claims no superiority over us'. Philip evidently discovered from Livingstone that Moffat had been blackening his character in England, and decided to repay the compliment before Moffat could get back to Africa from his London fund-raising trip. The young missionary had soon sucked in Philip's stories about Moffat being a scandalmonger and trouble-maker, so much so that within weeks Livingstone was writing to friends telling them that 'Mr Moffat is not on speaking terms with the Griqua Town missionaries and takes another route when visiting the colony to avoid seeing them. They in their turn *hate* the bretheren in the colony and amongst the whole there exists a pretty respectable amount of floating scandal one against the other.'[1] Livingstone was next shocked to hear the rumours that a number of missionaries outside the colony had taken native mistresses and he condemned the whole situation as 'most disgraceful'. Even if scandalous behaviour could not easily be proved, one thing Livingstone was sure of was the genuine hatred felt by Moffat, and the missionaries beyond the colonial borders, for the missionaries working on the older, more settled stations within the colony. Those at Kuruman and Griqua Town did not get on together, but they were united in their scorn for men who called themselves missionaries and worked in established communities within a few days of Cape Town. In the distant missionaries' view, that was not mission work, but a life like that of a provincial minister in England.

Livingstone might gasp with indignation at the squabbles and hatreds of his new colleagues, and make much of his own determination not to quarrel, but before he had even reached Cape Town he had already taken a lasting dislike to William Ross, a London Missionary Society artisan travelling out to South Africa on the same ship. Ross's wife had been constantly seasick and Livingstone had tried his medical skills to bring relief; all he brought was a husband's fury and accusations that the young man had designs on Mrs Ross. Livingstone told a friend indignantly that he would rather have flirted with his grandmother than with Ross's 'blooming bride of 34 or 5'.[2] From then on Livingstone wrote off Ross as a man with 'an exceedingly contracted mind', whose opinions should receive no more attention than an illiterate Hottentot child's. Ross repaid Livingstone by suggesting that he was unmarried because no girl would look at such a disagreeable young man. Livingstone, not to be bested, had countered by pointing to 'all the silly married people . . . as proof of how easy it is to get noosed'. For a while there was a chance that Ross might stay in Cape Town and Livingstone was delighted, especially since Ross might become the minister at Philip's old church, where the congregation had proved themselves unworthy of 'a good pastor' by forcing Philip to resign because of his championship of the slaves. But in the end Ross came on to Bechuanaland to remain, for many years to come, a constant subject for scorn and ridicule in Livingstone's letters.

Already depressed by Philip's gloomy picture of missionary arguing, Livingstone was made still more apprehensive when Philip told him that a local missionary committee was being planned to run the affairs of the missions north of the Orange river. Philip's claim that Moffat was behind it would prove fictional, but whoever was responsible, the very idea shocked Livingstone and brought out all his Independent fervour. After what he had heard about his future colleagues, Livingstone was already convinced that to have to do anything at their instructions would be agony. 'I shall yield cheerful obedience to the committee in London [the Directors of the Society],' he told a friend, 'but to a presbytery of missionaries I cannot; for take us as a body we are really a bad set.'[3]

On 16 April Livingstone and Ross once more boarded the *George*, this time bound for Algoa Bay, 450 miles to the east of the Cape. From there they were to collect their oxen and waggons for the journey north. On parting from them, Dr Philip told them that their most important task was to live in peace not with the natives so much as with fellow-missionaries. With a temperament like Livingstone's, and an inherent belief in the superiority of his mind over other people's, this was going to be uphill work.

Kuruman, the most remote mission station in southern Africa, was between five and six hundred miles north of Algoa Bay. Travelling in South Africa was slow and expensive; standard transport was the lumbering ox waggon, costing £40 to £75, while the dozen oxen needed to pull it came to about £3 each. A day's progress was rarely more than ten miles and, in sandy or very rocky country, sometimes less. Livingstone's journey to Kuruman took him the best part of two months; but provided there was enough water on the way for the oxen, and the roads were reasonably flat, travelling by waggon could be pleasant enough. The waggons themselves were miniature houses with large chests at the front and back for daily supplies such as tea, coffee, rice and so on, and smaller lockers down the sides for cutlery and china. In the middle of the waggon, boxes were stored, and over them a stretcher was placed with bedding laid on top of that. The traveller only pitched a tent if he was stopping for several days or if there were too many people in one waggon to make sleeping inside it comfortable. Other provisions, such as meal, would be hung suspended in large canvas sacks and still more could be roped under the waggon itself.

The driving itself would be done by two or three natives with long whips made of giraffe or rhinoceros skin.

From the very beginning of the journey, in spite of the unwelcome company of Mr and Mrs Ross, Livingstone was delighted by African travel. After the strict routine in Ongar and London, the complete freedom of stopping where and when he wanted to, lighting a fire and cooking when he was hungry, and looking across miles and miles of thinly populated country, seemed to mark a complete break with his cramped and regulated past existence. At times the roads were so bad that Livingstone feared the waggon might tip over and crush them all, and, at others, steep hills alarmed him in case the oxen stumbled and let the waggon run forward out of control.

For several days Livingstone thought the scenery not unlike Scotland, only hotter, but as he came closer to Kuruman and Bechuanaland the country began to change and he saw for the first time the endless vistas of rock, sand and lifeless scrub that he was to become so well accustomed to. Cutting across the sun-baked table-land were broad dried-out river beds filled with boulders, which posed terrible problems to the oxen; and the only relief on the horizon would be low, flat-topped ranges of hills with strange crumbling sides, like cake roughly cut with a blunt knife. The Dutch called them kopjes. Where trickles of water appeared in the river beds, acacias grew, and around them low scrub with villainous 'wait-a-bit' thorns. Near water there would also be a variety of grasses and

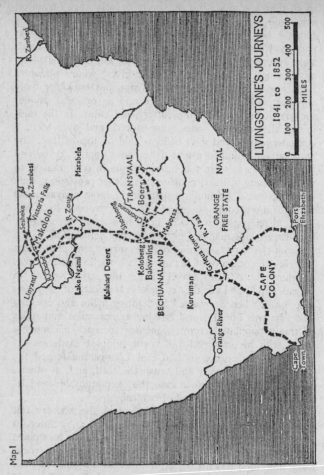

aloes with fleshy, purple-blotched leaves and spikes of
waxy red or yellow tube flowers. Occasionally near river
beds were small fan-palms with sage-coloured spiky fronds,
and huge gouty baobab trees with their broad distended
trunks and spindly branches, bare for all but two months
of the year.

In the spring or after the rains, the river beds would
fill again briefly and the grass grow green, while water-

melons would rapidly ripen and straggling gourds revive. There would be lilies too, white and pink, and the mopane trees would put out new, tender pinkish-blue shoots, but soon everything would return to the old parched greyness and the rocks and sand once more would dominate the landscape.

Throughout his time in Bechuanaland, Livingstone was amazed at the quantity of wild life capable of supporting itself in such apparently unpromising terrain. Spiders, scorpions, ants, lizards and frogs were all numerous, and herds of giraffe would scud across the plains to feed on the scarce foliage of the acacias. Antelopes, wildebeests, blesboks, springboks and pallahs were to be seen in large numbers, and further north the lion and rhinoceros were still abundant and the distinctively marked zebra was often to be found.

When Livingstone arrived at Kuruman on the last day of July, the south African winter was nowhere near over and the country would remain parched and dreary for fully another three months.

> All around is a dreary desert for a great part of the year, enough indeed, from its nakedness and sand, to give its people most of that opthalmia with which they are so often afflicted. There is not a tree near the station which has not been planted by the missionaries. Low stunted scraggy bushes, many of them armed with bent thorns villainously sharp and strong are the chief objects which present themselves to the eye.[4]

Livingstone had not expected Kuruman to be an aesthetic paradise but he *had* expected the place where Moffat had laboured for twenty years to be large, densely populated, entirely Christian and within reach of other heavily peopled areas. Moffat himself had spoken of the smoke rising from the fires of a thousand villages to the north. Livingstone was horrified to find that almost all his hopes had been false and the mental picture of the place which he had treasured for so long was a grossly distorted image. To start with Moffat seemed to have misled people about Kuruman's size: it was no more than a small village. That in itself would not have mattered if there had been native villages clustered around, but there were no such settle-

ments, and most estimates of the population for twenty
miles around did not exceed a thousand. If most of these
thousand people had been Christians, Livingstone might
have felt his disappointment less keenly, but the vast majority, while often wearing crudely made European clothes,
had never been baptized. Moffat's native congregation
amounted to about 350, an impressive figure, but of these
just under forty were communicants. Forty Christians
made in twenty years by the most famous missionary in
southern Africa—Livingstone was staggered. He wanted
to write home to the Directors of the London Missionary
Society to tell them that they had been duped, but as he
told a friend, 'If I wrote home to the Directors they won't
believe me for I am a nobody in their eyes.' But, novice or
not, he could not endure saying nothing and wrote telling
the Directors that Kuruman could never become populous and would probably lose people in the future, since
the Bechuanas were cattle-farmers and would inevitably
choose better watered and more fertile places to graze
their oxen and sheep.[5] Livingstone was telling the truth
but the Directors were not alarmed; nobody could seriously expect them to believe that their most publicized
African mission station was an arid, under-peopled village
that might soon be deserted. Generously they put down
Livingstone's complaint to youthful enthusiasm.

When Livingstone had finished torturing himself with
the problems of cattle grazing and population, his mind
usually returned to the question of conversions. He concluded, logically enough, that there must be some explanation for the tiny number of native converts. The missionaries must have been going about things the wrong way.
On his way to Kuruman he had passed through Griqua
Town and had met the missionaries there. He had found
out that the reason why the Kuruman missionaries disliked their neighbouring colleagues was the Griqua Town
policy of using native teachers for effecting conversions.
In Moffat's view no natives had been trained sufficiently
to enable them to give a faithful and accurate version of
the Gospel, or to make them more than purveyors of
falsehood. Livingstone nevertheless was certain that the
Griqua Town Mission had found the answer. It seemed
obvious to him that the natives would resist Christianity
much less if it was offered to them by people with black
skins like their own. Then Christianity would not simply

appear as one of the white man's customs.[6] In theory Livingstone was absolutely right, but in practice he would soon find that suitable native teachers were very hard to find.

Livingstone undoubtedly got a far worse impression of Kuruman than he would have done had Moffat been already back from England. The almost total paralysis in the place had a simple cause: Moffat was the driving force and Moffat was not there. The trouble was that the Directors had left no instructions for what ought to be done with Livingstone; he was expected patiently to await Moffat's return. Nobody had the faintest idea when that return might be: maybe the end of the year, maybe the end of the next. Livingstone very much resented the implication of the Directors' refusal to issue him with instructions. It seemed that the worthy men in London believed that nobody could do anything in Africa without Moffats' guidance. 'I did not come to be suspended on the tail of any one,' Livingstone wrote home bitterly. He also made up his mind that he would never stay at Kuruman whatever he was told to do.[7]

Disappointed already, the waiting and sitting about increased Livingstone's bitterness and frustration. It was not long before he discovered that the tribes living roughly a hundred miles from Kuruman to the north had developed a dislike and scorn for the people of Christian-dominated Kuruman. The reason was that these more distant tribes had only been preached to a few times and their impression of Christianity was the usual distorted version: that the white man's religion was just a trick to get them to give up their wives. Livingstone became certain that this attitude would soon poison the minds of tribes living two and three hundred miles north of Kuruman. It therefore seemed imperative for a missionary to make contact with these untouched people before that happened. There was also a danger that if missionaries did not reach them soon, traders would get there first and give them quite the wrong impression of what white men wanted. Livingstone wrote telling the Directors this, but no satisfactory reply came. Resigned and by now thoroughly disgusted, all Livingstone could do was try to cure minor native ailments and sit learning Sichuana.

Livingstone's real misery during his early days in Bechuanaland has not received much attention in the past, for

Livingstone in later published accounts of this period of his life did not make much of his disappointment, largely out of respect for Moffat's feelings. But his initial disillusion was to be an important early determining factor in his life. If twenty years' hard work by Moffat had only produced Kuruman, Livingstone came to feel that he would have to spend the next twenty years of his life working in a different way. With the shock of disappointment still fresh, he was not yet sure how his own future would differ, but differ in some way he knew it would have to.

Had Livingstone been shown figures for conversions in other South African missions before he left England, he would have realized that Moffat had achieved as much at Kuruman as any other missionary elsewhere, inside or outside the colony. Ignorance of the problems that men like Moffat had faced, coupled with a previously uncritical acceptance of missionary propaganda at home, had made Livingstone incapable of objective judgment of reality when he saw it. The Hebrew, Greek and theology learned at Ongar had done nothing to offset the stories of African missionary successes which Livingstone had so eagerly read about in the *Missionary Magazine* and the *Evangelical Magazine.* Both these publications had been far more concerned with missionary fundraising than with truthful reporting. Had it been admitted that most missionaries laboured for years before achieving anything at all, and that Africans only tolerated missionaries because they could mend guns and bring beads, the public would not have dipped their hands in their pockets. Instead there had to be reports of instant success or spectacular failure, accompanied if possible by martyrdom. When missionaries returned to harangue the faithful, the heads of their Societies would not have thanked them if they had painted bleak pictures of failure and isolation. Accurate information about natives and conversion were not to be had from missionary sources in England. The only alternative source of information on Africa available to Livingstone in England had been the writings of travellers like Park, Clapperton and Lander. Unfortunately these books had been written for entertainment and, while they made the public gasp with stupefaction at the hilarious absurdity, barbarity of pure nonsense of native customs, they had been worse than useless for a reader wanting to discover more about the African's way of life and the problems which it might pose to missionaries. Park and the rest of them used native customs out of context simply as extravaganzas—vignettes of local colour to add spice to already spicy stories.

Nothing that Livingstone had been told or been shown to read had given him any idea of what Moffat had been through after his arrival at Kuruman in 1821. For a start Moffat had needed to gain the tribe's consent to settle with them, then he had to grapple with building houses for himself and his fellow-workers and with starting gardens and planting crops and vegetables. With no knowledge of the native language he had had to reduce it, write it down and finally work out its grammar. Completely cut off from the outside world, he had needed to return to Cape Town for supplies when they ran out, and this journey had each time taken six months there and back. Much of his time had to be devoted to daily agricultural tasks, mending waggons, making ploughs or attending to animals. No thought could be given to conversions till he was sure that he had mastered the native language. His wife had lived an equally hard and difficult life; in addition to the usual tasks like cooking, washing and mending, she had been obliged to make clothes, and learn how to manufacture soap and candles. Making cheese and butter had also occupied her time. Frequent pregnancies and inadequate medical attention had weighed heavily on her. It is not hard to imagine what such isolation could do to people over long periods of time; cut off from their own society and usually facing total indifference on the part of the natives, it is a wonder that Moffat persevered for eight years to make his first converts. Livingstone had imagined converts being made after a short struggle and had never thought about the possibility of their backsliding. Moffat could have told him that it was almost impossible to tell whether a conversion was genuine or not. Conversions could simply be the result of native gratitude for agricultural improvements or a desire to please the 'gun mender'; which is the role the missionaries were often given. Add to these difficulties the low rainfall and frequent cattle disease, and Moffat's achievement can be seen in perspective. Livingstone would get that perspective later, but by that time his mind was moving in other directions.

Before Moffat returned to Africa, and before Livingstone made any independent moves of his own, the young missionary had written a confidential letter to his sisters in Scotland telling them: 'I would never build on another man's foundation. I shall preach the gospel beyond every other man's line of things.'[8] There is certainly nothing in this that suggests that he had already become primarily interested in exploration, but it does pose a difficult question. If Livingstone chose a tribe that was *then* beyond other men's lines of operation, would he remain content to stay there if other missionaries started to outdistance him? Livingstone often repeated this phrase about working in more remote places than everybody else, so it is significant, and pointed to an ambition to excel personally: a very questionable motive for a young man ostensibly about to begin a grinding and largely frustrating life of humble service with a single tribe. There are other clues in letters of this date that again indicate thinking quite opposed to conventional missionary aims. Livingstone told a friend that he had heard that there was a large lake hundreds of miles to the north, which 'everyone would like to be the first to see'.[9] 'Everyone', Livingstone admitted in the same letter, included himself.

Livingstone had been at Kuruman only a month when to his amazement and delight he heard that Rogers Edwards, the missionary with whom he was temporarily lodging, had just gained permission from the Directors to make a journey of several hundred miles to the north of Kuruman with a view to selecting a site for a new mission station. Edwards asked Livingstone if he would like to come too, and understandably the younger man leapt at the offer. In direct contrast to his initial reaction to Ross, Livingstone had liked Edwards from the beginning, considering him 'an excellent friend'.[10] Edwards was in his late forties and had been at Kuruman almost as long as Moffat himself. Unlike Moffat, however, Edwards had been an artisan missionary all those years and had never been promoted to the post of full missionary. He had disliked being what he called 'Moffat's lackey' and saw the chance of forming a new mission as his last chance to gain promotion.

The journey that Edwards and Livingstone made between September and December 1841 was to lead Livingstone to undertake two more trips on his own between April 1842 and June 1843. The three journeys together paved the way for the selection of a site for the new mis-

sion and its inauguration by Livingstone and Edwards in
August 1843. During this two-year period Moffat remained
in England and the Directors did not send Livingstone any
further instructions; neither did they give their permission
for him to join with Edwards in starting the new station
till July 1843, when Livingstone had already made definite
plans to do so.

The three journeys were all to the north-east, and the
farthest Livingstone travelled from Kuruman was 500
miles as the crow flies. The main tribes he met were the
Bakhatla, 250 miles north-east of Kuruman; the Bakwains,
a tribe split under two rival chiefs, and situated 60 miles
north-west of the Bakhatla; and the Bamangwato, 150
miles north of the Bakwains. The Bamangwato had already
been visited by two travelling ivory and skin traders,
Wilson and Hume, in the early 1830s. So, while Livingstone met many natives who had never seen a white face
before, he was not, strictly speaking, breaking into totally
unexplored country. The main importance of the three
trips to him, apart from the ultimate foundation of the
new mission, was the knowledge they gave him of the
difficulties he would face when he began his own work as
a missionary. What he discovered was anything but encouraging and led him to view Kuruman with a less critical
eye.

To begin with Livingstone realized that travel in Bechuanaland could be a lot less comfortable than his journey
up to Kuruman. Any journey undertaken between November and January—the hottest time of the year—was a real
physical ordeal in a countryside with very little water.
The waggon oxen might have to go two days without water
in temperatures well over 100° Fahrenheit, and the same
would apply to human beings if a known water-hole turned
out to be dry. On his first trip to the north, Livingstone
described the heat as so great that 'the very flies sought
the shade and the enormous centipedes coming out by mistake from their holes were roasted to death on the burning
sand'.[11] The scenery, for the most part, was as uninspir-
ing as that around Kuruman, and, as Livingstone mourn-
fully acknowledged, Bechuanaland was no more populous
further north. 'We travelled over hundreds of miles of
dreary wilderness, not a soul appearing in sight'.[12] There
were few compensations, but Livingstone did at least see
his first elephants and marvelled at the digestive powers of

an animal that could eat branches as thick as his thumb and 'covered with large strong thorns more than an inch in length'.[13]

At first, native reactions to the arrival of so strange a visitor as a white man amused Livingstone. He noted how his straight hair was a source of fascination and incredulity, and laughed when a native woman touched his nose 'to make herself sure that it really was so far elevated from the level of my face as it appeared to be and was not like her own little flat thing'.[14] Livingstone was also entertained by native fascination with European technical gadgets like watches and cutlery. 'Show one a looking glass,' he told a friend, 'and he will almost go into convulsions at his own image.'[15] But while European strangeness led the natives to show Livingstone respect, their automatic assumption that he was 'a great wizard . . . possessed of supernatural power . . . capable of even raising the dead'[16] did not please him at all. He realized that, while this kind of hold over the people was useful as a means for persuading them to dig watercourses and build small dams, it was a terrible barrier to any form of religious teaching. Even at Kuruman he had seen people hiding under the benches in the chapel to avoid the preacher's eye and sometimes rushing out of the building screaming with fear.[17] He was often horrified to hear natives calling him by the Sichuana word for God, a title frequently given to chiefs.

When he tried to get across to natives the idea of praying to an unseen deity, and knelt down to show them the position in which Christians prayed, he was greeted with delighted laughter. Livingstone's head bowed to the earth convinced the watchers that he was talking to a god who lived under the ground. His first attempts to explain to them in Sichuana about the coming of Christ and His great sacrifice made no impression at all. On his second journey, full of optimism, he had taken the two most reliable native Christians in Kuruman to preach to the northern tribes. The result had been no better, and although the preachers had managed to collect an audience, interruptions, sometimes ten minutes long, had quickly brought the instruction to a halt.

Livingstone did a little better when talking to individual chiefs in private. Sekhomi, chief of the Bamangwato, when told that Christianity could change people's hearts, imme-

diately expressed interest. Sekhomi explained to Livingstone that for a long time he had been afflicted by violent
and quite unpredictable fits of rage. Christianity, he felt,
might cure him. Livingstone did his best to point out that
the gospel was not a medicine, but Sekhomi brushed this
explanation aside. If Christianity would stop his rages, he
would accept it straight away, if only his white visitor
would stop making excuses and give him the magic drink.
His heart troubled him, Sekhomi went on: 'I wish to have
it changed by medicine, to drink and have it changed at
once.'[18] Further attempts at reasoning got Livingstone
nowhere.

With Sechele, chief of part of the divided Bakwain
tribe, Livingstone at least managed to get over the idea of
Christianity as something to be understood rather than
eaten or drunk. Sechele in fact embarrassed him by asking
some extremely difficult questions. Why was it, the chief
enquired, that Europeans had not tried to convert Africans sooner, since they had known for centuries that
Christianity brought great benefits? 'My ancestors are
gone,' he continued, 'and none of them knew anything of
what you tell me. How is this?'[19] Livingstone later
remarked: 'I thought immediately of the guilt of the
church, but did not confess.'[20] At the time he made
excuses about Africa being a faraway country and very
difficult to travel in. Sechele was not impressed.

Reactions to Livingstone ranged from superstitious
dread to sceptical indifference, and made him decide that
a new approach to Africans was called for: a far less
humble way of dealing with them. Later he told friends
that the results were gratifying: 'I make my presence with
any of them a favour, and when they show any impu-
dence I threaten to leave them, and if they don't amend
I put my threat into execution. By a bold free course
among them, I have not had the least difficulty in managing even the most fierce.'[21]

All this did not however bring him any closer to explaining the Christian faith although he did manage, by pointing out the personal advantage, to persuade several tribes
to dig small irrigation canals from distant streams to help
their crops. At this early stage he began paying natives
for work and always tried to find a poor individual who
would 'esteem employment a favour'.[22] Payment would
be in tea, coffee, sugar or beads. By making himself use-

ful as an agricultural adviser and general handyman, and by doling out rewards, Livingstone gained some popularity and standing, but this very popularity made him uncertain, when natives listened to his preaching, whether they were simply doing so to encourage him to stay with them long enough to give more technical help. As time passed he became sure that in their eyes he was somebody to be exploited by a little politeness.

Nevertheless there were small compensations, as when the Bakhatla allowed him to see their iron-smelting process: a sight never before witnessed by a European. Before the natives would reveal these mysteries Livingstone was asked whether he had recently had sexual intercourse. Indignantly he told his questioners that he was unmarried, and when they were still unsatisfied, he tried to explain his views on fornication and adultery. At last they were convinced and he was taken to see the smelting; his hosts apologized for the questions but pointed out that the presence of anybody who had had intercourse within the past month would spoil the iron. The Bakhatla in fact showed Livingstone such friendliness that he felt safe to ask their chief, Moseealele, whether he would consent to have a missionary settle with him. Moseealele, recognizing that a missionary would possibly attract traders and would certainly bring a knowledge of gun-mending, agreed at once. Livingstone, still uncertain of the Directors' intentions, was not able to say when he and Edwards would come, but at least the chief's consent had been given.

Back in Kuruman in June 1843, with these three preparatory journeys behind him, Livingstone was left to ponder the vast difficulties that lay ahead. In July he heard from the Directors, who at last agreed to his joining in the formation of a new mission station but suggested that the move should not be made till Moffat came back. Livingstone, having just experienced the heady freedom of travelling hundreds of miles with only three native attendants, was not pleased by this check. He was still more distressed when he read that the Directors intended Moffat to organize a local committee as soon as he returned. The committee would discuss whether the site Livingstone proposed was suitable. Feeling as he did about committees, and having, as he put it, 'not the least confidence in the wisdom either collective or individual of our South African bretheren',[23] Livingstone decided that to wait for Moffat's

return would be to court endless delay and quibbling.
Perhaps the committee might wreck the whole scheme.
This thought was more than Livingstone could endure. He
imagined that unless he could get out of Kuruman before
Moffat got back, he might have to spend years as Moffat's
'lackey' just as Edwards had done. He confided his fears
to Edwards and reminded him that both their futures were
bound up in the new venture. Edwards was frightened of
doing anything that might give the Directors offence but
eventually he confessed that Livingstone's reasoning was
sound. Unless they left soon, both men knew that the
weather would become too hot for them to build huts on
their arrival at Moseealele's.

Livingstone and Edwards planned to leave Kuruman for
the north-east in early August. As they were preparing to
go, three young Englishmen arrived; they were on leave
from postings with British regiments stationed in India and
had come to South Africa for some hunting. When they
asked to come north too, the two missionaries raised no
objections, so Livingstone got his first close view of members of the British upper class. Although he disapproved
of the three men's pointless killing of game, he liked them
as people and did not react like a man with a social chip
on his shoulder. He liked best Captain Steele, the current
aide-de-camp to the Governor of Madras. Steele was apparently 'well versed in the classics & possessed of much general knowledge'.[24] Livingstone later corresponded with
him. While Livingstone was never exactly a social climber,
he had considerable respect for people who were 'well
bred' and tended to keep up with them far longer than
with his humbler acquaintances of earlier years.

Once the party arrived among the Bakhatla, the three
hunters went off alone, and Livingstone and Edwards
attended a meeting that Moseealele had called to inform
his people of the missionaries' intended settlement and to
gauge his subjects' feelings. After some discussion, Moseealele gave his formal consent. The April 1844 edition of
the *Missionary Chronicle*, true as ever to its unfailing
standard of inaccuracy, depicted this event with Livingstone and Edwards both wearing top hats and frock-coats.

The Bakhatla had independently made up their minds
to move to the spot which Livingstone had selected for
the new mission, so there was no argument on that score.
The missionaries bought the land they intended to live on

and cultivate; they could have had it for nothing, but they
insisted that unless they paid they would be beholden to
the chief. Moseealele did not mind either way. As far as
he was concerned a man who asked for land became his
vassal whether he gave gifts or not. Nevertheless Livingstone and Edwards drew up formal title deeds for their
new property and got the chief to make his mark. The
area bought was a mile and a half in width and two in
length; it was purchased with a gun, some powder, lead
and beads. The legal formalities over, the missionaries set
to work to build a large hut: no less than fifty feet by
eighteen. This would one day be the chapel, they hoped.
Neither man, however, was under any illusions about why
they were wanted. Livingstone's analysis was as follows:
'They wish the residence of white men, not from any
desire to know the Gospel, but merely, as some of them
in conversation afterwards expressed it, "That by our
presence and prayers they may get plenty of rain, beads,
guns &c. &c." '[25]

The Bakhatla also rather optimistically believed that the
missionaries might in some inexplicable way be able to
help them if they were attacked by the Boers or the Matabele, who were then fighting each other for possession of
the Transvaal just to the east. But whatever the reasons
behind the Bakhatla's desire for missionaries, Livingstone
was satisfied that Mabotsa, the site of the new mission,
was a more fertile and better watered place than Kuruman. The presence of wild fig trees even led him rashly
to tell a friend that he believed 'all kinds of tropical fruits
might be cultivated with ease'.[26]

So in August 1843, two years after his first arrival in
Bechuanaland, Livingstone was about to embark on missionary work of his own. He had shown he was ambitious,
and to date he had achieved his desire to live and work in
a place 'beyond every other man's line of things'. In his
ignorance he had scorned Moffat's achievement; now he
would be able to discover whether he could do any better.

5

A False Start: Mabotsa, 1844–1845

Before looking in detail at Livingstone's missionary work, it is necessary to have a picture of the people he was trying to convert: their numbers, beliefs and tribal organization. To date, in explaining the minute number of converts, I have concentrated on the physical difficulties that faced the early missionaries: their isolation, agricultural tasks and problems ranging from the reduction of a native language to the building of a house. All these activities dissipated energies and contributed to their failure, but the primary cause always lay with the Africans themselves.

Livingstone's estimate for the population of Bechuanaland was thirty thousand, and although it was a conservative guess, he was probably not more than ten thousand out. There were eight or so major tribes, all of the same Bechuana or Tswana stock, and the numbers of each ranged from two to seven thousand. Livingstone worked first with the Bakhatla and then with the Bakwains and they accounted respectively for 2,000 and 3,500 people.[1] The primary activity of these tribes was cattle-farming, with agriculture coming a poor second, maize and sorghum being the principal crops. The only agricultural implements were hoes and primitive ploughs. A very low annual rainfall guaranteed disappointing results. The Bechuana tribes lived in towns or villages and these centres remained occupied for many years at a time. When Livingstone visited Shoshong, the capital of the Bamangwato, he found over 3,000 people living there. Mabotsa was rather smaller with 400 huts and a population of about 1,500. The Bechuanas paid the price for keeping their established villages; as the cattle-grazing around them diminished, they had to move their cattle further away to distant cattle posts. Cattle might be grazing over fifty miles away before the people would accept a move as inevitable. Crops, too, were often grown many miles away. As a result people were often travelling backwards and forwards between their villages and the grazing pastures and gardens. These absences were naturally a hindrance to consecutive missionary teaching sessions. Dress was fairly uniform: a leather or fur cloak or kaross worn over a leather apron. Ivory or copper rings and ornaments were often worn and most people smeared their skins with a mixture of grease and a metallic powder called *sibilo*. Men and women divided their tasks: the men tending the all-important cattle—milking was a male job—preparing leather, sewing clothes, and when necessary making war, while the women grew the crops, fetched water and fuel, cooked, looked after the children and built the houses.

Tribal chiefs were hereditary rulers and in Bechuanaland, at least, the succession passed to the first son of the chief's principal wife. The chief had religious as well as temporal duties. He was often the tribe's rainmaker: a much respected office in a country with very little rain. Rather surprisingly constant failure did not make the people doubt their rain-maker's powers. Without his work they believed no rain at all would fall. The chief also performed the rituals connected with sowing and harvest, with moving a village and going to war. As head of the tribal government he had the last word on policy decisions; he acted as judge in all disputes and distributed the land for use by his subjects. Land was freely given on a basis of tenure rather than possession. The chief was also responsible for looking after his people's interests and safeguarding them, as much as he could, against famine. The poor turned to him for help and he always had to feed numerous relatives. His generosity was taken for granted and to maintain it he needed all the dues and privileges he received in exchange for his allocation of land. His powers were tempered by his being the representative of the people and the living embodiment of the tribal will. He usually took advice from a circle of advisers before making vital decisions.

The heart of the missionaries' difficulties lay in the enormous differences between the social, moral and economic requirements of nineteenth-century industrial Britain and those of a small African tribal community. Victorian virtues such as work, punctuality, thrift, monogamous marriage and personal ambition were all vices which a good African tribesman wanted to avoid. In a tribal community men and women certainly worked, but they did not do so to grow rich or to build up a surplus of food. Work was limited to providing the necessaries of life and setting aside a small communal store of food to protect the tribe against drought and famine. A man who attempted to keep for himself a surplus of food to sell at a profit would have been ostracized for an antisocial act. Each man depended on his neighbour; and in a society where there were no exchanges of goods made on a money basis, it was advisable to be generous if your own crops were fruitful, for the next year they might fail and you would be dependent on another's generosity. The whole tribe was a closely-knit, interdependent community based on a comprehensive set of mutual obligations. These obligations to be generous and to think more of the tribe's security than his own did not weigh heavily on a man, since he knew that by fulfilling them he was acting in a correct and moral way. Thrift and personal ambition would have been directly counter to all his beliefs about the collective benefit of the society of which he was a member. Besides, to become wealthy and to hoard grain was a dangerous course to pursue: such people were often accused of witchcraft.

Economic competition and other ideas associated with capitalism were quite alien to tribal societies. The small scale of the communities and the lack of external markets meant that each society operated as a self-sufficient unit. Competition would only have been possible with outsiders; but with vast distances separating tribes, and the lack of any means of carrying goods except on the backs of oxen or on the heads of men and women, external trade rarely developed. When the missionaries accused the Africans of being lazy and not helping themselves to gain the good things in life by working hard, there was complete incredulity. The missionaries talked about factories and steam engines, but to people who had never seen a house bigger than a hut or any form of transport more sophisticated than a waggon, these stories sounded too far-fetched to be taken seriously. Besides, the Africans were content with the beads, glass, guns and other oddments that the missionaries and traders brought with them. The missionary could give his pupils no better proof of the technical superiority of the European than his pocket watch and his magnifying glass. The natives were impressed, but not impressed enough to wish to change their culture. The missionary was isolated and therefore helpless.

Polygamy was a worse stumbling block than work. At

least the missionary could claim some rewards for work and thrift, even if they were thought to be illusory. On the subject of polygamy, the African was convinced that the white man was mad. It was as clear as day that to be satisfied with only one wife was to court social and economic disaster. While economic competition was alien to a tribal community, competition among the various headmen for influence within the tribe was quite legitimate. Such influence could only be acquired by a man with many dependants, and the best way to obtain dependants was to beget them. One wife could only have a limited number of children; the implication was obvious: a man who wanted influence had to have many wives. These wives would also be able to grow more food than would be needed even by the enlarged family, and this would enable the head of the family to give feasts to gain prestige. With luck, if his feasts were impressive enough, he might be able to attract the dependants of other headmen. His generosity would not only advance his own position but would help his tribe. Generosity might not bring an individual short-term profit, but it would certainly bring long-term social benefit. A man would be unable to honour all his obligations if he had only one wife. The chief was always particularly conscious of this. In a technically primitive society he could not show his primacy by living in a house very different from those of his subjects, nor could he demonstrate his superiority by amassing an impressive range of possessions. His position depended solely on the extent of his largesse. Generosity was the basis of tribal security. It would have been completely undermined had nuclear families been substituted for large, interdependent kinship groups. Therefore the missionary who told Africans that polygamy was sinful was laughed at and ignored. In their circumstances the tribesmen knew that monogamy would have brought them disaster.

Obviously, with such different values, the missionaries were completely unable to get across the Christian idea of sin; nor where men thought of their well-being in terms of their community was it possible adequately to explain a concept like individual salvation. Even the notion of Christian equality was repugnant to most Africans; to the chiefs it sounded like open sedition. They might have viewed it with less alarm had they known that most European rulers were nominal Christians. The idea of the resurrection of the dead was almost as bad as the notion of equality. An African chief was not ready to be convinced that those he had killed in battle might rise again.

Grounds for misunderstandings between missionaries and their pupils were too numerous to be conveniently listed. Some, however, were particularly marked. Africans gained a reputation for lying and boasting that was partly due to the fact that a man who had inherited rights, from, say, his grandfather, would not find it odd to speak in the first person and use the present tense for things his grandfather did. Again, myth and tribal history were closely interwoven, and in a society with no written records, discrepancies of dating events were inevitable. Africans also got a reputation for imprecise thinking because of failure to give precise instructions to travellers. Sometimes the reason was that they had never travelled far from their home village, and anyway, as often as not, they failed to see the point of geographical discovery. A pond was water and so was a large lake. Who but a fool would risk life and limb to gaze at gallons of water? They also probably felt that it was unreasonable for strangers to expect from them a great deal of information about their locality before they had got to know them.

Then there were occasions when missionaries witnessed fights and protracted quarrels over apparently trivial incidents: a gift not given, a spear taken from its owner or an obligation waived. But it was on these courtesies that the whole society depended. A spear could symbolize the link between father and son, just as the giving of cattle formed a physical manifestation of the new status of a man and woman after marriage. Rituals, too, were deplored by missionaries, and one reason was the obscenity of some of them. On most occasions rituals portrayed behaviour that was to be frowned on. Thus rebellion would be the theme of rituals of national unity, immorality the subject of rituals enjoining proper behaviour, and so on. This ritual licence was and is believed to bless the participants and those who allow the licences. Tensions could be released and the statement of conflicts render them harmless and subordinate to existing tribal values.

Europeans also found it almost impossible to grasp African attitudes to ownership and could not understand how matters could run smoothly without enforceable rules. Indeed, often disputes over the ownership of cattle were

simply insoluble; two or more men might have different
rights over the same beast, and still others rights over the
offspring. Then there were different claims to succession
to the chiefship and no easily apprehended hard and fast
rule. It really is neither true nor fair to see these early
missionaries as men successfully deluding helpless natives
with a powerful alien culture. While the missionaries were
alone and had no help from their own society, they had
no hope at all. In their own terms they acknowledged
that, short of direct intervention by the Holy Spirit, their
prospects were extremely bleak.

In this impossible situation it would have been strange if
the missionaries had not worked out two main methods
for comforting themselves. The first was to subscribe to
an unquestioning faith in God's Providence. Death and
failure could not be understood by mere mortals but God
undoubtedly had a plan too large for any individual to
understand. If failure came, it was obvious that God was
holding things back for a good reason. Perhaps he was
aiding other men's efforts elsewhere. They believed in 'sowing seed that would not bear fruit in their own lifetimes'.
The ways of God might be slow but they were also sure
and in the end Christianity would triumph everywhere.
The second major source of comfort came from stressing
and exaggerating the supposed depravity of the natives.
The Negro was congenitally indolent, he lied, smelled,
rarely attained intelligence greater than that of a fourteen-
year-old white child. His nudity and tribal customs were
barbarous and his use of women as labourers was disgraceful. His anger and grief were displayed, just as with
children, in sudden bursts, and even his good qualities
usually went to extremes, so that obedience became ser-
vility, generosity indulgence and limited intellect deceit.
Even those missionaries who retained their philanthropic
love for the 'noble savage', and managed to some extent
to continue to love the man while hating his habits, were
inevitably patronizing. Phrases such as 'the poor African',
'the untaught child of nature' and the 'humble Negro',
who might be 'raised' with God's help, were all designed
to bolster up the missionary's morale and persuade him
that until the African grew from childhood to maturity
he would not be able to appreciate the gift of true religion.

Robert Moffat exemplified the total condemnation
school. Every missionary, he wrote, would have to get

accustomed to the natives' 'ignorance, their degradation and their wallowing in wickedness'.[2] By the middle of 1842, Livingstone, taking his cue from his predecessors, was writing equally ringing denunciations: 'The population is sunk into the very lowest state of mental and moral degradation, so much so indeed it must be difficult or rather impossible for Christians at home to realise anything like an accurate notion of the grossness which shrouds their minds.'[3]

But by the middle of 1844, after only a year at Mabotsa, Livingstone was writing about Africans with a perception greater than that shown by any previous observer. First of all he realized, accurately, that Christianity was a direct threat to tribal society on every level. Christianity, he wrote, 'appears to them as that which will reduce them & overturn their much loved "domestic institutions" '.[4] It was a crucial observation and, having made it, Livingstone came to other logical conclusions. He decided that missionaries had failed in the past by too readily condemning what they did not understand. The *boguera* or initiation rites had previously been treated as barbarous black magic and a perverted religious ceremony. Livingstone soon saw that the *boguera* was 'more a national civil rite than a religious observance'. 'Those who have gone to the circumcision together,' he wrote, 'are bound into a cohort under one of the chief's sons or brothers for ever afterwards and have to render service, go wherever he is sent, do whatever he likes under pain of death.'[5]

In other words tribal unity and survival depended on the continuation of the *boguera* and, having grasped this, Livingstone knew that former attacks on it 'had been a great hindrance to the spread of Christianity'. He went as far as to say that he did not consider that 'Christianity gives any licence for assaulting the civil institutions of man',[6] and included polygamy in this. Almost every other missionary working in Africa pronounced with absolute confidence on the wrongs of polygamy, but Livingstone said, 'We cannot call it adultery,' and admitted that whenever he thought about the subject he felt confused and perplexed.[7] Whereas missionaries in the past had always believed that the marriage gift of cattle by the groom to his wife's family constituted bride-buying', Livingstone saw that it was more a pledge of good faith for the future, and the physical manifestation of a change in relationship. Although the system complicated cattle ownership, he was aware that the gift of cattle made for ties between families, and encouraged husbands not to desert their wives, since if they did they lost the cattle, which had not been given absolutely, but were on loan.

At Mabotsa Livingstone soon learned that the usual missionary sermons, based on common texts like 'God so loved the world' (John 3:16), were quite useless and equivalent to delivering an address in Greek.[8] Conventional Christian words and images had to be thought out afresh to be made intelligible. For a start the Sichuana word for love, he discovered, made no distinction between sexual and spiritual love, and Bechuanas always understood it in the sense of *eros* rather than *agape*. The Sichuana word usually employed by missionaries for 'holiness' was used by Bechuanas to describe 'a nice fat ox or cow. Beauty is nearest the word in our language but not that exactly'.[9] Similarly the missionary translation of 'sin' was in Sichuana equally applicable to cow dung. There was no Sichuana word that directly translated meant 'soul'; the nearest the missionaries could get was a word used to describe breath, air or steam from a boiling pot.[10]

Livingstone's father used to drive his son into bitter rages when he talked about useful sermons he had heard in Hamilton. 'We don't preach to Scotchmen', Livingstone wrote back scathingly. The Bakhatla were not people to appreciate Scottish theological quibbles.

Moffat and his colleagues had always claimed that the Bechuanas had no idea of God or a supreme being. Livingstone soon felt convinced that ancestor worship did not preclude the idea of an overall deity, nor belief in a future existence.[11] He did not, as many missionaries did, claim that the Africans refused the gospel because of stupidity; in fact he believed that, in what they knew about from direct experience, natives 'showed more intelligence than is to be met with in our own uneducated peasantry'.[12]

Livingstone had no training or background reading to make him so responsive and it is truly remarkable that even when he made no impression on the Bakhatla he retained his liberal beliefs. It would be seven or eight years before he became convinced that every tribal custom, good or bad, would have to give way to British values if Christianity was to make any headway. Only a society in disintegration would prove responsive to an alien reli-

gion. But in 1844, at Mabotsa, Livingstone was still a long
way from these later beliefs. The Bakhatla's indifference
to his teaching did, nevertheless, drive him to the borders
of despair. For a time he found consolation in studying
plants and animals, finding in them proof of God's
'wonderful intelligence and design'. Only this pursuit, in
his view, saved him from callousness and melancholy.[13]
But there were times when even he admitted that the
habits of ants and scavenger beetles failed to make up for
his isolation. While Edwards, his fellow-missionary, was
married, he was not. He wrote to all his friends asking
them to write as often as they could, but a letter could
take from four to six months to reach England and as long
again for the reply to come back. Often he implored his
family to write more letters and, after one such request,
he described his isolation hauntingly:

Next month I expect to receive letters from home.
What are you all doing? is a question that I sometimes ask myself, but no answer but the still deathlike
quietness which you can almost hear in this wide
wilderness land. Here in the evenings I hear the bleat-
ing of sheep & goats, the lowing of oxen & the jabber
of the Natives mingling with the yell of the jackal &
howling of the wolf. Occasionally the Natives dance &
screech their own wild unearthly music the greater
portion of the night . . . I have written very often to
you, but if I don't get letters from you I suppose I
shall get tired by & by.[14]

Back in 1840, while still in London, he had written to a
friend telling him that if he married it would be only to
'render me most useful, but whether', he went on, 'my usefulness will be augmented by getting a wife, I really don't
know'.[15] Again, before leaving Kuruman for Mabotsa, he
had written to another fellow-student from Ongar days,
firmly repudiating any hints that he was thinking of marriage. 'You thought I should turn foolish at the Cape, what
nonsense, man. Do you think I would take a thing in hand
and not carry it through?'[16]

At Kuruman, with his journeys and inflated hopes to
take the edge off his isolation, it had been easy to sneer
at the settled comforts of marriage as weak-minded escap-
ism, but at Mabotsa, with the daily indifference of the

natives and no diversions in prospect, he was left far more
time to contemplate his personal loneliness. In the few
letters he received from home, he was asked about whether
he intended to get married. Some friends even sent him
some baby clothes to give him the right idea,[17] but even
when he knew that he wanted a wife, it was not easy to
find one. Apart from missionary daughters, there were no
white women in Bechuanaland, and even they, knowing
the privations of the missionary life, were many of them
not prepared to spend their whole lives facing hardships.
Anyway Livingstone was not keen to marry into a missionary family. In his view, as he told a friend, 'daughters
of missionaries have miserably contracted minds, colonial
ladies worse and worse. There's no outlet for me when I
begin to think of getting married but that of sending home
an advertisement to the Evang. Mag. And if I get very
old it must be for some decent sort of widow.'[18]

The half-joking tone could not disguise his real distress.
Missionaries often did advertise in missionary publications,
and the unions that followed were hardly guaranteed success from the outset. A well-meaning missionary couple
had sent their daughter to see Livingstone while he had
been at Kuruman, and when nothing had happened, the
honest people had started to make enquiries about his
female correspondents in England; these efforts included
opening some of his letters, and keeping those written to
Mrs Sewell, the elderly woman who ran the boarding-
house where he had lodged in London. Mrs Sewell was
assumed to be some young widow.[19]

Three miserable months passed at Mabotsa, during
which Livingstone and Edwards finished the large hut they
had begun on their first visit, completed a ditch and
watercourse and built one more hut besides. In late
October news came from Kuruman that Moffat was at
last on his way up from the coast. Livingstone and
Edwards knew that they would have to go south to meet
him and explain why they had not waited till his arrival
before beginning their new mission. On his way to Kuruman, Livingstone felt apprehensive about the coming meeting; he remembered what Dr Philip had said about Moffat
and had not entirely got over his own feeling that the
founder of Kuruman had deceived the Directors about
the population of Bechuanaland. Rumour, of the usual
bitter missionary sort, had it that Moffat had been spoilt

by the praise lavished on him in England. It was also said
that he was returning a rich man, having made a fortune
out of his recently published book, *Missionary Labours
and Scenes in Southern Africa*. This was untrue, as was
the allegation that he had bought so much in England that
his luggage weighed fifty tons.[20] Livingstone was nevertheless inclined to fear the worst. He had already written to
his parents telling them to ignore Moffat's book as it was
bound to be full of lies.

But just as he had been forced to admit that he was
gullible to believe all he heard about Philip, Livingstone
was soon admitting that he had been a credulous idiot to
have misjudged Moffat too. The rapport between the two
men was immediate and it marked the beginning of a long
friendship. Moffat at forty-eight was still a visually impressive figure, with his long black beard streaked with grey
and his commanding height of over six feet. He had a lot
in common with Livingstone: both had come from poor
Scottish families and both had educated themselves in the
first place through their own efforts. Moffat's absolute conviction and his inflexible refusal to see anything good in
African society must have distressed Livingstone, but he
had to concede that Moffat was respected by large numbers of natives, many of them not Christians. Moffat's
most extraordinary success had been with the universally
dreaded Mosilikatse, the tyrannical paramount chief of
the Matabele. Moffat had already visited Mosilikatse twice
at his kraal, in what is now Rhodesia. On each visit he
was able to criticize an autocrat who normally killed people for saying much less. In fact Mosilikatse had tears in
his eyes on both occasions when Moffat had left him.
Livingstone felt the power of Moffat's presence at once
and described how excited he had been on first seeing
Moffat's waggon, how his horse had raced across a wide
plain under the burning sun as if 'at Ascot or the Derby',
and how once they had started talking, they had not
stopped for many hours.[21]

Livingstone had ridden down south almost as far as the
Vaal river to meet Moffat. It took them a week or so to
return to Kuruman, where they arrived on 13 December.[22] Livingstone, to his great relief, very soon learned
that Moffat was not so opposed to native teachers as he
had been led to believe, nor, it appeared, was he in favour
of a committee. But there were pleasures other than eager

discussion to be had at the Kuruman home of Mr and
Mrs Moffat. The Moffats had two daughters of marriage-
able age, Ann and Mary. Livingstone only stayed at Kuruman for two weeks, but during that time he managed to
make some headway with Mary, who, although by no
stretch of the imagination beautiful, was compliant and
good-tempered. Livingstone knew that a man in his position could not afford to be fussy. Although he had now
made up his mind that Miss Moffat had better become
Mrs Livingstone, he decided that he ought to ask her
formally on his next visit to Kuruman.

Shortly after Christmas, Livingstone was on his way
back to Mabotsa, where he experienced far less pleasant
embraces. As early as 1842 he had seen 'a woman actually devoured in her garden' by a lion, and had noticed
that there was a plague of these animals at Mabotsa.
Nevertheless he had always remained unworried by the
thought of personal danger from them, and had assured
friends in England that 'the sense of danger vanishes when
you are in a country of lions'.[23] On 16 February 1844
Livingstone was working in the ditches of the watercourse
when some natives came screaming to him to help them
kill a lion that had just dragged off some sheep. As Livingstone put it later: 'I very imprudently ventured across the
valley in order to encourage them to destroy him.'[24] It
was not Livingstone's only mistake; he went with only one
gun and with no armed native at his side. He fired both
barrels at the lion but only wounded him. As he vainly
tried to reload, the lion leapt on him and, catching him
by the arm, shook him 'as a terrier dog does a rat'.
Livingstone's upper arm was splintered at once; the lion's
teeth made a series of gashes like 'gun-shot wounds'. Livingstone was only saved by the sudden appearance of
Mebalwe, an elderly native convert whom Livingstone had
brought from Kuruman as a native teacher. Mebalwe,
seeing that his master would be dead within minutes unless
he acted, snatched a gun from another native, loaded and
fired both barrels. The gun misfired but the lion was
diverted at the crucial moment and bounded off to attack
his new assailant. The luckless Mebalwe was badly bitten
on the thigh and another native who tried to help him
was in turn bitten on the shoulder. At this stage however
the lion suddenly dropped dead, killed at last by the
wounds initially inflicted by Livingstone.

In letters written afterwards, Livingstone was extremely reticent about his terrible injuries; this was doubtless partly to avoid worrying people and partly so as not to advertise his own carelessness. In fact he was extremely ill for weeks, too weak to move his limbs for a while. The wounds suppurated for several months. The long-term effects were not as bad as might have been expected and Livingstone was subsequently able to shoot, lift heavy weights and do everything that he had done before. His only limitation was the inability to lift his left arm higher than the shoulder. It is hard to imagine the agony he must have suffered without anaesthetic and without the help of another doctor. He had to supervise the setting of the badly splintered arm himself. Nevertheless he made an astoundingly fast recovery and within three months was working cautiously on the lighter tasks involved in building his house. Then in early July he left for Kuruman and a short period of convalescence. His stay was almost three weeks and during this time he proposed to Mary Moffat and was accepted.

1. Encounter with a lion

Sophistication was certainly never one of Mary's qualities, and if her manners were a little rough that was to be expected. She had lived all but four of her twenty-three years in Africa. During all that time, apart from occasional visits to the Cape, there had been no social life worth the name; no balls, carriage rides or outings. But what she lacked in refinement, she made up for in other ways. She was literate and had been taught by her mother all the household tasks a missionary's wife ought to be able to manage; ranging from making clothes to making candles and soap. She would never be homesick for England, since Africa had always been her home, and that was a considerable advantage. Livingstone was also convinced that having a wife would help his missionary work; she could run an infants' school and would diminish the suspicions which Africans unfortunately felt about a bachelor missionary questioning native women on fornication and adultery. Discussions of sexual ethics with African women would obviously be easier for Mary than for her husband. Mary's presence would also go some way towards cutting out any missionary gossip about him finding consolation with African women. All single missionaries were suspected by the married ones of carrying on with natives.

The marriage was one of convenience and both recognized this. Livingstone might know that he would be better looked after than hitherto, but there were advantages for Mary too. Her mother was a domineering woman and it was a relief to her daughter to escape from the house at Kuruman to a home of her own. Like Livingstone she had also had very little choice of partners; added to that she was fat and plain and probably felt fortunate to be getting married at all. Moffat's other two daughters eventually married missionaries too.

Livingstone treated his impending marriage with a matter-of-factness that seemed to border on indifference. He could not have been more impersonal in announcing it to the Directors of the Society, even if he had tried:

> Various considerations connected with this new sphere of labour, and which to you need not be specified in detail, having led me to the conclusion that it was my duty to enter into the marriage relation, I have made the necessary arrangements for union with Mary, the eldest daughter of Mr Moffat, in the beginning of January 1845 . . . and if I have not deceived myself I was in some measure guided by a desire that the Divine glory might be promoted in my increased usefulness.[25]

Writing to a friend shortly to begin a missionary career in India, Livingstone advised him to choose a wife before leaving, on the grounds that the missionary he would otherwise have to lodge with would think him inferior. Livingstone also suggested the best sort of woman for the job: 'a plain common sense woman, not a romantic. Mine is a matter of fact lady, a little thick black haired girl, sturdy and all I want.'[26] For some other friends, he compared his wife with a mutual acquaintance but added that Mrs Livingstone was 'a great deal stouter'. In later life Mary grew extremely fat but it is interesting that this should already have been such a feature in her early twenties. A couple of years later Livingstone was writing to the same people asking them to send some dress material. He told them not to worry much about what they sent, and then described Mary: 'She is a good deal of an African in complexion, a stout stumpy body so you will have no difficulty in selecting the proper sort of thing.'[27] There are no photographs of Mary prior to 1857 and these certainly show that Livingstone's descriptions were fair; by then she was a stout, heavy-jowled woman, slightly coarse-featured and with a large nose. Even so, Livingstone's mother might have expected her son to open his heart to her on the subject of his new bride. Livingstone, however, had no intention of gushing about Mary. All he felt able to say was: 'My wife is amiable & good tempered, and my new connections pious, which you know to be the best certificate of character.'[28]

Poor Mary Livingstone was not to have a happy married life. Had she known Livingstone's views on marriage before their wedding, she might have had second thoughts. 'I have never found two agreeing unless one were a cypher,' Livingstone later told his brother-in-law, J. S. Moffat.[29] Livingstone was not joking either; he believed without question that in all working relationships one person had to dominate the other person or persons absolutely, whether man, wife or fellow-missionary. It was a belief that would have much to do with his failure as a leader of Europeans, and to a large extent accounted for his later preference for travelling only with Africans. Livingstone felt that the one mistake he would never make in his marriage was to expect too much of his wife.[30] In the romantic sense he kept his word and certainly never gave her an idyllic role she could not live up to. But, considering her appearance, he cannot be given much credit for this achievement. In other ways he expected a great deal too much. As the old trader Aloysius Horn put it much later, 'dragging that poor Mary Moffat along until she was forced to a long rest in her grave'.[31] But Mary Livingstone's suffering was still in the future when she married David Livingstone on 2 January 1845.

Livingstone had become engaged to Mary in May 1844 and then returned to Mabotsa for five months to finish the house he and Mary would live in. This early separation was the first of many. The letters Livingstone wrote to Mary, during it, were pleasant, affectionate even, but they contained very little of his thinking on missionary topics. These he reserved for a couple of friends made at Ongar, and for his father-in-law. Later he would confine his serious thinking to letters written to more famous men, and Mary would never be told about his plans for commerce and colonization, when his mind started moving in those directions. Nor were his letters to his wife ever so gay or amusing as those sent to male friends. The disparity in the respective intellectual gifts of husband and wife sometimes worried Livingstone. A lack of communication between Mary and himself is hinted at in a letter he wrote to a friend just a few months after the marriage. 'This is private. I reflect on no one, but there is guilt. I tell you my sorrows although I have a wife.'[23] This single enigmatic sentence stands in isolation, and is made no clearer by the context. The 'guilt' could have been over some wish that he could enjoy prettier women, but it is certain that Livingstone found it distressing to have to talk about problems and 'sorrows' to people other than his wife. There exist only a handful of letters written by Mary herself, and none of these are particularly revealing about the personal aspects of her marriage; they all deal with physical rather than mental hardships.

Livingstone's own feelings about marriage fluctuated. He told J. S. Moffat some ten years later that if he could begin again it would be on a mission station alone with his wife. But at other times he regretted the loss of independence and advocated an isolated, celibate missionary life. His reading about the work of the Jesuits in foreign mission fields made him confess that 'although quite happy and contented in the married state I should like to commence being more of a Jesuit . . . O that I could begin again.'[33] He did not, of course, mean that he would have preferred to have been a Roman Catholic missionary, but that he would rather have stayed celibate.

After their wedding the Livingstones spent January and February of 1845 in Kuruman. During this time Livingstone had a row with his father-in-law about the possible foundation of a seminary for native teachers. Moffat and his colleagues felt that there was insufficient zeal among existing converts to make such an institution viable. Livingstone countered that if they went on with the present system of Bible classes, there would never be enough zeal. He went on openly to criticize the set-up at Kuruman, and, as a result, made himself extremely unpopular. Later he realized that, had he attempted to win over one or two of the older missionaries and suggested that one of them should run the new seminary, he might have got somewhere, but instead his own championship of the idea merely appeared as a challenge to the existing order and an implied criticism. Livingstone was also accused of having ambitions to run the seminary himself and thus attract the attention of the Directors. Before that, many of the other missionaries had come to dislike Livingstone because of his openly expressed hostility to the committee. They were not fools and could see that his real objection was to his fellow-workers themselves. The young man's journeys, and his setting up of the new mission before being finally authorized to do so by the committee, gained him a reputation for ambition and 'the wrong kind of ambition' at that.[34]

Livingstone's scathing attacks on William Ross, who had travelled out to Africa on the same ship, gave early indication of Livingstone's tendency to judge harshly and on little evidence. His ready acceptance of unfavorable reports of Philip and Moffat confirmed the feeling that eagerness to condemn others might be a serious defect in his character. This was further supported by events during 1844 and 1845.

On his return to Africa, Moffat was accompanied by a young missionary called Walter Inglis, who had been a fellow-student of Livingstone's at Ongar. Before Inglis arrived, Livingstone had written to the Directors telling them that he would prefer to work at Mabotsa with a young man like Inglis, rather than with an older man like Edwards. Nevertheless Moffat told Livingstone that Inglis had many faults and would probably not make a good missionary. Livingstone immediately wrote to his parents telling them: 'Inglis I suspect won't do for Africa . . . he will be a curse.' In the same letter Livingstone denounced those who had lied about Moffat's character without evidence. He seems to have been quite unaware of his own hypocrisy. Livingstone had denounced Moffat as eagerly as anybody and was now maligning Inglis before he even re-met him in Africa. Ironically Livingstone's attack was due to Inglis's objections to the committee. The arguments which now struck Livingstone as examples of 'ridiculous intellectual pride' were almost identical to his own earlier complaints about the committee. Livingstone's attitude to Inglis showed a complete inability to see faults in himself, even when he himself was guilty of failings he happily condemned in others.

But it was not to be Inglis who would provoke Livingstone to display all the worst aspects of his character, but Edwards. Within weeks of his return to Mabotsa at the end of March 1845, with his new bride, Livingstone was to show himself capable not only of hypocrisy and self-righteousness in his dealings with colleagues, but also of lies and double-dealing.

Between August 1843 and December 1844, in the months when Livingstone and Edwards were at Mabotsa together, their relationship had steadily deteriorated but with few outward signs. On two occasions there had been rows over trivial incidents that led Edwards to claim that Livingstone was attempting to undermine his authority over the Bakhatla by taking the side of natives whom Edwards had censured for various reasons. It was unfortunate for Edwards that he chose two minor incidents with which to challenge Livingstone; for it gave the younger man no difficulty at all in representing Edwards as a small-minded idiot who could work himself into a frenzy over trivial disagreements. This was precisely the line Livingstone took when he wrote a 9,000-word letter to the Directors, telling them about Edwards's unstable temperament. In this gigantic letter of self-justifications, Livingstone cannily relegated to a very secondary position the real cause for tension. Behind all Edwards's hostility lay an absolute conviction that Livingstone was attempting to claim all the credit for the foundation of the new mission.

Edwards had good grounds too. A letter written by Livingstone in 1843, for publication in the *Missionary*

Chronicle,[35] had not included a single mention of
Edwards as co-founder of Mabotsa. Edwards was not
unaware that Livingstone had told several missionaries at
Kuruman that the choice of site was entirely due to his
own preparatory journeys. Edwards quite justifiably considered that had he not taken Livingstone with him on his
journey of 1841, Livingstone might never have made his
subsequent trips. Also Livingstone had tried to persuade
the Directors that on this first journey he and Edwards
had not visited the Bakhatla at all. This was a lie designed
to cut Edwards out altogether. The two men had gone to
the Bakhatla together on that first occasion, and afterwards Edwards had written to the Directors proposing a
mission among the Bakhatla near Mosega. Mabotsa was less
than thirty miles from Mosega. Soon Livingstone was even
claiming that Edwards had never wanted to found another
mission anyway. Edwards did not see Livingstone's letters
to the Directors but he guessed at what Livingstone was
up to, partly through what he heard from other missionaries and partly from the accounts of the foundation of
the station, which Livingstone had sent home for publication.

Livingstone's attempt to make the Directors see him as
an innocent wounded by the sudden tantrums of a mad-
man was by no means the result of naïvety. He cannot
have failed to realize how important Mabotsa was to
Edwards; it represented his last chance to establish himself as an independent missionary, his final opportunity to
escape from a life dominated by Moffat. Nor, knowing
Edwards's feelings about Moffat, could Livingstone have
been surprised that Edwards was distressed to see Mary
Moffat at Mabotsa. It almost seemed as though Moffat had
established spies to report back to Kuruman. Livingstone
must surely have known that to avoid serious trouble with
Edwards he would have to display great tolerance and
forbearance. In the event, when Edwards first did lose his
temper, Livingstone made sure that the row boiled up
into something serious enough to create a lasting rift.

The worst aspect of Livingstone's behaviour was his failure to tell Edwards that he intended leaving Mabotsa anyway. This decision had been made while Livingstone was
at Kuruman just after his wedding. Before returning to the
Bakhatla he had written to some friends telling them that
Mabotsa was too small to provide two missionaries with

work. He went on to say that he did not fancy working
with another man, for he wanted to be responsible for
introducing the gospel to a tribe 'wholly by my instrumentality'. He concluded with the statement that he would
leave Mabotsa 'as soon as possible'.[36]

Had Livingstone told Edwards that he meant to go anyway, all Edwards's suspicions and worries would have
melted away. Livingstone must have known this too, and
yet it was months before he finally got round to telling
Edwards. When the older man then suggested that he
would never have quarrelled had he known, Livingstone
used the admission as clinching proof that Edwards had
never had a leg to stand on.[37]

Livingstone later argued that his long letter to the
Directors vilifying Edwards was made necessary by a letter
Edwards had written laying charges against him. There is
little doubt but that Edwards wrote such a letter; Livingstone said he saw it. Nevertheless Edwards never sent it,
and his next letter to the Directors, written a year after
the quarrel, hardly mentioned Livingstone at all. Although
at the time Livingstone claimed that he felt degraded by
the whole unpleasant business, he later wrote dozens of
letters to Moffat filled with bitter remarks about Edwards.
The matter even seemed to give a spur to other animosities, and led Livingstone to attack the Rosses again. Not
even the death of Mrs Ross was to make him relent.
'Mrs Ross is gone,' he wrote. 'No loss certainly, not even
to her own children.'[38] He went on telling tales to the
Directors too, until they finally had to tell him to learn the
meaning of the word 'charity' and to stop expecting them
to take his word as gospel when he himself was one of
the parties concerned.[39] Yet not even this stinging rebuke
could stop him telling discrediting lies about Edwards.
Soon Livingstone was claiming that Edwards had never
helped him with his house-building in spite of the injuries
to his arm caused by the lion. At the time he had told
Mary the truth; that Edwards was unable to assist because
of an injury to his hand.[40] Edwards said that he had done
everything he could to nurse Livingstone after the lion
accident, going so far as to build an extra room on to his
own house specially for the invalid. Livingstone however
told Moffat that he had had difficulty in getting Edwards
or his wife to dress his arm 'even when crawling with
maggots'.[41] On the whole Edwards's version is easier to

believe, since Livingstone did not complain about this neglect till after the quarrel. It is quite inconceivable that a man with Livingstone's temperament could have remained silent about such brutal treatment for such a long time.

The accusations and spite were not all on Livingstone's side, however, since Mrs Edwards took it upon herself to write to Mrs Moffat telling her that her son-in-law was 'shabby, ungentlemanly and unchristian'.[42] On Livingstone's side it can also be claimed that the long time-lag between his first visit to the Bakhatla with Edwards and the establishment of the mission three years later suggests that Edwards had really played a subsidiary role. But, whatever the facts, Livingstone's behaviour throughout the whole affair brought him little credit. Past biographers have glossed over the whole incident and have therefore not only distorted Livingstone's character but have also ignored an important contributory cause for his later decision to leave Bechuanaland: namely his complete inability to live and co-operate with other missionaries.

After the row it was quite evident that the Livingstones and the Edwardses could no longer remain on the same mission station. Since Livingstone intended to leave anyway, it would have been grotesquely inconsistent if he had suggested that Edwards ought to clear out. Livingstone has been said to have left a well-established and thriving mission to his disagreeable fellow-missionary, simply out of the goodness of his heart;[43] nothing could be further from the truth. Livingstone was relieved to be going because the Bakhatla had already shown definite signs that they cared not a damn for Christianity. Livingstone had met Sechele, chief of half the Bakwain tribe, on two of his early excursions from Kuruman. Sechele had impressed him by his intelligence and seemed a more likely candidate for conversion than the chief of the Bakhatla. Sechele had also recently moved to a place called Chonuane, only forty miles north of Mabotsa. Having asked Sechele if he would have him, and having received a positive invitation, Livingstone began making preparations for his move. He ought to have asked the Directors' permission first, but since their reply would almost certainly take a year to come back, Livingstone decided to move first and explain later.

6

Livingstone and the Boers:
Chonuane, 1845–1847

The rapidity of Livingstone's move to Chonuane was
understandable, given the state of his relations with
Edwards, but the choice of site could not have been
worse. Sechele had already discovered this but had not
wanted to discourage such potentially useful visitors as
the Livingstones by telling them about his difficulties. Of
course Sechele was no more keen to become a Christian
than the chief of the Bakhatla had been; he merely wanted
a gun mender and technical adviser.

Shortly after his arrival at Chonuane, Livingstone wrote
proudly to friends, telling them that he was now the most
remotely situated missionary in southern Africa, living at a
place which was 'a blank on the map'. His excitement was
nevertheless short-lived. The water supply was bad at the
best of times and for most of the year dried up entirely.
The year 1845 had also seen a severe drought and most
of the corn had been ruined. Sechele had been compelled
to plant crops forty miles away from his village, and
had recently heard that these new plantings had been
wrecked by a herd of buffalo. It was not many months
before Livingstone had to resort to bringing corn from
Kuruman: a humiliating experience since many native
women in Kuruman suggested that Mary had been starved
by her new husband.[1]

Food and water shortages were bad enough in themselves, but the Livingstones also had to foot their removals
bill and pay expenses connected with building a new house,
a chapel and a school. Mrs Livingstone was by now expecting her first child and her husband was £30 in debt: an
unhappy situation for a man earning only £100 a year.
In spite of the hard labour that he had to put in on the
new buildings, Livingstone was determined, in the face of
what seemed to be a hopeless situation, to put a brave
face on it. The Bakwains, he assured Robert Moffat, were
altogether a superior tribe to the Bakhatla and the prospect for conversions was infinitely brighter. Sechele was

in every way a most superior African, with hardly a
barbarous habit to his name. None the less Livingstone
had to admit that Sechele had shown no interest in
Christianity. Other signs were a little better and Livingstone clutched at any causes for optimism, however slight.
Sechele's desire to possess various types of European goods
sent Livingstone into rhapsodies. 'That he is desirous of
civilization I think we may conclude since he sent out
goods with us [on a journey to Kuruman] to purchase a
mattress—4 lanterns—6 candle boxes—a baking pot, a
smoothing iron, a table, & soap.'[2]

Since cleanliness was next to Godliness, in the view of
many missionaries, a desire for it was an excellent indication of better things to come. Its application also had
directly practical results. Since the Bechuanas used grease
in lieu of clothing, ticks, fleas and lice bred on them
prodigiously. Many of these parasites found their way on
to the missionaries as well. Washing with soap would
with luck do much to eliminate this curse.

Sechele had already deserted grease for the sartorial
pleasures of European clothing, and had already managed
to get hold of a few old coats, one of them red. At
Livingstone's request, the Moffats kindly sent up a red cap
to match and some shirts and handkerchiefs. Livingstone
also sent some hartebeest skin to Kuruman, to have it
made up into a suit for the chief. Henry Methuen, an
English traveller, was to see Sechele at about this time,
and his description did not say much for Mrs Moffat's
skills at making up hartebeest suits. Sechele's trousers,
Methuen wrote, were 'too short, his coat too tight, and his
stockings the colour of the soil around. He walked amongst
his admiring subjects with conscious superiority, but,
despite his efforts to conceal it, looked ill at ease in the
tramels of civilized dress.'[3]

Other hunters and traders remarked on Sechele's
bizarre combination of clothes. On one day he was to be
seen in 'moleskin trousers,' a duffel jacket, a wide-awake
hat, and military boots',[4] the next 'in a suit of tiger-skin
clothes made in European fashion'.[5] Nor did he see anything incongruous in wearing an 'immense Mackintosh
overcoat with huge water-boots' on a boiling hot day. Yet,
in spite of the amusement he sometimes afforded, almost
all paid tribute to his good looks, bearing and intelligence.
Livingstone too was well aware of the comic aspects and,

while applauding Sechele's vigorous washing habits, also appreciated their humour.

> You would be amused [he tells a friend] to see his royal highness . . . a king standing up to his knees in water and two persons scrubbing his royal person all over. As a preliminary to his washing his wardrobe himself. It takes a whole day to wash an old red coat and a few other duds the which if sold to a Jew in London would not realise 5/-. His wives too are fond of European clothing.[6]

But Livingstone soon had undeniable cause for rejoicing. Sechele had an astounding aptitude for learning, and incredibly made such progress in learning to read that he 'acquired a perfect knowledge of the alphabet, large small and mixed, in two days'.[7] Within a month he was spelling words of two syllables and asking questions about England. Soon he was compiling his own spelling books and persuading his five wives to read with him. In time three of them became Livingstone's best pupils; but for pure eagerness Sechele knew no rival. It did not take him long to get through all the Moffat translations Livingstone had brought with him, and so he then started to read the same material over again.[8]

Not only did Sechele enjoy reading; he wanted to possess books, and Livingstone was asked to write for 'a Testament of the imitation Russia, a brownish colour' and for selected translations by Moffat. Yet in spite of Sechele's keenness, he did not give up his wives and made no moves to show that he might wish to be converted. He often told Livingstone that he could not understand 'why I should persist, as he says, with tears in my eyes, to entreat his people to believe, seeing they don't want to hear about futurity'. Livingstone's only answer was to 'point to my works and ask if I am a fool'.[9] Sechele also helpfully suggested a more effective way to get converts: 'If you like, I shall call my head men, and with our whips we will soon make them all believe together.'[10]

The offer was rejected. Sechele himself continued in most of his old beliefs, still considering it 'highly meritorious to put all suspected witches to death'. On one occasion he asked Livingstone whether he would be saved if he 'acted justly, fairly avoided fighting, treated both his own people and strangers kindly, killed witches, & prayed to God'.[11] It was a fair question too, since he believed that killing witches was a necessary social duty. Witches could kill people or cause them serious inconvenience, and so they were clearly better out of the way.

Livingstone did, however, secure one early success by persuading Sechele to give up rain-making for a while. It was nevertheless a success which he later regretted for the whole Bakwain tribe blamed Livingstone for the prolonged drought which followed Sechele's decision. In the end Sechele was obliged to make rain again.

Just when Sechele was making such excellent headway with his religious reading, Livingstone's hopes received a severe setback. For twenty years Sechele had ruled over only half the Bakwain tribe. The split had taken place during Sechele's childhood and had come about as a result of his father's murder. After a period of chaos Sechele found himself an exile, and two of the conspirators who had planned his father's murder divided the tribe and became chiefs of the two respective sections: Bubi took one and Molese the other. Eventually in 1829, at the age of nineteen, Sechele managed to oust Molese, but Bubi retained his hold over his part of the tribe. This was still the situation when Livingstone arrived at Chonuane in 1845. In August that year, Sechele sent Bubi a gift of gunpowder. Bubi, suspecting that this unexpected present was enchanted, set about dissolving the charm. The method he chose was to pass hot embers over the gunpowder. The result was an explosion that killed him. After his death many of his subjects went over to Sechele but many stayed with Bubi's successor, Khake. Livingstone managed to dissuade Sechele from attacking Khake till very near the end of 1845. He argued that Sechele might lose a lot of the cattle he had spent so long rearing and might even come off worse in the fight. Besides that, many people might be killed on both sides. Out of respect for Livingstone, Sechele tried diplomacy. This merely led Khake to accuse him of cowardice. Then one day Livingstone saw Sechele's warriors arming for what he was told was an elephant hunt. Towards evening Livingstone emerged from his house to see 'the wounded carried past to the town' and this was 'soon, followed by the sounds of heathenish joy mingled with the loud wailing of those who had lost their friends'.[12] Probably not many more than fifty were killed but that was still a significant loss for a tribe numbering less than four thousand, in all.

Livingstone's prestige suffered greatly, for it was widely known that the chief had ignored his missionary's advice. In the eyes of most of the Bakwains their chief had been right, for by fighting he had united his tribe. Although Sechele remained affable towards Livingstone and went on with his reading, the numbers attending public worship fell off dramatically. Since people had only ever come to hear Livingstone preach because Sechele had told them to, Livingstone was left to draw his own conclusions. Sechele in fact started making rain again soon after his victory over Khake. There were few natives in the village at a given time anyway, for most of them were walking backwards and forwards between their homes and their distant crops and cattle. A mere trickle came to hear Livingstone preach and most of these were women who had been threatened by the man who called them together. His usual method was to yell out that he would knock down any woman failing to come to the meeting place.[13] Those who did hear Livingstone's exhortations delivered 'again and again in the plainest language' were quite indifferent. 'They seem dry bones indeed,' Livingstone wrote despondently.[14]

This repeated failure seemed to point more and more to the necessity for giving native teachers a proper trial. Livingstone had also been stung by a letter from the Directors, sent in December 1845, alluding to his 'former' interest in native agency and suggesting that he should think about it sufficiently to put it into action.[15] This reproach could not have pleased him when he thought of his efforts to get a native seminary started at Kuruman. But it was quite true that, with his two moves and the quarrel with Edwards, he had had little time to think about settling either of his two native teachers with another tribe. Livingstone brought both men from Kuruman to Mabotsa and thence to Chonuane. Of the two, only Mebalwe has already been mentioned; the other was called Paul. Neither had received any real training as Christian teachers but, in view of their white colleagues' lack of success, it is doubtful whether more instruction would have improved their chances. Both men had been among Moffat's early converts. Mebalwe had not only saved Livingstone's life but had since made himself quite invaluable

as a general handyman. Livingstone was therefore very
reluctant to think of settling him with some distant tribe;
instead he decided that Paul ought to begin independent
missionary work first. With this end in view, Paul and
Livingstone set out in July 1846 on the first of two
journeys which together would occupy the best part of
eight months. They did not go without some trepidation,
for a couple of months earlier the commandant of the
Boers settled in the neighbouring Transvaal had sent Livingstone a note informing him that any future missionary
expansion should not take place without prior permission.[16] Livingstone had sent a civil reply telling the commandant that his intentions were entirely innocent and
could only meet with the approval of all good Christians.
The Boers, with their allegiance to the Dutch Reformed
Church, were, after all, nominal Christians. Their church
did not however recognize the equality of black and
white.

The Boers were not primarily worried about missionary
expansion as such. Missionaries had so few successes that
the Boers often used to suggest they would do better trying
to convert baboons.[17] Nevertheless the Transvaal Boers
had other reasons to feel concerned, for they remembered
the days before they had trekked out of the colony; then
the political pressure exerted by the missionaries had
compelled the Cape Government to condemn the Boers'
use of forced labour and their indiscriminate seizure of
native land. In the mid 1840s the Boers saw Livingstone's
plans to introduce native teachers into the Transvaal as a
political rather than a religious move. The native teachers
would report back to Livingstone on the Boers' treatment
of Africans, and Livingstone would then publish the
reports and do his best to force the British Governor at
the Cape to end his policy of *laissez-faire* towards the
Boers beyond the borders of the colony. If Livingstone was
successful, some Boers even believed that Britain might
attempt to incorporate the Transvaal and Orange Sovereignty into the Cape Colony. If that happened there
would be all the old legal difficulties about blacks being
the equals of the whites; there would also be restrictions
placed on the confiscation of native land, and in general a
return to the bad old days.

Since Livingstone knew that making converts was nigh
impossible, even in favourable circumstances, it might

well be asked why he decided to try and settle native
teachers to the east of Chonuane in the Transvaal, adding
Boer opposition to all the usual problems. The Boers
thought the answer was simple: Livingstone was a political
trouble-maker. Livingstone himself saw things differently.
He could not settle native teachers to the west of Chonuane because of the Kalahari Desert; to the north the
Bamangwato were too far away and were in any case an
isolated tribe; to the south the Bakhatla already had a
mission at Mabotsa. The east, Livingstone argued, was the
only option left to him. One further question remains, and
that is how Livingstone could have been naïve enough to
suppose that the tribes in the Transvaal would listen to
native teachers when these same teachers had been
ignored by the residents of Mabotsa and Chonuane. The
truth was that Livingstone was far from confident of
success, but with personal failure as a missionary staring
him in the face, the settlement of native teachers in the
densely populated Transvaal seemed the last positive move
he could make. He comforted himself by thinking that
Paul and Mebalwe would do better on their own, away
from any white missionaries—his idea being that only
when Africans saw native teachers as Christians in their
own right, and not as the puppets of a resident European,
would they make progress.

The two journeys Livingstone made in the second half
of 1846 were not encouraging. He found that between a
hundred and two hundred miles east of Chonuane there
were certainly lots of natives, many more than in Bechuanaland, but the Boers had already started to set tribe
against tribe and had themselves raided tribes, taking vast
numbers of sheep and several hundred captives at a time.
Livingstone concluded that neither Paul nor Mebalwe
would be able to make headway under such circumstances; they might even be killed.

Livingstone soon discovered to his disgust that the captives taken by the Boers on their raids were usually young
children, who then became 'apprentices'. The barest legal
formalities were gone through to declare the children
orphans and once done, the child worked for his master
for nothing for the next twenty years. The younger the
children were when captured, the better. Older ones might
remember their homes and therefore try to run away.
What made this look still more like slavery was the com-

mon practice of exchanging 'orphans' for a transfer fee of about two guineas. The original cost of registering the child as an 'orphan apprentice' on the *landrost* did not come to more than is 6d, so the profits to be made were substantial. As late as 1865 three children could be bought for 'two white blankets',[18] which for about fifty years free labour was not a bad bargain. Livingstone admitted that physical maltreatment of 'apprentices' was not the rule and that many of the emigrants regretted what was going on, but there was still a prevailing feeling that labour was merely in exchange for the natives remaining in the country where they were settled.

The Boers knew very well that the less the Cape Government found out about their system of 'apprenticeship' the better. Therefore they made up their minds to keep Livingstone out. With this end in view they accused him of providing the Bakwains and the Bakhatla with guns and thus creating a dangerous situation on the western border of the Transvaal. When the charge was made public, Livingstone denied it emphatically and wrote to a Cape Town newspaper challenging the Boers to publish their evidence; "if you can prove that I either *lent* or *sold*, or *gave* a gun to Sechele', he told the Boers, 'I shall willingly leave the country.'[19]

The Boers claimed that Livingstone had supplied the Bakwains with five hundred guns and a cannon; a ridiculous exaggeration. But Livingstone was also being less than truthful when he suggested that the Bakwains could not muster more than five guns between them. He himself had supplied them with many more than that as his letters to his father-in-law bear out. As early as February 1846 Livingstone was writing to Robert Moffat telling him that Sechele 'is greatly in love with your rifles'.[20] A month later Moffat was told that a Scottish big-game hunter, Gordon Cumming, had left a 'good deal of powder' under Livingstone's care 'with liberty to assist any of the people with it'.[21] Letters from Livingstone to Moffat in March and November 1848 refer to guns sent from Kuruman to Sechele's people.[22] Livingstone later wrote to Joseph Sturge, a leading Quaker and pacifist, justifying arming Africans and saying that he loved peace so much that he would be quite prepared to fight for it.[23] He was certain that if the Boers knew that the Bakwains were armed they would not come and take captives from Sechele. It was a balance-of-power theory that was later proved mistaken.

By early 1847 Livingstone knew that the Boers would never tolerate any native teachers in the Transvaal; he was therefore thrown back on Chonuane again with no better prospects of success than he had had in 1845. Livingstone now had to face the idea of spending the rest of his life with the Bakwains, making thirty or so converts, if he was lucky. It was not a pleasing prospect for an ambitious man in his early thirties, and Livingstone squirmed and wriggled to try and find a let-out. As in his early days at Kuruman, he once more began to doubt whether he could endure the conventional static missionary life with its scant and ill-recognized rewards. With the settlement of native teachers temporarily out of the reckoning, it was hard to think of any way to exercise his ambitions for working beyond every other man's lines. Gradually he began to persuade himself that the abandonment of a tribe *before* making conversions might be a positive and not a negative step. Could a missionary, he asked himself, be reasonably expected to stay with a single tribe for more than ten years if that tribe showed no interest? Moffat would have pointed out that there would only be progress *after* ten years; but Livingstone preferred to ignore such inconvenient thoughts. He made up his mind that if a decade passed and the Bakwains were still resistant, he would 'move on to the regions beyond'. In ten years he would have told them all he could, so it would be their fault if they did not listen: 'now is their opportunity, and if they do not learn, the guilt will be on their heads'.[24] Having thus easily salved his conscience, Livingstone adapted the old missionary formula of 'sowing seed not to bear fruit in a single lifetime' for his own ends. He suggested that seed could be sown just as effectively in years as it could be in lifetimes. The missionary ought not to waste seed on barren ground but should eventually leave a tribe who consistently refused to listen and move on to another tribe whose people might be more deserving and receptive. These were convenient views to hold for a man who had once wanted to discover the lake to the north and who had found such pleasures in travelling. That this thinking contained a stinging irony, either did not occur to Livingstone or, if it did, did not bother him. His new ideas were tantamount to the suggestion that a missionary who might otherwise fail to convert one tribe in a lifetime, should somehow, by some mysterious process, succeed in converting many tribes by briefly saying his piece and passing on to 'the regions beyond'.

At any rate in 1847, after less than two years with the Bakwains, Livingstone knew that he would have to stay a little longer if he wished to avoid the derision of all his colleagues. Whether Livingstone or Sechele liked it, the Bakwains were to have one last chance; but the continued drought and the drying up of all springs within reach of Chonuane meant that that chance would have to be given somewhere else. Another move had to be made. This time it was to a place called Kolobeng, forty miles to the north-west. The Directors of the London Missionary Society had only just written accepting Livingstone's move to Chonuane. When they heard about the next move, they wrote with weary tolerance: 'We hope we may now regard you as permanently settled, knowing well the disadvantages attending frequent changes of this nature.'[25] They would not have been so polite had they known that Livingstone's thinking was gradually leading him to consider 'permanent settlement' unacceptable.

7

The Only Convert: Kolobeng, 1847–1849

Although Kolobeng had a better water supply than Chonuane, in other ways it was hardly more comfortable or more attractive: perched, as an English hunter later put it, 'in naked deformity on the side of and under a ridge of red ironstone'.[1] There were woods several miles away but most of the surrounding country was as bleak and arid as any in Bechuanaland. Wild animals were numerous but this was no great advantage, for quite often a buffalo or rhinoceros would charge through the new settlement terrifying the women and children.

Moving had become almost second nature to the Livingstones, but it was no less exhausting for all that. In fact, for Mrs Livingstone, now the mother of two children, it was far worse. Robert had been born early in 1846 and Agnes was just three months old when the Liv-

ingstones' waggon rumbled out of Chonuane for the last
time. Mary Livingstone's life had been hard even before
the arrival of children, and she had needed all the skills
her mother had taught her. In addition she had had to
run an infants' school with numbers sometimes rising to
eighty. Native mothers used the school as a child-minding
facility, and of course it was never much more than that.
Mrs Livingstone was hard put to keep order let alone teach
anything. In less than a year after the arrival at Kolobeng,
Mary was pregnant again and so the school had to be
abandoned. Livingstone called her frequent pregnancies
'the great Irish manufactory',[2] a description which probably amused him more than his wife. Another son,
Thomas, was born in March 1849; a daughter, Elizabeth,
who survived only a month, in August 1850; and a further
son, William, in September 1851. To have five children in
six years is an ordeal today, but for Mrs Livingstone,
constantly on the move and always overworked, it was
nearly fatal. Livingstone told Robert Moffat that Mary was
often in pain and usually tired, but that, he remarked com-
placently, 'is hardly to be wondered at, for she has much
work on her hands'.

Mary had other problems too. Her family lived in a
crudely made hut for a year after their arrival at Kolobeng; it took that long for Livingstone to build a stone
house, nor did he find the work easy. Once he nearly
broke his bad arm, when he slipped and found himself
dangling by it from a beam. Then he fell off the roof
while thatching. Next he cut himself badly with an axe;
and all the time he was working, the incessant rays of the
sun split his lips and burned his face so much that it
became cracked and pitted with scabs.[3] And all the while
the small hut they lived in was purgatory: too hot in
summer and painfully cold in winter. Livingstone, even
when being humorous about a very distressing period,
could not disguise the discomfort: 'A year in a hut through
which the wind blew our candles into glorious icicles (as
a poet would say) by night, and in which crowds of flies
continually settled on the eyes of our poor little brats by
day.'[4]

Livingstone never wrote much about the arrival of the
'brats' and usually greeted Mrs Livingstone's deliveries with
a bare record of the date and the intended name of the
child. His parents, if they hoped for more information,

never got it. Livingstone did however make a concession
to his father, when he told the old man that his first
grandchild might have been called Neil 'if it were not such
an ugly name'.[5] Livingstone did grudgingly consent to call
his eldest daughter Agnes after his mother but could not
help adding that it was 'not a pretty name'.[6] As the children grew, their father was still sparing with descriptions,
and so Janet, his sister, wrote begging him to say more
about them. Her reward was one sentence about Robert
'singing at the top of his voice' and Agnes trying to bite his
leg. Livingstone, evidently pleased with such expansiveness,
added a sentence to let his sister know how lucky she was:
'You see I am making an effort to please you.'[7] Usually
when Livingstone wrote anything more about his family, it
was to bemoan their sad state. 'One does not know how
our children may turn out,' he told his parents comfort-
ingly. 'Ours are surrounded by heathenism. It is very difficult to keep them from contact with it.' The children still
managed to treat their spiritual danger lightly. Robert had
seen Livingstone baptize Mrs Livingstone's latest arrival
and promptly 'went out and came in again with some
water on his face and said, "Papa, I have baptised
myself"!'[8]

The Livingstone children had few toys, and those they
did have came from the Livingstone seniors in Scotland.
Since Neil Livingstone now earned rather less than he had
done when his son had been in England, the flow of toys
was like the Kolobeng river: erratic. A lack of toys was
not all the children had to put up with. Often they cried
with hunger and on one occasion, when all the corn failed,
Mary had to take them three hundred miles south to Kuruman. After their departure Livingstone dug up some tiny
potatoes and ate them. When he had enjoyed these tiny
vegetables, which he had previously described as being the
size of marbles, he regretted not digging them up before
the children had left. 'They would have enjoyed them so
much.'[9] The Livingstone diet was at the best of times
bizarre; often the whole family would sit down to a feast
of locusts, which, Livingstone assured friends in England,
were not unlike shrimps and excellent with wild honey. The
Baptist's food, he added, maintained a delicate alimentary
balance: 'the former is excessively constipating, and the
latter has quite the opposite tendency'.[10] The children
particularly relished a species of caterpillar and a large

frog called *matlametlo*. Livingstone enjoyed the frog too
and thought it looked and tasted just like chicken. Diet
was not all that marked off the Livingstone children from
their contemporaries in Britain. They grew up bilingual,
and, to their father's alarm, their Sichuana was soon better
than their English.

When the outer walls of the house had been built and
the roof was at last in place, Livingstone started to think
of possible improvements. He placed antlers on the walls
and rather shamefacedly ordered a sofa from Cape Town.
Mrs Livingstone was soon proudly playing her part in
making the house habitable. To outsiders her methods
might have seemed strange, especially when she came to
clean the floor. Her proceedings were the same her mother
had boasted about twenty years before. 'We all smear all
our rooms with cow dung once a week at least . . . It lays
the dust better than anything, kills the fleas which would
otherwise breed abundantly, and is a fine clear green.'[11]
The fleas often made Livingstone wish that he had a bath
and he wrote to his sisters asking if they knew of any
way whereby one might be sent from Scotland in pieces,
to be soldered up on arrival. But no bath ever arrived and
perhaps it was just as well for they would have felt guilty
about wasting valuable water. The last improvements
Livingstone made for the house were the doors and
window frames. Strangely, he left the outside door to the
very end. Before it was in place Mrs Livingstone showed
she was equal to any emergency, as her husband recorded:
'A big wolf came . . . & took away a buffalo's skin from
the door. Mary wanted me to go and see whether the
room door were fastened, but . . . I advised her to take a
fork in her hand and go herself, as I was too comfortably
situated to go myself.'[12]

Mary's tasks were all-embracing. At Chonuane she had
learned something of dentistry, and Livingstone amusingly
described her successful efforts at pulling out one of his
teeth with a pair of 'shoemaker's nippers'.

> Every pull was like a haul at my entrails . . . Another
> wrench and I roared out 'murder'. It came a little
> farther, but was still sticking doggedly. Another trial
> of the nippers, forceps, &c. . . . completed the first
> attempt at dentistry. We were a pretty sight in our
> ghostly dresses, I on the floor & Mary standing over

me. It was dreadful. 'Teeth drawn at Chonuane 1/- each.' Mouth rinsed out afterwards with dirty water *gratis*.[13]

The Livingstones usually got up at dawn, had family prayers, breakfast and then school for anybody prepared to come. The rest of the morning Livingstone devoted to manual work—sawing, ploughing, smithy work and anything else that needed doing. Mary would spend her morning cooking, sewing and looking after the children. Lunch would be followed by a short rest, and after that Mary went to her infants' school and Livingstone went on with his manual tasks till about five o'clock. After that he generally went into the town to talk to anybody who felt like it, milked the cows, and finally went to the chief's house to pray and give him special instruction. He would arrive home at 8.30, worn out. In letters to friends be bemoaned the fact that so much of his day was given to agriculture and so little to real missionary work. 'As I write now my hands have the same aching sensation I had when spinning. My mind is often so exhausted by sympathy with the body I cannot write in the evenings, and this is the only time I have.'[14]

The help given by a native couple made matters a little better, but not much. Livingstone's ten cows were quite inadequate to give them milk all the year round, and even when seven were simultaneously in milk, he claimed they produced no more than one would back in Scotland. The reason was that grazing was bad because of the same drought that had afflicted them at Chonuane. The situation was so serious that trees started to die and the corn failed completely. Potatoes withered and so did all the other vegetables. Worse still the Kolobeng river had 'dwindled down to a dribbling rill' and was therefore useless for irrigation. A year later it had dried up altogether, and in the meantime the fish had started to die and 'the hyenas from the whole country round collected to the feast, and were unable to finish the putrid masses'.[15] Livingstone measured the temperature three inches under the soil and found that it was 132° at midday. Less than two inches of rain had fallen in two years. An increasing number of people believed that Livingstone's presence was responsible. Sechele kept the Livingstone family going by sending them what food he could spare. Livingstone got used to the drought, the fleas, the chirr of the crickets, the endless zebra meat that Sechele sent, and he even became hardened to his children's emaciated faces. But he could never get used to the Bakwains' indifference to the gospel. Every evening he wrote in his journal, and to keep his spirits up tried every form of self-deception. 'It seems very unfair,' he wrote, 'to judge of the success of these [missions] by the number of conversions which have followed.' That was how he had judged Moffat, but now it was another story. Conversions themselves were not what really mattered, Livingstone went on; the real significance of missionary work lay in the fact that missionaries 'are diffusing a knowledge of Christianity throughout the world'. Livingstone concluded the passage almost in a pleading tone: 'No mission which has His approbation is entirely unsuccessful. His purposes have been fulfilled if we have been faithful.'[16]

At other times Livingstone was anything but sure that remaining faithful was enough; on those occasions he comforted himself with reading about failures in the Bible. Noah and Isaiah, he was thankful to record, had both considered their achievements negligible, so too had Jeremiah and Ezekiel. Paul had spoken the truth when he had written: 'All seek their own, not the things of Jesus Christ.' But in the end no comparisons or comforting arguments helped Livingstone in his unhappiness. Yet strangely, at this very moment when almost the whole Bakwain tribe were showing complete indifference, Sechele, their chief, sent his brother to see Livingstone with the request that Livingstone should establish an evening prayer-meeting in Sechele's house for the whole of the chief's family. Livingstone could hardly believe it when Sechele told him that he 'knew he was living in sin, but though he had not given up those with whom he sinned [his wives], he wished to pray in his family'.[17] The chief's conversion now seemed a distinct possiblity and Livingstone watched him eagerly for signs. Glistening eyes were, he felt sure, excellent external evidence of a change of heart; and, as Livingstone told Moffat, Sechele's eyes had often glistened after his request for an evening prayer-meeting.

But glistening eyes did not remove Sechele's problems. A Bechuana chief who opposed his people's wishes ran a real danger of deposition, and Sechele, who had endured a childhood and adolescence in exile, knew what that meant.

He was well aware that all his headmen and advisers hated the idea of Christianity. Under normal circumstances polygamy presented any chief wishing to be a Christian with impossible problems, but for Sechele they were worse than usual. Two of his five wives were the daughters of under-chiefs who had been directly responsible for rein-stating him after his exile. Rejection of these wives would therefore make enemies of several of the leading families in the tribe. This dilemma led Sechele to ask Livingstone whether it might not be a good idea for him to go to England for a period of several years, ostensibly to study but really to give his wives a chance to forget him and remarry. Livingstone saw the sense in this suggestion, but knew that it would be too expensive to be practicable.[18] In fact he sympathized deeply with Sechele and considered his superfluous wives to be his best pupils. More perplexing still was the thought that if Sechele rejected them, he would be left with his principal wife, who was one of the tribe's most staunch opponents of Christianity. Livingstone described her as 'about the most unlikely subject in the tribe ever to become anything else than an out-and-out greasy disciple of the old school'. Sechele was frequently compelled to ask her to leave prayer-meetings because she had come without a gown and was therefore indecently dressed. Then, Livingstone observed, 'away she would go with her lips shot out, the very picture of unutterable disgust'.[19]

Livingstone had never been certain whether missionaries could condemn a custom that was socially approved by the tribal society, and was now even less sure what course Sechele should follow. He was even doubtful whether he ought to refuse Sechele baptism if the chief asked to be baptized before he had disowned his wives. In August 1848 Sechele came and asked for advice. Livingstone did not feel able to give it and merely pushed the responsibility back on to the chief by telling him to look in the Bible for guidance. When Livingstone learned that Sechele had decided on rejection, he told the chief to treat his wives gently 'for they had sinned in ignorance'. Sechele announced his intention to become a Christian and give up his wives on Monday, 7 August 1848. It was not, as Livingstone confessed in his journal, a happy day.

Great commotion in the town. All seemed to be in
perplexity. Complete cessation of work. Women all
remained at home, although on every other lawful
day they are seen going to the gardens in crowds.
The men seemed downcast and dismayed. A large
meeting in the khotla [meeting place]. Many spoke
fiercely, so much so as to surprise the chief himself.
Next morning he resolved to call the people together
generally to explain his conduct, and say if they
wished to kill him to do so immediately.

Sechele's bravery must remove all doubts about the
genuineness of his conversion. What had tilted the balance
for him in favour of Christianity will never be known, but
in view of the danger and inconvenience he caused himself, to say nothing of the suffering inflicted on his wives,
it was little short of miraculous that he decided to take the
plunge. Livingstone, without doubt feeling guilty about the
rejected wives, went to see them all to try and soften the
blow. He started with Makhari. 'Poor thing, she was
melted in tears, could not speak but with a choking voice.
Offered me back her book, "as she must now go where
there is no word of God". Wished that they could have
remained in the town that they too might be saved, but
Makhari has no relations. She was much loved and worthy
of it.'[20]

His meeting with Mokokon was equally distressing and
she told him, 'while the tears chased each other down her
cheeks . . . she could not leave us and her child'. The other
two wives showed their grief with violent anger.

On 10 August Makhari left, leaving her Bible behind.
That night a large *picho* (meeting) was held to intimi-
date Sechele and it was proposed that he should at least
allow his wives to remain in their old homes. He com-
promised and allowed them all the possessions from their
former homes and gave them new clothing, but they were
still to go to their parents or families. Mokokon stayed at
Kolobeng because she had no parents to go to.

Throughout September the opposition to Sechele's
impending baptism went on unabated. Livingstone shared
this unpopularity. Many suggested that it was a pity the
lion had not killed him at Mabotsa; but the main onslaught
was aimed at the chief who had to endure 'very bitter
curses' that would formerly have been punished by

death.[21] Hostility increased as the day of the baptism grew closer and in the end what ought to have been the most joyful and triumphant day in Livingstone's missionary life, turned out to be an ordeal. Two religious ladies in Birmingham had sent out two chairs for Sechele and these were used in the ceremony. So too was a long cloak that had been ordered from Scotland. But the details of the ceremony paled before the large crowd of spectators, most of them in tears. Afterwards Livingstone tried to find humour in what had been at the time a depressing experience. 'The old stereotyped case-hardened characters were weeping to see him "so far left to himself"—After the meeting we heard of an old man wiping off the stream from his cheek saying—"this beats the putting away of wives hollow" "What shall we do?" Another old gentleman said to me "You might have delayed till we got rain." '[22]

The belief that Sechele had become the white man's creature was common and the rumour, or, as Livingstone put it, the 'satanic suggestion', was widespread that baptism meant 'being caused to drink men's brains'.[23]

Three months after his baptism, Sechele was still standing up to his people's taunts and appeared to be making good progress. To Livingstone's delight he began learning English. He had already been introduced to English books in translation when Moffat had sent his Sichuana version of *The Pilgrim's Progress*. Sechele had enjoyed it, for, as Livingstone noted, 'some parts of the Pilgrim's experience and his are exactly alike, and make him extol the wisdom of Johane Bunyana'.[24] His interest in European merchandise also continued, and a jug, representing the Duke of Wellington's head, became one of his most precious possessions. It was not till five months after the baptism that Livingstone noticed that Mokokon, Sechele's rejected wife who had been allowed to remain, was showing symptoms that looked unpleasantly like pregnancy. Livingstone made a terse note in his journal for 7 March 1849: 'Symptoms of pregnancy discovered in Mokokon. Enquired of Sechele. Confessed he had been twice with her . . . about the beginning of January 1849.'[25]

The blow to Livingstone was devastating. Sechele made no excuses and gave him an honest account of what had happened. Writing to Moffat, Livingstone admitted how deeply hurt he was. 'The confession loosened all my bones.

I felt as if I should sink to the earth or run away . . . no one except yourselves can imagine the lancinating pangs. They fell on the soul like drops of aqua fortis on an ulcerated surface.' Sechele said he was deeply sorry and asked how he could obtain forgiveness. Although Livingstone cut him off from fellowship, the congregationalist's name for church membership, he could not help acknowledging that Sechele's lapse 'had required no effort such as going to another man's wife . . . He had become so accustomed to their customs it was like his ordinary food.'[26] Sechele's fall from grace was not the only one at this time. Livingstone had always looked on the families of Paul and Mebalwe as irreproachable. Now he discovered that one of Paul's sons, Isak, had been regularly committing adultery and had got another man's wife pregnant. Paul had hidden this from Livingstone and Mebalwe, who had also known, had remained equally silent. Livingstone subsequently found out that many of the Bakwains had shared Isak's guilty secret and had laughed at the missionary not to have guessed. Livingstone sent Sechele a note: 'My heart is broken. First Isak, then you. I can no longer be a teacher here.'[27]

Livingstone's attempt to make Sechele believe that the lapses were entirely responsible for his determination to leave the Bakwains, was convenient rather than truthful. Livingstone's first mention of plans not to stay with the tribe for longer than a given period had been made at Chonuane two years before, in March 1847. Later in that same year he had written to Robert Moffat suggesting that the two of them should attempt a journey to the unknown lake to the north. This plan had fallen through, partly through lack of funds and partly through Moffat's determination to press on with his translation of the Bible. Nevertheless Livingstone was not beaten; in June 1845, while still at Mabotsa, he had met an English hunter and traveller, William Cotton Oswell: a man with a bent for exploring and money to indulge it. So late in 1847 Livingstone wrote to Oswell in an attempt to persuade him to come to the lake. At first there had been no response because Oswell had been in England and India during 1847 and 1848; but in early 1849, the time of Sechele's lapse, Livingstone received a letter from Oswell saying that he and a companion, Mungo Murray, would arrive at Kolo-

beng at the end of May that year, and that the three of
them would then attempt to reach the lake.

Nevertheless Livingstone's determination to reach the
lake—called Ngami by the natives—was a symptom rather
than a direct cause of his now clearly formed conviction
that he would very soon end his stay with the Bakwains,
and with it his own static missionary life. The question
still remains as to precisely what stage Livingstone's ideas
and plans for the future were at in the middle of 1849.

In 1847 he had been toying with the idea of itinerant
missionaries 'diffusing a knowledge of Christianity'. But,
as I have already suggested, the vagueness of the terms
emphasized rather than disguised the fact that Livingstone
was looking for some comforting formula to help him
through a difficult and depressing period. In the same way,
when Livingstone wrote to the Directors of the London
Missionary Society in May 1849, on the eve of his departure for Ngami, his suggestions for a new kind of missionary work were uneasy and confused. He explained the
difficulties he had been having with the drought and argued
that, since the Boers had prevented him settling native
teachers to the east, the only direction for future expansion
was the north. He briefly mentioned Sechele's lapse but
gave it no weight. Instead he suggested that the real reason for a series of journeys to the north was the fact that
the Bakwains would not be persuaded to believe 'precipi-
tously' and that in the meantime thousands of precious
souls to the north were perishing. 'It is therefore,' Livingstone went on, 'imperatively necessary to endeavour to
extend the *gospel to all* the surrounding tribes. This . . . is
the only way which permits the rational hope that when
people do turn to the Lord it will be by groups.'[28] The
hope was anything but rational and was based on wilful
self-deception. There was no evidence at all to support
the belief that occasional visits to distant tribes would
make them 'turn to the Lord by groups'. Flying visits
could never be more successful than long years with a single tribe. Livingstone was inventing excuses partly to
deceive himself and partly to fool the Directors into thinking that he had hit on a viable new missionary policy.
His allusion to the 'perishing thousands' fitted in nicely
with his previous complaints about the size of Bechuanaland's population, but it was also a blind, for he had
already suggested that the *diffusion* of a knowledge of

Christianity was almost as valuable as conversion itself. Having thus relegated conversion to a position of reduced importance, he could hardly logically claim to be so alarmed about the spiritual future of the unconverted, or reasonably suggest that thousands were perishing. This argument led him into other contradictions for he had moved away from strict Calvinism in his late teens and early twenties, and when he shortly came to write about his initial missionary impulse, he was to ascribe it to a desire to work for the 'alleviation of human misery', rather than to any longing to save perishing souls.[29] In fact, when he set out for Lake Ngami in June 1849, Livingstone was thankful for a long journey in which to try and clarify his thoughts.

The contradictions I have pointed out are certainly glaring, but it would be wrong not to acknowledge that Livingstone was less certain than his colleagues about the ideal form of missionary work, because, ironically, he possessed a far greater insight into the basic causes of tribal rejection of Christianity. Unlike his colleagues he had understood the role of the *boguera* or initiation rites; unlike them he had not been happy about voicing an outright condemnation of polygamy. He had never considered tribal marriage to be 'bride-buying'. This more liberal approach laid him open to problems unguessed at by the type of missionary who automatically castigated every native custom and belief. Livingstone often repeated the phrase 'Jesus came not to judge', and insisted that missionaries ought 'to follow His example, neither insist upon their rights'. Yet unless the missionary did judge and condemn, his own position became untenable, for his very presence implied a criticism——he had a message for the 'benighted', to tell them about the one true faith in Jesus Christ. In addition that faith was antithetical to almost every tribal custom and belief.

Livingstone realized this and cast about for a way out of the impasse: a method of changing tribal society without compulsion. He came to believe that if only he could make the Bechuanas understand the technological superiority of Europeans, he might be able to persuade them that a change in their own society would be to their advantage. He tried to explain the benefits of wider trade and better communications and to convince them that selling skins and ivory to Europeans and to distant tribes would bring them greater wealth, and in the end enable them to increase their range of production. He soon realized that it was easier to have the idea than to explain it.

> It is extremely difficult to explain to the people of this country the use of money or machinery, or of any of the sciences as sources of pure intellectual pleasure. If they can count as many as serve in all their simple transactions, which can almost always be effected on the fingers, what need is there for the rules of proportion &c.? The art of writing is very curious, but of what use is it to those who can send all their messages viva voce and who have all their family and connections within five minutes walk of their own residence, and will have so little news to communicate.[31]

When Livingstone tried to explain the workings of steam-engines and cotton mills, he was met with blank incomprehension. People who had never even seen two-storey houses were not going to be taken in by far-fetched stories about things called steamships and trains. The unpleasant truth soon became apparent to Livingstone that the natives were content with what they had and were not going to put themselves out to facilitate changes they thought unnecessary. They obtained guns, beads and brass wire from missionaries and traders, and that was quite good enough. As Livingstone observed, 'As there is no pressing necessity apparent to those whose wants are few, they take the world easy.'[32]

So Livingstone's dilemma grew worse. While the natives were satisfied with their existing society and contrived to survive and be happy, it was hard to claim that occasional tribal war and regrettable customs like witchcraft and infanticide gave anybody the right to contemplate under-mining the whole system. Livingstone even had moments when he doubted whether natives derived any benefit from contact with Europeans. While maintaining that mission-aries could do good, he criticized the Cape Government and the Boers for their treatment of Africans. 'If natives are not elevated by contact with Europeans,' he wrote, 'they are sure to be deteriorated. It is with pain I have observed that all the tribes I have seen lately* are under-

---

* He was referring particularly to the tribes in the Transvaal.

going the latter process.'[33] This was an especially unwelcome observation for Livingstone to have to make, given his feeling that only with a greater knowledge of European economics and customs were the natives likely to take more kindly to Christianity. In fact Livingstone's conclusions had forced him into a position in which the logical response would have been an argument in favour of leaving the Africans to their own devices. This, however, was a course he found quite unacceptable, for, believing that he had a mission to spread Christianity, he could not allow himself to be dissuaded by mundane facts and apparently insuperable problems. His own Christian faith was of supreme importance to him and he wanted others to be able to share it. In 1849 he was uncertain how it could be done, but he knew that he must go on trying.

In the meantime, if a journey to the unknown lake did not solve anything, it might provide him with hints for a new approach. He would also be able to review his situation and his ideas away from the depressing indifference of the Bakwains.

PART TWO

Achievement

8

North to the Zambesi, 1849–1851

Between 1849 and 1851 Livingstone made three long journeys north of Kolobeng, and these, especially the third,
irrevocably altered the direction of his life and gave a
definite form to his so far incoherent ideas. Between June
and October 1849, he travelled over three hundred miles
north-west of Kolobeng to Lake Ngami in the extreme
north of modern "Btoswana—formerly Bechuanaland. His
second trip, also to Ngami, took place between April and
August 1850 and achieved no more than the first. On the
third crucial journey, Livingstone reached the upper Zambesi, almost exactly in the middle of south-central Africa,
in the area of the Barotse valley. This was two hundred
miles north-east of Ngami and at a place where the modern Caprivi Strip—part of South West Africa—divides the
northern boundary of Botswana from the south-western
border of Zambia.

Before describing these journeys, it is important, in
view of Livingstone's reputation for being the first European to penetrate south-central Africa, to record what, if
anything, was already known about the area he was to
visit. Lake Ngami itself had often been visited by natives
from the south, but Livingstone's journey of 1849 is the
first recorded visit by any European. Two attempts had
been made in the 1830s, and on both occasions the Kalahari Desert had defeated the explorers. Ngami however
was a minor affair compared with Livingstone's arrival on
the upper Zambesi in 1851, and there he had definitely
been anticipated by other Europeans—the Portuguese.

The Portuguese colonies of Angola on the west African
coast and Moçambique on the eastern side of the continent
had been established during the sixteenth century and
were, of course, well known to Livingstone and his contemporaries. Nevertheless the extent to which individual
Portuguese explorers had penetrated the interior was far

less widely appreciated. Their efforts inland from Moçambique were better known than similar attempts made from Angola. While, for instance, it was known that Lacerda in 1798 had travelled six hundred miles north-west to Tete in Moçambique to Lake Moero, very close to the southern end of the then unknown Lake Tanganyika, it was almost entirely unknown in Britain that Rodrigues Graça in 1846 had reached south-western Katanga from Angola. While Graça's journey had been north of the area Livingstone was to reach in 1851, another Portuguese trader, Silva Porto, had reached the upper Zambesi, between 1847 and 1848, at almost the very spot where Livingstone first saw that river. Therefore Livingstone's generally accepted claim that the Portuguese never imagined the Zambesi to flow from so far to the west was false. When Livingstone later met Porto and other Portuguese traders on the upper Zambesi in 1853, he would inaccurately pronounce them Portuguese half-castes in order to defend his position as the only true European to have been in the area. By the late 1840s the Portuguese knew that the large river Porto had reached from Angola was without doubt the upper reaches of the Zambesi they knew in Moçambique. For three hundred years the Portuguese had possessed detailed knowledge of the Zambesi up to six hundred miles inland from the east coast. They had merely never filled in the 400-mile gap between Porto's discoveries and their furthest progress up the river from Moçambique.

The Portuguese, while being the only Europeans to precede Livingstone, were not however alone in their prior penetration of south-central Africa. During the first decade of the nineteenth century, two native traders had travelled from Angola to Tete in Moçambique. Since the only records of these journeys were to be found in Portuguese periodicals and archives, the general public in Britain and other European countries outside Portugal knew nothing of them. British geographers who did read the relevant papers were often sceptical because the journeys had been so badly documented. But, as will be seen, they had other reasons also for acclaiming Livingstone as the only European to have made important discoveries in south-central Africa.

Livingstone, on his £100 a year salary, would never have been able to make his three journeys between 1849 and 1851 had it not been for the generosity of William

Cotton Oswell, who accompanied him on the first and third trips. At first sight it would seem most improbable that a man with Livingstone's vocation and background should have taken to somebody from the upper class, whose life had been mainly taken up with pig-sticking, boxing, racquets and cricket. Educated at Rugby and Haileybury, Oswell had entered the Indian Civil Service, but had retired after ten years for a life of leisure and the delights of African travel and big-game hunting. Oswell, however, was no mindless young man with a private fortune and little else. He was exceptionally generous, modest and completely lacking in personal ambition. These last two qualities provide the key to the success of his relationship with Livingstone, who had already proved himself incapable of suffering any European whose views conflicted with his own. Livingstone liked to get his full measure of praise for what he did, and Oswell conveniently never saw fit to press his own claims. Oswell's companion, Mungo Murray, who also came on the 1849 journey to Lake Ngami, was a man of similar character, who preferred doing things to talking about them afterwards.

The importance of Oswell's contribution to the first trip to Ngami can be gauged from the fact that he brought to Kolobeng, for the journey, twenty horses, eighty oxen, two waggons and enough supplies to keep three Europeans and eight Africans in gunpowder, bullets, tea, coffee and sugar for a year. The party that left Kolobeng for Ngami on 1 June 1849 was a large one, for it included not only Oswell, Livingstone and Murray, with their dozen African drivers and attendants but also thirty Bakwains sent by Sechele to bring back any ivory they might find near the lake. J. H. Wilson, a trader centred on Kuruman, had asked to come too and had been accepted as one of the party. Wilson, like Sechele, wanted to get his hands on some of the copious stocks of ivory supposed to exist in Ngamiland.

Previous travellers had failed to reach Ngami because of the Kalahari Desert, which started to the west of Kolobeng and extended two hundred miles to the north. These early expeditions had, however, been made at the wrong time of year, for the Kalahari is not a desert in the strict sense of the word, because during the rainy season water is retained in the sun-baked hollows and does not dry up till several months afterwards. At this time water-melons

and red cucumbers are an added source of moisture. The
Bushmen managed to find waterholes and extract enough
liquid to survive by sucking it up from under the ground
with the help of long hollow reeds; some antelopes, notably
the eland, lived there too without apparent ill-effects. But
all this said, the Kalahari was a nightmarish place to cross,
even at its outermost extremities, and the oxen which
drew the party's waggons on several occasions had to
travel seventy miles without water, a distance that could
take three days or more, in areas where the soft sand
bogged down the axles. When the oxen seemed in danger
of dying there was no alternative but to send them back
as much as twenty miles to the last wells, leaving the waggons where they were till the beasts returned refreshed.

There were other problems besides water shortage. On
a flat plain, which stretched as far as the eye could see,
and where the only landmarks were occasional stunted
trees or bushes, it was easy to alter course without noticing
it. Even Bushmen guides often lost the track they were
attempting to follow. Throughout their time in the Kalahari the travellers were deceived by mirages caused by
large dried-out pools covered with a thick salt deposit.
The heat was so intense that the oxen could only travel
in the evening and very early morning.

Five weeks after leaving Kolobeng, they reached the
river Zouga and enthused about the large trees and thick
vegetation on its banks. The Zouga was flowing from a
west-north-westerly direction and the travellers had no
doubt but that its source lay in Lake Ngami. Their sole
remaining task was to trace it there. This was to prove a
straight-forward journey of three hundred miles. Before
they arrived at the lake, they discovered that another river
flowed into the Zouga from the north.* Livingstone was
now firmly convinced that the area to the north of the
Zouga would contain a major river network. In his view
this completely eclipsed the impending discovery of the
lake itself. So when Livingstone stood on the shores of
Ngami he was unimpressed and made no plans to walk
round it or to ask the natives more than a few questions
about its depth and extent. It was in fact shallow and,
including the surrounding marshes, was about seventy
miles long. While Oswell made detailed enquiries, Living-

* The Thamalakane, a tributary of the Okavango.

stone, still in a state of great excitement, thought about the river system to the north. He had not read about Graça or Porto and therefore genuinely believed he had hit on important new information on the nature of south-central Africa. Never having read any Portuguese periodicals, nor having met any well-informed British geographers, Livingstone was sure that he was on the verge of proving that central Africa was a well-watered, fertile land instead of being, as popular fancy had it, a desert as large as the Sahara.

So while Livingstone ignored Ngami he asked a great many questions about the area to the north, and the answers confirmed what he already firmly believed. He therefore decided to set out at once for the area to the north-east. Unfortunately the Zouga had to be crossed first, and the chief of the principal tribe round Ngami gave orders that the white men should not cross. The chief knew the direction Livingstone was planning to go in and knew that if the white man went about two hundred miles north-east, he would reach Sebitoane, chief of the far from pacific Makololo. The chief of the Ngami people not only feared an attack by Sebitoane but also believed that the white men would make matters worse by selling guns to the Makololo. Livingstone and Oswell tried to argue, but in vain—no canoes were forthcoming. Livingstone started to build a raft but the wood was too heavy and sank by its own weight. He then tried a lighter wood but this turned out to be wormeaten and absorbed the water like a sponge. The river at this point was about fifty yards across. 'I could easily have swam across, and fain would have done it, but landing stark naked and bullying the Bakoba for the loan of a boat would scarcely be the thing for a messenger of peace, even though no alligator met me in the passage.'[1]

So when Oswell offered to return to the Cape and bring up a collapsible boat on his next trip in slightly under a year's time, Livingstone agreed to give up for the present. Their journey to date had taken much longer than Livingstone had anticipated and he was worried about his wife and children, who had gone to stay with his father-in-law at Kuruman but would soon be returning to Kolobeng.

The return journey was uneventful and Kolobeng was reached on 9 October. Livingstone lost no time in sitting down to write letters to the Directors of the London Missionary Society, his parents and Robert Moffat, informing them of his discovery. Before leaving he had told his brother Charles that Oswell might well get the credit for the journey, and now after his return Livingstone vigorously set about stating that although the finance had been Oswell's, the motive power behind the whole trip had been his original suggestion. Livingstone warned his parents that 'others less closely connected may be more highly favoured', and suggested that Oswell and Murray 'could never have reached this point without my assistance'. But Livingstone felt that the people he really had to impress were the Directors of the London Missionary Society; he had not asked their permission to leave his post at Kolobeng and was uncertain what their reaction would be. Livingstone decided the best approach was to play down the purely exploratory goal of reaching Lake Ngami and concentrate on the river system to the north, the revelation of which, in any case, he considered the most important result of his journey. This network of rivers he went on: '. . . opens out the prospect of a highway capable of being quickly traversed by boats to a large section of well-peopled territory . . . I do not wish to convey hopes of speedily effecting any great works through my poor instrumentality. I hope to be permitted to work as long as I live beyond other men's line of things and plant the seed of the gospel where others have not planted.'[2]

Working beyond everybody else and disseminating the word in some general and unspecified way were old ideas. What was new in Livingstone's thinking was the idea of using rivers as *highways* to open up the continent. Once this notion had gripped Livingstone's imagination, he would never get free of it. Rivers would bring him spectacular success and bitter failure.

In fact Livingstone need not have worried greatly about the attitude of the Directors. Arthur Tidman, the Foreign Secretary of the Society, realized at once that if the discovery of Ngami was given publicity it would encourage public generosity. He published Livingstone's account of the discovery in the March 1850 edition of the *Missionary Magazine*, and when the Royal Geographical Society decided to award Livingstone one half of the year's Royal Premium—the far from regal sum of £25—Tidman went along to collect it on behalf of the intrepid Dr Livingstone. The prize would be good for quite a few donations to the missionary cause. The Royal Geographical Society had also seen the advantage of publicizing the discovery of the lake. Founded in 1830, this body had been incompetently run for some years by a group of naval officers and was only just becoming what it had been intended to be: a society for the promotion of geographical discovery and for providing those interested in geography with published accounts of new discoveries. In recent years the Royal Geographical Society's financial fortunes had been so bad, that, to the horror of many members, the Board had decided to allow women to attend some lectures and had started organizing social entertainments to attract more members. The Society's new president, the well-known geologist Sir Roderick Murchison, knew, like Tidman, that subscriptions to any sort of society were the result of advantageous publicity. Making the work of individual explorers as widely known as possible was therefore one of Murchison's policies. Tidman, for his own financial reasons, had no objection to Sir Roderick publicizing Dr Livingstone's work, although the Directors of the London Missionary Society had no intention of starting new and costly ventures in central Africa. They were, in spite of all their talk of success, none too impressed by the state of the mission stations in Bechuanaland.* But if Livingstone wanted to go off travelling they were prepared to let him, especially since he had found a rich man to pay for most of it.

In spite of Livingstone's fears that Oswell might get all the credit, neither Oswell nor Murray wrote home for some months after reaching Ngami and in the meantime Livingstone gained most of the recognition. He alone caught Murchison's eye. Livingstone would remain unaware of this eminent man's interest until seven years later, when Murchison intervened decisively in the missionary explorer's life. By that time, under Murchison's guidance, the R.G.S. had become an influential body, with close links with the Government and the Admiralty developed for the one purpose of sponsoring specific exploratory expeditions.

From the moment Livingstone had returned to Kolobeng from his first journey to Ngami, his only thoughts

---

* In late 1849 and early 1850 J. V. Freeman, a Director of the L.M.S., visited Bechuanaland and was dismayed by the lack of missionary progress.

were to get back to examine the country further north. The hottest season of the year was upon him, however, and he knew that it would be madness to attempt a crossing of the Kalahari till the spring of the following year, 1850. The results of this second journey north were nil, and this was because Livingstone in the first place decided not to wait for Oswell to join him, and in the second decided to travel with his family. This trip between April and August 1850 is interesting only because it sheds light on Livingstone's character.

The reason why Livingstone decided not to wait for Oswell is simple: he could not bear the thought of anybody else getting the credit for penetrating further north than Ngami—he was not yet aware of the complete success of his attempt to gain all the praise for the first journey. Livingstone later tried to excuse his behaviour in leaving Kolobeng before Oswell got there by saying that there had never been any prior arrangement between them. He told his father-in-law, Moffat, that Oswell had asked to come but that he had refused to let him.[3] This was clearly a lie, since when Oswell did reach Kolobeng, shortly after the Livingstones had left, he brought the promised boat with him. He would hardly have gone to the trouble if there had been no previous agreement. Besides Livingstone had recently accepted £40 from Oswell to defray expenses. Not only does Livingstone's action look like ingratitude, it also appears to have been extremely foolish. He must have realized that, if the recalcitrant chief at Ngami did not change his mind about a crossing of the Zouga, no further progress would be possible without Oswell's boat.

If Livingstone's behavior towards Oswell is confusing, his attitude to his family is many more times extraordinary. For a start the children were very young: Robert was four, Agnes three, and Thomas only one. Apart from that, in April 1850, Mrs. Livingstone was five months pregnant, and it could not have taxed her husband's medical knowledge to work out that she would probably give birth on the journey home, probably in the desert. Mrs Livingstone was used to Africa and had a strong constitution but, even so, Oswell's description of Livingstone's decision to take her as 'rather unwise' was a remarkably charitable understatement.

The Livingstones managed to get to the Zouga without

mishap, but there for the first time Livingstone encountered the tsetse fly. As soon as the oxen had been bitten, they began to sicken and die. The tsetse were unknown south of the Kalahari but had long been known to the natives of central and eastern Africa as a menace which made long journeys with animals a hazardous business. But Livingstone soon gained experience of a far more serious problem. Earlier travellers, such as Park and Lander, had suffered a great deal from 'fever' during their travels in west Africa near the Niger. Livingstone had read about malaria in medical periodicals and therefore knew that quinine was then the only effective remedy. Mercifully he had had the foresight to bring some with him in 1850, for within days of their arrival at Ngami, his children had contracted fever. Livingstone's attitude to their suffering was remarkably clinical. 'It is an interesting fever,' he told Robert Moffat. 'I should like to have a hospital here to study it. In Morukanelo [a native driver] it was continued fever. Thomas had it in the remittent form, & Agnes in the intermittent. In some it was simple bilious fever. In others it chiefly affected the vascular system of the abdomen . . . The source is no doubt marshy miasmata.'[4]*

This apparently detached observation must have amazed Robert Moffat, nor, in view of his daughter's advanced state of pregnancy, could he have been amused by Livingstone's light-hearted mention of another incident. The tribes round Ngami snared game with deep pitfalls. One day Livingstone and Mary were travelling in the waggon when it 'turned clean over in a pitfall'. Mary, Livingstone went on, had often feared being crushed in this sort of accident, 'but when it came could not help saying to herself, "Is this all?" '[5] Livingstone told his own parents that the mosquitoes were so bad that 'I could not touch a square half-inch on the bodies of the children unbitten after a single night's exposure'. Added to that, the children had no vegetables for over four months.[6] The children soon became so weak that Livingstone knew that any thought of going on north from Ngami would have to be abandoned. Ironically, just before the children had taken fever, the Ngami chief had agreed to let Livingstone cross the Zouga in exchange for Livingstone's best gun.

---

* Malaria was not known to be connected with the anopheles mosquito till the end of the century.

After recrossing the Kalahari, where on one occasion
they went without water for two days, the Livingstones
arrived back at Kolobeng. It was mid-August. Mary's
baby was already overdue. A week later she had a daughter. It is hard to imagine the strain of going through the
last months of pregnancy, in a jolting waggon, eating an
unbalanced diet, drinking too little water, experiencing terrible heat. Mrs Livingstone had not been able to think only
of herself, for Thomas and Agnes had had to be nursed
constantly since both were too weak to stand unassisted.
Already enfeebled, the Livingstone children soon caught
a bronchial infection that was widespread among the Bakwains at the time. In turn the new baby succumbed to it
and very soon died screaming. The final scream haunted
Livingstone for a long time afterwards but he still managed to clear his conscience with chilling ease. 'It was the
first death in our family,' he wrote, 'but just as likely to
have happened if we had remained at home, and we now
have one of our number in heaven.'[7] Naturally he had not
paused to ask himself whether the other children would
have caught the infection and passed it on to the baby if
they had been in good health. It is doubtful whether Mrs
Livingstone viewed with such apparent equanimity the loss
of a child that she had carried at such cost to herself.
That cost was not just weariness either. She herself then
became ill with shivering and earache, which Livingstone
put down to a rotten tooth. Soon however the right half
of Mary's face was paralysed. 'The affection,' Livingstone
confessed, 'causes considerable deformity, especially in
smiling.'[8] What Mrs Livingstone had to smile about is hard
to imagine; but happily the paralysis had eased within a
couple of months.

At Mary's mother's insistence the whole family went
down to Kuruman to convalesce from November 1850 to
February 1851. The children enjoyed their first fresh fruit
in months, but for the adults it was a tense and disagreeable time. The Moffats had discovered that Livingstone
was planning yet another journey to the north, and once
again intended taking his family. Mary Moffat was violently opposed to this. She was unimpressed by her son-in-
law's argument that if Mary stayed at Kolobeng, while he
went off again, the Bakwains might move to a better-
watered spot in his absence. Mrs Moffat easily countered
this by suggesting that the obvious course would be for

Mary and the children to stay on at Kuruman. To this
Livingstone had two unconvincing replies: in the first place
if he left Mary behind other missionaries would say that
he could not stand her company, and in the second that
she would be better off with him since he was her doctor.
While missionary gossip seems a quite inadequate excuse
for risking four lives, his idea that his wife and family
would be better off with him in a fever-ridden region
seemed to give too much credit to his medical powers.
But in early April Mrs Moffat discovered that her daughter was pregnant yet again, and this time she wrote to
Livingstone telling him precisely how she felt about his
endangering Mary's life.

> My dear Livingstone
> Before you left the Kuruman I did all I dared to do
> to broach the subject of your intended journey, and
> thus bring on a candid discussion, more especially
> with regard to Mary's accompanying you with those
> dear children. But seeing how averse both you and
> Father* were to speak about it, and the hope that
> you would never be guilty of such temerity (after the
> dangers they escaped last year). I too timidly shrunk
> from what I ought to have had courage to do. Mary
> had told me all along that should she be pregnant
> you would not take her, but let her come out here
> after you were fairly off. Though I suspected at the
> end that she began to falter in this resolution, still I
> hoped it would never take place, i.e. *her going with
> you*, and looked and longed for things transpiring to
> prevent it. But to my dismay I now get a letter, in
> which she writes, 'I must again wend my way to the
> far Interior, perhaps to be confined in the field.' O
> Livingstone, what do you mean? Was it not enough
> that you lost one lovely babe, and scarcely saved the
> other, while the mother came home threatened with
> Paralysis? And will you again expose her & them in
> those sickly regions on an exploring expedition? All
> the world will condemn the *cruelty* of the thing to say
> nothing of the indecorousness of it. A pregnant woman
> with three little children trailing about with a com-
> pany of the other sex, through the wilds of Africa,

* Robert Moffat.

among savage men and beasts! Had you *found a place*
to which you wished to go and commence missionary
operations, the case would be altered. Not one word
would I say, were it to the mountains of the moon.
But to go with an exploring party, the thing is preposterous. I remain yours in great perturbation.

M. Moffat.[9]

This letter increased rather than lessened Livingstone's
determination to take Mary. He had been at great pains to
try to explain to the Moffats that what seemed to be 'an
exploring expedition' was nothing of the sort: it was
opening the way to thousands of natives waiting to
become Christians. He had also tried to put across his
idea that finding a place from which to commence 'missionary operations' had to take second place till he had
discovered more about the network of rivers. The idea of
hundreds of missionaries punting their way up malarious
rivers and bringing the gospel to a land lying on the
wrong side of a sizeable desert seemed unrealistic to the
Moffats, who had worked hard to make their thirty converts and had found little time to experiment with
'navigable highways' or 'introducing the gospel into a new
land'. It should be added that although Moffat had made
two long journeys to the Matabele in the area of modern
Rhodesia, these had been his only major excursions from
Kuruman in twenty years. In the past, Livingstone admirers have tried to make the Moffats out to have been conservative die-hards, who could not see the worth of a new
and far-sighted approach even when it was pushed in their
faces.

In the meantime, to get over what Livingstone regarded
as an unjustified personal attack by Mrs Moffat, he began
reflecting on the worth of sacrifice as proof of a real
Christian vocation. 'It is a venture to take wife & children
into a country where fever, African fever, prevails. But
who that believes in Jesus would refuse to make a venture
for such a Captain?'[10]

Livingstone often thought of missionaries as members of
an army with Christ as their Captain or General. Sometimes he developed the argument that if soldiers died for
the Queen, missionaries ought to be prepared to die for
Christ. The parallel was none the less misleading, for not

even the most bellicose soldier would have thought of sending his small children into the firing line.

By April 1851, with his pregnant wife and his scarcely recovered children, Livingstone was once more ready to set out on his third and, as it turned out, his most important journey made from Kolobeng. This time he had had the sense to wait for the ever-forgiving Oswell, who had gone on a few days ahead to dig out the wells in the Kalahari. This service undoubtedly reduced the children's sufferings at the beginning of the journey. On the way, however, Livingstone learned that three other Europeans were attempting to reach the area he was aiming at—this trio consisted of J. H. Wilson, the same who had gone to Ngami on Livingstone's first visit, Sam Edwards, the son of Livingstone's former missionary colleague, and J. Leyland, an English naturalist. At once Livingstone was determined that at all costs these men should not beat him to his goal. He discovered at the Zouga that it was possible to reach the country of the Makololo, his intended destination, by striking due north instead of going west to Ngami and then north-east after that. There was however one difficulty: there would be very few wells on the direct route and many of these might be dried up; it had been an unusually hot summer.

Livingstone was prepared to take the risk. As usual it was his family who suffered for it. Not long afterwards they had to go five days without water, and as Livingstone, with his unique gift of being humorous after the event, put it, 'the less there was of water, the more thirsty the little rogues became'. He did, however, concede that the possibility of the children 'perishing before our eyes was terrible'.[11]

When they did finally reach water, it was stagnant and full of rhinoceros dung. But people with swollen lips and blackened tongues were not inclined to be fussy. As Livingstone wrote with typical stoicism: 'No one knows the value of water till he is deprived of it . . . I have drunk water swarming with insects, thick with mud and putrid with rhinoceros urine and buffaloes' dung, and no stinted draughts of it either.'[12]

By mid-June the party had travelled 170 miles from the river Zouga and had now reached the river Chobe, which Livingstone would later learn was a major tributary of the Zambesi. Across the Chobe, Livingstone knew from the reports of the natives near Ngami, lived Sebitoane, the chief of the Makololo. Since Sebitoane's tribe commanded the area north of the Chobe, Livingstone knew that he had all but achieved his object. Since the waggons were too large to transport across the river on native canoes, Mrs Livingstone and the children were left while Livingstone and Oswell went some twenty miles upstream to the place where local natives assured them Sebitoane was temporarily settled.

Sebitoane received his two white visitors with visible emotion, but his pleasure at their arrival had nothing to do with Livingstone's statement of the aims of his visit: 'the preaching of the gospel' and the Makololo's 'elevation in the scale of humanity'. In fact the chief of the Makololo wanted guns; he had been fighting almost constantly for the last thirty years, so his desire was understandable. White men were usually reputed to bring guns, so they were welcome. As Livingstone admitted, 'He had the idea that our teaching was chiefly the art of shooting.'[13]

Since the Makololo will feature prominently in Livingstone's life during the next ten years, it is necessary to say more about them. A tribe of the southern Sotho group, they had been driven from their home, in what was to become the Orange Free State, during the great Zulu emigration that took place in the first three decades of the nineteenth century. In the early 1820s the Makololo had been forced east into Bechuanaland but had then been driven north by the better armed Griquas after a battle near Kuruman in 1824. They had continued northwards and had finally reached the Chobe. During the next ten years they established themselves as overlords of the Barotse valley and the Batoka Plateau further along the Zambesi to the east. Their position however was still not secure, for they were threatened by the Matabele, one of the Zulu tribes which had originally forced them out of their true home. The Matabele, under their chief Mosilikatse, had themselves been forced north out of the Transvaal by the Boers into a region which today lies near the town of Bulawayo in modern Rhodesia. This was three hundred miles to the south-east of the Makololo, but still too close for comfort, since the Matabele had sent a number of raiding parties in recent years. To protect themselves the Makololo had withdrawn to the area between the Chobe and the Zambesi, for the two rivers afforded excellent protection. Unfortunately the surrounding swamps left the Makololo in the worst kind of country for malaria. They were in fact in a death-trap and knew it. Apart from guns they saw another way of returning to the more healthy territory which they had been compelled to leave: diplomacy.

Sebitoane had heard about the extraordinary affection Mosilikatse, the Matabele chief, had developed for Robert Moffat, who had already twice made the 600-mile journey from Kuruman to Mosilikatse's kraal. The Makololo chief had also learned, through messengers sent down to Sechele, that Livingstone was Moffat's son-in-law. Sebitoane therefore reasoned that if Livingstone came to live with him, as his missionary, Moffat would use his influence on Mosilikatse to stop him attacking the Makololo. There is no evidence that Livingstone fully appreciated this reason for Makololo helpfulness before 1853.

Although the Makololo were full of wounded indignation at the Matabele's attitude towards them, they were none too pacific themselves; their standard tactic with their enemies was to entice them on to islands in the Chobe or Zambesi and kill them all when they had nearly starved. During his visit Livingstone heard that one of Sebitoane's wives had eloped, taking nine attendants with her. The wife and eight servants were stabbed to death when caught and the ninth servant was only spared because Livingstone begged for her life. The Makololo also smoked cannabis and ate half-cooked meat, both unpleasant habits in Livingstone's eyes.

Although he had been delighted by Sebitoane's extraordinary eagerness to keep him and Mary as his teachers and missionaries, Livingstone's principal aim was to get to the great river which he had heard lay a hundred miles to the north. His plans to get there were, however, suddenly disrupted when Sebitoane unexpectedly died of pneumonia. It was not therefore till the end of July that Livingstone and Oswell were able to set out for their objective. Livingstone's arrival on the banks of the Zambesi near the town of Sesheke, on 4 August 1851, was to prove a turning-point in his life. Both he and Oswell were stunned by the size of the great river; neither had seen anything like it before. The river was between three and five hundred yards across and was flowing fast

although it had been an unusually dry year. The two men
persuaded an old native to take them out on to the river
in his canoe. Livingstone, oblivious of Silva Porto's discoveries, was so moved by the thought that he and Oswell
were the first white men ever to have seen this mighty
river, that he was close to tears. Only 'the fear that the
old man who was conducting us across might ask, "What
are you blubbering at? ain't afraid of these alligators, are
you?" made me hold my tears for some other occasion'.[14]
It is quite clear that if the two men did not at once connect their river with the Zambesi that flowed into the sea
in Moçambique, they made the deduction soon afterwards,
having questioned the Makololo closely. Oswell sent home
a sketch map with the river flowing downstream past the
Portuguese settlement of Tete on the lower Zambesi.
Although Livingstone had heard that there was a massive
waterfall eighty miles to the east, he soon resumed his
reverie of a navigable *highway*. If this river, as seemed
clear beyond doubt, did flow on for a thousand miles to
the east coast of Africa, would it not be possible for
traders and missionaries to come up it as far as the great
falls? There might of course be other lesser falls, but
Livingstone preferred not to think about them. His dream
of the Zambesi as a God-given highway into the interior
had already begun to take solid shape in his mind.

This idea could never have had such a momentous
impact on Livingstone's thinking had he not made a further discovery on his return to the Makololo's town of
Linyanti on the river Chobe. Livingstone's attention was
drawn to the clothing worn by some of the Makololo:
many were dressed in cloaks made of European cloth,
either cotton or baize. One or two even proudly sported
dressing-gowns. Livingstone lost no time in making enquiries about the suppliers of these items, and soon discovered that they were a tribe known to the Makololo as the
Mambari. From what he learned, the Mambari came from
a place far to the west: actually the area around Bie in
central Angola, six hundred miles north-west of Linyanti.
Livingstone next made the disquieting discovery that the
Mambari acted as middlemen and agents for Portuguese
and half-caste traders living in Angola. Worse still, these
traders—'either true Portuguese or bastards'—had themselves come to the Makololo's country to deal in slaves.
The slave-trade had therefore already penetrated into the

interior far further than anybody in Britain had previously believed.

The abolition of slavery throughout the British Empire in 1833 had cut by a half the number of slaves crossing the Atlantic, bound mainly for the West Indies. But just under twenty years later, when Livingstone first reached the heart of south-central Africa, some sixty thousand slaves were still crossing annually from west Africa to Brazil, Cuba and the southern States of America. This was in spite of the presence of a British blockading squadron on the west African coast which accounted for no less than a sixth of the Royal Navy's total strength. Although nations such as Portugal, Spain and France had officially outlawed the trade, in practice they turned a blind eye to its continuation, neither imposing stiff enough penalties nor making any efforts to apprehend slave-traders.

Livingstone's realization that the slave-trade had reached the upper Zambesi, did not lead him to abandon his now rapidly hardening conviction that the area dominated by the Makololo could become a thriving new mission field. In fact the presence of slave-traders made him still more determined that the region should be occupied by missionaries without delay. Even when he conceded to himself that missionaries on their own would be unable to cope with the usual problems of native indifference and the slave-trade as well, he was not downcast; he felt sure that a straightforward way to defeat the slave-trade had already been devised.

In 1840, while studying in London, Livingstone had visited Exeter Hall to hear the famous Thomas Fowell Buxton speak about the benefits 'legitimate commerce' could bring to west Africa. The central idea had been that the African would no longer sell his fellow-men to slave-traders if he had an alternative means of acquiring European cloth, guns and trinkets. If 'legitimate' traders pressed into the interior and offered to exchange cloth and guns for wax, palm oil and ivory, chiefs would have this alternative and the slave-trader would therefore be 'cut out'. The problem had always been how traders could be persuaded to penetrate hundreds of miles into an unknown continent where the tsetse fly ruled out carriage by waggon and oxen, and where malaria frequently killed those foolish enough to hack their way through tropical rain-forests. The difficulties posed by the environment would also cut profits considerably. Buxton's great idea of Christianity and Commerce forging into the 'Dark Continent', and together bringing civilization and the end of the slave-trade, had not therefore been taken up. Livingstone felt that his magnificent Zambesi would solve the communications problems that had bedevilled all trading efforts in west Africa.

Unfortunately the situation on the upper Zambesi was rather more disturbing than Livingstone had at first realized. Soon he discovered that the Makololo themselves were eager slave-traders too, and sold members of their subject tribes to the Mambari without any compunction. Recently Sebitoane had gone on a slave raid with the Mambari and had handed over two hundred captives in exchange for the cattle taken on the foray. Livingstone had to acknowledge that the Makololo were not averse to slavery because they operated a system that 'cannot be called slavery, though akin to it'.[15] Livingstone's previous assumption that the Makololo were a simple and untouched people, without any of the vices of the already contaminated Bechuanas, now had to be dropped. To soften the blow, Livingstone tried to convince himself that the Portuguese and the Mambari had only arrived the year before and had therefore not had time completely to corrupt the Makololo. He was wrong, for Silva Porto had reached Barotseland in the mid-forties and the Mambari probably ten years before that. It was not long before Livingstone admitted his mistake and wrote of the 'perpetual capturing and sale of children' from subject tribes as a crime which made the external slave-trade 'appear a small evil in comparison'.[16]

Had Livingstone not already committed himself mentally to a mission station in Makololo country, he might have acknowledged that the Makololo themselves would be unlikely to abandon their old and deeply ingrained habits for the sake of a few traders and missionaries. But Livingstone had made up his mind: traders and missionaries would come up the Zambesi in boats from the east coast to a point as far west as the great falls. Of course if the missionaries were going to have any hope of success, the operations of the traders would have to be substantial. One or two men buying ivory in exchange for cloth were not going to be able to dissuade the Makololo from selling slaves to the Portuguese and the Mambari. Only widespread European intrusion would have any effect at all.

Livingstone's position was painfully ironic; he had come hoping to find an untouched people, and having found that they had already been corrupted by external influences, was now advocating far more contact with outsiders. In the past he had usually felt that individual traders were interested only in profits and did not care in the least if the natives were robbed and exploited. He had also noted that as often as not the natives were made worse rather than better by contact with Europeans. Now he was arguing in a very different way and one that made nonsense of much of his earlier tolerance of native customs and institutions. But in his determination that the new area he had discovered should become his own mission field, Livingstone was prepared to forget his old strictures on traders. By using calming phrases like 'legitimate commerce' and 'Christian traders' he managed for a while to square his conscience.

But in the long term Livingstone wanted rather better justification for his new thinking than a few catch phrases. If traders were going to come and undermine tribal society in central Africa, Livingstone had to persuade himself that he had formerly been wrong to see any advantages in tribalism. The central problem which any Christian critic of tribal organization faced was the fact that the whole system was based on collective generosity rather than on private ownership and personal wealth: a far more 'Christian' society in that respect than capitalist nineteenth-century Britain. The trade which Livingstone would be recommending would be based on capitalist economics: the sale of surplus goods at a profit to outsiders rather than distribution of the surplus among the producers. This was hardly consistent with the Christian teaching of the vanity of all worldly wealth and goods. To counteract unpleasant thoughts like these, Livingstone set about convincing himself that tribal generosity was not generosity at all. He began by asking himself whether Western concepts like individual freedom and personal choice could mean anything in a tribal society. Since tribal organization was conservative and the social structure static, he decided they could not. Having satisfied himself on that score by pointing to the permanent social inferiority of the

Makololo's subject tribes, he went on to draw his next conclusion. If freedom of choice did not exist, then tribal generosity could not spring from any real or freely made decision; instead it was simply a reflex action dictated by custom, the need to survive and the hope of future benefits. 'Every action and all public movements,' he concluded, 'are made under stern compulsion . . . the entire system is one of selfishness.'[17] Livingstone added further condemnations of tribalism. All the members of tribes were so busy fulfilling their mutual obligations that they had no time to devote to any kind of advances, either collective or personal. Only private ownership of land, Livingstone argued, would free people from their dues and services to the chief, which he expected in return for the allocation of land. If feudalism had survived in England there could never have been any progress because the major part of the population would have remained tied to the land.

So, ignoring the fact that tribalism served the present needs of the people and enabled them to survive famines and to operate in a country were trade with distant tribes was made impossible by the nature of the terrain, Livingstone went on to contrast African poverty with British industrial wealth. His object was to persuade himself that Africans could only benefit from wide-scale European intrusion. Thus he unthinkingly endorsed the common mid-Victorian equation of industrialism with progress and 'civilization'. There was no mention now of contact with Europeans making Africans worse, instead he wrote confidently that Africans would only become civilized 'by a long-continued discipline and contact with superior races by commerce'.[18] Conveniently setting on one side his own miserable childhood, Livingstone enthused about the great advantages enjoyed by the inmates of British workhouses, who had 'glass windows and chimneys', not to mention 'soap and clean linen', all usually way beyond the reach of African chiefs. In Britain, Livingstone went on rhapsodically: 'Surgical operations are performed without pain, fire is obtained instantaneously, and travellers are conveyed on the ocean and on the land with a celerity which our forefathers could not comprehend and which Africans now consider fabulous.' In short: 'The world is rolling on to the Golden Age.'[19] Livingstone was not unusually gullible to have had thoughts like these; many of his contemporaries were convinced that through reforms and representative institutions the injustice which rapid industrialization had brought about would soon be swept away. Because Livingstone had left England in the early forties he would not see the continuance of the old poverty and exploitation which he himself had suffered.

This optimism helped Livingstone to justify his new determination that European commerce should invade Africa, not merely as a weapon against the slave-trade but as a means of undermining tribal society. The theory was that when the natives' tribal collectivism had been weakened by Western trading methods, they would be in a more receptive state of mind to appreciate the alien Christian faith. Yet Livingstone could not entirely escape the implications of his new philosophy, as he admitted when he wrote about 'the advance of ruthless colonists' as a 'terrible necessity'.[20]

Livingstone had abandoned much of his earlier thinking largely because of his passionate desire to make the area between the Chobe and the Zambesi a viable field for missionary work. He had felt that God had directed him north from Kolobeng to this region, and his discovery of the upper Zambesi had strengthened this belief. The fact that the Makololo spoke Sichuana was an added reason for his feeling that a mission with them could succeed. His conviction was so fixed that he would ignore or underestimate all the problems associated with his chosen field. Apart from the problems posed by the slave-trade and the Makololo's involvement in it, there was malaria. Livingstone told the Directors of the London Missionary Society that traders, if they came up the Zambesi during June, July and August, would not get fever. Livingstone's son, Thomas, had fever throughout June and July. In any case Livingstone's plans for the region depended on traders and missionaries being able to live there all the year. That would only be possible if a healthier and preferably higher adjacent area was found. Then the Makololo would have to be persuaded to move, and that of course would depend on the attitude of the Matabele. The greatest imponderable of all was whether the Zambesi would be navigable from the coast. If the river should prove impassable because of rapids or sand banks, then few traders would come to the area, for they would never be prepared, in sufficient numbers, to endure the long and perilous overland journey from the Cape to the upper Zambesi. Living-

stone had suggested that a brisk trade could be done in
ivory, but indiscriminate slaughter of elephants would soon
put an end to it. Apart from ostrich feathers and wax, he
had few ideas for the establishment of longer-term trade.
Instead, with typical optimism, he had suggested that
since gold had recently been discovered in South Africa, it
might be found further north. God, he claimed, would do
for central Africa something 'just as wonderful and unexpected as the discovery of gold'.[21] This prediction was
mistaken.

Livingstone's determination to leave Bechuanaland and
to gain the distinction of being the man who, hundreds of
miles beyond every other man's lines, began successful
missionary operations in Makololo country, led him to turn
his thinking upside-down and encouraged him to see circumstances not as they were, but as he wanted them to
be. This trait would enable him to press on where others
more logically minded would have given up, but it would
also pinpoint many inconsistencies in his ideas and pave
the way for future disappointments. At a later date it
would also lay him open to charges of deliberate misrepre-
sentation.

Before Livingstone started south again in August 1851,
he had none the less made two realistic decisions. He
would return as soon as possible to the Zambesi, in the
first place to see whether he could find a healthy spot for
a mission and trading centre, and in the second to reach
the coast either to the east or west, to see whether the
Zambesi was a realistic *highway*.

By September, Livingstone and his family had reached
the river Zouga and there they had to wait a month, while
Mrs Livingstone gave birth to her long awaited child. The
Livingstones called their new son William Oswell* after
their friend and benefactor. During this inevitable period
of delay Livingstone wasted no time in writing numerous
letters which would be ready for despatch when he got
further south. The most important was to the Directors.
In it he outlined his new plan for sending his wife and
family back to England while he took a closer look at
central Africa and tried to open a direct way to the coast,
which would be far shorter than the 1,300-mile trek from

---

* Livingstone sometimes called him Bill or William but more often
Oswell.

the Cape to Makololo country. Livingstone told the Directors flatly that if they would not support Mrs Livingstone and the children in England, he would still go north 'no matter who opposes'.[22] When Livingstone finally put his wife and family on to a ship bound for England in April 1852, he had still had no reply from the Directors and so could not have been sure whether they would help Mary or not. Livingstone could not have been expected to take his family back to the Zambesi—by 1851 even he had seen that their health and lives would be endangered by a prolonged stay—but his failure to wait and hear what provision the Directors would make was typical of his attitude to wife and children. When they became a hindrance to his cherished plans, his family, and not the plans, had to be sacrificed. Although Livingstone said that parting with his children was 'like tearing out my entrails',[23] they would be the ones to suffer four years of poverty and helplessness, and not he.

Livingstone arrived at Kolobeng on 27 November 1851 and found that the Bakwains had moved on in search of a better-watered place. The sight of the deserted village neither surprised nor distressed him; in fact, if anything, it pleased him. The Bakwains' move could be added to the list of excuses he had already worked out for leaving Sechele and Bechuanaland for good. So he told the Directors that since Sechele had deserted Kolobeng and would probably have to move on from the new site he had chosen higher up the Kolobeng stream, there could be no justification for trying to build up a new settlement with the Bakwains. Livingstone argued that all the houses he would be expected to erect would be a wasted labour.

He made other excuses too: the Boers and the drought had prevented the Bakwains accepting the Word, and would continue to do so. The tiny population of Bechuanaland gave no scope for settling native agents in any numbers, while the area near the Zambesi was populous and fertile and offered far better prospects. All the reasons Livingstone had given for leaving Bechuanaland had been false except the last. Had he wished to stay with the Bakwains, nothing would have stopped a man of his determination moving with them many more times and building new houses on each occasion. Nor would he have given in on account of the drought if he had wished to remain with them. The Boers had not yet directly threatened the existence of Kolobeng, and at their closest were between three and five days' journey to the east. Besides, if Livingstone had really expected the Boers to attack Sechele he ought to have stayed with him to act as his ambassador and diplomatist. Nor could Livingstone truthfully claim that the size of Bechuanaland's population gave him a good reason to leave. He had failed to convert even a small part of that population and his claim that there were insufficient tribes to send native teachers to was equally misleading. He would have been more honest if he had admitted that there were too few native teachers to send to any tribes. Mebalwe and Paul had been thought by Moffat to be the best native teachers in Bechuanaland and Livingstone had lost faith in both of them.

It is significant that at this stage Livingstone did not include the Bakwains' failure to be converted as a reason for leaving them. He realized that if he did, the other missionaries would accuse him of quitting because of failure. Only three years later would he confess to a friend that of all his reasons for leaving the Bakwains 'the principal one was determined hostility to the requirements of the gospel'.[24] But in 1851, precisely because he wished to create the impression that he was not leaving the Bakwains because of their lack of faith, Livingstone assured the Directors: 'I by no means give up the hope that they will be converted.'[25]

There can be no doubt however that although missionary failure had originally driven Livingstone north, his principal motive in 1851 for leaving Bechuanaland was his feeling that there was far more exciting work to be done among the Makololo. Bechuanaland could never offer the thrilling prospect of traders sailing hundreds of miles along a navigable river, nor could it ever give scope to Livingstone's abiding ambition to 'preach the Gospel beyond every other man's line of things'. He sensed that his ideas on commerce and Christianity might have a revolutionary impact on Africa, far greater than anything that an individual missionary working with one tribe could ever hope to achieve. Missionary work in the conventional sense was often dull, usually disappointing and never very successful. Livingstone had now chosen a far more attractive role, that of a man who opened the way for others, who would then follow and establish missionary and trading settlements. Then Livingstone would go on and open

up more territory, and so on. The important thing was
that he should lead and others follow. It was the ideal
formula for the personally ambitious missionary.

Livingstone was not the first nor the last religiously
motivated man to see his own wishes and personal prefer-
ences in terms of the dictates of Providence, and to justify
them accordingly. In his situation it seemed crystal clear
that unless a new conception of missionary work in Africa
was formulated, no significant number of Africans would
ever be converted. Therefore any moves that he could
make which might radically alter the situation throughout
the continent was surely in God's best interests. That they
were also in Livingstone's best interests was more than
coincidental, for when Livingstone had claimed, after Lake
Ngami had brought him a measure of recognition, that
he had been 'regardless of the fame of discovery',[26] he
had been less than truthful. His efforts to claim as much
of the praise as he could for that discovery hardly accord
with self-effacing modesty. Livingstone himself was uneasy
about being ambitious, and although he often denied that
he was, sometimes admitted his obsession with doing things
and getting to places first. 'Perhaps it arises from ambition,' he told the Directors, 'but it is not of an ignoble
sort.'[27] At other times he was a great deal less certain,
and although suggesting that all his actions were ultimately
intended 'for the benefit of Him to whom I have dedicated
my all', he admitted that there was 'much impurity in
my motives' and confessed that he mistrusted his ambition.[28] If he mistrusted it, his fellow-missionaries were
open in their condemnations. They did not, as Livingstone
put it, 'hesitate to tell the natives that my object is to
obtain the applause of men'. They also suggested that
Livingstone had stopped being a missionary and was now
simply a traveller. This last jibe really went home. 'A few
as I understand in Africa in writing home have styled my
efforts as *wanderings*,' he complained. 'The very word
contains a lie coiled like a serpent in its bosom. It means
travelling without an object, or uselessly . . .'[29]

For somebody who had thought about bringing social
change to Africa as thoroughly as Livingstone had done,
the charge was clearly maddening. But the other missionaries can hardly be blamed. Moffat never really forgave
Livingstone for abandoning Sechele 'at the time he
required the most watchful eye and encouraging voice of

his missionary'. All this, Moffat went on, was 'notwithstanding the importance of Mr Livingstone's discoveries'.[30]

By 1852 Livingstone had certainly ceased being a missionary in any sense that the members of the London Missionary Society could accept, but that still did not make him purely a traveller. Quite what he was is impossible to define; he had become part social theorist, part explorer, part missionary propagandist, part trading expansionist, part anti-slavery proponent. Many of his aims appeared to outsiders to be inconsistent. But force of circumstance and his own experiences, since his arrival in Africa eleven years before, had slowly combined together in Livingstone's mind to form a strange mixture of ideas both contradictory and complementary. How such unlikely components would hold together, only the future would tell, but in 1852, as Livingstone stood poised to set out on what would prove to be his greatest feat of exploration, he had persuaded himself, albeit by some fairly startling mental gymnastics, that hold together they would.

9

Return to Linyanti, 1852–1853

On 16 March 1852 the Livingstone family arrived in Cape Town, having come directly from Linyanti. The journey of roughly fifteen hundred miles had taken six months, including stops at the river Zouga, at Kolobeng and Kuruman. Livingstone had not seen a town for twelve years, and at first he found stairs so strange that he had to come down them backwards. He also had difficulty in expressing himself in English; at Kolobeng he had spoken Sichuana almost the whole time. The family made a bizarre spectacle entering Cape Town in their waggon, with the children's clothes in rags and the parents hardly better dressed. Only through Oswell's generosity was Mrs Livingstone saved having to take her children home looking like paupers. He gave Livingstone £200 to buy his whole family an entire new wardrobe. Livingstone, who had always thought the missionaries in the Colony pampered, was enraged to see them and their children wearing smart and expensive clothing, and fumed about 'the utter respectability' of the citizens of Cape Town for ever 'exchanging their how-d'ye-do's, their noddings, curtsyings and ministerial breakfasts'.[1] There is no record of what the would-be socialites of the town thought of this weird-looking man with his deeply tanned face and uncouth manners.

From the moment he arrived at the Cape Livingstone's one thought was to get a passage for his wife and children as quickly as possible, so that he could head north again. To his irritation he had to wait till late April before they could be got on to a ship bound for England. Livingstone was grieved at parting, but he could reflect with pride that the unique work he was about to begin more than compensated for a little personal sorrow. His advice to his children was to consider Jesus, rather than himself, as their father from now on. 'I have given you back to Him and you are in His care.'[2] Privately Livingstone admitted 'my children are become absolutely vagabonds', beggars dependent on the charity of the Directors of the London Missionary Society: a body of men more used to receiving money than handing it out. But Livingstone's most frequently repeated worry was not what would become of his wife and children, but that they might forget him.

When Mr and Mrs Moffat had asked Livingstone what plans had been made for their daughter and grandchildren in England, their son-in-law had had to confess that he had no idea, but he added with more bravado than realism 'that if they [the Directors] crimp my wife and family they will hear thunder'.[3] The Directors in fact heard nothing from Livingstone for several years and in the meantime Mrs Livingstone had begun a miserable four and a half years of poverty and homelessness.

She began by staying with her husband's parents, and his two spinster sisters, in Scotland. In the early 1840s the Livingstone seniors had moved into a tiny house in Hamilton. It is not hard to imagine the impact of the arrival of a strange daughter-in-law and four children, none of them older than seven, on a religious and meticulously ordered Scottish household. The children had been allowed to play in the open air most of the day with few restrictions, and much of their young lives had been spent with their mother and father travelling hundreds of miles by waggon. The contrast with their new environment could not have been more startling. Mary Livingstone, too, was ill-suited for her new role; and her strait-laced parents-in-law's constant meddling with the children soon drove her into rages. Within six months the situation had become unbearable. Mary left the house and told the Livingstone seniors that they were not to enquire after her and not to try and contact the children. Neil Livingstone told the Directors of the London Missionary Society that owning to his daughter-in-law's 'remarkably strange conduct', he 'had resolved to have no more intercourse with her until there is evidence she is a changed person'.[4]

After leaving Hamilton, Mary and the children lived a wretched nomadic existence. Sometimes they stayed a few months in rented rooms, sometimes with friends her father had made during his last visit to England between 1839 and 1843. Mrs Livingstone moved from Hamilton to Hackney, from Hackney to Manchester and from Manchester to Kendal. Finally she spent some months at Epsom. To start with she was sustained by the hope that her husband would return after two years, but as three and then four years passed she began to despair, until she scandalized people by making bitter remarks about missionaries. The Directors never gave her enough money and she was for ever writing grovelling and apologetic letters begging for more. 'I would beg of you to be lenient with me, I don't attempt to justify myself. I may not have been so discreet in the use of my money.'[5] She had not been discreet either. Mrs Livingstone had begun to drink. It was a habit she did not break till her death ten years later. Innocent observers often wondered why she so often had to borrow money. Had those same observers known what sort of a life she had to lead, with her four children, whose father was to become a total stranger to them, they would have been neither surprised nor censorious about her drinking. Poor woman, she became seriously ill in 1854 and could not afford to pay for medical attention. Only a doctor's offer of free treatment saved her. In her misery she wrote to her husband begging him to return. It was two years before his refusal came back and by then he was on the way home. She did receive a few letters from him, sent when he was in the Portuguese colonies of Moçambique and Angola, but they could not have comforted her much. The tone was usually harsh. 'Hope you give much of your time to the children,' he wrote self-righteously on one occasion. 'You will be sorry for it if you don't . . . I have nothing worth writing, having no news. I write only because you will be anxious to hear from me.'[6]

Four years later, on his way back to England his ship was delayed by a storm, and so Mrs Livingstone had to wait still longer for him. Her husband did not write a consoling letter, but instead told her that 'patience is a great virtue', and added that the captain of the ship bringing him home had 'been six years away from his family, I only four and a half'.[7] During his time in central Africa, Livingstone had been concerned that his children should not be spoiled, and in case they should think themselves hard done by, he told them stories of worse suffering. 'I saw a poor woman in a chain with many others, up at the Barotse . . . See how kind Jesus was to you.' But they should not, he warned, presume on that kindness by doing 'bad things', for then 'Satan will have you in the chains of sin, and you will be hurried on in his bad ways till you are put into the dreadful place which God hath prepared for him and all like him'.[8] One can hardly imagine Livingstone's children eagerly awaiting such letters. Sometimes he gave them advice which would have meant something to adolescents in their late teens. But for children between six and nine it could not have been cheering to read letters containing information like the following: 'I have no money to leave you. Each of you must work for himself in the world . . . the sooner you learn the better.'[9]

With his wife and children out of the way, Livingstone began getting his supplies together. He also learned how to take accurate geographical observations using a chronometer watch and a sextant. His tutor was the Astronomer Royal at the Cape, Sir Thomas Maclear. For the rest of his life, Livingstone would send Maclear observations and maps to check, and would give him details of his new schemes and ambitions. Livingstone also arranged to have his photograph taken for the first time. He sent his brother Charles two prints and added a note saying 'the ugliest is most like the original . . . a little pedantic looking'.[10] It is sad that Livingstone so rarely joked like this in his letters to Mary and the children.

The thought of leaving Bechuanaland filled Livingstone with joy. One of the advantages that pleased him most was that he would be leaving all his old missionary colleagues

behind, escaping 'their envy and backbiting'.[11] On 24
May he heard from the Directors of the London Missionary Society, who suggested that he ought to perform his
exploration with another missionary. One of the men they
suggested was William Ross. Livingstone wrote back telling them that in twelve years Ross had learned no
Sichuana and was so bad-tempered that his coming would
be disastrous. William Ashton, one of Moffat's colleagues
at Kuruman, had also been suggested as a possible companion. 'You might as well recommend the Lieutenant
Governor as Mr Ashton,' Livingstone assured the Directors. 'He will not go unless forced to it by some agency
more potent that moral suasion.' Ashton, he added, had
been frightened of travelling further than eighty miles
from Kuruman.[12] In short Livingstone had no intention of
letting any other missionary share in the glory of what he
felt sure would be his greatest achievement. In fact the
Directors' motives for suggesting that Livingstone travelled with a companion had been impeccable; they had
simply considered that two men would have a safer journey than one, on the general principle that, unless both got
malaria simultaneously, one would be able to look after
the other. The dangers Livingstone faced were, after all,
very real. Of the early explorers, Park, Clapperton and
Lander had all died in Africa; while the death-rate on the
four expeditions sent from Britain between 1816 and
1841 to examine the rivers Congo, Zambesi and Niger had
been over sixty per cent. All these expeditions had been
total failures due to malaria. Yet the Directors of the
London Missionary Society had never tried to dissuade
Livingstone from setting out. If he died on his journey he
would become a martyr and that would be useful for gaining subscriptions; if he succeeded, that too would stimulate
public generosity. The Directors, unknown to Livingstone,
had no intention of carrying ambitious operations into
tropical Africa. Their policy had always been one of
cautious advances into the interior along a linked chain
of mission stations. In 1849 John Freeman, one of the
Directors, had come out to Bechuanaland and had not
been impressed by what he had seen. His feelings had been
that until the position there had been improved, no further
plans could be considered for southern, let alone central,
Africa. Of course the Directors realized that if Livingstone came home safe and successful, he might attempt to

force the Society into premature advances into unsuitable territory. But Tidman and Freeman felt that they would be able to face that problem if and when it came. In the meantime, whatever happened, they felt confident that Livingstone's travels would provide financial benefits. They had therefore been happy to tell Livingstone that his wife would be supported till his return.

Livingstone finally left Cape Town on 8 June, and, after a series of minor accidents to his waggon, arrived at Kuruman on 29 August. He wanted to head north as soon as possible, but he had only been at Kuruman a few days when news came in that the Transvaal Boers had attacked Sechele near Kolobeng, killing sixty Bakwains and losing thirty-six of their own number. The Boers gave several reasons for the attack. They claimed that Sechele had harboured the chief of the neighbouring Bakhatla, who had refused the Boers free labour, and they also used Sechele's refusal to surrender his firearms as an excuse. The attack had really been a punishment for Sechele's rejection of a Boer demand to stop British hunters and ivory traders passing through his territory, to the north. The Transvaal Boers believed that unless they stopped these men getting through, there was a real danger that the British might in the end encircle them and begin settlements to the north, in the area of modern Rhodesia.

In the attack Sechele lost three thousand cattle, eleven horses, forty-eight guns and two hundred women and children as captives. Livingstone's house at Kolobeng was sacked. It might be thought that Livingstone's automatic reaction would have been sympathy for Sechele; he had after all risked universal unpopularity by his acceptance of Christianity. But Livingstone was unmoved. The Boer attack, he wrote in his journal, was not in the least mysterious, it was simply the result of the Bakwains' refusal of the gospel. 'God had dealt graciously with them for years and now suffers them to feel the rod of his anger.'[13] The other missionaries suggested that if Livingstone had still been with Sechele, he would have been able to negotiate with the Boers on the chief's behalf.

Livingstone saw matters differently. Had he been with Sechele, he argued, he would probably have been killed. God had clearly not intended him to die till he had achieved some more important work. It was this idea of the Providential role he had to play that kept Livingstone in Kuruman for another three months. Normally far from cautious, Livingstone considered it would be foolish to move north until the Boers had returned to their homes. Otherwise they might teach him a lesson for having sold guns to Sechele.

Livingstone's three months at Kuruman were unhappy for more reasons than the attack on Kolobeng. During this time he stayed with his parents-in-law, neither of whom approved his plans. Livingstone had earlier written to Robert Moffat asking him to stop Mrs Moffat giving 'soft-headed' advice, but she went on referring to her son-in-law's intended journeys as 'wanderings' and suggested that his going north again was a tempting of Providence rather than a true response to God's wishes. Mrs Moffat felt convinced that Livingstone was going to his death and naturally she was alarmed about the prospects for Mary and the children if this happened. Her continuing complaints led to ugly scenes, with Livingstone saying that people who confined their actions to a narrow field were showing their lack of faith. 'Commit thy way unto the Lord, and He shall direct thy steps. Is this all gammon?'[14] he asked angrily. Both Livingstone and the Moffats were thankful when he finally left Kuruman on 14 December.

Livingstone had not gone far when he met an angry Sechele heading south determined to take his complaint to the Governor at the Cape, and if need be to the Queen herself. Livingstone told him he 'might as well have remained at home'.[15] By the Sand River Convention of 1852, the Governor of the Cape had relinquished all pretence to any authority north of the river Vaal. Sechele however went on his way, but only as far as the borders of the Colony, where he was compelled to turn back because his resources had been exhausted. Two years later Moffat visited the Bakwains. Their feelings were bitter and Sechele's younger brother said scornfully: 'The teachers prayed, and where are they now? Look where we are and what we are by taking such advice.'[16] Livingstone never saw Sechele or the Bakwains again after 1852. For the next seven years the Makololo would be the focal point of his hopes.

As Livingstone pressed on to the north, he thought of the two main purposes of his current endeavour: to find a suitably healthy place in Makololo country for the establishment of a mission and trading centre, and to open a

viable route to the east or west coast along the Zambesi.
The essential preliminary to both operations was the trip
to Linyanti, for from there he would begin his real work.
The journey from Kuruman to Linyanti was a dull necessity for Livingstone, since he had covered the same ground
in 1851; nevertheless it needs mentioning, for on it he
displayed for the first time a number of the characteristics
which were to make him such an unusual explorer.

He set out with three native drivers and a travelling
companion, George Fleming. While Livingstone had
refused European company, Fleming was considered suitable since he was black: being in fact a West Indian half-
caste who had been sponsored by a Cape Town merchant
to start an ivory trade with the Makololo. While any
European might have annoyed Livingstone by expecting to
have his opinions considered, George from the beginning
knew that his role was distinctly that of a subordinate.
Nor was George going to come further than Linyanti.

By the second week of March 1854 the party had
crossed the river Zouga and were soon travelling into
country where malaria was common. Although to most
observers it would have been quite obvious that the illness
was serious, since it had soon smitten down every member
of the party except Livingstone and one native boy, Livingstone maintained that their complaint resembled 'bilious
attacks more than fever'.[17] When he at last had to recognize that perspiring, fainting, violent pains in his head,
neck and stomach, coupled with frequent vomiting, was
not the same as a bilious attack, he still complained that
his attendants kept 'on pretending to great illness when
weakness alone remains'.[18] When George suggested that
they were all going to die, Livingstone could 'scarcely
avoid a guffaw' at such spineless sentiments and finally
did break out laughing at George's 'utterly mock cadaveric
face'.[19]

This almost total inability to appreciate or sympathize
with other people's physical sufferings owed a lot to Livingstone's tough and gruesome childhood in the mills. There
was however nothing hypocritical about Livingstone's heart-
lessness; he would be irritated and ashamed by his own
incapacity when laid low by fever, talking about his lack
of pluck and being *unmanned* by the disease. Yet he
would force himself to keep going, even when suffering
repeated intermittent attacks. His great will-power was to

save him from death many times. A man without such reserves would have given up and died. In his early days in Bechuanaland the natives had laughed at Livingstone and suggested that the heat and the lack of water would soon 'knock him up'. 'This,' wrote Livingstone, 'caused my highland blood to rise, and made me despise the fatigue of keeping them all at the top of their speed for days together, and until I heard them expressing proper opinions of my pedestrian powers.'[20] This determination was a key both to his own personal prowess as an explorer, and also to his later failure to travel happily with other Europeans; he expected them to be capable of his own exceptional endurance and despised them when they were not. Few other men possessed Livingstone's greatest personal advantage. 'If God has accepted my service,' he wrote confidently, 'then my life is charmed till my work is done.'[21] Already the belief was forming that he was God's chosen instrument for opening up Africa to the healing light of the gospel. Unless God's desire for the whole world to become Christian changed radically, Livingstone could feel certain that he would not be allowed to die until he had achieved something significant. Given the heavy mortality of previous explorers, this was a comforting belief to hold.

On the journey to Linyanti Livingstone also began to make up for his previous inattention to detailed natural observation. From now on his notebooks and diaries would be full of longitudes and latitudes, altitudes and figures for rainfall. The reason for this change in Livingstone's approach to accurate recording of his travels is in part due to a rebuke he received from the Directors for not having made more notes about Lake Ngami, and also to the influence of Thomas Maclear, the Astronomer Royal at the Cape. But Livingstone's powers of description were not confined to scientific figures and cartography. He described even the arid country of Bechuanaland with a love and wealth of detail that owed much to his belief that all creation was an expression of the Creator's purpose.

The noon tide quiet of nature—the herds retire to sleep in the thickest shade, but amid the apparent silence there is a stifled sound—murmurs—a continual hum of insects which fills the lower strata of air ... myriads of insects crawl on the ground & flutter

round the plants scorched by the heat of the sun. A
confused noise issues from every bush, from the
decayed trunks of the trees, the fissures of the rocks
& from the ground . . . it is a voice that proclaims to
us that all nature breathes—that in a thousand forms
life is diffused in the dry & dusty soil, as in the bosom
of the waters and the air that circulates around us.[22]

Nothing was too small to escape his attention and he
gave many hours to studying the behaviour of the white
ant. His main preoccupation was to find out how they
communicated. 'At some of their operations,' he wrote,
'they beat time in a curious manner. Hundreds of them are
engaged in building a large tube, and they wish to beat it
smooth. At a signal they all give three or four energetic
beats on the plaster in unison . . .' He then went on to
describe how the white ant broke down wood and thus
helped to enrich the soil. During the journey north to Linyanti, Livingstone noted down hundreds of facts, ranging
from the strange attraction the camp-fire at night had for
toads, to similarities in the diets of elephants and bushmen:
they both enjoyed eating the bole of young palmyra trees.
The extent and detail of Livingstone's scientific and
descriptive observations made him unique among contemporary explorers.

By 23 April the party was within striking distance of
the Chobe, which they soon discovered had burst its banks,
flooding most of the adjacent low-lying country. This
forced them to travel for hours at a time through waist-
deep water. Soon Livingstone's guides deserted, and his
people refused to go any further. For the first time he
proved his exceptional powers of endurance when he and
one other man set off alone to try to find a way through
the swamps. The reeds were so high that it was impossible
to see more than a few feet ahead and progress could
only be effected by 'putting a staff against the reeds &
pressing against it with all our might; when it reached the
water we mounted on it & bent it down further'. Nor
were reeds the only difficulty; 'bramble papyrus, nearly as
thick as the wrist, vines and sedgy grass bound together
by a kind of creeper'[23] all had to be flattened or hacked
through. Soon Livingstone's canvas trousers were in ribbons
and his knees and hands were bleeding and lacerated.
Hippopotami posed yet another threat in the flooded val-

leys. It took Livingstone and his companion two days to force their way through the swamps to the river Chobe itself. For some time afterwards the native who had accompanied Livingstone had to walk with a stick, so badly had his legs been injured.

The Makololo themselves were incredulous. They had assumed the swamps to be impenetrable at the point Livingstone had come through them. The Matabele had certainly never managed to get past them. Livingstone was told that it was as though he had 'dropped from a cloud'.[24] The Makololo soon suggested a better way in which the waggons could be brought to the river without going through the swamps, and on 3 May the whole party crossed the river, waggons and all, on dozens of canoes lashed together into vast floating platforms. On 23 May Livingstone entered Linyanti in his waggon, watched by the entire population of the town: six thousand people. The first phase had ended and the real work was about to begin.

10

From Coast to Coast, 1853–1856

To avoid confusion I am beginning this chapter with a brief summary of Livingstone's movements between May 1853, when he arrived at Linyanti, and May 1856, when he embarked for England from the east African coast near Quilimane in Moçambique.

There are three distinct phases. The first, beginning in June 1853, was taken up with Livingstone's search for a malaria-free site for a trading centre and mission on the upper Zambesi. This quest was in the Barotse valley, due north of Linyanti, and took Livingstone three hundred miles north-west up the Zambesi. Having failed to find a suitable site, Livingstone returned to Linyanti in September 1853, ready for the second phase. This was his attempt to open a viable path for traders to follow into the interior from the west African coast. Livingstone set out west from Linyanti in November 1853 and, after a journey of over a thousand miles, reached the Atlantic port of Loanda, in Portuguese Angola. Dissatisfied with this route, the indomitable man prepared for phase three. Leaving Loanda in September 1854, Livingstone retraced his steps to Linyanti and from there set out, downstream along the Zambesi, for the east African coast, which he reached near Quilimane in Portuguese Moçambique in May 1856. His journey from Loanda to Quilimane had been little short of 2,500 miles, and was the first authenticated crossing of

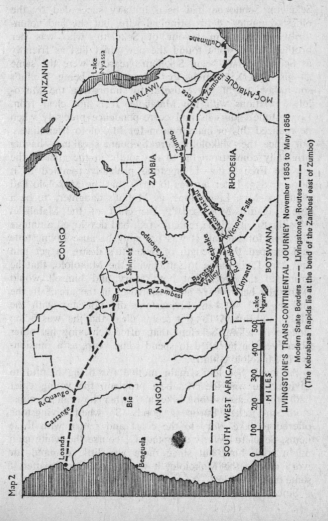

Map 2

LIVINGSTONE'S TRANS-CONTINENTAL JOURNEY November 1853 to May 1856

Modern State Borders ——— Livingstone's Routes ———

(The Kebrabasa Rapids lie at the Bend of the Zambesi east of Zumbo)

the continent from coast to coast by a European. From Quilimane, Livingstone sailed for England, where he arrived on 9 December 1856. From the day he had left the Cape in 1852 to the day he sailed from Quilimane in 1856 he had travelled almost six thousand miles.

In the spring of 1853 Livingstone found that the Makololo had a new chief, a young man of nineteen called Sekeletu. Sebitoane had been initially succeeded by the oldest daughter of his principal wife, but she had voluntarily abdicated in favour of Sekeletu, who was her brother. Livingstone found the new chief just as friendly as Sebitoane had been. Sekeletu's reasons were the same as his father's: namely that Livingstone, being Moffat's son-in-law, might prove useful for improving the Makololo's relations with the Matabele. It is not clear from Livingstone's journals and correspondence precisely when he realized this primary reason for Makololo friendliness, but since the Makololo were Sichuana-speaking—having originally come from far to the south, in the area of the Orange Free State—Livingstone probably tumbled to it during 1853. Later he was to write that the Makololo had plans for Mrs. Livingstone, as Moffat's daughter, 'to be a shield against Mosilikatse',[1] the chief of the Matabele. Mosilikatse, it will be remembered, had developed a unique affection for Moffat. It was probably because Livingstone had grasped the strength of Sekeletu's desire to get him and Mrs Livingstone to settle with the Makololo, that he promised the chief that both Mary and himself would eventually begin work as missionaries in the area.[2] In the end, as will be seen, Livingstone did not stay with the Makololo. But in 1853 it seems clear that he was being sincere in telling Sekeletu that, after achieving his other objectives, he intended to spend some years as a missionary in Makololo country.

Although Sekeletu's main motive for being helpful to Livingstone was the Matabele problem, the young chief had other reasons too. Like his father he wanted guns, cloth and other European goods. So when Livingstone offered to take ivory to the coast and return with these items, Sekeletu eagerly accepted. Of course the white man might trick him, but since there was little demand for ivory among the Makololo, it would not much matter if some tusks were lost.

Since Livingstone completely depended on Makololo

porters for his journey to the coast, it is not surprising that he gave Sekeletu an inflated idea of the benefits which trade would bring. His plan was to promise Sekeletu considerable future rewards and thus to persuade the chief to give him the free labour of a number of men for a couple of years. It is quite clear that he was completely successful, for the Makololo came to believe that he had unique commercial abilities. This point was proved beyond all doubt by the way they treated James Chapman, an ivory trader, who managed to reach Makololo country from the Cape in the summer of 1853. Chapman was told bluntly that the Makololo would do no trade with him, since Livingstone had 'promised them all the good things of the earth, rain, corn, cattle &c. . . . and that they would have nothing to do with anyone but Nake (as they called Dr Livingstone)—he was their trader— who would give them two barrels of powder, a large heap of lead, and sundry other articles, for a small tusk of ivory.'[3] Chapman argued bitterly that if Livingstone really wanted the Makololo not to trade with the Mambari and the Portuguese, he should not have given them such high hopes. Their rejection of southern traders, Chapman went on, would merely leave the tribe more dependent on the slave-trade than ever. Although this was partly sour grapes, there was much truth in Chapman's argument. Livingstone himself had to admit that there were some disadvantages in a close alliance of commerce and Christianity, for the Makololo soon believed that simply by listening to the words of the Bible they would overnight acquire everything they wanted materially. But Livingstone still reckoned that this was a small price to pay for Sekeletu's complete co-operation.

At the end of June, Livingstone, accompanied by Sekeletu and two hundred men, set out on the hundred-mile trip north from Linyanti to the Zambesi. There they all embarked in a fleet of thirty-three canoes and headed north-west up the river, bound for the Barotse valley. Livingstone eventually went three hundred miles upstream from the point of embarkation. His aim on this journey, which lasted till mid-September, was to find a suitable site for a mission and trading post. He failed in his objective, but other factors contributed to the acute depression he felt on his return to Linyanti.

On his visit to Linyanti in 1851, Livingstone had been

shocked to find that the Makololo sold members of their subject tribes to the Mambari, but he had considered this their solitary fault. Largely through wishful thinking he had built up a mental picture of them as unspoiled noble savages ripe to receive the gospel. His first shock on his journey up the Zambesi in 1853 was that they seemed very much more bloodthirsty than any tribe in despicable Bechuanaland. Conversation as a rule took the form of boasting about the number of men an individual had killed. Livingstone was often told about battles, and the Makololo, to make the story really live, would usually 'imitate the death cry of the victim, a fine joke apparently from the hearty laugh, exhibiting immense mouths, white teeth and glistening eyes'.[4] Sekeletu himself often behaved badly. One day Livingstone was about to preach when the chief and forty of his subjects started 'dancing and roaring at the top of their voices'.[5] Services were treated with derision, and were usually punctuated by the coughings and sneezings of those smoking wild hemp. As soon as Livingstone finished speaking, the chief would generally call for a sheep, which would then be roasted and eaten within half an hour. Then, less than an hour after Livingstone had been talking about God's infinite goodness in sending His only son to redeem their sins, the Makololo would be dancing to the music of the court musicians, whose antics Livingstone considered 'the most ungraceful I have ever seen. I was sorry to see any of our human family so degraded.'[6]

Worse was to come. Livingstone had only been travelling with Sekeletu for a couple of days, when a cousin of the chief, a man called Mpepe, attempted to assassinate Sekeletu. Mpepe was foiled because, at the very moment planned for the attack, Livingstone unwittingly sat down between the chief and his would-be murderer. Afterwards nobody was quite sure why Mpepe had not cut down Livingstone first and then killed the chief. Mpepe's aim had been to usurp the chiefship for himself, and the plot seemed even more sinister to Livingstone when he heard that Mpepe had been in league with the Mambari. The incident therefore worried him not only because he had been in such personal danger but also because it proved that the Makololo were politically unstable. Livingstone felt that he might labour to open up a trade with the coast, only to find while he was away that Sekeletu had been deposed.

Meantime his successor might (as Mpepe had planned)
have formed an exclusive trading arrangement with the
Mambari.

After the abortive assassination attempt Mpepe was
summarily stabbed to death and members of his family
rounded up and killed. Livingstone was a reluctant witness
to the murder of Mpepe's father and uncle. 'The men,
both upwards of fifty were paralysed with terror . . . the
two were led forth with a man on each side and one
behind each with a battle axe in hand, to execution. They
were led slowly to the river, there hewn down and their
bodies disposited by means of a canoe in the middle of
the river to be the food of alligators.'[7] 'I am forced to
witness, and protest almost in vain,' Livingstone wrote in
anguish.

In the Barotse valley, where the Makololo were the
overlords of a number of subject tribes, Livingstone noticed
that the people dreaded their oppressors. The Makololo,
Livingstone soon confessed, 'never visit anywhere but for
the purpose of plunder and oppression. They never go anywhere without a club or spear in hand.'[8] 'Nine weeks,' he
told a friend, 'hearing their quarrelling, roaring, dancing,
singing and murdering, have imparted a greater disgust at
heathenism than I ever had before.'[9]

In early July, to add to Livingstone's depression, he met
Silva Porto, the famous Portuguese trader who had
reached the upper Zambesi before him. Early in the same
year Porto had been appointed by the Angolan Government to attempt a trans-continental journey from Angola
to Moçambique, but had been prevented getting beyond
Barotseland by illness and tribal disturbances.* When Livingstone met him, he had been trading in slaves and ivory.
Livingstone hated the idea that he had been outdone by
another European, so he conveniently classified Porto as a
half-caste. This would be his usual method of dealing with
other Portuguese when he met them deep in the interior.
In this way he protected his own claim to have been the
first true European to reach the upper Zambesi. Although
Livingstone detested the slave-trade, he was aware that
Porto could give him useful information about the best

* Two of Porto's African attendants did complete the trans-continental journey; after passing the southern end of Lake Nyassa
they reached the east African coast at Kilwa.

route to Loanda in Angola. So the two men dined together, Porto 'swilling' Livingstone's wine as well as his own. Livingstone departed with some geographical tips, two Dutch cheeses, some preserved pears and a cauliflower: all gifts. Porto had erected a stockade near by to contain several hundred slaves. Livingstone had seen a line of chained captives led inside.

In late August, Livingstone met two Arabs who had made an epic journey from the island of Zanzibar, fifteen hundred miles to the north-east. They were assessing the slave and ivory potential of Barotseland. These men later went on to Angola and then recrossed the continent to Moçambique. a journey even more formidable than the one Livingstone was about to undertake. Livingstone's depression deepened. He was now in no doubt that far from having reached a virgin land he had arrived at a place where 'the slave trade seems pushed into the very centre of the continent from both sides'.[10] In fact Arab slaving operations would remain confined to the area hundreds of miles to the north-east, around Lake Nyassa, and to the regions immediately north of that. For the next ten years, as will be seen, Livingstone was to be far more concerned with Portuguese slavery than with Arab activities. Only when he started exploring around Lake Nyassa in 1863 did he realize the extent of the east African slave-trade. Since the British had never participated in the centuries-old Arab slave-trade, it was not a subject that pre-occupied them overmuch till Livingstone's revelations in the 1860s.

Livingstone's last disappointment on his journey through Barotseland was due to his complete failure to find any place free of malaria. He himself had never had malaria before late May 1853, and his first experience of the disease did much more to persuade him that it was serious than his previous observations of other people's sufferings. Between May and September, Livingstone had suffered eight attacks of fever. His tongue had been painful, his face had come out in boils, he had constantly wanted to urinate and his head and stomach felt as though they were exploding. Worse than that, 'the fever frequently affects the bowels, producing bloody stools and great pain . . . The people report the whole country as excessively sickly, and the appearance of the Makololo as contrasted with the aboriginal inhabitants fully confirms this assertion.'[11] As

Livingstone acknowledged in his journal, 'The prospects for these dark regions are not bright.'[12] In 1851 he had confidently told the Directors that traders would be able to come to Barotseland between June and September in perfect safety. During these months he had had fever once every couple of weeks. He was extremely alarmed at the thought that if traders came they might die and 'then others might esteem it a tempting of Providence to follow'. Of course he could have made a clean breast of it by telling the Directors the real state of affairs, but that would certainly have prevented any future efforts being made in the area. He could also have told them that the Makololo were more savage than any of the tribes to the south, but this too would have made his earlier pronouncements look like foolish over-optimism. Instead he decided to play down all the difficulties, including the firm foothold the Mambari and the Portuguese had established. So while Livingstone admitted to the Directors that he had not yet found a healthy locality for a mission, he informed them that he would 'not give up the case as hopeless'; instead, he went on: 'I have decided to try and fulfil the second part of my enterprise, viz. to open up a way to the coast.'[13] Realizing that he would have to say a little more about fever, he assured the Directors that none of his party had died of it, and 'if I had been able to regulate my diet, &c., I should not have been subjected to so many attacks'. The frequent wettings he had endured while travelling by canoe he added as another reason for the frequency of his own bouts of fever.[14] He concluded his letter by suggesting that he might well find a healthy spot east of Linyanti at a later stage. In his journal he told the truth: 'We must submit to malaria and trust in God for the rest.'[15]

So when Livingstone returned from Barotseland and the Zambesi to Linyanti in September 1853, he faced an insoluble dilemma. Having failed to find a suitable place for missionaries or traders to settle in, even if he did then manage to open a suitable route from the sea, it would still not justify him in recommending widespread European penetration of the interior. This was a crucial setback, for all his plans had hinged on the establishment of European trade in south-central Africa. Without commerce there could be no curbing of the slave-trade and no economic subversion of tribal society. Missionary success, Livingstone was certain, depended on those two preconditions. Otherwise missionaries would risk their lives to achieve less than they had in Bechuanaland. With good reason Livingstone wrote miserably: 'I am at a loss what to do.'[16]

Yet there was one thing he could not do, and that was to give up. He had given all his energies to convincing the Directors, his wife, his parents-in-law and his missionary colleagues that the only real hope of missionary expansion lay in the north. If he backed down he would be accused of loss of faith and held up to universal ridicule. There was nothing else for it but to try to open a path to the coast, regardless of whether anybody would want to follow it once they knew the dangers they would face in Barotseland and the adjacent country. It would have helped Livingstone if he had not known that Porto had travelled from Loanda to Linyanti several years before. His own trip to Loanda would not even be unique. But unique or not, he knew that he would be praised for it and that in itself would do something to take the edge off his sense of failure.

Of course Livingstone could have chosen to go to the east coast first, instead of deciding, as he did, to go west to Loanda. In many ways his choice was surprising. Had he gone east to start with, he could have followed the Zambesi all the way to the coast, and would thus have been able to pioneer a route that offered water transport for traders throughout its length. He gave various reasons for preferring the west. In the first place he said it was nearer —in fact the difference in distance was marginal, and in any case, since he would be going up the Zambesi against the current, the time involved would be greater. Another reason he gave was that there were Englishmen in Loanda. As he would soon discover, there was only one Englishman there.[17] It is probable that he was also influenced by the fact that Porto had already successfully made the journey. Livingstone's choice of Loanda itself is rather confusing. It was far further north than the port of Benguela on the same coast and was therefore much further from Linyanti—Loanda was north-west, Benguela west. Livingstone argued that Benguela lay on the main slave route to the coast and that, if he followed that path, he would encounter suspicion and hostility from the tribes on the way. He must however have known that Loanda received as many slaves as Benguela.[18] Although he did not say so, he was probably influenced in favour of Loanda because the Zambesi flowed from north-west instead of west. This would place Loanda closer than Benguela to the highest navigable section of the river.

As Livingstone sat in Linyanti planning his journey during September and October 1853, he must have reflected that the signs were not propitious. His attacks of fever had left him thin and weak and he also suffered badly from a common concomitant of malaria: giddiness. 'Everything,' he wrote, 'seemed to rush to the left, and if I did not catch hold of some object I fell heavily on the ground.'[19] Meanwhile, as he waited for his health to improve sufficiently for him to depart, he failed to persuade Sekeletu to take some lessons in reading. The chief's only concession was to appoint some of his subjects as guinea pigs. If reading had no terrible effect on them he might try it himself later, but if they decided to abandon their wives, as Sechele had done, he was not going to look at a book. Livingstone could only accept this, for he depended on Sekeletu completely for the goods and men he would need on his journey. The chief finally decided to loan Livingstone the free services of twenty-seven men, only two of whom were true Makololo, the rest being drawn from subject tribes like the Barotse, Batoka and Ambonda. Sekeletu was also prepared to lend his own canoe. He gave Livingstone several riding oxen and as much food as could be carried. Livingstone also received some ivory as a gift and took some more to sell in Loanda for Sekeletu. The amount of ivory that could be taken was none the less minimal, for twenty-seven men could barely carry all the supplies and trade goods needed to accomplish such a long journey.

And in spite of this, Livingstone was still dangerously underprovisioned. His beads, cloth and wire would not be enough to pay for food on the way, let alone sufficient to meet demands for payment for granting passage. There could be no guarantee that, even if food were available and themselves able to pay, the villagers would part with it; then all twenty-seven men and Livingstone himself would have to rely on his shooting skill, which, giddiness and fever apart, had not been improved by the lion's smashing of his arm. Nor could he allow Makololo to help him, since they were notoriously bad shots, and his ammunition and powder supplies were small.

When it is remembered that later explorers, such as Stanley, rarely travelled with less than two hundred porters, carrying enormous quantities of food and trade goods, the size of Livingstone's following is seen in proper perspective. Later Livingstone was to make a virtue of necessity by suggesting that 'the art of successful travel consisted in taking as few "impedimenta" as possible'.[20] The fact remains that had he been able to afford it, he would have taken more trade goods, more ammunition, more food and, to carry these, more men. He would also have provided himself with a watertight tent rather than the small and leaky one he was obliged to take. When he was on the point of departure he noticed that somebody had stolen all the medicines he had prepared. Even the traveller who claimed to believe that travelling light was the best way, admitted: 'This loss cripples me sadly.'[21] It is a striking token of Livingstone's bravery or foolhardiness that, with most of his quinine gone, he was still prepared to go on. Loanda was a thousand miles to the north-west, and once the twists and turns of the Zambesi and dozens of other diversions had been taken into account, that distance was likely to increase by a half. In modern terms the journey ahead of Livingstone would take him for a quarter of the way along the Zambesi through south-western Zambia. Then near the borders of modern Angola—nineteenth-century Angola was far smaller—he would have to leave the Zambesi and strike out overland for the remaining three-quarters of the way. This part of the journey was to prove the hardest.

When Livingstone left Linyanti, on 11 November 1853, he took little, but still everything he possessed. An inventory included a rifle and double-barrelled smooth-bore gun, a small collection of spare shirts and trousers, his Nautical Almanac, Thomson's Logarithm Tables and his Bible. He had a tiny tent, a sheepskin blanket, a rug and no ' "nicknacks" advertised as indispensable for travellers'. All this, including ammunition, beads and a little sugar, coffee and tea, fitted into four tin chests. His more precious possessions were carried separately: a sextant made by Troughton and Sims of Fleet Street, a chronometer watch with a stop second hand made by Dent's of the Strand, an artificial horizon, a pair of compasses, a thermometer and a magic lantern. Most of these had been bought with his prize money awarded by the Royal Geographical Society.

On 19 November he and his men embarked on the Zambesi at Sesheke, and from then on, while he was travelling by water, a routine was established. The party would rise at five in the morning and while Livingstone dressed, coffee would be made. After coffee and the loading of the canoes, all would embark. 'The next two hours are the most pleasant part of the day's sail. The men paddle away most vigorously; . . . they often engage in loud scolding of each other, in order to relieve the tedium of their work. About eleven we land, and eat any meat which may have remained from the previous meal, or a biscuit with honey, and drink water. After an hour's rest we again embark and cower under an umbrella. The heat is oppressive.'[22]

Two hours before sunset they would stop for the night, have coffee again and, if no animal had been shot, eat a piece of coarse bread made of maize meal. After this sparse supper, a routine worthy of a far larger expedition would begin. First of all, wrote Livingstone:

> . . . some of the men cut a little grass for my bed, while Mashauana [the head man] plants the poles of the little tent. These are used by day for carrying burdens . . . The bed is made and boxes ranged on each side of it, and then the tent pitched over all. Four or five feet in front of my tent is placed the principal or kotla fire . . . Each person knows the station he is to occupy, in reference to the post of honour at the fire in front of the door of the tent. The two Makololo occupy my right and left, both in eating and sleeping, as long as the journey lasts. But Mashauana, my head boatman, makes his bed at the door of the tent as soon as I retire. The rest, divided into small companies, according to their tribes, make sheds all round the fire, leaving a horse-shoe shaped space in front sufficient for the cattle to stand in . . . The sheds are formed by planting two stout forked poles in an inclined direction, and placing another over these in a horizontal position. A number of branches are then stuck in the ground in the direction to which the poles are inclined, the twigs drawn down ot the horizontal pole and tied with strips of bark, long grass is then laid over the branches in sufficient quantity to draw off the rain, and we have sheds

open to the fire in front and secure from beasts
behind. In less than an hour we were usually under
cover.[23]

Free at last from the chatter of his now sleeping men,
Livingstone would sit up for an hour or more writing in
his journal by the light of the fire. Around him was the
silence of the forest, only broken by the occasional howl
of a hyena and the croaking of frogs.

By day, although the Barotse valley was unbearably
hot and humid, Livingstone took pleasure in making notes
about plants, flowers and birds. Fishes also received attention, but one variety was most unwelcome: 'a striped fellow having a most formidable row of teeth outside his lips
sometimes leaps into the canoe'.[24] But the Zambesi itself
impressed Livingstone most.

> The river is indeed a magnificent one, often more
> than a mile broad, and adorned with many islands
> of from three to five miles in length. Both islands
> and banks are covered with forest, and most of the
> trees on the brink of the water send down roots from
> their branches like the banian . . . The beauty of the
> scenery of some of the islands is greatly increased by
> the date palm, with its gracefully curved fronds and
> refreshing light green colour, near the bottom of the
> picture, and the lofty palmyra towering far above,
> and casting its feathery foliage against a cloudless
> sky.[25]

The river was low and progress through the occasional
rapids was difficult. Sometimes the rocks produced steep
falls, but generally they merely caused the water to race
and boil through narrow gaps. The rocks themselves interested him, some being covered with a small, hard aquatic
plant, and others coated with a shining black glaze. During
his attacks of fever the rapids were formidable obstacles,
even though they were going against the stream. 'The
people have often to jump out and drag the canoe, and
the fall is so much the stern goes under, the water above
filling the canoe before they can bring up the after part
to the higher level.'[26]

If the canoe was allowed to come broadside to the
stream, approaching rapids, there was great danger of a

capsize. Navigation would have been easier in the middle of the river where there was deeper water, but Livingstone's men were too wary of hippopotami to risk this. They knew very well that in a river full of crocodiles, it was as well not to end up in the water.

Throughout the second half of December, Livingstone was ill with fever, but he forced himself to go on travelling. The narrow canoe became a nightmare for a man whose heart raced uncomfortably all the time and who was constantly having to be sick. Livingstone was either shivering or sweating, and vomiting was accompanied by painful diarrhoea. In these circumstances the endless singing and chatting of his attendants nearly drove him mad. 'I was so much pained by the obscene talk of our people I often wished to remove myself beyond hearing.'[27] In a canoe that was hardly feasible.

By the end of 1853, Livingstone had reached the point where he had turned back after his first examination of the Barotse valley earlier in the year. Here the Kabompo river flowed into the Zambesi from the east. Livingstone mistook the Kabompo for the upper reaches of the Zambesi and assumed as he continued north-west that he had left the main Zambesi and was following a new river, called the Leeba by local natives. In a sense this mistake was unimportant, for since Livingstone was still on the Zambesi, which he now called the Leeba, he went on mapping its course, albeit unwittingly. Livingstone was soon delighted by a sudden change of scenery, when the forests gave way to country more like 'a carefully tended gentleman's park' than anything he had previously seen in Africa.

By the end of the first week of January 1854, Livingstone had travelled sixty miles upstream from the junction with the Kabompo. The Zambesi was now much narrower and Livingstone could see that it could not be long before he would have to leave the canoe and go on overland. They were now passing through the territory of a tribe called the Balonda. Many of the Balonda underchiefs were women, and it was at the village of one such lady that Livingstone spent the night of 6 January. The chief's name was Nyamoana, and this formidable lady decided to detain Livingstone longer than he wanted to stay. She also told him not to go any further by canoe, for if a bad cataract did not stop him after a few miles, an extremely aggressive tribe called the Balobale certainly would. Livingstone told her he was not worried by aggressive tribes and insisted that he wanted to follow the river as far as he could before travelling by land. Nyamoana listened politely and told him she would not give him permission to go further. What she wanted was to get Livingstone to make a small diversion to the north-east to visit her brother Shinte, the paramount chief of the Balonda. The argument went on and Nyamoana was soon backed up by her twenty-year-old daughter, Manenko, who arrived from her village while discussions were in progress. The two women, having failed to convince Livingstone that he ought to abandon the river, set to work on his followers instead and soon had them thoroughly scared of being butchered by the fierce tribe ahead. Livingstone, however, would not give in and the issue was finally resolved by Manenko resorting to force. When Livingstone gave orders to load the canoes, she instructed her people to stop this operation. Since Livingstone was hopelessly outnumbered he had to submit, to the relief of his men. Manenko was amused by Livingstone's irritation, and, putting a hand on his shoulder, 'put on a motherly look, saying, "Now my little man, just do as the rest have done." '28

This was one of the very few occasions when Africans managed to change Livingstone's plans. He never took kindly to being thwarted, and the irony of having to do the bidding of a young woman smeared with fat and red ochre, and covered only by a profusion of ornaments and charms, did not escape him. He described her condition as one of 'frightful nudity' and deplored the thin strip of leather, less than three inches across, that was all that hid her genitals. His Makololo had in the meantime started to have dreams that told them not to go on, but they still proved amenable to a firm scolding. When all was ready for departure, Manenko's period started and another delay had to be endured. At last on 11 January the whole party set off. 'Manenko was accompanied by her husband and her drummer; the latter continued to thump most vigorously, until a heavy drizzling mist set in and compelled him to desist . . . On our Amazon went, in the very lightest marching order, at a pace that few of the men could keep up with.'29

Although Livingstone did not know it, he could not

profitably have gone more than another sixty or seventy
miles by river, for then the Zambesi would turn north-
eastwards towards its source 150 miles in that direction.
He had therefore all but reached the river's most westerly
point. Nor would the diversion to Shinte's town be a
severe inconvenience, for it was more north than east
and lay only twelve miles east of the Zambesi. At Shinte's,
Livingstone would be roughly eight hundred miles from
Loanda, which lay in a west-north-westerly direction.

As Livingstone and Manenko trudged the thirty or so
miles to Shinte's the full fury of the rainy season set in,
and Livingstone was happy to ride an ox rather than
trudge through the mud. Not so Manenko, who, rather
than appear feminine, strode ahead on foot. The country
had now become dense jungle and progress was reduced to
a crawl as the men worked with axes to cut through the
thickly entwined creepers and undergrowth. Paths seemed
to have been obliterated by climbing plants that had wound
themselves round 'gigantic trees like boa-constrictors'. The
light was dim and the damp gloominess of this shut-in
green world did nothing for the morale of Livingstone's
men. He himself was suffering from fever again: a condition which constant rain and a diet of manioc roots or
tapioca did not help.

On 15 January they arrived outside Shinte's town, and,
to Livingstone's annoyance, Manenko waited there till she
could exchange messages with her uncle. But neither the
pouring rain nor anything that he could say would make
her consider altering the normal procedure for entering
the town. Only at midday on the 16th were they able to
move on.

Livingstone heard that: 'Shinte had been employed during the night in passing from the court of one wife to
another till the morning dawned . . . Solomon,' he concluded, 'must have been in a similar predicament with his
outrageous female establishment.'[30]

Shinte was the most substantial ruler Livingstone had
come across since leaving Sekeletu, and the size of the
welcoming ceremony was an indication of this. A thousand
men in all were present, including a number of musicians,
several Mambari and two Portuguese, whom Livingstone
as usual described as half-castes. One of the Portuguese
was dressed in a blue frock-coat with epaulettes and had
brought, to add to the general noise, 'his drummer and a

key bugler making as much music as they could out of very old instruments'. 'The space allotted for Kotla* was at least one hundred yards apart, and two evergreens stood gracefully in the centre. Under these sat Shinte, clothed in a large kilt, the principal colours of which were scarlet and blue edging; he had a checked jacket on and a profusion of iron and copper leglets, his head covered with 'a helmet of beads and goose feathers.'[31]

2. Livingstone's reception at Shinte's

Livingstone sat under a tree forty yards from Shinte, while the purposes of his visit were explained by a spokes-man of Nyamoana. The connection of trade and the word of God was usually mixed up, and Jesus turned into a kind of medicine for acquiring cloth, rifles and beads. But Livingstone, who could not speak the Balonda's language, cound do little about this. His declared desire for peace was treated with scepticism on account of his travelling with two Makololo. Nevertheless Shinte was glad that he had come, and in the middle of the night of the 18th he had his guest woken up and asked to come to see him. Livingstone, who was in the sweating agonies of an inter-mittent fever, refused and the meeting took place the fol-lowing day at ten o'clock in the morning. This formal meeting was less significant than one that took place during

* The meeting place.

the night of the nineteenth. Shinte wanted to present Livingstone with a small girl, and when he refused, had a second larger one fetched, thinking his visitor had been dissatisfied because of the first one's size. One night Shinte came to Livingstone's tent and looked with astonishment at his hairbrush, thermometer and matches:

> Then, closing the tent, so that none of his own people might see the extravagance of which he was about to be guilty, he drew out from his clothing a string of beads, and the end of a conical shell which is considered, in regions far from the sea, of as great value as the Lord Mayor's badge is in London. He hung it round my neck and said, 'There, now you *have* a proof of my friendship.'[32]

Livingstone was touched by this generosity but was still depressed to note the readiness with which Shinte and his under-chiefs sold men to the Mambari or the Portuguese. He estimated that the slave-trade had been actively prosecuted in the region for fifty years. He saw further evidence of this in the extreme subservience of the Balonda to those in authority: a habit cultivated, he supposed, so that they might avoid being sold. 'The inferiors in meeting their superiors in the street at once go down on their knees and rub dust on the upper part of their arms, clapping their hands till the great ones have passed.'[33]

He was too ill during his stay at Shinte's to do much preaching but he did try his magic lantern on a large audience. The result was not happy. The first picture was of Abraham about to slaughter Isaac.

> The Balonda men remarked that the picture was more like a god than the things of wood or clay they worshipped. I explained that this man was the first of a race to whom God had given the Bible we now hold . . . The ladies listened with silent awe; but when I moved the slide, the up lifted dagger moving towards them, they thought it was to be sheathed in their bodies instead of Isaac's. 'Mother! Mother!' all shouted at once, and off they rushed helter-skelter, tumbling pell-mell over each other, and over the little idol huts and tobacco bushes; we could not get one of them back again.[34]

The task of explaining that the lantern itself was not supernatural proved too difficult. The balonda had already been told by the Mambari that English cloth came out of the sea and that the white men did too. Since they only had a dim idea of what the sea might be, these stories made their ideas of white people still more fantastic. Livingstone therefore in producing his matches, hairbrush and lantern, inevitably appeared as a magician—an impression that his constant mention of the Son of God coming down to earth and dying for everybody did nothing to dispel. The idea too that 'words' could be contained in writing seemed almost more extraordinary than the lantern itself. When Livingstone wrote up his journal crowds often collected around him to watch the strange process.

His own followers were no more receptive to his religious instruction than the Balonda, and the Barotse contingent stuck unflinchingly to their belief of metamorphosis into animals, regardless of anything he could say. They also seemed confused by their present instructions not to molest anybody. 'Going in a peaceful manner is so strange they are disposed to follow the dictation of every one we meet.'

By the end of January he was on the move again, once more in pouring rain. His guns and surgical instruments were soon rusty and everything from his tent to his clothing became damp and mildewed. By 14 February he was seventy miles north-west of Shinte's and had reached the next town, named after its chief, Katema's. Here the slave-trade's influence was still more marked and he learned with horror that potential slaves were often acquired by chiefs selecting a family or village with few or no connections elsewhere, and, after killing the headmen, selling all the women and children. He was also told that when a local chief died, 'a great number of people are slaughtered to accompany him'.[35] His attempts to tell them about Christian charity were useless and largely incomprehensible because of bad interpreters. After one sermon, he discovered to his disgust 'that my "words of God" meant "words of rain"'. Katema himself would only listen to compliments anyway, so a few major mistakes of translation in Livingstone's preaching hardly mattered to him.

By late February the party were most of them ill and thoroughly fed up with the dark rain-forests. They had other difficulties too. Only by accepting guides from each village, was Livingstone able to allay the suspicions of the people he was now passing, and these guides often took them to villages they did not want to visit, and deliberately detained them. Livingstone was still six hundred miles from the coast and was alarmed that already the slave-trade had completely undermined the usual tribal hospitality. Food was no longer given as gifts but had to be paid for. Since Livingstone's party had little to exchange, they often went hungry. Livingstone seemed unaware of the irony that the African's insistence on payment was one of the commercial habits he had hoped would break down the tribal structure. His complaints about their meanness in withholding food was a good example of his ability to adopt a double standard when it suited him. Nevertheless the commercial habits of these tribes were not of the 'legitimate' or Christian kind he had envisaged. The natives frequently asked for *hongo*, or payment for the right to pass through their territory. The demand was usually for a slave. The slave-trade had also undermined usual standards of honesty and fair play. Fines were often extorted by tricks. On one occasion a knife was planted on one of his men and cloth demanded as recompense. Soon all the beads and cloth had gone and Livingstone was reduced to parting with his shirts.

As they travelled west, the forests became slightly less dense but the rains had flooded the valleys they were crossing, forcing them to wade and swim across the worst streams and gullies. In such circumstances Livingstone and the men held on to the tails of their surviving oxen. Once Livingstone lost his grasp, and his men, who had already reached dry land, leapt in again to save him. He was amused that they were surprised he could swim and also touched by their loyalty. It was the only pleasing incident for many weeks.

The people they were now among were the Chiboque, whose manners, in Livingstone's view, matched their appearance: their teeth were filed into points and many had straws thrust through the cartilage of their noses. The Chiboque were the first people seriously to threaten the lives of Livingstone and his followers. In spite of his weakness and fever Livingstone responded with the same courage he so often showed. Ill-feeling had been provoked on both sides by failure to give presents of a suitable size. The demands being made on Livingstone were far more than he could meet and he was determined, at whatever cost, never to sell any of his own people.

> We heard some of the Chiboque remark, 'They have only five guns;' and about midday, Njambi* collected all his people and surrounded our encampment. Their object was evidently to plunder us of everything. My men seized their javelins, and stood on the defensive, while the young Chiboque had drawn their swords and brandished them with great fury. Some even pointed their guns at me, and nodded to each other, as much as to say, 'This is the way we shall do with him.' I sat on my camp stool, with my double-barrelled gun across my knees and invited the chief to be seated also.

The Chiboque were claiming that one of Livingstone's men had spat at one of them. After this incident had been explained as an accident, the old demands for a man or an ox were made. Finally these were changed to demands for guns. Livingstone was told this was what they usually got from the Mambari and they were going to get the same from him. His followers, whose nerve was now starting to crack, begged him to give some shirts and they offered to give some of their own beads. But this attempt to come to a settlement only made the Chiboque demand more and more. 'A shout was raised by the armed party, and a rush made around us with brandishing of arms. One young man made a charge at my head from behind, but I quickly brought round the muzzle of my gun to his mouth, and he retreated.'

In the meantime some of Livingstone's men had crept round behind the chief and his headmen and were now able to threaten them with their spears. In this more advantageous position, Livingstone asked once again why they wanted to shed blood when all he wished was to pass on his way peacefully. All the time he was acutely conscious that if the Chiboque used their guns, he would be their first target. 'But I was careful not to appear flurried, and, having four barrels ready for instant action, looked quietly at the savage scene around.'[36]

* A Chiboque chief.

Eventually the demands for guns and slaves were dropped, and an ox was asked for instead, with the added promise that if this gift was made, they would provide anything asked for. Livingstone decided to lower the tension by giving in and parting with an ox. The Chiboque broke their part of the bargain by giving very little in return, but at least no lives were lost. Very few later travellers displayed the same restraint in similar circumstances. But although Livingstone was not angry with the Chiboque personally, his depression increased. This would be the treatment that European traders would have to cope with if they came into central Africa from the west coast. He had no doubt at all that the Chiboque's behaviour was entirely due to the slave-trade. A single chief, provided he had a few guns, could give asylum to slaves and thus beggar an individual slave-trader. The slave-traders knew this and therefore yielded to the demands of every chief for cloth, beads and guns. The Mambari could content themselves with the thought that whatever they paid out, they would still make a decent profit in Angola. This new African rapacity was likely to be worse for the introduction of missions and trading centres than any of the old tribal habits he had so much deplored. This was not a pleasant thought to entertain when immediate difficulties were so great. Demands for oxen, slaves or ivory went on, and Livingstone soon feared that the trip might have to be abandoned. One resort was to travel by night but this was not easy in swampy forests. Livingstone was now emaciated and very weak. On average he fell off his ox three or four times a day and his bottom was covered with sores caused by constant riding. His men had now given up all hope of reaching the sea and started accusing Livingstone of having invented it. In order to quell a mutiny he had to threaten to shoot several of his followers. Immediately after this they were lured to a nearby village and robbed there. To crown it all they were then accused of stealing from a couple of slave-traders working in the area. The injustice and wearisome inevitability of the demands for recompense took Livingstone to the brink of despair. 'We came here against our will, the traders were called here without our knowledge or wish, yet all was laid gravely to our charge. After talking nearly the whole day we gave the chief an ox, but he would not take it but another.'[37]

On 2 April they were at last on the edge of the Portuguese settlements and on that day the party slaughtered their last spare ox. Livingstone had now parted with all his clothes, save those he stood up in; his razors, spoons, beads and cloth had gone some weeks before, but at long last the forests were thinning out and they stepped out of the darkness on to a wide plain: the valley of the river Quango. This river had to be crossed, and once more the demands for *bongo* started, backed up by a few inaccurate volleys of rifle fire. But deliverance was at hand in the shape of a young Portuguese sergeant of militia. Angola had been reached. Loanda was four hundred miles to the west.

Ever since its foundation in the early sixteenth century, the prosperity of this Portuguese colony had depended on the continuance of the transatlantic slave-trade. Most slaves leaving Angola were ferried straight across to another Portuguese colony: Brazil. In 1815 the Portuguese had yielded to British pressure and agreed to limit their shipments of slaves, from their possessions in Africa, solely to Brazil. The agreement was broken, and when in 1839 the British Government decided to use force to stop all exportation of slaves from Africa, whether to Brazil or anywhere else, Portuguese Angolans realized that the days of their prosperity were numbered. Nevertheless they still managed to smuggle out twenty thousand slaves a year—a quarter of their previous total. In 1850 the British Government authorized the Royal Navy to seize and search suspected vessels within Brazilian territorial waters. This was the death-blow for the Angolan slave-traders. By 1854, the year Livingstone arrived in Angola, the number of slaves exported numbered less than a couple of hundred.

The effect on the Angolan economy was disastrous. Britain had been able to abandon the slave-trade with negligible financial consequences, largely due to her rapidly expanding industries, but the Angolans had not even developed their agriculture let alone started on ambitious projects like cotton-spinning. Most of the Portuguese Angolans lived on the coast in Ambriz, Loanda or Benguela, where they were vainly striving to start cotton-growing and other activities to replace the slave-trade. All trade in the Portuguese African colonies was hampered by the metropolitan country's refusal to allow in foreign capital and by a protectionist policy. Portugal would not promote emigration schemes to bolster the tiny European population in Angola, nor would they invest capital. The result was a general sense of demoralization. Most of the white inhabitants had originally come out with the one intention of making some quick money and then returning home. Their hopes had gone very sour on them. In the interior Portuguese occupation was nominal rather than real. Livingstone reached his first Portuguese settlement fifty miles west of the river Quango, three hundred miles from the coast. This was the military and trading post of Cassange, with a total white population of fifty. Cassange was linked with the coast by a line of a dozen similar fortified trading posts. Life in these remote outposts was worse than at the coast. Fever, tribal raids, an almost total absence of roads and the indifference of the Angolan Government left these distant settlers without hope or incentives. Their most profitable activities were journeys into the interior to buy ivory and slaves, who would be sold not for export but for domestic use in one of the coastal towns. The central government had recently decided to curtail this one lucrative pursuit on the grounds that such expeditions into the interior might provoke incidents with distant tribes and thus create a border problem. In fact the traders knew that there was no real border; and since the central government could not count on law enforcement even on the coast, they were not likely to be able to do much about the situation four hundred miles inland.

It took Livingstone no time to point out most of the faults of the colony and his scorn increased when he heard that many of the white inhabitants had been transported there as convicts. He deplored the lack of European women but was impressed that the Portuguese who had half-caste children treated them with the same consideration as their white offspring. There was in fact, as Livingstone noted, far less racial prejudice in this former stronghold of the slave-trade than there was in the Cape Colony. But this liberality was in his view more than offset by the apparent apathy of most of the settlers. He wrote confidently that, had Britain originally colonized Angola, it would now be producing as much cotton as the southern states of America. Nevertheless there was one Portuguese virtue he could not deny and that was their hospitality.

It is miraculous that Livingstone was welcomed so

warmly at Cassange and at all the other Portuguese settlements where he stayed on the way from the Quango
river to Loanda. The British Navy had wrecked the economy of the colony, and here was an Englishman, who
called himself a missionary but probably was an agent of
the British Government, snooping around, taking longitudes and latitudes, and making numerous notes about
everything he saw. The Portuguese never did really believe
that Livingstone was a missionary but they still fed him,
gave him new clothes, took him into their houses and
treated him as a friend. Livingstone gratefully acknowledged each individual act of kindness, but did not change
his broader views about Angola being a corrupt and
unprogressive place.

Livingstone stayed at Cassange from 12 to 21 April.
Cassange, he soon discovered, was typical of most inland
trading posts which he passed through on his way to
Loanda. Of the fifty Europeans there, most were officers
in the Angolan militia. Since they were hardly ever paid,
these men also worked as traders, employing native agents
and middlemen, like the Mambari, to make journeys into
the interior to buy slaves and ivory. Sometimes the Portuguese took time off to go into the interior themselves. The
soldiery at Cassange mainly consisted of native /levies,
whose loyalty was questionable and whose discipline nonexistent. The soldiers were there largely to give credibility
to Portugal's claim to have established their authority over
an area extending three hundred miles into the interior.
They were also supposed to be watching against incursions
by hostile tribes. None of the officers were married to
European wives and therefore all the children were halfcastes. Nevertheless life at Cassange was not without some
compensations; the gardens around the town were full of
many different kinds of fruit and the lush grass suited
cattle. Ivory trading also brought some of the inhabitants
a decent profit. Had they not been so prone to regular
bouts of malaria, the residents of Cassange would not
have found too many reasons to bemoan their lot, unprogressive and corrupt though they were.

Strengthened by cheese, milk and meat, Livingstone
made good progress from Cassange and by the end of the
first week of May had travelled another two hundred
miles to Ambaca, the next Portuguese settlement of any
size. His host there was a man called Arsenio de Carpo,

whom Livingstone found exceptionally kind and pleasant. Later he changed his mind when he heard that Carpo had killed his father some years before and had also been convicted of fraud. Shortly after leaving Ambaca on the final 150 miles of his journey, Livingstone's health cracked up and he was prostrated by almost continuous attacks of fever. His followers were also becoming more and more apprehensive. Perhaps, after all, Livingstone would turn out to be a particularly plausible slaver who would sell them all as soon as they reached the coast. But Livingstone managed to reassure them. Twenty miles outside Loanda, Livingstone's condition worsened and he began to wonder whether he was going to live. His fever was so bad that he could not summon enough strength to stay on his ox for more than ten minutes at a time. He was also suffering from chronic dysentery. When Livingstone was carried into Loanda on 1 May 1854, he seemed very close to death.

He had heard at the Cape that there were a number of Englishmen in Loanda but his men soon found that there was only one: a Mr Edmund Gabriel, whose impressive official title was Her Majesty's Commissioner for the Suppression of the Slave Trade in Loanda. From Livingstone's later letters, nobody would have guessed how ill he had been on his arrival. Certainly none of his correspondents would have thought he had been all but given up for dead by Gabriel. Livingstone was a profuse letter-writer and was extremely regular in making entries in his journal. He was to keep up his journal till a few days before his death in 1873. But from 24 May to 14 June he was evidently too weak to write anything. As long after his arrival in Loanda as 4 July, he was unable to write a full-length letter and had to dictate one to Edmund Gabriel so that the Directors would know that he was alive. Only in early August, two months after his arrival in the town, was he able to write a letter unaided.

As usual Livingstone's motives for playing down his sickness had little to do with a desire to save his friends and family unnecessary worry. It was his old device for making conditions appear less malignant than they were. Soon he was telling the directors that had his party travelled in the dry, as opposed to the rainy, season he would not have suffered nearly so much. Then if he had been able to take more food and changes of clothing, things

might have been different. Even so he could hardly deny
that his journey had been hard. The problems, even when
understated, seemed formidable enough: dense rain-forests, swamps, hostile tribes, slave traders and fever were
difficulties which even in watered-down language were not
likely to encourage traders to believe that an ideal route
into the interior had been found. Livingstone told the
Directors that he intended to retrace his steps to Linyanti
and then attempt to reach the east coast. The reason for
this new journey, he assured them, was not that the route
he had 'opened' was impossible but that a way to 'the
Eastern coast may be less difficult'. 'If I succeed,' he went
on, 'we shall at least have a choice.'[38] A little later Livingstone was telling a friend: 'The path we have already
opened has many advantages.' When listed they were not
impressive. The principal one was that the Portuguese
coastal towns were in regular communication with Cassange and that this gave traders a good start. He did not
go on to emphasize that Cassange was still almost a
thousand miles from Linyanti. Later on in the same letter,
Livingstone's enthusiasm was even greater. 'The only fault
of the new path is, it admits of conveyance by human
labour alone. The forests and boggy rivers present insur-
mountable obstacles to waggons.'[39] Having stressed over
and over again that he had not set out as a mere traveller,
in order to justify himself, Livingstone had to pretend that
his trip had had some practical result. He might try and
fool others, but he could not fool himself; his journey, he
knew very well, had established beyond doubt that commercial operations in the interior could never be begun on
any scale from the west coast. Unless he was to content
himself with the glory of being the first British explorer to
have reached the west coast from Barotseland, he was
going to have to return to Linyanti, to find a better route
to the east coast along the Zambesi. Providence, he had
told everybody, had favoured missionary and commercial
operations in Makololo country. An east coast route was
the only chance he had left to prevent others suggesting
that he had been deluded and that his interest had always
been primarily in exploring. His position would have been
happier if Porto, and another Portuguese trader Caetano
Ferra, had not previously made the journey from the coast
to Barotseland. There is no denying that Livingstone's success in reaching Loanda, under-provisioned, ill-equipped

and completely dependent on the voluntary labour of
twenty-seven natives, had been a magnificent achievement.
But since it had disproved almost everything Livingstone
had wished to demonstrate, it was not simply self-effacing
modesty that made him feel he would have to do better.
His decision to try to reach the other side of the continent
is none the less remarkable for that. The journey from
Linyanti to Loanda had nearly killed him; now he was
going to attempt not only to repeat that journey but also
to go on another thousand miles east of Linyanti.

3. Loanda

While he was at Loanda, Livingstone refused a passage
home to England in a British warship. Later this was seen
as a mark of his true heroism, but more than that it
proved, according to most of his biographers, that rather
than abandon his faithful Makololo porters he was prepared to undergo the horrors of the 'dark continent' once
more. The fate of the Makololo who had come with him
was in fact a very low priority. He would take them back
to Linyanti because he needed them. When he arrived in
east Africa in 1856, he was happy enough to sail for England, leaving his 'faithful' Makololo at Tete for four years.
He had promised to return for them within a single year.

Livingstone's four months in Loanda were marred by
his repeated attacks of fever. He was lucky that three
British warships of the blockading squadron were in harbour, for without the attentions of the doctor of H.M.S.
Polyphemus, he might have died. Mr Cockin, however,
prescribed and made up pills of opium, opium supposi-

tories, calomel and quinine. The treatment was successful,
for by August Livingstone was able to take the Makololo
aboard another British warship, the *Pluto*. Since the Makololo had never seen any ship larger than a canoe, they
were amazed. The ship's cannons were fired in their honour, and when they had understood the destructive potential of such weapons they begged Livingstone to let them
take one back to Linyanti to fire at the Matabele. Livingstone had never before managed to get across the idea of
European technological superiority. These warships did
more to support what he had said than months of explanation. From then on, wrote Livingstone, 'I rose rapidly in
their estimation . . . and always afterwards they treated
me with the greatest deference'.[40] The *Pluto*'s captain was
a Commander Norman Bedingfeld, whom Livingstone took
a liking to. Two years later he was to regret he had ever
met the man.

Even when Livingstone was well, there were problems
that weighed on his mind and gave him no peace. Once he
got back to Linyanti, there was no knowing whether Sekeletu would allow him to take men with him for his proposed journey to the east coast. The thought of travelling
1,300 miles over Africa only to be told that further
progress was impossible, was a terrifying prospect. Livingstone would have felt more secure had he made a profit
with Sekeletu's ivory but he had had to sell most of it on
the way to buy food and to pay *hongo*. There was another
nasty consideration: even if Sekeletu ordered men to
accompany him, they might well desert after being told
about the hardships their companions had endured on the
way to the west coast. It is possible that thoughts like
these made Livingstone wonder whether he had made the
right decision in refusing a passage home in one of the
warships. The majority of Englishmen would, in all likeli-
hood, never have heard of Silva Porto and Caetano Ferra,
nor would they probably understand that, in Livingstone's
terms, his journey had been a failure. The directors of
the London Missionary Society would do all they could
to announce his return as a triumphant occasion. He
would be able to lecture all over the country and raise
thousands of pounds for the Society. If the Royal Geographical Society had awarded him half the annual Royal
Premium for reaching Lake Ngami, they too could be
expected to do more this time. Since Livingstone liked

praise and must have known that he would have received plenty had he returned, his sense of personal failure and disappointment must have been very great to have stopped him. In fact he had become completely obsessed with the idea of opening a *highway* into the interior. Without that highway there would be no commerce, without commerce there would be no social change and without that there would be no diffusion of Christianity. If the highway was found, Livingstone was convinced that not only African history but the future of Christianity itself would both be altered beyond recognition by his discovery. If he could hold out that prospect on his return to England, that would be something immeasurably greater than anything he had so far achieved. He might die in the attempt, but even if it was a gamble, the stakes were unusually high, and Livingstone felt that he had an advantage which few gamblers possess: his life was 'charmed' till his work was done. God must want Christianity to come to central Africa, so Livingstone would live. Such was his conviction. It did not however stop him seeing the dramatic elements in his decision. 'I will open a way to the interior or perish,' he told his brother impressively.

Before he left for the interior again, the Board of Works in Loanda donated a colonel's dress uniform and a horse for Sekeletu and clothing for all Livingstone's men. In addition they were all bought muskets, which meant that, in one respect at least, the expedition was better supplied now than when it had started. Official generosity did not, however, impress Livingstone much. He reckoned that if he had not unexpectedly approached Angola from the east, but had instead come by sea, matters would have been very different. Livingstone felt that because the Portuguese would know that Gabriel had informed the British Government of his arrival in Angola, 'they could not for shame refuse me a passage back. But it is ten to one if they would allow me to land a box of bibles at Loanda.'[41]

Livingstone left Loanda on 20 September 1854 and within a month was a hundred miles inland. He had had the offer of European company but had as usual turned it down. His proposed companion had been an Austrian botanist, Dr Walweitch, currently working for the Angolan Government. But, wrote Livingstone, 'as it appeared evident to me this plan would afford Dr Walweitch an oppor-

tunity of availing himself of all my previous labours . . .
without acknowledging his obligations to me in Europe, I
considered it would not be prudent to put such a strong
temptation in his way'.[42] If Livingstone found his precious
highway, nobody else was going to be in on the act.

Livingstone made very bad progress during the first
months of his trip back to Linyanti. Numerous officers at
the various militia posts detained him to give them treatment for fever, and then in mid-December, still only two
hundred miles from the coast, he heard that the ship
carrying the letters he had written in Loanda had been
wrecked. This detained him for a further two weeks, while
he re-wrote everything, and he was not on his way again
till New Year's Day 1855. While he was doing this rewrit-
ing, letters from Gabriel reached Pungo Adongo, where he
was staying. Enclosed was a copy of a letter from Lord
Clarendon, the Foreign Secretary, expressing pleasure at
Livingstone's safe arrival, and a cutting from *The Times*,
dated 8 August 1854, describing Livingstone's journey as
'one of the greatest geographical explorations of the age'.
Livingstone transcribed the cutting into his journal but
made no comment.

By 2 February he had reached Cassange; a distance of
just over three hundred miles had taken him four months.
He had completed the entire journey from Linyanti to
Loanda in six. It was probably this prolonged stay in the
decaying Portuguese settlements that temporarily made
Livingstone revert to his old liberal attitudes towards the
Africans. If Angola was an example of what white settlers
had achieved in the course of three hundred years, could
elaborate claims really be made for European civilization?
It was an embarrassing question, made more acute by
Livingstone's conviction that the nearer the Portuguese
borders he had travelled on his journey out, the worse the
natives had become and the more greedy their demands.
This was hardly an example of natives being 'elevated' by
a 'superior race'.

It is a peculiar paradox that, at the beginning of a journey intended as the first stage in the break-up of tribal
society, Livingstone should once again have been writing
about Africans with sympathy and understanding.

> With a general opinion they are wiser than their
> white neighbours. I think this good opinion of our-

selves is very·general in the world. Each tribe has a
considerable consciousness of goodness, or following
its own interests in the best ways. Austria would find
its own counterpart in every dirty little village in
Africa. In Africa, however, they have less of what the
Germans call philosophy to uphold their views; less
diplomacy, protocols, & notes. They go direct to the
point, and in so doing shew a more philosophic spirit
than the Germans. They have few theories but many
ideas . . . There is no search after the supreme good,
such as we are to believe the ancient philosophers
engaged in, but which were perhaps rather a search
for what words more could flow from the pen to
produce the impression among his contemporaries,
who might read his endless rhapsodies unfathomable
and pronounce their author to be a profound remarkable man . . . But the African cares not at all for
these utterly inane speculations. The pleasures of animal life are ever present to his mind as the supreme
good, and but for his innumerable phantoms he would
enjoy his luscious climate as well as it is possible for
man to do.[43]

Yet he was to go even further than this, in what
appeared to be a flat contradiction of much of what he
had written between 1851 and 1853. Then he had compared the state of the inmates of workhouses and the lot
of African chiefs and had confidently stated that in every
respect the British poor were better off. Now he made a
very different comparison in which the Africans came off
best. "To one who has observed the hard toil of the poor
in old civilized countries, the state in which the inhabitants
[of Africa] live is one of glorious ease . . . Food abounds
and very little effort is needed for its cultivation; the soil is
so rich that no manure is required.'[44]

In other ways, too, he decided that Africans could learn
nothing from Europeans: 'Africans are not by any means
unreasonable. I think unreasonableness is more a hereditary disease in Europe than in this land.'[45] It was almost
as though Livingstone could divide all his thoughts into
different and unconnected compartments. Sometimes he
would emphasize only Europe's technological prowess,
sometimes he would see only the social problems. Africans

were either miserable savages capable of selling their own
women and children to heartless slavers, or they were
unspoiled and innocent people living in a worldly paradise.
His judgment, inevitably, was often influenced by the conditions of travel and the state of his health. At the beginning of his journey back to Linyanti his health was good,
and in the dry season the going was firm. The quality of
the light, the gentle warmth of the air and the sense of
freedom that travelling gave combined to lead Livingstone
into writing passages of lyrical description that owed more
to his aesthetic feelings than to moral or economic judgments.

> How often have I beheld, in still mornings, scenes the
> very essence of beauty, and all bathed in a quiet air
> of delicious warmth! Yet the occasional slight motion
> imparted a pleasing sensation of coolness as of a fan.
> Green grassy meadows, the cattle feeding, the goats
> browsing, the kids skipping, the groups of herdboys
> with miniature bows, arrows and spears; the women
> wending their way to the river with watering pots
> poised jauntily on their heads; men sewing under the
> shady banians; and old grey-headed fathers sitting on
> the ground, with staff in hand, listening to the morn-
> ing gossip.[46]

Yet within weeks it is hard to believe that Livingstone
had ever written such words. As the plains gave way to the
forests, and his health again began to deteriorate, the old
condemnatory tone once more took over. After being
attacked again by the Chiboque, and having discovered
that most of the forest tribes were idolators, Livingstone
used the scenic beauty of Africa, not to show the happiness of the African's life but as a contrast to point out
his spiritual degradation. 'How painful is the contrast
between the inward gloom and the brightness of the outer
world, between the undefined terrors of the spirit and the
peace and beauty that pervades the scene around.'[47]

A little later Livingstone was transcribing into his journal, under the heading 'Prospects of the Negro', his belief
in progress and the coming of the 'Golden Age' through
the works of inventors, reformers and missionaries. Everything, he repeated, was hopeless for Africa unless there

was 'contact with superior races by commerce'.[48] The Africans, he went on, are 'inured to bloodshed and murder,' and care for no god except being bewitched'. They were cowardly and through their constant use of cannabis could not form 'any clear thought on any subject'.

By mid-March, Livingstone's fever had become more serious and the rate of travel had sunk to below seven miles a day. The countryside was so badly flooded that at times they had to dig trenches around the spot where they proposed to sleep so that some of the water would drain off. Three months later, Livingstone was in the Balonda country. He had partially lost the sight of one eye through walking into a jutting out branch and his hearing was failing due to repeated doses of quinine. To add to his misery he was vomiting blood. At this time Livingstone had to put down another mutiny among his followers. He did so by hitting the leading trouble-maker on the head with his revolver. Given his weakness it was quite an achievement. Livingstone did not see it in that light. The infliction of any corporal punishment, whether premeditated or not, always disgusted him. These were awkward views to hold when passing the Balonda, who, Livingstone felt, would strip harmless travellers of everything they possessed unless they showed a willingness to fight.

By late July, Livingstone had reached the northern end of the Barotse valley. Linyanti lay three hundred miles to the south-east. Many of his men came from Barotseland, and as they came closer to their homes, many heard that their wives had remarried in their absence. To Livingstone's dismay few seemed depressed, even when some former wives arrived with tiny infants fathered by other men. Their attitude was that there were lots of women about and that they would soon have more wives than they had had before they set out. Clearly Livingstone had not managed to persuade them that monogamy was the best form of marriage. In fact none of his religious teaching had had any effect on the men, even though he had been with them almost two years. They had admired the large houses in Loanda and had been impressed by the British warships but, contrary to Livingstone's theories, this had not made them any more interested in Christianity. James Chapman, the trader who visited the Makololo in 1853 and then again in 1862, said that one of the tribe's favourite pastimes was imitating Livingstone reading and singing psalms. This would always be accompanied by howls of derisive laughter. The Makololo's word for psalm-singing, *bokolella*, meant to bellow like a bull.[49] During the whole of Livingstone's association with the Makololo he made no converts.

The party reached Linyanti on 13 September 1855, having been away for two months short of two years. The men who had come with Livingstone were soon boasting shamelessly about their experiences, talking about the large ships which had eaten 'black stones'—there was no coal in Barotseland—and showing off their new clothes. Dressed in red caps and red and white jackets, 'they tried to walk like the soldiers they had seen in Loanda . . . and excited the unbounded admiration of the women and children'.[50] Sekeletu was also pleased with his colonel's uniform, and from then on wore it on special occasions until it fell to bits. Livingstone was immensely relieved that Sekeletu did not seem annoyed or surprised that he had not brought back more cloth and guns. In fact the chief was delighted that his white man had returned at all. When Livingstone explained to him that he intended to go down to the east coast, Sekeletu seemed as eager as ever to help him. This time, he said, he would lend Livingstone over a hundred men and would send much more ivory to be sold at the coast. In exchange Livingstone undertook to bring back a long list of goods that included guns, bullets, revolvers, shirts, blankets, soldiers' uniforms, cutlery, an iron rockingchair and a pair of spectacles with green glass in them.[51] The agreement was that Livingstone should bring back the men and the goods within two years. After that Sekeletu believed that Livingstone and his wife, the all-important daughter of Moffat, would come to live on the Zambesi. This would enable the Makololo to move away from the swamps without fear of the Matabele. It was this thought above all that persuaded Sekeletu that Livingstone was worth helping. Sadly for Sekeletu, time would show that Livingstone had used him and not the other way round. It would be five years before the two men met again and by that time Livingstone's interests would have shifted yet again. The Makololo were no longer God's chosen tribe. Livingstone gained fame and recognition for the journeys he made between 1853 and

1856. Without the help of the Makololo he could not have made them. Sekeletu and his tribe gained nothing; in fact in the end they lost by their association with Livingstone. Already cut off behind the Chobe river, in an unhealthy place, and with little security, their reliance on Livingstone led them to reject the few traders who fought their way up to the Zambesi from the south. When no trade came up the Zambesi from the coast, as Livingstone had promised it would, they were more isolated than before. Unable to leave their swamps for fear of the Matabele, the true Makololo were dying out through fever, bringing the 'day closer when their numbers would prove insufficient to keep down their vassals. Livingstone was their last chance for getting out of an impossible situation. They did everything they could for him and in the end he let them down. When Livingstone left Linyanti for the east coast in November 1855, the Makololo were eight years from extinction. Sekeletu died in 1863 and the Makololo's Barotse vassals seized the opportunity of a disputed succession to overthrow their overlords and butcher them all. It would be too much to suggest that Livingstone was responsible. But Sekeletu was probably right in thinking that Livingstone could have helped them to return to a healthier area without danger and could thus have saved them and their tribe.

Back at Linyanti, as well as planning the next stage in his journey, Livingstone wrote letters home. He was still worried in case his illness at Loanda had given the Directors the idea that missionaries ought not to work in central Africa. During three years Livingstone had had twenty-seven attacks of fever, but he still told the Directors jauntily: 'I apprehend no great mortality among missionaries, men of education and prudence who can, if they will, adopt proper hygienic precautions.'[52] Within a few years such dangerous false optimism would lead to tragedy.

On 3 November Livingstone and his 114 porters set out for the Zambesi. His plan was to follow the river right down to its mouth on the east coast, just south of the Portuguese town of Quilimane. This intended journey was roughly a thousand miles, three or four hundred less than his journey to Loanda. In modern terms for half the way he would be travelling along the Zambesi where it divides Zambia and

Rhodesia; for the rest, he would be following the river through Portuguese Moçambique to the sea. Theoretically Livingstone could have followed another route to the coast, that used by the Arabs he had met in 1853. This would have meant following a more northerly route taking him to the east coast via Lake Nyassa. His navigable highway fixation inevitably ruled out this second option.

In late November, five years after he had first heard about the great falls east of Sesheke, Livingstone reached the falls of Mosioatunya or 'the smoke that thunders'. Livingstone was impressed, but a waterfall, even the most spectacular in the world, did not thrill him to the extent the Zambesi itself had done in 1851. It was very fine to look at, but beyond that it had no useful function. Livingstone's description, on reaching what is still considered one of the great scenic wonders of the world, is so miraculously precise and flat that it is worth quoting. The lack of adjectives is an outstanding feature.

> The falls are singularly formed. They are simply the whole mass of the Zambesi waters rushing into a fissure or rent made right across the bed of the river. In other falls we have usually a great change of level both in the bed of the river and adjacent country, and after the leap the river is not much different from what it was above the falls; but here the river, flowing rapidly among numerous islands and from 800 to 1,000 yards wide, meets a rent in its bed at least 100 feet deep and at right angles with its course, or nearly due east and west, leaps into it, and becomes a boiling white mass at the bottom ten or twelve yards broad.'[53]

An indication of how little Livingstone cared about his 'discovery' was his complete underestimation of both the height and width of the falls. The actual width is 1,900 yards, double his figure, and the height varies from two to three hundred feet, again double his estimate. Livingstone only wrote his famous set pieces about the falls on his return to England, when his publisher John Murray suggested it would be a good idea. And so various famous phrases were written like: 'scenes so lovely must have been gazed upon by angels in their flight'. Nevertheless Livingstone could see that although the falls would not help him

in any practical way, they might still serve a purpose. He
would call them the Victoria Falls, which might help
interest the British public in the area where they were
situated. For some time he had been thinking of calling
some geographical feature after Her Majesty and this one
was eminently suitable.

Immediately east of the falls the Zambesi loops to the
south before flowing on east and then north-east. This arc
was roughly 250 miles in length. Livingstone decided to
travel on north of the river, cutting out the loop altogether. His decision owed nothing to a desire to reach the
coast speedily. He had heard that the area north of the
Zambesi and just east of the falls was high, fertile and
healthy. It might be the place he had so long hoped to
find for missionary and trading settlements. As Livingstone
pressed on eastwards across the Batoka Plateau, he
became more and more convinced that he had made a
crucial discovery. The plateau was relatively high and,
although it was well watered by streams, it was not
swampy. Because of the height, the temperature was cooler
than in the river valley. The area seemed suitable for
cattle and supported sizeable trees. In a state of euphoria
Livingstone tramped on, marking detailed notes of all the
favourable characteristics he could find. Of course he
knew that the Matabele lived due south, across the Zambesi, but he was not going to let this worry him yet. Nor
was his faith in the area shaken by the Batoka themselves,
whom he considered even 'more degraded than the
Barotse', and the Barotse had never impressed him much.
The Batoka, he fumed, are lacking in 'all self-respect,
savage and cruel under success, but easily cowed and
devoid of all moral courage'.[54] Almost everything they
did he found repellent, but he singled out their mode of
greeting strangers for special abuse.

> They throw themselves on their backs on the ground,
> and rolling from side to side, slap the outside of their
> thighs as expression of thankfulness and welcome,
> uttering the words, 'Kina bomba.' This method of
> salutation was to me very disagreeable, and I never
> could get reconciled to it. I called out 'Stop, stop! I
> don't want that;' but they, imagining I was dissatis-
> fied, only tumbled about more furiously, and slapped
> their thighs with greater vigour. The men being

totally unclothed, this performance imparted to my mind a painful sense of their extreme degradation.[55]

Yet no habit nor custom was sufficiently distasteful to discourage Livingstone from believing that he had found an area where Europeans could live in central Africa. Not even an attack by a frenzied native with an axe shook his faith. The Batoka Plateau was the place; the centre from which trade and Christianity would together send out cleansing waves in wider and wider circles till the whole area had been purged of the slave-trade and tribal barbarism. There was however one more problem left. The Batoka Plateau at its most easterly point was eight hundred miles from the mouth of the Zambesi. For traders to come, the Zambesi would have to be navigable for almost a thousand miles. It was therefore to the Zambesi that Livingstone now gave his undivided attention.

At the beginning of the year 1856 he had crossed the Batoka Plateau and rejoined the Zambesi on the eastern side of the loop, at a point a hundred miles from the Moçambique border, where the river begins to flow due east. Just as when he had been approaching Angola native hostility had suddenly increased, now, as Livingstone came closer to the deserted Portuguese settlement of Zumbo, the same pattern began to repeat itself. Just outside Zumbo the river Loango flows into the Zambesi from the north. Livingstone realized at once that without the help of local tribes and the loan of canoes he would be unable to cross. It was a most unfortunate moment to be so dependent. Recently the people had been behaving very suspiciously 'collecting from all sides and keeping at a distance from us though professing friendship'.[56] Livingstone knew that when his men forded the river they would be split up and therefore at the mercy of the local natives. He was also alarmed when these people refused to tell him why the Portuguese had left Zumbo. After prolonged discussions with the chief, Livingstone was offered two canoes for the crossing. This would mean numerous trips to transport his 114 men. It now seemed certain that an attack would be made when they began crossing. It was now evening and so no move could be made till the following day. In such circumstances Livingstone derived inner strength from comparisons which many of his former missionary colleagues would have thought blasphemous: 'See, O Lord,' he wrote, 'how the heathen rise up against me as they did to Thy Son'.[57] For a time he toyed with the idea of evading his enemies by crossing during the night, but at last he rejected this plan. Was that the way any Instrument of God's Providence should behave? 'I will not cross furtively by night as intended. It would appear as flight, and should such a man as I flee? Nay, verily. I shall take observations for lat. & long. tonight, though they may be the last. I feel quite calm now, thank God.'[58]

This mixture of bravery, pride, faith and obstinacy was typical of the man. But Livingstone's decision owed a lot to another cause; by risking his life he was showing his absolute faith in Providence. If God wanted him to live, then God's will would be done. Death would prove that God no longer needed him. 'If I am cut off . . . my efforts are no longer needed by Him who knows what is best.'[59] A belief that God controlled every event might seem to provide an insurance strong enough to exclude all fear. In a sense this may explain some of Livingstone's outstanding bravery; but it should also be kept in mind that when setbacks occurred, the man, who believed he had a providential role to play, was faced with something far worse than physical fear: a sense that God might not after all have intended him to follow the course he was pursuing and that He had rejected him.

The following morning the signs were as ominous as before. The women had been sent away and large numbers of armed men appeared. Although two canoes had been promised, only one was provided and this seemed more alarming because two further canoes were tied to the bank near by. Getting all the goods, cattle and men across in a single canoe was a lengthy and nerve-racking experience. Livingstone decided that he should be the last to cross. Surrounded as he was by natives with their spears at the ready, he showed no fear and started to talk to them, showing his watch, lens and compass 'to keep them amused until there remained only those who were to enter the canoe with me'. Afterwards he bore them no malice for having behaved so threateningly, suggesting that they had probably been afraid he might play them some trick.

It was late January when Livingstone passed Zumbo. He was now about five hundred miles from the mouth of the Zambesi. The reason why the Portuguese had left this area was obvious: the natives had forced them out. Twenty miles beyond Zumbo at a place called Pangura, Livingstone made a decision which would later bring him more grief than any he had yet made. He heard from a local chief called Mpende that the Zambesi flowed on due east for seventy miles and then turned sharply south-east. That being the case, if Livingstone headed south-east at once he would be able to cut off a corner and reach the Portuguese settlement of Tete much more quickly. Mpende's direct route to Tete was fifty miles shorter than the bending course of the Zambesi. Livingstone would not have been influenced by distance alone; for somebody who had travelled thousands of miles, 200 as opposed to 250 miles was not a significant difference. Mpende also told him that if he tried to follow the Zambesi he would have to cope with a hilly and rocky path. Livingstone, who was not feeling strong, considered this last piece of information and decided to cross the Zambesi and do as Mpende suggested. On the southern bank Livingstone expressed himself 'most sincerely thankful' that matters had turned out as they had. The irony of these words would only become apparent two years later.

By leaving the Zambesi at this point, Livingstone failed to discover the Kebrabasa Rapids, which were finally to wreck his hopes of the Zambesi becoming a navigable highway. Had he seen these cataracts in 1856, he would have been saved the ignominy of building up false hopes only later to have to admit to the public and the British Government that he had been deceived.

When he did reach Tete, Livingstone made enquiries about the section of the Zambesi he had not seen. 'I was informed of the existence of a small rapid in the river near Chicova; had I known of this previously, I certainly would not have left the river without examining it. It is called Kebrabasa and is described as a number of rocks which jut out across the stream.'[60] It is most puzzling that Livingstone managed to leave Tete with the impression that Kebrabasa posed so slight a threat to future navigation of the river. A number of Portuguese living in the town had seen the devastating series of cataracts that extended along the river for thirty miles. Perhaps Livingstone never spoke to these men, or if he did, he heard what he wanted to hear rather than what he was told. He was determined that the Zambesi was going to provide a navigable highway to the Batoka Plateau and nobody was going to persuade him otherwise.

His own scientific calculations about the Zambesi certainly show a marked propensity for wishful thinking. He must have felt slightly uneasy at Tete, for he wrote down a list of figures in his journal designed to prove by the speed of the river's flow that there were no steep drops between the Victoria Falls and Tete. Unfortunately all his deductions were based on the false assumption that the speed of the river was the same for nearly a thousand miles. He also ignored the vast differences in heights that he had previously noted: 3,702 feet at Linyanti and 1,537 feet a hundred miles west of Zumbo. Livingstone had also made a crucial omission. Normally at significant points he estimated the height of a place by measuring the boiling point of water with a special thermometer. When he left the Zambesi at Pangura he had not done this. If he had, he would have discovered on his arrival at Tete that he was six hundred feet lower than he had been at Pangura. The only conclusion he could have drawn from such a figure would have been that the rapid at Chicova could not be small.[61] But oblivious of this, he wrote to the Directors with his usual confidence, telling them that 'the only impediment' to navigation of the Zambesi was 'one or two rapids, not cataracts'.[62]

After the abandonment of Zumbo, Tete had become the most westerly Portuguese settlement in Moçambique. Out of a total population of 4,000, only 350 of the inhabitants of Tete were not slaves. Of these 350 only thirty were true Portuguese. The town had been established in the early sixteenth century, mainly on the false assumption that large quantities of gold and silver could easily be extracted from the neighbouring countryside. When this hope proved an illusion, the residents had been left totally dependent on the slave-trade and various subsidiary pursuits like the sale of gold dust, ivory and coffee. Angola had always been far better placed for participation in the slave-trade; closer to Brazil and Portugal than Moçambique, the Angolans had soon cornered most of the lucrative trade in men. Economic decline in Moçambique had therefore been more gradual, but because there had never been the wealth that Angola had once enjoyed, Livingstone was far more horrified by the decay and stagnation. The Angolans had had comparatively little trouble with native tribes, but

the Portuguese in Moçambique were often forced to buy
off tribes whom they could not militarily defeat. Then
there was another separate problem; over the years the
Portuguese Government had made grants of land to individual families living in Moçambique. In order to defend
their interests these landowners had raised private armies.
Within a hundred years the original Portuguese families had intermarried with natives and had become half-
castes, often adopting native names. When the Portuguese
authorities had attempted to curb the power of their
former subjects they were beaten back and defeated by
them. One of these landowners, Antonio Vincente da
Cruz, more commonly known by his native name Bonga,
had sacked Tete three years before Livingstone's arrival;
and, until 1870, when the authorities were forced to come
to terms with him, he was to remain a consistent thorn
in their sides.

Livingstone's remarks about the Portuguese in Angola
had been scathing; in Moçambique, they were to be openly
hostile. The reason for his former tolerance had been his
knowledge that penetration of the interior from Angola
was impossible. On his arrival at Tete he was convinced
that the Zambesi would be navigable, and thus he came to
believe that British traders and missionaries would only be
prevented from sailing up the river if the Portuguese Government raised objections. Since the Portuguese were
notorious protectionists, Livingstone's serious doubts, as to
whether they would ever allow the Zambesi to become an
international waterway, were understandable. It was also
unlikely that a Catholic nation would willingly bend over
backwards to be helpful to Protestant missionaries. Livingstone must have realized at the outset that Portuguese
recalcitrance might defeat all his plans, but, as with almost
every other problem, he had refused to face it until he was
forced to do so.

The condition of the inhabitants at Tete also posed an
awkward question which some thoughtless people might
ask Livingstone on his return to England. How was it, if
the Zambesi was such an ideal commercial waterway, and
if the potential of central Africa was really so attractive,
that the Portuguese had not made anything of it in their
three hundred years of residence? Livingstone gave one
answer, the only answer he could give. The Portuguese
were a decadent, lazy, spineless lot, who were rotting

with venereal disease and drink. One Englishman was worth dozens of them. Rather surprisingly he would get away with this flimsy argument when he returned home.

Livingstone gave no credence to the possibility that the Portuguese might have been defeated by factors like the climate, malaria and the nature of the terrain. Nor did he ask whether the Zambesi itself was everything that it appeared to be. The Portuguese could have told him that the sand bars at the mouth were a death-trap and that shifting sand and mudbanks in the river itself made navigation an extremely difficult business for most of the year. But instead Livingstone concentrated on Portuguese shortcoming to explain every failure. The reasons why they had not progressed were simple, he asserted: there were not enough white women, the authorities were corrupt, the population had neglected natural assets such as coal, iron and gold. This neglect, he went on, had nothing to do with their physical circumstances, but was due to their sad addiction to slavery. Of course in many respects Livingstone was right. The colony needed more colonists with their wives and families. But the Portuguese at Tete knew that these settlers would not come until conditions improved. They also knew that conditions would not improve till new settlers came. Their situation was impossible. Knowing, as they did, that colonists would not come to Africa, they viewed as insanity suggestions that they should abandon their only source of labour: their slaves.

Livingstone had arrived in Tete during the first week of March 1856. He stayed till the end of April and during that time was entertained as hospitably as he had been anywhere in Angola. The commandant of the garrison, Major Sicard, was particularly kind. He had not willingly spent nearly two months as Sicard's guest but had been ill on his arrival at Tete and then had had a further relapse during his stay.

From Tete, Livingstone intended to go on down the Zambesi by canoe; this would clearly be impossible with all his Makololo attendants. Considering that he had characterized Tete as a moral sink, it may seem surprising that Livingstone made up his mind to leave his followers there. There was, however, very little else he could have done. The expense of bringing over a hundred Africans to London would obviously have been far too great, so the Makololo had to remain somewhere in Moçambique.

Sicard had promised to allocate them land and see they did not starve, so Tete was probably as good a place as any. Having promised the Makololo that he would return to take them home within a year, Livingstone set off downstream in a canoe with eight of his original followers. The remaining 270 miles to the sea were easier than any previous part of his journey. But for much of the way Livingstone was very ill with fever, so ill that when, on 25 May, he arrived at Quilimane, within a few miles of the coast, he gave instructions for the sale of Sekeletu's ivory in the event of his death. Rather surprisingly he recovered within a few days and was contemplating the satisfying news that warships had been calling at the mouth of the Zambesi every few months to enquire whether anything had been heard of him. These calls had been made as the result of a letter written by Gabriel to the Foreign Secretary giving him approximate dates between which Livingstone might be expected to arrive on the east African coast. The visits of these ships were a sure sign, if Livingstone needed any after reading what *The Times* had had to say in 1854, that when he returned home it would be to a hero's welcome. But before that there were to be more trials.

At Quilimane, Livingstone heard that H.M.S. *Frolic* had recently sent a brig over the bar at the mouth of the river to enquire about him. This vessel had capsized in the surf that always pounded the bar and all eight crew members were drowned. This was distressing news. Livingstone did not however equate this tragedy with the unsuitability of the mouth of the Zambesi for shipping. He preferred to see it as a chance accident. Before Livingstone reached England the sea was to claim another victim. He had only intended to take one native home with him and had chosen for this honour his right-hand man and interpreter, Sekwebu. Unfortunately the same rough seas that had drowned the sailors were still raging when Livingstone and his companion were ferried out to the *Frolic* on 12 July. Sekwebu, who had never seen the sea before and whose only experience of boats had been in canoes on the *Zambesi*, was terrified by the large waves that broke over the pinnace and seemed about to swamp her. Sekwebu's next ordeal was being hoisted aboard the *Frolic* in a bo'sun's chair. It was not many days later that Sekwebu's mind broke under the strain of such novel circumstances. When *Frolic* anchored off Mauritius, Sekwebu leapt down into a boat that had been launched. When Livingstone clambered down after him, Sekwebu backed towards the stern, screaming: 'No, no! It is enough that I die alone.' After a great deal of persuasion Livingstone managed to get him back on board. The officers annoyed Livingstone by saying that mad savages ought to be put in chains. He argued that Sekwebu would immediately assume he had been made a slave and that feeling would probably make him mad for life. The officers gave way. That evening Sekwebu tried to stab one of the sailors and then leapt overboard. The last Livingstone saw of his interpreter was his head and arms as he gripped the anchor cable and 'pulled himself down hand under hand'.

More bad news was to come. At Cairo, Livingstone learned that his father had died. But this was nothing compared with a blow that he had already sustained in Quilimane. The Directors of the London Missionary Society had written a letter that seemed to negate everything he had been attempting to achieve.

> The Directors, while yielding to none in their appreciation of the objects upon which, for some years past, your energies have been concentrated . . . are nevertheless restricted in their power of aiding plans connected only remotely with the spread of the Gospel . . . Your reports make it sufficiently obvious that the nature of the country, the insalubrity of the climate, the prevalence of poisonous insects, and other adverse influences, constitute a very serious array of obstacles to missionary effort; and even were there a reasonable prospect of these being surmounted—and we by no means assume they are insurmountable— yet, in that event, the financial circumstances of the Society are not such as to afford any ground of hope that it would be in a position, within any definite period, to venture upon untried, remote, and difficult fields of labour.[63]

Livingstone was bitterly angry that the Directors had declared themselves in favour of the journey when he had set out and yet now were telling him that it was out of

the question for his explorations to be followed up. The
Society must have known before he left that central Africa
would remain an 'untried, remote and difficult field of
labour' whatever he managed to achieve. Distance alone
made that certain. While his colleagues had accused him
of being a traveller rather than a missionary, Livingstone
had always derived comfort from his belief that at least
the Directors understood his aims. But now it seemed
that they had ben as blind as everybody else. It must have
been especially galling to Livingstone that although he had
played down every difficulty, he had still not prevented the
Directors taking alarm. The truth seemed to be that the
London Missionary Society had encouraged his journeys
as a fund-raising stunt and nothing else. This was a very
painful discovery, and Livingstone's sense of disappointment was almost too great for fame to appease. He had
argued that he had never been concerned with geographical discovery as an end in itself, and now, by their attitude,
the Directors had made it appear to everyone that all
his work had been simple exploration with no further practical application.

When Livingstone landed in England on 9 December
1856 he was famous, but he was also angry and sick at
heart.

Before describing Livingstone's hero's reception in England, it is important briefly to summarize his achievement
to date. His work between 1853 and 1856, as I said at the
beginning of the chapter, can be seen in three distinct
phases. The first phase, during 1853, had been taken up
with Livingstone's search for a healthy place from which
to begin trading and missionary operations in Makololo
country. In all respects this phase was a failure. Livingstone not only found no suitable location but also discovered that the Mambari and Portuguese were well established and that the Makololo themselves were far from
pacific and unspoiled individuals. The second phase of his
work, which lasted from late 1853 to mid-1854, had thus
started in unfortunate circumstances. Livingstone had had
to face the thought that even if he opened a way to the
interior from the west coast, traders and missionaries would
not be able to stay in any safety in central Africa. His
route to the west coast seemed to him quite impracticable,
and this added to his feeling of failure. The next phase

had been the most important. Between 1854 and 1856, Livingstone had crossed the continent from Loanda to Quilimane. This journey, he believed, had led to the discovery of an ideal place for the settlement of missionaries and traders: the Batoka Plateau east of the Victoria Falls. Livingstone had reached the east coast firmly convinced that the Zambesi would turn out to be a navigable highway to the plateau. During this period he had come to the conclusion that the existence of coal and iron in western Moçambique was a sign that south-central Africa could be developed on European lines and that traders would not in the end have to depend on a transitory commerce in ivory, wax and ostrich feathers. He was also certain that cotton, coffee and sugar could be grown in vast quantities on the Batoka Plateau. Of course the success of any such ventures would depend on the viability of the Zambesi, but Livingstone, who had narrowly missed discovering the impassable Kebrabasa rapids, considered the river's navigability to be a foregone conclusion. In his own estimation a worse problem was posed by possible Portuguese objections to the opening of the Zambesi as an international waterway. Nevertheless Livingstone did not see this as a permanent obstacle. He supposed that if he could prove what a rich field south-central Africa could become for industry and commerce, the British Government might lean on Portugal to persuade her to abandon her protectionist policies. An objective judge might have reckoned that the Zambesi, until properly charted, and the attitude of Portugal were alone enough to place sizeable question marks over Livingstone's ultimate plans. In fact it could well have been that Livingstone would never have become a national hero if the public had chosen to assess his achievements between 1853 and 1856 in the light in which he saw them: as means to an end.

In 1854 Livingstone's trip to Loanda had been hailed by Sir Roderick Murchison, of the Royal Geographical Society, as 'the greatest triumph in geographical research which has been effected in our times'.[64] A number of British papers, including *The Times*, had reiterated this view. Ironically Livingstone had seen this journey as a failure. When he arrived at Quilimane, as the first European to have crossed the continent from coast to coast, he knew that his journey had been a great geographical feat, but his main preoccupation was with far wider objectives. Once again, when he was hailed as the greatest British explorer since the Elizabethans, his own most cherished aims were not being put under scrutiny. His fame was entirely due to his exploration and not to any prospects it might hold out for Africa. Livingstone realized this on his arrival in England and, in his attempt to stress his own estimate of his achievement, greatly exaggerated the potential and accessibility of the areas he had 'opened up'. As will be seen, many of his future difficulties and failures stemmed from this.

4. 'Boat capsized by an hippopotamus robbed of her young'

Finally, if one views Livingstone's great journey in the light in which most of his contemporaries saw it, as an amazing feat of exploration, there can be no doubt that he deserved all the praise he got. He had suffered over thirty attacks of fever during three years, had repeatedly risked his life and had continued when everything appeared hopeless. He had achieved the trans-continental journey, a feat never before accomplished by a European, with the slenderest of resources, and with no more than his salary of £100 a year had relied on the assistance of a native chief. His observations and cartography were infinitely superior to anything produced by the Portuguese, who had preceded him in south-central Africa but had never crossed the continent. It is true that the fact that Arabs had crossed from Zanzibar to Benguela between 1853

and 1854, and that two native traders had travelled from
Angola to Moçambique during the first decade of the
century, had not been taken into account by many of
Livingstone's public admirers in 1856, but even if these
previous journeys had been known about and acknowledged, it seems unlikely that Livingstone's fame would
have been much affected.

PART THREE

Fame

National Hero: the First Visit Home, 1856–1858

During the time Livingstone spent in England, between December 1856 and March 1858, he received a measure of praise and adulation which, even in view of his impressive geographical achievement, strikes one today as excessive. The Royal Geographical Society gave him their gold medal, as did most similar organizations on the Continent, he was granted the freedoms of half a dozen major cities, became an honorary D.C.L. of Oxford University and finally had a private audience with Queen Victoria. His book, *Missionary Travels and Researches in South Africa,* published in November 1857, sold seventy thousand copies, making its author rich as well as famous. A further two thousand guineas came his way through public subscription funds raised on his behalf in Glasgow and London. After a few months he was so well known in London that he had to be careful where he went in case he was mobbed. On one occasion he narrowly escaped being crushed by a large crowd in Regent Street. In church, if he was recognized, the service would break up in chaos, with people clambering over the pews to try and shake his hand.[1]

There is no one reason that accounts for Livingstone's sudden emergence as a national hero. On one level his trans-continental journey seemed to his contemporaries to be a feat comparable in modern terms with a landing on the moon. Few people in Britain knew about previous Portuguese discoveries, largely because the Portuguese had never wished to interest other European nations in Africa. Their own decaying colonies could hardly cope with competitors, so most of the records of earlier exploration remained in libraries and archives in Lisbon. In 1856 the commonly-held British view of south-central Africa, outside professional geographical circles, was of a dry and useless area not unlike the Sahara. Nor did geog-

raphers see fit to disillusion the public. Their own calling
would become much more significant if British explorers
were praised to the skies. Livingstone's description of
rivers and forests in central Africa therefore struck most
newspaper readers as an incredible 'discovery'. As one
journalist put it: 'Europe had always heard that the central
regions of southern Africa were burning solitudes, bleak,
and barren, heated by poisonous winds, infested by snakes
and only roamed over by a few scattered tribes of un-
tameable barbarians . . . But Dr. Livingstone found himself in a high country, full of fruit trees, abounding in
shade, watered by a perfect network of rivers.'[2]

But Livingstone was not simply praised as an explorer.
The Livingstone myth was in the making. He became for
many a great missionary too. One paper's description of
him was typical. Having portrayed him as 'this truly
apostolic preacher of Christian truth', the editorial went
on: 'Seldom have savage nations met with the representative of English Civilization in such a shape. He came not
for conquest or for gold, but for the love of his fellow
men.'[3] Most papers called him a 'devoted' or 'humble
missionary', not for a moment trying to establish what
form his missionary work had taken. The rapidly expanding penny press therefore carried to the public the vague
but unchallenged statement that Livingstone had been a
great missionary. It was an image of himself which, for
all its inaccuracy, Livingstone did not see fit to contra-
dict; nor did the Directors of the London Missionary
Society breathe a word about his solitary convert who had
lapsed. The more it was assumed that 'this truly apostolic
preacher' had converted thousands of savages, the more
donations could be expected from the public.

So Livingstone was not merely seen as a kind of Victorian astronaut but also as a saintly and entirely dedicated missionary. Since the missionary societies had never
made it their business to tell people that conversions took
decades of hard work with a single tribe, most people
found perfectly acceptable the idea of Livingstone making
conversions after a single sermon.

Much of Livingstone's initial publicity sprang from the
determination of various interested parties to make him
famous. Sir Roderick Murchison, the President of the
Royal Geographical Society, had hailed the discovery of
Lake Ngami in 1849 as part of a conscious drive to inter-

est the public in exploration and explorers. A famous Livingstone could be a great financial asset to the R.G.S., attracting subscriptions from hundreds of new members. The London Missionary Society, with a current overdraft of £13,000, also had high hopes of what could be done by comprehensive publicity. Murchison, however, had beaten them with the first move, by arranging an official reception for Livingstone at the R.G.S. headquarters in Savile Row on 15 December. He had invited as many eminent people as could be squeezed into the building, and the press had naturally been informed. The Directors of the London Missionary Society held a similar gathering the following day, with no less a figure than Lord Shaftesbury in the chair. Next a series of public lectures was arranged for Livingstone throughout the country. With his weathered face, and his strange, almost foreign, manner of speaking, Livingstone was sure to be a success.

In 1856 the religious fervour that had gripped the nation during the fight against slavery was no longer so marked. But the expanding middle class, whose money had been made in the still growing industries, kept up religious appearances. It had been quickly discovered that Christian virtues could easily be exchanged for business virtues; abstinence, diligence, an exemplary home life and a weekly confrontation with the Maker could produce rewards in this life as well as the next. Meanwhile guilt could easily be assuaged by occasional charity. Strangely this decline in pure religious standards and the coupling of divine and economic virtues made Livingstone still more popular. His life itself was a comforting justification of the *status quo*. The boy from the mills, who had made good by self-help, thrift and determination, could be seen as a living proof that exceptional men could overcome their origins, however disadvantageous. But Livingstone's real balm to the consciences of godly industrialists was his argument that Christianity could only make any headway in Africa with the help of commerce. Commerce and Christianity, he told numerous audiences, together became civilization. There could have been no more comforting thought for the Christian mill-owner, as he watched his work-people toil, than the idea that they, under his guidance, were working for civilization and Christ. Livingstone's projection of the image of industrial Britain as the universal ideal flattered many of his fellow-countrymen so much that they never stopped to examine the equation too carefully. They did not, however, leap at the opportunity of investing in a remote and so far untried market. Livingstone's appeal for traders to risk their lives and capital fell on suddenly deaf ears. Even philanthropy expected its guaranteed five per cent.

Livingstone, as befitting his modesty and reticence— both virtues attributed to him by the press—acted his role well and wrote letters to friends telling them what a bore 'this lionising is',[4] and claiming that he would far rather be having quiet meals with a few acquaintances than be feasting with the Lord Mayor.[5] Be that as it may, he went out almost every evening to dine with members of 'the best society' and had 'invitations every day'.[6] He had taken the pledge at Ongar as a student but, now that he was famous, he proved that he could drink with anybody; and, as his brother, Charles, remarked of one evening: 'We had wines, claret, port, champagne, porter &c. which were most excellent & so did David.' Livingstone's feeling was that there was no harm in private drinking with the well-to-do; public abstinence was only useful as an example to the poorer classes.[7] Livingstone thoroughly enjoyed his new life, and his much-vaunted claim that he disliked publicity comes strangely from a man who insisted on wearing a distinctive peaked cap wherever he went.

With all this frenzied activity it is not surprising that Livingstone's wife and children, who had spent four and a half miserable years of separation, saw little of the national hero. Livingstone, however, was always ready with a little joke about it. When he went to lecture in Dublin, he wrote home to his wife jocosely: 'I am just admiring what a good husband you have got. No sooner does he land in Ireland than he sits down & writes to his wife. Well he is a good fellow after all.'[8] Good fellow or not, when he left for Africa again, he wrote to his eldest son Robert, admitting: 'While I was in England I was so busy that I could not enjoy much the company of my children.'[9]

Without doubt, most can be learned about Livingstone's character at this time through a close examination of the manner in which he left the London Missionary Society and entered Government employment. In the past it has always been assumed that Livingstone parted cordially with the Society, having magnanimously forgiven the Directors their thoughtless letter which he had received at

Quilimane. The facts do not support this interpretation. Livingstone, it has previously been acknowledged, lied on occasions during the Zambesi Expedition between 1858 and 1863, but the strain and the climate and dozens of other problems can be named as mitigating factors. It has not, however, been suggested that before that, he was prepared to falsify and distort in order to get his own way. Duplicity and ruthlessness are by no means uncommon in exceptional men, but when they occur in the personality of a man usually considered to have been honest to a fault and gentle in his dealings, it does call for remark. In order to begin a full explanation of the negotiations on which Livingstone embarked with the London Missionary Society, the British Government and Sir Roderick Murchison, during his time in England, it is most advantageous to begin with the far from happy situation of his missionary employers.

Dr Tidman, the Foreign Secretary of the London Missionary Society, had thought a great deal before sending the letter that had so much offended Livingstone. Tidman's motives had been straightforward. Having seen the way the press reacted to Livingstone's arrival in Loanda in 1854, he and his fellow-Directors had realized that if Livingstone ever returned home alive, it would be as an extremely famous man. While this would be excellent from the point of view of fund-raising there were other dangers. For a start Livingstone might try to put pressure on the Society to send missionaries to the areas he had travelled through. The public might support Livingstone in such rash expansionist ideas and the whole thing might get out of control. It therefore seemed obvious to Tidman that he had to tell Livingstone that he should not think that forward moves in Africa would be made on any scale in the near future. The Society's £13,000 overdraft was an extremely good reason for wanting to squash ambitious schemes at the outset. But having discouraged Livingstone, Tidman then had to try and hang on to him. If Livingstone left the Society before his name could be used for fund-raising, a unique opportunity would be lost. Unfortunately for Tidman, he had forgotten that Livingstone had already shown a paranoid hatred of criticism after the minor trouble with his colleague Rogers Edwards, twelve years before. Nor had any of the Directors supposed that Livingstone, prior to the offending

letter, had any ill-feeling towards the Society. Had they
known how wrong they were, Tidman would have played
his cards very differently.

While at Tete in early 1856, Livingstone had written to
Edmund Gabriel moaning about the dismal prospect that
lay before him on his return to England. The Directors,
Livingstone told his friend, would force him 'to go through
the country . . . lecturing and imparting information as a
means of exciting more liberality. Now I cannot speak
English in public, nor am I willing to be a public beggar . . . The most disagreeable thing I anticipate is haggling about money.' 'My wife,' he went on, 'thinking to
leave in 1854 for the Cape, asked something to furnish an
outfit for the voyage, she had been visiting some rich
Quaker friends and the paltry £30 was refused because
some of these *financiers* believed she must have got presents during her visits. Expect me to go begging after
that.'[10] Livingstone's feelings towards the Society had
been ambiguous as early as 1853, for in September that
year he had told his family that 'if the Society should
object [to his plans] I would consider it my duty to withdraw from it'.[11] Tidman's letter had not therefore suddenly suggested novel ideas.

But Tidman's real gamble had been that Livingstone
would remain financially dependent on the Society for
some time after his arrival in England. None of the Directors had had any idea that Livingstone had already opened
an extremely confidential correspondence with Sir
Roderick Murchison. A letter from Sir Roderick had also
reached Livingstone at Quilimane in the same batch as
Tidman's. Murchison's praise was so rapturous that Livingstone had at once begun a long reply. Having gone over
all his reasons for supposing that Africa would turn out to
be a trader's paradise, he told him about his position with
the London Missionary Society.

I suspect I am to be sent somewhere else, but will
prefer dissolving my connection with the Society and
follow out my own plans as a private Christian. This
is rather trying, for, the salary being professedly
only a bare subsistence (£100 per annum), we have
in addition the certainty of education for our family
and some provision for our widows . . . Should I be
unable to return I hope you will direct the attention

of travellers to developing the rich resources of the country.[12]

This was a direct appeal for help and an open intimation that if Murchison found alternative employment, Livingstone would probably take it. From the moment he received this letter Murchison did everything in his power to see that Livingstone became financially independent. On 5 January 1857 Murchison had arranged a meeting, at the Mansion House, to inaugurate a testimonial fund for Livingstone. And that evening, deciding still more could be done, Murchison wrote to Lord Clarendon, the British Foreign Secretary, on his protégé's behalf. Sir Roderick referred to the speech he had made at the meeting earlier in the day and asked, tongue in cheek, to be forgiven for having said that Clarendon was a wholehearted Livingstone supporter. 'I ventured to say that I hoped that you might make good use of the man who knows more African languages than any other European and who seemed to have such a happy way of carrying on an intercourse with the natives along our frontiers.'[13]

The Directors of the London Missionary Society would not have got wind of these overtures to the Government, but they must have known that with mounting public interest they could not remain inactive much longer. They were also extremely worried about the Mansion House subscription fund. In their view the Society ought to be getting the money, and not Livingstone himself.[14] But the fact that Livingstone was getting it gave them proof that he would not be financially dependent on them for as long as they had hoped. According to Livingstone they actually tried to stop him getting any more donations.[15] But whatever clandestine efforts the Society made, if any, on 12 January the Directors held a special meeting with Livingstone as their honoured guest. Tidman had already told Livingstone that, with the Society's funds in such a state of imbalance, he could not contemplate new missions, but Livingstone was unmoved. At the meeting he told the Directors that they ought to send a mission to the Batoka Plateau and claimed that the Makololo would willingly move to that area as soon as such a mission was established. Livingstone went on to explain that a mission should also be started just to the south, with the Matabele, so that the Makololo mission would not be threatened. Livingstone had evidently explained about the influence Moffat had with the Matabele, for the board minutes for the meeting stated: 'That in his [Livingstone's] judgment the result would be promoted by the residence of himself and Mrs Livingstone amongst the Makololo and with God's blessing almost certainly secured were Mr Moffat to commence a Mission at the town of Moselekatsee, the chief of the Matabele.'[16]

So at this stage, a day after Murchison had written a second letter to Clarendon suggesting a meeting with Livingstone, the Directors of the London Missionary Society had been led to believe that if any mission to the Makololo went ahead, Livingstone would lead it. Livingstone had also acknowledged the reasons why it was crucial that members of his or Moffat's family should be attached to each of the two missions. Yet Livingstone must have known about Murchison's efforts to interest the Foreign Secretary, Lord Clarendon, in employing him. Oblivious of all this, the Directors, assuming Livingstone had meant what he said, submitted his proposals to the Southern Committee of the Society, which duly reported on 22 January. The committee recommended the Society to go ahead with the two missions, on condition that Moffat, or a member of his family, should head the Matabele Mission, and they went on to propose that 'A missionary be appointed *to assist Dr. Livingstone in the organization of the intended mission** among the Makololo'.[17]

The words in italics have in the past been taken to mean that the committee understood that Livingstone's role was now simply to be one of organization and not participation.[18] Yet since it had been stressed how important Dr and Mrs Livingstone's personal presence would be as recently as 12 January, it is inconceivable that this single weakly phrased sentence would have been the only mention of such a momentous alteration of plans. The minutes would certainly have included any refusal by Livingstone to fulfil his earlier promise. The obvious meaning of the wording is that Livingstone was to have a missionary helper to assist with organization of the mission prior to the actual departure. In view of Livingstone's other engagements there was nothing surprising in such an arrangement.

* Author's Italics.

The Directors believed this was the position anyway. At the Society's General Meeting on 14 May, they included a resolution adopted at a meeting of the Town and Country Directors on 10 February. The resolution begins: 'That two new Mission Stations should be opened—the one among the Makololo, north of the Zambese, *under the charge of Dr. Livingstone*,* assisted by another missionary; and the other among the Matebele . . .'[19]

A mission over a thousand miles in the interior of Africa could hardly have been *under the charge* of anybody if he were not physically present. Livingstone attended the meeting on 10 February so he could well have objected to the form of words if he had chosen to. In fact he 'expressed his entire concurrence'. Nor at the General Meeting in May did he deny that his wife and he would be joining the Makololo Mission. His lack of objections taken with his previous assurances, written from Africa, that, should a mission ever be set up among the Makololo, he and his wife would go 'whoever remains behind', must have left the Directors firmly convinced by May that even if the mission was a risky one, at least Livingstone would be there.

The amazing fact is that by May, when Livingstone had given firm assurances to the Directors, Murchison's clandestine efforts with the British Government had entered a crucial phase, and Livingstone knew very well that he would be offered employment of some sort. It might be argued that his double-dealing with the Directors served them right for having failed initially to see the long-term possibilities opened up by his journey. Or the whole confusion might be put down to a strange and inexplicable mental block on his part or on that of the Directors. The matter cannot however be dismissed lightly, since the implications do more than touch on Livingstone's truthfulness. When the Makololo Mission finally arrived at Linyanti without him, six out of the nine European members died of fever. Furthermore, afterwards Livingstone denied any responsibility for the tragedy. Since so much is at stake, it is necessary to examine Livingstone's approaches, through Murchison, to the Government more closely, taking careful note of dates. Only in this way can it be seen whether he deliberately misled the Directors.

* Author's Italics.

From the moment Livingstone realized his popularity, he had encouraged all Murchison's approaches to the Government and had expressed wry amusement at the Directors' hasty moves to change the impression they had made before. Two weeks after his arrival in England he had written to Sir Roderick from the Ship Hotel, Charing Cross, stating magnanimously:

> I have no wish to take any public advantage of their mistake, for such I now suppose they feel it to be . . . But you will perceive the reason why I said I should be willing to adopt the plan you suggested of a roving commission . . . I have not the slightest wish or intention of giving up working for the amelioration of Africa. I have devoted my life to that and, if I could be put into a position where I could be more effective and at the same time benefit my children by giving them a good education, I should think it my duty to accept it.[20]

So Livingstone had determined five months before the London Missionary Society General Meeting in May to leave them if a good enough offer was made. But it was not simply because he did not wish to 'take advantage' of them that he remained silent for so long, even after he was almost certain Clarendon would employ him. In fact, on 15 April, a month before the General Meeting, he had written to Murchison, and this letter goes some way to explain why he wanted to say nothing to the Directors till later. He told Sir Roderick that he wanted to delay putting in a formal application for government employment till nearer the time of his departure, not because he intended to refuse it and not because the suggestions Clarendon had already made were unacceptable. 'I fear if I got it [a government job] now, my friends of the Mission House will make use of the fact to damage my character in the public estimation by saying I have forsaken the Mission for higher pay. I have refused to take any more from them, and wish to do my future work in as unostentatious a way as possible.' He went on to say that he had suggested, and Clarendon had approved, 'a consulship to the Makololo and other central African tribes' which 'would enable me to do all I wish for both them and English Commerce'.[21]

Livingstone therefore appeared to be deceiving the Directors deliberately to safeguard his reputation. It might be claimed that his 'consulship' would not conflict with his position on the Makololo Mission, but this argument does not stand up to close examination. In the first place he would inevitably be away from the mission for long periods of time, charting the Zambesi and making commercial treaties with numerous tribes along it; and, secondly, he had already told Murchison in a letter, intended to be sent on to Clarendon, and dated 26 January, that roving government employment would enable him 'to effect a much greater amount of good than I could do by settling down for the remaining portion of my life with any one of the small tribes which are dotted over the country'.[22] Again in this same letter he referred to his fear that he would be accused of leaving the Society 'for the sake of filthy lucre'.

There was one other important motive for leading the Directors up the garden path, as he explained to Maclear in May: 'I am not yet fairly on with the Government but am nearly quite off with the Society.'[23]

But really, as his letter to Murchison of 15 April (quoted above) showed, he was as sure about the Government as he could be and had, at his own wish, postponed an official announcement of his appointment. Two letters prove beyond doubt that an appointment had been decided on by Clarendon by the first week in May; the first was written by Livingstone's brother, Charles, who told his wife that Livingstone had already 'concluded to accept Lord C's offer and has accordingly written him and the matter will be decided soon'.[24] This letter was dated 5 May, and the following day Murchison wrote to Clarendon suggesting a salary of £500 per annum for Livingstone; so by then the only questions left to be answered were practical: what sort of expedition should Livingstone lead and how much money should be laid out? Already Livingstone had told Clarendon what he intended to do: to open the Zambesi for commerce, to start cotton-growing and to try and work with the Portuguese to establish 'legitimate commerce' strong enough to drive out the slave-trade. He was not being unconsciously naïve in suggesting that the Portuguese would co-operate, but was eager to avoid mentioning difficulties to Clarendon at such an early stage.[25]

Meanwhile Tidman and his colleagues proceeded cautiously. Their appeal for funds for the two missions had only been started in March and the target of £5,000 would not be reached for some months. This, combined with Tidman's desire to make sure that Livingstone was going to stick to his word, accounts for his putting off writing to Robert Moffat till 4 April. Moffat was sent a copy of the Board Minutes for the meetings attended by Livingstone on 12 and 22 January, which, as will be remembered, set out the importance of Livingstone and Mrs Livingstone being with the Makololo Mission and stressed the need for a simultaneous mission to the Matabele. Moffat was now to visit the chief of the Matabele and to 'devote about a twelvemonth' to preparing the ground for the mission. 'No step to be actually taken.'[26] Tidman's motive for delaying everything was not just natural prudence. He had never been in favour of any mission to the Makololo, without the prior establishment of a chain of missions to connect it with the coast, and he probably hoped that, as time passed and the funds came in, Livingstone would grow impatient and go back alone, either with or without the backing of the Society. If that happened, a lot of money would already have been raised, the missions could be shelved and the Society would no longer be in danger of having to run its operations at the dictation of Dr Livingstone or public pressure. In this way it might appear that Livingstone had left the Society because he was too impatient to wait for reasonable preparations to be made. Thus the Directors would be able to part with him without their reputation suffering. Much of this is hypothetical, but without such motivation it is very hard to explain Tidman's delay of over two months before writing to Moffat. Of course it is just possible that Livingstone told Tidman about his government appointment in May and colluded with him to keep the matter secret so that Tidman's fundraising would not be impeded and his own reputation would not be damaged by remarks to the effect that he was leaving the Society hastily without giving the proposed missions a chance. But this last seems doubtful since neither man could risk this kind of deception ever becoming public.

From May to October, Livingstone had no dealings with Tidman, and Tidman did not contact Livingstone. Tidman's reasons would have been that the fund had not

yet reached the target and that nothing could be done
until Moffat reported on the attitude of the Matabele.
Livingstone in the meantime was working night and day on
his book *Missionary Travels*, for John Murray.

There is no evidence that Livingstone told the Society
of his real intentions till October, five months after
Clarendon had made his offer of government employment.
But on 27 October there was a meeting at the Mission
House and Dr Tidman read to a stunned board of Directors a letter from Livingstone, stating that 'although he
declined to receive pecuniary support from the Society,
and would probably in future sustain some relation to the
British Government, he would, there was every reason to
believe, render the Directors his best assistance in the
establishment of a Mission north of the Zambezi'.[27]
Regrettably Livingstone's letter is not in the London Missionary Society archives. Although many of the Directors
were distressed, Tidman probably did not share their feelings. He had never been in favour of the proposed
missions and now it seemed to him that after a decent
pause he would be able to scrap the whole scheme. After
all, acceptance of Livingstone's proposals had depended on
his leadership, and clearly this could no longer be counted
on. And so it was that in February 1858, over a year
after the proposals had been accepted by the Society's
Southern Committee, Tidman had still not selected candidates for either mission. By this time Tidman obviously
felt that since Livingstone had let the Society down, he
would not have the gall to tell the Directors that it was
their duty to proceed with the missions. But Livingstone
did have the gall. On 22 February an astonished Tidman
read a letter from Livingstone, asking when the missionaries for the Makololo and Matabele were leaving Britain.
Livingstone's tone was threatening. 'Abundant funds having
been furnished* for all that is needed on the case . . . I
should be glad to be assured that the intentions of the
friends in subscribing so liberally are likely soon to be
realised.'[28]

The implicit blackmail was clear: if the money was
used to clear the Society's overdraft and not for the purpose for which it had been ostensibly raised, there might

---

* £6,400 had been raised by the end of 1857. £1,400 more than the
target.

be some awkward questions asked in public. Tidman was trapped and knew it. On 27 February he wrote to Livingstone claiming that a party would leave in May. He added that there had never been any intention of shelving the project. Subsidiary evidence for doubting Tidman's word is strong. John Moffat, Livingstone's brother-in-law, had understood, as early as the middle of 1857, that he was to go either to the Matabele or the Makololo, but the delays and changes of plans that he was still being subjected to in early 1858 hardly indicated a determination to proceed on Tidman's part. Robert Moffat himself, after his return from the Matabele, was also chafing at the total lack of information from the Directors.

On 6 March Livingstone wrote to Tidman, at last telling him what his true position was in relation to the Makololo Mission.

> Should they [the missionaries] come through Mosili-katse's country to the Zambesi to a point below the Victoria Falls where our steam launch will be of any service to them, my companions will readily lend their aid in crossing the river . . . It might be better to go by Lake Ngami, as that is the only known opening Northwards; on every other point Mr. Helmore* can be trusted in implicitly.[29]

It is not difficult to imagine Tidman's feelings on reading this. He had not wanted to embark on any mission to the Makololo and had been pushed into it against his will, on condition that Livingstone was leader. Livingstone had kept him in the dark about his other plans for five months after those plans had produced results. Now, a year after the mission had been approved, Livingstone had pressurized the Society into going ahead, while blandly informing them that the most they could expect him to do would be to help the missionaries cross the Zambesi, if by chance he happened to be at the right place at the right time. How much this 'assistance' was worth could be seen at a glance. He had suggested that the missionaries went to Makolololand via Lake Ngami. This route would

---

* Holloway Helmore (1815–60), missionary at Likatlong in South Africa since 1839. In 1858 he was appointed leader of the Makololo Mission.

mean that they would cross the river above the Victoria Falls and not below them. Thus Livingstone would not be able to help even if this steamer ever got to the Falls.

Livingstone's part in the planning of the Makololo Mission has not previously been adequately dealt with, because it has always been assumed that the Directors were quickly disabused of the idea that Livingstone would have personal charge of the mission. The evidence quoted above proves this to have been false.

Before resuming a strict chronology and completing the record of Livingstone's negotiations with the Government, it is best to continue with the Makololo Mission and try to determine how much responsibility Livingstone must bear for the tragic outcome of that project. Because the disaster occurred in 1860, two years after Livingstone left England as leader of the government-financed Zambesi Expedition, it has usually been dealt with briefly *en passant*, during a description of the events of the expedition. But this placing inevitably tends to isolate the mission from its conception in London during 1857, and therefore tends to blur the part Livingstone played in forcing the mission on, even after he had dissociated himself from it.

I 2

The Price of Optimism: the Makololo Mission, 1857–1860

The Makololo Mission was dogged from the very beginning by false expectations. In *Missionary Travels* Livingstone had deliberately written about the Makololo in a much more favourable light than he had in his private correspondence. The bad treatment meted out to their vassals was glossed over and the constant raids on neighbouring tribes made light of. He had also played down his own sufferings from fever, partly through modesty, and partly to avoid the implication that he considered missionary work to be a sacrifice. Nevertheless his predominant motive for appearing optimistic about the conditions in south-central Africa had been the fear that if he did not, the area would be abandoned as hopeless.

The Directors however had plenty of evidence from his

letters to show that any mission would be fraught with dangers; indeed it had been these very dangers that had initially put them off. It is therefore all the more remarkable that they allowed a mission consisting of two missionaries, their wives and four young children to go ahead. It is true that Livingstone had written: 'I apprehend no great mortality among missionaries, men of education and prudence who can, if they will, adopt proper hygienic precautions.'[1]

But in the same letter he had talked of his own attacks of fever and the constant vomiting of blood. This was hardly the only reference to the severity of fever. The Directors had been told that the Makololo themselves were dying out because of it. The unhealthiness of Linyanti itself had led him to suggest that a move to the Batoka Plateau was indispensable. The Makololo themselves would nevertheless have to be persuaded to move, and, as Livingstone himself had told the Directors in 1853, this would be hard 'Because the vicinity of Mosilikatse renders it impossible for Makololo or any other tribe to reside there. A change may yet be effected among the Matibele which would change the present aspect of affairs.'[2]

It could be claimed that the problem had been solved by the proposed mission to the Matabele, but it would still take a year or two, after the start of that mission, for the Makololo to judge whether the Matabele had reformed. Therefore if a party went to the Makololo at the same time as the party to the Matabele, it might still be several years before the move to the Batoka Plateau could be effected. During that time the missionaries would be constantly exposed to fever. Even though Livingstone was confident that he himself could persuade them to move, he had still told the Directors late in 1855: 'I feel a difficulty as to taking my children there, without their own intelligent self-dedication. I can speak for my wife and myself only.'[3]

It is therefore puzzling that the Directors ever allowed the missionaries to set out for Linyanti with their wives and children. They could well have insisted that the men went on alone first, till the move to healthier ground could take place. The truth seems to have been that they trusted the missionaries to judge for themselves. They should have confided in Robert Moffat more and trusted in his judgment.

Regrettably Moffat had been told little and believed himself responsible only for the Matabele Mission. Tidman had not thought fit to tell him that Livingstone had opted out of the Makololo Mission till two months before the missionaries were due to leave England. On 19 April 1858 Moffat wrote acidly to the Directors: 'Of course I had not the slightest idea of being of use to the missies [missionaries] for the Makololo who it was taken for granted would go with Livingstone himself.'[4]

Moffat had heard, only a couple of weeks before writing this letter, that Livingstone had left the Society and was to lead an expedition up the Zambesi. His immediate thought, he told the Directors bluntly, was that it was madness for the missionaries to go overland, especially after what Livingstone had told them about fever, the tsetse and the lack of water crossing the Kalahari. The obvious course was for them to go with Livingstone and to approach Linyanti via the Zambesi. Livingstone could have told him that the Portuguese would not allow more than the basic personnel of the expedition to pass through their territory, but Moffat could hardly have known this without being told. Between April and July 1858 Moffat wrote repeatedly to the Directors trying to get them to abandon the Makololo Mission for the time being. 'I have my fears, and feel my mind beset with difficulties connected with the Mission to the Makololo which I cannot overcome.' Moffat went on that unless he or Livingstone visited the Makololo in person the tribe could not be expected to move from the malarial area around Linyanti to the healthier Batoka Plateau. Either Moffat or Livingstone would have to come to convince them they were safe from the Matabele. 'All this,' Moffat continued, 'makes it a serious matter to recommend three missionaries and their wives to proceed at once to Linyanti,' where fever might in a few months 'prove fatal to some if not all'. Moffat ended his letter by begging the Directors to put off the mission until Livingstone had first arrived at Linyanti and persuaded the Makololo to move.[5]

The Directors could hardly accede to this since the last letter they had had from Livingstone had given them no idea when Livingstone might be at Linyanti or anywhere near it. The Directors had never wanted the mission to get under way, but now that it had, they had to think of the effect on public opinion if they pulled out at the eleventh hour. But one aspect of their behaviour remains a complete mystery. They had been given definite information in Livingstone's letter of 6 March 1858 that he would help the Makololo missionaries only if he happened to be at the Victoria Falls at the right time. It is therefore completely confounding that in 1859 all the Makololo party, and Moffat himself, still believed that Livingstone would meet them at Linyanti. It was this misapprehension, which at this stage was not Livingstone's fault, that contributed so much to the deaths of so many of the party. A single example will be enough to show that the missionaries really did believe Livingstone would meet them at Linyanti.

One of the party, John Mackenzie, who, luckily for him, did not go with the rest because his wife was due to have a child and was ill as well, was later to claim with absolute certainty that the leader of the party, Helmore, was sure Livingstone would meet them.

> Above all his [Helmore's] great thought was to be at Linyanti in time to meet Dr. Livingstone there. He knew enough of the natives to be aware that a stranger would not be likely suddenly to acquire such influence with the chief and people as would be necessary to induce them to change their residence. Hence the importance of being introduced to the tribe by Dr. Livingstone as his friend. On no account must the Doctor reach Linyanti, and find that Helmore had not arrived.[6]

So Helmore, who knew that to be safe he should wait another nine months or so, set out at the worst possible time of year and arrived at Linyanti in February, a month notorious for fever. This would never have happened had he not been terrified of missing Livingstone. Within two months of their arrival, Helmore and Mrs Helmore were dead. So too was the other missionary wife, Mrs Price, and five out of a total of seven children. Roger Price and two of Helmore's children were the sole survivors.

The deaths themselves need not be gone into except to say that, although Price thought they had died through poison, he was almost certainly wrong. Fever accounted for all the symptoms mentioned. But the missionaries had some reason to suspect foul play. From the time of their arrival, the Makololo did not disguise their bitter disappointment that neither Livingstone nor Moffat had come. From their point of view these strangers were no earthly use to them as protection against the Matabele. They had not even brought guns to trade with.

Sekeletu had expected his relationship with Livingstone to make him rich, and now it seemed all it had brought was a sickly group of people who only wanted to talk of God. As Price said later, Sekeletu was angry that Livingstone had not brought his men back; he had promised to do so within a year and now four had passed, and these missionaries could not even tell him when the Doctor was likely to come. The Makololo had repeatedly turned away traders from the south in order to wait for the traders who, Livingstone had promised, would soon come paddling up the Zambesi. Had Livingstone thought about Sekeletu's feelings earlier, he would have warned the missionaries that they might encounter hostility. But, shortly before leaving for Africa, he had told Tidman that there was no point in his meeting Helmore as he had nothing to tell him.[7]

The Makololo had reason to be bitter, but nothing can excuse the way they treated Price when he, his dying wife and the Helmore children tried to leave Linyanti. Sekeletu took away Helmore's waggon and refused to allow them to cross the Chobe till they had parted with most of their supplies and clothing. They were all ill and now had to attempt a journey of over a thousand miles with hardly any food or provisions. Had Mackenzie not met them on the way, all might have died like the rest. The Makololo provided guides who then deliberately led the party into the tsetse fly so most of the oxen were lost. The last straw was that after Mrs Price's burial, the Makololo exhumed her, cut off her head and took it to Sekeletu. At the time of her death, Mrs Price had been so thin that she had had to put plaster over her joints to stop the bones breaking the skin. The suffering they all endured can hardly be exaggerated. One child died begging for water that was never fetched, another died unnoticed by his father, who was also near death. The last letter Mrs Helmore ever wrote was to her daughter Olive in England, telling her that she would soon be with them all in Africa. 'Lizzie says I am to tell you to bring some comfits, little baskets &c that we may have a Christmas Tree the first

Christmas you are all at home.'[8] By the time Olive read the letter her mother was dead.

The Makololo Mission had already ended when Livingstone decided to take Sekeletu's men back to Barotseland in April 1860. He had only been prompted to take them back then because he could do no more on the lower Zambesi until a second steamer came from Britain, so it was chance that dictated the exact time he chose. To be fair, had he not encountered the horrifying obstacle of the Kebrabasa Rapids he might well have arrived very much earlier.

He did not hurry once he set out, and again he cannot be blamed. He felt that his last letter to Tidman, the one written on 6 March 1858, had made it clear that he could guarantee nothing. On 9 August he reached the Victoria Falls and stopped for several days to reassess his previous measurements. Several weeks later he reached Sesheke, where he heard what had happend at Linyanti. When the initial shock had passed, Livingstone realized accurately that many people were going to accuse him of partial responsibility for the disaster. He set to work at once to try and forestall any such criticism. His letter to Tidman could hardly have been more irritating to the recipient, had he deliberately written it to annoy him. Tidman, too, was aware that he himself was likely to be blamed, and was as sensitive as Livingstone to possible criticism. The letter opened with conventional expressions of sorrow and then went on: 'The poignancy of my unavailing regret is not diminished by remembering that the very time when our friends were helplessly perishing we were at a lower and much more unhealthy part of the river, and curing the complaint so quickly that in very severe cases the patient was able to resume his march on foot a day or so after the operation of the remedy.'

As though to rub in the irony of this, Livingstone went on to tell him that he had first tried quinine as a remedy as early as 1850 and that it 'has been successful in every case of African fever met with since'. Tidman might well have been wondering why Livingstone had not told him more about the remedy while he was in London. Livingstone's answer was that he had included a sentence about it in *Missionary Travels* 'towards the end' and that he had kept quiet about it because it was bad medical etiquette to publicize anything till a proper trial had been given it.

Worse was to come. 'From all I could learn the Makololo took most cordially to Mr. Helmore—they wished to become acquainted with him, a very natural desire, before removing to the Highlands, and hence the delay which ended so fatally . . . The Makololo are quite ready to remove, they are perishing themselves . . .'

This claim that the Makololo had met the missionaries with friendship and had agreed to remove once they got to know them, was in direct conflict with all Price's evidence. He had claimed that the Makololo had absolutely refused to move, and had ordered the party to stay, when they asked permission to leave for the healthier highlands to wait there for Dr Livingstone. Tidman was more enraged still that Livingstone had not mentioned the fact that Sekeletu had robbed Price of almost all he possessed. Livingstone's final thrust had been aimed at the Directors themselves. He stated that he hoped that the Society would not be cowardly enough to leave this field because of an initial setback.[9]

Livingstone's praise of Helmore may have been due to genuine admiration, but Tidman would have had no doubt that Livingstone was commending him because he was dead and would therefore be unable to say anything unpleasant about the Makololo. Price, on the other hand, who had survived and was doing his utmost to discredit Livingstone's 'faithful' tribe, was soon to be abused at every possible opportunity.

On 5 July, Tidman replied to Livingstone's letter, pointing out that the Makololo had not been prepared to leave, and expressing anger that he had been told nothing of 'an antidote of known efficacy' for fever. He also suggested that Sekeletu had misrepresented the case to avoid Livingstone's displeasure. This letter and its implications were, Livingstone thundered in his reply, 'perfectly astonishing'. Sekeletu had treated him just as well as ever, although he was suffering from a serious skin disease. Furthermore the chief was unpopular, but nobody, not even a member of a subject tribe, had ever suggested that Helmore had been disliked. The real trouble, he went on, was that Price had been unpopular, and with reason. On one occasion he had kicked a man, on another tied a Makololo to the wheel of his waggon and had even threatened people with his revolver. If Price had been robbed, how was it, he asked, that his own waggon and its contents had not been pilfered

although he had been away four years? The truth was
clearly that Price had provoked them. Livingstone ended
by again asking the Directors not to give up. 'I still feel
convinced that a flourishing mission might be established
by a judicious missionary.'[10]

Price himself was horrified that Livingstone had accepted
Sekeletu's story rather than his own and wrote to the
Directors on 20 July 1861 suggesting that the final proof
of whether the Makololo had intended to move would be
their actual removal. Livingstone however would have
claimed that even if they did not move (and they did
not) it would be because the missionaries had given them
up.

There is no proof that Price bound a man to a waggon
wheel or that he kicked anybody. The revolver incident,
he explained to Tidman, in a letter written on 4 November
1861, had occurred after he had first been threatened. In
any case, had Price been suffering from fever at the time,
he might well have been delirious. It should be remembered that Livingstone himself had had to threaten to shoot
some of his men on his journey to Loanda. Livingstone's
anger with Price was not really concerned with any actions
of his, but was due in the first place to the failure of the
mission. Price, as the only adult survivor, bore the brunt
of his displeasure.

Livingstone's vilification of the Makololo missionaries
was not only due to his fear that, unless he could prove
them responsible for their own deaths, he might be blamed.
He was really trying to excuse his own failures by condemning Price and his colleagues. By 1860 Livingstone
had discovered the impassable Kebrabasa rapids and therefore knew that the Batoka Plateau and the Makololo could
never be linked with the coast via the Zambesi. That was
the real drawback to any future missionary or trading
efforts in south-central Africa. Now Livingstone took the
deaths of the missionaries as an excuse. He claimed that
the Makololo and the surrounding tribes would be abandoned, not because of Kebrabasa but because no traders
or missionaries would dare go to them after a handful of
stupid and culpably negligent men had allowed themselves
to die. Furthermore, Price's *lies* about the Makololo being
robbers would alone be enough to discourage potential
traders. Livingstone had, he argued, laboured for years to
open the interior, and now a group of incompetents had

wrecked it all. Livingstone's agonizing time on the lower Zambesi during 1858 and 1859 may partially explain his callousness, but it cannot justify his deliberate distortions. Another cause for his violent reaction was his by now bitter hatred of the Directors of the London Missionary Society. A few months before learning about the Linyanti tragedy, Livingstone had written to his brother-in-law, John Moffat, telling him how the Directors had tried to defraud him out of the money raised for him in London by Murchison, and how they had even made efforts to get a bookseller to sue him for a £40 debt. 'Were I disposed I could tell a tale,' he had ended darkly. A year later Livingstone's disgust with the Society had increased even more; he had heard that one of their agents, a Mr Farebrother, was going 'about the country telling at public meetings that I am morally responsible for the loss of the missionaries at Linyanti'. The missionaries, Livingstone went on, were entirely to blame for what had happened to them. 'Helmore did not write to me even. I think they wanted to do it all themselves and have it to say they did not require any aid from me. A precious mull they made of it.'[11] As will be remembered, Helmore's most cherished desire had been to meet Livingstone at Linyanti.

When anybody suggested that he had had anything to do with the deaths, Livingstone denied it furiously. His sister Janet was bold enough to ask him why he had not kept in touch with the Society. His answer, as usual, was that neither Helmore nor Tidman had ever seen fit to write to him. In fact, as will be remembered, just before leaving for Africa, Livingstone had written to Tidman telling him that there was no point in him meeting Helmore because he had nothing to tell him.

Janet had also reproached her brother for giving the missionaries a false picture of the problems they would face. This, too, Livingstone vigorously denied. 'I gave information according to the varying phases of my experience. If life was in danger I committed it as I always do to the Divine keeping. If reputation and usefulness among the heathen were endangered by false brethern* I spoke of it even as St Paul did long before me.'[12]

When Livingstone wrote his own official account of the disaster in his book *Narrative of an Expedition to the*

---

* By this he meant Price.

Zambesi he took only two pages to do so. These pages are full of inaccuracies and false implications. Livingstone could not bring himself to name Price, except as 'the missionary associate of Helmore', even though Price had now married Mrs Livingstone's sister Bessie. He referred to the party as nine Europeans which, although accurate numerically, is not the same as two missionaries and their families. The deaths of children would have been seen as a tragedy but the deaths of 'five Europeans' gave the impression that all were adults, and their extinction would thus only have excited from the public a slightly contemptuous pity for human weakness. As it was, he cut the number of European dead down from six to five. He also claimed, quite incorrectly, that the whole party had been on the point of leaving for the Batoka Plateau and had only been prevented by fever. Ths missionaries had not been at death's door when they arrived, and yet Livingstone laboured to make it appear that the journey was almost as much responsible for their demise as the fever. In his account he made no mention of his own part in getting the mission set up, and at no point did he admit that at one time he had been appointed to lead the mission. The theft of the missionaries' goods was of course omitted and Livingstone even implied that Price had *given* Helmore's waggon to Sekeletu, with no consideration for the interests of Helmore's orphan children. Some of these slips may be thought to be due to faulty native information, but Livingstone's final criticism of the party leaves little doubt that the distortion was deliberate: 'Had it been possible for one with the wisdom, experience and conciliating manners of Mr Moffat to have visited the Makololo, he would have found them easily influenced to fairness, and not at all the unreasonable savages they were represented to be.'[13]

In a sense this statement was true, but not quite in the way that Livingstone intended. The Màkololo wanted a member of the Moffat family to live with them, so naturally they would have behaved better had Moffat himself come among them. Livingstone's real fault in the matter was not that he did not turn up in time to cure the missionaries—he could well have arrived at Linyanti before their arrival and been no use—but that he encouraged the Makololo Mission to go ahead when the original guarantee of success had been withdrawn. The success of the

Matabele and Makololo Missions had always hinged on there being a member of the Moffat family in each party. When he and Mrs Livingstone withdrew, the grounds on which the missions had been accepted by the London Missionary Society had been nullified. Livingstone admitted as much to his sister Agnes. 'I was sadly blamed for not bringing Mrs L. as all believe that the presence of one of Mr Moffat's family would secure them from attack by Mosilikatze.'[14]

To Janet he also admitted that the Makololo were 'naturally dissatisfied with their men being so long away'. In view of this his scathing remarks about the missionaries were even less pardonable. But having said this, it must again be stressed that he was not directly responsible for the loss of life. He had told Tidman he would probably not be any help to the party, and yet this information was not passed on; both Price and Helmore believed that Livingstone would be at Linyanti to meet them. Tidman had also been warned several times by Moffat about the idiocy of sending the party before the tribe had removed, and yet he had weakly yielded to possible public disapprobation and had let the thing go on.

After the disaster Livingstone asked why no doctor had gone with them. In the first place Tidman had thought the mission would have a doctor in the shape of Livingstone himself, but, after he had finally made his intentions clear, no second doctor was appointed. Maybe had Livingstone given more time to the planning of a scheme he had forced into being, Tidman would have made sure a doctor was sent; but he still ought to have realized the necessity for one, even without any outside advice. Livingstone's letters to him had played down the severity of fever, but the picture that emerged had still been bad. As it was, the supplies provided for the missionaries were inadequate, as Mackenzie told the Directors, in a letter written in October 1859, several months before the missionaries died. 'It was the opinion of Messrs Helmore, Price & myself that in the *supply of medicines* there was a deficiency.'[15]

So Livingstone, the Directors and the Makololo were all to blame in various ways, but Livingstone comes out of the affair worst of all. He unleashed all the fury of his own already frustrated hopes on to men and women who had given their lives in an attempt to bring Christianity to an area he had now given up. He knew that no mission in

Barotseland could survive without river communication
with the coast, and by 1860 he knew such communication
was impossible, but when Price said all this in Cape Town,
Livingstone did his best to discredit him with accusations
of lying and cowardice. It was the old story, Livingstone
had been wrong and could not bring himself to say so.
Instead he argued that if better men went, they would
succeed where Price and Helmore had failed. To prove his
point he cited examples of success following over forty
deaths in the west-coast mission stations at Gabon. But a
coastal mission was of course a completely misleading
comparison.

His refusal to acknowledge the truth of a word Price
was saying was nothing less than a calculated attempt to
cover up for his own miscalculations about the Makololo.
On his trip to Linyanti in 1860 he had found that the
Makololo were dying out at an astounding rate and that
Sekeletu had effectively lost his grip over his subject tribes.
He did not mention this in any of his letters, but those
written by his brother Charles, who was with him, put the
matter beyond doubt. Charles told a friend:

> I have no doubt he [Sekeletu] treated the mission
> body badly . . . I suspected at the time that he stole
> from Mr Price . . . Mr Price was no doubt very
> much frightened and they seeing this took advantage
> and plundered him. I believe they would have treated
> us the same way had we been afraid of them . . .
> There were not more than fifty men alive of the true
> Makololo; soon they will all be dead. I presume that
> the kingdom of Sebitoane is all in pieces now.[16]

Charles wrote this letter in 1862, and at that date the
Makololo had three years left before their total extermination during an uprising of their Barotse vassals. What was
obvious to Charles ought to have been obvious to his
brother and should alone have stopped him vilifying
Price and suggesting that other men ought to go to Linyanti to try again. Livingstone's readiness to believe that
Europeans were more often at fault than Africans was
probably admirable, but on this occasion it cannot disguise
one of the worst blots on his reputation. He had deliberately maligned innocent people for whose deaths he had
been partially responsible, in order to escape the slur of

having misrepresented the true situation in Barotseland. He never showed regret for this behaviour nor did he ever exhibit any trace of remorse for having maliciously maligned and slandered Roger Price, a man who had just suffered the horrifying personal tragedy of losing his wife and only child—a tiny baby. There are other blots on Livingstone's reputation, but because none would be greater than his response to the Makololo disaster, I have dealt with this previously neglected episode at some length.

Now it is possible to return to 1857 and the culmination of Livingstone's negotiations with the British Government.

13

Her Majesty's Consul

In this chapter I will try to explain how Livingstone, still a missionary in name if not in fact, became the leader of a government-sponsored expedition to Africa, and I will also attempt to show what he hoped to achieve in his new position. But before doing so it is essential to note the radically new direction Livingstone's thinking had taken since he had returned home at the end of 1856. Unfortunately for Livingstone's hopes, his new ideas were completely at variance with contemporary Government thinking on colonial affairs.

During his trans-continental journey, Livingstone's plans for south-central Africa had rested on a loosely thought-out voluntary scheme whereby European traders penetrated the area west of Portuguese Moçambique and began commercial operations there. The idea had been that these traders would 'cut out' the slave-trader and undermine tribal organization, thus leaving individual Africans in a suitably confused frame of mind to listen to alien Christian teaching, which they would previously have rejected. Livingstone had never thought about the need for a co-ordinating central authority for these random international trading efforts. He had envisaged the work being done by the individual enterprise of numerous philanthropic businessmen with limitless time and capital to invest. Nevertheless, by early 1856, while he was at Tete, Livingstone had started thinking more realistically. He had realized that the whole project depended on Portuguese willingness to allow the Zambesi to become an international waterway. The more he had thought about it, the more certain he became that there was little chance of the Portuguese giving permission without some firm prodding. In fact he thought it might be necessary to boot the Portuguese out altogether. The booting would of course have to be done by the British Government. Since Portugal, a spent force though she might be, was still Britain's 'oldest ally', there were clearly going to be some diplomatic problems. But Livingstone talked the matter over with Sir Roderick Murchison. Having persuaded Murchison that the Batoka Plateau could produce crops of cotton larger than the southern states of America, and having impressed upon him the enormous profits that English businessmen could make, if the Government led the way, Livingstone suggested that Murchison should sound out Lord Clarendon cautiously. Sir Roderick duly took the bull by the horns and in May 1857 wrote a letter to the Foreign Secretary. Clarendon was told about the amazing prospects that central Africa held out for every sort of commercial operator, and Murchison went on to restate the arguments about legitimate commerce defeating the slave-trade. Everything, Clarendon was informed, depended on Britain's determination. Then Sir Roderick spelled it out: 'Either England and her ally Portugal may be made one for this great object, or the latter country might readily part with her Colony of Quilimane and Tete, etc., useless to her, but which in our hands might be rendered a paradise of wealth.'[1]

Lord Clarendon however doubted whether Portugal would 'readily part' with her 'useless' colony, and politely ignored the suggestion that he should try a little persuasion. Meanwhile rebuffs did not stop Livingstone developing his ideas.

> That you may have a clear idea of my objects, [he told a friend], I may state that they have something more in them than meets the eye. They are not merely exploratory, for I go with the intention of benefitting the African and my own countrymen . . . All this ostensible machinery [the planned expedition and its members] has for its ostensible object the development of African trade and the promotion of civilization, but I hope it may result in an English

colony in the healthy highlands of central Africa. (I have told it only to the Duke of Argyll) . . .'[2]

Since Britain had plenty of overseas colonies by the middle of the nineteenth century, Livingstone's reticence about his colonial ambitions will seem theatrical and absurd unless more is said about the attitudes of politicians and public to the British Empire at that time. The Empire certainly existed, and had done for decades, but in general it had not come into being as the result of any unified or planned Government policy. Britain's West Indian possessions owed their existence to the initial efforts of individual British planters and slave-traders. Australia, until the 1840s, had meant no more to Britain than a suitably remote location for convict dumping. The North American colonies and Canada had been started by the arrival of English emigrants who had left their homes to escape religious discrimination and persecution in the seventeenth century. The Cape Colony again demonstrates the random nature of the causes for the Empire; that had been taken from the Dutch because of the tactical advantage it offered Britain during the Napoleonic Wars. India had become 'British' because the London-based East India Company had started trading operations there in the seventeenth century, and had later successfully defeated Dutch and French rivals. In short, there had never been a deliberate policy of annexation by superior might with the object of increasing Britain's power and influence. Coaling bases here and there, the odd island like Mauritius, were taken to provide ports for the Royal Navy, but in 1856 no politician and few members of the public would have been prepared to express any feelings except horror towards those who advocated large colonial advances. The reasons for this were practical rather than moral.

Mid-Victorian Britain did not need wider possessions to increase her wealth or power. Since she had a wider share of world shipping than any other nation and could out-manufacture and out-export all potential rivals, free trade and a policy of colonial *laissez-faire* suited her interests better than any more overtly assertive policies. Livingstone had seen this in South Africa. In 1852 the British Government had given independence to the Boers north of the Vaal and Orange rivers, rather than embark on expensive and probably unremunerative advances.

But one other crucial consideration militated against
Livingstone's hopes for a British colony, or colonies, in
central Africa. His contemporaries, when they heard the
words 'The British Empire', did not think of multi-racial
subject nations bowing to a central imperial power. Their
pride in Empire was not the late-Victorian love of prestige
and power, but more a pride in the idea that British men
and women had settled in distant and previously thinly
populated parts of the world, and were there reproducing
all that was best in the British way of life—a free press,
trial by jury and government by representative institutions.
Most of Livingstone's fellow-countrymen during the 1850s
saw Empire as the link of common nationality that bound
together, more by voluntary union than by power, a mother
country and her white settled, and soon to be self-governing, colonies overseas. In this *family*, the West Indies and,
above all, India were seen as strange anomalies simply
because they, unlike for example Canada, Australia and
New Zealand, had large 'native' populations and were not
predominantly 'British' and white. The problems encountered in India, where a handful of whites were vastly outnumbered by the indigenous coloured population, had
taught British governments to think twice before contemplating committing themselves to any new colonies where
the whites could only ever be a minority. The Indian
Mutiny would shortly justify this caution. In fact, until
Disraeli's long period in office in the 1870s, the British
Empire and the Indian Empire were often spoken of as
two separate entities. So in 1857 the prospects for new
colonies were bad everywhere, but in a *black* continent
like Africa they seemed hopeless.

'Imperialism' is often loosely used almost as a synonym
for Victorian, but in fact its use as a laudatory description
of indiscriminate colonial annexation did not gain general
acceptance till the late 1870s and early 1880s; and by then
Livingstone had been dead the best part of a decade. But
though he did not live to see the European partition of
Africa, Livingstone was one of imperialism's earliest
prophets and advocates. From the mid-1850s he began
writing about the British as a 'superior race' with a divine
mission 'to elevate the more degraded portions of the
human family'.[3] British businessmen, he averred, were 'the
most upright and benevolent in the world',[4] and it was
upon such men, he claimed, 'that the hopes of the world

for liberty and freedom rest'.[5] The British colonist in Africa would elevate and civilize by his very presence. This idea of 'superior' moral values bringing the right to govern alien races would be a common imperial theme in the 1880s and 1890s, but in 1857 Livingstone was voicing ideas that even the morally fervent found rather embarrassing. Livingstone was not oblivious of the public mood nor of the Government's attitude on these matters; for that reason he had not risked writing to Clarendon himself about ousting the Portuguese, but had got Murchison to do it for him. Livingstone knew that if he was to gain a Foreign Office appointment and Treasury money to support any new African venture, he would have to tread gingerly. He would certainly not be able to mention his colonial ambitions for the time being.

Past Livingstone biographers have usually accepted Livingstone's own assessment of his reasons for becoming a government employee. He claimed that the Directors of the London Missionary Society had attempted to confine missionary operations within too narrow limits and had therefore forced him to choose another employer. In fact the Directors, as has been recorded, had granted, reluctantly it is true, all that Livingstone asked. As representatives of a missionary society they could have done no more than give their permission for the inauguration of two new missions in south-central Africa. Yet Livingstone turned it all down. It is hard not to believe that once again his missionary disappointments with the Bakwains played an important part in his decision, and his letters to Murchison make it plain that the minimal salary paid to missionaries was another important consideration. But the principal reason was that his thinking had taken him so far from 'missionary work', even in the widest possible interpretation of the words, that a settled life with the Makololo and their scattered subject tribes could no longer have satisfied his new ambitions. Convinced, as he now was, that individual traders could not, unassisted, undermine tribal salary, he wanted organized colonization to do this work, which he saw as an essential prelude to Christian success. If he settled with the Makololo, he would not be able to do much to hurry along such grandiose schemes. Colonists would only come if they and their sponsors were convinced that central Africa would prove profitable and relatively accessible. Livingstone would therefore have to

prove that the area was commercially viable and that
steamers could sail up the Zambesi without hindrance.
When all this had been established, the British Government might then exert pressure on the Portuguese to
make the Zambesi international, and they might eventually oust the Portuguese altogether.

Commercial prospects could only be assessed by expert
judgments on the Batoka Plateau's real potential for growing sugar, wheat, coffee and cotton. The quality and
quantity of the coal and iron-ore in western Moçambique would also have to be estimated. Livingstone would
not be able to perform this work alone, so he would need
an expedition, and that could not be mounted without government aid. The Government could not, however, be told
of the ultimate end Livingstone had in view. Instead he
represented his ostensible objects to Clarendon as a desire
to promote international trade and to increase scientific
and geographical knowledge. An understandable subter-
fuge, given the circumstances.

In May 1857, Sir Roderick had managed to persuade
the Foreign Secretary to offer Livingstone employment as
a British consul with a roving commission extending
throughout Moçambique to the areas west of it. A salary
of £500 per annum was agreed in the same month. No
detailed plans had been made and Livingstone's demands
to date had been cautious to the point of cowardice. He
had not made any mention of an expedition with a steamer
and other European members, but had confined his
requests to two simple cotton gins, two or three iron
ploughs and two small rollers for extracting the juice from
sugar cane. Knowing his objects, it is hard to believe that
he was being sincere in telling Clarendon that he wanted
'a small beginning with a view of making greater efforts as
the prospects open out'.[6] Livingstone clearly had wanted
to secure a definite offer of employment before stepping
up his demands. Even later he preferred to gain concessions from Clarendon by the representation of third
parties. For example, when he lectured before the British
Association at Dublin that August, he gave his listeners
such an alluring description of the commercial prospects
of the Batoka Plateau, and represented the Zambesi as
such an ideal waterway for shipping, that General Sabine,
soon to be the President of the Royal Society, asked him
whether he would object to an official petition from the

British Association to the Foreign Secretary on the subject of providing Dr Livingstone with a steamer for his next venture. Livingstone of course did not decline. Later he spoke to the Manchester Chamber of Commerce and so impressed the businessmen in his audience with the possibilities of African cotton, that they too decided to ask the Government to assist Dr Livingstone to the full. Clarendon inevitably took note of these men's opinions.

After the offer of employment in May 1857, no more official moves were made till the following October. This long gap can be explained partly by Clarendon's preoccupation with the Indian Mutiny and by Livingstone's commitment to the writing of his book *Missionary Travels*, which was not finished till October. Publication in a blaze of publicity may have stimulated government activity on Dr Livingstone's behalf at that time. At any rate in that month Clarendon began a correspondence with Livingstone and the British Ambassador in Lisbon over the role of the Portuguese in any future expedition. Livingstone could sense that the Foreign Secretary was worried at the thought of possible diplomatic complications and wrote to him proposing a combined effort by Britain and Portugal 'to establish new stations on the higher portions of the Zambesi for the purpose of developing the rich revenues of the country'.[7] Of course he knew very well that such an overture would be rejected out of hand by Lisbon. The suggestion was aimed more at Clarendon than the Portuguese. Livingstone was eager to make his plans seem entirely innocent. Perhaps Clarendon was satisfied by this ploy, for on 11 December 1857, the Chancellor of the Exchequer announced to the House of Commons that the Treasury intended to vote £5,000 for Dr Livingstone 'to embark on a voyage of discovery upon the Zambesi'. The commercial prospects were made much of and almost every statement made by the Chancellor was greeted by cheers. The following day Livingstone attended a reception at 10 Downing Street, and was told by the Prime Minister, Lord Palmerston, that preparations for a full-scale expedition would be set in motion at once.

Neither Palmerston nor Clarendon hoped for a great deal from the expedition they had sanctioned. They did not want new colonies and they did not want any diplomatic wrangling with the Portuguese. But Livingstone was a national hero and they would not lose in popularity by supporting him: £5,000 was not a heavy price to pay. Besides, it was just possible that there might be some commercial advantages in it, even though the Portuguese themselves had never benefited much. With luck the expedition might make some new discoveries, and that would bring the Government a little reflected glory. Logically Clarendon could not really have refused Livingstone backing, since in 1856 he had contributed funds to assist two young army officers, Richard Burton and John Speke, to strike inland from Zanzibar to find a large lake rumoured by missionaries to lie hundreds of miles due west, in the interior. The two men would discover Lake Tanganyika in February 1858. Livingstone, by the way, would not learn about this achievement till several years later. In 1857 he did however know that Burton and Speke were in Africa and he was eager to get back to forestall them in case they started operations further south.

Clarendon's first move towards the creation of the Zambesi Expedition was a letter of instructions to Captain Washington, an influential Admiralty official, asking him to draw up a few alternative plans. Washington lost no time in doing so and by the end of December there were two suggested schemes on the Foreign Secretary's desk. Both of these were for ambitious projects, not unlike the 1841 Niger Expedition that had involved a number of ships and two hundred men. This was not at all what Livingstone had in mind and he immediately rejected both plans on the grounds that such large parties would prove unwieldy and unmanageable. A week later, on 7 January, he put forward his own much more modest scheme, which Clarendon at once accepted. In the past it has generally been argued that Livingstone had never wanted to go to Africa with any sort of expedition, but had been swept into it against his will and as a result of his popularity. This does not accord with the facts. Had he wished to go out alone rather than with an expedition, he would never have made such deliberate hints in his speeches at Dublin and Manchester to attempt to get his audiences to put pressure on Clarendon, nor, once the expedition was in being, would he have written telling a friend that he had set up everything primarily to encourage future colonization.[8] The fact that he was able within a week to tell Lord Clarendon how many people he wanted, and to name all but one of them, is hardly good supporting evidence for a claim that he was hustled into a scheme he had never really wanted.

The expedition Livingstone outlined was to consist of seven Europeans, including himself, ten natives, a paddle-steamer of shallow draught and an iron house in sections. Livingstone indicated what he wanted the six other Europeans to do, in the way of agricultural and mineral experiments and in charting the Zambesi; these men were to include an economic botanist, a geologist and a naval officer. Since Clarendon had been told what Livingstone's ostensible aims were, Livingstone did not bother to repeat them in detail; instead he gave a brief itinerary, which was to be accomplished, he hoped, within two years.

He intended to reach Tete as quickly as possible and then to proceed to the Kebrabasa Rapids 'to discover whether the launch would be able to steam up there when the river is high'. Having proved the Zambesi to be navigable, the next step would be to steam on upstream to the Batoka Plateau, erect the iron as a centre for stores, and begin agricultural experiments aimed at proving that enough sugar and cotton could be grown to make the area a commercial paradise. Meanwhile some expedition members would go on to explore the upper reaches of the Zambesi.

This was a breathtakingly simple schedule of operations that impressed Clarendon by its cheapness. There was however one imponderable: Livingstone had never seen the rapids he hoped so confidently to ascend 'when the river is high'. Since the area below the rapids was notorious for malaria, the success of the Expedition depended on getting beyond them to his much-vaunted Batoka Plateau. The steamer could clearly not be taken to pieces and carried without wheeled transport, pulleys and a large number of mules or oxen. When he had first visited Tete, Livingstone made some enquiries about the rapids, but they had not been exhaustive. It was well known in Moçambique that the cataracts were impassable, for the Portuguese Minister of Marine and Colonies told the British Ambassador in Lisbon, towards the end of 1858, that native canoes always had to be carried overland at Kebrabasa.[9] But if Livingstone worried about the crucial gamble he was taking he did not show it. In any case the matter was now in Captain Washington's hands and not his. In fact Washington had approved plans for a steamer before Livingston had told him how many men he wanted. In spite of this the steamer was no liner: 75 feet in length and 8 feet in beam. She was built by the Macgregor Laird yard at Birkenhead in little over a month.

Once stores and equipment had been dealt with, there were only a few loose ends left. These however included the thorny question of the attitude of the Portuguese to the expedition. Ministers in Lisbon had read transcripts of Livingstone's English speeches with less amusement than anger. It was obviously unpleasant for them to have to read thousands of words about all the marvellous economic possibilities of their African colonies, which they had failed to realize because of addiction to the slave-trade and official corruption and ineptness. The Portuguese Government was not unnaturally suspicious of a British government-sponsored expedition that claimed only to be seeking new geographical and scientific information. They were not fools and saw clearly enough that the commercial part of the expedition's programme would eventually lead to requests for the Zambesi to be opened to international shipping. That might even lead to other European nations staking territorial claims in Moçambique. In almost every way the Portuguese disliked the new expedition right from the outset. They did not want foreigners prying into their undoubtedly decaying colony, nor did they want to stir up the philanthropic British fervour that had destroyed their lucrative transatlantic slave trade. Nevertheless it would be unwise to forbid the expedition altogether. Britain was an extremely powerful nation.

So the Portuguese accepted the inevitable and did their best to smile graciously. But, while promising Livingstone all the help they could give him, the Government in Lisbon took steps to try and preclude the making of any later territorial claims. On 4 February a royal decree came from Lisbon, stating that: 'The name of Zambesia shall be given in all official documents to all the territories to which the Crown of Portugal has a right in the valley of the Zambezi from the mouth of that river to beyond the fortress of Zumbo.'[10]

This was rather better than might have been expected. After all, a western limit had been set to Portuguese territorial ambitions and the boundary was not beyond

Zumbo,* which the Portuguese, as Livingstone knew, had once occupied. The Portuguese, however, followed up this moderate statement of their position with the outright refusal of a Foreign Office request. Clarendon had wanted Livingstone's consular appointment to be for the whole of Moçambique, including Sena and Tete. The Portuguese, however, would only give their exequatur for Livingstone for Quilimane—their reason being, they said, that Quilimane was open to foreign trade but that Sena and Tete were not.[11]

Livingstone wrote angrily to Clarendon telling him that this must be challenged since it implied that the Portuguese had authority over the independent tribes along the river and the right to exclude international trade from the Zambesi. Clarendon remonstrated but was not prepared to make an issue out of the Portuguese attitude. In 1855, as the Foreign Secretary remembered very well, Anglo-Portuguese relations had been very severely strained and he did not wish to open up old wounds. In that year the British Government had asked Portugal to act against all ships taking slaves to the French islands in the Indian Ocean, particularly to the island of Réunion. The Portuguese had responded at once by seizing a French ship, the *Charles et Georges*. French Government action had been the immediate despatch of gunboats to Moçambique. The Portuguese had appealed to Britain, only to be told that they would have to submit to the French demand, since the British Government were not prepared to go to war over such a small issue. It was this memory that led Clarendon not to press the Portuguese too hard about the freedom of the Zambesi and the precise extent of Dr Livingstone's consular authority. Livingstone felt that to leave matters like this was a bad policy but he could not persuade Clarendon to protest any further.

But Anglo-Portuguese relations were never the real problem which Livingstone faced in March 1858 as he prepared to sail for Africa. He himself had created far more formidable difficulties. All these centred on his own exaggerated accounts of what might be expected from the regions he was going to. Sir Roderick Murchison, normally a calculating and sober individual, had spoken of the Batoka Plateau becoming 'a paradise of wealth'. Similar

---

* Two hundred miles west of Tete.

assurances had been made by Livingstone to businessmen
up and down the country. He was already pledged to
brush aside trivial obstacles that had held up the spineless
and supine Portuguese for three centuries. Naturally the
public took note of these fair words. Livingstone had got
his expedition together by painting glowing pictures of vast
cotton fields and huge mineral resources. Now he was
saddled with enormous public expectations. He had promised miracles and he would have to perform them, if he
wished to remain a national hero.

PART FOUR

Reversal

14

The Zambesi Expedition Sets Sail

The Zambesi Expedition set sail from Liverpool in the Colonial Office steamship *Peal* on 10 March 1858. Flurries of snow stung the faces of the more intrepid members of the party who had stayed on deck to see the coast of England out of sight. Within an hour or so the ship was pitching violently and most of them were below, very sick. Among those afflicted in this way were Mrs Livingstone and her youngest son, six-year-old Oswell, who had been so named after William Cotton Oswell, Livingstone's former companion and benefactor. Already Livingstone had been heavily criticized for letting his wife and young son come out to face possible death from fever, but after her previous experiences of life alone in Britain, Mary Livingstone was ready to endure whatever the Zambesi might do to her. The other children had been left to the tender mercies of their devout grandparents and a succession of guardians. Livingstone had set aside £5,100 of his earning from *Missionary Travels* to provide for them.[1]

By the time the ship was off west Africa and heading south for the Cape, everybody had stopped being sick except Mrs Livingstone. Livingstone soon knew why. Mary was pregnant again. This news stunned her husband, but not because of her grief that she would now have to be left at the Cape to have the baby at Kuruman. Livingstone was more concerned with the inconvenience to himself. 'This is a great trial to me,' he confided to his journal, 'for had she come with us, she might have proved of essential service to the expedition in cases of sickness and otherwise.'[2] Another consideration worried Livingstone too: people would think him a fool for having got her pregnant at such an awkward time. So in most of his letters he referred to her condition as an 'illness'.

Several of Livingstone's colleagues guessed what was the matter with Mary and were not sorry that she would have to stay behind. Africa, they felt, was no place for a woman. One of these was Livingstone's second-in-command, Commander Norman Bedingfeld, R.N. Bedingfeld had impressed Livingstone when he had met him briefly in Loanda in 1854, but at that time Livingstone had not made enquiries about him. Later Livingstone discovered that he had been twice courtmartialled and once dismissed from his ship for 'contempt and quarrelsome conduct towards a superior officer'. When Captain Washington, of the Admiralty, warned Livingstone about Bedingfeld's record and advised him not to take him, Livingstone brushed this well-meant warning aside as a piece of interference.[3] He would regret it later.

Dr John Kirk, who at twenty-five was ten years younger than Bedingfeld and twenty years Livingstone's junior, was to be the only person to leave the expedition with an enhanced reputation. Kirk, a Scot, had done medical work in the Crimea and was an experienced botanist and a doctor of medicine. He had been recommended by the Director of Kew and two Edinburgh professors. Unlike all his colleagues, Kirk would prove consistently reliable and hardworking. He also had the good sense to confine his complaints to his journal. His official designation was economic botanist, although he was expected to help Livingstone with medical duties.

Richard Thornton, the geologist, was even younger than Kirk; in fact he was not yet twenty when the expedition sailed. Sir Roderick Murchison had described him as one of the most brilliant students ever to pass through the Royal College of Mines, but Livingstone would make little use of him. Thornton, like Bedingfeld and Thomas Baines, the artist and storekeeper, would be dismissed. Baines, with the exception of Livingstone, was the oldest member of the party. At thirty-eight he was an experienced man too. He had left England for South Africa as a young man and, after working in Cape Town for a while as an ornamental sign-painter, he had been employed by the army as an official war artist during the 1850–53 Kaffir War. From 1855 to 1857 he went, again as an official artist, on a government-sponsored expedition to northern Australia. His work had been highly praised and in 1857 he was made a Fellow of the Royal Geographical Society. He was an easygoing, modest man, eager to work hard when the occasion demanded it. But, although all the others liked him, he would fall foul of Livingstone.

George Rae, the engineer, like Kirk managed to stay the course. Perhaps it helped that he had been born at Blantyre like Livingstone. He was to prove competent at his job, and the dourness which most of his colleagues disliked did not distress Livingstone, who hated idle social chatter. Rae shared another characteristic with Livingstone: he took to heart gossip that reflected badly on colleagues and tended to use it to his own advantage.

Livingstone's most startling appointment had been his choice of his younger brother Charles. Livingstone had not seen him since 1840, when Charles had sailed for America to get an education there. Quite by chance, Charles had returned, as he thought, for a brief trip to England in 1857 and had been offered a job as the Zambesi Expedition's 'moral agent'. This post had been created for him by Livingstone, who wanted him mainly as a personal assistant to support him in any troubles that might erupt with other members of the party. Charles's qualification to be a 'moral agent'—Livingstone never described what the job involved—was his theological education at Oberlin College, Ohio, and his subsequent ordination as a nonconformist minister. Livingstone justified his appointment to the Foreign Office on the grounds that Charles knew about the relatively new pursuit of photography and also claimed that life in America had taught him all about cotton. In fact he knew little about either. Nevertheless he had roughed it in America and had worked hard to pay for his education. Livingstone's letters to Charles before 1857 had been almost paternal, and he had helped his younger brother with money from time to time. Nothing in their past relationship gave any hint of the ascendancy which Charles was soon to establish over his older brother with such distressing consequences. Livingstone ought, however, to have known that since Charles had married only a few years before and had three children aged five, four and one, he might have personal problems to face which would make him a very difficult companion. Later Charles would write miserable letters to his wife, begging her to write more about the children, and repeatedly asking for more photographs of them all.[4] Livingstone's later reliance on Charles would be due to his own incapacity to lead Europeans.

Livingstone himself would in many ways prove to be the weakest link in the party. Needless to say, his weakness would not be physical. He would simply prove a disastrous leader. Had the British Government thought about it, a man who had just passed four years entirely without European company was hardly an ideal person to lead, live and work with six other men in claustrophobic proximity. No previous experience had prepared him for it. The nearest he had been to living and co-operating with a fellow-countryman in the past had been during his time with Edwards at Mabotsa. That was hardly an encouraging precedent. With the exception of his wife and family, whom he had seen little enough of, Livingstone had done his best to avoid Europeans when there was any chance of doing so. His success with William Cotton Oswell was due to Oswell's exceptional tolerance and his ability, as he put it, to 'agree to differ'. Agreeing to differ would not be enough to keep together an expedition where success would depend on agreement and close co-operation. Livingstone's iron will and incredible powers of endurance were paradoxically to prove counter-productive, since they set him apart; a leader needs to be able to identify with his men and share their experience. Livingstone underestimated his own uniqueness and expected the same physical and mental dedication from the others. He had always been limitlessly patient with natives but had never missed an opportunity to condemn weakness or stupidity in Europeans.

His years alone had made him self-sufficient and disinclined to talk unless he had something specific to say. To men unused to these long silences, they seemed to indicate aloofness and a lack of warmth. He had not lost the 'rusticity' of manner that his tutor Richard Cecil had noticed twenty years before, and while this had not mattered during his previous journeys, it was to be a severe handicap now. He could not make jokes when things went wrong nor encourage his party by showing that he appreciated what they did, nor could he laugh at himself. The wit so often displayed in his letters and journal was confined to paper and formed a contrast with his brusque and inarticulate manner of speaking. He felt criticism more keenly than most men and knew that as leader he was more exposed to it than anybody else, and this added to his self-consciousness. His moods seemed unpredictable, since he would often keep a grievance to himself for weeks and then blurt it out when the others had forgotten the circumstances. The same attributes that had made him successful as a lone traveller were often those that made him a failure when journeying with others. He had always hated any kind of restriction and had never been constrained on his epic journey; he had rested when he decreed and set out when he was ready. Now there would be countless checks and delays: the steamer had to get steam up; the others had to pack up their gear and finish what they were doing; and for any smoothness of operation each member had to know what the others were up to. Tragically Livingstone believed that men worked best when left most to themselves; this policy was laudable in many ways but inevitably led to confusion and misunderstanding when time was limited and aims changing. Perhaps his most crucial mistake was not to realize that since the leader would get most of the credit if the expedition was a success, he could not expect his men to push themselves to the same limits of endurance as he pressed himself. Instead he was aware only that if the expedition failed he would be blamed and get no credit for having exerted himself more than everybody else.

Five days out from Liverpool the whole party was assembled to hear Livingstone read out the Foreign Office Instructions to the Expedition. Livingstone had drafted them himself and they certainly did not read like most government documents of the day. Full of exhortations to the party to use their 'moral influence' on the natives to show them how 'a superior race' behaved, the instructions stressed the importance of 'a well regulated and orderly household of Europeans setting an example of consistent moral conduct'.[5] The terrible arguments and squabbles that were not far away would make almost every word ring with irony. Having outlined the scientific and geographical aspects of the work ahead—he kept his colonial ambitions to himself—Livingstone went on to advocate a deliberate policy of paying natives for any work done, thus helping to break down the chiefs' expectations of the free labour of their people.[6] Thus individual Africans might learn to see their prospects as individual rather than collective. With his usual habit for wanting the best of both worlds, Livingstone told his colleagues that they should not pay for gifts of food since it would be 'impolitic to allow the ancient custom of feeding strangers to go into disuse'.

On a more personal note, Livingstone turned to personal hygiene and admonished his companions to defecate with faultless regularity. Constipation, he warned them, should be avoided, if necessary by the constant use of laxatives. Livingstone's own bowel problems, the result of numerous attacks of dysentery on his trans-continental journey, made him almost obsessive on the subject. His companions would notice that the state of his bowels affected his moods considerably. Livingstone ended by warning everybody that he had powers of instant dismissal and could change the aims of the expedition if he thought it expedient. Each individual member of the party was issued with personal instructions about his duties, and these were often very precise. Kirk's duties covered seventeen densely-written paragraphs and contained a vast number of matters, to be attended to in the fields of botany and zoology.

As the *Pearl* steamed south, Livingstone had no inkling of what lay ahead. He was pleased with his colleagues and wrote telling a friend that all 'seem to me to be of the right stamp'.[7] This was still his view when they sailed into Table Bay on 21 April.

While it was gratifying to Livingstone to find many of those who had once laughed at him for his uncouthness and poverty falling over themselves to be agreeable, his meeting with Robert Moffat, then in Cape Town waiting for the Makololo missionaries, was far from happy. Moffat was angry that Livingstone was not going with the new missionaries and felt that he had deceived the London Missionary Society. Worse than that, Livingstone, during his time in England, had persuaded Moffat's son John to leave the Society and set up as an independent missionary. To get him to do so, Livingstone had promised him a salary and a lump sum of £500. John had accepted. Moffat felt that John had also betrayed the Society, and taken the education and training they had given him only to ditch them when he reached a useful age. Then there was the general sadness about Mary Livingstone. When she watched the *Pearl* sail from Cape Town, it would be four more years before she saw her husband again. Ahead of her lay a year in Kuruman and nearly three in Scotland with her disagreeable in-laws.

The *Pearl* sailed for the mouth of the Zambesi on 1 May 1858.

15

The Rocks in God's Highway, 1858

On 14 May the *Pearl* anchored off the maze of sand-banks and mudflats that formed the mouth of the Zambesi. The night before, there had been a storm which had come at a very bad time for Livingstone: during a severe attack of dysentery. 'Nothing can exceed the discomfort and pain', he wrote in his journal, 'when one is obliged to hold on with all his might to prevent being pitched off the closet.'[1] It was a bad beginning.

Most of the party were surprised to see a far from inviting coastline: monotonous mudflats and mangrove swamps stretched as far as the eye could see, and the river mouths were obstructed by dangerous sandbars, pounded by heavy surf and tall breakers. Livingstone believed there were four channels but all the charts were inaccurate and there were no local pilots to offer advice. During the next two weeks two separate attempts were made to enter the Zambesi proper, and both failed. Tempers became frayed and the Kongone mouth, discovered at the end of the first week of June, was found only just in time to prevent serious quarrelling.

Livingstone's plan was to get everybody up to Tete in one trip in the *Pearl*. This would mean that the party would not need to split up and it would also cut out dozens of separate journeys in the expedition's small steamer in order to get stores up-river. From Tete, Livingstone proposed to sail on in the smaller vessel, past the Kebrabasa Rapids to the Batoka Plateau, where the agricultural experiments were to begin. For a short time all went according to plan. The metal parts of the steamer were soon taken off the *Pearl* and bolted together by George Rae, the engineer. Livingstone called the vessel the *Ma-Robert*, because that had been the Makololo's name for Mrs Livingstone, and literally meant 'mother of Robert'. Robert was the name of Mary's eldest son.

Within a week, navigation had become slow and hazardous and by 16 June it was clear to everybody that the *Pearl*, a steamer 160 feet long, was not going to be able to go further. Livingstone's much-vaunted river was shallow and had channels that shifted from month to month. The *Pearl* had been loaned to the expedition by the Colonial Office and therefore no risk could be taken with her. The river was falling and if she went further she might be stuck for six months or more. The blow was stunning to Livingstone's hopes of getting the party through the malarial lower reaches of the river quickly. He did not confess to anybody how completely he had depended on this quick beginning. Now the iron house for stores would have to be set up barely fifty miles from the sea and all the stores brought up to Tete in the small *Ma-Robert*; the job, Livingstone knew, could take months, during which time no scientific work could be done. In the meantime morale and health would suffer.

The conditions faced by the party during the first few months of the expedition were entirely new to most of them and far worse than anything they had expected. All had read *Missionary Travels*, and because Livingstone had omitted almost every unpleasant feature of African travel, they had come out expecting adventure, even danger, but certainly not the continual debilitating hardships they were soon enduring. After the departure of the *Pearl*, the *Ma-Robert* was always over-crowded due to the greatly increased quantity of stores she had to carry. Consequently everybody was squeezed into close proximity, at a time when many were experiencing fever for the first time. The temperature was usually more than 100°F and the only place to escape the sun was the tiny cabin of the steamer, which, although in the shade, still heated up like an oven. Tropical rain was almost as bad as the sun, and in severe storms water would pour through the decking of the *Ma-Robert*, soaking men, stores and food. Because the river itself was much shallower than expected, and the steamer considerably overloaded, the vessel was perpetually grounding on sandbanks. Hours of almost every day were spent dragging the boat along with ropes and winches: back-breaking work under the blazing sun. Mosquitoes, ticks, tropical ulcers and an unfamiliar diet

Map 3

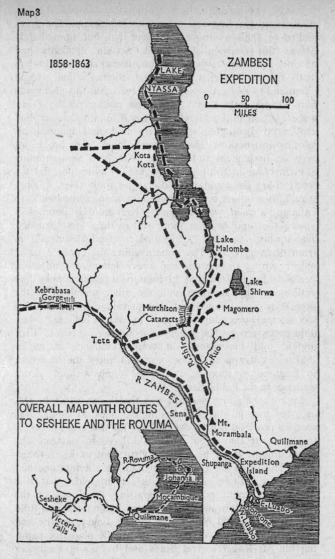

were other causes for irritation and distress. If serious arguments had not broken out it would have been a miracle.

Barely two months after entering the Zambesi, Livingstone faced the first real test of his leadership. The *Pearl* had to go, there was no doubt about that, but, immediately before this decision was made, certain incidents had produced an ugly situation. Commander Bedingfeld had justly felt that, in view of his instructions, he had overall command of navigation and he believed that this also made him responsible for the *Pearl*. The master of the *Pearl*, a mere officer in the Merchant Navy, Captain Duncan, had challenged Bedingfeld's authority and had ignored his piloting instructions. Eventually a violent row broke out between Bedingfeld and Duncan, with both men shouting at each other in front of Livingstone. Livingstone did the worst thing he could have done: he took sides. Livingstone's lower-class origins made him more sympathetic to Duncan, a man with a similar background. Bedingfeld sensed this and became more rather than less arrogant. The upshot was that Livingstone rebuked Bedingfeld in front of everybody.[2] The same evening the enraged naval officer wrote Livingstone an angry letter of complaint. Bedingfeld suggested that Livingstone's public rebuke had undermined his standing with the other members of the expedition and pointed out that private consultation was the normal procedure adopted by senior officers when differences arose. The letter went further: 'I trust,' Bedingfeld told Livingstone, 'if your confidence in me is shaken, as it appears to be, you will allow me to return to England as soon as it can be done without inconvenience to the Public Service.'[3]

Livingstone's first reaction was that he should take this as a resignation and send Bedingfeld back to England as soon as possible. But he decided against this since he knew that without Bedingfeld he would have to navigate the river himself. Later he made a virtue out of his forbearance. The truce did not last long. Earlier Livingstone had promised, without a word to Bedingfeld, that the *Ma-Robert* would pilot the departing *Pearl* out of the river. When Duncan came to see Bedingfeld and told him this, the naval officer was bitterly angry that he had not previously been warned. He had made plans for painting the *Ma-Robert*'s rivet heads and for doing a number of minor repairs to fit out the vessel for the series of journeys to Tete which she would soon be making, carrying heavy loads. Since the expedition at the time had a naval pinnace, Bedingfeld argued that this could be used to pilot Duncan to the mouth. When Duncan heard these arguments he simply told Bedingfeld that he should do what Dr Livingstone said. Again shouting began, and again Livingstone had to intervene. Ironically Livingstone did not want to have to keep his rash promise, but he was prepared to do anything rather than admit that Bedingfeld had been right.

Bedingfeld wrote to Livingstone with all his arguments against the *Ma-Robert*'s intended journey, only to hear from his leader that Duncan had decided to go down with the pinnace after all. Had Livingstone acknowledged that he ought to have told Bedingfeld his plans in advance, and had he decided to have a quiet chat with him, everything could have been patched up, for a time at least. But Livingstone's next letter to his naval officer was the last straw. Knowing Livingstone's gift for sarcasm, it seems quite impossible that he did not intend to annoy Bedingfeld with the gratuitous addition of some personal advice, offered by way of a parting shot.

> A pretty extensive acquaintance with African Expeditions enables me to offer a hint which, if you take it in the same frank and friendly spirit in which it is offered, you will on some future day thank me and smile at the puerilities which now afflict you. With the change of climate there is often a peculiar condition of the bowels which makes the individual imagine all manner of things in others. Now I earnestly and most respectfully recommend you try a little aperient medicine occasionally and you will find it much more soothing than writing official letters.[4]

Bedingfeld described this letter as 'the most insulting I ever received' and suggested it would have 'been better addressed to a child'. He wrote back telling Livingstone once again that he would 'gladly return to England', as soon as Livingstone could replace him. 'In the meantime,' he added, 'I will do my best to carry out your wishes as far as I know them.' Bedingfeld, like most officers in the services at that time, was a snob and, as he told Livingstone, he had never been so hurt as when the opinions of Duncan, 'who was behind a counter and a steward's boy, long after I obtained my first commission', had been

preferred to his own.[5] Livingstone could only have been
wilfully blind not to recognize these feelings. Bedingfeld
had just abandoned the command of a large warship with
several hundred men under him to take up the command
of a tiny vessel like the *Ma-Robert*, and Livingstone had
not even consulted with him about what that vessel ought
and ought not to do. Livingstone appeared almost deliberately to have made Bedingfeld's position untendable. He
might however have delayed dismissing the man if the
Ma-Robert had performed as expected during the next
few weeks.

It was soon apparent that the *Ma-Robert* was a very
dubious vessel. Her consumption of wood was outrageous,
being several tons a day, and, to make matters worse,
steam could only be raised satisfactorily on very hard
woods like ebony and *lignum vitae*, both of which took a
long time to chop up. Fuel was sometimes consumed at
such a rate that a day and a half's wood cutting would
not be enough to keep the boilers going for one day's
steaming. There were other faults too: the ship's feed
pipes often became choked and the cylinders and boilers
were always giving trouble. Livingstone was soon describing the *Ma-Robert* as 'a wretched sham vessel' with an
engine 'evidently made to grind coffee in a shop window'.[6]
Mr Laird the builder had of course had no idea that his
steamer would have to carry loads in excess of ten tons
several hundred miles up a shallow river against the current, but that did not stop Livingstone accusing him of
greed, deceit and incompetence.[7] Laird had used a new
kind of steel in thin sheets to build the hull of the
steamship, and here all Livingstone's criticisms were
sound, for this steel sheeting had not been properly tested
and soon started to rust through in a honeycomb of holes
that had to be plugged with clay. In short the *Ma-Robert*
was a disaster. But Livingstone did not only blame the
builder; he blamed Bedingfeld too, for he had been the
only member of the expedition present at the vessel's
trials. Livingstone accused Bedingfeld of having been
duped by Laird into believing that steam raised on coal
had actually been raised on wood. Bedingfeld retorted
that he had seen wood put in with his own eyes. Bedingfeld did not make Livingstone's temper any sweeter by
suggesting that he ought to have seen that the engineer had
also gone on the trials. The row over the *Ma-Robert*

finally made Livingstone decide to get rid of his naval officer.

There was a problem however. Bedingfeld had not resigned; he had merely said that he would continue serving until replaced. The onus was therefore on Livingstone to dismiss him. This he did not wish to do in case there was a full Admiralty investigation. He got round this difficulty by claiming that Bedingfeld's letter of a month before—it was now late July—had been the equivalent of a resignation. Bedingfeld, when he learned what Livingstone intended doing, went round the other members of the expedition asking them to let him have written confirmation of the fact that he had offered to serve until replaced. Only Thomas Baines obliged him and for that perfectly honest service Baines became the next object of Livingstone's hatred.[8] Meanwhile Livingstone obliged Bedingfeld to proceed overland to Quilimane to await a passage on the next ship that called.

It is undeniable that Livingstone's treatment of Bedingfeld was colossally inept. But few members of the party were sad to see him go. Kirk usually summed things up correctly, and his opinion goes some way towards justifying Livingstone's apparently irrational behaviour. Bedingfeld, wrote Kirk, 'seems to have expected to live the life of a Man of War Commander and no idea of being a subordinate. He also feels that he has done nothing but act sailing master of the launch; but I do not see much desire for scientific observations and of surveying. He has no more knowledge than any other one with a little common sense.'[9] Yet Kirk's words also point up a lack of foresight in Livingstone's planning of the expedition. Bedingfeld never really did have any role except acting as 'sailing master of the launch'. Once, Livingstone had imagined him making charts of the river, but since it had been discovered that shifting sandbanks altered all the channels dozens of times within a single year, such charts would have been useless. It should be added that Bedingfeld went on to become an Admiral, retiring at his own request in 1877; so he could not have been the idiot Livingstone claimed he was. The Bedingfeld affair did great harm to the morale of the party at a time when unity would have helped them surmount a series of initial disappointments.

Throughout July, August and September the *Ma-Robert*

chugged up and down the Zambesi in a painfully slow series of five separate trips to drop off supplies upstream at Shupanga, Sena and Tete. Only in November had all the supplies been removed from the temporary base near the river mouth. It was six months after the *Pearl* had first anchored off the Zambesi that the whole party were reunited at Tete. By then morale was low and early eagerness had gone for good. Most members of the expedition felt that Livingstone had deliberately deceived the Government about the Zambesi. Miles below Tete they had spent days aground on sandbanks while all of them sweated with winches and cables to get the *Ma-Robert* off. Sometimes 150 miles from the sea the river had been less than two feet in depth at its deepest point. The *Ma-Robert* drew three feet. Livingstone had often driven his companions into a frenzy with the contradictory instructions he gave them for refloating the vessel; in fact 'the Doctor', as Kirk put it, was 'nothing more than a landsman out of his element'.[10] Three days aground was not uncommon, nor was it unusual for the vessel to have to be dragged two hundred yards across mud and sand. To add to the miseries of the party, many of them were suffering from malaria for the first time. As usual Livingstone was distant and unsympathetic. He described delirium, giddiness and vomiting in his despatches as an illness no worse than the common cold. In view of his problems with Bedingfeld, the *Ma-Robert* and the Zambesi, he had not felt inclined to worry about 'trivial' ailments.

In Tete, during the first week of November 1858, there was one thought which above all others occupied Livingstone's mind: the 'small rapid' he had missed on his way to the coast in 1856. All Livingstone's plans, both immediate and distant, depended on the steamer being able to sail past the Kebrabasa Rapids on to the Batoka Plateau. In the short term, if the *Ma-Robert* failed to get through, the basic aim of the expedition to examine the agricultural and mineral potential of the plateau would be vitiated. But, worse than that, all plans for traders to reach the Makololo and the new missions from the coast would have to be abandoned. That in turn would rule out his long-term dream of the Batoka Plateau becoming a British colony. Quite apart from these terrifying possibilities, the effect on Livingstone's reputation if the rapids proved impassable would be dramatic. All his optimistic forecasts for south-central Africa had hinged on his claim that the Zambesi would be navigable as far as the Batoka Plateau. During their first few days at Tete, Kirk noticed his leader's preoccupied state and was worried to hear Livingstone talking about blasting a way through if need be.[11] None of the party knew much about explosives, and Kirk found it strange that, although Livingstone had made light of the rapids in England, he now spoke about the possibility of getting army sappers sent out.

In spite of his troubles, Livingstone could at least enjoy his reunion with the Makololo whom he had left at Tete in 1856. They were genuinely delighted to see him and showed no irritation that he had returned a year later than he had promised. Yet even this reunion brought Livingstone some worries. The Makololo seemed to enjoy living with the decadent Portuguese, and some of them even suggested that they did not want to go back to Sekeletu.

On 8 November Livingstone, Kirk and Rae set out for Kebrabasa in the *Ma-Robert*, leaving Charles, Thornton and Baines in Tete recuperating from fever. After a day and a half's steaming, the Zambesi began to narrow rapidly until it was soon only thirty yards across. The current had soon become much faster and the *Ma-Robert*'s progress against it was reduced to a crawl. On each side of the stream, sheer black rocks rose up to form cliffs several hundred feet high. The steamer managed to pass the first small rapid she came to, but at the second, the force of the current swung her bows round on to a rock, holing her above the water line. It was a depressingly bad start.

The next day Livingstone and Kirk set off on foot over rough, rocky country to see what happened further upstream. By mid-afternoon they came to a point where the river split into several channels and the two men separated to examine a channel each. A little later Kirk was looking down at the water pouring over a ledge 'at a considerable angle and becoming a mass of broken water at the bottom'.[12] Livingstone's cataract was as bad, with a fall of eight feet within twenty yards. Towards evening they came to two more rapids which were rather worse. Kirk's view was that when the river was in flood, the speed of the current would be so great and the pull of the eddies so strong, that no steamer could hope to pass up or down in any safety. Livingstone disagreed. 'I believe,' he

wrote in his journal, 'when the water rises about six feet,
the cascades may be safely passed. If not, then at flood,
when the water is spread over all the dell.'[13] Livingstone's
optimism rested on the assumption that the river would
rise enough after the rains to burst its rocky banks and
thus reduce the speed of the current. Kirk's opinion,
which would prove correct, was that the banks were quite
steep and high enough to contain an enormous amount
more water; enough perhaps to rule out flooding altogether. That being the case, the water would come down at
a speed too great for any steamer to combat. With so
much depending on getting past these obstacles, Livingstone would not admit defeat yet. Already he began thinking up excuses to use at a later date. One useful one that
came to mind was the power of the *Ma-Robert*. He would
argue that a more powerful vessel could do what Mr
Laird's 'sham vessel' could not. Since local natives said
that there were other rapids many miles further on, Livingstone decided to return to Tete again to collect the
other members of the party, before coming back to Kebrabasa for a thorough survey. On 13 November, five days
after setting out, the *Ma-Robert* dropped anchor off Tete.

No sooner was he back than Livingstone began making
feverish enquiries about Kebrabasa, and the answers he
got soon established that his efforts in 1856 to get hard
information about the rapids had been far from exhaustive. One man arrived saying that he had seen the rapids
beyond the minor falls Livingstone had just examined. This
Portuguese trader, José St Anna, confirmed Kirk's view
that Kebrabasa was far worse when the Zambesi was in
flood. Natives, he said, tried to get down from time to
time in canoes, and never lived to tell the tale. Even an
empty canoe had failed to make it, being smashed to
matchwood after a few miles. Livingstone did not say a
word about his fears to anybody, but confessed in his journal: 'Things look dark for our enterprise. This Kebrabasa
is what I never expected. No hint of its nature ever reached
my ears.'[14] He also began looking for ways to justify his
earlier optimism. The thought that he had gained such
popularity because of exaggerated claims tortured him,
and he now tried to delude himself and others into believing that he had written his book and given his lectures
against his will. 'The honours heaped upon me were not of
my own seeking,' he wrote hopelessly. 'They came unbid-

den.'[15] Recently he had heard from Thomas Maclear, at
the Cape, that Bedingfeld was doing his best to blacken
his name. Livingstone did not have to rack his brains to
see what men like Bedingfeld could do with a piece of
ammunition so damning as failure to pass the rapids.
Livingstone therefore tried to prepare himself for future
criticism. 'I expected snarling after I was gone,' he told his
brother-in-law, John Moffat; 'I did not seek their praise,
nor do I much care for their frowns. All came unsought.
I have had abuse before.'[16] And when he had had abuse
he had over-reacted like a wounded child.

Before the end of November the whole party had left
Tete for a thorough survey of the rapids, and although
Thornton and Baines were still ill, they too were forced
to come. Clambering over large boulders was not ideal
treatment to mete out to convalescents and soon the sick
men were holding up the party. Charles Livingstone however was the main offender. According to Kirk, 'more than
half the time is occupied allowing Mr L. to have a little
snooze every half hour'.[17] While Livingstone criticized
Baines and Thornton, he ignored the constant delays
caused by his brother. It was the beginning of a favourit-
ism that was to break up the last remnants of the expedition's unity. Baines became Livingstone's whipping-boy for
every failure and soon Livingstone was claiming that he
had failed to issue the Makololo with proper rations. In
fact he himself had given Baines no instructions on the
matter, but Livingstone was not swayed by such facts.
Baines he felt had betrayed him in giving Bedingfeld written
confirmation of his agreement to serve till replaced. Kirk
was angry that Baines was being picked on, especially
since Baines was so much harder-working than Charles
Livingstone.

Soon the going was so hard that Charles and Thornton
had to stay behind. The banks of the river were formed
from a mass of rocks and boulders heaped one on top of
the other in a crazy jumble of stone. Some boulders were
thirty feet high and all were smooth and covered with a
black glaze that made them slippery. The sun was so hot—
Livingstone's thermometer gave readings up to 130°F—
that if anybody left his hand on a rock for more than a
few seconds, the skin was badly burned. This of course
made climbing difficult and even more hazardous. On 30
November the Makololo, who were acting as porters,

refused to go on. Their feet were a mass of burns and blisters. Yet, incredibly, after some hours of arguing, Livingstone managed to persuade them to make one last effort.

They had now travelled for four days without seeing any worse rapids than Livingstone and Kirk had encountered on their first visit, and every hour Livingstone's hopes began to rise. The rocks he had seen already it *might* be possible to get rid of by blasting. A powerful steamer *might* then be able to get through. Before long Livingstone decided that the worst rapids had already been passed and that they might as well return to the steamer. Everybody with him was thankful for the decision. His spirits were much higher than they had been for weeks.

They had been clambering homewards for a couple of hours when one of the Makololo casually mentioned that he had heard something from some local natives near the place where they turned back. Livingstone said that any detail was interesting, and so in a matter-of-fact way the man told him that some miles further upstream there was supposed to be a fearful waterfall as high as a tree and so dangerous that anybody, even a man 'perishing with thirst . . . would retire in fear from it'.[18]

Livingstone listened in stunned silence, furious that, at the very time when his spirits were rising, this man had known something that would destroy all his hopes with a few words. After yelling at the offending Makololo for having kept such crucial information to themselves, he rounded on the rest of the party. They could all stay where they were, he did not care what they did, but he would go on alone to finish the job. Now that defeat seemed a foregone conclusion, Livingstone found the sight and company of his companions unendurable. They would complain about fever and the heat and the rough going while what was really at stake was the future of central Africa. After a pause Kirk said that he was quite able to go on, and asked Livingstone whether he could reasonably expect everybody to sit idly 'smoking their pipes' while their leader went 'off alone on difficult service'.[19] Livingstone took Kirk's point and agreed to accept him if he volunteered. Kirk did so at once.

During the next couple of days the two men experienced worse conditions than ever and Livingstone described keeping going as 'the hardest work he had ever had in his whole life'. The boulders were just as bad, and in addition they were soon coping with thick scrub. Then the hills got higher, and in order to proceed a quarter of a mile, they often had to cross valleys with a drop of several thousand feet in the middle. On 2 December they reached two more rapids, but these were clearly not what they had set out to find. Later that day, after clambering up an almost perpendicular cliff, the two men were rewarded with a sight that made Livingstone's blood run cold. Below them was a waterfall thirty feet high with the water thundering over it at less than 30°. Kirk was now satisfied that to think of getting past such an obstruction was lunacy. For a while Livingstone was unable to say anything, but then to Kirk's amazement he suggested that if the water rose eighty feet after the rains, even this waterfall might not prove an insuperable barrier. But Livingstone must have known in his heart that such claims were futile. He did not admit as much publicly for a very good reason: if he did the news would get back to England and thence to the Foreign Office. The Foreign Secretary might then feel impelled to consider whether it was right for an expedition to continue when its ostensible aims had become impracticable. It was for this reason that Livingstone wrote to the new Foreign Secretary, Lord Malmesbury, on 17 December, telling him: 'We are all of the opinion that a steamer of light draught would pass the rapids without difficulty when the river is in full flood.'[20] When Kirk saw this despatch he could not believe his eyes. Since Livingstone knew that within a year or so the already rusting *Ma-Robert* would be finished, he decided that it would be an ideal time to persuade them with his criticisms of the *Ma-Robert* that only his 'tin kettle of a steamer' had prevented the party reaching the Batoka Plateau as planned. Of course he did not tell Lord Malmesbury that when the new steamer came, whatever else he used it for, it would not be to get past Kebrabasa. Now Livingstone knew he would have to play for time in the hope of making face-saving and prestigious new discoveries before eventually being forced to admit to a crushing initial failure. Just to make sure that those in touch with the Foreign Secretary would back up his version of events, Livingstone wrote them confident letters. In one to Maclear he said: 'I have not the smallest doubt but a steamer of good power could pass up easily in flood.'[21]

In the long term, however, these optimistic lies were not going to solve anything. If Livingstone hoped to justify his request for a new steamer at some future date, he would have to prove that there was work for the steamer to do. In fact Livingstone had made up his mind before getting back to Tete that from now on his energies must be devoted to a different area altogether. The Zambesi and the Batoka Plateau were to be deserted for another river: the Shire.

The Shire flowed into the Zambesi from the north at a point roughly one hundred miles from the coast. Livingstone was not sure that it was navigable, but he knew that if it was not, he might as well cancel the order for the new steamer and disband the expedition. The Shire offered the only possible alternative open to him. The whole venture was a gamble but Livingstone was comforted by the memory of what he had been told in 1856 by a Tete trader, Candido José da Costa Cardosa. Candido claimed that the Shire was fed by a vast lake which could be reached directly from Tete in forty-five days' march. At the time Livingstone had been sufficiently impressed to draw a map based on Candido's information.[22] Livingstone now decided that he would not take the overland route from Tete but would try, if he could, to reach the lake via the river Shire. If the lake really was a large one he would be able to keep quiet about Candido's previous discovery and claim it for the expedition and himself. A major geographical find would do a lot to make up for Kebrabasa.

Of course Livingstone's new decision to abandon the upper Zambesi was a volte-face more extreme than any he had contrived in the past. By turning to the Shire he was abandoning the Makololo, abandoning the Batoka Plateau and abandoning God's Highway: the Zambesi itself. The new direction he was taking was tantamount to an admission that all but the very last part of his trans-continental journey and his previous trip to Linyanti had been fruitless. He was now preparing to devote himself to an area which was at no point further than four hundred miles from the east coast.

Many men would have been unable to adjust to such a sudden and fundamental change, but Livingstone was made of sterner stuff. If everything he had said and done in the past seemed to be contradicted by the plans he had now started to lay, he would still go on. But he would do much more than that; Livingstone would even manage to persuade himself that the hundreds of thousands of tons of rock, blocking the river he had once thought the answer to every African problem, had been placed there by God for an excellent reason. God had obviously intended him to turn his attention to the areas from which the Shire flowed. God's plan had evidently never included the Mako-lolo, nor the Batoka Plateau nor the Zambesi. There was, however, an alternative theory to explain the existence of Kebrabasa: that God had rejected the services of his chosen Instrument, David Livingstone. Not unnaturally Livingstone preferred the other interpretation. He sustained himself with the thought that although a lot had changed, he might well be able to find a new area just as suitable for a British colony as the Batoka Plateau. There would be another promised land.

16

Colonial Dreams: the Shire and Lake Nyassa, 1859–1860

Between December 1858 and November 1859, the Zambesi Expedition would record its only positive achievements, and yet, ironically, Livingstone's notorious over-optimism and ambitious new schemes would nullify these successes and sow the seeds of future disintegration and collapse.

On 20 December 1858 Livingstone, Kirk and Rae left Tete in the *Ma-Robert* on the beginning of the 200-mile trip down the Zambesi to the point where the Shire flowed into the Zambesi from the north. The Shire joins the Zambesi roughly a hundred miles from the sea, having flowed three hundred miles south from its source in Lake Nyassa. On New Year's Day Livingstone entered the Shire and was delighted to find the river broad and deep. The only disadvantage appeared to be a thick aquatic weed which tended to clog the paddle-wheels. As they steamed north, it was not long before Livingstone began to imagine rice, cotton and sugar-cane growing on the flat plains that extended for miles on both sides of the river. Soon he had even persuaded himself that the Shire's potential might be as great as the Nile's. But since the country was flat and had a tendency to flood, Livingstone had to admit that there was a fair chance that it would be unhealthy. Other more obvious disadvantages soon became apparent.

On the Zambesi itself, natives had often come running to the steamer simply to gaze at such a strange-looking boat, but on the Shire many natives ran away and those who came near were clearly hostile. On several occasions arrows were fired at the steamer and Livingstone had to ask Kirk to fire warning shots at the aggressors. It became quite usual to see large crowds of natives running along the banks shouting to the steamer to stop and pay them dues for passage. Livingstone refused these requests and risked the showers of poisoned arrows rather than set a precedent that might convince the natives that they could prevent people passing if they wished.

In spite of the hostility of the inhabitants of this new region, Livingstone was still enthusiastic about the river Shire. By the end of the first week of January 1859 they had steamed over a hundred miles without grounding once. Of course the *Ma-Robert* was not heavily loaded and the river was high after the rains, but Livingstone was not one to let considerations like that qualify his optimism. On 9 January, however, they encountered an obstacle that no wishful thinking could remove: the first rapid in a chain of cataracts extending for thirty miles. Livingstone named these rapids the Murchison Cataracts.* After several days' depression his spirits began to rise again with the thought that a smaller vessel, made in portable sections, might be carried past the rapids at a later date. For the present the only way to make further progress was on foot. For the time being, however, Livingstone decided to postpone further exploration in the hope that a few months later the natives would have become accustomed to the steamer, and would therefore be less hostile. Before steaming south again Livingstone made enquiries about the area to the north and heard that it was a high, fertile country with hills and a great lake. As soon as he heard about these fertile hills Livingstone convinced himself that he had

* Not to be confused with the Murchison Falls in Uganda.

found a substitute for the Batoka Plateau. Once he had come to this conclusion nothing would change his mind.

Livingstone's next visit to the Shire was in mid-March. His companion was Kirk. Because Rae the engineer had pronounced the *Ma-Robert* unsafe for further service, due to thousands of leaks, the Doctor had left him behind. As they steamed closer to the Murchison Cataracts, Kirk noticed how preoccupied Livingstone was and wondered why, but as usual the leader of the Zambesi Expedition kept his thoughts to himself. In fact he was beginning to believe that the area they were going to would be the ideal situation for a British Colony. They had not seen the region which Livingstone would call the Shire Highlands but already he was building up grandiose dreams for the future. On the banks the natives screamed and fired off occasional arrows as they had done the previous January, but Livingstone took little notice. Even when somebody on the bank was seized and eaten by a crocodile, the Doctor remained impassive, as his journal shows: '21st. March 1859. A woman was taken off by an alligator [*sic*] near to where we anchored, and we saw him dragging her up to a quiet spot to eat her. A relative, probably her mother, stood wailing on the bank. Started at 8½ A.M. Cut wood.'[1]

At the Murchison Cataracts, Livingstone and Kirk set off on foot. They had heard that before reaching the great lake, they would discover a smaller one, forty miles north of the cataracts. They were now entering country dominated at a tribe called the Ajawa, who acted as middlemen for Arab slave-traders operating further north. Soon Livingstone had no doubts about why the Manganja people on the banks of the Shire had been either frightened or aggressive: the slave-trade had reached the upper Shire. The Ajawa were no more friendly to Livingstone than the Manganja had been, but instead of firing arrows at him they gave him guides who turned out to be local lunatics.

On 18 April, after three weeks' walking round in circles, they reached Lake Shirwa and looked out across its blue waters to the mountains beyond. When they paddled in the cool water they were attacked by thousands of leeches. Shirwa was seventy miles long and thirty wide but the natives assured the white men that the great lake to the north was many times larger. Since Livingstone reckoned that the 'discovery' of this lake would be a major achievement for the expedition, he decided that he ought to try to map the lake and stay there for some time. This would mean a return to Tete for the other members of the party and for more supplies. It was therefore late August when he once more set out north from the Murchison Cataracts.

The first hundred miles of the 200-mile journey to Lake Nyassa took all of three weeks, and by the time the expedition members started to climb into the Shire Highlands they were already exhausted and irritable. Livingstone was in a terrible mood, largely because it was dawning on him for the first time that the slave-trade was already firmly established in the area. When they passed through villages, the people ran into their huts, 'the children screamed in terror, and even the hens would fly away and leave their chickens'.[2] Soon by the side of the path Livingstone saw piles of slave-taming sticks, with forked ends for securing the captive's neck. A little later he met a large slaving party led by Arabs. Evidently one of the main Arab slave routes passed just south of Nyassa. It was hardly a good omen for Livingstone's hopes for the area. He knew it as well; so much so that when he reached the southern shore of Lake Nyassa—the second largest lake in Africa—it was a distinct anticlimax. He recorded the moment in ten words: '17th. Sept. Reached Lake Nyassa from which the Shire emerges.'[3]

In fact as Livingstone gazed out over the waters of the vast lake, he felt no elation or sense of triumph. The mountains rising high above the blue water were very fine, and there could be no doubt that the natives were right in asserting that Nyassa extended several hundred miles to the north, but still Livingstone felt no pleasure. The embarrassing fact, as he very well knew, was that he was not the first European to have reached Nyassa. The Tete trader, Candido José da Costa Cardosa, had told Livingstone in 1856 that he had reached a very large lake about three hundred miles from Tete, on a trading expedition some years before. The lake, according to Candido, was the source of the Shire. Livingstone had written this information into his journal, with a map.[4] After his arrival at Nyassa, Livingstone did his best to make it appear, from certain inconsistencies in Candido's descriptions, that the trader had been to a different lake altogether. But try as he could, Livingstone could not suggest what other lake he could possibly have seen. All Candido's information ruled out Lake Shirwa. But Livingstone was successful in getting himself accepted as the 'discoverer' of Nyassa, and not one of his previous biographers has refuted it.[5]

But the fact that Livingstone had been beaten to Lake Nyassa was not his major worry. Ever since he had first heard about the Shire Highlands and the region around Nyassa, he had been determined that this would be the new area for traders, settlers and missionaries, which he had once thought lay in the Batoka Plateau. But the problems in this region were immense.

In 1840 the Sultan of Muscat had moved his court from Muscat and Oman to Zanzibar, the administrative centre of his east African coastal possessions. By the end of the decade his Arab subjects, in eager pursuit of slaves and ivory, had penetrated inland beyond Lake Nyassa as far west as Katanga. Nyassa itself, soon lay directly on the slave route from Katanga to the coastal town of Kilwa, and slave parties were either ferried across the lake in dhows or marched just south of it. In the Shire Highlands the Arabs acquired their slaves through African middlemen, the Ajawa, who had recently moved south from their original home just east of Nyassa. Livingstone had first realized the role played by the Ajawa at the time of his visit to Lake Shirwa. But he had not fully appreciated that the Ajawa were not merely selling members of the more numerous Manganja tribe to the Arabs, but were attempting to establish their own tribal dominance throughout the Shire Highlands. Thus tribal war added to the disruption caused by the slave raids. But Livingstone was alive to another problem: he had heard on arrival at Nyassa in September 1859 that the area to the north was being devastated by an exceptionally aggressive tribe called the Mazitu, a part of the Ngoni people.*

As if these problems were not enough, there was one further serious threat to any future exploitation of the Shire Highlands: the area could only be reached via the river Shire, which in turn could only be entered from the Zambesi. The future of the Shire Highlands therefore rested on Portuguese goodwill, since the Zambesi could be

* One of the Zulu tribal groups that had left Natal in the early nineteenth century, in the same mass emigration that had forced the Makololo northwards; the Ngoni had gone as far north as Lake Victoria, but by the 1850s had headed south again.

closed to foreigners by orders from Lisbon at any time.
By the middle of 1859, as Livingstone was well aware,
there was very little goodwill left. As Kirk observed in
January that year, 'There is some undercurrent of opinion
among the Portuguese which has no love to the Doctor.'[6]
There were many reasons for this. From the beginning,
officials in Lisbon and Moçambique had suspected Livingstone's motives. They had read copies of the speeches he
had made in England during 1857 and could not see how
his encouragement of British trade in Africa could work
without British territorial claims being made. The Portuguese were also stung by criticisms of the administration of
Angola and Moçambique, made by Livingstone in his book
Missionary Travels. A further cause for irritation had been
Livingstone's suggestion that prior to his own discoveries
very little effort had gone into the exploration of the
interior. During 1859 Livingstone heard that the official
Portuguese *Boletim* and the *Almanaque de Moçambique*
had included essays and maps claiming that most of his
discoveries had been anticipated by Portuguese explorers.[7]
The truth of much of what the Portuguese claimed did
not make Livingstone any more favourably disposed
towards them. The Portuguese meanwhile went on suspecting that Livingstone had territorial ambitions and had
been sent as a colonial agent of the British Government.

The Portuguese, to forestall any future British advances,
decided to make their position plain by building a customs
post at the junction of the Shire and the Zambesi and a
fort at the Zambesi's Kongone mouth. Livingstone interpreted these defensive measures as a deliberate attempt to
obstruct him. It underlined for him the deplorable fact
that Portugal had the whip hand as regards the Shire Highlands. The best policy Livingstone could have adopted
would have been one of diplomatic conciliation, but instead
he made no secret of his now bitter feelings towards
Portugal, and his letters and journals gave constant proof
of a passionate dislike verging on obsessive hatred. He
described Portuguese morality as 'worse than Sodom and
utterly bad and abominable' and suggested to friends that
the Portuguese only hated him for his 'standing protests
against vice and uncleanness'.[8] But that, as he told another
correspondent, was hardly surprising since the Portuguese
were nothing more than 'an utterly effete worn out used
up syphilitic race'.[9] Portuguese morality in Moçambique

was certainly far from exemplary and venereal diseases
troubled most of the whites in the country, but their dislike of Livingstone and the expedition, as Kirk noted, had
nothing to do with Livingstone's moral censure. The cause
was more fundamental. The members of the expedition
were intruders in a foreign country. The Portuguese, Kirk
felt, had been remarkably tolerant to allow the expedition
to come to Moçambique in the first place. The British
would never have contemplated allowing a German or
French party into one of their overseas colonies.[10] Apart
from this major conflict of interests, there was another
significant cause for mutual friction: the Portuguese in
Moçambique were beginning to expand rather than con-
tract their external slave-trade.

By the early 1850s the British Navy's activities had
virtually destroyed participation in the transatlantic slave-
trade by Angola and Moçambique. In the late 1850s and
early 1860s, however, demands for slaves by the plantation owners on the French islands in the Indian Ocean
once more stimulated the Portuguese in Moçambique to
renew their old pursuit. Since domestic slavery had never
been abolished in the colony, old habits were resumed
with few pangs of conscience. The Portuguese Government in Lisbon condemned all external slave-trading, but
officials in poverty-stricken Moçambique, who remembered how Britain had yielded to France over the seizure
of the *Charles et Georges*, were determined to turn a blind
eye to the new traffic. In fact, as Livingstone soon discovered, the Governors of Tete and Moçambique were soon
both playing a leading part in the trade. These gentlemen
made it quite clear to Livingstone that, while it was true
that there was an official ban on the export of slaves, this
was virtually unenforceable since the laws of the colony
allowed parties of slaves to be moved by land without
hindrance. In fact anybody who hindered them was breaking the law.[11] Livingstone was not slow to realize that
since he had just pioneered a new route up the Shire, the
Portuguese might soon start slaving operations on the
lower reaches of that river. When that happened, as Livingstone feared it would, the Shire Highlands would suffer
from Portuguese raids from the south, Arab raids from
the north and general Ajawa disruption in the middle.

By the end of 1859 Livingstone needed few prophetic
gifts to be able to see that, whatever the agricultural

and climatic advantages of the Shire Highlands, no future occupants, whether traders, colonists or missionaries, were going to have an easy time. Past biographers have claimed that the difficulties in the Shire Highlands which destroyed the Zambesi Expedition in 1862 and 1863 could not have been foreseen in 1859. This is quite untrue. Livingstone was aware of all the problems from September 1859, but played them down because he felt that if the Shire Highlands had no future, all the work he had so far done from 1853 onwards in south-central Africa would have been wasted.

Had Livingstone believed that there was another less ravaged area within reach, he would undoubtedly have explored it before attempting to press a case for occupation of the Shire Highlands, but he was certain that there would never be any alternative in south-central or south-eastern Africa. River transport was essential to success since the tsetse fly ruled out land transport by oxen. Livingstone dismissed areas to the north for a number of reasons. To start with, he knew that the Arab slave-traders operating from Zanzibar and Kilwa would pose far greater problems than the small-time Portuguese slavers of Tete and Quilimane. Then, Speke and Burton were travelling in the area due west of Zanzibar, and Livingstone had no wish to work in any place where he had been preceded. Finally, Livingstone was still bent on proving that rivers could be highways from the coast into the interior; further north there was no suitable river.

So, having made up his mind that the Shire Highlands was the only place for future exploitation, both Christian and colonial, Livingstone had to think of ways in which action could be taken quickly enough to anticipate further deterioration. He decided that, in these circumstances, he could no longer keep his colonial plans a secret and in March 1859 he had started a correspondence with the Foreign Secretary, in which he proposed a scheme for government-sponsored emigration and the creation of a new colony. Livingstone knew that these proposals cut across the declared objects of current British foreign policy. He was therefore painfully aware of the need to put forward strong arguments to justify his suggestions. Unfortunately he was faced with an impossible dilemma. If he asked for colonists, simply on the grounds that the Shire Highlands was an ideal location, in terms both of climate and agriculture, he would be rejected out of hand. The Foreign Secretary would point out that there were many similar areas in the world, which by the same argument ought also to be occupied. If such a policy were followed to its logical conclusion Britain would find herself embarked on a massive series of annexations. If, on the other hand, Livingstone tried to persuade the Government to send colonists to prevent the area being engulfed by Portuguese and Arab slave raids, and to avert the annihilation of the Manganja by the Ajawa, the Foreign Secretary would probably argue that however morally impeccable were the aims of such a venture, it would still be madness to expose a handful of settlers to anarchic conditions, which they would be unable to control without the help of troops.

So Livingstone had to try to have his cake and eat it. The area would have to be represented as ideal and peaceful at present, but menaced by certain threats which would bring disaster unless colonists arrived soon. This was all right as far as it went, but Livingstone's situation was not quite that straightforward. He wanted the Foreign Office to grant an additional request, which would involve him in admitting that the Arab slave-trade was already a serious menace. Livingstone could see that until the Arab slave routes across Lake Nyassa, and just to the south of it, were blocked, there could be no real stability in the Shire Highlands. The only way, it seemed to Livingstone, to sever these routes was to employ an armed steamer on the upper Shire and Lake Nyassa itself. This vessel could then patrol the crossing places, capturing dhows and freeing slaves. Since Livingstone did not wish to pay for such a vessel out of the profits of his book, he could only ask the Foreign Office to ask the Treasury to vote the necessary funds. But the matter did not stop there, for this steamer would have to be built in portable sections which could be carried thirty miles overland, past the Murchison Cataracts. That in turn might involve the Government in the added expense of sending out a company of sappers to build a road so that the parts of the steamer could be conveyed on carts. The whole business would clearly be expensive. But in any case Livingstone's arguments fell between two stools. The extent and severity of the east African slave-trade, in one sense, offered Livingstone his only realistic weapon for enlisting government assistance.

But if he used it too much, and admitted how bad conditions were already, he would have no hope of trying to persuade potential colonists to risk their lives. In trying to have it both ways, Livingstone could neither present the slave-trade as sufficiently horrific to justify direct government action, nor could he depict the Shire Highlands as a suitably safe and stable area where colonists would have a real chance to prosper.

Since Livingstone either had to take his despatches to the mouth of the Zambesi, to leave them at an agreed place where Royal Naval warships could collect them every three months, or had to trust Portuguese traders to convey them to the same spot, the Foreign Secretary did not receive any of the despatches penned by Livingstone in 1859 till early the following year. In April 1860, Lord John Russell, the new Foreign Secretary, sent the Prime Minister, Lord Palmerston, copies of Livingstone's proposals.[12] Palmerston returned them with a note: 'I am very unwilling to embark on new schemes of British possessions. Dr L's information is valuable, but he must not be allowed to tempt us to form colonies only to be reached by forcing steamers up cataracts.'[13] Russell therefore wrote to Livingstone, suggesting that his colonization scheme was 'premature', and telling him that he would be unwise to be optimistic over his chances of persuading the Treasury to pay for a portable steamer. Livingstone's request for sappers was rejected outright on financial grounds. Russell also suggested that Livingstone would do well to tone down his criticisms of the Portuguese, since the British Government had no desire to become embroiled in a diplomatic crisis with Lisbon.[14] Livingstone would not receive this dismissive despatch until early 1861. In the meantime his conviction that colonization would prove the answer to every evil grew stronger month by month.

Between February and November 1859, Livingstone wrote a series of letters to his friends Sir Thomas Maclear and Sir Roderick Murchison, repeating again and again that there was one 'subject which becomes every day more impressed upon my mind . . . It is that the interior of this country ought to be colonised by our countrymen . . . I see more in that for the benefit of England & Africa than in any other plan.'[15] Six months later it was the same story: 'I am becoming every day more convinced that we must have an English colony in the cotton-producing districts of Africa.'[16] He stressed how Britain would thus be spared the guilt of using the slave-produced cotton of the southern states of America for her textiles industry, and listed other commodities which could be produced cheaply: coffee, sugar, indigo and fibrous tissues such as sisal. There would be, he claimed, 'immense commercial benefits for England'. He did not admit that his desire to found a colony had been stimulated by the real fear that without one the Shire Highlands would descend into a state of anarchy and chaos. But he had had this in mind when he had begged Sir Roderick to do all he could to persuade the Foreign Secretary to back the venture.

At first Livingstone's plan was to have a small colony, but as the months passed his ideas became more and more ambitious. 'The soil is so rich,' he told his son Thomas, 'that it could support millions of people where now there are just thousands or hundreds.' Livingstone soon felt that he had discovered a remedy for England's problems as well as Africa's. If large numbers of the British urban poor emigrated to Africa they could begin new lives, no longer 'crowded together in cities . . . in close ill-ventilated narrow lanes'.[17] He had evidently forgotten his old ideas about the inhabitants of poor-houses having more benefits than African chiefs and, now that necessity demanded it, he also conveniently mislaid his former fears about African character suffering from 'intercourse with the lower ranks of our own population'.[18] These new settlers would consist of 'Christian families' and would be members of the 'honest' and not the 'blackguard' poor.[19] Before long Livingstone would realize that this sort of mass emigration would not work in Africa and he came to abandon his idea of new lives for the poor. The 'lower ranks' would, after all, not be able to elevate the Africans, and it would be detrimental for white men to compete in manual labour of 'any kind' with the natives: 'But they [English colonists] can take a leading part in managing the land, improving the quality, increasing the quantity and extending the varieties of the production of the soil; and by taking a lead too in trade and in all public matters, the Englishman would be an unmixed advantage to every one below and around him, for he would fill a place which is now practically vacant.'[20]

This sort of colonization, with the whites simply as leaders, could be effected with far fewer colonists, and therefore seemed more practicable. But even though Livingstone was sometimes confused about what British colonies in Africa ought to be like, he was convinced that without them there would not take place the massive social changes that were needed to make the natives susceptible to Christianity. In the short term he also knew that unless colonists came to the Shire Highlands quickly, all hopes for the area would have to be abandoned.

Throughout 1859 and 1860 Livingstone prayed that the Government would back his proposals. But during this time of waiting he was not inactive, for he set in motion a definite chain of events which he would later bitterly regret having started. During 1857 he had made speeches at Oxford and Cambridge, appealing for young men to dedicate themselves to a life of service in Africa. During the first months of 1859 he heard that, due to his appeal, a combined Oxford and Cambridge Universities Mission had been formed, with Durham and Dublin also joining the venture. In March 1859 Robert Gray, the Bishop of Cape Town, had written to Livingstone telling him about the determination of the Universities Mission to begin work in central Africa. Gray went on to ask what area Dr Livingstone would recommend as a suitable field for these men.[21] The decision was a difficult one for Livingstone. In his view the Shire Highlands needed colonists and not just an isolated group of missionaries, who would be able to do little about the serious problems which would face them there. On the other hand if Livingstone told the Bishop of Cape Town that the Shire Highlands was not a suitable area for missionaries, this news would get back to London and the Foreign Office, and would probably put paid to any plans for a colony. So on 31 October 1859 Livingstone wrote to the Bishop telling him that the Shire Highlands would prove an ideal location for a mission.[22] Livingstone knew that he was taking a risk, but could not see any way out. If the Government agreed to send colonists, there would be no risk at all; if not, then the missionaries might have a hard time. How hard, Livingstone did not dare think. Had he done so he might have spared himself the disasters of 1862 and 1863.

The arrival of the Universities Mission in early 1861 would mark the beginning of a new and crucial phase in the history of the Zambesi Expedition, but, before going on to deal with this period, it is important to describe the complete disintegration of the morale of the expedition itself during 1859 and 1860.

In 1858, Bedingfeld's dismissal, the inadequacy of the *Ma-Robert*, the depth of the Zambesi and the obstructions at Kebrabasa had dealt morale some heavy blows. The discovery of the Shire Highlands and Lake Nyassa, in the following year, ought to have improved matters, but in fact the situation had worsened critically. The principal reason was Livingstone's inability to share his feelings and his hopes with his colleagues. Kirk noticed that as soon as Livingstone's health suffered he became impossible, and even his normally excellent relationship with Africans deteriorated. 'He knows how to come round niggers very well, but if his digestive system don't go all right, he loses his diplomatic power wonderfully.'[23] Livingstone himself knew that he was prone to moods of manic-depression, when 'cheerfulness vanishes and the whole mental horizon is overcast with black clouds of gloom and sadness'. In such a state, he acknowledged, 'the liveliest joke cannot even provoke the semblance of a smile'.[24] In this state Livingstone would say nothing for days, even weeks, at a time, but would stare in front of him with a fixed expression, sometimes humming to himself. For his companions such behaviour was strange and alarming. Kirk could not bear being on deck with his leader when he was in a depressed mood and would be forced to go down to the cabin to escape him, but that was as bad, if not worse. Kirk wrote miserably about 'being alone in the cabin for four months with millions of cockroaches and not a single companion to speak to'.[25] The cockroaches were a nightmare and no trivial cause for complaint. They bred, as Kirk said, in millions in the warm dark hold of the *Ma-Robert* and ate into botanical specimens, food, candles and anything they could find. They bit humans too, 'nibbling at the legs by night and making sores'. Livingstone trapped two in a bottle on one occasion to see how fast they reproduced and discovered to his horror that from two of the female's egg cases, seventy-eight young ones appeared. Livingstone adopted a tame mongoose as a counter-measure and introduced several species of spider, but all to no effect. But Livingstone usually made light of mere physical discomfort. He noticed that the mongoose was losing weight, although eating thousands of cockroaches. 'This would be invaluable to fat young ladies,' he wrote in his

journal. It was a pity he never joked with his colleages
but kept his humour confined to his writing. Yet Livingstone did sometimes worry about the state of his mind.
He realized that only constant physical activity was any
use against his depression, and yet, as he confessed, when
he was active his powers of sympathy diminished and his
'heart became cold and dead'.[26] Ironically at this time,
when all communication with his staff broke down completely, he wrote advising his eldest son, Robert, to 'be
natural in everything. Let your smile be pleasant and easy.
Seldom show that you are displeased for very often the
cause of displeasure may be a mistake you have made
yourself.'[27] Yet being 'natural' and smiling pleasantly were
things Livingstone himself never mastered. All through
1859 he was troubled by unpleasant forebodings. If chaos
did come to the Shire Highlands, might it not be a judgment on his usefulness to God? The Kebrabasa Rapids had
been a severe shock, and Livingstone did not like to imagine whether he would be able to remain sane if more setbacks hit him. 'This heart is sometimes fearfully guilty of
mistrust,' he confided to his journal. 'I am ashamed to
think of it.'[28]

Meanwhile his colleagues, cut off from their leader,
struggled with repeated attacks of fever and laboured to
keep the *Ma-Robert* afloat. Livingstone never praised their
efforts nor gave encouragement; in his heart of hearts he
wanted to get rid of all of them and would have done
so if he could have managed it without the Foreign Office
knowing. 'All the exploration effected would have been
better done alone, or with my brother.'[29]

His undiminished faith in his brother soon led him into
direct conflict with other members of the party. The
troubles that eventually led to the dismissal of Baines and
Thornton dated back to the time the two men spent at
Tete with Charles Livingstone in late 1858. Unfortunately
this trio spent many months together in 1859 too; most of
the exploration up the Shire was done by Livingstone,
Rae and Kirk on their own.

Charles Livingstone was far more religiously narrow-
minded than his brother, and tended to dislike anyone
who did not share his theological interests. Neither Baines
nor Thornton had any interest in religion at all; both were
sociable, outgoing men with more interest in present enjoyment than future salvation. Charles shared his brother's

hysterical hatred of the Portuguese and was horrified to see that Baines and Thornton got on well with these 'degenerate' companions. When they went to drink wine with individual residents of Tete, Charles considered that they were doing something almost as sinful as participating in an orgy. Baines and Thornton soon disliked Charles considerably for his attitude to men like the Commandant of Tete, Major Sicard, who had consistently shown members of the expedition kindness and courtesy. Both men found Charles's habits infuriating. The younger Livingstone paid a great deal of attention to his appearance and rarely ventured out of doors without a felt hat or umbrella.[30] They were also irritated by Charles's constant complaints about the food, and his employment of a washerwoman to launder his own clothes with especial care.[31] But worst of all was Charles's assumption, that, since he was officially ranked higher in the expedition's chain of command, he could expect Baines and Thornton to run around doing whatever he asked them to. Baines was particularly annoyed by this since he was ten years older than Charles. Eventually he told Charles 'that he had not come as his servant but as an officer that had duties of his own to attend to'.[32] After this incident Charles wrote telling his wife that Baines was disagreeable and 'exceedingly stupid'.[33] Then relations became so strained that Charles moved to a room at the other end of the expedition's house in Tete. Soon he regretted this action, since when callers came they went to see Thornton and Baines and always left him alone. The other two men often received gifts of fruit, meat and poultry from the Portuguese, and Charles of course got nothing. This made him feel vindictive and jealous. Soon he was bribing natives to spy on his two colleagues and to report back anything discreditable that they might see.[34] Gradually Charles became convinced that Baines and Thornton were hard drinkers who attended Portuguese 'orgies'. The natives were ready to tell him anything he wanted to hear, since the more damning their stories, the more cloth they were paid.

Since the Portuguese were always friendly and often came with presents, Baines, as storekeeper, felt that it was only right that he should occasionally give them small gifts like a little sugar or a tin of sardines in return. Baines considered that it was essential to be sociable so that the Portuguese continued to look favourably on the expedition. When Charles heard about these presents and also discovered that Baines had painted the portraits of several Portuguese friends, using the expedition's artist's materials, the younger Livingstone felt that he had a case to accuse Baines of giving away supplies that did not belong to him. Charles was very soon convinced that a lot of sugar had been stolen. Since Baines had been given no place to lock up stores, it was hardly surprising that some pilfering took place. But there was no shred of evidence to accuse Baines of theft; and yet that was the accusation Charles made publicly in front of his brother in June 1859.

As usual Livingstone believed what his brother told him, but, while condemning Baines behind his back, did not order an investigation. Kirk thought that some stores probably had been squandered but blamed Livingstone whose 'own utter want of method in these matters would completely confound anyone in keeping exact lists'.[35] Livingstone decided that it suited his own interests best to claim that Baines had 'made away with expedition goods' while suffering from brain fever.[36] Livingstone did not much care about a few pounds of sugar, but he still remembered that Baines had taken Bedingfeld's side, and was eager to suggest to the Foreign Office that Baines's testimony was worthless since he was mentally ill. Of course Baines suffered from fever like all the others, but there was never any suggestion by anybody except Livingstone that he might be liable to occasional insanity.

While Charles had done his best to turn his brother against Baines, he had also worked hard to discredit Thornton. Thornton's sin in Charles's eyes was that he 'sneered at Scotchmen' and laughed at religiously-minded men for their seriousness.[37] Livingstone did not care for being laughed at, but he hated indolence much more than insolence. Thornton had been asked to excavate a shaft into a coal-seam near Tete, to a depth of thirty feet. In six months the young geologist had only achieved fifteen feet. Thornton had often been deserted by his native attendants, whose language he could not speak, and he had suffered so much from mosquito bites that his legs had become a mass of festering sores. He had also suffered constant attacks of malaria and some painful boils on his feet. In spite of all this he had extracted five tons of coal for the *Ma-Robert*'s boilers. This was much less than Livingstone had hoped for and he soon pronounced Thornton 'insufferably lazy'.[38] The young man excused himself on the grounds of his illnesses, but Livingstone still decided to dismiss him, having, as he put it, made 'every allowance for your suffering from prickly heat and other little ill-nesses'. After his dismissal Thornton decided to stay on and pay for his own keep. Within a few months Livingstone noticed to his annoyance that Thornton was working much better and making good progress. Thornton was only twenty-one and Livingstone had left him entirely to his own devices from the moment the expedition had arrived in Africa. Had he taken more interest in the young man, there can be no doubt that he would have got some good work out of him. Livingstone was forced to admit his mistake when he accepted Thornton back as a member of the expedition two years later. The precise part Charles Livingstone played in Thornton's dismissal is not entirely clear, but it is certain that Thornton himself felt Charles had been responsible. Thornton's sisters, Helen and Octavia, both referred to 'Mr Charles Livingstone's brutal-ity' and suggested that their brother had been 'foolish and imprudent to irritate Mr C.L.'.[39]

Thornton was sacked on 25 June 1859, and, after this success, Charles Livingstone once more turned his atten-tion to Baines; by July he had managed to persuade his brother to dismiss his artist and storekeeper. No new evi-dence had been produced, and when Kirk, much against his will and on Livingstone's orders, searched through Baines's boxes in late October and went through his store-keeping books, Charles's claim that Baines had stolen a quarter of the expedition's total sugar stocks was proved false.[40] Kirk discovered that butter had been badly accounted for and that one cask of sugar could not be traced. There was one piece of canvas in Baines's personal luggage which he could not explain how he came to possess. But since this article was not worth more than a few shillings, it did not strike Kirk as very important. At the end of his search, Kirk wrote that there was 'no expedition property which I can claim at once'.[41] All the Portuguese at Tete firmly asserted that Baines was inno-cent of all charges of theft.

Livingstone was acutely embarrassed by Kirk's lack of condemning evidence. He had already sacked Baines and felt that he could not retract now. Instead he suggested

that Kirk had been deceived and that Baines 'had cooked
the book of store expenditure, making it appear as if 4 lbs
of sugar had been consumed per day'. Livingstone rejected
the sworn statements of the Portuguese on the grounds
that all the residents of Tete were too degenerate to be
capable of knowing the difference between truth and falsehood.

Baines was given a hearing of sorts by Livingstone and
Charles, but since both his accusers refused to accept his
denials of the charges made and would not return to Tete
for a proper re-examination of the evidence, the artist was
condemned without any chance of proving his innocence.
When Livingstone was later accused of having refused a
proper trial, he replied that there had been no judge and
jury within a thousand miles and that he had spared Baines
the ignominy of additional publicity by refusing a full
enquiry.[42] Although Livingstone made much of his desire
not to blacken Baines's character, he wrote to numerous
friends in England telling them about Baines's stealing,
'drinking & debauchery'.[43] When he wrote his official *Narrative* of the expedition, Livingstone did not once mention
Baines by name and refused to acknowledge that Baines
had drawn most of the pictures which appeared in the
Narrative as illustrations. During the time that remained
to Baines on the Zambesi, Livingstone isolated him from
the rest of the party so that he could not contaminate
anybody. Livingstone evidently saw nothing inhuman in this
for he wrote almost with pride: 'I do not allow Baines to
our table but send him a good share of all we eat ourselves. He lives in a whaler, with a sail as an awning over
him.'[44]

When Baines was put on to a warship bound for England on 7 December 1859, all his possessions were still at
Tete. He never saw most of his paintings again, and had
Kirk and Rae not given him money and clothing, he would
have left with nothing but the clothes he stood up in.

At the end of 1859 Livingstone may have congratulated
himself on purging the expedition of evil-doers, but in all
respects his position was unenviable. He had lost half of
the six European colleagues he had come out with, the
Ma-Robert was leaking like a colander and could not be
expected to float more than a few months, no letters had
been received from the Foreign Secretary in response to
Livingstone's request for a new steamer to replace the

Ma-Robert and it seemed unlikely that the Foreign Office would send their reaction to his plans for the Shire Highlands for another six months or a year. Meanwhile George Rae, the engineer, was talking about resigning, and Livingstone was losing all control over his native crew. After Kirk had been attacked by a member of the crew with an iron bar, Livingstone had lost his temper and, in an undignified fury, jumped into the water to beat the offending man with a cook's ladle. Shortly afterwards Livingstone had to quell another near-mutiny by hitting the ringleader with a stout piece of wood. Kirk was horrified when his leader, normally so restrained and tolerant where natives were concerned, told him 'to break their heads if they did not do as I told them'.[45]

All these troubles were at their worst in mid-December 1859, when Livingstone and the remnants of his party came down for supplies to the Kongone mouth of the Zambesi after their journey to Lake Nyassa. For a week or so Livingstone remained in a state of complete indecision. There seemed little or nothing he could do. Until a new steamer came he was helpless, and even then there would be little to be done until the Foreign Office either sanctioned or refused his other plans. The Universities Mission would not be arriving for another year and so that project offered no immediate hope for profitable work. Yet Livingstone's great strength was his ability to ignore present difficulties even when they seemed quite overwhelming. In late December he told his colleagues that instead of sitting around for most of the coming year, they would employ 1860 in taking the Makololo back to their chief. He had promised Sekeletu that his men would be back by 1858, and now that there was nothing else to do, Livingstone felt able to honour his promise. Livingstone also made another rather more important decision. He told George Rae that he was to embark on the next warship for England and that on his arrival he should supervise the designing and building of a portable steamer for the upper Shire and Lake Nyassa. If the Foreign Office would not pay, Livingstone said that he would spend all the rest of the profits from *Missionary Travels*, up to six thousand pounds, on the vessel. There is no denying that this was a brave and magnificent gesture, once more proving Livingstone's total commitment to the Shire Highlands. But Livingstone had now set himself an almost impossible task for the future. The parts of this portable steamer would have to be carried past the Murchison Cataracts for thirty miles, and that would only be possible if a road was built. In any case, vast numbers of natives would be needed, not only as labourers on the road but also as porters to manhandle the parts of the steamer past the cataracts. Carts would be needed too. In view of events that followed in 1863, it is hard to believe that Livingstone could ever have given much serious thought to the practical details of such an ambitious operation. But in his desperation to create circumstances in the Shire Highlands suitable for the establishment of a colony, Livingstone was prepared to defy odds which appeared, to a rational observer, to be hopelessly against him.

Rae was sent back to England according to plan, and in early 1860 Livingstone, Charles and Kirk set off for Tete from the mouth of the Zambesi. The idea of taking the Makololo home was excellent from Livingstone's point of view, since it conveniently filled in time that would otherwise have been wasted, but the Makololo themselves had settled in well at Tete and many elected not to return. When Livingstone left for Makololo country, in May 1860, he did so with roughly sixty out of the original 114. According to Charles Livingstone thirty of these had deserted to return to Tete before Livingstone had got them as far as Kebrabasa. Livingstone blamed their behaviour on the Portuguese who had 'perverted' them. Charles thought this ridiculous and said that they 'could hardly have learned anything bad which they did not know and practice before they left their own country'.[46]

Livingstone would not return to Tete from Makololo country till the end of November 1860. The importance of this trip was not the homecoming of some thirty Makololo, but Livingstone's discovery of the deaths of six of the nine European members of the London Missionary Society mission to the Makololo, which he himself had set in hand in 1857. Since I have dealt fully with this episode in Chapter 12, little more need be said about it now; but two points are important. The discovery of the deaths and Livingstone's realization that the Makololo were disintegrating as a tribe, confirmed his conviction that all hopes for the future lay in the Shire Highlands. Secondly, the actual journey to Sekeletu's town was important, since on it a series of rows broke out between Charles and David

Livingstone. These disagreements ended their close relationship and left Livingstone completely isolated.

The trouble had really started when Charles made it perfectly clear to his brother, before leaving Tete, that the trip was a waste of time and energy. Livingstone never liked his plans to be challenged and could sense that Kirk agreed with Charles. Only two of the men being taken back to Sekeletu were true Makololo, and all the rest were members of subject tribes. The Makololo never treated their vassals well and it seemed to Kirk folly to risk a great deal of hardship and fatigue simply to take thirty natives back to central Africa when twenty-eight of them probably did not want to go. Kirk however had the sense not to argue. Charles was less self-controlled and on 13 May Livingstone was transcribing some hurtful things his brother had said to him. 'My brother informs me that the members of the Expedition did not get orders what to do, and were always at a loss how to act . . . All were willing and anxious to help if I only could have told them. He never told me before.'[47]

Livingstone was completely confounded by this since Charles had taken such a leading role in the dismissal of Baines and Thornton. In the past Livingstone had believed that whoever else might fail him, Charles would not. Thus, in spite of a mass of evidence to the contrary, Livingstone had suggested that Charles was the only ideal travelling companion in the party. When he found that Charles was repaying such loyalty with criticism, Livingstone was astounded. Without his famous brother's recommendation, Charles would never have gained a job on the expedition in the first place. Livingstone at once accused him of ingratitude and treachery. Not satisfied with this, Livingstone sat down to write an assessment of Charles in his journal. 'As an assistant he has been of no value. Photography very unsatisfactory. Magnetism still more so. Meteorological observations not creditable, and writing in the journal in arrears. In going up with us now he is useless, as he knows nothing of Portuguese or the native language. He often expected me to be his assistant instead of acting as mine.'[48]

Kirk claimed that the first violent row between the brothers broke out over 'an old pillow which had rotted in the ship, like many other things'.[49] The triviality of this is a good indication of the state of mind the two men were

in. Livingstone had accused Charles of deliberately destroying the pillow without considering to whom it belonged.
The result had been a long argument with 'Mr C. L. using
most improper expressions to a superior officer, and Dr L.
saying that he had been a failure from the beginning and
that the only mistake made was in bringing him out'.[50]
Worse was to come.

For several weeks Charles sulked and occasionally mut-
tered about his brother being 'no Christian gentleman' and
being employed 'in the service of the Devil'. Then one
day Charles, who had recently fallen six feet into an elephant pitfall, lost his temper with the headman of the
Makololo and kicked him with all his strength. Since they
were now within days of reaching Sekeletu's town, this was
not a sensible thing to do. Sekeletu would not be pleased
to hear that his men had been beaten up on their way
home. Livingstone flew into an uncontrollable rage and
Kirk confessed that he then listened to 'the most abusive
filthy language ever heard in that class of society'. During
this scene the headman had nearly murdered Charles, and
the two brothers had come to blows. Kirk wrote coolly in
his journal:

> I trust that if I am sent on an overland trip, I may
> not have C.L. for a companion, for if he can break
> out and abuse, tearing with nails so as to draw blood
> and tear clothes, saying his brother was serving the
> Devil, indulge in epithets such as 'the cursing consul
> of Quillimane', repeated over and over again, act
> before the men in such a way as to make them look
> on him as mad, which if I could only say that I
> thought he was, would be the most charitable thing I
> could do. But under one who loses his temper so sud-
> denly so as to change from joking to kicking with
> iron nailed boots the chief man sent by a proud
> powerful savage chief, . . . is one on whom no reli-
> ance can be placed. Nothing but the high personal
> regard for Dr L. averted bloodshed in that case.
> The spear was poised and needed only a stroke of the
> arm to send it to the heart. I never expected so much
> moderation from savages.[51]

From the time of this incident all order and discipline
broke down and it was with the greatest difficulty that Liv-

ingstone prevented the whole party disbanding *en route*. That evening Livingstone wrote down sadly some of the insults his brother had thrown at him: 'Manners of a cotton spinner, of the Boers', 'that I had cursed him, that I had set the devil into him . . . and repeated again and again that I had cursed him', 'seemed intent on a row. Would be but a short time in the Expedition: regretted that he was on this journey. Would rejoice when he could leave it.'[52] At last, too late to remedy things, Livingstone realized that Charles had probably slandered other members of the party without grounds. In the meantime, Livingstone knew that he could not dismiss Charles without appearing a fool. From July 1860 till the middle of 1863, when Charles returned to England, Livingstone saw him and talked to him only when he could not avoid doing so. From now on Livingstone felt entirely alone.

The trouble with his brother evidently did little for Livingstone's judgment, for on the way back to Tete he decided to try and shoot the first rapids at Kebrabasa. Charles and Kirk were too tired and disenchanted to argue. During the attempt Kirk's canoe was upset and he himself nearly drowned. Livingstone emerged on the other side of this first section of the Kebrabasa rapids wet but unharmed. In his journal Livingstone dismissed this incident, which had nearly cost his botanist's life, in a few sentences.

The three men were back at Tete by the end of November, and there Livingstone was handed a mail-bag containing the Foreign Secretary's answer to his suggestions for the development of the Shire Highlands. While Livingstone was dismayed that his colonial plans had been rejected out of hand, he could comfort himself with the news that Lord Russell had agreed to prolong the expedition for a further period up to three years. The steamer to replace the *Ma-Robert*, he was told, had started from England earlier the same year, which meant that she should already be at the mouth of the Zambesi. The Foreign Secretary had refused an additional vessel for Lake Nyassa, and so Livingstone realized that the ship Rae had gone to order would have to be paid for with the remains of his book money. He had known that this was a distinct possibility from the beginning.

The most important news Livingstone received was from the organizers of the Universities Mission, who wrote tell-

ing Livingstone that the first members of the mission could
be expected at the Zambesi mouth during January of the
New Year. After the Foreign Secretary's flat rejection of
plans for a colony in the Shire Highlands, Livingstone could
not help being alarmed about the prospects of the new
mission; none of its members had been prepared in any
way for the problems they would shortly have to face. Livingstone had recommended the mission to come to the
Shire Highlands because, had he done otherwise, his earlier
optimism about the area's glorious future would have
seemed grotesquely inconsistent, and all future efforts in
the region would have been blighted. But without the help
of colonists from the beginning, Livingstone realized that
life for the missionaries would be far from simple. This was
a Church of England mission that had been inaugurated
with a great deal of publicity. If a disaster like that at
Linyanti happened to these members of the Established
Church, it was going to be a lot harder to explain away
than the deaths of several nonconformists and their children. Livingstone could see that his future reputation to a
large extent depended on what would happen to these men
whom he had been obliged to summon to the Shire Highlands.

With the Portuguese and Arab slave raids, and the inter-
tribal conflict between the Ajawa and the Manganja very
much in mind, Livingstone decided at once to try and
qualify some of his earlier unrestrained enthusiasm, just in
case anything went wrong at a later date. He wrote to the
Secretaries of the Mission telling them that, while the
country was healthy and fertile, the missionaries should
expect some hostility and suspicion from the natives on
account of the slave-trade.[53] He wrote in similar terms to
the Bishop of Oxford, informing him that, although the
area held out 'glorious prospects' 'there are difficulties,
no doubt—an unreduced language, and people quite ignorant of the motives of missionaries, with all the evils of
its being in the slave market. But your university men are
believed to possess genuine English pluck, and will, no
doubt rejoice to preach Christ's Gospel beyond other men's
line of things.'[54] Having gone some way towards redress-
ing his formerly unblemished picture of the Shire Highlands, Livingstone went on to assure the Bishop of Oxford
that the missionaries would have nothing to fear from

malaria, which, if treated correctly, was no worse than a common cold.

Even after this spate of letter-writing, Livingstone was still uneasy. But he felt elated as well as fearful. He had heard that the Universities Mission was to be headed by a Bishop, and Livingstone realized that the creation of a bishopric in an area that was not a British possession was equivalent to a quasi-claim over that territory.[55] For this reason the British Government had been against the consecration of a bishop as leader of the new mission; in the eyes of the Foreign Secretary it had set a dangerous precedent. Livingstone was delighted for the very reason that distressed Lord Russell so much: namely that, if the bishop was hindered by Portuguese or Arab slave-traders, there might be a massive upsurge of public feeling in favour of annexing the area. Yet Livingstone could see that if harm came to the bishop, public anger might turn on the man who had sent him to so difficult a region. Missionary failures could lead to a revulsion against sending more men to an area which had proved fatal to others. As Livingstone left Tete in early December and headed down river towards the mouth of the Zambesi, to meet the newcomers, he knew that a great deal hung on the success or failure of the new bishop and his colleagues: not just the fate of the Zambesi Expedition and the Shire Highlands, but the kind of attitudes the British Government and public would entertain towards colonial expansion in Africa for maybe the next twenty or thirty years.

17

Death of a Fighting Bishop

The first members of the Universities Mission arrived at the Kongone mouth of the Zambesi at the end of January 1861 in two ships of the blockading squadron: H.M.S. *Sidon* and H.M.S. *Lyra*. Livingstone, Charles and Kirk had spent a wet and gloomy month, in a group of damp, mosquito-infested huts, waiting for the new arrivals. A few days before reaching the mouth, the *Ma-Robert* had done what she had promised to do for some months: she had gone to the bottom. Fortunately the crew had enough warning to get out most of the supplies and goods. Before leaving Tete, Livingstone had selected a fresh crew to man the new steamer that was expected to arrive at the same time as the missionaries. This crew had been chosen from among those Makololo who had preferred to remain in Moçambique rather than return to Linyanti. The sight of the *Sidon* with the *Pioneer*—the *Ma-Robert's* replacement vessel—in tow did much to raise the spirits of the small reception party after their miserable month of waiting.

The missionaries' first impressions of the Zambesi delta were none the less far from favourable. They were surprised to see the *Pioneer* almost capsize crossing the bar, especially since they had heard that the Zambesi was such an excellent waterway. The naval officers on both the warships found their confusion entertaining and told them with lugubrious relish that eight or nine men had already lost their lives on the bar coming and going on Dr Livingstone's business. One of the missionaries was soon writing bitterly in his journal that 'nothing could be more impracticable for ordinary commercial purposes' than the Kongone mouth.[1]

Yet Livingstone, on his affable best behaviour, soon reassured the newcomers. Kirk was equally friendly, and even Charles, who had already decided on theological grounds to despise the Church of England men, managed to conceal his true feelings. Bishop Mackenzie was an energetic and hearty man in the best traditions of muscular Christianity. He had had a brilliant career at Cambridge, where he had taught theology and mathematics. He had then gone to work among the Zulus as a missionary in Natal, soon rising to the rank of Archdeacon of Natal. He had recently been consecrated Bishop in Cape Town. Kirk at once dubbed this prematurely-bald prelate, with his luxuriant sideboards and easy manner, 'a trump of a fellow' and Livingstone, with rare generosity, pronounced him 'A 1'. Livingstone was also delighted with the other members of the party and wrote to the Foreign Secretary telling him so: 'I hail their arrival with very great satisfaction for they seem to have sound practical views of the work before them, and during our short intercourse have shown that they have no nonsense about them.'[2]

At this stage Livingstone had not become acquainted with the extremely High Church views of the Bishop and his Deacon, Henry Rowley. But he had genuinely taken to an Anglican priest, H. C. Scudamore, and to a young man designated as 'lay superintendent', Horace Waller. His judgment was later shown to be sound; Waller became one of his greatest friends, and Scudamore, while he lived, worked with tireless unselfishness. Both men were Low Church, unlike Mackenzie and Rowley. Another member of the party, Lovell Procter, made no marked impression on either Kirk, Charles or Livingstone. In addition to these men, the mission included a carpenter called Gamble, and Adams, a cockney labourer, whose official title was 'agriculturalist'. A doctor, John Dickinson, and another young clergyman, Henry Burrup, were expected to come out shortly.

In spite of all the initial goodwill, discords were not long in coming. Mackenzie had expected to be taken to his new mission field without delay. He was therefore more than surprised when Livingstone told him that he would have to wait three months. Livingstone wanted to explore an alternative route into the Shire Highlands before taking the missionaries anywhere. The Doctor had never been entirely satisfied with the river Shire, partly because the upper reaches became very shallow in the dry season, but mainly because the Portuguese could prevent entrance via the Zambesi, if and when they might wish to do so. Recently Livingstone had made up his mind that the river Rovuma, which flowed into the Indian Ocean some six hundred miles north of Quilimane, had its source in Lake Nyassa and would therefore prove an ideal *highway* into the Shire Highlands. The Rovuma's main advantage was its situation outside the northern limits of Portuguese Moçambique.

Mackenzie was not impressed when Livingstone claimed that the Portuguese would become obstructive unless another way into the Highlands were found. The Bishop had previously been promised that there would be no interference; in fact he had letters of recommendation from the Portuguese Government and had been assured of complete co-operation. Apart from that, Mackenzie had always understood that the Shire was an ideal river with no navigation problems at any time of year. Livingstone did not want to admit that he had deceived anybody in the past, and instead suggested that it would be best for the Bishop to wait a few months while the Rovuma was explored, since the Mission as yet had no doctor. Again Mackenzie was puzzled. Since Livingstone would be with his party till they were settled, Livingstone and Kirk would be their doctors. Besides, Livingstone had suggested that fever was easy to treat and no more serious than the common cold. Livingstone eventually had to admit that another important reason for wishing to avoid the Shire was the existence of widespread fighting on its lower reaches. He blamed the Portuguese slave raids for this and conveniently omitted mentioning the primary cause: the Ajawa.

Eventually Mackenzie reluctantly gave in and agreed to wait three months. He knew very well that if any misfortune did befall his men, and it was subsequently discovered that he had rejected Dr Livingstone's advice, there would be some unpleasant recrimination in Britain. This did not stop him telling Livingstone that in his view the delay would mean a loss of morale and possibly the cooling of public enthusiasm for the venture at home. The Mission had been launched with official fanfares by Brougham, Gladstone and Dr Wilberforce, and Mackenzie was terrified by the thought of failure. 'I am afraid of this,' he wrote; 'most works of this kind have been carried on by one or two men in a quieter way, and have had a quieter beginning.'[3]

The missionaries had been surprised in the first place that Livingstone was putting so much faith in the Rovuma's potential. They had heard from their naval friends that the river had been surveyed by a naval officer, Commander Owen, and found to be navigable by steamer for only forty-five miles.[4] Captain Crauford of the *Sidon* told Mackenzie that when the river was low, and it was in the first quarter of the year, Livingstone could not expect to get more than thirty miles upstream. Crauford was right. When Livingstone met the missionaries again in April, they had ceased to think of him as quite the man of judgment they had been led to believe he was.

The party steamed into the Zambesi on board the *Pioneer* on 1 May 1861 and the bonhomie of January was very much a thing of the past. Livingstone had offered to do all he could for the missionaries, and now he had been landed with the job of transporting them around with all their gear. He had been quite firm with their organizers when he had suggested that they bring their own vessel, but, although the appeal for the venture had reached £20,000, no steamer had been ordered. He had

been surprised and irritated that they should have tried
to thwart him in his plan to explore the Rovuma, and felt
that they had no right at all to try to dictate what he did
when he was doing so much for them. In the meantime
he had been having naval troubles. The *Pioneer* had
arrived with a master, Mr May, who thought that he was
to succeed Bedingfeld. Livingstone assured him that he
was mistaken, whereupon May resigned. So now Livingstone was in charge of the *Pioneer*, plus his own expedition, plus, for the time being, the missionaries. Morale
among his own men was no better than usual, and Kirk
was particularly depressed by a typical piece of his leader's thoughtlessness. Livingstone had not told him that he
had asked for another medical officer and botanist to
come out with the *Pioneer*, but now, without any warning,
a Dr Meller had arrived. Kirk immediately liked Meller
but still felt that his appointment was a slap in the face.
Meanwhile Charles was doing his best to try to set the Low
Church section of the mission against the High Church
section. Worse still, all the missionaries, except the irritable Rowley, had now suffered from fever and had discovered it to be a far worse affliction than a 'common
cold'. Rowley described this part of their venture well:
'Fever still prevailed among us, and from the foul and
crowded state of the little ship, this was not to be wondered at. At most there was but healthy accomodation for
twenty people on board the *Pioneer*, and there were forty-
eight . . . The deck was blocked up with boxes, bales, and
sacks of coal. The saloon and after-cabin were offensive
with the odour from the mass of stuff stored in them.'[5]

On 8 May, when they were steaming through the delta,
Mackenzie wrote telling his sister that they would all be
at the Murchison Cataracts within seventeen days.[6] The
estimate was sadly optimistic. A week later the *Pioneer*
went aground, and for the next two months it was rare
when she was not being dragged along by anchors and
ropes. Livingstone had asked the Foreign Office to see that
his new vessel should draw no more than three feet, but it
was hardly surprising that, overloaded way beyond any
limit that had been envisaged, she should draw over five
feet. At the end of June, when all the ship's capstans
had been ripped out of their mountings by the strain put
on them in pulling the *Pioneer* across sandbanks, Livingstone was soon landing surplus stores in a vain attempt to

lighten ship and get the draught down to three feet. After this, progress became a little faster, and by 8 July they were a few miles below the Murchison Cataracts.

It says a lot for the characters of the missionaries that, after their disappointment over the initial delay due to the Rovuma, they did not criticize Livingstone for mis-informing them about the navigability of the Shire, nor for suggesting that the Shire valley was well populated, when in fact it was not. Although most of them suffered badly from fever, Procter particularly, they pulled hard at the ropes and rarely became irritable or depressed. Much of the credit must go to Mackenzie, who, unlike Living-stone, was a born mixer and a man quite able to combine an almost feminine gentleness with masculine heartiness. Even Charles Livingstone liked him. Mackenzie never minded seeming ridiculous and was quite happy to take a bath in full view of everybody in the space under one of the paddle-boxes. On one occasion the paddle-wheel started to turn suddenly, and he was 'like a squirrel in a cage, his clothes all went and his cassock, he rushed out without clothes crying to the seamen to save the cassock'.[7] Only Rowley had serious misgivings about the future. The state of the river Shire proved to him that communication with the sea was going to be very difficult in future, and, in his view, virtually ruled out any traders following in their footsteps. But the rest, like Waller and the Bishop, still trusted Livingstone, if not as a miracle-worker, at least as a man who would guide them to a safe and peaceful place from which to begin missionary operations.

The mood on 15 July was one of almost unalloyed optimism, as the whole party, led by Livingstone, set off on foot from a village just below the Murchison Cata-racts. Mackenzie summed it up in a lighthearted descrip-of them all:

> You would like to see our picturesque appearance on the march . . . Livingstone in his jacket and trousers of blue serge and his blue cloth cap. His brother, a taller man, in something of the same dress. I with trousers of Oxford grey and a coat like a shooting coat, a broad-rimmed wide awake hat with white cover, which Livingstone laughs at, but which all the same keeps the sun off. *He* is a salamander.[8]

However, after 'a few hours of the seventy-mile march towards Magomero—the village chosen by Livingstone as the new mission site—the good spirits started to decline. The porters were soon slacking, and Mackenzie, who was unused to this normal hazard of African travel, made matters worse by prodding dawdlers with his crozier. But real trouble was not far off.

Livingstone and the Bishop had already argued about whether missionaries should carry arms, and although Livingstone had managed to win over all the other members of the University party to the view that arms were the best means of deterring attack, Mackenzie had only reluctantly given in. Thus, as he marched, he was painfully aware of the incongruity of carrying a double-barrelled gun in one hand and his bishop's crozier in the other. But the events of 16 July were to banish his pacifist leanings for good; on that day he and his companions saw their first slaving party.

There were eighty-four slaves, many of them women and children, with their hands tied and their necks secured to forked wooden taming-sticks. The missionaries were euphoric as they watched most of the slave drivers run away at the appearance of the combined Christian party. Clearly the hand of God was behind it. Livingstone remained less rapturous. He put down the flight of the slavers to the warlike gestures of his Makololo crew, who were now accompanying him as porters. Waller at once started to cut through the ropes that bound the captives and Mackenzie listened in horror to the interpreted story of one woman whose baby's brains had been dashed out in front of her eyes. No shots had been fired, but the Bishop had already made up his mind that 'in such cases it is right to use force, and even fire if necessary to rescue captives'.[9] Livingstone was not so concerned with the rights or wrongs of firing or not firing. He had just seen among the slavers a couple of former slaves from Tete. Portuguese slaving operations had already reached the heart of the Shire Highlands. The implications were not pleasant for the future of the Mission. Livingstone had been warned by the Governor of Tete that it was illegal to interfere with slave caravans. The Bishop's letters of recommendation from the Portuguese Government were not likely to be much use from now on. Livingstone could also see that if Mackenzie went on freeing slaves, he would have to feed them all. Already he had made himself responsible for eighty-four people before he had even planted any crops. Yet the issue, as Livingstone could see, was not a simple one. If the slavers were allowed to continue operations with impunity, there was going to be no peace in the area in future. News soon reached the combined party that there were other slave caravans in the area, and so, on Livingstone's instructions, his men split up to search these other slavers out. Soon a further fifty-seven people had been freed.

On arrival at Magomero it soon became apparent that the Portuguese slavers were a comparatively small problem when set beside the series of raids recently carried out in the area by the Ajawa. More raids were planned, so Livingstone and Mackenzie were told. While Livingstone had told Mackenzie about the Portuguese slavers, he had not warned him about the role the Ajawa played as Arab middlemen. Nor had he admitted that the Ajawa were fighting a tribal war against the Manganja. But there was no time for retrospective explanations or calm deliberation. By 22 July the rumours of nearby Ajawa attacks had hardened to certainty, and it was clear that the Ajawa had more aggression in mind. A raid was planned on a village some ten miles away. Livingstone and Mackenzie set out in that direction with most of their party, a group of armed Makololo and some of the local Manganja people. Soon they were passing through burned-out villages and could see in the distance another village still burning. As they marched closer they could hear shouting and the noise of women wailing for their dead men-folk. The Bishop suggested that the whole party pray, and so they did. When they got up from their knees, it was to see a long line of Ajawa warriors and their captives coming round the hillside to their right. The Ajawa headman stood up on a conveniently placed ant-hill to get a good view of the opposition, and decided that it was negligible. When Livingstone attempted to talk peacefully, this was taken as confirmation that the strangers were too cowardly to fight. Soon Livingstone and Mackenzie found themselves the prime targets of a deluge of poisoned arrows, fired with uncomfortable accuracy—one fell right between them.

The aggressors now advanced to a distance of fifty yards and seemed to be preparing to charge. A Manganja near Livingstone doubled up with an arrow through his

5. Missionaries buying food at Magomero

arm. Livingstone gave the order to fire, and the Bishop, not wishing to fire himself, handed his weapon to the Doctor, who promptly started to blaze away. In later accounts of the engagement Livingstone did not mention the number of Ajawa killed, but Kirk reckoned it to have been six. None of Livingstone's party were hit, although one Manganja was killed and several others wounded. Livingstone estimated that the Ajawa had had four guns, although their use of them had been far from expert. The Doctor finally led his party into the Ajawa's town and set fire to it.[10] As he was later to tell his son Robert, it was the end of 'a hungry, fatiguing and most unpleasant day'. For the Mission, this foray had momentous consequences.

Livingstone now realized that the Mission's position was an extremely dangerous one. He cursed himself for having got mixed up in a situation where he had been obliged, for the first time in his life, to shoot Africans. The whole incident, he felt, might be taken as a precedent by the Bishop for future occasions. That the Ajawa would want revenge Livingstone had no doubt. The missionaries might have secured the lasting friendship of the Manganja but they would undoubtedly never make any headway with the Ajawa, who would probably become the dominant people in the area before long. Livingstone did not tell Mackenzie about another unpleasant thought that was passing through his mind. No one side in any African tribal conflict ever had a monopoly of right, and it was ten to one that the Manganja would sell Ajawa into slavery if they got the chance.

Mackenzie was at first inclined to move to a more peaceful region further south, but Livingstone was against this for two reasons: in the first place Magomero was in an ideal defensive position, being on a peninsula formed by a stream, and in the second the Ajawa would soon take their revenge on the local Manganja, who would be without a place of refuge if the missionaries moved away. There were disadvantages at Magomero too. It lay in a hollow, and water drained into rather than out of it. This would pose health problems since the excrement of 150 people would not be carried away by the stream. But Livingstone dismissed this difficulty, and, having promised to leave the Bishop two sailors, who had come out with the *Pioneer*, as helpers, he recommended the building of a defensive stockade and prepared to leave. He wanted to make a thorough survey of Lake Nyassa to see whether the Rovuma really did flow out of it.

On 25 July Livingstone invited the local Manganja chiefs to meet him at Magomero. He then made a formal speech. Mackenzie was certain that in it he pledged himself and the Mission to assist the Manganja against the Ajawa. Livingstone later denied this, and Waller, the only other European witness to the speech, besides Mackenzie, thought that this help was to be purely defensive.[11]

Before Livingstone left Magomero for Nyassa, Mackenzie asked him in some perplexity what he meant by defence. When they had killed six Ajawa they had been defending themselves, and yet they had had no alternative other than a counter-attack. Livingstone admitted that it was a thorny question, but advised the missionaries that whatever the circumstances they should on no account become involved in a tribal war. He warned Mackenzie that Manganja chiefs would ask for help. 'You will be oppressed with requests,' Livingstone told him, 'but don't go.' This advice was good but hardly much use. The missionaries had already been committed to the Manganja cause by the events of 22 July. If they gave refuge to the Manganja, the Ajawa would automatically view the missionaries as their enemies. Since Livingstone had suggested that Mackenzie ought to provide refuge, it was futile his telling the Bishop to avoid taking sides. Had Livingstone discussed the issue in greater detail before he left, he would probably have realized that the missionaries would lose even the slender hold they now had over the Manganja if they sat back while the Ajawa destroyed village after village. Such apparent indifference would hardly bring in converts. The missionaries could not see that there was a great difference between releasing slaves and preventing their capture. Both actions constituted active intervention. So the Universities Mission was a confused and worried body of men when Livingstone set out north at the end of July 1861. None of them could speak any native language, they had 150 people to feed and no crops sown, and on top of all this, they faced the possibility of involvement in a major tribal war. They could afford to forget minor irritants like Portuguese and Arab slavers.

Livingstone was away at Lake Nyassa till mid-November, and during that time he achieved little that he wanted to. He mapped, with remarkable accuracy, two hundred miles of the west side of the lake, but on the east side he did not find any outlet that could have been the Rovuma. In fact the Rovuma's source was some forty miles to the east of Nyassa. Livingstone had hoped to reach the northern end of the lake, but he was forced back by famine and tribal disturbances before reaching his goal. All in all, this trip consisted of three and a half very depressing months. From the number of dhows they had seen crossing Nyassa, Livingstone and his companions had little reason to doubt the fact that the lake lay in the path of a major Arab slave route. They were equally distressed at the havoc caused by the aggressive Ngoni at the northern end of the lake and, even further south, they had passed through villages littered with 'skeletons and the putrid bodies of the slain'.[12] When Livingstone reached the *Pioneer* below the Murchison Cataracts in early November, he badly wanted good news. Instead he heard to his horror that Bishop Mackenzie had made two separate attacks on the Ajawa. Apparently the missionaries had driven away the Ajawa without waiting to be attacked. Instead of wondering whether Mackenzie had had any alternative, and without blaming himself for having brought the mission to such a chaotic place, Livingstone at once concluded that the missionaries had deliberately flouted his advice. Livingstone's immediate thought was not for the welfare of the Bishop and his men but for his

own reputation at home. His journal makes this very
plain. 'People,' he wrote, 'will not approve of men coming
out to convert people shooting them. I am sorry that I am
mixed up with it, as they will not care what view of my
character is given at home.'[13]

Livingstone's assessment of public feeling was soon to
be proved correct. As soon as he heard about the attacks,
he felt he must see Mackenzie as soon as possible to stop
him sending home information about recent events. So
when the Bishop arrived at the *Pioneer* on 14 November,
Livingstone lost no time in telling him that 'it would be
as well if they agreed to say as little as possible about it at
home'. Mackenzie then told him that letters about the
fighting had already been despatched to the coast. These
letters did not contain just casual references to the recent
brushes but full and detailed accounts.[14] Worse still, Livingstone heard that Rowley had sent an article to a Cape
Town newspaper claiming that the attacks had been in
response to Dr Livingstone's first fight with the Ajawa.
This information ended any chance there might ever have
been of Livingstone showing the missionaries understanding and sympathy. Now his only interest was to see that
people in England should know that he dissociated himself
from the Universities Mission.

During the next few days Livingstone wrote numerous
letters putting all the blame on Mackenzie and stressing
over and over again that his own earlier fight had been
forced upon him and had therefore set no precedent. He
made a special point of telling the Foreign Secretary that
he would 'keep carefully aloof from the policy adopted
by this new mission'. It did not seem to have occurred to
Livingstone that by damaging the Mission he was also
damaging his own hopes for the Shire Highlands. His best
course would have been to sit down with Mackenzie and
work out some very convincing justifications. Instead his
condemnations of the Mission virtually brought to an end
public subscriptions in England, and therefore crucially
endangered the party's further existence. When, some time
later, Livingstone realized that he had been lumped with
the missionaries whether he liked it or not, his defence of
Mackenzie came too late to redress the earlier damage. In
November 1861 he had felt able to treat the missionaries
badly because he had recently heard that the Free Church

of Scotland had arranged for one of their members to come out to pave the way for another mission.

In fact Mackenzie *had* gone against Livingstone's advice, but he had seen no alternative. While he had realized that Christian missionaries damaged their peaceful image by fighting, he had seen at the same time that no successful mission could be established in an area where anarchy prevailed. Since there was nobody else to establish order, Mackenzie had taken the task upon himself. Livingstone refused to listen to this justification and told the Bishop bluntly that he could no longer expect much help from the members of the Zambesi Expedition, who had more important jobs to do than getting improvident missionaries out of scrapes. This was bad enough, but Livingstone added that Mackenzie ought to have come out with a steamer for the mission, since the *Pioneer* would no longer be able to act as their private 'passenger ship'.[15] It was true that Livingstone had suggested to the organizers of the mission that a steamer ought to be sent out, but since one had not arrived, his threat to leave the missionaries to their own devices made them feel that very soon they would have no contact with the outside world.

Livingstone had further reasons to be uneasy. Before he had realized quite how gruesome conditions in the Shire Highlands were, he had agreed to the idea of Mackenzie's elderly spinster sister coming out to help at Magomero. At the same time Livingstone had sent word to his own wife in Britain telling her that, when George Rae returned to Africa with the new portable steamer, she could come too. Mrs Livingstone, it will be remembered, had been forced by her pregnancy in 1858 to stay in South Africa for a year, and had then had to return to Scotland to stay with her husband's parents for a further three years. Again, earlier in 1861, Livingstone had approved Mackenzie's permission for the young bride of Henry Burrup, a new recruit to the Mission, to come out at the same time as Mrs Livingstone and the Bishop's sister. All these females were expected within a month or two. Livingstone, after the fighting with the Ajawa, was now extremely uneasy about the future fate of Mrs Burrup and Miss Mackenzie. If these miserable women managed to die at Magomero, that really would spell the end of everything.

Although Livingstone had sanctioned the plan earlier, he now tried to push the full responsibility on to the missionaries by suggesting that they were too feeble to go on without feminine encouragement. 'Most high church people lean on wives or sisters . . . I would as soon lean on a policeman.'[16] But whatever his feelings, Livingstone knew that he was going to have to co-operate with Mackenzie to get these new arrivals to Magomero. In fact he did not expect the exercise to inconvenience him a great deal, since his next plan was to take the portable steamer he was expecting up past the Murchison Cataracts to Lake Nyassa. But, since the ladies would probably arrive early in the following month, when the Shire was low, the *Pioneer* would not be able to get up very far. With this in mind Livingstone told Mackenzie that he would have to meet the steamer on New Year's Day 1862 at the point where the river Ruo flowed into the Shire: this was 130 miles south-east of Magomero. Livingstone also suggested to Mackenzie that he would have to open up a route overland from Magomero to this point so that the ladies and several tons of supplies, expected by the missionaries, could be safely conveyed to the mission from the mouth of the Ruo. To start with the Bishop had wanted to come down to the mouth of the Zambesi to welcome his sister, but Livingstone had eventually persuaded him that to leave Magomero at such a potentially explosive time would be madness.

When the *Pioneer* left for the sea on 15 November, Mackenzie no longer entertained any illusions about Livingstone's sanctity. The Bishop was saddened and apprehensive. As Rowley remarked, from that time Mackenzie seemed 'to lose much of that bright hopefulness which had distinguished him above all other men'.[17] He would never regain it.

During the next two months, fate would deal both Bishop Mackenzie and Dr Livingstone a series of blows as swift and gratuitous as any sequence of disasters in a Hardy novel.

As soon as the *Pioneer* left, the Bishop hurried back to Magomero, where he immediately gave instructions to two of his colleagues, Procter and Scudamore, to go south to open a suitable path to the Ruo. The two men had only been travelling for a couple of days when they were attacked by hostile villagers and narrowly escaped with their lives. Most of their African attendants were taken captive. The missionaries were therefore faced with another moral and practical dilemma. If they rescued the captives and chastened the aggressors, they might unleash a host of new troubles. On the other 'hand if they left things as they were, the route to the Ruo would remain blocked. Again Mackenzie had little choice. Within a couple of days he was setting out south at the head of a hastily assembled punitive expedition. There was no fighting when they reached the village, for the inhabitants fled at the appearance of the Christians, but Mackenzie's followers still plundered the place and set fire to all the huts. Nevertheless an hour or so later the villagers rallied and counter-attacked; one of the Bishop's native followers was killed in the fighting that ensued. The attack had solved nothing, for now all the surrounding people would be hostile. The Bishop was therefore obliged to return to Magomero to try to reach the mouth of the Ruo via the Shire. By now Mackenzie was hopelessly behindhand in his plans to reach the agreed meeting place by New Year's Day. In fact it was already 2 January when he got back to Magomero. There he decided that he and Burrup, who had recently joined the Mission, should leave at once for the Shire and then go downstream in a canoe.

Unfortunately neither man was in good health, and both were suffering from diarrhoea when they began their journey in teeming rain. The other missionaries had begged the Bishop to wait before starting, but he had not listened. He had been badly shaken by Livingstone's attitude in November and he was scared that if he failed to reach the Ruo within a 'few days, he might forfeit for ever any further assistance from the unpredictable explorer. By 9 January, after a week's travelling through non-stop rain, the two men procured canoes for their journey downstream. As the days passed, Mackenzie became totally obsessed with the idea that Livingstone might not wait for him.

By the merest of coincidences Livingstone had actually been at the place where he had arranged to meet Mackenzie on the appointed day. But he had not had Miss Mackenzie with him, nor Burrup's young bride, who had been expected to arrive at the same time. In fact the Doctor had not been down to the sea at all. He had spent the month and a half since he had said goodbye to the Bishop, dragging the *Pioneer* through mud and sand. Things had

been so bad that it had taken three weeks to get the
vessel over one bank. While he had cursed the Shire and
the *Pioneer* and his crew, he had had little time to think
of the Bishop, whose thoughts were at that time exclusively directed towards him. Livingstone's main worry was
not that Mackenzie might have to wait for weeks at the
Ruo mouth but that the ship bringing Mrs Livingstone and
the other women might arrive at the Kongone mouth and
leave before he could get there. He was also horrified at
the thought that his precious portable steamer, which Rae
had gone to collect two years before, might be taken
away for a further two months while the ship that had
brought her as yet unassembled parts went north to Zanzibar to take on more coal and supplies.

When he finally arrived at the Kongone mouth on 10
January, a month later than planned, it was to hear that
the brig *Hetty Ellen* with the steamer and his wife on
board had called three weeks earlier and had been forced
by heavy seas to sail again. 'Always too late,' Livingstone
lamented in his journal.[18] In a state of abject depression
the party prepared for a long wait till the ship returned.

On 11 January, the day after Livingstone had arrived at
the mouth, Bishop Mackenzie and Henry Burrup came to
the point where the clear waters of the Ruo joined the
muddy currents of the Shire. The two missionaries had
endured the most appalling journey. Several days before,
their canoe had filled with water and they had lost all their
medicines. They had also suffered terribly from dense
clouds of mosquitoes; but both men were elated to have
arrived at the rendezvous alive. At once they started making enquiries about Dr Livingstone. To their horror they
discovered that the *Pioneer* had last been seen steaming
downstream. Their immediate assumption was that he had
come and not waited for them. Further questions however
seemed to prove that the steamer had not come up the
Shire but had only gone down. The two men knew about
the sandbanks and came to the right conclusion. In one
way this was comforting: at least they had not been too
late and could not be blamed on that account. In another
respect the situation was potentially calamitous: they
would have to wait in a notoriously unhealthy low-lying
area for as long as it took Livingstone to return. Nevertheless they were certain that Livingstone would by now

have met the ladies and would be back within the next ten days. Mackenzie was in a dilemma about whether he ought to return to his post or whether he ought to wait. But his certainty that Livingstone would soon be back decided him. Medicine or no medicine, they would stay. Their only misgiving was due to their discovery that the Doctor had not left any letter for them. But he would be with them soon; the lack of a letter could not mean that he was not thinking about them.

The local chief of the area gave them a bare and damp hut on a small island off the Ruo mouth, and there the two men lived, and it was there that Mackenzie wrote his last letter: pathetically an appeal to the boat clubs of Oxford and Cambridge for funds for a steamer.[19] As the days passed his remaining optimism started to drain away. He began to feel that he would never see his sister, never see a steamer belonging to the Mission, never return to Magomero. Twice every day Mackenzie went to the southern tip of the island and strained his eyes to catch sight of the *Pioneer*. But the scene was always the same: the tall reeds and the basking crocodiles, and no steamer. Burrup and the Bishop passed the time translating into Greek St Paul's letter to the Romans—'O wretched man that I am! Who shall deliver me from the body of this death?'[20] The days went very slowly.

By 18 January, Burrup's diarrhoea had worsened and the Bishop was also suffering from the same complaint. Soon fever came too. After this neither man could communicate with the other. The Bishop imagined that he was back at Magomero with his sister and that new stores had arrived. The three natives who had accompanied them treated them with great kindness. On 24 January, Mackenzie's condition worsened and he began to bleed profusely at the nose and mouth; soon he was in a coma and was breathing with difficulty. By the 31st he was very close to death but Burrup had not quite given up. To his horror, that same day the chief came and told him that the Bishop must be moved, because if he died in the hut there would be a taboo on it afterwards. In the end, after vain protests that taxed his declining strength to the utmost, Burrup agreed that Mackenzie should be moved to a less important hut. The movement caused fresh bleeding and by noon the end seemed close.[21]

On this same day, 31 January, Dr Livingstone sighted two ships off the East Luabo and experienced the most intense relief that he had felt for a long time. The vessels had not gone off for two months but only for three weeks. Through a telescope he could see that the largest of the two vessels was a man-of-war and that she was running up a signal: ' "I have—steamboat—in the brig—" to which we replied, "Welcome news" Then "Wife—aboard". With "accept my best thanks" concluded this conversation.'[22]

On board too was Burrup's bride of less than a year and Miss Mackenzie, both desperately eager to get to Magomero to be united with their men. Kirk described Mrs Burrup as 'full of life' and a young lady who delighted 'to talk nautical and jump about'. Miss Mackenzie, he saw, as 'an old invalid who had followed him [the Bishop] through some sort of fanatical infatuation'.[23] The women were attended by a couple of maids: Jessie Lennox and Sarah, whose surname nobody ever mentioned. On the voyage Mrs Livingstone had written a jocular letter to a friend in England describing 'the regular cargo of ladies' going out to the Zambesi. 'We shall take Livingstone by storm. I just fancy his surprise when he sees what a lot of women have come upon him.'[24] But the number of ladies was not to be his only surprise during the next two months.

At roughly the time Livingstone was exchanging signals with H.M.S. *Gorgon*, Bishop Mackenzie's laboured breathing stopped. Burrup was soon surrounded by the local natives, who implored him to bury the body at once to avoid enchantment. He was hardly able to stand but he and his African followers wrapped the body in cloth and, having placed it in a canoe, took it to the mainland; there among the tall reeds they cleared the ground beneath a mimosa tree and dug a grave. When they had finished it was almost dark. The first Bishop of the Central African Mission had been dead three hours. Burrup had his prayer-book with him but he could not see to read. Instead he repeated what he could remember of the burial service. The grave was left unmarked.

Burrup's supply of cloth was now all but exhausted and the sick man realized that soon he would not be able to buy food. There was therefore no question of remaining to wait for Livingstone. He would leave a letter and return to the mission. On 14 February, Burrup was carried into Magomero, a dying man. Three months before, he had been strong, athletic and confident. Now the young missionary was little more than a skeleton. He died on 22 February of a combination of dysentery and fever.

After Burrup's burial, Rowley wrote with understatement worthy of Livingstone: 'The probable arrival of the ladies was now a great anxiety to us.'[25]

While these tragic events were unfolding, Livingstone had no time to give much thought to the two men, who, for all he knew, were still waiting for him. Ever since the *Hetty Ellen*, escorted by the warship H.M.S. *Gorgon*, had anchored off the mouth of the Zambesi on 31 January 1862, Livingstone's life had become a nightmare. His object was to transport his new portable steamer as quickly as possible to the Murchison Cataracts and thence to Lake Nyassa. First the steamer would have to be assembled for the trip up the Shire; then she would have to be dismantled for the overland journey past the Cataracts, and finally she would have to be reassembled again on the other side. In ideal circumstances such an ambitious project would have been difficult to achieve in a year, but now Livingstone's circumstances were far from ideal, and speed was all important to him. Unless he could get his steamer into the Shire within a couple of months, the river would be low again and the attempt would have to be abandoned till early the following year, and that in turn would mean that the steamer would not be floating on Lake Nyassa till the end of 1863. By then the extended time limit, which the Foreign Office had granted the Zambesi Expedition, would have been exhausted. The thought of being recalled before being able to use his steamer to cut the Arab slave routes across Nyassa and to the south of it into the Shire Highlands, after spending so much time and money in the attempt, caused Livingstone acute anxiety. What he now needed above all else was a calm atmosphere and a united, well-organized band of helpers. At this crucial time he was in fact surrounded by disunity, chaos and confusion.

In addition to her normal complement of expedition members, the *Pioneer* was now going to have to carry upstream five women and their luggage, another missionary and his possessions, the numerous metal plates of the unassembled steamer and thirty tons of stores for the Mission. Livingstone was clearly never going to be able to load everything on to the *Pioneer* without the help of sailors from H.M.S. *Gorgon*, and even then the operation would have to be well planned and executed. The man chosen as Livingstone's principal helper was Assistant Paymaster W. C. Devereux of the *Gorgon*. Devereux had an exceptionally orderly mind and almost everything he saw offended him: the heaps of baggage without inventories, the lack of discipline and the general feeling of disorder. He considered Livingstone and the organizers of the Universities Mission to be criminally irresponsible men who, 'not content to push part of their people blindfold and almost purposeless into the wilds of South Africa, add to their distressing position by allowing a lot of helpless females in their blind devotion to accompany them'.[26] Devereux was even more sceptical about Livingstone's chances of getting his portable steamer on to Lake Nyassa. 'If the Engineer [Rae],' wrote Devereux, 'carries all safely to its destination and floats the "Lady Nyassa", as his piecemeal steamer is called, on the lake, he will deserve a monument in the Institute of Civil Engineers; but I am afraid the obstacles will even overcome his energy, and that pieces of the steamer will be left here and there—small memorials, monuments of a great but wild endeavour.'[27]

Devereux was soon saying even more critical things. He claimed that he had 'never seen such constant vacillations, blunders, delays, and want of common thought and foresight as is displayed on the *Pioneer* . . . I have rarely, if ever, seen a man so easily led as Dr Livingstone.'[28] But although he probably had plenty of justification for such remarks, the parts of the *Lady Nyassa* were loaded on to the *Pioneer* within a week, with as much of the Mission's stores as could safely be stowed aboard. On 8 February the *Pioneer*, listing dangerously to port, with one paddle-wheel all but submerged and the other hardly touching the water, started up-river.

As might have been predicted, the considerably overloaded vessel made slow progress, and her increased draught caused her to ground frequently. The seventy-mile trip upstream to Shupanga, where it was planned to assemble the *Lady Nyassa* for the first time, took from 8 February to the end of the month, and during that time Livingstone had to endure more than the agonizing delay itself. For a start Mrs Livingstone was no longer the placid and tranquil lady he remembered from the last time they had been together for any duration at Kolobeng. In the intervening decade little had happened to Mary to make her sweet-tempered and optimistic. She had had to shoulder the responsibility for bringing up a large family completely without her husband's assistance, and had suffered a great deal from the behaviour of Robert, her eldest son, who had become quite unmanageable. In order to rejoin her husband she had had to leave her little daughter, Anna Mary, who was not yet four, with Livingstone's family in Scotland. The other children also had to be left behind, either with relatives or at boarding schools. Mary felt that her husband's conception of his divine duty had destroyed any happiness which she and the children might ever have had. Now in 1862 she had few kind words to say for missionaries or mission work. In Livingstone's eyes this was a terrible state of affairs, but worst of all was his growing feeling that Mary had lost her faith. It was not long too before Livingstone heard some unsavoury rumours about his wife.

Expedition gossip had it that James Stewart, the good-looking young representative of the Free Church of Scotland, sent out to plan another mission for the Shire Highlands, had had an affair with Mrs Livingstone. The idea, on the face of it, was preposterous, for Stewart was a sensitive and handsome man of thirty, while Mary, at forty, was, in Kirk's eyes at least, 'a coarse vulgar woman' and extremely fat as well.[29] Nevertheless Rae's stories that Stewart had visited Mrs Livingstone's cabin at night on the boat coming out were true. Stewart, however, had never been summoned for the purposes Rae imagined. Mary in fact was a heavy drinker, who, Stewart later acknowledged, often drank enough 'so as to be utterly besotted at times'.[30] During these bouts of excessive drinking Mrs Livingstone sometimes became hysterical and on such occasions Stewart had been summoned by Mary's maid to go and calm her mistress down. Stewart, who had some medical knowledge, usually administered some laudanum and then went back to bed. He certainly never enjoyed these nocturnal visits and normally returned to his cabin 'with feelings', as he put it, 'which I am not disposed to chronicle'.[31] Mary had distressed Stewart in other ways too. Her need to drink led her to borrow money from him; and when Stewart finally refused any more, she treated him to a stream of angry abuse. Afterwards Stewart often noticed her proneness to 'queer and disagreeable moods; dull, dumpy and discontented'.[32]

While Livingstone never believed that anything improper had taken place with Stewart, his wife's drinking was a fact that he could not deny even to himself. It was an added burden to him at a very difficult time. His peace of mind was further disturbed by the internal bickerings and hatreds in his now greatly enlarged party. The Bishop's sister, Miss Mackenzie, had taken a dislike to Mrs Livingstone, since she considered Mary's criticisms of missionaries in general to be an implied attack on her brother and his colleagues. Charles Livingstone was also in an intractable mood and hated Stewart, whom he considered an impostor. 'What is this Mr Stewart?' he wrote home to a friend, 'None of us like him. Is he a humbug, or does he really intend to be a missionary? . . . We have no room for these missionaries. They eat up all our nice things and we can't get them replaced. They take care of their own boxes as this Stewart tried to do by turning our boxes out into the rain.'[33] Charles became so enraged by the loss of delicacies like jam and dates that he thought of placing rat-traps in the galley to discourage 'pilfering parsons'.[34] Conditions on board the *Pioneer* were bad enough without personal animosities.

The Doctor and Mrs Livingstone occupied the after-cabin, but the portholes could not be opened because the steamer was so low in the water; instead a hole had to be made in the deck to let in air, but even then, as Charles noted with relish, 'the unfortunate couple are nearly melted'.[35] Miss Mackenzie, Mrs Burrup and the two maids lived in an improvised tent on the deck and had little privacy from curious sailors. Neither Livingstone, nor even Captain Wilson of the *Gorgon*, who had agreed to come to Shupanga with fifty men in three boats, to help offload the sections of the *Lady Nyassa*, seemed able to discipline the sailors. The bluejackets were soon drinking large quantities of a powerful Portuguese brew, *agua ardente*, which they nicknamed 'hoggy-dent'—Livingstone called it 'vile spirit secretly sold'. The men also went out on numerous sexual sorties, to the horror of James Stewart, who noted breathlessly in his journal that 'one woman was abused five times'. Livingstone's stoker on the *Pioneer* had already fathered several little half-castes. Drinking became such a problem that eventually Livingstone and Wilson had to agree to put anybody found drunk on to half pay.[36]

Meanwhile the delay, the disorder and the quarrelling wore down Livingstone's patience and made him snap at everybody, including Miss Mackenzie, who described him as 'abrupt and ungracious'.[37] James Stewart, who had hero-worshipped Livingstone ever since reading *Missionary Travels*, was shocked at the Doctor's sudden explosions of bad temper. Soon Stewart was writing in dismay, after hearing Livingstone abusing his crew: 'I could hardly have credited that Dr L. would have said "Go forward, you useless trash!" '[38]

Everybody was heartily relieved when Shupanga was reached and some of the stores could be temporarily put ashore; work could also begin on the *Lady Nyassa*. Shupanga was reached at the end of February; two weeks before that, Captain Wilson and Kirk had volunteered to take Miss Mackenzie and Mrs Burrup on ahead in an open boat to meet their men-folk at the mouth of the Ruo. It was not to be a pleasant journey. Miss Mackenzie was soon ill with fever and took up most of the stern of the small boat. Kirk soon loathed the sight of her. 'If she decided to shift her position, she had to get assistance and have herself supported with pillows.'[39] Before the elderly invalid could be persuaded to wash or change her clothes, a special 'bower or shelter had to be constructed'.

When they reached the Ruo there was no sign of anybody, and the natives denied ever having seen Burrup or the Bishop. On 3 March, just below the Murchison Cataracts, Kirk and Wilson heard that the Bishop was dead; poor Mrs Burrup had to wait another week before hearing that her husband too had perished. There was no question of the two women going to Magomero.

Kirk, Wilson and the two ladies, who were now prostrated with grief and exhaustion, arrived at Shupanga on 14 March. When Livingstone heard the news that the Bishop was dead, he sat in the small, dimly-lit cabin of the *Pioneer* with his head in his hands and murmured: 'This will hurt us all.'[40] After Mackenzie's attack on the Ajawa, Livingstone's first reaction had been to work out how he might dissociate himself from any blame. The present situation seemed to him to call for similar tactics. Livingstone had no illusions about the reaction there would be in Britain to this double tragedy. A great many people were going to say that Dr Livingstone had lured a group of godly men to their deaths by duping them into believing that central Africa was a healthy and idyllic area. In the outbursts of indignation the fact that the two men had died in notorious low-lying marshy country, and not in the Shire Highlands, was likely to be overlooked, and if that happened all chances of trade, or colonization, either with or without the Government's aid, would disappear for good. With this in mind, as well as his reputation, Livingstone sat down to blame the dead men for what had happened to them. Early the following day he was writing a despatch to the Foreign Secretary telling him that 'coarse living and rash exposure have ended in the sad loss of life'. Livingstone wrote to most of his friends telling them the same: if Mackenzie had taken reasonable care of his health he would not have died. His attacks on the dead Bishop almost equalled the libels he had penned after the Linyanti missionaries had died. With characteristic callousness he told his brother-in-law, John Moffat, that 'the effect will be better men will come to the work'.[41] When James Stewart offered his condolences, Livingstone informed him that in future no missionary would feel inclined 'to come for a lark or to make a good thing of playing the missionary for a few years and then reaping laurels'.[42] This attack, on the man whom he had once called 'the best of the bunch' and 'A 1', cannot be excused by Livingstone's misery about the future. Mackenzie had been sincere and selfless; nor would he ever have taken the risks he had done if Livingstone had not threatened to stop helping the Mission in November 1861. Even when Livingstone wrote to a cousin of the Bishop, General Hay, he implied that Mackenzie had died because he had been late at the meeting place and because he had stayed there rather than returning to Magomero or pushing on downstream after the *Pioneer*, once he knew that she had been detained.[43]

The missionaries still left at Magomero might have expected some sympathy from the man who had led them to the Shire Highlands, but Livingstone, just in case Mackenzie's death might be taken as an excuse for the survivors to leave the country, gave them a stern lecture: 'Remember pray, that the eyes of the most influential people in England are upon you, and should anything prevent you doing your duty manfully you will be set down as a parcel

of canting hypocrites that ought never to have been entrusted with anything.'[44]

Livingstone did not, of course, care what the most
influential people in England thought of the missionaries,
but he knew that they would not think much of his powers
of judgment if the members of the Universities Mission
had to leave their 'ideal and fertile' location in order to
save their lives. Livingstone concluded his savage letter by
suggesting that he had told Mackenzie not to 'go down to
the Ruo and explore upwards' on account of the rains at
that time of year. Since he had also told the Bishop that
the route would have to be pioneered by 1 January, it is
hard to see how he could have avoided doing so outside
the rainy season. In any case Mackenzie had come down
to the Ruo via the Shire and had not explored 'upwards'.
It had certainly not been Livingstone's fault that the two
men died, for the swamping of their canoe and the loss of
their medicines had seen to that, but his many letters of
self-justification and recrimination, all devoid of real grief
at the loss of a man whom even Charles Livingstone had
felt able to like, point up once more that central defect
in Livingstone's character: his virtual inability to respond
to the suffering of others.

Livingstone could argue that he was thinking of the
future of Christianity in the area for centuries to come,
and could therefore not sympathize with men who had, by
their deaths, done positive harm to the Christian prospects
of a large region. But that was hardly enough. In 1859
he had known that missionaries who came to the Shire
Highlands, as an isolated group of men, would face the
most fearful problems posed by the Ajawa and the Arab
and Portuguese slavers. But now he turned even the problems to his advantage by employing that argument in which
he firmly believed: settled African tribal communities
were confident and rejected Christianity out of hand. In
the Shire Highlands where all was anarchy, the Manganja
ought to have been in an ideal psychological state to
receive the gospel. Christianity could have given them
something to cling to when all else fell apart around them.
Livingstone argued that the missionary prospects had been
excellent because many of the freed slaves had been
orphans and would not therefore have been taught tribal
traditions by their parents. It was only Mackenzie's idiotic
attacks on the Ajawa, and his needless death, that had pre-

vented thousands of conversions. With more justification
Livingstone claimed that if Mackenzie and Burrup, once
they had found out what had delayed the *Pioneer,* had not
stayed so long at the Ruo mouth, but had instead returned
at once to Magomero, they would not have died. The
Shire Highlands was, unlike the river Shire itself, a relatively healthy area. Livingstone's knowledge, that the
Highlands would now be represented as a malarial death-
trap, increased his bitterness towards the dead men.

Only when Livingstone heard, early in 1863, of a packed
meeting that had taken place during the previous summer
at the Sheldonian Theatre, in Oxford, did he begin belatedly
to defend the missionaries. At that meeting, Dr Pusey, and
various equally eminent High Churchmen, had attacked
Dr Livingstone and the missionaries for using firearms,
even in self-defence, for by doing so they had denied
themselves that most prestigious of Christ's rewards: a
martyr's death. This inanity at last forced Livingstone to
admit to Horace Waller, one of the missionaries who by
now had become a personal friend: 'I thought you wrong
in attacking the Ajawa . . . because I thought you had shut
yourselves up to one tribe, but I think differently now and
only wish they would send out Dr Pusey here.'[45] Livingstone also paid glowing tribute to 'the good and noble
bishop Mackenzie', but this change of heart came over a
year too late. By then Livingstone's earlier attacks on the
Mission had turned too many people against the missionaries for the mood to be reversible. Already influential men
like Murchison and Admiral Washington, of the Admiralty,
had resigned from the Universities Mission Committee.
When Livingstone saw that there was a danger of the Mission being withdrawn, he fought against it, for at last he
had grasped the fact that such a move would destroy all
his hopes, whether for traders, colonists or missionaries, to
come to the Shire Highlands. As will be seen, he failed to
undo the earlier damage he had done.

18

Disaster and Collapse: the End of the Zambesi Expedition, 1862–1864

Bishop Mackenzie's death did not change any of Livingstone's plans. In March 1862 he was still determined to get the *Lady Nyassa* up past the Murchison Cataracts to the lake after which she had been named. At Shupanga, Livingstone was three hundred miles from his objective and by the end of March the river had started to fall. There was no question of getting the steamer up to the cataracts in pieces on the *Pioneer*; that would mean weeks, maybe months, aground in the Shire. The new steamer would have to be towed up by the *Pioneer*, having been partially assembled at Shupanga. The engineer, George Rae, estimated that it would take him at least two months to bolt the hull together, and by then the *Pioneer*, even without any kind of load, would be unable to get up the Shire beyond the Ruo. Livingstone was forced to admit that the *Lady Nyassa* would not reach the Murchison Cataracts till early the following year. It was worrying enough for him that by then the extended period granted to the expedition by the Foreign Office would almost be exhausted, but equally distressing was the fact that the delay would force him to spend months on the lower Zambesi in far greater danger of malaria than he would have been in the Shire Highlands. He had never been personally afraid of fever—he was rarely afraid of anything —but he was badly scared by the thought that his wife would be exposed to fever for a long period. Partly for this reason, and partly because he hated inactivity, Livingstone decided that he would remain at Shupanga only until the hull of the *Lady Nyassa* had been put together; then, with Mrs Livingstone and the rest of the party, he would sail to the island of Johanna, six hundred miles north-east of Quilimane, to get fresh supplies to last into 1863. After that, leaving his wife safely on Johanna, Livingstone intended to spend a couple of months making one more effort to get up the river Rovuma. By the time he returned to the Zambesi, the river would be high again and he would be able to tow the *Lady Nyassa* up the Shire to the Cataracts without difficulty. This then was the long-term plan.

When Livingstone knew that the Bishop was dead he decided to take the bereaved women down to the mouth of the river himself, to put them on to the *Gorgon* for the return voyage to England. This trip should have been accomplished in a couple of weeks, but when the *Pioneer* reached the Kongone mouth it was discovered that the *Gorgon* had been forced by dwindling stocks of coal to sail for the port of Moçambique. This meant that for the next two and a half weeks Livingstone and his wife were forced to remain in the notoriously malarial Zambesi delta, awaiting the *Gorgon*'s return. Even then there was yet another delay caused by the inefficiency of the *Pioneer*'s engineer, Hardesty, who had allowed the feed pipes to become blocked. Thus it was not until 14 April that the steamer was back at Shupanga. Livingstone dismissed Hardesty, but the damage had been done. For over a month the whole party had been exposed to malaria in the worst part of the river.

Mrs Livingstone had been worried and out of sorts ever since James Stewart had foolishly told her what people were saying about them both. On 21 April, less than a week after her return from the Zambesi delta to Shupanga, she fell ill with fever. From the beginning Livingstone took her complaint seriously but he was not badly worried till the 24th. Stewart had seen her the day before and had thought drink was the root of the trouble. But by the 25th there was no doubt that her condition was serious; soon she was tormented by terrible spasms of nausea every quarter of an hour. The following day there was still no improvement and she was moved from the *Pioneer* to the one stone house in Shupanga. Kirk and Livingstone used every method they had learned to try and reduce the fever, but even the most massive doses of quinine seemed to have no effect. By now her mind was wandering; her thoughts were filled with her distant children. Robert, her eldest son, had rejected any efforts made by his teachers and had become a problem child. Often she mentioned him. Then she wept about her baby daughter, who had been left in Scotland. Later she burst out: 'See, see Agnes is falling down a precipice.'[1]

Livingstone stayed by her bed day and night, vainly trying to feed her. She could not even keep down slices of melon. Early on the morning of the 27th she started moaning uncontrollably and could hardly drink water from a spoon. At 3 a.m. Livingstone got Kirk out of bed and he arrived to find her in a half comatose state. She could not swallow any longer and so medicine could only be injected. By dawn the coma had deepened and her face and skin were becoming tinged with yellow. Kirk was distressed but not in any way emotionally involved. He wrote coolly in his journal: 'The state of her mind has been such as to predispose her to any disease while her indiscretions in eating and drinking previously have been such as to undermine her health.'[2] He was sure that she would have been more likely to rally had Stewart not told her about the rumours going around. It seemed unlikely that she would live beyond midday, but she did. Livingstone had remained hopeful until she lost the power to swallow. After that his self-control cracked and he started to weep. At 6 p.m., scandal or no scandal, he summoned James Stewart from the *Pioneer*. The man had been his wife's friend and she had been fond of him. When Stewart arrived he saw Livingstone 'sitting by the side of a rude bed formed of boxes, but covered with a soft mattress, on which lay his dying wife . . . The man who had faced so many deaths, and braved so many dangers, was now utterly broken down and weeping like a child.'[3] Stewart found his own eyes filling. Livingstone asked him to say a prayer, while he and Kirk knelt. Afterwards her breathing became laboured and irregular. Livingstone once more broke down and, taking his wife in his arms, choked: 'My dearie, my dearie you are going to leave me . . . Are you resting on Jesus?' He was uncertain whether she had heard what he said because the quinine had deafened her. But she had looked upwards when he had spoken and took this to mean that she had understood. Later he very much regretted not using writing to communicate with her during these last few hours. He knew quite well that she 'had fallen into a gloomy desponding state' and it haunted him to think that she might have died without faith. Just after seven he kissed her and she did not respond: 'lying with her mouth a little open she gently shut it and breathed her last'.[4]

During the night Rae made a coffin and Kirk and Stewart washed the body and wound it in cloth. The local Portuguese begged to be allowed to fire a salute at the funeral the following day, but Livingstone refused. Although he was dropping with tiredness, he spent much of the night going through her things. The thought of her dying without believing in God agonized him. He gained some consolation when he found a short prayer among her papers: 'Accept me Lord as I am, and make me such as thou wouldst have me to be.'[5] Surely, Livingstone argued, there were plenty of examples in the lives of saints and other pious people when a time 'of religious gloom or paroxysms of opposition & fierce rebellion against God found vent in terrible expressions—these were followed by great elevations of faith'. But his doubts persisted. A few days before, she had said gloomily 'that she would never have a house in this country'.[6] At the time he had thought she was just being despondent and had joked about it. Now he wondered whether she had felt that she would soon die and had been using a religious metaphor. All the hardships she had endured in Britain, the journeys across the Kalahari, the long separation at the beginning of the expedition, now seemed real to Livingstone for the first time. Providence might have led him but that did not redress her suffering. He wrote to his mother telling her: 'There are many regrets which will follow me to my dying day. If I had done so and so &c. &c. . . .'[7] In his journal he reproached himself as bitterly: 'My heart smites me that I did not talk seriously on that [her doubts] and many things besides.'[8] One of the 'many things' was the fact that Mary had had no home for the last ten years of her life and had had no settled environment in which to bring up the children. In the depths of his grief Livingstone at last seemed to understand what his children had lived through. His wife's death left him a more understanding father, and from then on the tone of his letters to the children became more personal and less homiletic. He told each one of their mother's death and in none of these letters did he attempt to cloak his grief with conventional phrases of religious consolation. He started his letter to Oswell:

> With many tears running down my cheeks I have to tell you that poor dearly beloved Mama died last night about seven o' clock . . . She loved you dearly and often spoke of you and all the family, especially little Baby . . . She gave me the comb and toothbrush you kindly sent me. She was collecting some curiosi-

ties for you. There are two ostrich eggshells and other shells she brought from Moçambique . . . You must all love each other more than ever now.[9]

In his journal he wrote: 'For first time in my life I feel willing to die D.L.'[10] James Stewart noticed a distinct change in the Doctor's manner during the next few weeks. 'Dr L. pecularily communicative and agreeable. His recent loss seems to have had some effect of a softening kind on him.'[11]

The day after her death Mary Livingstone was buried at noon under the shadow of a massive baobab tree. She was only forty-one years old. The day was misty and the sky heavy and leaden. Livingstone asked Stewart to conduct the service and he was proud to do so. Four sailors carried the coffin to the grave and afterwards mounted guard over it to protect the body from wild animals till a stone cairn could be built.

That afternoon Rae went on working on the *Lady Nyassa* and Kirk attended to three members of the *Pioneer*'s crew, who were all dangerously ill with fever. Ironically, one of them was Hardesty, the engineer, whom Livingstone blamed for delaying their progress. But, unlike Mrs Livingstone, Hardesty recovered, as did the other two sick men. To the accompaniment of the banging of bolts, the screaming of delirious men and the distant howling of hyenas, Livingstone went on sorting his wife's papers and clothes. He felt overcome with doubts and regrets. Perhaps she ought never to have come. Perhaps once he had known that there would be so many delays before the Highlands could be reached, he ought to have sent her home. But, as he told his mother, 'it would have broken Mary's heart to have sent her away then'. He had known, too, that, while at Kuruman in 1859, she had often been taunted by other missionaries' wives with words like: 'O she is not good—she is here because her husband cannot live with her.'[12]

For the first time he began to have doubts about what God intended him to do. 'There is something I have to do or be; such I take to be the meaning of this dispensation. I wish I could find out.'[13] In his despondency he remembered saying to her, after they had shared a joke just before she became ill, 'We old bodies ought now to be more sober.' She had replied, 'Oh no, you must always be

as playful . . . I would not like you to be as grave as
some folks I have seen.'[14] To Livingstone that conversation seemed a very long time ago.

When, months later, Livingstone started to receive letters of condolence, he was not blamed for encouraging
his wife to join him. Dr Tidman, alone, could not deny his
true feelings; the deaths at Linyanti were too recent: 'As
it is easy to be wise after the event, the thought might
occur to some persons that, if your dear wife had remained
in England, her life might yet have been spared to her
family and friends.'[15]

After his wife's death, Livingstone was eager to get away
from Shupanga, but knew that he would not be able to do
so till the *Lady Nyassa* was launched. Although Rae was
working hard, this event would not take place for a
further two months. During this time Livingstone made a
couple of trips down to the mouth for mail and supplies
but otherwise had to remain inactive, a situation which
always depressed him.

At last, on 23 June, the *Lady Nyassa* was ready for
launching. The operation was a shambles and the steamer
nearly sank stern first during it, but before sunset, after
twelve hours of constant heaving and shoving, she was
forced down into the water over rollers made from the
trunks of palm trees. Livingstone felt that there should be
some sort of celebration, so he fired off a couple of
rockets, one of which disappointingly sped along the
ground into the river. A bottle of wine was opened and
glasses raised to a future in which only Livingstone
claimed to have any confidence. Most of the party doubted
whether the new steamer would ever reach the Murchison
Cataracts, let alone the lake. Nor was the *Lady Nyassa*
anywhere near completion; a lot of fitting out would have
to be done before she could be towed.

Mrs Livingstone's death had not altered her husband's
determination to go to Johanna for stores and then to
take a final look at the Rovuma. The previous survey had
been enough to convince Charles and Kirk that any further
effort in that direction would be futile. But both said
nothing. Kirk badly wanted to object, but felt that if he
did 'all former services would be lost sight of' by Livingstone.[16] Every logical fact supported the view that the
Rovuma could not be navigable for more than a hundred
miles at the very most. Quite apart from previous surveys,

the height of Lake Nyassa, 1,200 feet above sea level, and the distance of the lake from the sea, three hundred miles, made it a foregone conclusion that there would be cataracts somewhere along the course of the river. But after his loss Livingstone was less concerned with logic than with remaining active during the months that remained before he would be able to get the steamer up the Shire. Whenever circumstances had threatened to crush Livingstone in the past he had fought back by forcing himself to go through with some physically gruelling exploring. Now in his personal misery he would try the same remedy on the Rovuma. His companions had noticed that, since Mary's death, Livingstone's manner had softened a little, but they had also observed that his previously inflexible determination had hardened into an obsessive, almost masochistic desire to push himself to the limits of human endurance. The journey up the Rovuma during September and November 1862 would highlight this trait which was to become central during the remaining years of Livingstone's life.

There was so little water in the Rovuma that, from the beginning, it was obvious that Livingstone and his companions would have to go up in two open boats. They got off to a bad start when Rae flatly refused to travel in the same whaler as Charles Livingstone. After a reorganization, Livingstone and Charles were put in one boat and Rae and Kirk in the other.

After five days it was crystal clear to Kirk that there was no point in going any further; the river was already a maze of shoals, and the main channels never more than a foot deep. But Livingstone seemed oblivious to this. When the water dwindled to a few inches he was quite undeterred and began hiring natives to carry the boats over distances of anything up to half a mile. Kirk was soon writing in his journal: 'I can come to no other conclusion than that Dr L. is out of his mind.'[17] Had Kirk been able to see the sort of letters his leader was writing at this time, he would have been still more worried. Livingstone was now in a strange fatalistic frame of mind, as he confessed to Robert and Mary Moffat. 'It is probable,' he told them, that. 'I may fall in establishing a new system on that great centre of slaving, Lake Nyassa.'[18] Over and over again the thought of impending death appears in his journal at this time. 'Am I to be a martyr to my own cause?' he was soon asking himself. 'I begin to think that I may not live to see success. Am I to experience that this cause is to be founded on my sacrifice and cemented by my suffering? Every covenant was ratified with sacrifice . . . I hope this may be compensated if I die by my death.'[19]

As another week passed and Livingstone forced the boats on over the sand, Kirk wondered whether Livingstone had any idea of the dangerous situation they would all be in if the water fell too low for them to get back to the coast. They had already been fired on by natives and had had to return fire, killing two men in the process. A return to the sea on foot would now be extremely hazardous. 'Dr L. is a most unsafe leader,' Kirk noted in his journal, and added, 'It is useless making any remark to him.'[20]

During the evening of 26 September they at last came to a cataract, and there, to the amazement of Livingstone's companions, he began making arrangements for the boats to be carried up over the rocks. But to everybody's intense relief, the following day he changed his mind and gave the order to turn back. The safety of his followers had not influenced his decision. His only reason for returning was his fear that if they did get stuck, he might miss the next flood season in the Shire and Zambesi and thus fail to get the *Lady Nyassa* up to the Murchison Cataracts.

The journey up the Rovuma had not increased Livingstone's knowledge. At best the continual labour of struggling up a useless and shallow river had kept his despair at bay. Unfortunately it had determined the rest of the party to leave Africa as soon as they could decently do so.

Before they reached Shupanga again, in mid-December, George Rae had told his leader that he would resign as soon as the *Lady Nyassa*'s engines were installed. If he did so, Livingstone knew that there would be no hope of getting the steamer past the Murchison Cataracts. He had no choice but to swallow his pride and allow Rae to be as abusive and insubordinate as he wished. Soon Rae was writing the sort of letters to Livingstone which would have led to instant dismissal in the days of Bedingfeld and Baines. 'I have decided,' the engineer told his leader in early January, 'not to go on board the *Pioneer* again unless duty calls me. Therefore I wish you to give me my provisions on board the *Lady Nyassa* and a boat for the use of the *Lady Nyassa*.'[21]

Livingstone objected, but Rae got his way and ate all his meals away from the rest of the party. In other ways discipline had reached a new nadir. On the way back from the Rovuma, Livingstone had been obliged to issue a Public Order prohibiting his officers from striking native crew members without permission.[22] Charles had already started writing to friends telling them that in his view the Government ought to recall the expedition before it fell to bits of its own accord.[23] When the *Pioneer* left Shupanga on 11 January 1863, with the *Lady Nyassa* in tow, only Livingstone himself felt that there was any point in continuing. The Zambesi Expedition was entering its last phase.

To start with, Livingstone and his party made excellent progress; after ten days steaming up the Shire they had reached the junction with the Ruo. But a few days later, in early February, the *Pioneer* and the *Lady Nyassa* became firmly imbedded in the mud and sand of the river bottom. The next few months were to be the worst any member of the party had ever known.

The previous year there had been a terrible drought in the Shire Highlands and on the lower Shire, and the low rainfall, besides ensuring that there was much less water in the river than usual for the time of year, had also caused all the native crops to fail. The whole area was gripped by the worst famine any of the natives could remember. Up river, the missionaries, themselves without adequate stockpiles of food, had looked on helplessly for many months as men and women scrabbled for roots to eat. All the natives whom Livingstone and his colleagues now saw had swollen bellies, skeletal limbs and dull, dead eyes. The famine had been made far worse by the continuing aggression of the Ajawa, whose raids had diverted the people's attention from agriculture at a time when they had a chance to save a small percentage of their corn and crops. The dead soon littered paths and fields and nobody had the energy to bury them.

As February dragged on, and Livingstone and his unwilling companions forced their steamers upstream at the pitiful rate of a mile a week, they soon saw very real evidence of the severity of the famine. Bodies began to float past them downstream. The natives knew that it was easier to dump a dead relative in the river than to dig a grave. Livingstone counted thirty-four corpses in three days. It was not an edifying sight to see crocodiles tearing at bloated stomachs and fighting each other to get more of an arm or leg. Soon fever added to the misery of those aboard the *Pioneer* and the *Lady Nyassa*. Livingstone's orders were disobeyed by everybody. Several of the members of the Mission, which had now moved out of the Highlands down to the river, came to see if they could help the *Pioneer*'s crew; they went away disgusted. As Waller put it 'the discontent and murmurs are sickening: it is a ship divided against itself, plank by plank'.[24] Rowley was even more depressed by what he saw: 'The officers are all but in rebellion, and the Dr daily becomes more incapable of self-control. A catastrophe, or tragedy I fear is not far off.'[25] But tragedy, when it came, struck the missionaries and not the expedition men. Within a month Scudamore, who, with the exception of Mackenzie, had always been the most popular of all the missionaries, died in agony from ulcers on the neck and chest. Shortly afterwards Dickinson, the doctor to the Mission, died of fever. Livingstone with characteristic brevity summed up his life in a sentence: 'a very weakly subject but very religious and resolved to brave out the fever which he had perpetually'. Livingstone was genuinely grieved at the loss of Scudamore, but his final observation on both deaths was predictable: 'This will be another blow to our work.'[26] Nor could he help telling the three survivors of the once seven-strong mission that nobody would have died if they had remained in the Highlands. Poor Rowley had tried to explain that they had been driven out of Magomero by famine and the Ajawa.[27]

On 10 April the two steamers at last lay at anchor below the Murchison Cataracts. The last sixty miles had taken them ten weeks. Before Livingstone could make any preparations for the next stage of the work, the dismantling of the *Lady Nyassa*, another death occurred. In the summer of the year before, Richard Thornton had agreed to rejoin the expedition on condition that he was allowed to continue working independently. Livingstone, who had wanted to add Thornton's geological notes to the expedition's scientific data, had agreed to this. Since his dismissal in 1859, Thornton had taken part in an expedition to Mount Kilimanjaro, led by the German explorer, Baron von der Decken. The young man had also worked hard on his own account and had filled dozens of notebooks with scientific observations. He had been working near the mission in early 1863 and, on discovering how little food they had there, offered to travel overland to Tete to bring back goats and sheep. He kept his word and returned to the mission on 13 April, but the journey had over-taxed his strength and he died five days later of fever and dysentery. Livingstone had witnessed so many deaths that another was no matter for unusual concern; just one more unpleasant event that might be placed to his account at a later date. Once again he showed little sorrow, just a puzzled contempt for human weakness. 'Thornton was a fool and went off to Tete to buy goats for the lazies though he had my written orders to geologise in a healthy quarter . . . Folly killed him.'[28] This was a pretty bleak, uncharitable obituary for a young man of twenty-five who died trying to help three men who had just suffered the loss of four companions. But Livingstone, who considered that the fallibility of his colleagues had played a major part in the expedition's failure, was in no mood to be charitable. *He* had not died, *he* had not stopped working nor asked to go home. After Kebrabasa he had redoubled his efforts rather than admit defeat. He had met the death of his wife with the same determination to go on, whatever the cost. Why, he asked, should others be pitied when they succumbed to a disease that he had lived through and fought off so often? Only the weight of so many failures and disasters can explain Livingstone's contempt for those who died. To view death as a voluntary act of surrender is never the sign of a healthy mind, and when Kirk, on the journey up the Rovuma, had described Livingstone's head as 'not of the ordinary construction but what is termed cracked',[29] he had not been exaggerating. The disappointment at Kebrabasa, the disaster of Linyanti, the chaos in the Shire Highlands, the death of the Bishop and the loss of his own wife, had in the end numbed Livingstone to all normal human emotions except one: the dull anger of despair.

Livingstone would later recover his power to feel emotions, but in the spring and summer of 1863, drained by the loss of Mary, and recognizing for the first time that complete failure was now inevitable, the sight of other human beings only sickened him. When Charles and Kirk asked permission to leave, a week after Thornton's death, Livingstone did not withhold consent. 'It would be well to get rid of them all and have no more,' he wrote, and added that all his white colleagues had never been more than 'a complete nuisance'.[30] When Kirk left, after six years of loyal service in hellish conditions, Livingstone did not thank him, and when he did finally sit down to write a brief note of thanks, Kirk had gone and the moment had passed. Kirk wrote bitterly to a friend:

> I find that in an underhand way Dr L. has given me no cause to thank him . . . He is about as ungrateful and slippery a mortal as I ever came in contact with, and, although he would be greviously offended to think that anyone doubted his honesty, I am sorry to say that I do. I think the explanation to be that he is one of those sanguine enthusiasts wrapped up in their own schemes whose reason and better judgment is blinded by headstrong passion.[31]

When Charles and Kirk left for the coast, George Rae was the only original member of the party left with Livingstone. There was one other officer, Lieutenant E. D. Young, who had been in charge of gunnery on the *Gorgon* and had stayed on with the expedition after the other sailors had left in April the previous year. In Young's opinion the thirty-mile road, which would have to be built before the pieces of the *Lady Nyassa* could be transported past the Cataracts, would take a year to construct and would need the constant work of a hundred natives during that time. There were barely twenty natives who could be relied upon to work for a week, let alone a year. The famine had left all the people too weak to devote any of their time to anything other than the search for food. Cloth could not buy the services of starving men. Livingstone by now realized that his own food supplies would not last more than two months, at the end of which he would be forced to go to Tete or the coast for more supplies. Once down the Shire he would never get up again. Failure he could see was certain. On 17 April he wrote in his journal: 'If the Government looks on this as I do we may expect to be withdrawn.'[32]

But Livingstone would not publicly admit that he had given up. He wanted it to appear that when the order of recall came, it alone had stopped him achieving the successful launching of the steamer on the lake.* So, to the amazement of Rae and Young, Livingstone gave orders for the *Lady Nyassa* to be taken apart for the land journey past the Cataracts. Livingstone himself, with the handful of natives he could persuade to work for him, started on the road, felling trees and rolling large rocks out of the way. At the same time he wrote a despatch to the Foreign Secretary claiming that he was still determined to get the steamer up to Nyassa, but painting such a bleak picture that Lord John Russell would have no alternative but to recall the expedition at once. In the past Livingstone had always minimized problems; now he laid them on thick, going so far as to admit that the Shire Highlands, that ideal place for a British colony, had become 'a desert strewed with human bones'.33 Livingstone explained about the famine and suggested that he would soon have to abandon his work for several months to go down to the coast for supplies. Livingstone would not have felt happy if he had not excused himself for failing to predict the present situation in the Shire Highlands. He therefore suggested that, although the famine and the Ajawa had both been severe problems, the major part of the blame for the chaos and death should rest with the Portuguese. In fact the Portuguese slave raids had depopulated the lower Shire, but were not a crucial factor in the Highlands. The missionaries, when Livingstone tried this argument on them, were not impressed, and replied that the famine and the Ajawa had done all the damage. Livingstone merely repeated his argument: 'They [the Portuguese] have cleared this valley of people—I put it on them because famine from drought never utterly exterminates.'34 Writing to his daughter Agnes, Livingstone used the same excuse. 'Half of the labour and toil I have undergone would have left an indelible mark on any part of Africa not subject to the Portuguese.'35 Livingstone now knew that people in Britain would say that the Zambesi Expedition had been a failure from beginning to end, and he badly needed a public scapegoat. The Portuguese would serve very well. His only regret was that he had not abused them rather more often in his letters to the Government written during 1860 and 1861.

---

* His last biographer George Seaver accepted that, given a month longer, Livingstone could have launched the *Lady Nyassa*. Seaver did not see Livingstone's journal for 1863.

In fact Lord John Russell did not in the end need Livingstone's despatches, written during 1863, to convince himself that the expedition ought to be withdrawn. The deaths and dismissals had already persuaded him that nothing more would be achieved, and on 2 February he had issued the order of recall. The despatch did not reach Livingstone at the Murchison Cataracts till 2 July, when Adams the cockney labourer from the mission, appeared on the shore and yelled: 'Hallo you *Pioneer* chaps—no more pay for you after December. I brings the letter as says it.'[36] It was hardly the sort of dignified announcement of the termination of six years' work which Livingstone would have wished.

The reason Adams had known the contents of the despatch was simple. It had been brought up from the coast by the new Bishop who had been sent to replace Mackenzie. Bishop Tozer had felt little compunction in reading Livingstone's official papers, since the future of the expedition would crucially affect the future of the Mission. For a start, once the expedition left, the Mission would have no link with the coast, and the naval warships that had called regularly at the Kongone mouth to collect official despatches would no longer come. From the beginning Tozer was convinced that the Mission would have to be withdrawn. He had not discovered that Scudamore and Procter had died till he arrived on the Shire, but when he did so, his determination to pull out became total. To avoid accusations of cowardice he decided to give the Mission a final trial further south, on a mountain near the junction of the Shire and the Zambesi. This effort was to be a brief prelude to later withdrawal.

It was unfortunate that Livingstone so quickly got wind of Tozer's intentions, for with the collapse of the expedition the Doctor had decided that the Mission offered the 'one ray of hope' in an otherwise hopeless area.[37] Livingstone did not seem for a moment to be aware of the incongruity of his new love for the Mission. The truth was that he wanted the missionaries to stay on, not because he thought they could achieve anything, but because he felt that their continued presence in Africa would help him to claim, on his return to England, that he had left behind a stable and flourishing Christian community in the Shire Highlands. His vitriolic response to Tozer's plans was therefore no objective judgment but the last flashes of anger and disappointment at the loss of all his earlier hopes. If Tozer was going to leave, then Livingstone would add him to the other excuses for his own failure.

Livingstone in 1859 had described Mount Morambala, where Tozer re-established the Mission, as an ideal 'sanatorium', which the Portuguese had been mad not to utilize.[38] As soon as the new Bishop went there, the mountain changed its character and became 'a mountain 4000 feet high, where clouds rest perpetually at some seasons and the condensed vapour drips constantly through the roofs of huts.'[39] In the past Livingstone had not noticed that Morambala had a thin and scattered population, but now he blamed Tozer for not having come to that conclusion after a single inspection. Tozer had actually asked Livingstone whether he considered the mountain to be a suitable spot for resettling the Mission, and had been told that, although not as good as the Shire Highlands, it was not a bad choice. It was, as it turned out, a terrible choice since, as Livingstone had observed with after-the-event wisdom, the clouds *did* rest 'perpetually at some seasons' and the water did drip through the roofs.

Tozer was soon writing angrily to the Bishop of Cape Town, telling him what he thought of Dr Livingstone. 'The idea of making a Portuguese sanatorium here, is a good specimen of the way in which Livingstone leaps to any conclusion he may wish to see adopted.' The criticism was a just one. Once Livingstone decided he wanted to achieve a particular aim, he would at once throw all his hopes and energies into the venture without pausing to consider at the outset whether it was practicable. This trait, Tozer went on, made the Doctor 'a very dangerous man'.[40] But, as Baines, Thornton or Bedingfeld could have told Tozer, to criticize Dr Livingstone was a hazardous undertaking. When Livingstone knew Tozer had set a date for leaving Africa, he wrote to the new Bishop telling him that he, Livingstone, would make him regret this decision 'till his dying day'.[41] Livingstone at once embarked on a campaign of character assassination worthy of any of his previous efforts.

While claiming that he would 'not say a word in public to injure them [the missionaries]',[42] Livingstone roundly condemned Tozer in his published account of the expedition, *A Narrative of an Expedition to the Zambezi*. The fact that Tozer intended to withdraw the mission to Zanzibar suggested a suitably invidious comparison. 'The mission in fleeing from Morambala to an island in the Indian Ocean,' thundered Livingstone, 'acted as St Augustine would have done, had he located himself on one of the Channel Islands, when sent to Christianise the inhabitants of central England.'[43]

Not content with blackening Tozer in the eyes of the public, Livingstone next informed the Foreign Secretary that the new Bishop had been lacking in mental and physical courage and had been a classic case of a man whose 'zeal had collapsed'.[44] Members of Livingstone's family were told that Tozer had been a weak-minded, two-faced creature, fit for 'nothing but walking about in slippers made by admiring young ladies'.[45] The Zambesi Expedition ended as it had begun, with bitterness and recrimination.

Livingstone would have been happier if he could have pulled out at once, having received his recall orders, but he could not get down the Shire till the end of the year when the waters rose again. To pass the time, and to show that, while others might die or go home, he at least still had plenty of energy left, he spent September and part of October in walking seven hundred miles along the western shores of Lake Nyassa and back again to the Murchison Cataracts. It was a remarkable feat, for by then Livingstone was ill and emaciated, so bad in fact that, a month before, Lieutenant Young had written that 'he could never remember having seen a man fail in health and appearance in so short a time as the Dr'.[46] But Livingstone was to provide still more remarkable proof of his tenacity and endurance before he returned to England.

At the mouth of the Zambesi, in early February 1864, Livingstone handed over the *Pioneer* to Lieutenant Young to sail her to the Cape. He himself wanted to sell the *Lady Nyassa* at the nearest port where buyers might be found. Zanzibar, nearly a thousand miles to the north, was the closest possible market. A long sea voyage would be a dangerous undertaking in a small steamer that had been designed for lake and river use rather than as a sea-going vessel. But, in spite of the fact that his crew was untrained and too small, Livingstone made up his mind to risk it. When he arrived at Zanzibar in April and found no buyer, he made an even more remarkable decision; he would sail his tiny forty-foot ship two and a half thousand miles across the Indian Ocean to Bombay, where he was told he would have a better chance of selling her. Not even the desertion of his long-suffering engineer, George Rae, could change his mind. Nor was he daunted by the information that the monsoons would break in roughly three weeks. But although he had only been able to carry enough coal for five days' steaming, Livingstone made it to Bombay, mainly under sail, in forty-five days. As his insignificant vessel entered the harbour, the first monsoon rains started to fall and the gales broke the following day. When Livingstone stepped ashore and walked slowly through the busy docks, nobody took any notice of him. It was not surprising; only madmen crossed the Indian Ocean from Africa in small ships at that time of year. At the Customs House, Livingstone asked if the Governor was in town. On being told that he was not, the leader of the Zambesi Expedition wandered into the Court House to listen to a few cases while he waited till the city magistrate could see him. It was a strangely banal ending to six horrifying years.

Livingstone embarked for England on 24 June and was back in London by the end of July.

On 20 January 1863, the editor of *The Times* had assessed the results of the Zambesi Expedition as follows: 'We were promised cotton, sugar and indigo . . . and of course we got none. We were promised trade; and there is no trade . . . We were promised converts and not one has been made. In a word, the thousands subscribed by the Universities and contributed by the Government have been productive only of the most fatal results.'

All this was perfectly correct. In 1858 Livingstone had promised that the Zambesi would prove navigable as far as the Victoria Falls, and that a brisk trade would soon be developed with the Makololo and the tribes living on the Batoka Plateau. He had suggested that traders and missionaries would be able to live in perfect safety in central Africa and would have no difficulty in communicating with the coast. Livingstone had argued that the real importance of his great trans-continental journey was that it had drawn his attention to the enormous Christian and commercial potential of the Batoka Plateau. With the discovery of the Kebrabasa Rapids in the first year of the expedition, all

his optimistic plans lay in ruins.* In 1859 he thought that
he had found in the Shire Highlands a suitable alternative
for Christian and commercial exploitation, and since this
region seemed to offer Livingstone his last chance to justify earlier rash promises, he committed himself to it
totally. His almost simultaneous discovery of serious problems: Arab slave raids and the tribal war between the
Ajawa and the Manganja, did not lead him to qualify his
new optimism. As a result, when the Universities Mission
came out, they faced a situation with which they were
unable to cope. The complete anarchy in the Shire Highlands in 1863, and the missionaries' decision to withdraw,
set the seal on the Zambesi Expedition's failure.

Given the vast distances travelled and the enormous
amount of energy expended, this judgment inevitably
seems harsh, especially since the Zambesi Expedition had
made important discoveries. For a start it had proved
beyond doubt that the Zambesi was useless for navigation
beyond Tete. The Shire Highlands had been found to be
accessible only via the river Shire, which was shallow
and treacherous for six months of the year above the junction with the Ruo. Important new facts about the Arab
slave routes across Nyassa had also been brought to light.
And although the lake itself had previously been reached
by Candido, the Tete trader, Livingstone had fixed its
position accurately for the first time, and had produced a
reliable map of its southern and western shores. In fact,
had Livingstone set out with the limited, but still significant, aim of finding out with scientific objectivity about
the geographical problems of south-central and south-eastern Africa, with related facts on the number and disposi-
tion of tribes and their relations with the Arabs and the
Portuguese, he would have returned home disappointed
but satisfied that he had brought back the information he
had set out to provide. As it was, Livingstone came back to
England unable to claim any credit for the expedition's
only achievement: its negative discoveries. Yet by promising too much too soon, he had in the end denied himself

---

* In 1973, 100 years after Livingstone's death, the Portuguese are
building a vast dam across the rapids. The power from it will enable
them to mine vast deposits of gold, copper, iron, asbestos and
graphite found in the Tete area, where Livingstone set his geologist
to work. Thornton's notes, written in a bizarre personal shorthand,
have not yet been deciphered.

this one chance to salvage a little glory from the ruins. Instead he was left with the feeble and untrue excuse that the malice of the Portuguese and the cowardice of the missionaries had robbed him of success. Nor would this be enough to convince many people that the expenditure of £50,000 of Government money and the loss of a dozen lives had been satisfactorily justified or explained by Dr Livingstone.

And yet the restatement of obvious failure is not enough. The disconcerting fact remains that without his over-optimism, and without the determination that his work should have more far-reaching effects than the increase of geographical knowledge, Livingstone would never have crossed Africa, and would certainly never have been able to summon up the superhuman tenacity and endurance which had alone kept his deeply divided and disillusioned expedition in being. Livingstone had often treated his subordinates abysmally, had lied and shown unbelievable insensitivity, but his indestructible strength of will, which Kirk had at times felt to be not far from insanity, had kept the party pressing on after crippling disasters and set-backs. And there is a still more important consideration regarding Livingstone's false expectations: unless he had formulated plans for the colonial occupation of Africa, at a time when the prospects for such moves were negligible, his later influence on the course of African history would have been no greater than that of any other explorer. But in 1863, after all his earlier overtures to the Government had been rejected, and when he had been bluntly told that it was out of the question for him to take possession of discoveries in the Queen's name,[47] he predicted that, what-ever the present administration said, there would one day be British colonies in central and eastern Africa. Then he proceeded to describe the colonial system which would become the pattern for the British African Empire fifteen years after his death. On the ship going home he developed his idea of a small minority of whites, not vying with the natives in manual labour, but taking 'a leading part in managing the land . . . taking a lead too in trade and all public matters', and filling an organizing role 'which is now practically vacant'.[48] He also wrote, early in 1864, with an apparently insane disregard for the facts that had ruined all immediate hope of the Shire Highlands being occupied: 'Viewing calmly all the circumstances . . . I could not conceive of a sphere in which the missionary prospects would be more inviting than that which has now been abandoned . . . I have no doubt that it will be done though I may not be alive to hear of it . . . the future will justify my words & hopes.'[49]

Had history disproved his boast, it would be possible to condemn Livingstone for another piece of characteristic over-optimism and leave the matter there. But incredibly history *did* vindicate Livingstone's claim. Less than a decade after his death, Nyasaland became a British Protectorate, and, as will be seen, this would be the result of Livingstone's posthumous influence. But in 1864 it would be misleading to believe that Livingstone was entirely confident in his predictions; not even he possessed that degree of self-confidence. At the time that he was writing optimistic letters about his certainty that the future would prove him right, his journal tells a different story: 'I shall have nothing to do at home,' he wrote miserably on the crossing to Bombay. 'By the failure of the Universities Mission my work seems vain. Am I to be cut off before I can do anything to affect permanent improvement in Africa? I have been unprofitable enough . . .'[50]

Certainly Livingstone had good reason to be alarmed about his immediate personal prospects. All his work from 1851, when he had seen the upper Zambesi for the first time, to early 1864, when he sailed from Zanzibar, had been undertaken on the assumption that his explorations would produce practical and tangible results. Yet his experiences during the Zambesi Expedition had made it impossible to think realistically of traders, missionaries or colonists settling in the foreseeable future in any of the areas he had 'opened up'. From 1859 onwards, because he knew that isolated groups of men would face problems too formidable for them to overcome, Livingstone had put all his faith for future progress in Africa on colonization; in his view, that alone would break up tribal societies and leave the natives responsive to Christian teaching and European commercial habits. But in 1864, with the Government still adamantly opposed to any colonial expansion anywhere in the world, it was going to be quite impossible for Livingstone to go on suggesting that he was 'opening the way for others'. Colonists were not going to come without government aid, and no missionary or trader was

going to catch the next boat for Africa after reading about
the fighting, the deaths and the terrible communications.
Livingstone had to face the fact that, unless he thought up
a brand-new justification, if ever he went back to Africa it
would be as an explorer, no more, no less.

Nor did his difficulties end there. If he returned, it could
obviously not be to Moçambique nor to any adjoining
area. The Portuguese, after what he had said about them,
were most unlikely to let him in again, and anyway, since
Livingstone had claimed that the Portuguese presence by
itself made all constructive moves impossible, he could not
logically give either the Shire Highlands or the Zambesi
another chance. This was a very serious state of affairs,
for it cut him off from all the areas he had previously
explored. If he returned to Africa, he was going to have to
start in a new area and abandon any idea of utilizing any
of the work he had done in the last ten years. It was a
daunting prospect, and even more so now that he had spent
the remainder of his money from *Missionary Travels* on
the *Lady Nyassa*. Nor would he be able to count on the
Foreign Office or the Treasury to back him again. On the
way back to England he wrote to Waller, of the Universities Mission, saying: 'I don't know whether I am to go on
the shelf or not. If I do, I make Africa the shelf.'[51] But
defiant statements were easier to write than to act out.
Charles Livingstone thought that his brother's situation
would be best remedied by marrying a rich, religious
widow and living a life of prosperous retirement augmented by the profits of another book.[52]

But Livingstone, although he had no certain plans, did
not intend getting another wife. He had told a number of
friends after Mary's death that he had abandoned all
thoughts of a permanent home, more than ever now that
three of his children were nearly grown up. Livingstone had
spent over twenty years in Africa, most of them travelling,
and this nomadic existence had left him with little taste for
settling down. His experiences of the company of his
fellow-countrymen on the Zambesi Expedition had not
increased his desire to live a close domestic life in Britain.
He longed to be able to recapture the happiness and
freedom of his journey across Africa, and that could only
be done in the company of Africans. *They* would not
question his decisions nor ask for their opinions to be con-

sidered. With them, acting as the well-behaved children of
a benign if paternalistic leader, Livingstone felt he might
begin achieving things again in Africa. Precisely where in
Africa he was uncertain. When he would return and how,
were equally vexing questions, but the most puzzling question of all was what he would do when he got there.

PART FIVE

Rejection

19

The Last Visit Home, 1864–1865

When Livingstone reached London in July 1864, there were
no banquets and official receptions as there had been in
1856; and although one evening he was invited to dine
with the Prime Minister, Lord Palmerston, and on another
occasion took tea with Mr Gladstone, Livingstone could
soon sense that these invitations had been prompted by
dutiful courtesy rather than by any real enthusiasm. At
eighty, Lord Palmerston was struggling with failing sight
and hearing, and had insufficient energy to interest himself
in concerns other than vital policy decisions. At the time
of Livingstone's return the Prime Minister was facing a
serious European crisis provoked by the Prussian invasion
of Schleswig-Holstein. Not surprisingly Lord John Russell,
the Foreign Secretary, was also preoccupied by events in
Europe and could scarcely find time to see or discuss the
future of a man who had just returned from leading an
inglorious African expedition.

Lord John had never struck even his friends as the
possessor of a warm personality, and Livingstone, when he
met him on 26 July, was badly shaken by Russell's 'very
cold manner'. There was really no reason why the Foreign
Secretary should have been affable. Lord John had not
merely been annoyed by criticisms of the Zambesi Expedition in the press and by the complaints of High Churchmen blaming Dr Livingstone for the failure of the
Universities Mission; the Foreign Secretary had been far
more acutely embarrassed by Livingstone's constant outbursts against the Portuguese. Not only was Russell
opposed to unnecessary diplomatic entanglements, but he
resented Livingstone's attitude to the nation which had,
after all, given permission for the expedition to enter the
Zambesi. Apart from that, Prince Albert had been enraged
by criticisms of his cousin the King of Portugal; and
Russell, who did not get on with Victoria, had no desire

to add more fuel to the Queen's hostility. The Prince Consort, by refusing to become Patron of the Universities Mission, had already made quite plain his views on Dr Livingstone. There were other reasons for the Foreign Secretary's 'very cold manner'. The Admiralty had reported adversely on the Zambesi Expedition and had claimed that all naval support had been carried out at a cost in cash and lives far too high to justify the negligible results. The Treasury too had censured Livingstone for costing the nation an extra £3,000 by failing to evacuate by the end of 1863.[1]

Nevertheless Russell did not wish to turn away with nothing a man who had suffered a great deal of personal hardship. He told Livingstone that if he intended to return to Africa, the Government would pay £500 towards the cost of his supplies, provided he did not go near any territory where the Portuguese claimed direct or indirect authority. The Foreign Secretary then made it clear that there was no question of any regular salary, the £500 was all that he could offer. Livingstone left Russell's office trembling with anger and wounded pride. No expedition lasting two years could possibly be mounted on less than £2,000 and the Government was only going to provide a quarter. His anger was all the more intense because he was well aware that Russell knew that, after the Government's refusal to contribute towards the cost of the *Lady Nyassa*, he, Livingstone, had had to find the money himself. Livingstone had also taken deep offence when the Foreign Secretary had told him to moderate any remarks he might make in public about the Portuguese, and not to tell anybody about the £500 grant 'because so many people will bother the Foreign Office'.[2] In fact Russell had one person in mind: the Portuguese Ambassador. After his interview with Lord John, Livingstone thought only of the snubbing he had been treated to; he never acknowledged that Russell could have dismissed him with no offer of any sort and would have been able to justify such an action without difficulty.

Since there were no banquets and few requests for lectures, there was nothing to keep Livingstone in London for more than a few days. In the street he was occasionally recognized, but generally by 'imbecile old ladies'.[3] In early August, Livingstone left for Scotland where he was relieved to discover that popular support had not dimin-

ished so much as in the south. The main purpose of his
journey north was not the pursuit of cheering crowds, but
to spend some time with his neglected family. He had
seen none of his children for nearly seven years and the
youngest, five-year-old Anna Mary, who had been born in
Kuruman in 1859, he had never seen. Agnes, the eldest
daughter, had only been with her father for six of her
eighteen years. How pathetically out of touch he had
become can be seen from a letter written to Agnes just
before his arrival in Scotland. 'I have some "sweeties" for
you . . . I did not know what else to buy,'[4] he told his
daughter, who was no longer a child but a young woman.
Livingstone's time in his parents' small house in Hamilton
was not happy. His mother was evidently dying and her
mind was deranged. She did not recognize her son but
talked to him as though he was one of his own children.
Often she would ask him what had happened to his
brother, meaning his eldest son Robert. The old woman
could hardly have asked a more painful question.

Robert's life is really the story of Livingstone's tragic
failure as a parent. Born in Bechuanaland in 1845, Robert
had shown signs of rebellion at the tender age of four,
when what had probably been no more than healthy independence had been called by Livingstone 'excessive obstinacy'. As his father had done before him, Livingstone
tried to beat his son into submission, but the remedy
increased rather than diminished the complaint. Robert
had been seven when he and the rest of the family were
sent back to England in 1852, while Livingstone tramped
his way across Africa. Until his father's return in 1856,
Robert had shared his mother's wretchedly poor existence,
moving from room to room, from town to town. When
Livingstone had set off on the Zambesi Expedition, the care
of his children was shared by a board of trustees and Livingstone's spinster sisters in Hamilton. The 'aunts' were
narrow-minded, and their constant resort to the strict discipline enjoined by the elders of their church was hopelessly
inappropriate treatment for a strong-willed boy brought
up on an African mission station, where, away from his
father's eye, he had enjoyed a great deal of freedom.
From the age of twelve he was sent to a series of boarding schools in Scotland and the north of England, but he
would not work and often ran away, thus provoking stern
letters from his father, commanding him to end his 'vaga-

bond ways'. But homiletic letters could not give Robert the sense of love and security he needed. With his mother dead, and never really knowing his father, it was not surprising that Robert was considered difficult by his schoolteachers. At the age of eighteen he announced that he was not prepared to submit to any more education. So the same year, 1863, Livingstone reluctantly agreed to his coming out to the Zambesi to discuss his future with a view to some sort of apprenticeship. Unfortunately the trustees knew nothing about Africa and made no arrangement for Robert to get anywhere further than Natal. His father had believed that plans would be made for him to come up with Bishop Tozer, but nothing of the sort had been envisaged, and Robert arrived in Natal penniless and with no better prospect of getting to the Zambesi than he would have had thousands of miles away in London. When Robert's grandmother, Mary Moffat, heard about his situation she was beside herself with worry. Not so Livingstone, who had told Kirk, when he had left the expedition, that if he saw Robert and found out that no passage would be possible, Kirk was to tell Robert 'he must work his own way in Natal'.[5] Livingstone's feeling was that Robert, by refusing an education, had condemned himself to a life of manual labour.[6] In a letter to a friend written in November 1863, Livingstone admitted, 'often conscience accused me of being deficient in my duty to my children'.[7] It was sad that he never told Robert as much; more often he accused his son of deliberate laziness and a liking for 'bad company and drink'. From the end of 1863, till he returned to England in the summer of 1864, Livingstone heard no more about Robert.

But, by 28 July, he had had more news of his son, for on that day he wrote to Kirk, telling him: 'My heart is rather sore—that bad boy has got into the American army and will be made manure of for those bloody fields.'* How Robert had entered the Northern forces against the Confederates, Livingstone had no idea, until he received a letter from his son in October. This was a striking and moving letter, not simply because Robert addressed his father as 'My dear Sir' and ended 'your quondam son Robert', but because the young man emerges not as the delinquent his father considered him, but as gentle, hon-

* The American Civil War lasted from April 1861 to May 1865.

ourable and brave. After explaining how he had been kidnapped in Natal and later impressed into the American army, Robert went on to describe two skirmishes and one battle which he had been in; another battle, he went on, was imminent: 'I have never hurt anyone knowingly in battle, have always fired high, and in that furious madness which always accompanies a bayonet charge and which seems to possess every soldier, I controlled my passion and took the man who surrendered prisoner.'

Robert admitted that he regretted throwing away his chance of an education and wished that a 'craving to travelling' had not led him astray. He concluded: 'I have changed my name for I am convinced that to bear your name here would lead to further dishonours to it.' Then, almost as an afterthought, he added that he was at present in a military field hospital suffering from exposure.[8]

Only a few months before, Livingstone had written to his son Thomas, telling him that Robert was only interested in making capital out of having a famous father, 'but when they see he has nothing in him he will be despised and be fit only to drive a "cuddy and a cart" '.[9] Robert was wounded in a skirmish at Laurel Hill, Virginia, and taken prisoner. He died in a prison camp in Salisbury, North Carolina, on 5 December 1864; a few days later he would have been nineteen. He had, as Livingstone so delicately suggested, been 'made manure of for those bloody fields'. The lesson, however, was not lost on Livingstone, for he never pressed Thomas or Oswell to take up any particular career unless they wanted to do so.

But Livingstone's real efforts to make up for his past failures as a parent were directed at his eldest daughter, Agnes. Agnes was to have everything which had been denied the others. Nothing, Livingstone decided, was to be too good for her. He thought of sending her to a £150-a-year finishing school in London and finally chose a still more expensive option. She could go to Paris to improve her piano-playing and her French. There she could also take lessons in riding and drawing if she wished. Only 'injurious' French novels were to be forbidden her. It is more than ironic that while Livingstone was making such lavish plans for his eldest daughter, his eldest son lay dying, but even if Livingstone was sentimental about young girls, his real affection for Agnes cannot be denied. The large number of letters he wrote to her until his death are proof of that.

From September 1864 to April 1865, Livingstone and Agnes stayed at Newstead Abbey, the Nottinghamshire country home of William Webb, a former big game enthusiast, whom Livingstone had met in Bechuanaland through William Cotton Oswell, his first travelling companion. Livingstone's days at Newstead were among the happiest in his life and, while there, he was affectionate, unassertive and kind. Nobody who met him then could have believed him capable of callousness or lying. Dr Livingstone was always ready for a joke and delighted Mr and Mrs Webb by his constant attentions to their children. Ethel, their youngest, was a particular favourite, and Livingstone was always bringing down the wrath of her nanny for handing the child illicit scones and jam. He often went for walks with the children and one day got so involved in a game of blindman's buff that he blundered into the edge of a stone mantelpiece and cut his forehead. It was at this time that he confided more regrets to his friends over his inattention to his own children. 'Oh why did I not play more with my children in the Kolobeng days? Why was I so busy that I had so little time for my bairns?'[10] He tried hard with little Anna Mary, but his youngest daughter did not like being kissed by this strange man with a moustache who seemed to spend so many hours writing. Livingstone gave her a black doll, but she would have preferred a white one, as she admitted later.

Her memory of Livingstone endlessly writing was correct. At Newstead her father set about his second book, *A Narrative of an Expedition to the Zambezi and its Tributaries*. The *Narrative* was entirely for public consumption and glossed over all the problems and troubles which Livingstone had faced. But there was one obstacle the author did write about at length. In spite of Lord John Russell's warning, Livingstone savagely attacked the Portuguese and once more suggested that every failure could be pinned on them.

In September 1864 Livingstone broke off his writing to go to Bath for the annual meeting of the British Association. He had been invited to address the members of his favourite subject: the Portuguese slave-trade. It was an opportunity too good to be missed; and yet other aspects of the Bath meeting did not please him. In 1856, at the

Association's meeting in Dublin, he had been the only explorer of note, the undisputed star of the show, but now there were others with a title quite as good as his. The main attraction at Bath was not to be his vitriolic attack on the Portuguese, but what was expected to be a violently heated debate between Richard Burton and John Speke on the probable location of the source of the Nile. Before Livingstone came to Bath he was hoping to return to Africa, if he could raise enough money to do so through his new book and the generosity of public or private patrons, but he had not come to any conclusions about what he would do on arrival, or where he would head for. Although Livingstone did not acknowledge it at the time or afterwards, the Speke-versus-Burton Nile controversy marked the beginning of his own passionate interest in that river, and consequently changed the course of his life.

In 1856, with the backing of the Foreign Office and the Royal Geographical Society, Speke and Burton had set out into the interior from Zanzibar in an attempt to reach a large inland lake which numerous Arab and native traders had visited. The two men stood on the shores of Lake Tanganyika in February 1858, over a year before Livingstone reached the more southerly Lake Nyassa. On the way back to Zanzibar Speke had made a detour north of his own and had arrived at the southern shore of a vast lake which he named Victoria Nyanza.* From the great height (3,700 feet above sea level) and apparently gigantic size of this lake, Speke at once decided that he had found the source of the Nile. Burton, who was irritated beyond measure not to have accompanied Speke, dismissed contemptuously his companion's excited claims to have solved the world's greatest geographical mystery. Undismayed by Burton's hostile response, Speke had returned to the northern side of his lake in the summer of 1862 and had found an outlet, which he called the Ripon Falls. This discovery he was certain clinched the matter. It did not. In March 1864, Samuel White Baker, who had met Speke and his new travelling companion, James Grant, in 1863, north of the Victoria Nyanza, discovered another large lake, 150 miles north-west of Speke's. Baker now claimed that this lake, which he called Lake Albert, was the *true* source. He had also found a spectacular waterfall

---

* See Map 5 on page 395.

on the eastern side of the lake, which he was to name the Murchison Falls. Whether this waterfall was fed by the same river that began at Speke's Ripon Falls, Baker did not know, nor could he claim with any certainty that the large body of water that flowed out of Lake Albert at its northern end was the Nile. That claim could only be substantiated by tracing that river north and seeing where it went. It was also impossible for Speke to make absolute claims for his lake until he had travelled north from the Ripon Falls far enough to be able to prove the Victoria Nyanza's connection with the lower Nile.

Thirteen years later it would be discovered that Speke had been right and that the waters leaving the Victoria Nyanza at the Ripon Falls were the most southerly source of the Nile. In fact the Nile begins in the Victoria Nyanza and, after joining Lake Albert at the Murchison Falls, flows on out of the northern end of Albert as the Nile proper. Lake Albert is therefore at best a secondary source.

In September 1864, the extent of Baker's discovery was not yet known, and, in any case, when it was the following year, there was still no certainty that Baker's Albert or Speke's Victoria were individually or jointly responsible for the lower Nile. Even before Lake Albert was found there were other very plausible alternatives to Speke's lake being the source, and Burton was prepared to put forward all of them in September 1864 at Bath.

For a start Burton would be able to argue that since Speke had not circumnavigated his lake, he could not even reliably claim that the water he had seen in 1858 was part of the same lake which contained the Ripon Falls. But, more tellingly, Burton could suggest quite plausibly that Lake Tanganyika might be the source of the Nile. A river might well flow out of the northern end of Tanganyika, and then, following a course to the west of Speke's lake, it could join the Nile several hundred miles north of the Victoria Nyanza. If that was so, any connection of Speke's or Baker's lakes with the Nile would become irrelevant, since Lake Tanganyika was so much further south.

Livingstone was briefed by Sir Roderick Murchison on all the arguments likely to be employed during the great debate, and Livingstone's interest was soon keenly aroused, and not simply because it was common knowledge that the two men hated each other. Livingstone was beginning to

form his own ideas, and once that happened he always
wanted to act them out. The day set for the eagerly anticipated geographical slanging match was 16 September. But
the ticket-holders would never have their fun. At 4 p.m.
on the day before, John Speke, out shooting on his uncle's
estate just outside Bath, clambered over a low wall. Before
he reached the other side his gun went off, blasting a gap-
ing wound in his chest. Speke died shortly afterwards.
Although there was a lot of talk about suicide, the evidence was far from conclusive. Eearlier in the day Speke
had appeared as keen as ever to defend his claims against
Burton. This tragedy increased rather than diminished
public speculation about the Nile's source.

It is more than likely that Sir Roderick Murchison asked
Livingstone, while he was in Bath, whether he would like
to be sponsored by the Royal Geographical Society to
solve the riddle of the central African lakes once and for
all. But in September 1864 Livingstone was not ready to
commit himself. A straightforward search for the source
of a river, albeit the longest in the world, was not going
to be enough to persuade the public that he was returning
to Africa as a missionary. Besides, if an announcement
was made so soon after the Bath meeting, it might appear
that Dr Livingstone was a little over-keen to compete with
others for the greatest of all geographical prizes. There
was no doubt that Livingstone already wanted to compete,
none at all, but he was not quite ready to announce the
fact. He had never liked the idea of other men working
beyond his lines and the thought of outsmarting them all
gave him a great deal of pleasure.

In the past, Livingstone's determination to secure the
credit for geographical discoveries had been emphasized
again and again by his bitter attacks on those claiming
that others had preceded him. Speke himself had suggested that Dr Livingstone had never given Portuguese
explorers enough praise, and for this insolence Livingstone
declared that his young critic had 'such slender mental
abilities that silence in this & other matters would have
better become him'. After Speke's death, Livingstone wrote
patronizingly of him as 'a poor misguided thing with such
an intense desire to please that I always pity him'.[11] Had
Livingstone been indifferent to Speke and Burton as men,
it is possible that the source of the Nile might not have
become so important to him, but from the time of the

Bath meeting he became personally as well as scientifically involved. Soon he was writing with derision about Speke's theories.

> Speke gave the best example I know of the eager pursuit of a foregone conclusion. When he discovered Victoria Nyanza . . . here were the headwaters of the river of Egypt and no mistake. Though he saw that the little river that issues thence would not account for the Nile, he would not let it be doubted even in his own mind . . . and invented a 'backwater' to eke out his little river.[12]

When Livingstone heard about Baker's Lake Albert in 1865, he decided that the Nile source probably lay southwest of Lake Tanganyika. His theory was that these sources drained into Tanganyika and that a river, issuing from the northern end of Lake Tanganyika, joined the southern end of Lake Albert and flowed on north as the Nile proper. If this was so, Speke, Burton and Baker had all been working several hundred miles too far north; it was an idea that gave Livingstone grim satisfaction. With all the available knowledge in 1864 and 1865, Livingstone's theory seemed rather more likely than Speke's. After all, on the face of it, it seemed most unlikely that the Nile, which flowed for four thousand miles, much of the way through the largest and driest desert in the world, could be supplied from one outlet, the comparatively small Ripon Falls.

But derision of Speke and geographical interest were not enough to make Livingstone obsessively interested in outsmarting rivals. His bitter hatred of Burton was what swayed the balance. Almost everything about Burton distressed him: his view of travel in Africa as an entertainment rather than a mission, his undisguised contempt for conventional morality and conventional people, his preferring Arabs to Africans and his frequently expressed conviction that it was useless to try and change Africans. The last of these failings was in Livingstone's eyes the most serious. To suggest that Africans were "unprogressive and unfit for change' was bad enough, but to Livingstone even this seemed trivial in comparison with Burton's further claim that religion was the 'mental expression of a race'. From this premise Burton had gone on to argue that it was crass wishful thinking to believe that the 'Bible *made* England, or the Koran Stambul'; the truth, he asserted, was that the higher or lower state of a race predetermined their religion.[13] Thus to attempt to force upon Africans a creed belonging to a different race was about as sensible as trying to graft a cat's head on to a dog's body. Christianity, Burton had claimed, could not achieve in decades what could only come about through generations of social change.[14]

This sort of thinking undercut every argument that Livingstone had ever utttered and he hated Burton for it. Burton had also attacked missionaries, largely because he considered, for the reasons given above, that their work was based on a completely false assumption. In 1860 Burton had accepted a Foreign Office consular appointment in west Africa, and there he became convinced that missionaries were badly selected, meddlesome and ignorant. Certainly it would have been strange if Burton, an intellectual snob who prized only the bizarre, had taken to worthy Christians from the lower middle class. In September 1864 Burton had been in England on leave but he had not confined his attentions to the Nile question. In the spring of the following year he had appeared as a witness before a House of Commons Select Committee on West African Settlements. The Committee's job had been to recommend the Government either to devote more money to bolster up existing private British enterprises in the area or to pull out altogether. The Committee in the end opted for the latter course. The Government in fact just left matters as they were. Livingstone felt that Burton's evidence had done a lot of damage and had set back for years any hopes of a more positive British policy towards colonization. Burton had derided the economic potential of West Africa and had claimed that the missionaries there were doing more harm than good. Livingstone was angry enough to write a sympathetic letter to Dr Tidman with condolences for the 'lies' and 'aspersions of that beastly fellow Burton against the missionaries on the West Coast'. 'Burton,' Livingstone had gone on, 'seems to be a moral idiot. His conduct in Africa was so bad that it cannot be spoken of without disgust—systematically wicked, impure and untruthful.'[15] Livingstone was referring to the rumours that Burton had often failed to pay porters and had travelled with a harem of African women to serve his sexual needs. Burton, who liked shocking people, did little to dis-

pel these rumours. Later Livingstone wrote: 'I don't like to
face people who were witnesses of his [Burton's] bestial
immorality.'[16]

I have described Livingstone's personal dislike of Speke
and Burton in some detail since no previous biographer
has devoted any space at all to what in my view seems to
be an important motivating factor for Livingstone's search
for the Nile source. His idea was that if he could prove
the geographical theories of both men to have been wrong,
thus making their discoveries seem insignificant, it would
be a victory for his own views, on the benefits of trade
and Christianity, over Burton's pessimistic assumption that
Africans were immutably 'unprogressive and unfit for
social change'. If there were ever going to be British
colonies in Africa it was vital that men with views like
Burton's should be silenced.

Yet Livingstone was aware that his personal feelings
could hardly be used publicly to justify his eternal claim
that he was more than an explorer. To persuade anybody
that he was still a missionary would take more than that,
but until he had worked out supporting arguments, Livingstone was not going to risk admitting that he was planning to return to Africa to find the source of the Nile.
For a start, as Livingstone told Sir Roderick Murchison, a
purely geographical task would mean moving swiftly across
country with no time to appear to be planting the seed of
the gospel in the natives' minds. Unless he stayed for several months at a time in individual places, not even the
most gullible of his supporters would believe that he was
converting anybody. This problem appeared to be insur-
mountable, but there was another factor which saved
Livingstone: the Arab slave-trade.

Before 1865, Livingstone had concentrated most of his
vitriol on the Portuguese trade, but from the autumn of
1861, after his first extensive survey of Lake Nyassa, he
had realized that the Arab trade was a far more serious
problem. There were two reasons why Livingstone had
not given it more attention; in the first place, since Arab
slave raids had been concentrated in the area north and
west of Nyassa, they could not be used as an excuse to
explain the chaos in the Shire Highlands. The Portuguese
were far better scapegoats. Livingstone's second reason for
reticence on Arab slaving was the fact that he could
hardly speak about it without reference to his own failure

to launch his steamer on Lake Nyassa; his purpose, it will be remembered, had been to cut the main southern Arab slave routes. But now, in early 1865, Livingstone realized that if he went to the area just south of Lake Tanganyika, to search for the source of the Nile, he would find himself in the heart of Arab slave-trading activities. This then provided him with the ideal justification. He would not only be looking for a river but would be reporting back on the slave-trade too. Perhaps his information might even prove horrific enough to persuade the Government to intervene directly in central Africa. Livingstone was very pleased with the idea and went on to argue that a search for the Nile's source, if successful, would greatly strengthen his anti-slavery diatribes. 'The Nile sources,' he told a friend, 'are valuable only as a means of enabling me to open my mouth with power among men. It is this power which I hope to apply to remedy an enormous evil [the slave-trade]. Men may think I covet fame, but I make it a rule not to read aught written in my praise.'[17]

Although in 1865 the Arab slave-trade was a convenient excuse, during Livingstone's last journey it became much more than that, and in time it would be hard to judge whether the search for the Nile's source or his desire to expose the slave-trade was his dominant motive.

When Sir Roderick wrote to Livingstone on 5 January 1865, formally inviting him on behalf of the Royal Geographical Society to return to Africa to clear up the mystery of the source of the Nile, he had felt able to accept. With his justification now fully thought out, Livingstone had applauded the decision of the Council of the R.G.S. to send him out, and suggested that the Society had chosen 'the true scientific way of settling the matter'.[18] Had they selected Burton or Baker for the same task, Livingstone would have thought the decision anything but the 'true scientific way'. Nevertheless the R.G.S. only offered £500, which Livingstone thought mean, and he did not take kindly to some written instructions ordering him to make regular observations of longitude and latitude. He felt that for £500 he could hardly be expected to sit for weeks at a time in given positions to wait for cloud conditions to allow him to make accurate astronomical observations. But this was a mild irritant compared with the Council's request to be shown all his personal notes on his return. It was a pity that he did not have it out with them at the time, but as usual he kept his resentment to himself and harboured a grudge that would become little short of obsessive within a couple of years.

With £500 from the R.G.S., Livingstone knew that he would need £1,500 more. If he took the money Russell had offered, he would have to raise only an extra £1,000 to have enough to last him two years in Africa. But this money still had to be found; it is therefore astounding that when, in early 1865, Lord Palmerston (who had always been more sympathetic to Livingstone than Lord John Russell had) sent his unofficial political agent, Mr Lionel Hayward Q.C., to visit the Doctor at Newstead, Livingstone failed to take advantage of it. Alas, Mr Hayward's discreet approaches were too discreet for Livingstone to understand them. Hayward asked whether Lord Palmerston could be of any assistance. Livingstone was puzzled. The Foreign Secretary had told him with painful precision what the Government would and would not do for him. Rather than risk a second rebuff, Livingstone told Hayward coldly that he could ask Lord Palmerston to persuade the Portuguese to open the Zambesi to international shipping. Naturally enough Palmerston let the matter drop. Since the Zambesi was unsuitable for navigation, the Prime Minister could not understand why Dr Livingstone had asked for such an impractical favour. A few hundred pounds or a K.C.B. would have been a different matter. It took Palmerston's death in October that year to wake up Livingstone to the opportunity he had missed, not through pride or altruism but through naïvety. Unhappily he confessed the truth to a friend: 'Lord Palmerston sent Mr Hayward, a Queen's Council, to ask "how he could aid me for he was most anxious to be of service to me." Most unaccountably it never once glanced across my mind that he meant anything for me or my children.'[19]

Having missed this opportunity, Livingstone had to avail himself of Russell's £500. He therefore wrote to the Foreign Secretary and on 11 March was invited to meet Austen Layard, the Permanent Under-Secretary at the Foreign Office. Layard was friendly and courteous. He confirmed that Livingstone could have his £500 and would be given the honorary rank of Consul with certain exemptions from normal duties. As a rule British consuls had to be settled in one country, where they were meant to look after the interests of British subjects in that country, and to report back to the Foreign Office in London on developments both domestic and external that might be of interest to the British Government. After chatting to Layard for a while, Livingstone left in a far better mood than he had been in after his interview with Russell. It was therefore a sickening shock, when he received his Consul's commission and instructions dated 28 March 1865, to read a separate enclosure signed by Russell: 'Whilst I have been willing to obtain the grant of £500 from the public funds . . . I wish you distinctly to understand that you are not to receive additional consular salary for the service in which you are now engaged, and that your consular appointment gives you no future claim on Her Majesty's Government for a consular pension.'[20]

Livingstone had not expected either a salary or a pension, but he was mortally offended that the refusal had been put in writing and in such dismissive terms. Quite apart from this, Livingstone felt that if his appointment was renewed beyond the two years, a situation might arise when he ought to get a pension. Thus a definite rejection in 1865 might later be taken as final, even if circumstances changed. But the general tone of the instructions seemed to Livingstone to be brusque and aggressive. 'You will distinctly understand' was a phrase used on several occasions, and he was warned not to 'make any promise to, or to enter into any arrangement with, chiefs, which might form an embarrassment to Her Majesty's Government'. He was ordered not to allow himself to be made a prisoner, since, if the Government were unable to punish the offenders, the safety of other explorers might be put in jeopardy. Altogether it was a chilling document.

These instructions, drawn up by a Foreign Office Official, Mr Murray, and signed by Russell, Livingstone was later to describe as 'the most exuberant impertinence that ever issued from the Foreign Office'.[21] Whenever Livingstone felt depressed or ill on his last journeys, he remembered this communication and it cut him to the heart. Over and over again he referred to it in the letters written between 1870 and 1872, five to seven years after it had been sent. Livingstone tried to soften the blow by believing that Murray had been solely responsible and that Russell had signed it without being aware of the contents.

On receiving his commission, Livingstone wrote to Sir

Roderick Murchison, who in turn wrote to Lord Clarendon, who had been Foreign Secretary at the beginning of
the Zambesi Expedition, and who would hold the same
post again when Russell succeeded Palmerston as Prime
Minister. Both men thought the Foreign Office's attitude
had been 'ungracious and unjust',[22] but their thoughts did
not change the matter or increase by a single pound the
size of the grant. Ironically Russell, on first reading the
despatch Murray had composed, suggested to Layard that
it ought to be shown to Murchison before being sent.
Unfortunately, for some reason Layard did not take this
advice.[23] Murchison, on hearing from Livingstone, wrote
to Russell telling him how upset Livingstone was, and on
26 April the Foreign Secretary sent a note to Murray. 'Dr
Livingstone is much distressed at a letter he has got from
me saying his present consular appointment is not to count
towards a pension—I never intended this and I wish the
letter to be withdrawn, as he is a regular Consul, only to
fifty black chiefs instead of to one white one.'[24]

But strangely nothing was done about the pension. In
fact Livingstone was not granted a Civil List pension till
19 June 1873. He had by then been dead nearly two
months. The amount the Government decided on was
£300. Why Russell's note was never acted on, it is now
impossible to discover; although it seems extraordinary
that nothing was done. On 23 May Livingstone even wrote
to the Foreign Secretary returning the despatch and asking him to change the last clauses, since Sir Roderick
Murchison and Lord Clarendon had assured him they no
longer 'express your Lordship's view'.[25]

In mid-August of 1865, just after Livingstone had left
the country for Africa, Lord John belatedly sent the
deeply wounded man a letter which made matters worse
rather than better. Livingstone wanted an apology more
than anything else and an assurance that the present
refusal of a salary and pension would not be binding on
future administrations. Livingstone described the contents
of the Foreign Secretary's letter to a friend: 'Lord Russell
says that he intended to give me £500 a year if I settled
anywhere. My position he said was somewhat anomalous
in not being stationary.'[26] This seemed to Livingstone to
be nothing more than a macabre joke on Russell's part.
The Foreign Secretary knew that Livingstone had agreed
to search for the source of the Nile for the R.G.S. and

had received £500 for that purpose. Russell must therefore also have realized that Livingstone could not settle down without abandoning the work he had gone out to do.

Livingstone's memory of Russell's 'very cold manner' and the 'impertinence' of Mr Murray were to be major factors in his later decision not to return to England, while he still could, in 1872. He was determined never to return until he had finished his work and found the source of the Nile. Then Russell and the rest of them would be sorry for treating him so badly.

One person who treated Livingstone well in 1865 was James Young, the inventor of paraffin, whom Livingstone had first met as a student in Glasgow. Young gave Livingstone the extra £1,000 which enabled him to set out. During March, April and May 1865, when Livingstone was obsessed with money and his relations with the Government, it is hardly surprising that he neglected other important matters. He was not with his mother when she died in May, nor did he find time to have an operation for the severe piles and haemorrhoids that had plagued him on the Zambesi, causing loss of blood and constant diarrhoea. It is a sad irony that Livingstone, who had never lost an opportunity to tell others how to look after their bowels, should have failed to look after his own. The operation was not considered dangerous and yet a hatred of inactivity, coupled with a terror of possible statements in the press that he was too old and ill to return to Africa, made him decide against it. It was to prove a fatal mistake.

PART SIX

Atonement

20

Nyassa to Tanganyika, 1866–1869

Livingstone's life, as he prepared to leave England for the last time, had already been shot through with many ironies: the missionary who made but one convert who lapsed, the expedition leader who hoped to navigate a river blocked by impassable cataracts, the guide who led two missions to disaster, the father who never knew his children. But the greatest irony of all was yet to come, for in the end the image of Livingstone, which his contemporaries would retain and cherish, owed nothing to these failures. The Livingstone myth rested entirely on the last eight years of his life, and its power was such that to this day, if Livingstone has a popular image, it is of an old and saintly man wandering meekly through the wilds of central Africa, cut off from the outside world for years at a time, pursuing an almost mystical quest, in which a search for the Nile's source is somehow merged with the nobler but apparently hopeless objective of ending the slave-trade with prayer and gentle persuasion. Livingstone's isolation and ill-health, his setbacks and disappointments, his refusal to come home while life remained, and finally his lonely death, earned him more posthumous praise than he had ever known during his lifetime. For the public at large, a lifelong pilgrimage had ended in glorious martyrdom.

More recently the verdict has been suicide brought about by a fatalistic obsession with the pursuit of an unattainable visionary goal.[1] But Livingstone was neither a mystic nor a visionary;[2] his thought had always been very much of the world—commerce, trade, economics, practical, if currently impracticable, measures for breaking down tribal structures and finally introducing Christianity. Certainly he had seen, and still saw, himself as an instrument of God's Providence, but it was a providence that he interpreted in easily explicable terms—the Zambesi had been a highway for trade, the Shire Highlands a place for a British colony. When Livingstone had crossed Africa, and, later, when he had struggled on the Zambesi and the Shire, circumstances had thwarted him, but he had known precisely what he had wanted to achieve. The trouble with his last journey was that circumstances had robbed him of a definite set of aims, and old ideas did not fit the new situation he would face in east Africa.

In the past, Livingstone had always been able to suggest that he was opening the way for others, and even in the dying days of the Zambesi Expedition, when he realized that nobody would follow his lead, he had comforted himself by claiming that 'better men' would succeed where amateurs and bunglers had failed. Now that he was planning to go to the centre of Arab slaving activities, he no longer felt that he could claim that anybody ought to follow until the trade itself had been crushed. In 1865 he knew, for example, that over 20,000 slaves were exported annually from Zanzibar; this was surely the tip of an iceberg which would sink any efforts by colonists or missionaries, however determined. As Livingstone admitted to Kirk, at the end of March 1865, 'The slave trade must be suppressed as the first great step to any mission—*that* baffles every good effort.'[3]

So, now that he no longer felt able to recommend traders, missionaries or colonists to follow his lead, Livingstone had to face the fact that, unless he could really hope to defeat the slave-trade single-handed, he was returning to Africa simply as an explorer. And of course he knew that only whole-hearted and determined government action could make any impression on the east African slave-trade. So the question was whether any information he could obtain would push the Government into such action. Livingstone had always been an incurable optimist, but on this subject he saw no reason to be hopeful.

British Government thinking on the slave-trade in Africa was founded on a dogmatic distinction between the west and east coast trades. The west coast slave-trade, so ran the official argument, had been a special case of moral obligation, an atonement for the guilt of heavy British involvement, but the east coast trade had always been an Arab, and never a British, affair. There was therefore no similar moral obligation for any British government to take upon themselves sole responsibility for east African anti-slavery measures. Nor had the Government any

desire to alter the *status quo* in east Africa. They had an
excellent relationship with the Sultan of Zanzibar and felt
that France or Germany would be the only beneficiaries if
this friendship was ended as a result of Britain leaning too
hard on the Sultan. In fact, the Government argued, the
slave-trade in east Africa had already been limited by
treaties with the Sultan. In 1845 one had been signed
restricting all movement of slaves to the area within the
Sultan's east African possessions. And this, in theory if not
in fact, had stopped the export of slaves to Saudi Arabia
and the Persian Gulf. In 1864 a further treaty had banned
the movement of all slaves by water during certain
months of the year. The fact that thousands slipped
through the blockading net was known to the Government,
but they were still not prepared to act. This being the
case, Livingstone realized that it was most unlikely that
any new information on the slave-trade, relayed by him to
the Foreign Office, would have any effect on government
policy.

It is only against this background that the apparent
indecisiveness of Livingstone's plans and motives on his
last journey can be understood. Believing, as he did, that
colonization alone could bring about conditions in Africa
suitable for the spread of Christianity, and knowing that
colonists could not prosper till the slave-trade was suppressed, Livingstone's realization that the Government
intended no further anti-slavery moves in east Africa,
during the foreseeable future, gave him a terrible feeling
of impotence even before he left England. He wanted to
believe himself more than an explorer, but if his efforts to
bring social change, by encouraging others to act, seemed
doomed to automatic failure, he would soon be unable
to claim, even to himself, that he was anything else. Only
once this central dilemma has been appreciated can it be
seen how easy it was for him to use the search for the
Nile's source as a compensation for all other problems.
Eventually, to persuade himself that his task was not simply geographical, he would see the Nile as more than a
river, its source as more than a physical lake or spring.
His search had to be dignified as a divine mission. But in
1865 this conception of his work still lay several years in
the future. On 13 August, the day Livingstone left England for the last time, the thought of going back to Africa
was enough to lift depression. He felt the same excitement

that had driven him to the north from Kuruman twenty-
five years before. In Africa he could regain his old sense
of freedom, the knowledge hat he was going beyond other
men's line of things. This time there would be no white
companions to delay or irritate him. Alone once more
with a band of Africans, he believed that he stood on the
threshold of new achievements that would dwarf his trans-
continental journey. His feelings at this time are best
expressed by a long eulogy upon African travel:

> The mere animal pleasure of travelling in a wild
> unexplored country is very great. When on lands of a
> couple of thousand feet elevation, brisk exercise
> imparts elasticity to the muscles, fresh and healthy
> blood circulates through the brain, the mind works
> well, the eye is clear, the step is firm . . . the mind is
> made more self reliant: it becomes more confident of
> its own resources—there is greater presence of mind.
> The body is soon well-knit; the muscles of the limbs
> grow as hard as a board, and seem to have no fat;
> the countenance is bronzed, and there is no dyspepsia.
> Africa is a wonderful country for appetite . . . No one
> can truly experience the charm of repose unless he
> has undergone severe exertion.[4]

In view of the terrible suffering and disappointment that
lay ahead, this passage must rank as the most ironic Livingstone ever wrote. But, as with the best tragic irony,
here too the tragic hero was utterly unsuspecting of his
fate.

Livingstone planned to return to Africa via Bombay,
since the *Lady Nyassa* had still not been sold and he hoped
finally to dispose of her. He also wanted to re-employ the
Africans he had taken over to India at the end of the
Zambesi Expedition. It was a wise decision. Four of these
Africans would be with Livingstone eight years later when
he died. Two, Chuma and Wikatani, had been among the
slaves freed by the missionaries back in 1861. Then they
had been boys, and on his arrival in Bombay in 1864 Livingstone had found them places in the Free Church of
Scotland Mission School. The other two, Susi and Amoda,
had first been employed by Livingstone at Shupanga to fit
together the pieces of the *Lady Nyassa*. Both men were

too old to go to school and so Livingstone had found them work in the Bombay docks.[5]

In Bombay, Livingstone stayed with Sir Bartle Frere, the Governor, a determined opponent of the east African slave-trade, which he knew a great deal about, since many Anglo-Indians from Bombay traded with the Zanzibar Arabs. Frere recommended Livingstone to choose some of his party from the government-run school for freed slaves at Nassick, where the pupils were given an elementary education and were also taught music and handicrafts. Livingstone did not then know that most of the school's pupils had ambitions that went beyond acting as porters on African expeditions. So he selected eight. Frere next suggested that Livingstone take a dozen Sepoys from the Bombay Marine Battalion, with an Indian *bavildar* or corporal in charge of them. This choice of men was almost as unwise as the selection of Nassick boys. Livingstone knew nothing about Indian customs, habits or temperament. Before leaving England, Livingstone had written to the British Consul at Johanna asking him to send ten Johanna men to Zanzibar to await his arrival. Although Livingstone gave careful instructions for the selection of these men, it was another strange decision, since the natives of Johanna had the reputation of being deceitful and lazy. In view of the problems Livingstone had experienced with his European staff on the Zambesi Expedition, it is surprising that he did not take rather more trouble in selecting his African and Indian followers for his last journey.

Livingstone intended to travel with a small party of sixty men—he already had thirty-five and intended to hire twenty-five more either at Zanzibar or on landing in Africa itself. Even if he could get his full sixty, this would be a party of less than half the strength usually employed by African explorers. Speke and Burton, for example, had never travelled with less than 130. Livingstone's decision to travel with few followers was due partly to his meagre funds, but owed a lot to his absolute confidence in his ability to handle natives. He also believed that to go in 'grande array' merely aroused hostility and caused greater demands for *hongo* or dues for passage. Apart from this he was convinced that the more men taken, the more there were to fall sick, and thus the more frequent the stop-

pages. Larger parties had to take more cloth and beads to
pay for food. Nevertheless the disadvantages of travelling
with few followers outweighed the advantages. The fewer
the porters, the fewer the trade goods that could be taken,
and therefore the shorter the time till the caravan had to
return to the coast to replenish its supplies. A white man
without trade goods was virtually helpless in central
Africa, and unless he could rely on his followers to go on
carrying these precious items, without deserting, his very
life was threatened. The loss of forty porters might not be
too much of a blow for a man with over a hundred followers, but for a man with only sixty, the same loss could
prove catastrophic. This meant that unless Livingstone
could guarantee his men's loyalty, he would soon be in
serious trouble. In retrospect it seems amazing that Livingstone was not frightened to be setting out with such a
small party, containing only four men he could be sure
of. The truth is that his confidence stemmed from a false
comparison. He was still thinking of his trans-continental
journey. But then the Makololo had been with him under
orders from their chief, and they themselves had believed
that they were working not just for their leader but for
the benefit of their entire tribe. Even then, with Livingstone's unique ability with Africans, he had at times nearly
failed to keep his party together.

6. Zanzibar

In late January 1866 Livingstone was at last in Zanzibar, poised to begin his work. During the next month and a half he was to gain a far more accurate and comprehensive picture of the slave-trade and Arab slavery. For a start Livingstone could see that the Sultan, who derived £20,000 of his annual revenue from the trade, was not going to give up such privileges without forcible encouragement; nor were his most important subjects. All the main firms in Zanzibar benefited from the trade in some way or other, and at a later date Livingstone was to discover to his horror that the firm of Jairam Sewji, where he went for his trade goods, employed a man, Ludha Damji, who also acted as the Sultan's Customs Master. Thus dues from the slave-trade were often diverted into Sewji's firm.[6] The truth was that there were no caravan suppliers who did not have a vested interest in the slave-trade. Their best customers were the leaders of slave caravans. But disgusted as Livingstone was by the slave market, he could not afford to offend the Sultan, since his Arab subjects had penetrated deep into the interior, where they had established large trading posts as far away as Ujiji on the shores of Lake Tanganyika. So Livingstone politely sipped sherbet with the Sultan and listened to a brass band playing tunes suitable for a British visitor: the 'British Grenadiers' and the 'National Anthem'.[7]

One of the great puzzles about Livingstone's behaviour on his last journey would be the way he travelled with, and became friendly towards, a number of Arabs whom he knew to be slavers. There is no completely satisfactory explanation, but it is important to realize that, while he was at Zanzibar, Livingstone learned to make a distinction between Arab slavery as an institution—the possession and treatment of domestic slaves—and the process by which natives were torn from their homes and subjected to terrible suffering on their land and sea journey to Zanzibar and more distant places in the Persian Gulf and Arabia. Once the slaves arrived at their destinations, they were treated without cruelty—better in fact than many employees of British industrialists. The reason, as Livingstone could see, was that Arabs were not thoroughly dominated by the profit motive, as were for example the plantation owners in the southern states of America, where slavery coexisted with European commercial habits. Livingstone expressed this well: 'When society advances,' he wrote, 'wants multiply; and to supply these the slaves' lot becomes harder. The distance between master and man increases as the lust of gain is developed.'[8] Livingstone realized how ironic it was that Arab slavery would become far worse if Western economics were adopted by Arabs and Africans. While this realization made Livingstone less antagonistic to individual Arab slave-traders, it increased his certainty that no European 'progress' could come to Africa until total abolition had been achieved. Thus he would often express a greater hatred of *domestic* slavery than the system warranted.

In his early days in Africa, Livingstone had tried for a while to judge African customs objectively. Now, judging Arab behaviour in the same way, he could see that it was about as useful to accuse an Arab slaver of immorality as it was to accuse a British capitalist of deliberate exploitation. It is also important to recall that since the early fifties Livingstone had known that Africans co-operated with slavers. Now he saw that Europeans too, by buying pianos with ivory keys and knives with ivory handles, were bolstering up the trade. The slave and ivory trades were closely related. Since the Arabs used slaves captured in the interior to carry their ivory, and since both tusks and porters were sold at the coast, an increase in the demand for ivory meant that more slaves were needed as porters, and thus more slaves were sold for export at the coast. These considerations, when taken together, undoubtedly made Livingstone less hostile towards individual Arabs, but this cannot explain how he managed to justify to himself travelling with men who, even if they treated their slaves well at home, subjected slaves captured in the interior to horrifying hardships on the journey to the coast.

Before Livingstone left Zanzibar in March 1866, he heard that Colonel Playfair, the British Consul and Political Agent at Zanzibar, was resigning. Since Livingstone knew that Zanzibar was going to be his only lifeline with the outside world, he was keen to try and get somebody he knew appointed for the job. He had resumed reasonably friendly relations with John Kirk in England, and tried to use his influence to get Kirk appointed. He failed, but finally succeeded in getting Kirk the job of Surgeon to the British Agency in Zanzibar, a stepping-stone to the Consulship.

Livingstone sailed from Zanzibar for the mainland on 19 March. The officers of H.M.S. *Penguin* could hardly have guessed that after they lost sight of Livingstone, as he marched inland from Rovuma Bay, only one white man would see him alive again.

Livingstone began his last journey with a disastrous tactical mistake, which he could have avoided had he taken Sir Roderick Murchison's advice. Both Livingstone and Murchison believed, mistakenly as it happened, that a river flowed out of the northern end of Lake Tanganyika and ultimately joined Baker's newly discovered Lake Albert. According to this theory, Lake Tanganyika, or more probably a river flowing into the lake from the south, would provide the key to the Nile's source. Since this theory cut out Speke, Burton and Baker, Livingstone was determined to believe it. Sir Roderick however sensibly suggested that it was imperative for Livingstone to check the connection of Lakes Tanganyika and Albert before searching for sources south of Tanganyika. But Livingstone had other ideas:

> Supposing that [he told Murchison], as I almost fully believe Tanganyika goes into Baker's lake, the discovery of this would leave the matter very much as it was before. The source would have to be sought for still . . . and I should be obliged to come away back to it in order to give a feasible account of the ultimate origin of the Nile. Much more time would be required for this than by my plan of going at once to the headwaters.[9]

This decision would account for many of Livingstone's future geographical misconceptions. By 1871 when he discovered that there was no connection between Lakes Tanganyika and Albert, his health had been severely undermined and his judgment had likewise been impaired.

During the next few years Livingstone would face few travelling conditions which he had not previously experienced on his transcontinental journey or on the Zambesi Expedition, nor would he meet tribes notably different from those he had encountered in the past.

Livingstone had landed just north of the Rovuma at a small port called Mikidani. His party consisted of thirty-five men—he had not yet managed to hire any more porters—and a bizarre assortment of baggage animals: three buffaloes and a calf, six camels, four donkeys and two mules. Livingstone's reason for bringing so many different kinds of animal was that he wished to find out if any one should prove immune to the tsetse fly. The immediate aim of the party was to head due west to Lake Nyassa, cross the lake in canoes and then head north-west for a lake called Bemba or Bangweolo, which Livingstone had first heard about during his second survey of Nyassa in 1863. Since then he had become convinced that Bangweolo would prove to be the source of the Nile. What Livingstone hoped to do was reach Bangweolo, trace a river north-east out of it into Lake Tanganyika and then proceed north triumphantly to Lake Albert and the Nile. Even if Livingstone's geographical assumptions had been correct, his task would still have been a terrifyingly difficult one.

As in the past, initial false optimism accounted for much of Livingstone's misery once things started to go wrong. From the day he landed, disappointments came in quick succession. He had hoped to add another twenty or thirty porters to his party at the coast, but he was assured by all those he asked that no local tribesmen would come with him for fear of being captured in the interior and sold into slavery. This was a damaging blow and meant that he had to leave behind stores that he could ill afford to lose. The first few weeks of travel were fraught with difficulties. He had landed, it appeared, at one of the few points on the coast where there was thick jungle. This had to be hacked through with axes, and the size of the camels meant that a much wider path had to be cut. The air seemed heavy and smothering and the constant work with the axes soon began to sap the morale of his polyglot following.

Ten days after leaving the coast he noticed that his sepoys were maltreating the baggage animals. Yet, although several animals had been overloaded so cruelly that they often stumbled and fell, Livingstone did not assert his authority firmly on this crucial first occasion. He noted in his journal: 'They assure me with so much positiveness that they are not overloaded, that I have to be silent, or only, as I have done several times before, express the opinion that they will kill these animals.'[10]

The matter was far more serious than the simple fact

Map 4

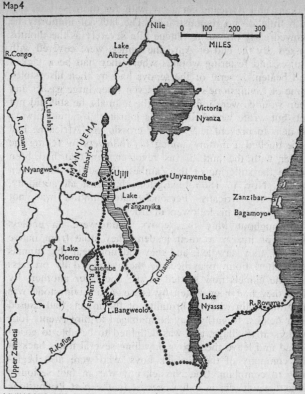

LIVINGSTONE'S LAST JOURNEYS Routes: March 1866–March 1869 •••••
July 1869–October 1871 ▪▪▪▪ November 1871–February 1872 ••••
August 1872–April 1873 ▬▬▬
(Livingstone's death occurred some distance S.S.E. of Lake Bangweolo)

of cruelty. If the animals died from maltreatment, the
experiment to judge their resistance to tsetse would be
vitiated; worse still, since the party was short of porters,
if the animals were lost more stores might have to be
abandoned. Overloading the camels and mules was therefore sabotage, but Livingstone had reacted with a mild
rebuke. It seems barely credible that this was the same
man who had disciplined Baines and Bedingfeld so severely
seven years before. Yet whereas he had always been prepared to blame Europeans on the slightest pretext, he let

Indians and Africans get away with far more serious sins with little or no remonstrance. The lack of authority he showed early on was to plague him severely as the months passed. By the end of April the camels were covered with bruises and festering wounds where they had been kicked and beaten. Several of the sepoys had by then also stolen some of Livingstone's clothing. Even when large gashes and deep wounds were inflicted on the animals, he still did not act, but wrote wretchedly in his journal: 'I cannot always be near to prevent it.'[11] On his crossing of Africa he had once quelled a mutiny among his followers by felling the leader with the butt of his revolver, but that had been before the suffering of the Zambesi Expedition had taken its toll. Now in 1866 Livingstone had lost all authority, even over Africans. Personal determination was not enough to keep his followers in order.

Throughout May the sepoys again were an endless source of misery to their leader. They stole from native villages, they dawdled, and they did not treat the animals any better. Four miles became the average daily progress and the camels now started to die one after another. By then they had been bitten by tsetse, and Livingstone was now uncertain whether brutality or the insects had caused their deaths. In early May he managed to hire twenty-four porters at a village, and was delighted to be able to go on ahead and leave the sepoys dawdling several miles back in the company of the Nassick boys, who were also beginning to complain. One Nassick boy was in fact seriously ill and would die in a few weeks. In the past Livingstone had always had difficulty in telling when illness was feigned or genuine. Not surprisingly a man who was dangerously ill resented being told he was shirking, and this lack of discernment was to prove yet another cause for ill-will.

Two hundred miles inland there was a great shortage of food, due in part to a severe drought, but made worse by Ngoni raids. Many people were starving and Livingstone could not help remembering the gruesome days in 1863 when the Zambesi Expedition was dragging to a close. Hunger made the men still more mutinous and in early June the twenty-four porters refused to go on. In order to save his party from starvation, Livingstone had to make a series of forced marches to get out of this famine-stricken country. At this time he wrote a reassuring letter to Agnes: 'I am very well but have lost some of that beastly fatness that threatened to swallow me up.'[12] He might have lost his authority over his men but he had not lost his powers of understatement.

On 2 June the Nassick boys and the sepoys offered money and cloth to the party's Somali guide, Ben Ali, to misdirect them all so that they could get back to the coast. Livingstone heard of the conspiracy but did nothing; until at last, on 4 June, he had to issue a long overdue ultimatum to the Nassick boys: either work or return to the coast. The incident that forced Livingstone to this step had been the adoption by the mission boys of a habit learned from the sepoys: the engaging of local natives to carry their loads for them on the understanding that the white man would pay for it all.

The problem of getting food was still serious, when Livingstone began to see the first signs of Arab penetration. Many people had guns; and occasionally piles of slave-taming sticks could be seen on either side of the path. The knowledge that he was entering a slaving country did something to revive the Doctor's firmness, and the next sepoy insurrection was met with a promise to flog any future offender. He kept his word and the next Indian to delay the party was given 'some smart cuts with a cane'. Livingstone always hated corporal punishment and noted in his journal: 'I felt that I was degrading myself, and resolved not to do the punishment myself again.'[13] Considering the disciplinary excesses of which almost every other explorer was guilty, Livingstone's forbearance was almost miraculous. Although he was almost certain that the sepoys were bent on turning both the Nassick boys and the Johanna men against him, he could still write patiently: 'I shall try to feel as charitably as I can in spite of it all, for the mind has a strong tendency to brood over the ills of travel.'[14]

During the period when internal tensions within the party were at their most acute, Livingstone saw evidence of far greater inhumanity than he had ever witnessed in the Shire Highlands. On 19 June he wrote: 'We passed a woman tied by the neck to a tree and dead, the people of the country explained that she had been unable to keep up with the other slaves in a gang, and her master had determined that she should not become the property of anybody else if she recovered after resting for a time.'[15]

7. Slaves abandoned

Other groups of corpses were found with remorseless regularity. Some had been stabbed to death, others shot and many had simply been left tied together to die slowly of starvation. Over and over again Livingstone was told that the Arabs often grew so enraged with slaves who became too weak to walk that they murdered them out of rage because their investment had not come up to expectation. When slaves were left alive, the local people often came and rescued them, fed them up and then sold them again. In fact it could be a profitable business to follow a slave caravan in the hope of taking over the rejects. Livingstone deduced this at a very early stage from the number of taming sticks he saw on the path, without bodies near them. His knowledge that Africans were as much responsible for the system as the Arabs had always horrified him. He spent many hours explaining to chiefs that 'if they sell their fellows, they are like the man who holds the victim while the Arab performs the murder'.[16] Livingstone pointed out repeatedly that they were under no compulsion to sell their people to a handful of alien intruders. He made little impression. The answers he got were predictable enough: ' "If so and so gives up selling so will we. He is the greatest offender in the country." "It is the fault of the Arabs who tempt us with fine clothes, powder and guns." "I would fain keep all my people to cultivate more land, but my next neighbour allows his people to kidnap mine and I must have ammunition to defend them." '[17]

Sickened though he was by African indifference to the

fate of people, often even of the same tribe, Livingstone did not for a moment turn against them. In 1851 he had discovered that the Makololo sold slaves to the Mambari, but he had gone on defending them long afterwards.

In June and July 1866 he might have tried to send out sensational reports to the coast of what he had seen, but he did not. Instead he wrote two cool and lucid despatches to the Foreign Secretary, setting out his arguments why the British restriction treaties, which legalized slavery within specified limits, could never work. When evasion of the blockade was so regular, he asked how the Foreign Office and Admiralty could countenance such vast expenditure to so little effect. He argued that the prohibition of all slave movements by sea would not create anarchy in Zanzibar, because slavery on the island need not be abolished as an institution. Once the supply was cut it would die slowly and peacefully. Domestic slavery was mild; only the export of slaves had to be ended. He had often heard the official government view expressed that if all sea-going movement of slaves was stopped to and from Zanzibar, many more markets would spring up on the coast, and thus the destruction of one big slave market would only produce a crop of little ones far more difficult to control. Livingstone's reply was simple. Slaves were only contained in Zanzibar because it was an island and they could not therefore run away. Any huge slaving emporium on the mainland would be untenable because it would be impossible to contain the slaves. Finally he made a number of suggestions about building depots for freed slaves along the coast, so that ships in the blockading squadron would not have to return to a distant port every time a slaving dhow was captured. He also suggested that it was imperative for British warships to be in Zanzibar harbour when the prevailing winds allowed the northern Arabs to come south.[18] Livingstone's proposals were workable and sound. When the slave market in Zanzibar was closed in June 1873, a month after his death, there was no anarchy in Zanzibar and no attempt was made by the coastal Arabs to set up large coastal markets. There is something enormously impressive about these despatches and the completely unemotional and logical way in which he martialled his facts at the very time when he was personally so deeply involved in the far from abstract misery of the slaves themselves. Livingstone had decided to tackle the

Foreign Office in their own impersonal terms. There is little overt anger, even against the Arabs, although at the time he was finding it very nearly impossible to buy food in exchange for cloth, since the Arabs had all but saturated the market.

By early July, Livingstone was within a hundred miles of Lake Nyassa and was leaving behind the famine-stricken, depopulated country. Now, instead of travelling across dried-up country with burned grass and stunted trees and shrubs, he was entering green undulating hills. The new country, although more pleasing to the eye, was not easy to cross. His weary followers found themselves endlessly climbing up to the tops of steep ridges and then descending to valleys with streams running down the middle. On one day they clambered into and out of fifteen such valleys.

Livingstone knew that his route into the interior was for much of the way identical with the southern Arab slave route from Lake Nyassa to the port of Kilwa on the coast. He had very much hoped to meet slave caravans returning from the interior, so that he could get an idea of their size, the areas the slaves had come from, the amount of ivory carried and any other information that might prove suitable for sending back to the Foreign Office. The Arabs, however, usually heard that he was approaching and took their caravan off in another direction for a day or two. The Arabs were certainly not frightened of a man with a small following, but since they knew from contacts at the coast that Livingstone was British, they had no desire to meet him. Although the Sultan of Zanzibar knew the advantages of British protection—he had twice been saved by the intervention of the Royal Navy, from *coups d'état* planned by his relatives—his subjects resented the existing British anti-slavery treaties. Most caravan leaders, as soon as they heard that Livingstone was British, felt convinced that he had come as a spy of the British Government. Nevertheless the fact that the Sultan valued British friendship ensured that none of his subjects, however distant, were likely to murder Livingstone. He was, after all, a potential nuisance rather than a serious threat.

On 14 July Livingstone came upon the first caravan that had not taken deliberate evasion action. The leader was an Arab called Seph Rubea, who, on hearing that Livingstone was short of food, had actually made a detour to

meet him and, as Livingstone put it, 'came forward like a
man and brother with an ox and big bag of flour'.[19] After
seeing the corpses of so many murdered slaves, it might
be thought that Livingstone would have refused the gift,
however altruistic the motives of the donor, but the hungry traveller took what was offered gratefully. He managed
to square his conscience easily enough; if he starved, he
would not be able to report on the slave-trade and these
reports were his only hope of getting the system stopped.
Besides, if he offended the Arabs by rejecting their hospitality, he would never be able to elicit information from
them. If the Arab slavers helped him it was because God
was making them the agents of their own ultimate destruction. Even so, Livingstone realized the ambiguity of his
position, and later, when he actually travelled with Arabs,
he would find it necessary to make a distinction between
the southern slave-traders on the Nyassa-Kilwa route and
the northern traders operating directly from Zanzibar in
the Lake Tanganyika region. 'If one wanted to see the
slave trade in its best phases,' he wrote the following year,
'he would accompany the gentlemen subjects of the Sultan
of Zanzibar. If he wished to describe its worst form he
would go with the Kilwa traders.'[20] It was true that in
general the Kilwa traders were worse, largely because
the Sultan of Zanzibar had less influence over them than
he did over traders operating from Zanzibar itself. Nevertheless it must have occurred to Livingstone that no Arab
was likely to murder slaves in front of him.

Yet, for a Kilwa trader, Livingstone thought Seph Rubea
to be an excellent man, and managed to learn a great deal
from him: namely that most of the slaves taken across
Nyassa came from the area south-west of Lake Tanganyika where Livingstone hoped to find the Nile source. Seph
also told Livingstone something that impressed him
greatly: one hundred Arabs had died on the Kilwa route
during the past year. Maybe, Livingstone reflected, similar
European sacrifices might be necessary before philanthropists managed to get the trade stopped. Since Seph seemed
friendly, Livingstone handed him the letters he had recently
written, including his despatches to the Foreign Office,
and asked him to see that they reached Zanzibar. Seph
kept his word.

A few days later, the sepoys, in line with their previous
behaviour, killed and ate the buffalo calf and then con-

cocted a story about it being eaten by a tiger. Livingstone asked whether they had seen the tiger's stripes. They eagerly assented. Since there are no striped tigers in Africa, Livingstone was unimpressed. The following day a sepoy threatened to shoot a Nassick boy and another stole a large number of cartridges and some cloth from the stores. At last Livingstone had come to the end of his patience, and he discharged them. They were given eighteen yards of cloth and left at a village to wait for the next caravan to the coast. The *bavildar* begged to be allowed to stay on, and Livingstone reluctantly agreed. He deserted some weeks later.

At the beginning of August, Livingstone's party—now reduced to twenty-three—started to climb into the tall mountains that flank Nyassa. On 6 August he could see the blue water of the lake, ten or so miles away. Two days later he was on the shore itself. 'The roar of the waves and a dash in the breakers was quite exhilarating.'[21] Less exhilarating was the failure of all his efforts to get a dhow to take him across the lake, so that he could head straight for Lake Bangweolo without having to skirt Nyassa to the north or south. But all the Arabs were convinced that if he got hold of a boat he would burn it on the other side. In vain he showed them a letter of commendation from the Sultan of Zanzibar. Unfortunately nobody was able to read it, or that was what they said. In fact these Arabs on the Lake knew more about Livingstone than those at the coast. Rumour of his freeing slaves in the Shire Highlands had long since reached them.

Unable to cross the lake, Livingstone rejected the shorter route round it to the north because it was rumoured that the Mazitu or Ngoni were ravaging the area. Instead he chose to go south and cross at the most southern point of the lake, where the Shire ran out from it. He reached the Shire in mid-September and it brought back bitter memories of past failure. 'Many hopes have been disappointed here,' he wrote. 'Far down on the right bank of the Zambesi lies the dust of her whose death changed all my future prospects; and now, instead of a check being given to the slave trade by lawful commerce on the Lake, slave dhows prosper.'[22]

At this time, one of the boys who had been with Livingstone since 1863 decided to rejoin his family in the Shire Highlands. Wikatani had been one of Mackenzie's favourites and had been rescued by Livingstone from the Ajawa. His loss was a sentimental rather than a practical blow. Although Amoda, Susi and Chuma would one day be the backbone of Livingstone's following, in 1866 they, like Wikatani, were still too young and unreliable to be much use. Already he had had to stop employing them as his personal servants because all his spoons and forks had been mislaid and he always had to repeat everything he told them, and rarely got breakfast when he asked for it. But he was still fonder of them than of any of the others, and, although all were inclined to sing and giggle more than he liked, Chuma was learning to read and began to show other hopeful signs that he would soon be useful.

A few days after Wikatani left the party, the Johanna men made up their minds to do the same. The reason they gave for refusing to go on was the news they received from an Arab that the country ahead was being pillaged by the Mazitu. The leader of the Johanna men, Musa, had been a constant trouble-maker aboard the *Lady Nyassa*. Even when Livingstone forced him to listen to a local chief, Musa would not accept that the Arabs had exaggerated the severity of the Mazitu raids to stop Livingstone's party going on. Musa would have none of it and remained determined to go. Although the sepoys had been without doubt the worse bane to date, and the Nassick boys a close second, the Johanna men had not been much better. They had stolen repeatedly from their loads and had recently started to dawdle. To do them justice, there were persistent rumours at the time that the Mazitu were in the neighbourhood, and while Livingstone knew why he was risking his neck, it is extremely unlikely that the Johanna men understood the purpose of either the fight against slavery or the search for the source of the Nile. As Musa said, 'I want to see my father, my mother, my child at Johanna. I no want to be killed by Mazitu'.[23] Short of threatening to shoot Musa if he deserted, there was nothing Livingstone could do to retain the ten Johanna men. In the end he had to accept their desertion, although he knew that it made his party dangerously small—eleven men in all.

Incredibly, although Livingstone faced a host of terrible problems, due to the loss of so many porters, he was still able to write serene passages of natural description.

The morning was lovely, the whole country bathed in bright sunlight, and not a breath of air disturbed the smoke as it slowly curled up from the burning weeds . . . The people were generally busy hoeing in the cool of the day. One old man was carefully paring a stick for stirring the porridge, and others were enjoying the cool shade of the wild fig trees . . . I like to see the men weaving or spinning, or reclining under these glorious canopies, as much as I love to see our more civilised people lolling on their sofas or ottomans.[24]

This passage evokes all the pleasure he had felt in his early travels and is the more poignant since the same day a series of thunder storms shattered the rural calm and turned paradise into a muddy hell, where paths disappeared under water and small streams became rivers. The rains would last for two months. Soon the old problem of food shortage was added to the 'excessively adhesive mud' and the waterlogged paths. Because of the Mazitu raids, people were frightened of Livingstone and his small party and were therefore even less willing to part with any precious food. Agriculture had been neglected due to the raids and in many places the villagers were living on wild fruits. The air was muggy and the clouds too thick for any accurate observations to be made.

On 6 December the only entry in Livingstone's journal was: 'Too ill to march.' The night before, the whole party had been badly wetted by a storm and had slept in soaking clothes. Bad health was now to be a recurrent problem. December passed miserably. The only food to be got was the indigestible native porridge that brought back Livingstone's old enemy, dysentery. He managed to buy four goats, but on Christmas Day they were stolen. Nevertheless he pressed on north-wèst and by the end of the year had crossed the Loangwa river, midway between Bangweolo and Nyassa.

On New Year's Eve he wrote: 'We now end 1866. It has not been so fruitful or useful as I intended. Will try to do better in 1867, and be better—more gentle and loving; and may the Almighty, to whom I commit my way, bring my desires to pass, and prosper me! Let all the sins of '66 be blotted out for Jesus' sake.'[25]

On 6 January the first serious mishap of the year occurred. They were clambering down the steep slopes of a ravine and the path was so slippery that two of the porters fell; one of these men was carrying the precious chronometers, without which no accurate longitudes could be taken. Livingstone, understanding as usual, wrote: 'This was a misfortune, as it altered the rates, as was seen by the first comparison of them together this-evening.'[26] Because the weather was so bad, and the clouds very rarely lifted, it was doubly important that the few longitudes he was able to take should be accurate. Unfortunately for the next eighteen months they would all be some twenty miles to the eastward in error, undoubtedly due to the damage to the chronometers.[27] These mistakes did not have any immediate effect, but errors of this nature usually built up, and could, over a long period of time, dangerously mislead the traveller who relied on his observations being accurate. Two weeks after this incident, the man carrying the party's medicine chest deserted. Livingstone thought this a far worse disaster than the damage to the chronometers; in fact he called it 'the sentence of death'. He was wrong; the real death sentence came when he returned to this same general area six years later, and relied on his previous observations to guide him.

In the short term, however, the loss of the medicines was a devastating blow. Precisely at the time when everybody's health was deteriorating, the drugs, which alone could check malaria and dysentery, had gone. In similar circumstances many travellers would have abandoned their immediate work and returned to the coast to get more quinine. But Livingstone would not even retrace his steps to Nyassa and the southern trade route to send to Kilwa for more medicines. He may have felt that he could not rely on the Arabs to transmit the message and then return with the drugs, but more likely he could not face the prospect of retracing his steps even for a mile. The thousand miles he had now travelled since leaving the coast had already taken him months more than he had expected. To struggle back for many days through the mud and the rain, feeling faint with hunger all the time, was psychologically out of the question. Soon Livingstone hoped to reach Lake Bangweolo, where he was certain he would find a large river flowing north to Lake Tanganyika. He would go on.

But the nearer they got to where Livingstone supposed Bangweolo to be, the harder the going became. The country was now an enormous swamp. On the evening of 16 January 1867 Livingstone recorded a typical day's march: 'The rain as usual made us halt early . . . We roast a little grain and boil it, to make believe it is coffee . . . Ground all sloppy; oozes full and overflowing—feet constantly wet. Rivulets rush strongly with clear water . . . Rivulets can only be crossed by felling a tree on the bank and letting it fall across . . . Nothing but famine and famine prices, the people living on mushrooms and leaves. We get some elephants' meat from the people, but high is no name for its condition. It is very bitter, but it prevents the heartburn.'[28]

In mid-January, Chitane, a little poodle Livingstone had bought in Zanzibar, was drowned. He had developed the greatest admiration for his dog and had often praised him for chasing off much larger curs in the villages they passed through. When all else had failed, Chitane had raised Livingstone's spirits by rushing tirelessly up and down the straggling line of porters. Fording a mile-wide marsh, waist-deep, nobody had noticed the little dog vainly struggling to keep up. In the weeks to come Livingstone often thought about his dead pet.

At the end of January, Livingstone crossed the Chambesi river, but did not realize that it flowed south-west into Lake Bangweolo. He had not been able to establish the precise position of the lake, and now, pressing on north, he had passed fifty miles to the east of it. By the time Livingstone realized his mistake a few weeks later, the lake lay one hundred miles to the south-west. Instead of retracing his steps, Livingstone made up his mind to continue his northward march, in the hope of finding the point where the river, which he assumed flowed north from Bangweolo, entered Lake Tanganyika. Livingstone would not now reach Bangweolo till July 1868, over a year later. Apart from the flooded state of the country, there was another reason why Livingstone decided not to retrace his steps to Bangweolo: by now he was seriously ill with what he suspected was rheumatic fever: 'Every step I take jars in the chest, and I am very weak; I can scarcely keep up the march, though formerly I was always first . . . I have a constant singing in my ears, and can scarcely hear the loud tick of the chronometer.'[29]

February 3rd brought the first gleam of hope he had known for months. He met a party of Arabs who were going to Bagamoyo on the mainland opposite Zanzibar. At last here was a chance to get letters to the outside world. Although he was not certain that the Arabs could be trusted, his packet did reach Zanzibar; one letter was to the Consul, Mr Seward. Livingstone asked for goods to be sent to Ujiji on Lake Tanganyika, where he hoped to be within a couple of months. Among other things he wanted coffee, candles, soap, sealing-wax, preserved meat, six bottles of port wine and, of course, medicines. He described his almost constantly gnawing hunger and ended: 'Don't think, please, that I make a moan over nothing but a little sharpness of appetite. I am a mere ruckle of bones, did all the hunting myself, and wet, hunger, and fatigue took away the flesh.'[30] Livingstone could of course have painted a far grimmer picture. He could hardly travel at all at this time, and although in early February he was only 150 miles from the southern end of Lake Tanganyika, he did not reach it till 1 April.

Once at Tanganyika, Livingstone was eager to head north, along the western shore of the lake, where he was convinced there would be an inlet. He was preparing to set out when he heard that war had broken out north and west of his position, between local tribes and several large parties of Arab traders. There was nothing else Livingstone could do but head south again, in the hope that he would soon be able to make a looping detour round the trouble spot. But he did not get far, for soon he was laid out by the worst attack of fever he could ever remember. It came suddenly: 'I found myself floundering outside my hut and unable to get in; I tried to lift myself from my back by laying hold of two posts at the entrance, but when I got nearly upright I let them go, and fell back heavily on my head on a box . . . some hours elapsed before I could recognise where I was.'[31]

Chuma and Susi, who by now had become devoted to Livingstone, hung a blanket across the door of the hut so that no inquisitive strangers could see his helplessness. His condition was extremely precarious for a full month, so bad that he was unable to make a single entry for April in his journal. Just before he fell ill, Livingstone had heard of a large lake, a hundred miles to the west, called Lake Moero, which he felt certain must be linked in some way with Lake Bangweolo. Now that he could no longer entertain the idea of finding an inlet on the western side of Tanganyika, Livingstone's new plan was to reach Lake Moero as soon as possible. But until he had found out more about the extent of the fighting between the Arabs and the local tribes, he did not feel able, with his tiny following, to risk travelling far to the west. Instead, as soon as he was strong enough, he set out south for the nearest Arab settlement, where he hoped to discover how serious the war was.

Livingstone joined the Arabs on 20 May and remained with them till August, waiting for the war to end. Although he was keen to get to Moero, he was happy to convalesce for a couple of months, with his well-supplied hosts, who raised no objection to his presence. It is worth noting that during July there was an earth tremor, which played further havoc with Livingstone's chronometers. The first accident to these instruments had made his observation for longitude twenty miles too far to the east. Now, after the tremor, when he reset them, a further error crept in, and from this time his longitudes erred in the opposite direction, being fifty miles out to the west. Now Livingstone would have seventy miles more of space on his map than was in fact there.[32] If the maps he had previously drawn were inaccurate, those he would shortly make would be far worse.

With peace finally agreed by the Arabs and their native adversaries, in mid-September Livingstone was at last able to set out for Lake Moero. Since a party of Arabs was going in that direction, he decided to take advantage of their supplies by travelling with them. The leader of this particular caravan was Tippu Tip, an ivory and slave trader, who would soon establish political and commercial control of the whole area through which they were now passing on their journey west from the southern end of Lake Tanganyika. Progress was very slow because Tippu was always stopping to make enquiries about ivory. The hundred miles to Lake Moero took well over a month. Livingstone stood on the banks of the Lake on 8 November.

Livingstone was not particularly elated after his 'discovery'. He knew that the Portuguese explorer Francisco José de Lacerda had died just south of Moero in 1799, and that since then three other Portuguese expeditions had reached the area from Tete. Livingstone's only real interest in Moero—itself a mere puddle by African standards, being seventy miles long and twenty wide—was its relationship to Lakes Bangweolo and Tanganyika.

Within a few days, with the help of native reports, Livingstone had made some important and entirely accurate deductions about the lake. He was convinced that a large river, the Lualaba, flowed out from the north-western corner of Lake Moero in a northerly direction. He also concluded that, to the south, Moero was linked with Lake Bangweolo by another river, the Luapula. Thus the ultimate source of the Lualaba, which was a colossal river, lay 150 miles south in Lake Bangweolo. All this information was correct, but Livingstone rather surprisingly did not immediately claim in letters or despatches that the Lualaba was the Nile and Bangweolo its source. When he did so the following April (1868) he was not in possession of very much more knowledge; in the meantime he had only verified that the river Luapula did indeed connect Lakes Moero and Bangweolo. From the moment Livingstone first heard about the Lualaba, he knew that his major task would be to find out where it went. Believing secretly, as he did, even in November 1867, that it was the Nile, he would now have to sort out whether the Lualaba continued its northern journey from Moero into Tanganyika, and then, through that lake and via a river at its northern end, to Lake Albert, or whether instead it joined Albert direct without touching Lake Tanganyika.

At the end of 1867 Livingstone was aware that there were two important tasks ahead of him. The first was to go south to Lake Bangweolo to verify that it was, as the natives claimed, the most southerly source of the Lualaba. The second was to follow the Lualaba north from Lake Bangweolo as far as it might be necessary to prove that it was the Nile. But unfortunately matters were not quite so simple. Livingstone's supplies were dangerously low, he had only nine followers left and he could not hope to take on more until he could promise payment with trade goods. As it was, he had insufficient cloth to buy food for the few men with him. He also needed medicines. Before leaving Zanzibar in 1866, Livingstone had wisely made arrangements for supplies to be sent to the Arab town of Ujiji, on the eastern side of Lake Tanganyika, for him to collect at a later date.

In December 1867, Livingstone could certainly not risk setting out on a long journey northwards down the Lualaba, until he had first picked up his stores from Ujiji, 250 miles north-east of Lake Moero. So much was clear. It still remained for Livingstone to make up his mind whether he should travel the 150 miles south to Bangweolo and 'discover' the Lualaba's source, before making his long detour to Ujiji. In the end Livingstone made no real decision, but came to the stop-gap conclusion that, in view of his low supplies, he ought to stay with Tippu Tip and his party for as long as possible. Tippu planned to go twenty miles south to the town of Chief Casembe, the principal trading centre of the area; after that, the Arab assured Livingstone, he would head back for Ujiji and, when he did, Livingstone would be welcome to come with him. Livingstone intended to defer a final decision about his intentions until he reached Casembe. There he meant to decide once and for all whether he would return north with Tippu or go on south to Lake Bangweolo. Livingstone wasted a month at Casembe and then discovered that Tippu was going on west to Katanga and not back to Ujiji. After yet another bout of indecision Livingstone decided to abandon Bangweolo for the time being and to head north with an Arab called Muhammad bin Salim, who intended to go straight to Ujiji. Unfortunately, by the time Salim and Livingstone left Casembe the winter rains had set in, and by the end of March 1868, after three months' travelling, the two men and their followers had only progressed fifty miles north of Casembe. Ahead of them the rains had turned the entire region between the point they had reached and Lake Tanganyika into an enormous and impassable swamp. Livingstone's failure to act positively after reaching Lake Moero had cost him five months. Now it appeared that his only course was to find a village and sit out the rains with Salim for another two months. Livingstone estimated that, as things were, he would not reach Ujiji before June and would therefore be unable to get back to the Lualaba until October or November; since he had only counted on being away from England for two years in all, and had already been in Africa a year and eleven months, this was an extremely depressing time.

Right through the losses, delays and desertions of 1866 and 1867, Livingstone had displayed a patience and tolerance which, if told about, any member of the Zambesi Expedition would have considered too unlikely to be credi-

ble. But although Livingstone's character had softened a
great deal in the past three or four years, the despair he
felt during the first three months of 1868 brought back
many old traits. Fearing that both time and money were
running out, Livingstone wrote bitterly to Sir Roderick
Murchison, attacking the Government for meanness and
dishonesty. He went over his treatment by Russell in
minute detail, telling Murchison that the 'impudent letter'
from the Foreign Office still 'gnaws at my heart on every
touch of illness or despondency'. Earlier grievances were
aired again and Livingstone argued that Prince Albert and
his cousin, the Portuguese King, had worked together to
destroy the Zambesi Expedition. Once Livingstone had
started pouring out a stream of bitterness, he could not
stop, and now he went on to attack the Council of the
Royal Geographical Society as well. They had given him
a pittance, he claimed, and afterwards expected all his
notes. This was just a plot to cheat him out of making
money from any book on his return. He reserved his most
biting criticism for the cartographer, John Arrowsmith,
and the Society's secretary, Francis Galton, who had both
instructed him to make regular observations. In view of
the dense cloud conditions Livingstone had faced during
the past few months, these orders seemed like a very bad
joke. 'Put Arrowsmith & Galton into a hogshead,' Livingstone told Murchison, 'and ask them to take bearings out
of the bunghole. I came for discovery and not for survey,
and if I don't give a clear account of the countries traversed, I shall return the money.'[33]

At precisely the time when Livingstone appeared to be
hopelessly lost in past grievances and quarrels, he suddenly
cast aside all previous indecision and told the astonished
Salim that he would not wait for the rains to stop but
would head south at once for Lake Bangweolo and return
north to Ujiji only when he had made sure of the Lualaba's source. With the country inundated, and food almost
impossible to obtain, this was a decision brave to the point
of foolhardiness.

On 13 April Livingstone told his nine followers to prepare to march. Salim argued with Livingstone and told
him that to attempt the 200-mile journey south before the
end of the rains would kill him and all his men. Livingstone
was unmoved by this warning and did not change his
mind when five of his followers refused to come with him.

The party of thirty-five was now finally reduced to four. When Livingstone had set out, Salim sent a messenger after him to make one last attempt to dissuade him from such a suicidal venture. Livingstone told this man 'to say to Mohamad [Salim] that I would on no account go to Ujiji, till I had done all in my power to reach the Lake I sought'.

And now the man who had written so bitterly to Murchison, such a short time before, forgave the five deserters completely. 'I did not blame them very severely in my own mind for absconding; they were tired of tramping, and so verily am I . . . Consciousness of my own defects makes me lenient.'[34]

During the previous year, Livingstone had felt unsafe to leave the shelter of Arab caravans. Then he had been able to count on nearly a dozen followers; now, with only four men, a few fathoms of cloth and no medicines, he was prepared to risk travelling two hundred miles through waterlogged country, in the worst of the rains, to an area said to be particularly unhealthy at this time of year. A little while before, he had written, 'It is needless to hide that I never travelled with less spirit.'[35] His recovery was little short of superhuman.

In the month that it took Livingstone and his four men to retrace their steps to Casembe's, *en route* for Bangweolo, they were often up to their waists in water for stretches up to four hours at a time; and, even when the water was shallower, 'black tenacious mud' clung to their feet, making walking a terrible effort. Unexpected areas of soft mud could unexpectedly plunge them up to their armpits in slime. Each step was usually followed 'by a rush of bubbles on the surface, which, bursting, discharged foul air of frightful faecal odour'.[36] Apart from midges and mosquitoes, they had to contend with leeches, which 'needed no coaxing to bite, but flew at the skin like furies'; with hands and fingers numbed by the water, these parasites were extremely hard to pull off.

But in spite of such dreadful conditions, Livingstone and his followers reached Casembe's after twenty-seven days' travelling. They had done well to average two miles a day. Livingstone left Casembe's and headed south on 11 June. This time he went with Muhammad Bogharib, an Arab trader, going to the Bangweolo district in search of ivory and copper. In spite of the fact that Bogharib also dealt in slaves, Livingstone soon grew to like him and during the next year grew so attached to him that later he would regret not having a photograph of the Arab as a memento. Bogharib proved more than a friend, for he shared his own food with Livingstone and personally nursed him when he was sick. As with all Livingstone's friendships with Arabs, it is hard to establish whether hypocrisy or a remarkably clear-sighted understanding of an alien culture played the most important part. Whatever the truth, Livingstone clearly made a distinction between the Arabs' acceptance of the slave-trade as a legitimate and normal form of commerce and their personalities as men. Nor did Livingstone feel uneasy about this, for he often praised Bogharib in letters, even when they were addressed to the Foreign Secretary.

By the beginning of July, Livingstone and Bogharib were within thirty miles of Lake Bangweolo, and native reports had soon absolutely confirmed Livingstone's opinion, formed seven months before at Lake Moero, that Bangweolo was the source of the Lualaba. Now that he knew that he would be at the Lualaba's source within a few days, Livingstone decided that, before that historic moment, he should abandon his secrecy and tell the world that the Lualaba was the Nile. Of course Livingstone could not communicate with the coast unless he happened to encounter a caravan bound for Kilwa or Zanzibar, but this did not stop him writing letters and despatches to be ready for sending when an opportunity occurred. Although Livingstone had not followed the Lualaba north, his assumption that it was the Nile was not as rash as later events made it appear. His confidence would have surprised no geographer possessed of the same information, at the same date.

Livingstone had located a very large river, flowing due north out of Lake Moero. Clearly this river's direction and size made it certain that it would enter the sea several thousand miles away. Even by the end of the sixteenth century the whole African coastline had been mapped with tolerable accuracy, and by 1868 Livingstone had no difficulty at all in concluding that, apart from the Nile, only one other African river could account for the Lualaba: the Congo. Livingstone felt able to reject the idea of it being the Congo on several counts. For a start the two hundred miles of the Congo, which had been navigated from the Atlantic, had taken explorers not east, nor southeast, but *north*-east; so unless the Congo completely changed direction and described an enormous south-easterly loop,* it could have no possible connection with the Lualaba. Another simple fact, which Livingstone thought was evidence against the Congo being the Lualaba, was that Lake Moero was 1,100 miles from the west coast and only 700 from the east. In 1868 the Congo was not known to extend further east than a couple of hundred miles, at which point it was flowing *north*-east, a direction which made any connection with Lakes Bangweolo and Moero—both over a thousand miles to the *south*-east—seem extremely unlikely.

On 8 July, still a few miles short of Bangweolo, Livingstone began a despatch, which he was certain would be the most important he had ever written. It was addressed to the Foreign Secretary, Lord Clarendon.†

> I may safely assert [wrote an elated Livingstone] that the chief sources of the Nile, arise between 10° and 12° south latitude, or nearly in the position assigned to them by Ptolemy . . . If your Lordship will read the following short sketch of my discoveries, you will perceive that the springs of the Nile have hitherto been searched for very much too far to the north. They rise some 400 miles south of the most southerly portion of the Victoria Nyanza, and, indeed south of all the lakes except Bangweolo.[37]

In a letter to Kirk, written the same day, Livingstone gave him the same information about the Lualaba being the Nile and then added, almost as an afterthought: 'I have still to follow down the Lualaba, and see whether, as the natives assert, it passes Tanganyika to the west, or enters it and finds an exit into Baker's lake [Lake Albert].'[38] In his journal at this time, Livingstone played down the immensity of the task that still lay ahead of him. 'I have no doubts on the subject [of the Lualaba being the Nile], for I receive the reports of natives of intelligence at first hand, and they have no motive for deceiving me. The best maps are formed from the same sort of reports at third or fourth hand.'[39] Even though Livingstone could back

---

* As indeed it does.
† Clarendon had once more become Foreign Secretary when Russell succeeded Palmerston as Prime Minister in October 1865.

up his suppositions with plausible arguments, this new admission, that he was prepared to base geographical theories partly on the testimony of third parties, marked a definitive move away from rigidly scientific deduction to something a great deal less precise. It was hardly a good augury for the future.

On 18 July, Livingstone at last arrived at Lake Bangweolo. It is important, in view of events that happened to Livingstone there five years later, to describe in some detail not only his conclusions about Bangweolo's connection with the Lualaba but also his estimate of the lake's shape and extent. After a couple of days Livingstone persuaded some local natives to take him out on to the lake in a canoe. The vessel, however, had been stolen and to his anger Livingstone had to be content with two days instead of four on the lake as agreed. In the short term this was no disaster. It merely meant that he mapped the lake wrongly. Livingstone had been taken out from the northern shore of the lake to one of four islands. Gazing south and east from this low island, he had looked across what appeared to be an uninterrupted stretch of water as far as the eye could see. Unfortunately his line of vision was restricted by the fact that the highest point on the island was only forty feet. He thus failed to see the beginning of a line of swamps just over the horizon. Had he seen them he would have realized that Bangweolo proper was a small lake and not the vast expanse of water he imagined it to be. His final calculation was that it was 150 miles long from east to west. Had the natives, who had stolen the canoe, been prepared to paddle on south-east for two hours more, he would have discovered how large his error was. Bangweolo was only twenty-five miles long, and most of the area Livingstone thought was water was, in fact, marsh and swamp. The high level of the water was partly responsible for his misunderstanding; in the dry season he would undoubtedly have recognized that two of the 'islands' were not true islands at all, but higher ground surrounded by marsh, and that the two others were larger than he had thought, and different shapes.[40]

The fact that he saw Bangweolo at the end of the rainy season was not his only reason for exaggerating its size. For his estimate, he had also relied on the longitudes he had taken in 1867 and in the summer of 1868. One set it will be remembered had been twenty miles out to the east,

the other fifty to the west. He thus added seventy miles
more to the lake's length than he would otherwise have
done. These errors did not affect his most important deductions about Bangweolo: that it was fed by the Chambesi,
which he had crossed on his way to Lake Tanganyika
in 1867, and that the Luapula left it for Lake Moero, after
which it became the Lualaba. All this was perfectly correct. The only trouble would come if Livingstone should
ever choose to return to the lake from a different direction and at a different time of year. Then he would not
recognize any of the landmarks he had seen on his first
visit, and his incorrect longitudes would lead him hopelessly astray into the swamps. But in late July 1868, Livingstone was unaware of his miscalculations and did not
have any intention of coming back.

Two days later, on 1 August, Livingstone rejoined
Bogharib at his encampment ten miles north of the lake.
Livingstone realized that until he had collected his supplies
from Ujiji he would be dependent for everything on his
Arab friends, and would therefore have to fit in with their
plans; but when Bogharib told him that he was planning to
visit Manyuema, the area west and north-west of Lake
Tanganyika, the very region through which, according to
native reports, the Lualaba flowed on its journey north,
Livingstone at once made up his mind to abandon Ujiji
for the time being.

By 22 October Livingstone and his Arab escort had
arrived at the point, a few miles west of Lake Moero,
where he had left Muhammad Salim five months before.
Salim was still there and another group of Arabs had
recently joined him; with the addition of Bogharib's men,
a vast caravan had been formed. Livingstone's five deserters who had stayed with Salim now begged to be taken
back and Livingstone agreed without hesitation. 'More
enlightened people often take advantage of men in similar
circumstances,' he wrote in his journal: 'I have faults
myself.'[41]

There was a delay of almost a month before the large
caravan set off for Manyuema, but at last in late November a start was made. Two weeks later a group of Arabs
in Bogharib's party took prisoners from a village in
reprisal for the loss of some runaway slaves who had been
sheltered by the villagers. This small matter soon led to
more serious trouble and the Arabs shortly realized that

if they wished to continue north to Manyuema they would have to fight their way past several hundred angry tribes-men. Since there were over a thousand slaves and a large amount of ivory at stake, the caravan leaders decided against such rashness and proposed instead to dispose of their precious merchandise at Ujiji on Lake Tanganyika and return to Manyuema for more ivory later. Livingstone was extremely disappointed as the caravan altered course from north to north-east, but there was nothing that he could do. Without supplies of his own he was helpless.

In early January 1869, the caravan was still sixty miles south-west of the point where the Arabs intended to cross Lake Tanganyika for Ujiji. Now the first of the rains began and, after his exploits of the year before, Livingstone's resistance to cold and damp was very low. Soon he was seriously ill. The entry in his journal for 7 January reads:

> Cannot walk: Pneumonia of right lung, and I cough all day and all night: sputa rust of iron and bloody: distressing weakness. Ideas flow through my mind with great rapidity and vividness, in groups of twos and threes: if I look at any piece of wood, the bark seems covered with figures and faces of men, and they remain, though I look away and turn to the same place again. I saw myself lying dead in the way to Ujiji, and all the letters I expected there useless. When I think of my children and friends, the lines ring through my head perpetually:
>
>> I shall look into your faces,
>> And listen to what you say,
>> And be often very near you
>> When you think I'm far away.[42]

But, in his delirium, lines from Tennyson could not comfort him when his thoughts turned to Robert's fate. His son Tom would now be approaching a vital stage in his career, and Livingstone was tormented by the thought that he would be unable to help him. He did not even know whether his son had got through the course he had started at Glasgow University a few years before. No letters from his family had reached Livingstone since he had left Zan-zibar in 1866. Trivial family details distressed him. Perhaps Tom would be refused jobs because of his appearance. 'He must get that front tooth out if it holds his lips apart, for that does not look smart & will be a drawback in any situation.'[43] So many people had told Livingstone that they would help his children in his absence, but they had probably done nothing. 'Again and again I have been left in the lurch,' he told a friend bitterly.[42]

Soon he was too ill to write and to think coherently. When he was conscious, one thought above all others gave him heart: at Ujiji there would be letters for him. During the long periods of delirium which he suffered throughout January and February, only Bogharib's devoted care and nursing kept Livingstone alive. Bogharib had a wooden litter made for Livingstone, and gave strict instructions that the sick man should be carried with the utmost care; but, even so, when the ground was rough, Livingstone was inevitably jolted from side to side, causing him, while conscious, terrible pain. Because he was too weak to move unassisted, when the sun shone, as it did when the rains temporarily let up, his face got badly burned; he found it too tiring to hold up a spray of leaves to shade himself.

At last in mid-February the caravan arrived at the western shore of Lake Tanganyika, but it was another month before the crossing had been made and Livingstone was carried ashore on the other side at Ujiji. Here at last Livingstone believed he would find stores, food and, most important of all, medicines and letters. An hour later he knew that three-quarters of his supplies had been pillaged. There was no food, no medicine and no letters. After three years' travelling, he was ill, weary and destitute. The only provisions waiting for him could have been packed into one chest: a little sugar, tea and coffee, some low-quality beads and a quarter of the cloth he had ordered in Zanzibar.

2 I

Fantasy in Manyuema, 1869–1871

Ujiji, situated seven hundred miles due west of Zanzibar, had been since the early 1840s a thriving Arab trading centre. From Ujiji's small harbour a procession of dhows crossed Lake Tanganyika, transporting caravans to the slave and ivory fields, west and south-west of the lake. In Ujiji itself the streets were rarely empty and, as a rule, groups of Arabs in white flowing robes, strings of slaves laden with grain and ivory, and flocks of sheep and goats on their way to market, all gave the place an air of activity and bustle. There were probably no more than thirty or forty Arabs living in the town, but whenever caravans passed through, their numbers rose to two or three times that many. Arab houses, called *tembes*, were built of mud but appeared substantial, with their central courtyards and separate rooms for the domestic slaves and the harem. Around these flat-roofed buildings was a jumble of native huts, some square but most beehive shaped. There were at least two thousand Africans living in Ujiji in 1869.

Livingstone, to start with, took in little of his new surroundings; the terrible loss of his supplies, coming on top of his severe illness, left him feeling helpless and broken. The fact that his own men had pilfered from their loads in front of him during his travels, should have prepared him for losses from supplies that had been at Ujiji for two years. Many of the Arabs who had helped themselves to Livingstone's cloth and beads had imagined that, since the owner of the stores had not come for so long, he must have died some time before.

As soon as Livingstone was well enough to be up and about, he could see that he had two choices. He could either go to Zanzibar and return with new supplies or he could try to get a letter to the coast asking Kirk, who was at present standing in for the Consul at Zanzibar, to send stores with the next caravan. There was really no certainty that this second method would be successful, since the goods might be stolen *en route*, and in any case there was a war raging between the natives and the Arabs east of Ujiji on the Zanzibar route. Livingstone decided against going to Zanzibar in person for a number of reasons. First of all the journey there and back would be fourteen hundred miles, and in his present state of health Livingstone believed that he ought to conserve all his strength for his geographical work. In addition he knew that, once at Zanzibar, pressure might be put on him to abandon his work in view of his failing health. Another consideration was his determination that, when he returned, it would be as the man who had once and for all proved that the source of the Nile lay not in the Victoria Nyanza, nor in

Lake Albert but in the area south-west of Lake Tanganyika. Then he would be able to show the Council of the R.G.S. and the officials at the Foreign Office that they had insulted and stinted the man who had single-handed solved the world's greatest geographical mystery.

Having decided not to go to Zanzibar himself, Livingstone made arrangements to travel to Manyuema with Bogharib in the late summer. Since Bogharib would provide all the supplies needed for that journey, Livingstone felt that he could afford to leave Ujiji for a time and return there late in 1869, by which time Kirk would have sent more supplies from the coast. Nevertheless getting letters out of Ujiji was not easy, since Livingstone had unwisely let the Arab residents know that he thought them all thieves and parasites—in his journal he called them 'the vilest of the vile'.[1] Livingstone wrote forty-four letters while he was at Ujiji, but only one reached the coast—fortunately it was the letter addressed to Kirk. The Ujiji Arabs had evidently believed that unless they destroyed Livingstone's letters, news of his losses would reach the Sultan of Zanzibar and lead to some unpleasant recrimination.

While waiting to leave for Manyuema with Bogharib, Livingstone remained at Ujiji convalescing during the spring and early summer of 1869. This gave him plenty of time to think about his theories concerning the central African lake and river system. Many of the Arab traders he spoke to at this time horrified him by suggesting that the Lualaba flowed north-west and not north-east and was therefore more likely to be the Congo.[2] Livingstone sidestepped this unwelcome idea by arguing with typical optimism that the amount of water leaving the northern end of Lake Moero suggested that the Lualaba was large enough to be able to divide further north and supply both the Nile and Congo.[3] Livingstone made a great many enquiries about the area west and south-west of Lake Tanganyika, and, piecing together all the information, came to the conclusion that there were three main interconnecting 'lines of drainage' in central Africa, running roughly parallel with each other from south to north. The western line originated, according to the theory, due west of Bangweolo and joined the central line of drainage somewhere north of Lake Moero. The central line itself ran from Lake Bangweolo, through Moero and then on north

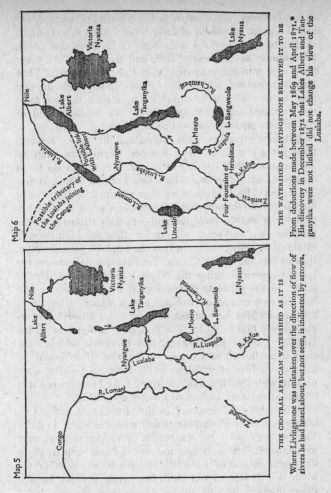

Map 6

THE WATERSHED AS LIVINGSTONE BELIEVED IT TO BE*

From deductions made between May 1869 and April 1871.* His discovery in December 1872 that Lakes Albert and Tanganyika were not linked did not change his view of the Lualaba.

Map 5

THE CENTRAL AFRICAN WATERSHED AS IT IS

Where Livingstone was mistaken over the direction of flow of rivers he had heard about, but not seen, is indicated by arrows.

* The principal evidence for this reconstruction is as follows:

(a) A rough sketch map sent by Livingstone to his daughter Agnes with a letter dated 12.12.71 (see Plate 23), in B.M. Ad. MS. 50184.
(b) The map facing page 448 of H. M. Stanley's *How I Found Livingstone*, London 1872. (Livingstone discussed the watershed in detail with Stanley, whose map is based on those conversations.)
(c) Two letters from Livingstone to Kirk, dated 30.5.69 and 14.5.71 respectively (both are published in *The Zambesi Doctors: David*

as the Lualaba. The eastern line, Livingstone believed, began at a point just north of Lake Moero, where the Lualaba split in two, sending the main body of its water due north, to continue as the central line, and the rest of its water north-east into the western side of Lake Tanganyika. Thus Lake Tanganyika and Lake Albert—Livingstone thought that the two lakes were connected by a river flowing from the northern end of Tanganyika to the southern end of Albert—formed the eastern line of drainage.

Although fundamentally mistaken, in some respects Livingstone's theories were correct. A modern map of Africa shows that Lakes Albert and Tanganyika do lie at opposite ends of a chain of lakes, but this chain is not connected. The Lualaba does flow northwards from Lake Moero for six hundred miles between the chain of lakes to the east and the river Lomani—a major tributary of the Lualaba—to the west. The major flaw in Livingstone's thinking was his conviction that the Lualaba was the Nile. It is in fact the upper Congo. Yet Livingstone's claims for Lake Bangweolo being the Nile's source did not depend solely on the ultimate destination of the Lualaba; he still had the eastern line of drainage up his sleeve. It was most unfortunate that he had not done what Sir Roderick Murchison told him to do in 1866 and gone straightway to the northern end of Lake Tanganyika to check whether the river there flowed into or out of the lake. If it flowed in, the eastern line of drainage could have no possible connection with the Nile, since it would have been proved that Lakes Albert and Tanganyika were not linked.

During his convalescence in the summer of 1869, Livingstone tried to determine which way the water in Lake Tanganyika flowed, but the results of his experiments were inconclusive. The only real test would have been to go to the northern end of Lake Tanganyika to see whether the water flowed into or out of it, but, while at Ujiji, Livingstone allowed himself to be discouraged by reports of

Livingstone's Letters to John Kirk 1858–1872, ed. R. Foskett, Edinburgh 1964).

(d) *The Last Journals of David Livingstone in Central Africa*, ed. H. Waller, London 1874, vol. 2, 49–50. Also two maps published with the *Last Journals*.

(e) Letter from Livingston to B. Frere, dated 27.11.70, published in *Proceedings of the Royal Geographical Society*, vol. xviii, 265–6.

tribal disturbances in the area. Thus when he set out for Manyuema in July, to try to determine where the Lualaba flowed to and whether it joined up with the Nile or the Congo, he felt that even if he came to no definite conclusion, he would still be able to return to Lake Tanganyika to find a river flowing out of that lake's northern end and running on north to Lake Albert; thus he would still be able to claim, if he also found that the Lualaba did send a tributary into the western side of Lake Tanganyika, that he had discovered a source of the Nile in Bangweolo, hundreds of miles south of the discoveries of Speke and Baker. This claim would not of course depend on the Lualaba itself being the Nile.

By the end of July 1869, Livingstone and Bogharib had crossed Lake Tanganyika and set out on their journey to Manyuema. By a typical piece of misfortune, Livingstone had landed less than twenty miles north of a small river— the river Lukuga—flowing *out* of the western side of Lake Tanganyika. If Livingstone had known the direction in which this river flowed, he would have realized that the river at the northern end of Tanganyika would almost beyond doubt flow into the lake and not out of it; and if he had made this discovery Livingstone would also have realized in 1869 that the eastern line of drainage had nothing to do with the Nile and that everything depended on the Lualaba.

Livingstone's aim in July 1869 was to pass through Manyuema as quickly as possible and, on reaching the Lualaba at a point roughly three hundred miles west of Ujiji, to trace the Lualaba north to establish whether it was the Nile or the Congo. Livingstone believed that he would be able to achieve this within six months, at the end of which he could return ot Ujiji. In fact a year later he was still only 150 miles west of Tanganyika and had failed to reach the Lualaba. His health had been a major reason for failure. He had thought that after his rest at Ujiji he was his old self again, but pneumonia had affected his lungs and he found even three hours' walking over dry and level country left him exhausted. When the rains came and the mud clung to his feet, he had to rest every few minutes. But, apart from his lungs, his resistance to fever had also lessened and soon he was also suffering from dysentery, accompanied by heavy anal bleeding. Then in July 1870 Livingstone was unable to move at all for three months. This time his complaint was ulcers on the feet. These terrible sores were probably due to the damp. The ulcers tended to spread and 'eat through everything—muscle, tendon, and bone, and often lame permanently if they do not kill'. 'If the foot were put to the ground, a discharge of bloody ichor flowed, and the same discharge happened every night with considerable pain, that prevented sleep.'[4]

Apart from ill-health and his old enemy the rainy season, other factors had contributed to Livingstone's slow progress. Manyuema had become an ivory boom area and hundreds of Arabs had flooded in to take advantage of it. Many of these newcomers were far more ruthless than Bogharib or the Arabs with whom Livingstone had travelled in the past. If villagers tried to get a decent price for their ivory they were often murdered and their villages fired. Soon there was widespread fighting throughout Manyuema between Arabs and natives. As a result Livingstone found it very hard to travel. He could not buy food, nor gain permission to pass through the territory of chiefs who had been attacked by Arabs. Without medicines and supplies, Livingstone was still more helpless when Bogharib went off trading on his own. By the middle of 1870 six of Livingstone's nine followers had deserted and he was down to three: Chuma, Susi and a Nassick boy, Gardner.

The ulcers on his feet kept Livingstone a virtual prisoner at the town of Bambarre, midway between Lake Tanganyika and the Lualaba, from July 1870 to February 1871. Inactivity had always depressed him and now he even began to wonder whether he was too old to complete his work. He knew that he looked ten years older than his fifty-seven years. 'I shall not hide it from you,' he told Agnes, 'that I am made very old & shaky—My cheeks fallen in—space round the eyes—the mouth almost toothless . . . a smile is that of a hippopotamus—a dreadful old Fogie.'[5] Livingstone also worried about his children, especially Tom and Agnes who might well be thinking of getting married. Livingstone had always professed himself completely disinterested where money was concerned but his advice to his children was chillingly practical and mercenary. Tom was told: 'On no account ought you to look to a girl however beautiful and loving if she or her parents have nothing.'[6] Agnes was warned about men who pretend to have money when really they were paupers:

'Wise people use the utmost precautions not to be taken in. Lawyers dig to the bottom of a man's affairs before they will allow a young lady to listen to the soft nothings of lovers or shams.'[7] This view of most suitors as parasites had a lot to do with Livingstone's personal feeling that he had been jilted by the Government and deceived by the R.G.S.

During his time at Bambarre, Livingstone realized that many tribes in Manyuema were cannibals and this depressed him still more, especially since one of his deserters, James, a Nassick boy, was killed and eaten. Yet Livingstone did not turn against the Manyuema tribes because of their habits. He saw many of them captured and taken away as slaves and his response was to write the most haunting of all his indictments against the slave-trade: 'The strangest disease I have seen in this country seems really to be broken-heartedness, and it attacks free men who have been captured and made slaves.'[8]

Many recently captured men seemed to waste away and die within weeks for no obvious physical cause. Livingstone talked to many of those in the first stages of this inexplicable disease, and wrote: 'They ascribed their only pain to the heart, and placed the hand correctly on the spot, though many think that the organ stands high up under the breast bone.'

As the months passed at Bambarre, Livingstone became an object of great curiosity to the local tribesmen, who would often try to steal into his hut for their first view of the white man. Eventually Livingstone had to eat in public to appease native curiosity. Then, seated at a solitary table in the centre of a roped-off enclosure, he would amaze everybody by eating elephant meat with a knife and fork. Crowds would also gather to see him write in his journal, but the greatest interest was aroused by the use of soap for washing his hair. The natives watched with horrified fascination as the lather formed while he rubbed his scalp. There was no doubt about it: the white man was washing his brain. But moments of occasional humour were too few to stop Livingstone entering a strange, almost dream-like state of mind. Pain, isolation and inactivity soon seriously affected his judgment and patterns of thought.

During his seven months at Bambarre, Livingstone read the Bible through four times, giving special attention to the Old Testament, with Exodus getting a minute examination. In the summer of 1869, he had asserted as geographical facts theories which he could not substantiate, but from July 1870 Livingstone's ideas passed into the realms of fantasy. He himself soon began to describe his thoughts about the Nile as 'waking dreams'. The horrifying pain Livingstone suffered with the ulcers on his feet, coupled with periodic attacks of fever and loss of blood, helps explain the strangeness of his new thinking. As Livingstone read and re-read Exodus he became mesmerized by the figure of Moses. On 25 August he wrote: 'One of my waking dreams is that the legendary tales about Moses coming up into Inner Ethiopia with Merr his foster-mother, and founding a city which he called in her honour "Meroe", may have a substratum of fact.'[9]

Reading this single entry the statement does not look too extreme, especially since it is qualified: 'may have a substratum of fact'. But during the next few months his journal is studded with references to Moses; like this one, written two months later:

> I had a strong presentiment during the first three years that I should never live through the enterprise, but it weakened as I came near to the end of the journey, and an eager desire to discover any evidence of the great Moses having visited these parts bound me, spell bound me, I may say, for if I could bring to light anything to confirm the Sacred Oracles, I should not grudge one whit all the labour expended.[10]

Ten days later he was writing a similar passage. A desire 'to confirm the Sacred Oracles' was a new strand and added a new obsession to existing ones. Ever since reading, at the age of nineteen, the works of Thomas Dick, Livingstone had abandoned a strict fundamentalist's approach to the Bible. He had not disapproved of Darwin's *Origin of Species by means of Natural Selection*, after that work was published in 1859. He had taken issue in minor points but had not attacked the major thesis.[11] In 1864 and 1865 he had deliberately avoided becoming involved in current arguments about the historical accuracy of the Pentateuch, and the reason had obviously been that he did not feel strongly on the subject. His knowledge of geology had alone been enough to tell him that the dates given in the Old Testament for the age of the world were hopelessly wrong. But now in 1870 and 1871, after four years in Africa, he had stopped thinking logically. His search for the source of the Nile had become no simple geographical task but a reaffirmation of faith, a quest which, if successfully accomplished, would 'confirm the Sacred Oracles'. Sick, destitute and helpless, Livingstone could not have continued unless he gave to his work a dignity which no geographical search could ever have possessed.

Almost every waking moment Livingstone thought about the Nile and all the men, long since dead, who had tried to fathom the mystery of its source. 'More than sixteen hundred years have elapsed since Ptolemy put down the results of early explorers; and Emperors, Kings, Philosophers—all the great men of antiquity longed to know whence flowed the famous river and long in vain.'[12]

The ancients of the classical world, as well as those of the Bible, became important figures in Livingstone's fantasy from the middle of August 1870. In that month two Arab traders came to Bambarre after a long journey that had taken them to Katanga and beyond. Their names were Josut and Moenepembé, and what they told Livingstone was to dominate his thinking in the few years that remained to him. Their information was that Lake Bangweolo was not the primary source of the Lualaba. While still at Ujiji, in 1869, Livingstone himself had come to the conclusion that the Lualaba was supplied not just by Bangweolo but by a western line of drainage as well; now, in the summer of 1870, these two Arabs confirmed this view. But they did much more than that. They told Livingstone that some miles south-west of Bangweolo were two sources which supplied an unnamed river—Livingstone soon called it the Lualaba west—which flowed north through an unvisited lake and joined Livingstone's Lualaba several hundred miles north of Lake Moero. Just south of the two sources, the Arabs went on, were another two sources, whose waters flowed south to become the upper Zambesi and its tributary, the Kafue river. In fact, broadly speaking, this information was correct. The sources of the Zambesi and Kafue rivers were within a hundred miles of two sources whose waters flowed north to join Livingstone's Lualaba several hundred miles above Lake Moero. So Livingstone was not gullible in believing the Arabs; it was the use he made of their information that was alarming.

Before leaving England in 1865 he had read all the classical allusions to the Nile's source, and one important reference was in Book Two of Herodotus' *History*. When Herodotus visited Egypt in the fifth century B.C. he made inquiries about the source of the Nile, and on his return home he wrote: 'Not one writer of the Egyptians or of the Libyans or of the Hellenes, who came to speech with me, professed to know anything, except the scribe of the sacred treasury of Athene at the city of Sais in Egypt.'[13] But the scribe made up for all the others: he said most specifically that at a point midway between two hills with conical tops 'are the fountains of the Nile, fountains which it is impossible to fathom: half the water runs northward into Egypt; half to the south'.[14] This detail, about half of the water flowing south and half north, immediately led Livingstone to the conclusion that the scribe of the sacred treasury had been right. The Arabs had spoken about a hill between the four sources, and one hill was not so very different from two hills with conical tops. Herodotus had only quoted the story because it was all he could discover about the source of the Nile, not because he had believed it. But, once Livingstone had listened to the two Arabs, he was convinced that the scribe had had access to definite information which had since been lost. In November, Livingstone told a friend: 'I feel so certain on the matter, that I have given English names to the fountains [sources] by anticipation.'[15] The four names he chose were those of Palmerston, William Cotton Oswell, James 'Paraffin' Young and Bartle Frere, the Governor of Bombay. The unvisited lake he called Lake Lincoln.* The only reason why Livingstone felt so sure that the Arabs had been right was the similarity between what they said and the story recounted by Herodotus. But soon Livingstone went even further in his reverence for classical accounts.

Livingstone had read Ptolemy's *Geography* and had carefully scrutinized his map of Africa. Ptolemy suggested that the source of the Nile consisted of two springs situated in a range of hills which he called the Mountains of the Moon. Once more the mention of twin sources left Livingstone still more convinced. Of course it was sad that

---

* President Lincoln had been assassinated in 1865.

Ptolemy had not known about the two sources flowing south, but Livingstone easily explained this away. 'He [Ptolemy] probably got information from his predecessors who inquired of men who had visited this very region, and mistakes were natural in oral information.'[16] But whatever his mistakes, Livingstone decided that Ptolemy's Lake Coloe 'is probably a more correct view of the Victoria Nyanza than that given by Grant and Speke'.[17]

Ptolemy, who lived in Alexandria during the second century A.D., had been a remarkable man, and his astronomical theories were accepted till the time of Copernicus and Kepler; but to take his maps of Africa seriously was madness. In fact by the end of 1870 the whole patchwork of Livingstone's thinking had become an impossibly intertwined web of fantasy and reality. The Arabs had not invented the sources west of Bangweolo, but of course they had nothing at all to do with the Nile. Livingstone had allowed his determination, that his Lualaba should not be the Congo, to make him clutch at every thread of information that made it seem probable that it was the Nile. Yet whatever his classical and biblical obsessions, Livingstone from August 1870 became convinced that, before he could conclude his work, he would have to visit the sources which the two Arabs had described. After he had managed to examine the Lualaba near his present position, he would return to Ujiji and then travel south to approach the four fountains via Lake Bangweolo. But his immediate problem was how to get from Bambarre to the Lualaba.

In late January 1871, when Livingstone had all but abandoned any hope of ever leaving Bambarre, ten men arrived who had been sent from the coast to Ujiji and then directed on from there to join him in Manyuema. Livingstone realized that his letter to Kirk had reached its destination after all. The ten men were mutinous and almost at once demanded higher wages; the supplies they brought were less than a quarter of what Livingstone had asked for, but they had come, and he now had some quinine, some sugar, coffee, tea and a few fathoms of cloth. At first the men refused to go any further, but when Livingstone threatened to shoot their two leaders they changed their minds. On 16 February 1871, after seven months' idleness, Livingstone and his party, now

numbering thirteen, marched out of Bambarre, heading
northwest.

In comparison with the trials he had experienced during
his previous attempts to reach the Lualaba, this last successful journey proved easy. By the end of March, after
six weeks' travelling, Livingstone reached the Lualaba at a
town called Nyangwe and gazed across its two miles of
slowly moving water. Soon after his arrival he once more
started hearing unpleasant stories that the Lualaba soon
bent westwards, and not eastwards as he hoped. At
Nyangwe itself the river's flow was due north. Livingstone
would obviously have to follow the river north to make
certain of its course, but at Nyangwe there was one
important experiment he could perform. His idea was that
beyond Nyangwe the Lualaba flowed north-eastwards and
joined the Nile at Lake Albert or just above it. For this to
be possible, the altitude at Nyangwe would have to be substantially higher than the altitude at Lake Albert. When
Livingstone gauged the height of Nyangwe with his boiling
point thermometer, he was horrified to find that it was
only 2,000 feet, the same height Baker had given for Lake
Albert. This should have told Livingstone that it was most
improbable that the Lualaba had anything to do with the
Nile, but by now he was too far gone in his certainty to
let a purely scientific fact change his mind. There was
another reason why he could not accept Baker's figures
or his own: Lake Tanganyika was 2,500 feet above sea
level and, that being so, the Lualaba, being lower, could
not send a tributary into the western side of Tanganyika.
The easiest thing to do was to reject all the figures. Nevertheless Livingstone was worried and acknowledged that if
the Lualaba joined the Nile it might very well be several
hundred miles north of Lake Albert, where the Nile's altitude would be lower.

The natives and Arabs at Nyangwe generally believed
that the Lualaba did ultimately flow westwards, but Livingstone never listened. He might have done so had he not
heard about a river called the Lomani a week after his
arrival in Nyangwe. The natives told him that six days
north of Nyangwe, the Lomani ran into the western side
of the Lualaba, having flowed parallel with the Lualaba
for several hundred miles. No native had any idea where
the Lomani's source was. Unfortunately Livingstone
thought he did: it was south of Katanga and in the region

of the four miraculous fountains with their central mound. The existence of the Lomani seemed to confirm everything the two Arabs had said. Obviously the Lomani was the river that flowed from the twin sources northwards into the unvisited lake—Lake Lincoln—and then joined the Lualaba several hundred miles north of Lake Moero. Without pausing to think again, Livingstone made up his mind once and for all: the Lualaba was the Nile because the Lomani's existence backed up the story the Arabs had told about the four sources. The Arabs had been right, it will be remembered, because their information had confirmed the report in Herodotus. The Lomani also fitted in with Livingstone's earlier idea of the three lines of drainage.

The information about the Lomani once more diverted Livingstone from the task he ought to have been contemplating. Before doing anything else he should have given all his energies to marching north to see whether the Lualaba began to flow to the west. Instead, considering it a foregone conclusion that the Lualaba was the Nile, he thought only of tracing the Lomani south to reach the twin sources. But in fact what Livingstone wanted soon became academic. The natives refused to let him have canoes to cross the Lualaba, and he would have to get to the western bank before being able to reach the Lomani. The natives persisted in refusing help for several months to come, and at last Livingstone tried to get the traders in the town to help him, but his old friend Bogharib was not there, and the Arabs in Nyangwe were not helpful. They believed that Livingstone had come to spy on their slaving activities and that he might well be interested in starting a European ivory trade west of the Lualaba, to rival their trade in Manyuema. By July, after three months in Nyangwe, Livingstone was desperate to get canoes, and offered Dugumbe, the leading Arab in the town, £400 and all his supplies at Ujiji if he would get him and his men across the Lualaba. Dugumbe was still considering this proposition on 15 July: the day a terrible disaster occurred in Nyangwe.

Ever since his arrival in the town, Livingstone had found consolation for his failure to get canoes in going to the busy market place to watch the activity and bustle. Almost everything about the scene there pleased him—the women with their earthen pots on their heads, children

8. The massacre at Nyangwe

carrying squawking hens, the disappointment on the faces of sellers who failed to convince potential customers of the value of a sheep or goat. On 15 July, as on every other market day, Livingstone wandered among the two or three thousand buyers and sellers and tried to forget his problems, but the day was hot and sultry and he did not stay more than an hour. As he was leaving, an argument over the price of a chicken broke out between a native and three armed Arabs. Livingstone heard shouting but thought nothing of it; haggling was often spirited. He had walked another thirty yards when suddenly two shots rang out behind him; a moment later screaming men and women were rushing past him. The three Arabs were now firing wildly into the backs of the fleeing crowd.

Many natives had come to the market in canoes, which they had moored in a small creek just below the town. Hundreds of people swarmed down into the creek at the same time and pandemonium broke out. Many canoes were swamped without leaving the shore, and others cast off without paddles. Many people tried to swim out to an island in mid-stream. At the height of the chaos another group of Arabs just above the creek opened fire on the already terror-stricken people. Only three canoes got away and all these were capsized by the frenzied efforts of those in the water to pull themselves aboard. Soon Livingstone could see a long line of heads drifting away downstream; very few of those who took to the water survived. That evening Livingstone wrote despairingly: 'No one will ever know the exact loss of the bright sultry summer morning, it gave me the impression of being in hell.'[18] The Arab estimate of four hundred dead was probably a couple of hundred too few.

When the shooting stopped, it was discovered that in the turmoil several hundred slaves had broken loose and had looted the market. On the other side of the river similar massacres were taking place and before long Livingstone could see plumes of smoke rising from burning villages. Dugumbe and his partners had launched a deliberate campaign of arson and murder to frighten the Manyuema into abject obedience to all Arab demands.

After what he had witnessed, Livingstone knew that he could never accept help from Dugumbe, even if the Arab offered a fleet of canoes for nothing. The work of a morning had destroyed all Livingstone's hopes of reaching the river Lomani. If he left Nyangwe without either tracing the Lualaba north or following the Lomani south, the pain and suffering of the past two years would have been for nothing, yet only with Arab help could Livingstone hope to do either of these tasks. His sense of outrage and disgust were too strong. Livingstone knew that he could never willingly depend on Arabs again. Only one course remained to him: the long return to Ujiji.

On 23 October, after three gruelling months travelling Livingstone reached Ujiji. A party of slave-traders with several hundred slaves and thirty tons of ivory arrived just afterwards. 'All the traders were returning successful,' he wrote miserably: 'I alone had failed and experienced worry, thwarting, baffling, when almost in sight of the end towards which I strained.'[19] But Livingstone was sustained by the knowledge that he would have supplies in sufficient quantity to finance a return to the Lomani and the four fountains of Herodotus.

Within a couple of hours of landing Livingstone realized with a sinking heart that the events of 1869 had repeated themselves. The supplies Kirk had sent from the coast had been stolen and sold off by the man who had brought them to Ujiji and by other Arab traders in the town. There was virtually nothing left out of £600 worth of goods. To the east of Ujiji the war still went on, and there could be no immediate hope of getting goods from the coast to replace those stolen. If Livingstone had not left a few yards of calico with one of the few Arabs in Ujiji

whom he could trust, he would have had nothing with
which to buy food.

There seemed no hope at all now. Livingstone had fled
from Nyangwe to escape having to rely on Arabs, and
now at Ujiji, unless help of some sort arrived within
weeks, he would have to ask for their charity. Livingstone's agony was all the more acute since he knew that
Sherif Bosher, the man who had sold off all his goods,
had invested the proceeds in ivory, which was still in
Ujiji under lock and key. Sherif however had bribed the
three principal men of the town, and all refused to let
him have the key so that he could reclaim what was right-
fully his.

All that Livingstone could do was to write to Kirk
explaining what had happened and asking for a further
lot of stores. The loss meant that he would be heavily in
debt but without more supplies he would starve. Reliable
reports of the fighting around Unyanyembe, to the east of
Ujiji, suggested that it would be hopeless for Livingstone
to attempt to get through to the coast with his handful
of followers. The prospect ahead of him was at least ten
months waiting at Ujiji with no certainty that Kirk would
manage to get a caravan through. During all that time,
Livingstone knew, he would have to exist on Arab credit.

Two days after his arrival at Ujiji, Livingstone was
amazed to hear that a white man had recently left Unyanyembe, two hundred miles east of Ujiji. Who this white
man was or where he was going, nobody had any idea.
His nationality was as much a mystery as his name. Livingstone, in spite of himself, could not help hoping,
praying that this stranger, if he existed, would come to
Ujiji. Without aid, Livingstone wondered whether he would
live long enough for Kirk to get supplies to him.

Livingstone only had to endure three more days' sus-
pense, and then at noon on what he reckoned to be 28
October, but was in fact a day in early or mid-November,*
shots were heard outside the town, shots not fired in anger,
but announcing the approach of a caravan. The rumour
spread rapidly that the newcomer was an Englishman and
soon crowds started to form outside Livingstone's house.
Livingstone could not believe anything he heard until Susi
dashed up to him gesticulating wildly and shouting: 'An

* See Appendix A.

Englishman coming.' In a few minutes the column of men had reached the centre of Ujiji and Livingstone could see that they were all dressed in long white robes and turbans, but, more remarkable still, they were carrying enough to sustain a traveller for years: tin baths, tents, saddles, a folding boat, an impressive array of gigantic kettles. Whoever the leader of this party might be, Livingstone knew that he was 'no poor Lazarus like me'. Then out of the advancing crowd stepped the white man himself; a huge native preceded him carrying the stars and stripes. The stranger was immaculately dressed in a freshly pressed flannel suit; his boots glistened and his helmet was a dazzling white. The crowd parted and Livingstone now moved towards the newcomer, who lifted his hat and said, as formally as he could, in a voice that none the less trembled with excitement:

'Dr Livingstone, I presume?'[20]*

9. 'Dr Livingstone, I presume?'

* See Appendix B.

22

Stanley and the Livingstone Myth

On 28 October 1869 Henry Morton Stanley, a young journalist on the staff of the *New York Herald*, had been summoned to an important meeting by the owner and editor of that paper, James Gordon Bennett Jnr, who was currently staying at the Grand Hotel, Paris. Bennett was an autocratic newspaper proprietor who rarely spoke to any of his journalists, so Stanley realized that something unusual was in the offing. Bennett, as Stanley's verbatim account of the interview shows, did not waste time in coming to the point and weighed in at once with a question:

> 'Where do you think Livingstone is?'
> "I really do not know, sir!'
> 'Do you think he is alive?'
> 'He may be, and he may not be!' I answered.
> "What!' said I, 'do you really think I · can find Dr Livingstone?'

And the answer of course was an emphatic *yes* from Bennett. When Stanley gasped that the venture would prove extremely expensive, his employer contemptuously brushed the objection aside:

> 'Draw a thousand pounds now; and when you have gone through that, draw another thousand, and when that is spent draw another thousand, and when you have finished that draw another thousand, and so on; but, FIND LIVINGSTONE.'[1]

It is no mean tribute to Bennett's journalistic sense that, at the time he was preparing his paper's greatest scoop, Livingstone, for the British public at least, was a forgotten figure. In December 1866 the Johanna men, who had deserted Livingstone near Lake Nyassa, had arrived in Zanzibar with a story that their master had been killed by natives in the interior. Although this report of his death was generally believed, when obituaries appeared in the British press in early March 1867 they were short and unemotionally factual. Only the Council of the Royal Geographical Society had reacted positively. Murchison had pressurized a reluctant British Government into voting £1,200 for an expedition to prove or disprove the story of Livingstone's death. E. D. Young, who had served with Livingstone on the *Lady Nyassa*, had been appointed as leader of this search party. During the autumn of 1867 Young had reached the southern end of Lake Nyassa and had collected evidence which proved beyond doubt that Livingstone had passed through that area and had travelled far to the north without meeting his death. Young's discovery was made public in January 1868 and in the same month letters from Livingstone reached the British Consulate in Zanzibar. By the end of 1868 no further news had been heard of Livingstone and again rumours that he had died began to circulate, but, as in the early months of 1867, there was little public reaction in Britain. After the disasters of the Zambesi Expedition, Livingstone's reputation had fallen so low that he was not considered newsworthy. Bennett however believed that a face-to-face interview by one of his journalists with this British explorer, who had not seen a white man for five or six years, could prove a story with such emotional and dramatic impact that the previous lack of interest in Livingstone would become entirely irrelevant. If Stanley managed to find Livingstone, Bennett was also convinced that the single incredible fact that a newspaper reporter had tracked down a man whom many supposed dead, in the heart of a vast and virtually unknown continent, would in itself create a sensation. It is important to stress at the outset that Bennett would completely change the British estimate of Livingstone. Stanley's mission would turn a once-adored but now forgotten explorer into the legendary figure the late Victorians enshrined.

When Stanley left James Gordon Bennett's Paris hotel room, he realized that if he found Livingstone he would be made for life, both financially and professionally. Socially, he knew, there would also be rewards, and for a man who had experienced an even harsher childhood than Livingstone's, this was an added spur.

Stanley had been born in Wales, the illegitimate son of John Rowlands, a Denbighshire cottager. Deserted by his

mother in his infancy, he had been looked after by two
uncles for a few years until, at the age of five, he had
been consigned to the St Asaph workhouse. For the next
nine years, according to his own later account, Stanley
suffered the constant brutalities and humiliations perpetu-
ated on all the young inmates by James Francis, the
master, who was later found to be insane and put in an
asylum. One of Stanley's best friends died after being
assaulted by Francis, and the most traumatic experience
of Stanley's youth was to see the bruised and battered
body of his friend in the workhouse mortuary. At the age
of fifteen, Stanley was driven by an unusually savage punishment to attack Francis and beat him unconscious. The
only course then open to him was to run away.

After rejection by most of his relatives, Stanley went to
Liverpool and signed on as cabin boy on an American
ship bound for New Orleans. In New Orleans, by an incredible piece of good fortune, he met and was later
adopted by a prosperous wholesale merchant, who took
him into his home and gave him his own names: Henry
Morton Stanley. For two happy years Stanley travelled
with his new father in the Mississippi valley, preparing himself for a business career, but in 1861 old Stanley heard
that his brother in Cuba was seriously ill, and decided to go
to him. It was a decision that cost him his life, for, shortly
after his arrival in Havana, he died of fever. Stanley would
not hear of this for several years, for in the meantime the
American Civil War had broken out. Since he was now
twenty-one, Stanley enlisted in the Confederate Army.
After a year's service he was captured and imprisoned in
shockingly insanitary conditions. A few months later he
agreed to join the Federal Artillery in exchange for his
release, but his fighting career was over; his health soon
cracked up and he was discharged.

In the autumn of 1864, he enlisted as a ship's writer in
the Federal Navy and his official accounts of the war at sea
off the southern coast impressed a number of newspaper
editors and encouraged Stanley to leave the navy and
take up journalism as a career. By 1868 Stanley had
attracted enough notice to get an offer of employment
from James Gordon Bennett of the *New York Herald*.
The *Herald*'s reputation was founded on its ability to
print sensational and scandalous stories, more with a view
to the number of papers sold than to the truth. But the

Herald also on occasions produced genuine scoops which astounded all rival editors. In his first year on the paper Stanley contrived just such a scoop.

At this time the British Government were known to be planning a punitive expedition into Ethiopia, where King Theodore had imprisoned the British Consul and a number of British citizens. Stanley reported Sir Robert Napier's campaign and managed to send home news of the British victory before any other reporter. Because of this success Bennett had decided to send Stanley on the far more challenging search for Livingstone.

Perhaps because a letter from Livingstone unexpectedly arrived in Zanzibar in the autumn of 1869—the one he had written to Kirk from Ujiji in May that year—Bennett decided against sending Stanley to Africa straight away. Instead he told Stanley that he should first send reports on other matters from Egypt, the Holy Land, Turkey, Persia and finally Bombay. This Bennett knew would occupy Stanley for a year by which time Livingstone would with luck be thoroughly *lost* again. In fact when Stanley eventually arrived at Zanzibar in January 1871, no further news had been heard from Livingstone. Bennett's instinct had proved correct.

From the time he met John Kirk, who had been the Acting British Consul in Zanzibar since June 1870, Stanley decided that Kirk was stand-offish, arrogant and unhelpful. Stanley's wretched childhood had made him almost as sensitive to possible insults as was Livingstone. Since Stanley's relations with Kirk would later prove a crucial factor in Livingstone's refusal to come home with Stanley, it is important to see how the trouble started.

Although Stanley had told Kirk that his sole purpose in coming to Africa was to examine the Rufiji—an insignificant river which flowed into the Indian Ocean a hundred miles south of Zanzibar—he felt that Kirk had seen through this ruse and realized that he had really come to look for Livingstone. Stanley was almost certainly right; Kirk was not a fool, and Stanley was hopeless at disguising his real intention. When Stanley asked Kirk what Livingstone's reactions might be if by coincidence 'I might stumble across him?', Kirk's reaction was to tell the journalist that Livingstone would probably be extremely angry to be 'found'. 'I know,' Kirk had continued, 'if Burton, or Grant, or Baker, or any of those fellows were going after him, and he heard of their coming, Livingstone would put a hundred miles of swamp in a very short time between himself and them.'² Later Stanley was to use this snatch of conversation as 'proof' that Kirk did not care whether Livingstone lived or died and that he had taken pleasure in putting obstacles in the path of somebody who was eager to help the Doctor. Apart from the fact that Stanley had not actually told him that he intended to find Livingstone, Kirk had a good many reasons for wishing to put the eager young journalist off. He remembered with painful clarity Livingstone's anger over articles that had appeared in the South African and British press during the Zambesi Expedition. During the years Kirk had been with the Doctor, Livingstone had given striking and repeated demonstrations of the fact that he hated travelling with Europeans, and in 1871 Kirk had no reason to suppose that an exception would be made for Mr Stanley of the *New York Herald*. Kirk might have lent a more sympathetic ear to Stanley had he believed that Livingstone was short of supplies; but between the end of 1869 and November 1870, Kirk himself had despatched three separate caravans with stores for the Doctor. The chances were that if Stanley did 'stumble across' Livingstone, the young journalist might well arrive having exhausted his own supplies and in bad health. Thus he could easily be a drag on Livingstone. The very idea of Livingstone being 'found' seemed idiotic to Kirk. In May 1869 Livingstone had written saying that he was about to set out for Manyuema; and Kirk was sure that, in due course, the Doctor would return to Ujiji, where he would write further letters explaining his future plans.

Unaware of any of Kirk's thoughts, Stanley assumed that the Acting British Consul had been unhelpful and dismissive as the result of a purely personal antipathy to him. But Stanley did not let his grudge against Kirk interfere with the preparation of what was to be an exceptionally lavishly equipped expedition. Before leaving Zanzibar a month after his arrival there, Stanley had spent £4,000. His purchases included nearly twenty miles of cloth, a million beads and 350 pounds of brass wire. Determined to be ready for anything, he also bought a couple of collapsible boats and took seventy-one cases of ammunition and forty guns. Stanley's stores eventually weighed roughly six tons. No European traveller in the history of African exploration had ever been so well provided. In contrast with the thirty-five porters Livingstone had led into the interior in 1866, Stanley set out with 192. He also took on two Europeans, W. L. Farquhar and J. W. Shaw. Neither of these two men survived the journey ahead of them.

Although Stanley headed inland at the front of a large caravan, success was far from guaranteed. A large party, without discipline and organization, could disintegrate more easily than a small expedition. Stanley soon proved that his abilities as an organizer were outstanding. The speed with which he travelled was proof of this. Whereas Speke and Burton had taken five months in the dry season to reach Unyanyembe, Stanley covered the same five hundred miles in just over three months, and in the rainy season too. Stanley's methods were not Livingstone's; his early years had persuaded him that 'the selfish and woodenheaded world requires mastering, as well as loving charity'.[3] And the way to master it was with the whip, which Stanley used a great deal on his journey to Ujiji. He was not ashamed to do so either, and later shocked many humanitarians in Britain by his jocular descriptions of floggings, which, he assured his readers, restored 'the physical energy of the lazily inclined' and encouraged them often 'to an extravagant activity'. On one occasion he was trying to slip past a hostile tribe by night, when the wife of one of his porters became hysterical and started screaming. Her distraught husband suggested decapitation as the best way to shut her up but Stanley resorted to his usual remedy: 'I asked her to desist after the first blow. "No!" She continued her insane cries with increased force and volume. Again my whip descended on her shoulders . . . Louder and louder she cried, and faster and faster I showered the blows for the taming of this shrew.'[4]

Supporters of Missionary Societies and members of philanthropic organizations in Britain were appalled by incidents like this, nor did Stanley appease them when he threatened to give them all 'seven tons of Bibles, four tons of prayer books, any number of surplices and a church organ into the bargain' if they could reach longitude 23° 'without chucking some of those Bibles at some of those negroes heads'.[5] In his defence, the punishment of one man, if it obviated a long delay, could mean that all the other members of the party got a decent period of rest before going on.

Stanley arrived at Unyanyembe, two hundred miles east of Lake Tanganyika, at the end of June 1871, having made excellent time, but now he was held up for three months by the war the Arabs were fighting with the natives living between Unyanyembe and Ujiji. Stanley's frustration was all the worse when he heard that a white man had either arrived at Ujiji, or was on his way there. Stanley attempted to fight his way past the trouble but failed; then, in early October, he set out on a long southern detour to avoid the fighting. On 3 November, with a much reduced party of fifty-four, Stanley triumphantly entered Ujiji.

Stanley was not a naturally religious man, and yet, as he had come closer to Ujiji, he began to see his journey as a pilgrimage: a divinely appointed task, and not merely as a journalistic assignment which would make him both rich and famous. Just before leaving Unyanymbe, he had written:

> I have taken a solemn enduring oath, an oath to be kept while the least hope of life remains in me, not to be tempted to break the resolution I have formed, never to give up the search, until I find Livingstone alive, or find his dead body . . . only death can prevent me. But death—not even this; I shall not die, I will not, I cannot die![6]

With thoughts like this, and an absolute conviction that the meeting with Livingstone would be the crowning moment of his life, Stanley could not, without risking terrible bathos, admit, even to himself, that there was any chance at all that Dr Livingstone might be anything other than a unique and saintly man. Stanley's 'solemn enduring oath' would seem pretty foolish if Livingstone turned out to be a garrulous and vindictive old man. In fact, by the time Stanley met him, the sufferings of the past five years had substantially softened Livingstone's personality and had taken the edge off his former acerbity. But even so, as will be seen, when Stanley noted unpleasing aspects in Livingstone's character, he tried first of all to persuade himself that they did not exist, and, when that failed, made up his mind that nobody else should know.

When Stanley actually entered Ujiji his nerves were on edge, and, in spite of his imminent triumph, he could not keep other thoughts at bay. Perhaps, after all, Kirk had been right about Livingstone hating publicity. There was a chance that the Doctor might slip away before he had given any interviews or said anything memorable. Even when he reached Ujiji, Stanley was still unsure; still could not believe that some untoward event might not snatch everything from his grasp. One side of him was ecstatic; 'what would I not have given for a bit of friendly wilderness where, unseen, I might vent my joy in some mad freak, such as idiotically biting my hand, turning a somersault, or slashing at trees'. But uncertainty remained: 'When the moment of discovery came, and the man himself stood revealed before me, this constantly recurring doubt contributed not a little to make me unprepared for it. "It may not be Livingstone after all," doubt suggested. If this is he what shall I say to him? My imagination had not taken this question into consideration before. All around me was the immense crowd, hushed and expectant, and wondering how the scene would develop itself.'[7]

Stanley knew that whatever he first said to Livingstone would be likely to go down in history. After all, his words would be the first a white man had spoken to the Doctor in six years. He was awed by his own sense of occasion in a way that Livingstone could not have understood. At all costs Stanley was determined that 'his face should not betray emotion, lest it should detract from the dignity of a white man appearing under such extraordinary circumstances'.[8] He tried to imagine what an upper-class Englishman would have said and done in the same situation. He had hated the reserve and sang-froid of Napier's officers in Ethiopia, but he had envied them too. Poise and understatement were great Anglo-Saxon attributes and he would emulate them. And so Stanley walked up to Livingstone at a steady pace, doffed his hat and said the four words which he was to regret for the rest of his life. The very people he had attempted to impress later found his formal greeting a ludicrous parody. If ever there had been an excuse for effusive behaviour, surely this had been it. The words Stanley had hoped would lend dignity to a solemn occasion were later hailed with explosions of laughter and disbelief. They were used in music-hall burlesques; friends or strangers greeted each other substituting their

own names for Livingstone's. 'Dr Livingstone, I presume?'
one dummy asked another in a fashion plate in the
October 1872 issue of *Tailor and Cutter*.[9] A mass of
advertisements came out using the phrase. Stanley himself
was often met with 'Mr Stanley, I presume'. But he could
never see the joke. The greatest irony of all was to be the
fact that later generations would forget almost everything
about the main achievements of the two men but would
remember the joke phrase. As recently as November 1971
it re-emerged in a cartoon television advertisement for
beer.

But in November 1871 Livingstone did not laugh, for as
he took Stanley's hand he felt tears coming into his eyes.
There can be no doubt that Livingstone had never been so
pleased to see a white face as he was to see Stanley's. He
was not exaggerating when he told Stanley: 'You have
brought me new life.'[10] Stanley, who could not immediately have appreciated the absolute despair Livingstone had
been in before his arrival, considered the Doctor's genuine and outspoken gratitude to be the first indication of a
saintly character. Of course Livingstone would have been
outrageously inhuman had he not responded emotionally
to Stanley's arrival; for the journalist had not only brought
food, medicines, supplies and a package of letters that had
been held up for months at Unyanyembe; he had brought
Livingstone the first proper accounts of what had been
happening in the outside world that he had heard for five
years. Livingstone was soon listening open-mouthed as
Stanley told him about the Franco-Prussian War and the
fall of Paris. Stanley filled him in on items of news ranging
from the inauguration of the trans-atlantic telegraph, and
the opening of the Suez Canal, to the death of the British
Foreign Secretary, Lord Clarendon. But undoubtedly the
information which Livingstone listened to with most attention was that, due to Sir Roderick Murchison's persistent
and determined efforts, the Treasury had at last agreed to
let him have more money for supplies. The sum voted had
been £1,000.[11] The knowledge that he had not been
entirely forgotten in England did not make him any the
less grateful for what he called the 'disinterested kindness
of Mr Bennett, so nobly carried into effect by Mr Stanley'.

Livingstone's belief that Mr Bennett had acted only out
of affection for him was of course a ludicrous overstate-
ment of his debt to the newspaper owner, but, from the

beginning, Stanley behaved with a kindness and consideration which gave the lie to almost all his previous behaviour. He divided everything he had brought into two piles and gave Livingstone one of them. He prepared food for the old man with his own hands and saw that he had four meals a day. In every way that he could think of he made life easier for the Doctor, whose health soon seemed to improve. Stanley did not minimize the dangers he had survived on the journey and Livingstone was duly appreciative of his 'truly noble braving of death & danger to serve me as a son might have done'.[12] In letter after letter Livingstone lavished praise on the newcomer. He told Agnes: 'He came with the true American characteristic generosity—the tears often started into my eyes on every fresh proof of kindness.'[13]

If Livingstone was grateful, so was Stanley. Each sight of Livingstone reminded him that he had succeeded. He lived from day to day dazed with pleasure, frequently enjoying little dialogues with himself: 'What was I sent for?—To find Livingstone—Have you found him?—Yes, of course; am I not in his house? Whose compass is that hanging on a peg there? Whose clothes, whose boots, are those? Who reads those newspapers, those "Saturday Reviews" and numbers of "Punch" lying on the floor?'[14]

Mutual gratitude is a good foundation for friendship, and the advantages the two men brought each other must have been an important reason for their getting on so well together. But there was more to it than that. Livingstone had always disliked all forms of pretentiousness and cant. Stanley was awkward, shy, defensive and given to bluster, but he was rarely pretentious or hypocritical. Livingstone almost certainly sensed his insecurity and knew how he felt, for his origins, although less traumatic than Stanley's, had been similar. Both men shared the same shyness and as a result were often thought brusque and rude. This could have led to violent misunderstanding but it did not, for they seemed to recognize the same traits in each other and to make allowances accordingly.

Livingstone was not, as Kirk had predicted he would be, offended when he discovered that Stanley was a journalist. He had always liked his work to be appreciated, and trusted Stanley to present his travels and efforts in a favourable light. It was highly gratifying to feel that Mr Bennett, thousands of miles away in America, had thought him important enough to spend £4,000 for an interview. He had felt that the British Government and people had forgotten him and it therefore touched him all the more to think that a foreign nation had not done the same. Ever since he had tried to persuade his parents to emigrate there in the 1840s, he had thought highly of America, and now his affection naturally increased. He was not in any way offended when he heard that Kirk had been saying that Stanley would make his fortune out of him. Livingstone's reply was characteristic: 'He is heartily welcome, for it is a great deal more than I could ever make out of myself.'[15]

Livingstone wrote two letters to Mr Bennett within ten days of Stanley's arrival and both were of course for publication. If Stanley and Bennett stood to gain, so he felt did he. He was able to put his views on the slave-trade before a vast audience and to give enormous publicity to the massacre he had witnessed at Nyangwe. Stanley's arrival could not have come at a better time from that point of view. In fact the publicity given to these and other letters written by him, and the general furore caused by Stanley's feat, were of crucial importance in the revival of public indignation in Britain and America at the continuation of slavery in east Africa. Graphic descriptions of a full-blown massacre, and not just a few isolated deaths, were just what the missionary and philanthropic pressure groups needed to spur the Government on to a policy of abolition rather than restriction. Livingstone also used the *New York Herald* to put over his arguments against notions of African racial inferiority.

> I have no prejudice against their colour; indeed, any one who lives long among them forgets that they are black and feels that they are just fellow-men . . . If a comparison were instituted, and Manyuema, taken at random, placed opposite say the members of the Anthropological Society of London, clad like them in kilts of grass cloth, I should like to take my place among the Manyuema, on the principle of preferring the company of my betters.[16]

Having said what he wanted to, Livingstone was quite prepared to please Stanley by writing a few whimsical passages about Manyuema women and their beauty:

'their charming black eyes, beautiful foreheads, nicely rounded limbs . . . But they must adorn themselves; and this they do—oh, the hussies!—by filing their splendid teeth to points like cat's teeth.'

Kirk had suggested to Stanley that Livingstone would dash off as soon as possible after being 'found', and had added that the old veteran hated publicity. When Stanley realized that Livingstone had no desire to try and get rid of him and was eager to co-operate in giving information about his travels to date and his plans for the future, the young journalist was so overwhelmed with gratitude and relief that he at once assumed that all the stories he had heard from Kirk and others about Livingstone's perverse antisocial behaviour had been malicious fabrications. Stanley made up his mind to remedy the situation once and for all; he knew that the despatches he would send back to the *New York Herald* would be published in other papers throughout the world. So Stanley set about canonizing Dr Livingstone: a figure 'without spleen or misanthropy', a man as near an angel 'as the nature of living man will allow'; not overtly or self-consciously pious either, but with quiet honesty. Nor was Livingstone gloomy or inward-looking, for he had a 'fund of quiet humour'. 'His gentleness never forsakes him; his hopefulness never deserts him. No harassing anxieties, distractions of mind, long separation from home and kindred, can make him complain . . . His is the Spartan heroism, the inflexibility of the Roman, the enduring resolution of the Anglo-Saxon— never to relinquish his work though his heart yearns for home.' This then was the picture of Livingstone which Stanley gave the world. He repeated it in speeches, articles, letters and finally gave it more permanent form in his world-wide best seller, *How I Found Livingstone*, published in England and America in 1872. But the lasting effect of Stanley's character study was its acceptance by almost all those who read or heard about it at the time, and by subsequent biographers.

Stanley cannot be accused of deliberate insincerity; the great personal meaning with which he had invested his meeting with Livingstone influenced him, to some extent unconsciously, and Livingstone's unfeigned gratitude and genuine liking for Stanley did the rest. Livingstone's infinite patience with all Africans, even those who had deserted him, also justifiably impressed Stanley. But after a couple of months with Livingstone, Stanley wrote in his diary: 'I have had some intrusive suspicions, thoughts that he [Livingstone] was not of such an angelic temper as I believed him to be during my first month with him; but I have been driving them steadily from my mind . . .'

A little later, however, Stanley was certain that his suspicions were well founded and that Livingstone by 'reiterated complaints against this man and the others' had proved that 'his strong nature was opposed to forgiveness'.[17] Livingstone had in fact been going over all his old quarrels that had taken place during the Zambesi Expedition. To be 'opposed to forgiveness' was hardly consistent with being as near an angel 'as the nature of living man will allow', but in subsequent despatches and articles Stanley made no qualification of his earlier rhapsodic praise for the saintly Doctor. Perhaps he disliked the idea of seeming to have been gullible, and he may also have realized that the story of the discovery of a forgotten saint made far better copy than any rather more truthful account would have done. The above extracts from Stanley's diary were only published five years after Stanley's death in 1909.

In fact Stanley became even more aware of the weaknesses in Livingstone's character when he came to talk to the Doctor about John Kirk. Stanley had disliked Kirk ever since their first meeting, and he had become convinced that Kirk had neither taken sufficient care in the selection of members of the caravans despatched with goods for Livingstone, nor taken routine precautions to see that these caravans had set off from the coast at once. Before Stanley's arrival, Livingstone had not found fault with Kirk; the Doctor had realized that, due to the war outside Unyanyembe and also as a result of successive outbreaks of cholera in Zanzibar and along the coast, assembling caravans at all could have been no easy matter during 1869 and 1870. Apart from that, as Livingstone knew, Kirk had to perform many routine duties as Acting British Consul at Zanzibar. Stanley's charges, apart from those already mentioned, were that Kirk had deliberately employed slaves as porters and had gone to Sewji's—a firm notorious for its association with slave caravans—to get supplies. Livingstone himself had also gone to Sewji's in 1866, largely because that firm had a virtual monopoly. Judged by the most exacting standards, Kirk might perhaps have done more for Livingstone, but short of having gone personally with the caravans to Ujiji, which he could only have done by abandoning his post at Zanzibar, he could never have guaranteed the safety of Livingstone's supplies. Even Stanley, with all his discipline, had lost many of his porters and a quantity of his stores on the way to Ujiji.

But the rights and wrongs of the arguments Stanley used against Kirk are not really of cardinal importance. The row between the two men brought in Livingstone, but is far more revealing of Stanley's character than Livingstone's. For this reason and because Sir Reginald Coupland dealt thoroughly with this episode in his book *Livingstone's Last Journey* (1947), I have confined myself to a short summary. What mattered was that Livingstone, usually inclined to believe that former friends had let him down, accepted Stanley's charges. Livingstone was soon writing letters to most of his correspondents, telling them no longer to refer to Kirk, as Sir Roderick Murchison did, as 'companion of Livingstone'. One friend was told that Kirk was 'too lazy and indifferent to serve David Livingstone',[18] and another, that the Acting British Consul at Zanzibar had inflicted on him 'a loss of two years time, at least 1,800 miles of tramp, and what money I don't exactly know'.[19]

Stanley, who had merely intended to discredit Kirk, had had no idea that Livingstone might begin to see the whole matter as a monstrous conspiracy against him, in which Kirk, the British Government and the Council of the Royal Geographical Society were all in league. Livingstone soon suspected that Kirk had been acting on instructions from the Foreign Office to force him home. The extra £1,000 grant had merely been a blind to deceive him into believing that the Government still supported him. The Foreign Office was clearly ganging up with the members of the Council of the R.G.S. who wanted him home to get their hands on his precious notes.

So when Stanley, who had noticed that Livingstone had by no means made a thorough recovery, attempted to persuade the old man to come home to recuperate, get some artificial teeth and build up his strength in England before returning to Africa for a final effort on the Lualaba, he was surprised and wounded that Livingstone refused even to consider the suggestion. Ironically Stanley remained unaware that his attack on Kirk had made Livingstone's refusal a foregone conclusion. Once Livingstone felt suspicious and persecuted there was no holding him and soon he was even suggesting that Kirk was trying to force him back to England so that he, Kirk, could 'finish up the sources'.[20] Livingstone had tried to persuade Kirk to come out to Africa in 1865, but since he could offer no salary, Kirk, who had then been contemplating marriage, had felt unable to accept. Livingstone now argued that Kirk had realized that he had made a sad mistake and was attempting, by unscrupulous means, to reverse it before it was too late.[21] In this state of mind Livingstone felt unable to trust anybody. In December 1871 he sent his daughter Agnes a rough map, incorporating his latest conclusions on the Lualaba, and told her solemnly: 'Now I entrust it to you, and if you betray my confidence I shall never trust you again—if Sir Roderick asks, say that all your letter is private and confidential . . . He is not too easily put off but be firm.'[22]

Sir Roderick had been almost entirely responsible for getting Livingstone his extra £1,000 out of the Government. Murchison had in fact blackmailed the Foreign Secretary, by telling him that he would publish the Foreign Office correspondence with Livingstone for 1864 and 1865. He had also told Clarendon that if no money was voted he would shame the Government by raising a public subscription fund.[23] Perhaps it was as well that Sir Roderick would never know that Livingstone had lost faith in him; he had been dead two months when Livingstone stopped trusting him.

Stanley had brought Livingstone new life and new hope and had saved him at a critical time, but the doubts he had raised in Livingstone's mind not only revived old traits like vindictiveness and mistrust, at a time when Livingstone seemed to have outgrown them, but also made sure Livingstone would never return to England to make a proper recovery before attempting to finish his work. Stanley, to make Livingstone feel still more indebted to him, had not minded letting the old man know that people in England did not care much about him. Livingstone had already suspected as much and it confirmed his feeling that if he came home without having proved that the Lualaba was the Nile, it would be to a life of disgrace and poverty. 'To return unsuccessful,' he told Agnes, would mean 'going abroad to an unhealthy consulate to which no public sympathy would ever be drawn'.[24] When the *Lady Nyassa* had finally been sold in Bombay, the money had been invested in a bank that failed. So now, unless he broke the trust he had set up for his children, Livingstone would have no money on his return. There would be no pension either. It would have to be death or success.

Stanley and Livingstone spent five months together in all. During November and December 1871 the two men did their only piece of mutual exploring and it proved highly significant. They travelled to the northern end of Lake Tanganyika and discovered that the river there—the Lusizé—flowed into the lake and not out of it. This finally proved that Lakes Tanganyika and Albert had no connection. Livingstone's eastern line of drainage had nothing to do with the Nile. Had he been aware of this on his arrival at Nyangwe in March 1870 he would undoubtedly have made more determined efforts to cross the Lualaba, even building a raft if all else had failed, but all the time he had believed that whatever the ultimate destination of the Lualaba and Lomani rivers, he still had the eastern line of drainage to fall back on. Now he knew otherwise. Everything depended on the Lualaba and the sources of the Lomani. On this trip Stanley was distressed at the numerous attacks of dysentery Livingstone suffered.

On 13 December the two men returned to Ujiji and two weeks later set off for Unyanyembe, Stanley on his way home, Livingstone to collect any supplies from Kirk's caravans that had not got through to Ujiji. Unyanyembe was reached on 18 February 1872, and once again Stanley vainly attempted to persuade Livingstone to change his mind about coming home. At last Stanley agreed instead to help Livingstone in any way he could. The two of them drew up a list of supplies which Livingstone would need for the long journey ahead of him, and Stanley promised to send everything with fifty porters as soon as he could after reaching the coast. These fifty men he swore would be free men and reliable too. As the time grew closer for parting, Livingstone tried to detain Stanley a little longer, till the rains ended, but Stanley, although in many ways reluctant to leave, was in others eager to get away: he

had yet to telegraph his news to the world, and he knew
that the longer he stayed with the Doctor, the longer Livingstone would have to wait for his fifty porters and the
supplies.

On the evening of 13 March all Stanley's preparations
for departure on the following day had been completed.
Livingstone handed over to him the letters he had written
while they had been together and, as a sign of his complete trust in Stanley, his journal. This was sealed with five
seals and marked not to be opened until his own return to
England or his death. In England it was to be entrusted to
Agnes. Livingstone did not waste words on the parting.
'Mr Stanley leaves,' was all he wrote. But there was no
doubt at all that he felt considerably more. In letters to
most of his friends he instructed them to treat Stanley with
friendship and kindness 'just as you would do to me'.[25]
In many letters he compared Stanley's behaviour to that
of an ideal son. As a great privilege Livingstone had confided to Stanley all his thoughts about the central African
river system. 'He has a clear idea of the geography,' Livingstone told H. W. Bates, the Assistant Secretary of the
Royal Geographical Society.[26] Stanley did not doubt Livingstone's conclusions, because Livingstone had visited the
Lualaba and he had not. Also, being a self-educated man,
and never having read any Ptolemy or Herodotus, Stanley
did not see anything strange in relying on their information.

The night before Stanley left, Livingstone's reserve
finally broke down completely and he 'poured out his
gratitude . . . uttered with no mincing phrases'. Stanley
was so touched that he wept openly like 'a child of
eight'.[27] The following morning their last breakfast was
sad and largely silent. Livingstone realized that Stanley
might well prove his last link with the outside world; the
job of tracing the Lomani north from its source and then
going on along the Lualaba would have taxed his endurance to the utmost twenty years before. So Livingstone,
to keep Stanley with him a little longer, accompanied him
for the first few miles of his journey to the coast. Stanley
also seemed to have a presentiment that they would never
meet again, and as they walked side by side, he 'took long
looks at Livingstone to impress his features thoroughly on
my memory'. When they parted and Stanley went on
alone, the journalist could barely keep back his tears, and

when Chuma and Susi ran up to him to kiss his hands, it was too much for him. 'I betrayed myself . . . "March! Why do you stop? Go on! Are you not going home?" And my people were driven before me. No more weakness. I shall show them such marching as will make them remember me.'[28]

Within a week of Stanley's landing in England on 1 August 1872, the story of his meeting with Livingstone had swept all other items off the main news pages of all the major papers in Britain. Whereas in March 1867, reports of Livingstone's death had been given barely half a column in most papers, now, throughout August and September 1872, it was not unusual to see two pages of ten full columns each, devoted exclusively to Livingstone. The main reason for this extraordinary volte-face was the realization, by most editors, of the fact that Mr Bennett had been aware of three years before, namely that a meeting between a journalist and a once-famous explorer, who had been seen by no member of his own race for five years, made an exceptionally good story. Stanley made it a much better story by turning up in Britain and claiming that Dr Livingstone was not only a great explorer, who had been forgotten by his own countrymen, but a near saint.

Just before Stanley had reached Britain, many papers had published articles insinuating, and some openly stating, that Stanley was a fraud and that he had not found Livingstone at all; all the information he claimed to possess could have been culled from despatches sent home by Livingstone in 1866 and 1867. On 2 August, the day after Stanley's arrival in Britain, the Foreign Secretary, in an open letter to *The Times*, had silenced all these critics by stating that all the despatches brought home by Stanley were without question genuine. Having previously cast doubt on Stanley the press now attempted to make up for their previous errors by accepting, without reservation, his glowing picture of Dr Livingstone. The editor of the *Standard*'s description of Livingstone, as 'the brave, noble hearted and heavenly minded Dr Livingstone', became typical.[29] The Foreign Office released passages from Livingstone's despatches, and the story of his losses, his suffering and his continuing efforts was published in most papers in his own words. The reaction of the editor of the *Morning Post* was re-echoed in every other paper: 'To those who live at home at ease, it may well appear marvellous that any human being would voluntarily undergo the hardships suffered by Livingstone, or could undergo them and live to tell the tale.'[30] The idea of a lonely man, surrounded by cannibals and slave-traders, floundering through swamps with ten-foot reeds, prostrated by fever, yet still forcing his way on through the 'dark continent', seemed so miraculous that most people never bothered to ask what he had been doing or whether he had achieved his objectives.

On the whole, when the press did touch on the value of Livingstone's discoveries they tended to accept that Speke and Baker had been wrong and that Livingstone had found the true source of the Nile. It would not be known positively that he had been deceived for another five years, and in the meantime the certainty of most geographers that the height Livingstone had given for Nyangwe meant that the Lualaba was the Congo, was disparaged by many journalists as an 'armchair opinion'. So for the last years of his life and the first years after his death, Livingstone's reputation as a great geographer was built up sufficiently for the subsequent revelation of his crucial error to have a comparatively minor impact. Livingstone's reports on the massacre at Nyangwe also made a deep impression and it was often said that 'even the discovery of the Nile is secondary to that far greater object—namely putting an end to the slave trade'. Livingstone's former dependence on the Arabs received little attention.

There can be no doubt that Livingstone got a great deal more coverage than he would have done otherwise through the series of acrimonious rows Stanley became involved in during his months in Britain. The worst of these quarrels was over a British expedition sent out to relieve Dr Livingstone in early 1872. This party had been planned by the Council of the R.G.S. on the assumption that Stanley would never manage to get out of Unyanyembe through the war to the west of that town. The Relief Expedition, for which £4,000 was subscribed, arrived on the African mainland to find that Stanley had forestalled them. The officers resigned and the venture was abandoned. No contingency plan had been made for what they should do if Stanley succeeded; his failure had been considered a foregone conclusion. Stanley felt that the officers of the expedition had been carelessly chosen and that the whole business had been badly planned. When he got to Britain he said this, and so became embroiled in an unpleasant quarrel with the Council of the R.G.S. This was widely reported and sides were taken. Most of the papers took the view that the expedition should have gone on and done something, as opposed to returning to Britain, having wasted £2,300 of the money which had been publicly subscribed. The press in general made this row an excuse to attack the British Government for having abandoned Livingstone in the first place; had they not done so, it was claimed, the Doctor would never have needed a Relief Expedition. Articles soon appeared castigating the Foreign Office for meanness and indifference to the fate of one of Britain's greatest men. The hypocrisy of these attacks went unnoticed. The press had, of course, been just as indifferent to Livingstone as the Government, before Mr James Gordon Bennett had decided to send Stanley to *find* Livingstone. It was a waste of time for the Foreign Office to issue statements saying that Livingstone, in addition to his £500 grant, had been voted £1,000, and that £1,200 of public money had been spent on the search party sent out in 1867. The press and public had made up their minds that a dedicated and godly man had been ignored by the people only because the Government had withheld information.

In 1864, after the Zambesi Expedition, Livingstone had been attacked in almost every national paper for having led innocent men to their death and having wasted a great deal of Treasury money on a venture which he ought to have known was doomed from the beginning. In 1872 Stanley wiped away the memory of Livingstone's earlier failures so effectively that today *his* picture of Dr Livingstone is still the accepted version.

There is one more important fact about Stanley's visit to Britain: he brought information about the slave-trade, in the form of Livingstone's despatches, at a crucial time. During 1871 a House of Commons Select Committee had been set up to review the problem of the east African slave-trade. The Committee had in the end come out in favour of total abolition of the seaborne trade. This conclusion was largely the result of evidence submitted by Kirk, Livingstone and Sir Bartle Frere—Livingstone's evidence, it should be added, dated back to the last despatches received in London prior to Stanley's visit: these had been written in 1867. Once the Select Committee had made its recommendations the Government was not bound to act on them, and, at the time of Stanley's arrival in Britain in August 1872, no final decision had been made. Livingstone's description of the massacre at Nyangwe, however, was an incredible piece of good fortune for the abolitionist lobby, and they used it most effectively. By the end of September 1872, Gladstone's Government had decided on the abolition of the sale of all slaves, whether for domestic use or for export. Sir Bartle Frere, the Governor of Bombay, was appointed to sign a treaty with the Sultan of Zanzibar to that effect. On 5 June 1873, after being threatened with a British naval blockade, the Sultan signed, and that day the slave market in Zanzibar was closed for ever. Frere himself was convinced that Livingstone's information had been crucial in provoking immediate Government action, and he ought to have known.[31] So while there can be little doubt, in view of the Select Committee's findings, that abolition would have come in the end anyway, Livingstone's information ensured that the process was not delayed. It was tragic that Livingstone himself never lived to hear about Frere's treaty.

23

The Last Journey, 1872–1873

As Livingstone waited at Unyanyembe, throughout the spring and summer of 1872, he knew nothing about the fame Stanley had brought him, nor did he have any idea of the impact his anti-slavery despatches had had. All that came his way, as he waited six weary months for the men and supplies Stanley had promised to send from the coast, was news that a Relief Expedition had been sent and had broken up after Stanley's arrival at Zanzibar. Livingstone's son, Oswell, had been a member of the expedition, and like the others had decided not to press on. His father was shocked by this, and, even when he knew that, since the others had resigned first, Oswell would have had to have gone on alone, Livingstone did not forgive him. As he told Agnes, her brother should have had 'the sense to come with me and gain a little credit that may enable him to hold up his head among men and not be merely Dr Livingstone's son'.[1] And when, several weeks later, Livingstone received two letters from Oswell, telling him that his prime purpose in coming to Africa had been to persuade his father to come home, an enraged Livingstone not only accused Oswell of cowardice and duplicity but also described his letters as 'the most snobbish and impertinent I ever received or read'. Oswell, he continued, was 'as poor a specimen of a son as Africa ever produced': a young man who 'does not think of supporting himself by his own labour' but prefers 'to run away home calling loudly for more money'.[2] Livingstone's old sisters, who also wanted a cash handout, were additional targets for his scathing pen. 'I devoted all my money to these neer do weels [sic] and they forget the hand that fed, clothed & lodged them & say I forgot them.'[3] Livingstone's extreme irritation is not hard to understand. He felt that at the moment when he stood poised to begin the most important and arduous of all his journeys, his family—Agnes excepted—far from encouraging him, were doing everything in their power to discourage him so that he would consent to come home and write another best-seller for them to live off. That they might have been genuinely worried that unless he returned home, Africa would kill him, just as it had killed his wife, did not seem to have occurred to him.

During his six months at Unyanyembe Livingstone had plenty of time to think not only of his ungrateful family, but also about his past and what he had so far achieved with his life. He recalled his failure to encourage traders and the Government's rejection of his colonial plans. For the first time in his life he could not help feeling that he had possibly been too ambitious. He thought back still further to his days in Bechuanaland and remembered the hopes he had once held of succeeding as an ordinary missionary. Now he wondered whether the conventional missionary approach might not have been the best. Missions could be established within a few hundred miles of the coast; that would be a beginning. Old ideas flooded back. Had he really ever given native agency a chance? Two missionaries in a place like Unyanyembe might be able to achieve something with the help of native teachers.[4] Magomero had failed because the communications had been too bad; the same difficulties would not be experienced in the area midway between Lake Tanganyika and Zanzibar. But this idea only stayed with Livingstone for a week or two; soon he was off on a new theory, as wild and impracticable as any he had ever dreamed up. On the west African coast successful missions had converted large numbers of Africans. If these men, or a proportion of them, could be induced to join a voluntary emigration scheme from west to east Africa, their influence might prove great enough to stop chiefs selling their people into slavery. Africans might be better for the job than whites: 'English people in a new country show themselves very often to be born fools.'[5] Soon Livingstone abandoned this idea too. But the real miracle is that, after all his previous rebuffs and disappointments, the man was still an optimist, still an idealist thinking of new ways of changing Africa. Livingstone had not succumbed to fatalism nor to blind acceptance of the escapist dream that Providence alone would sort out everything.

During this time Livingstone also thought about his immediate aims. Although his itinerary would be completely dominated by the geographical task ahead, he could not help believing that this work was far less significant than action taken against the slave-trade. 'What I have seen of this horrid system,' he told a friend, 'makes me feel that its suppression would be of infinitely more importance than all the fountains [sources] together.'[6] Yet if he abandoned his Nile pilgrimage, there was no knowing whether he would be able to do any more to combat the slave-trade in some other way. He would continue to write despatches, to keep up his journal and to hope that if he returned home the public would listen to him. If he could prove the Lualaba to be the Nile, he felt that his words would gain a prestige and authority which would otherwise be denied them. But later, as will be seen, when pain and illness once again began to destroy him, he reverted to his old obsession with the Nile as an end in itself: a compensation for every other failure. In his last weeks he would not be able to bear the memory of the deaths of Nyangwe, that 'come back unbidden, and make me start up at dead of night', without believing that his search for the source would in itself help end the slave-trade.

Waiting for Stanley's men, Livingstone wrote the words

that were to be cut into the stone that marks his grave in Westminster Abbey: 'All I can say in my lonliness* is, may heaven's rich blessing come down on every one— American, English, Turk—who will help to heal this open sore of the world.'[7]

Five days after Stanley had left, Livingstone had celebrated his fifty-ninth birthday with a reaffirmation of faith: '19th. March—Birthday. My Jesus, my King, my life, my all; I again dedicate my whole self to Thee. Accept me, and grant, O Gracious Father, that ere this year is gone I may finish my task. In Jesus' name I ask it. Amen, so let it be. David Livingstone.'[8]

And if he was to achieve anything like the task he had set himself within a year, Livingstone knew that he would have to be off soon, and so, as he waited and the days slipped by, he felt more and more impatient. The best months for travel were passing. But impatient though he was, Livingstone was once again excited and happy. The men would come and the supplies, and then he would redeem all past failures. In this mood he could write to friends jovially telling them 'that all past misdemeanors, faults, failings and nonsense are hereby condoned and obliterated . . . I feel inclined to proclaim an amnesty to all the world'.[9] When the cold east wind and sudden showers gave him a touch of fever, his optimism was unchanged. He wrote asking Horace Waller, his friend from the Universities Mission, to make preparations for his return home when he had finished his work: 'Will you speak to a dentist about a speedy fitting of arteficial teeth? I beg your aid to secure lodgings for me say anywhere near Regent's Park—comfortable and decent, but not excessively dear.'[10]

Often in the past he had thought he would not survive, but now he had no such presentiments. In another letter to a friend he spoke of the same foreboding he had known in the past and went on: 'it is weakened now, as I seem to see the end to which I have been striving looming in the distance'.[11] In that distance were the four fountains of Herodotus, the source of the Lomani, the Lualaba and finally, somewhere two or three hundred miles north of Lake Albert, the Nile. First, in order to get to the sources of the Lomani river, Livingstone knew that he

---

* On the stone 'solitude' replaced 'lonliness'.

would have to skirt Bangweolo's southern shore. But this did not distress him, even though he must have realized that unless he could leave Unyanyembe by June, he would arrive at Bangweolo in the rains. In his own view there was no need for alarm; he had been there before and knew the shape of the lake, or thought he did.

As April, May and June passed, and the men still did not come, inactivity at last began to undermine Livingstone's good spirits. Doubts reappeared. Livingstone began a despatch to the Foreign Secretary outlining the route he intended to take: south-west to Bangweolo and then west along the southern shore of that lake. 'Being then in Lat 12° the course will be straight west to the fountains of Herodotus. But what if these fountains exist only in my imagination! Then we shall see.' He never finished the despatch for it ended: 'In battling down the central line of drainage: the Lualaba—the enormous amount of westing it made caused me at times to feel as if knocking my head against a stone wall. It might be the Congo and . . .'[12] In his journal over and over again he began to express the same doubt. 'I know too much to be positive'; and positive he desperately wanted to be.[13] To take such risks and suffer so much needlessly would be ironic beyond endurance, but there could be no turning back. He had already expressed himself with too much certainty to feel able to climb down; besides Stanley's men would have left the coast weeks before. The case was beyond arguing now; only action remained, and he would go on, as he had always done. Two years before, in Manyuema, he had written to a friend: 'Had I known all the hunger, hardship, toil and time required, I might have preferred a strait-waistcoat to undertaking the task; but having taken it in hand, I could not bear to be beaten by it.'[14]

At last, on 9 August, an advance party of Stanley's men marched into Unyanyembe. Livingstone could not contain his excitement. 'How thankful I am I cannot confess,' he wrote in his journal.[15] Stanley had sent fifty-six men in all. They had been extremely carefully chosen and twenty had served on Stanley's journey to Ujiji. Six were Nassick boys, who had been members of the abortive Relief Expedition, and the rest had been taken on at Bagamoyo on the coast. The men had all been engaged to serve for twenty-five to thirty dollars a year each for two years. Stanley had written into their contracts that if Livingstone's

work should still be incomplete at the end of their term
of service they should stay with him till he had reached
a place where he could take on new porters. Stanley had
equipped each man with a musket and had provided ten
kegs of powder and three thousand bullets. Flour, sugar,
coffee, tea, numerous varieties of tinned food, a new
journal, a chronometer and a pile of Nautical Almanacs
made up a part of the stores the men came with. In addition there were two riding donkeys, hundreds of yards of
cloth and a slave chain, 'with which,' Stanley told Livingstone in a letter carried by the men, 'you may imprison in
iron collars any incorrigibles you may have'.[16] Livingstone, not surprisingly, never used the iron collars, but he
was touched by Stanley's letter which reflected the sharp
contrasts of the man himself, juxtaposing affection, exhor-
tation and self-interest in a single paragraph.

> My dear Doctor, very few amongst men have I found
> I so much got to love as yourself . . . England and
> America expect their people to do their duty. Do
> yours as persistently as heretofore & come back to
> your friends and country to be crowned with the
> laurel, and I will go forth to do mine . . . Do not for-
> get the *Herald* please. The *Herald* will be grateful to
> me for securing you as a Correspondent . . .[17]

As Livingstone surveyed his new party, the best
equipped he had ever had, he thanked God Stanley had
come and told Agnes: 'that good brave fellow has acted
as a son to me'.[18] It was not an overestimate. Livingstone
now had just over sixty men, including the five men who
had stayed with him since 1866: Chuma, Susi, Amoda and
two of the Nassick boys, Mabruki and Gardner.

A start was made on 25 August. Livingstone's intention
was to travel south-west till he hit Tanganyika, and then
to follow the lake south to its foot. From there he would
head south-west, skirt the southern shore of Bangweolo
and then march due west to Katanga and the four fountains. The first weeks of the journey were smooth in
comparison with his experiences in 1866 and 1869. Nevertheless a series of minor misfortunes would together prove
significant. First of all a case of dried milk was left behind
at Unyanyembe. Then his ten cows were allowed to stray
into a belt of tsetse and died as a result. Milk was the
only food which restored Livingstone's health when he had

dysentery, so these two misfortunes coming together did not augur well for the future. The tsetse fly also accounted for the expedition's best riding donkey, which was a severe loss.

In the past, rain and mud had been the greatest hindrance to travelling. Now heat proved almost as bad. Throughout September and October, Livingstone's journal was full of complaints about how the relentless sun sapped his strength and slowed down the pace of his men. The heat was so intense that the porters' bare feet were blistered and burned by the soil. In these conditions it was a mistake to hug the shores of Tanganyika, since this meant constant clambering up hills and out of valleys. But Livingstone was determined to map the southern part of the lake. He had suffered a minor attack of fever and severe dysentery before reaching the lake in early October, and the extra effort he forced on himself prevented a satisfactory recovery. It was a sadly typical error. By the middle of October he was admitting that he felt tired and ill, and that every effort was made only with the greatest difficulty. In his own words, he felt 'constrained to lie like a log'. The tiredness was due more to dysentery than heat, although he himself did not care to confess as much.

By the beginning of October they were nearing the southern end of the lake, and the hardships of climbing were over. The rains however were not far off and, although the going was easier, the country was thinly populated and food was hard to come by. On 9 November, Livingstone's old problem of anal bleeding stopped them all for a few days. It was a clear indication that, in spite of his recuperation during Stanley's visit, his recovery had been superficial at best. He knew the rains were coming and his previous journey to Bangweolo had told him that, even if he managed to avoid the worst swamps, he would still have to ford a multitude of small rivers and marshes. But severe bleeding was not going to deter him. It never seemed to occur to him that he should turn back. The basis for such incredible optimism was the list of his previous hardships. It was impossible for him to believe that anything he would encounter in the future could be worse than conditions he had already survived in the past.

As they pressed on south the food shortage increased, and it was probably because of this that he temporarily abandoned his original idea of passing to the south of Lake

Bangweolo. In fact his hand was forced on 3 December by a native guide who told him that if he continued south-west the food situation would get worse. Reluctantly he allowed the guide to take him to the western shore of Bangweolo. This journey of 170 miles was to take over a month, for by mid-December the full fury of the rains had once again transformed the country. For day after day the rain fell, sometimes in sheets, sometimes in a thin steady drizzle. Streams burst their banks, flat land became swamp and the party was held up for days on end trying to get canoes to cross the larger rivers. All this time, Livingstone was seldom dry. Often he slept on a wet bed.

Ironically when he did arrive near the western shore of the lake and the guide told him where he was, he refused to believe him. He was convinced he was on the north-eastern side of Bangweolo. This conviction was directly due to the faulty longitudes he had taken on his first visit to the lake in 1868. Those observations had been forty miles too much to the west and so now he reckoned he was far east of the position the guide claimed to have brought him to. He wanted to get to the southern shore of the lake to make sure there were no sources south of it, before heading for Katanga as planned. Local natives told him the best way round the lake was to head south-west. To Livingstone, who imagined himself north-east of the lake, a south-westerly course seemed madness. In his view it would take him into the lake itself and not round it. Ironically had the guide taken him a bit further he would have recognized where he was, for then he would have been almost at the point where he had reached the lake in 1868; but Livingstone was determined to take no further native advice. By trying to persuade him to go south-west, he was convinced that they had proved themselves eager to force him round the lake by the longest route. Instead he would head east and get round that way. It was to prove a disastrous decision.

Four years before, he had wrongly concluded that the lake was 150 miles long from east to west. He had been taken out in a canoe by natives who had turned back just too soon for him to see that Bangweolo was really only twenty-five miles of true lake and for the rest was marsh and bog. Most of this marshland was to the east of the true lake and this was the direction he was now heading in. The longer he went on, the more confused he became.

He expected water but found only endless reeds and mud. There was no high ground from which he might see any distance. By mid-January 1873 he had arrived at the north-eastern side of Bangweolo, the point which he had thought himself at weeks before. Now he believed himself safe to head south and thus skirt the lake. If he had then been as far east as he believed himself to be, this decision would have been all right. But south from the north-eastern shore of the lake led straight into the swamps, which stretched away almost a hundred miles to the south-east.

No landmarks that he had picked out on his previous journey were any use to him, for in the rains everything looked completely different. In early February the sky cleared enough for him to make new observations for latitude. Had he believed his new observations, all might have been well, but these new figures proved that the guide had not been lying and that he himself had been mistaken all along. This Livingstone would not accept. In his view the observations he had made in 1868, in far better conditions, were more likely to have been right. He concluded that water had wrecked the reflectors of his sextant and so ignored his new discoveries. From that time on he was doomed. For the next two months he would never again be sure where he was.[19]

By January of 1873 Livingstone's strength had reached a very low ebb. He was losing blood daily and with the constant cold and wet and the lack of milk and decent food there was no hope of his condition improving. The party rarely covered more than a mile and a half a day and even that was taxing their leader's powers to their limit. Hour after hour they all waded on through oozing mud and overflowing streams. The wonder is that few men deserted, but now all of them seemed tied to the lonely man and felt unable to abandon him. Often Livingstone had to be carried across streams and rivers on the shoulders of his men, but they did not complain. These rivers were usually pitted with deep hollows and were sometimes half a mile wide. As Livingstone wrote on 24 January: 'Carrying me across one of the broad deep sedgy rivers is really a very difficult task . . . The first part, the main stream came up to Susi's mouth, and wetted my seat and legs. One held up my pistol behind, then one after another took a turn, and when he sank into a deep elephant's footprint, he required two to lift him.'[20]

10. 'The main stream came up to Susi's mouth'

As though the cold and the rain were not enough, they were also plagued by leeches, and when they did find dry ground, it was usually occupied by red ants. One night, as he lay in bed, Livingstone was attacked by an army of them. 'The first came on my foot quietly, then some began to bite between the toes, then the larger ones swarmed over the foot and bit furiously, and made the blood start out. I then went out of the tent and my whole person was instantly covered as close as small pox.'[21] Amazingly Livingstone used this experience for scientific observation and described the shape and size of their mandibles and how they used their six legs to acquire leverage to bite. Nor was this an isolated example of his devoting time to minute observation. Whenever anything of interest occurred he noted it down, even something as apparently trivial as the appearance of a small frog. The following passage shows not only Livingstone's ability to forget himself in his appreciation of nature but also his complete lack of self-pity and complaining during these dreadful months.

> Caught in a drenching rain, which made me fain to sit, exhausted as I was, under an umbrella for an hour trying to keep the trunk dry. As I sat in the rain a little tree-frog, about half an inch long, leaped on to a grassy leaf, and began a tune as loud as that of many birds, and very sweet; it was surprising to hear so much music out of so small a musician. I drank

some rain water as I felt faint—in the paths it is now calf deep. I crossed a hundred yards of slush waist deep in mid channel, and full of holes made by elephant's feet, the path hedged in by reedy grass, often intertwined and very tripping. I stripped off my clothes on reaching my hut in a village, and a fire during night nearly dried them. At the same time I rubbed my legs with palm oil, and in the morning had a delicious breakfast of sour goat's milk and porridge.[22]

But miraculously stoical though he was, the steady loss of blood and increasing weakness soon affected his thinking again. From now on he became more and more obsessive about the Nile and Herodotus' four fountains. Hopelessly lost, and by now bleeding slowly to death, Livingstone began writing despatches to the Foreign Secretary— despatches that would never be sent. Livingstone wrote as though he had already made his discovery; pathetically, only dates and geographical positions are omitted.

I have the pleasure of reporting to your Lordship that on the,   I succeeded at last in reaching your remarkable fountains, each of which, at no great distance off, becomes a large river. They rise at the base of a swell of land or earthen mound, which can scarcely be called a hill, for it seems only about,   feet above the general level . . . Possibly these four gushing fountains may be the very same that were mentioned to Herodotus . . . The geographical position of the mound or low earthen hill, may for the present be taken as latitude,   and longitude,   . The altitude above the sea,   .[23]

Then, as if waking from a dream, he remembers that the discovery is not yet made but still cannot admit it. Instead he will keep the fountains and confess as a postscript that the sources may lead to the Congo and not the Nile. That was the old doubt that still haunted him, while he listened to the falling rain and heard the screaming of the fish eagle. All around stretched the flat deserted marshes and the unbroken lead-grey sky.

In late March he managed to get canoes to take his party on south-east through the marshy eastern stretches of the lake. In the end they would reach dry land; they

would have to. Sitting in the canoes it was still harder to
see where they were going and at this stage Livingstone
probably passed one of the islands he had seen from a distance on his first visit in 1868. But reeds blotted out the
view and on they went, punting six hours at a time. The
night was spent on a small treeless lump of land just above
the level of the water. 'No sooner did we land than a piti-
less pelting rain came on. We turned up a canoe to get
shelter . . . The wind tore the tent out of our hands and
damaged it too. The loads are all soaked, and with the
cold it is bitterly uncomfortable. A man put my bed into
the bilge, so I was safe for a wet night.'[24]

The following morning, suffering the agonies of internal
haemorrhage, he wrote defiantly: 'Nothing earthly will
make me give up my work in despair. I encourage myself
in the Lord my God and go forward.'

But a week more of punting in the constant rain, with
no proper food and no warmth, weakened him still
further, and by 10 April he had to admit the seriousness of
his position. 'I am pale, bloodless and weak from bleeding
profusely ever since the 31st. of March last: an artery
gives off a copious stream and takes away my strength.
Oh! how I long to be permitted by the Over Power to
finish my work.'[25]

At this time the canoes were abandoned and the party
went on again on foot. Two hours' walking made Livingstone dizzy and weak. Soon he was forced to lie down for
long periods after any exertion. He fought against being
carried, but there seemed no alternative; in the past he
had only been helped across rivers, now he would be carried across drier ground as well. But he still did not stop
making observations, and went on measuring rainfall in his
portable gauge, and noted down any forms of vegetation
he had not seen before. After a long description of a
species of fish and its feeding habits, Livingstone went on
to record how strange he found the voice of the fish
eagle. 'It is pitched in a high falsetto key, very loud, and
seems as if he were calling to some one in the other
world.' He had no presentiment of death and did not intend
any symbolism.

Now the party was moving south-west again, away from
the worst swamps, in a broad arc round the south of
Bangweolo. It was what Livingstone had initially hoped to

ATONEMENT

do in November and December the previous year. Now it
was mid-April.

Even in the face of his rapidly increasing weakness he
was inclined to make light of the agonizing pain he was
suffering: 'Very ill all night, but remembered that the
bleeding and most other ailments in this land are forms of
fever. Took two scruple doses of quinine and stopped it
quite.' The next day, 19 April, he wrote the greatest of all
his many understatements: 'It is not all pleasure this exploration.' The same day he confessed himself almost too
weak to hold a pencil. That Sunday, he managed to read
aloud some prayers to his men and to travel on a few
hours, crossing a small river in a canoe. 'The river,' he
wrote, with his old precision, 'is about thirty yards broad,
very deep, and flowing in marshes two knots from S.S.E.
to N.N.W. into Lake.'[26] This was the last detailed observation he made, although, while he could still write, he noted
the number of hours marched each day.

On 21 April he knew that he was too weak to walk
unassisted even a few steps, but he still tried to ride the
surviving donkey. It was no use, as he soon discovered.
After a few yards he fell to the ground exhausted and
faint. Susi at once lifted him, undid his belt and pistol and
picked up his scarcely recognizable consul's cap, the
insignia of office. His men then carried him back to his
hut. Death was near now, but Livingstone still refused
to recognize it. Back in the village he sent men to ask the
chief for guides to take him on further the following day.

Seeing that he would not walk again, but knowing that
he would not rest in one place, Chuma and Susi constructed a litter of *kitanda* for the remaining miles. Next
day they moved again as Livingstone recorded: '22nd.
April—Carried on kitanda over Buga S.W. 2¼ [hours].'

For the next three days they carried the dying man on
through the same flooded, treeless waste. On the 25th,
when they reached a village, Livingstone summoned a number of local men and with great difficulty asked them
whether they knew about a hill and four adjacent fountains. All shook their heads. They were not travellers and
all who used to go trading to the west were now dead.
Unable to conceal his grief, Livingstone dismissed them,
explaining that he was too ill to continue talking. If the
fountains existed, surely they would have known. Perhaps
he remembered his despatch to Lord Granville: 'But what

if these fountains exist only in my imagination!—Then we shall see.'[27] To have come so far and to have suffered so much for yet another disappointment seemed intolerable.

On the 26th he gave the first sign that he realized he was dying. Susi was instructed to count over the bags of beads and to see to the purchase of two tusks to exchange for trade goods on the way back to Zanzibar. Susi's assumption was that the Doctor now thought of returning to the coast himself, but the truth was far more likely that he was keen to work out whether his men would have enough supplies to reach Zanzibar without him.

On 27 April Livingstone made the last entry in his journal: 'Knocked up quite, and remain—recover—sent to buy milch goats. We are on the banks of the Molilamo.'[28]

Milk was all important, for when Livingstone was given mapira corn pounded up with ground-nuts, he was unable to eat it. By the next day no goats had been found and so no milk could be procured. Even so, Livingstone still wished to press on while life was left. Since by now he could not walk even to the door of his hut to reach his *kitanda* outside, he instructed the men to break down the wall of the hut and bring the litter up to his bed. Although all his followers knew that all further progress was hopeless, they honoured his wishes. He would have few more demands to make. So on the 29th they pressed on.

After several hours a substantial river had to be crossed, and, since none of the canoes were wide enough to take the *kitanda*, he had to be lifted bodily. The pain, as he was carried the few feet into the canoe, was excruciating and the slightest pressure on his back was too great to be endured. As would be seen later, there was a clot of blood the size of a man's fist obstructing his lower intestine.

Once on the western bank they approached the village of Chitambo, a local chief; they were seventy miles S.S.E. of the southern shore of Lake Bangweolo. As they carried him towards the small village he often had to beg them to stop, for the slightest jolt was anguish to him. When his pain was less acute, Chuma and Susi noticed a deep drowsiness stealing over him. Some of the men had gone on to build a hut for him in the village and it was nearly completed when Livingstone's bearers arrived.

His followers did what they could to make his final resting place comfortable. The bed was raised from the floor by sticks and grass and his medicine chest was placed by

11. The last entries in Livingstone's Journal. Incredibly, during the last week of his life, Livingstone was still making precise geographical observations: noting down thermometer readings for temperature, the width of rivers, their speed and exact direction of flow. From 22 April for four days he was too weak to write anything except the number of hours travelled: a total of $8\frac{1}{4}$ hours for the four days. In his pain and exhaustion he multiplied this figure by four to get 33 miles. But four miles an hour would be impossible in the circumstances. He was probably thinking back to the days when that had been his regular pace. The last entry on 27 April reads: 'knocked up quite and remain: recover sent to buy milch goats. We are on the banks of R. Molilamo'.

the side of the bed on a packing case. It was agreed that somebody should keep constant watch with him night and day.

On 30 April chief Chitambo came to pay a courtesy visit but Livingstone sent him away. He was too ill to speak. He dozed through the day, only occasionally troubling his people. On one occasion he asked Susi to hold his watch so that he could wind it, and, on another, asked why some men outside were shouting. Then, in the evening, he asked Susi suddenly: 'Is this the Luapula?'* Susi told him gently that they were in Chitambo's village, near

* The Luapula was the river linking Lake Bangweolo with Lake Moero and the Lualaba.

a small stream called the Lulimala. 'How many days is it to the Luapula?' he asked next. Susi told him three. A little later, as if in great pain, he half sighed 'Oh dear, dear!' and then fell asleep.

An hour later Susi was called to his bedside and asked by his master to boil some water. Next Livingstone asked him to bring his medicine chest. Susi did this and opened it. He had to hold a candle very near to Livingstone's face, for his sight was failing. With a terrific effort the Doctor managed to select a little calomel. Then he asked Susi to pour some hot water into a cup and to bring another empty one. When Susi had done this Livingstone murmured: 'All right: you can go out now.'

Shortly after this, Majawara, the boy left to watch, fell asleep. He did not wake for three or four hours.

At 4 a.m. he burst into Susi's hut, in terrible distress, begging him to come at once. Susi roused Chuma and three others, and the six of them went to their master's hut. The sky was faintly tinged with the first light of dawn. A dim glow came from the entrance of the hut; a candle stuck with its own wax on to the top of a box was still burning. To their amazement Livingstone was no longer in his bed. As he had felt death coming, with a final super-human effort, he had somehow managed to crawl from his bed into a kneeling position. For a moment Susi thought he was praying. The men did not go in at once but waited for some movement. When they saw none, one went in and touched the kneeling man's cheek. It was almost cold. David Livingstone had been dead for several hours.[29]

For the sixty Africans, who had followed Livingstone's instructions without question since leaving Unyanyembe the previous August, the sudden loss of their leader, so far from their homes, could have proved catastrophic. Certainly, had the party broken up and the trade goods been thoughtlessly sold off and plundered, it is doubtful whether any could have reached the coast; but, from the morning of Livingstone's death, Chuma and Susi acted with a calm decisiveness that no European could have bettered.

Susi knew that the easiest and safest course would have been to bury the body at the earliest opportunity and then to return to the coast. He was well aware of the powerful superstitions held by many tribes about corpses. At best, if they were discovered carrying a body through some villages, they would be fined heavily; at worst they might be attacked as witches. But Susi, who had been chosen to lead the party by common consent, needed no time to make up his mind what he wanted to do. Whatever the risks involved, Livingstone's body should be carried to the coast and shipped to England for burial. The fact that the others, the vast majority of whom had been engaged by Stanley, were all prepared to stand by Susi's decision, shows the hold that Livingstone had gained over them in a very few months.

It will never be known how these Africans really saw Livingstone. He never discussed his aims with them, nor asked their point of view, and yet without doubt they respected and admired him. They did not understand his geographical aims and certainly could never have appreciated why he had subjected himself to such suffering simply to find the source of a river and the direction in which it flowed. As one chief had once told Livingstone scornfully, when asked about a lake, 'It is only water—nothing to be seen'. Yet, despite their lack of comprehension, none of these men with Livingstone, during the last months of his life, left him. They too waded through the mud and the water, suffered rheumatism, sores, malaria and exhaustion. Susi, Chuma and Gardner had been with their leader every day since he had landed in Africa in 1866; they had stayed when all the others deserted, they had given up their own food so that Livingstone could eat, had carried him when he could not walk, had done their best to conceal his physical weakness from strangers. They had always known that Livingstone was not rich and could never make them adequate recompense for their service. The reason for their devotion was Livingstone's gentleness with all Africans. Most explorers kept their expeditions together by rigid discipline and frequent floggings, yet Livingstone had always worked on the principle that since his men were not slaves, they should be allowed to leave when they wished. It is a pathetic irony that, if Livingstone had shown his colleagues on the Zambesi a quarter of the tolerance and kindness that he reserved for Africans, he would have been a successful and popular leader of his fellow countrymen.

The day after Livingstone's death, Chuma went to see the local chief, Chitambo, and, hiding the fact that his master was dead, told him that the white man's followers wanted permission to build a place outside the village, since they did not like living among the huts. The chief gave his consent, and work began the same day. A group of huts was built within a palisade. Slightly apart from the domestic buildings, a separate hut was constructed. This structure was open to the sky at the top and had specially strong walls to keep out wild animals. Inside, the corpse was prepared for the journey. An incision was made in the abdomen, and the intestines and internal organs were removed, placed in a tin box and buried. Jacob Wainwright, one of the Nassick boys, sent out with Stanley's men, read the burial service as the box was lowered into the ground. When taking out the intestines Chuma and Susi noticed a clot of blood several inches in diameter obstructing Livingstone's lower intestine. Such a large obstruction must have caused him horrifying pain.

To preserve the body, the Africans first placed salt in the open trunk and next allowed the corpse to dry for fourteen days in the sun—the dry season was beginning. The body was moved a fraction once a day. Since the hut had no roof there was no need for this slightly macabre process to be public.

When the prescribed period was completed, the face was bathed in brandy, as an extra preservative, and when the body had been wrapped in calico and encased in a cylinder of bark, it was sewn into a large piece of sailcloth. Susi added the finishing touch when he tarred the whole bundle to make double sure that it was watertight. The whole operation was efficient and quick. Earlier Susi had asked Wainwright to write out an inventory of Livingstone's things to see that nothing was stolen.

Susi's abilities as a leader were confirmed by the speed with which he led his party to Unyanyembe—five months. During that time ten men died.[30] They suffered all the usual ravages of disease and on one occasion had to fight their way out of a hostile village. At Unyanyembe they met a group of Englishmen, who were leading out another Livingstone Relief party. This expedition was quite as unhappy as its immediate predecessor. Already one of its members, a grandson of Robert Moffat, had died of fever, and another, W. E. Dillon, would shortly blow his brains out. The leader was Lieutenant V. Lovett Cameron.

Cameron's immediate advice to Chuma and Susi was to bury the body. To their credit they politely refused and reiterated their determination to reach the coast. Cameron then looked over the boxes and took Livingstone's geographical instruments for the use of his own party. Susi was reluctant to part with these but felt unable to resist. Perhaps Cameron's overbearing manner partly prepared Susi for what was to come when he reached Bagamoyo in February 1874.

Chuma was sent on to Zanzibar and there he discovered that Kirk was in England on leave and that Captain W. F. Prideaux was acting for him. Prideaux, on hearing that Livingstone's body was at Bagamoyo, despatched a warship, H.M.S. *Vulture*, to collect the corpse. Although Prideaux was aware that these sixty Africans had performed an amazing feat, he was completely at a loss as to what should be done. He was only standing in for Kirk, and was too timid to risk sending any of Livingstone's men back to England with the body without first getting the consent of the Foreign Office. This, however, could never be achieved in time, so Prideaux decided that, rather than be blamed later for causing the Foreign Office unnecessary expense, he would pay the men—he had to do so out of his own pocket since Livingstone's last £1,000 had been spent—and send them to their homes. Prideaux in fact did not recover his money from the Government until 1877. But the sixty Africans who had risked so much were not in a position to understand the acting Consul's financial dilemmas. At great personal risk they had brought the body of a man, whom they supposed to be famous in his own country, to the coast, and they were being sent away with their wages. For Chuma, Susi and Gardner it seemed a ludicrous ending to eight years' service. By the time the Royal Geographical Society struck commemorative medals for the sixty men the following year, they had all dispersed and very few ever received this reward, which they would never have understood anyway; cloth, beads, rifles, cattle would have been fine—but a medal! Chuma and Susi in the end did gain by their association with Livingstone. A year later, James 'Paraffin' Young, who had given Livingstone such important financial aid, paid for his two most faithful followers to come to England to help edit the explorer's *Last Journals*, and fill in verbally any gaps in the narrative. After that they both returned to Zanzibar and became much sought-after caravan leaders.

One African attended Livingstone's funeral in Westminster Abbey and he ironically had only been with Livingstone since August 1872; but because Jacob Wainwright had been a pupil at the Church Missionary Society's Nassick School, the missionaries paid his passage to England as a fund-raising exercise. Chuma and Susi arrived too late to see Livingstone buried.

Had Livingstone known that his followers were never to receive any reward from the Government, he would not have been surprised; it would have been merely the last of many disappointments.

24

Livingstone and the British Empire

The morning of 15 April 1874 was wet and windy, but shortly after dawn crowds started forming round the docks and quays of Southampton. By eight o'clock the Mayor and Aldermen of the town, dressed in their fur-trimmed robes, stood assembled on the quay. Behind them a military band was waiting, and not far away a company of the Royal Horse Artillery prepared to fire off 21-gun salutes at minute intervals. A long procession of black-draped carriages was being lined up just behind the main quay, but few eyes were concerned with preparations on land; the crowd and the reporters, the official artists and photographers were all looking out to sea.

A few minutes before nine, the silhouette of a battered and insignificant-looking steamer was sighted at the mouth of Southampton water. The first of the salutes boomed out across the silent town, the band broke into the opening bars of the 'Dead March from Saul' and the telegraph operators started eagerly tapping out the news. Through binoculars it was soon possible to see on the deck a coffin draped with a Union Jack. Beside the Mayor and Alderman a small black boy had now taken his place and lifted up a placard decorated with sable rosettes and streamers, bearing the inscription: 'TO THE MEMORY OF DR. LIVINGSTONE, FRIEND OF THE AFRICAN'.

The body was conveyed from Southampton to London by special train, and that evening was examined at the headquarters of the Royal Geographical Society so that a positive identification could be made. After eleven months the features were unrecognizable, but the lump in the bone of the left humerus, which had been shattered by a lion nearly thirty years before, was perfect proof.

For the next two days the body lay in state at the R.G.S. building in Savile Row, and crowds filed past the coffin constantly. On 18 April burial took place in Westminster Abbey. The press acclaimed the hero and announced his virtues.

> Westminster Abbey has opened her doors to men who have played larger and greater parts in the history of mankind; but the feeling amongst many this-after-noon was, that seldom has been admitted one more worthy—one more unselfish in his devotion to duty—one whose ruling desire was stronger to benefit his kind and advance the sum of human knowledge and civilization—than the brave, modest, self-sacrificing, African explorer. The virtues which distinguished Livingstone are those which our country has always been ready to acknowledge, which our religion has taught us to revere, and seek to cultivate and conserve.[1]

Livingstone's bravery, endurance and self-sacrifice during his last years deserved tributes like this one. His dogged refusal to give up in the face of hopeless odds, his uncomplaining acceptance of agonizing pain and finally his lonely death, conjure up images so powerful that his contemporaries' adulation seems, in retrospect, the only possible response. That any man could voluntarily have undergone such hardship seemed, and still seems, so remarkable that to ask whether he achieved his aims or deceived himself appears in the end almost churlish. The fact that Livingstone in his last years had allowed himself to accept as true what he had wanted to believe, rather than what his scientific observations suggested, seems to call for sympathy rather than criticism. Those who wept in the streets on the day of his funeral did not know that the Lualaba was not the Nile—had they done so, it is doubtful whether they would have cared. Knowledge of Livingstone's mistake would only have deepened for them the pathos of his death. Very few found it necessary to examine his aims or to ask whether a search for the Nile's source had anything to do with missionary work or the spreading of Christianity.

In analysing the life of a great man—and Livingstone was undoubtedly great—there is always a basic problem: to be great is to be different, so ordinary criteria of judgment fall short. The point at which determination becomes obsession, and self-sacrifice self-destruction is very hard to estimate. Yet even if Livingstone's determination is called obsessive—and it was—it must be acknowledged that without this inflexibility he would never have left the mills, never have qualified as a doctor and never have ended his life in the swamps of Bangweolo; without it, too, he would have made a better husband and father, and a more approachable and likeable man. In the same way, had Livingstone been a precise and rational thinker rather than an idealist, he would never have attempted to cross Africa without backing or his own supplies, nor would he ever have managed to persuade the Government that he was the man to lead a full-scale expedition. Optimism enabled him to take on tasks which rational men would never have attempted; optimism also led to most of his disappointments and failures. Very often his best qualities were also his worst.

As a man, Livingstone had been marked for life by the harshness of his childhood. His efforts to leave the mills had been laughed at by other boys, and this had stiffened his determination rather than weakened it. Throughout his career, opposition and derision increased his efforts and strengthened his will. It is as true today as it was in the 1840s, that between the ages of eighteen and twenty-five most young men learn, through close contact with other people, to accept that earlier ambitions and ideals may have been pitched too high. They come to realize that there are limits to their own abilities, and in marrying, or forming close attachments, are forced to recognize that compromise and concession are vital for the success of any close relationship. Until he was twenty-seven, Livingstone had studied medicine and theology so intensely that he had never had time to make these normal adjustments, and as a result he would never really understand people. On arriving in Africa the ordinary human weaknesses of his missionary colleagues had seemed far worse to him than they would have done to anybody who had not suffered Livingstone's severely limited youth and young manhood. In southern Africa there was no opportunity for Livingstone to gain that knowledge of other people which he had failed to acquire in Britain. He rowed with his colleagues, Ross and Edwards, because he could not make any allowances for their failings, which were not extreme; in the end he even quarrelled with the Moffats, whom he had admired. His marriage, which was one of convenience, brought no change. He saw his wife's position as that of an inferior, rather than an equal partner, and he rarely found time to play with his children. The closest relationships he formed were by letter—friendships at a distance.

In the long periods devoted to travel—he spent four and a half years alone on his trans-continental journey—his isolation deepened, and he returned still less aware of normal human motives and feelings. His thinking, too, started to suffer, since for years at a time he had nobody with whom to discuss his hopes and ideas. By crossing Africa he had performed an almost superhuman feat, but he seems not to have realized his own uniqueness, and he expected others to be able to reach similar attainments. When his colleagues on the Zambesi fell ill, and could not endure hardships which he considered routine, he despised them for it. This scorn became so pronounced that in the end he was able to shrug off the deaths of the missionaries, whom he had encouraged to come to the Zambesi and the Shire Highlands, as just another form of spinelessness and lack of guts. Horror of failure, which he never felt able to discuss with others, led him to lie deliberately and to blame innocent people for situations for which his own over-optimism was alone responsible. People were judged not as human beings but for their use, or lack of use, in carrying out his plans; and however important his objects, the callousness resulting from this attitude must rank as his major defect. His loyalty to Africans and his faith in their capacities were limitless, but he was easily swayed, on the scantiest of evidence, into believing the worst of fellow-countrymen who had previously served him well. As a leader of Europeans he was indecisive, unpredictable and unjust.

Livingstone's yearnings for praise and recognition were very human weaknesses, especially in view of his struggle to get out of the mills. Even his frequent denials of ambition, taken side by side with his determined efforts to prevent others gaining any credit for discoveries, were not serious flaws, although they hardly rank as modesty and selflessness. Livingstone's love of fame never destroyed his real altruism. His frequent soul-searchings, about the purity of his motives and the ambiguity of his aims, are proof of that. He wanted to be thought well of, but, even if it led to self-deception, he had to be able to convince himself that his work had objectives beyond mere discovery.

The man's character and his aims can only be judged together, for his thinking was largely a product of his optimism and idealism. His whole life up to his arrival in Africa had been governed by his inflated hopes of missionary prospects there. When he saw the real situation, the shock was overwhelming, but, unlike most young missionaries, he had not accepted the inevitable limitations and compromises of conventional static missionary work. He needed definite hopes and aims and soon managed to supply new ones to replace those which circumstances had destroyed. Until his death, he had to convince himself that he was following a plan which would ultimately bring Christianity to vast new areas of Africa.

In the Zambesi he had seen a *highway* for traders and missionaries to use in a combined penetration of the interior. His thesis was that without commerce Christianity could not drive out the slave-trade and could not persuade the Africans to abandon old customs. The argument that good trade drives out bad is fallacious, but Livingstone's main hope was that if formerly self-sufficient tribes traded with each other, their isolation would diminish and they would thus become less conservative and more receptive to new ideas. The introduction of currency might break down the power of petty chiefs and teach men to see themselves as individuals rather than members of a collective whole. Finally, if trade brought prosperity, the Africans might associate their new wealth with the gospel. While Livingstone knew it was over-optimistic to think that those who accepted Christ would be able to build steam-engines as a result, he was prepared to overlook the fallacy for the sake of Christian expansion.

Soon the impracticality of the Zambesi as a *highway*, the climate and the harsh travelling conditions convinced Livingstone that private trade would be inadequate for the great task. Although in his early days in Africa he had felt that one race had no right to destroy the institutions

and way of life of another, and had seen much to applaud
in tribal society, from the late 1850s he correctly diag-
nosed the root cause for African rejection of Christianity:
tribalism itself. Colonization, he next maintained, would
not only give traders and missionaries security but would
force social change on the Africans, destroying their customs and institutions and so leaving them psychologically
prone to accepting a new set of beliefs. Colonization on
the pattern of a minority of whites ruling, albeit philan-
thropically, a vast majority of blacks, became his main
preoccupation. The failure of the Zambesi Expedition and
the withdrawal of the Universities Mission made colonization less likely but, in Livingstone's view, still more
indispensable. The Government thought otherwise and
gave Livingstone repeated proof of their thinking.

Government rejection of his colonial plans, the extermination of the Makololo and the chaos in the Shire Highlands spelt the end of Livingstone's conception of his role
as a divinely appointed guide for others to follow into the
interior. By the mid-1860s all Livingstone's ideas seemed
merely to have led him into a hopeless dead-end. Throughout his life, Livingstone had conveniently jettisoned old
plans and theories if they did not fit new circumstances—
realistic perhaps, but a habit which all too easily made
former protestations seem wild and insincere. In the end
Livingstone could no longer persuade himself that he had
a coherent and practicable set of aims. His search for the
source of the Nile was a purely geographical task, and
because he could not believe that anything he might say or
do could do much damage to the slave-trade, he had no
real compensatory motive. The fact that he had once
advanced radical ideas for 'progress' and change in Africa
merely sharpened his sense of failure and defeat.

But he remained convinced that colonization was the
answer, and in his attempt to convince people in Britain
that they had a 'mission' in Africa, he had gone much
further than he would have wished in endorsing the values
of a British industrial society, which, in the past, he had
acknowledged as leading to exploitation of the poor and
terrible social conditions. He also conveniently forgot that
his previous experience of settlers, both English and Dutch,
in southern Africa had convinced him that contact with
Europeans often made natives worse. Yet from the early
1860s Livingstone argued without reservation that the

effects of new settlers in central Africa would be entirely beneficial. As usual, adverse circumstances had brought about this volte-face, and his arguments were not saved from severe contradictions by his unworkable qualification that settlers should be Christian.

Yet if Livingstone's colonial ideas were at variance with much of his earlier thinking, he cannot be accused of being motivated by a desire to exploit Africans. Colonization might mean the destruction of tribal society, but Livingstone was realistic enough to see possible advantages. He had admired African generosity and the responsibility which chiefs took for their people's welfare, but he had also been aware since 1850 that Africans themselves were eager participants in the slave-trade. The way the Makololo had treated their subject tribes had also told him that tribalism was no guarantee of idyllic and unspoiled little communities. In fact Livingstone had still more substantial reasons for advocating European intervention. Pleasant though it might be to suppose that central and eastern Africa could have escaped all alien contact and thus have developed peacefully along traditional lines, it is not realistic. In the early 1850s Livingstone had met Arabs and Portuguese Angolan traders in Barotseland. In the late 1860s he had seen the Arabs extend their trading operations well into what is now the Congo. As the search for slaves and ivory went on and the gun frontier expanded, so too did wars. The circumstances which Livingstone encountered in the Shire Highlands in 1863 seemed to him to constitute unanswerable proof that the Africans in that area would be better off under a British administration. In view of the slave raids, the famine and the Ngoni incursions, it is hard to disagree.

Livingstone's appreciation of the seriousness of the conditions in the interior made his misery at the British Government's non-intervention all the more acute, and deepened his sense of failure. Of course, by ordinary standards his exploration made him unique, and placed him in a different category from all other nineteenth-century explorers. For a start he had spent not just a few years in Africa, like most of his rivals, but thirty, the first fifteen of them continuous. He had also operated in a far wider range of country than any other explorer: a vast area defined by places as far apart as Ujiji and the Cape from north to south, and Zanzibar and Loanda from east to

west. He had also done more than any single man to
break down Victorian stereotypes of the African, either as
the humbly kneeling slave of abolitionist propaganda, or
as the irredeemable savage described by many missionaries and travellers. But Livingstone's ambitions had been
far more extensive; his object had been to bring sweeping
social change to Africa, and in the year of his death the
chances for this seemed more remote than when he had
first come to the continent thirty-three years before.

As the Zambesi Expedition had drawn to its painful
and humiliating conclusion in 1863, and Livingstone had
watched the bodies of some of the thousands of Africans
who had died of starvation, floating down the Shire, he
had not given up his hopes for the Shire Highlands. The
slave raids, the famine, the Ngoni attacks and the deaths
of four out of seven missionaries had left him unmoved.
Even when the expedition had been recalled and the mission withdrawn, he had been able to write with apparent
conviction: 'Viewing calmly all the circumstances, I could
not conceive of a sphere in which the missionary prospects
would be more inviting than that which has now been
abandoned . . . I have no doubt that it will be done
though I may not be alive to hear of it . . . the future will
justify my words & hopes.'[2]

At the time these sentiments seemed yet another example of Livingstone's insane over-optimism. But, incredibly,
after his death the future *did* justify his words and hopes,
and, more surprisingly still, it did so through the efforts
of some of the people whom Livingstone had quarrelled
with and scorned. James Stewart, the young Free Church
of Scotland missionary, who had felt rejected by Livingstone on the Zambesi, played a leading part; and the
despised Universities Mission and the London Missionary
Society also contributed. Even Bedingfeld, as the Captain
of the British East African Squadron, and Charles Livingstone, as the British Consul on the west African island
of Fernando Po, returned to the continent they had hated.

The eulogies and tributes that followed Livingstone's
funeral did not have any effect on the way politicians
viewed Africa, but they did influence thousands of ordinary men and women to give money to any philanthropic
or missionary society with African connections. The *Daily
Telegraph* expressed the sentiments of the average mission-

ary subscriber in its obituary article: 'The work of England for Africa must henceforth begin where Livingstone left it off.'[3]

James Stewart was one man whom any observer of the later stages of the Zambesi Expedition might have thought would be violently opposed to beginning anything where Livingstone had left off. Before leaving Africa, Stewart had hurled his copy of *Missionary Travels* into the Zambesi with the words: 'So perish all that is false in myself and others.'[4] Yet, during Livingstone's funeral in Westminster Abbey, Stewart underwent a sudden and, as it seemed to him, miraculous change of heart. He shortly made up his mind to start a Free Church of Scotland Mission on the shores of Lake Nyassa. The name he intended to give this settlement was Livingstonia. The Free Church of Scotland gave their blessing, and Scottish businessmen donated the necessary funds. Stewart chose E. D. Young, who had been with Livingstone on the *Lady Nyassa* and had led the first Livingstone Search Expedition, to take out the first contingent. At this stage the Established Church of Scotland also decided to send a party. Soon their missionaries had started a mission in the Shire Highlands, named after Livingstone's birthplace, Blantyre. Blantyre is the present capital of Malawi. In due course the Free Church had also set up Livingstonia. Young had made all this possible by doing what he and Livingstone had failed to do in 1863—namely get a steamer overland past the Murchison Cataracts and on to the lake. Livingstonia and Blantyre were viable settlements by the early 1880s.

Missionaries were not the only men who came to Lake Nyassa in response to the appeals following Livingstone's death. In 1878, John and Frederick Moir, brothers who had previously been successful businessmen, founded the Livingstonia Central Africa Company—later to be called the African Lakes Company. The capital had been subscribed by James Stevenson and Sir William Mackinnon, like the Moirs both Scottish. These two shipping magnates would finally donate over a million pounds to African projects. Amazingly, within ten years of Livingstone's death, what Livingstone himself had predicted twenty years before had come to pass. Two Scottish Missions and one Scottish company were operating in the Shire Highlands and on the shores of Lake Nyassa. The area was not yet under British Protection. In 1887, however, the missionaries and the members of the African Lakes Company were attacked by Arabs in a series of well-planned raids. After a spirited campaign on their behalf in England and Scotland, a Protectorate was declared over Nyasaland in 1891. Livingstone's colony had come into being. But important events were not confined to one area.

In his lifetime, Livingstone had been powerless to dissuade the London Missionary Society and the Universities Mission from abandoning south-central and eastern Africa. As a direct result of his death they returned to it. The efforts in both cases were led by men who had been associated with the previous withdrawals. Bishop Steere, Tozer's successor, led the Universities Mission to a settlement on the eastern shore of Lake Nyassa, and Roger Price, the same Price whom Livingstone had so mercilessly lashed for cowardice at Linyanti, began the search for suitable sites for London Missionary Society settlements near Lake Tanganyika.

Livingstone's influence on the course of Stanley's life had by itself enormous consequences for Africa. After the death of his hero, Stanley resolved to trace the Lualaba north and finally finish Livingstone's work. Backed by the *Daily Telegraph* and the *New York Herald*, he did just this, in a feat of exploration that ranks with Livingstone's transcontinental journey. The result was to prove that the Lualaba was the Congo. During those years, between 1874 and 1877, Stanley's reports caught the imagination of King Leopold II of Belgium, who from the early sixties had been interested in acquiring colonies for his country. His search had then been in the Far East, where he had attempted to buy some of the Dutch possessions. His failure there disposed him to consider Africa, and Stanley's optimistic forecasts for what could be achieved in the Congo tipped the balance. When Stanley failed to interest the British Government in the country he had opened, he was persuaded by Leopold to work for him. The result was the foundation of the Congo Free State, eventually the Belgian Congo.

Stanley's journey had one other result of almost equal importance. Before following the Lualaba north and west, he circumnavigated Lake Victoria and proved once and for all that Speke's claims for the lake had been correct. On this stage of his journey, Stanley stayed with Mutesa, the Kabaka of Buganda, on the northern shores of Victoria. During this time Mutesa convinced Stanley that he wanted missionaries. The Kabaka's real desire was to gain protection against the Khedive of Egypt's ambitions in Equatoria. Nevertheless Stanley took him at his word and in April 1875 wrote an appeal, which was to be published in the *Daily Telegraph* later that year.

The consequences were momentous. The Anglican Church Missionary Society and the French Roman Catholic missionary order of White Fathers decided to make Uganda their African field. Before the arrival of these two parties, political intrigue was the order of the day in Mutesa's kingdom. A strong Arab faction had been established at his court for some years. Clearly the arrival of two rival groups of missionaries was going to bring quite unimaginable complications. Within a year both groups of missionaries saw what they had let themselves in for: religious groupings were adopted by members of opposing political factions. An alliance of one religious group with the Kabaka against the other could lead to the massacre of the adherents of the isolated party. To guard against this the missionaries armed their supporters and were soon able to put a thousand men into the field against all comers—whether the Kabaka, the Muslims or the opposing Christian party. Only a spark was needed to create an international incident. That spark came when Sir William Mackinnon's Imperial British East Africa Company entered Uganda with the primary object of forestalling a rival German company. The arrival of a British company in a country where the balance of power was almost equally divided between the armed supporters of French and British missionaries could only produce a crisis. The French, to protect their position, convinced the Kabaka that the British would depose him unless he was prepared to fight. An alliance was duly formed. This isolated the British missionaries and meant that if war broke out, the company would have to intervene on their countrymen's behalf. This was precisely wh t happened in January 1892. The pandemonium in Uganda itself, and the force of public opinion in Britain, led to its annexation in April 1894. The following year, to ensure that they had access to Uganda, the British Government annexed the territory later known as Kenya. With the addition of Rhodesia—the area comprising modern Zambia and (southern) Rhodesia—through the efforts of Cecil Rhodes, almost two-thirds of Britain's colonial empire in Africa had been secured.

The influence of Livingstone in Nyasaland and, through Stanley, in Uganda paved the way for still more annexations. The link is very clear, for had the missionaries not been inspired by Livingstone's death, and had the funds not poured in from Scottish philanthropists, there would have been no crisis on Lake Nyassa in 1887 and no war in Uganda in 1892. The presence of the missionaries and the operations of men like Sir William Mackinnon had created the situations which gave rise to annexation. The matter cannot be left there, however, for the 'Scramble for Africa', as the most popular current historical orthodoxy has it, was not influenced by individuals at all, but hinged entirely on British Government thinking that followed Britain's occupation of Egypt in 1882.[5]

The claim that Nyasaland and Uganda really precipitated the British Government into carving out a colonial empire in Africa might seem to be disproved by the fact that, five years before events in Lake Nyassa became critical, Gladstone had gone into Egypt. But Egypt was a special case in every way. Gladstone had occupied the country against his will, to protect British and French investments—primarily accounted for by Suez Canal shares—after the collapse of the Khedive's finances and government. Gladstone's intention had been to restore solvency and order within a year, and then clear out. It was a serious miscalculation, and one shared by the leader of the Conservatives, Lord Salisbury. In fact Salisbury did not abandon the idea of withdrawal till 1887. Britain's occupation of Egypt undoubtedly played a part in directing French and German eyes to Africa, but this did not worry either Gladstone or Salisbury.

In 1885, after Germany had declared a protectorate over a large slice of the Sultan of Zanzibar's mainland possessions, Gladstone's response was: 'If Germany becomes a colonising power, all I can say is "God speed her".'[6] There were many people in Britain who agreed with him. The Government's support of non-involvement, which Livingstone had tried to change in the late fifties and sixties, was still strong. In the same year, 1885, Lord Salisbury gained power and he did nothing to discourage Germany: quite the reverse in fact. In the following year he agreed to the major part of east Africa—an area roughly equivalent to modern Tanzania—becoming a German Sphere of Influence. Britain accepted the smaller area to the north —modern Kenya—as her sphere. Salisbury had no intention of doing anything with this sphere of influence, for in March 1887 he refused Government aid to Sir William Mackinnon's newly formed British East Africa Association. Mackinnon wished to develop the new area and stake claims in Uganda. This clearly showed that in March 1887 Salisbury was as opposed as ever to colonial advances in Africa. By the summer of 1888 he had changed his mind. The crucial question is: why?

The generally accepted view is that when, in the spring and early summer of 1887, Salisbury's attempt to negotiate his way out of Egypt with safeguards had broken down for good, the Prime Minister realized that, since Britain would be in Egypt for an indefinite period, he ought to annex Uganda so that no other nation could tamper with the sources of the Nile, which was of course Egypt's lifeline. The argument also goes that, since the building of the Suez Canal and the closer link with India which this made possible, British interests were also bound to increase on the African side of the Indian Ocean. The canal was opened in 1869, and so the attitude of Gladstone and Salisbury, as late as the mid-1880s, to German expansion in east Africa would seem to give the lie to this second argument. The fact that Uganda contained the source of the Nile would, however, have appealed to Salisbury as a possible reason for annexation, but it cannot have been as crucial as has been claimed. It was a full year, after the collapse of the Egyptian withdrawal negotiations, before Salisbury changed his mind about Sir William Mackinnon and gave the British East Africa Association his support and a royal charter. Had he been desperate to exclude the Germans from Uganda in 1887, he would have given Mackinnon his charter at once. The fact is that Salisbury made his decision over Uganda as a result of events in Nyasaland and the public reaction to these events in Britain.

In 1887, it will be remembered, the missionaries and traders on Lake Nyassa had been attacked by Arabs. When the news of these attacks became known in England and Scotland early in 1888, a vigorous campaign began with the single aim of forcing Salisbury into declaring a protectorate. In February 1888 the Member for Glasgow raised the matter in the Commons; in April supporters of the Scottish Missions, the Universities Mission and the African Lakes Company sent a deputation to see the Prime Minister. This was followed by a petition from a number of members of Parliament. August saw the formation by Scottish businessmen of a Nyassa Anti-Slavery and Defence Fund to buy arms for the missionaries. So, by August, Salisbury was under considerable pressure, but he was not eager to appear suddenly to change his mind or his colonial policy. Instead he praised the missionaries for their bravery and promised their supporters that he would ensure that the Portuguese did not hinder the import of arms. He also gave his word not to allow the Portuguese to expand into Nyasaland and the Shire Highlands. In September he gave Mackinnon's company its royal charter, in the full knowledge that Mackinnon's immediate aim was to secure Britain's position in Uganda. The timing of Salisbury's grant to Mackinnon cannot have been coincidental; the Prime Minister knew that there were missionaries in Uganda as well, and wished to close that country to other European nations to avoid a situation there different in kind from the crisis in Nyasaland but similar in that it would arouse the same public indignation over British subjects being left defenceless against aliens.

The Prime Minister had decided in July or August 1888 that both Nyasaland and Uganda would have to become British protectorates.[7] His reason had been the presence of the missionaries, and not the source of the Nile and Egypt.

Early in 1889, to justify his volte-face, Salisbury, knowing very well the sentimental attachment of Scots to Nyasaland and the Shire Highlands, on account of Livingstone, put it about in Scotland that he intended to cede the Shire Highlands to Portugal in exchange for Portuguese recognition of the rights of British subjects living on the shores of Lake Nyassa. The result, as Salisbury had calculated, was a massive vote of protest from Scotland. One petition the Prime Minister received had been signed by the majority of ministers in both the Established and Free Church of Scotland, asking incredulously how the Government could dare sign away David Livingstone's heritage. With this proof of public opinion, Salisbury felt able to reverse his previous policies without too many qualms. In 1891 he declared a protectorate over the whole area. By then his task had been made much easier by a Portuguese attempt to occupy Blantyre.

When the trouble broke out in Uganda in early 1892, Salisbury had an excellent precedent for declaring another protectorate, and his position was stronger still since the approaching bankruptcy of Mackinnon's company meant that company employees would have to withdraw, leaving the British missionaries to the mercy of the supporters of the French faction. But at this crucial moment Salisbury's government lost a general election and Gladstone took office.

During the next two years the Uganda issue almost split the Liberal Party wide open. Gladstone favoured a complete rejection of any further African advances; Rosebery, his Foreign Secretary, was determined that Uganda should become a protectorate. In April 1894 Rosebery got his way, but he could never have fought and won a battle to annex Uganda, had he not been able to utilize the public support whipped up by the missionary societies and individuals such as Henry Morton Stanley. So great was this support that a Liberal Government, committed to a policy of Home Rule for Ireland, was able paradoxically to create a new African colony. Afterwards Sir Edward Grey, justifying for the Government what appeared to be a Conservative and not a Liberal decision, said: 'If we had abandoned Uganda, we should have had month by month news of most sinister consequences reaching this country. The Government would have been assailed on all sides as being responsible.'[8] There could have been no clearer admission that the missionaries had brought about annexation; and the missionaries had gone there in response to the appeals following Livingstone's death.

And 1894, the year in which Uganda was annexed, was an important one in British colonial history. In that year Gladstone resigned and Home Rule for Ireland went with him. Gladstone had also failed to curb British naval expenditure, just as he had failed to curb expansion in Africa. With Salisbury's return to power in 1895, mid-Victorian liberal policies of isolation and *laissez-faire* had finally given way to assertive imperialism. Joseph Chamberlain took over the Colonial Office, determined to continue advances in Africa. By 1898 Nigeria had been acquired and the French thwarted. In the same year French ambitions on the upper Nile and their dream of linking their west African Empire with the Red Sea ended with Kitchen-er's victory over the Mahdist forces at Omdurman. The Sudan, like Egypt, had become British beyond dispute.

So, twenty years after Livingstone's death, those colonies which he had advocated to Palmerston and Russell as likely to be of mutual advantage to Britain and Africa had come into being. Livingstone's ideas had been expressed more than thirty years too soon. During his lifetime he had been defeated because most people thought of the Empire in terms of the white-settled territories such as Australia, Canada and New Zealand. Empire was generally understood to be the link between the mother country and the extended family of self-governing Britons overseas. Empire did not convey a picture of a small population of whites governing millions of aliens. In 1876 Disraeli's Royal Titles Bill had added the style of Empress of India to Queen Victoria's other titles. The move had not been popular. India was not a white-settled territory and was therefore considered alien; its singling out therefore seemed to many to be a slight on the real colonial empire.

Events in Africa between 1874 and 1894 forced a reassessment of what the Empire really was. The addition of new African colonies, peopled not by whites but by blacks, changed the whole balance of the Empire and inevitably altered the way people in Britain viewed it. This new view was significantly influenced by Livingstone's ideas and those of his missionary successors.

When Joseph Chamberlain, speaking after the annexation of Uganda in 1894, dilated on Britain's 'manifest destiny' to be a 'great civilizing power',[9] the sentiment echoed Livingstone's instructions to the members of the Zambesi Expedition: 'We come among them as members of a superior race and servants of a Government that desires to elevate the more degraded portions of the human family . . . to become harbingers of peace to a hitherto distracted and trodden down race.'[10]

The coupling of moral fervour with the right to power was implicit in much of what Livingstone had written about Britain's special duty and mission as a colonizing nation. He had suggested without reservation that on people of British stock depended the 'hopes of the world for liberty and progress',[11] and had claimed that the presence of Englishmen in Africa would be 'an unmixed advantage' to the Africans themselves.[12] These views were taken up and developed by the missionaries who went out to Africa, after and as a result of his death. The concept of a national mission to elevate other races was convenient moral justification for governments interested in expansive colonial policies for other reasons.

When Livingstone had spoken of his nation's mission to 'civilize' the underdeveloped nation of the world, Britain's industrial and naval supremacy had seemed unchallengeable. After Livingstone's death it was soon clear that other potentially stronger nations were yearly cutting back the industrial lead. Livingstone's ideas for African development had been straightforward: commerce mattered primarily as the servant of Christianity; British rule only as the prelude to a Christian society. For later imperialists the philanthropic and religious slant given by missionaries to the idea of Empire could work as a convenient cover for other motives for imperial expansion: the carving out of new markets; the exploitation of diamonds, gold and copper. With Germany, America and Russia growing stronger, it was hoped that a cohesive and centrally-dominated Empire would enable Britain to maintain her supremacy and counter the expanding powers of larger nations. This had never been part of Livingstone's plan. Mutual benefit, the spread of Christianity, and the 'diffusion of better principles' had been his concern when thinking of colonies, not the domination of vast areas for power and prestige.

The realities of the 1890s would have confronted Livingstone with the many paradoxes in his own thinking and would have forced him to a revision of many ideas. He had advocated British rule and settlement but had never specified how the potential rulers and settlers should be chosen, nor had he given any thought to the problems that would have to be overcome before a just multi-racial society could exist. With British rule, he had assumed that Christianity would come, and with Christianity in the aescendant there could be no injustice. It was the old optimism again, an optimism which all his previous experience of settlers should have led him to mistrust.

What Livingstone would have made of Africa today is a matter for speculation, but several facts are certain. He would have been grieved that British investment in her new African colonies had never been large, and that the industrial society which he extolled had never been exported. He would have been surprised to see that the decadent Portuguese had outstayed the British, and depressed that the descendants of the Boers, whom he had despised for what he called 'their stupid prejudice against colour',[13] had taken over the government of South Africa and maintained the old racism. It seems certain that, while he would have regretted the lack of progress made in the British colonies, he would have applauded Britain's withdrawal from Africa. In 1852 he had written with remarkable foresight:

> With colonies it is the same as with children—they receive protection for a time and obey from a feeling of weakness and attachment; but beyond the time at which they require a right to think for themselves, the attempt to perpetuate subordination necessarily engenders a hatred which effectually extinguishes the feeble gratitude that man in any condition is capable of cherishing.[14]

Undoubtedly Livingstone's greatest sorrow would have been that Africa never became a Christian continent.

APPENDICES

SOURCES

NOTES

APPENDIX A

The Date of the Stanley–Livingstone Meeting

Ian Anstruther, in his book *I Presume: Stanley's Triumph and Disaster* (London 1956), p. 198, n. 84, argues that 3 November 1871 is the correct date. The argument goes as follows: 'The 3rd was the date given in Stanley's first accounts of the meeting in the *Herald*, and the 10th did not appear until later. It will be remembered that Stanley became a week out in his dates after his attack of fever at Tabora, and it was this that caused the confusion. He did not discover this mistake until Livingstone pointed it out to him on what he believed was the 21st, eleven days after the meeting, by which time he had recorded the date of his arrival at Ujiji in his diary as the 10th. Because of the week's error, however, the actual date was the 3rd. The mistaken date of the 10th probably crept into his book (H.I.F.L.) because, working from his diary nine months afterwards, he forgot to make allowance for the error.' Anstruther may be right, but I do not think so. In the National Archives of Rhodesia is a letter written by Livingstone to Kirk from Ujiji during November; in this letter Livingstone says that he had thought that Stanley had arrived on 28 October but now knows that he was wrong. Livingstone's estimate was that he had been twenty-one days out. He made this calculation with the help of his nautical almanac and the arrival of the Muslim feast of Ramadan on 14 November. According to Livingstone, therefore, the meeting should have taken place on 18 November. Since Anstruther's date of 3 November depends on Livingstone having corrected him, the letter to Kirk must throw doubt on Stanley's recollection of the actual correction. Yet Livingstone's letter to Kirk is not reliable either, not least because Livingstone misdated it 1 November. This date is clearly wrong since in the letter Livingstone refers to the beginning of Ramadan on 14 November as having already occurred. Livingstone usually wrote letters to friends and family shortly after the occurrence of important events, even when there was no immediate way of sending letters to the coast. His letters to his daughter Agnes usually just pre-date letters to other correspondents. Livingstone's first letter to Agnes about Stanley's arrival is dated 18 November. I cannot honestly name a date but my feeling is that 3 November is too early.

APPENDIX B

'Dr Livingstone, I Presume?'

On 6 January 1972, in the issue of the *Radio Times* launching the British Empire Series, the following piece appeared:

> THAT HISTORIC REMARK: GRANDAD NEVER MADE IT! Sadly, it seems, Henry Morton Stanley probably *didn't* utter that famous quote: 'Doctor Livingstone, I presume?' Richard Stanley, the great man's grandson, says his father always told him that the remark was a quip based on a music-hall joke, or perhaps a quotation from Sheridan.

I wrote to Mr Richard Stanley about this and in his reply he stated:

> I made no such bold statement and, as is not uncommon in the popular press, I have been completely and utterly misquoted . . . However, my reference to Sheridan was not without foundation for if you turn to *School for Scandal*, Act V, scene 1, Joseph Surface greeting one whom he assumes to be a long lost poor relation (actually his uncle Sir Oliver Surface) says: 'Sir, I beg you ten thousand pardons for keeping you a moment waiting, Mr Stanley, I presume?' I always understood from my father that this famous statement may well have been based on a current saying of the day and I wonder whether in fact it could have been from this quotation. No doubt you know when *School for Scandal* was first published and that would decide once and for all whether or not my grandfather had this quotation at the back of his mind when he made this famous statement.

The School for Scandal was first performed in 1777 and first published in 1780, ninety-one years before Stanley's meeting with Livingstone. This must rule out Joseph Surface's remark as the basis for the famous utterance.

In *How I Found Livingstone* (1872), p. 411, Stanley admitted that he was confused and overcome with emotion at the moment of the meeting and had said the first words that came into his head. In view of the fact that these words .soon became a music-hall joke, greatly to Stanley's embarrassment,* it is not surprising that he thought of excuses like the one Mr Richard Stanley mentioned; but it is of course inconceivable that, at the culminating moment of his life, he should actually have chosen to swap literary allusions with Livingstone. Because the remark became such a joke, it would have been natural for Stanley to deny it publicly if he had really never made it. But he never did make a public denial, and when Lady Stanley edited *The Autobiography of Sir Henry Morton Stanley*, after his death, the famous words were repeated and justified on page 264 as follows: 'When the moment of discovery came, and the man himself stood revealed before me, this constantly recurring doubt contributed not a little to make me unprepared for it. "It may not be Livingstone after all," doubt suggested. If this is he what shall I say to him? My imagination had not taken this question into consideration before.'

* Ian Anstruther, *I Presume: Stanley's Triumph and Disaster* (London 1956), p. 146.

SOURCES

Manuscript

1. BODLEIAN LIBRARY, OXFORD. The Clarendon Papers Dep C 80. Letters from Lavid Livingstone and Sir Roderick Murchison to Lord Clarendon concerning the Zambesi Expedition.

2. THE BRITISH MUSEUM, LONDON. Ad. MS. 50184—Eighty-five letters from David Livingstone to members of his family. Also several rough drafts of Foreign Office despatches.

   Ad. MS. 37410—Letters written to Edmund Gabriel 1854–55.

   Ad. MS. 38991—Layard Papers. Several letters from Lord John Russell to A. Layard concerning Livingstone's finances in 1865.

3. LIVINGSTONE MEMORIAL, BLANTYRE. Miscellaneous Journals, Diaries and Notebooks, including the originals of the *Last Journals* and a manuscript copy of *Missionary Travels*. Most of the letters formerly at Blantyre have now been deposited in the National Library of Scotland.

4. LIVINGSTONE MUSEUM, ZAMBIA. Miscellaneous letters to friends: James Young, W. C. Oswell, A. Sedgwick, etc. Charles Livingstone's letters to his wife: 1857 to his death.

5. LONDON MISSIONARY SOCIETY, LONDON. David Livingstone's Missionary Correspondence 1837–58. (Most of this sequence has been published in *Livingstone's Missionary Correspondence 1841–1856*, ed. I. Schapera, London 1961). Letters from Livingstone to the L.M.S. concerning the Makololo Mission 1860–62. Miscellaneous letters to friends: D. G. Watt, M. Prentice, H. Drummond. Letters from Mrs Livingstone to the L.M.S. 1852–5. Neil Livingstone's letters to the L.M.S., 1838 and 1853. R. Moffat's letters to the L.M.S. Helmore Papers concerning Makololo Mission. Lane Papers: letters to E. Gabriel. Moir Papers: miscellaneous.

6. NATIONAL ARCHIVES OF RHODESIA, SALISBURY. The most important letters in this large collection are those written by Livingstone to Sir Thomas Maclear and Sir Roderick

Murchison 1855–68. Also miscellaneous letters to Kirk, the Foreign Office, etc. Charles Livingstone: letters to F. Fitch. James Stewart: Correspondence. J. T. Baines: private correspondence. R. Thornton: family letters.

7. NATIONAL LIBRARY OF SCOTLAND, EDINBURGH. Wilson Collection: letters from Livingstone to his family. Miscellaneous letters to friends: including Sir Thomas Maclear, Sir Bartle Frere, B. Pyne, Dr Tweedie, H. Dickson, G. Drummond, M. J. Dyke, etc. Various maps, notebooks, journals, including an unpublished private diary for the years 1861–3. Harryhausen Collection of Stanley letters, including several to Livingstone.

8. PRIVATE COLLECTIONS. Harryhausen Collection: family letters, mainly 1860–67. Pyne Collection: letters written by Livingstone from Bechuanaland to B. Pyne. Miscellaneous letters in the possession of Mr Quentin Keynes.

9. PUBLIC RECORD OFFICE, LONDON. Livingstone's Government Correspondence: F.O. series 2/49B, 63/842, 63/871, 63/894, 84/1249, 84/1265, 97/322, etc. Many of Livingstone's later despatches from 1866 can be found in the *Proceedings of the Royal Geographical Society*; originals of most of these are in the P.R.O.

10. RHODES HOUSE, OXFORD. Waller Papers: eighty-five letters to H. Waller 1862–72. Various letters to John Kirk and miscellaneous letters.

11. WELLCOME MEDICAL LIBRARY, LONDON. Miscellaneous letters.

Published Works

I. LIVINGSTONE'S BOOKS, JOURNALS, LECTURES AND LETTERS

CHAMBERLIN, D., (ed.), *Some Letters from Livingstone 1840–1872*, London 1940.

FOSKETT, R., *The Zambesi Doctors: David Livingstone's letters to John Kirk 1858–1872*, Edinburgh 1964.

LIVINGSTONE, D., *Missionary Travels and Researches in South Africa*, London 1857.

LIVINGSTONE, D. and C., *Narrative of an Expedition to the Zambesi and its Tributaries*, London 1865.

MONK, W. (ed.), *Dr. Livingstone's Cambridge Lectures*, Cambridge 1858.

SCHAPERA, I. (ed.), *David Livingstone: Family Letters, 1841–1856*, London 1959, 2 vols.

SCHAPERA, I. (ed.), *Livingstone's African Journal, 1853–1856*, London 1963, 2 vols.

SCHAPERA, I. (ed.), *Livingstone's Missionary Correspondence 1841–1856*, London 1961.

SCHAPERA, I. (ed.), *Livingstone's Private Journals 1851–1853*, London 1960.

WALLER, H. (ed.), *The Last Journals of David Livingstone in Central Africa*, London 1874, 2 vols.

WALLIS, J. P. R. (ed.), *The Matabele Mission: A Selection from the Correspondence of John and Emily Moffat, David Livingstone, and others 1858–1878*, London 1945.

WALLIS, J. P. R. (ed.), *The Zambesi Expedition of David Livingstone 1858–1863*, London 1956, 2 vols.

I have also quoted from letters appearing in: *The Proceedings of the Royal Geographical Society*, vols xii, xiv, xvii, xviii; *The Atlantic Monthly*, July 1922; *The Christian World*, February 1933; *The Congregationalist*, October 1925; *The Cape Town Mail* 26.4.1853.

2. BIOGRAPHIES AND OTHER WORKS

ADAMSON, W., *Life of Fergus Ferguson*, London 1900.

ANSTRUTHER, I., *I Presume: Stanley's Triumph and Disaster*, London 1956.

BENNETT, N. R. and YLVISAKER M. (eds.), *The Central African Journal of Lovell J. Procter 1860–64*, Boston 1971.

BLAIKIE, W. G., *The Personal Life of David Livingstone*, London 1880.

CAMPBELL, J. R., *Livingstone*, London 1929.

CHADWICK, O., *Mackenzie's Grave*, London 1959.

CHAPMAN, J., *Travels in the Interior of South Africa*, London 1868, 2 vols.

COOLEY, W. D., *Dr Livingstone and the Royal Geographical Society*, London 1874.

COUPLAND, R., *Livingstone's Last Journey*, London 1945.

COUPLAND, R., *Kirk on the Zambesi*, Oxford 1928.

CUMMING, R. G., *Five Years of a Hunter's Life in the Far Interior of South Africa*, London 1850, 2 vols.

DEBENHAM, F., *The Way to Ilala: David Livingstone's Pilgrimage*, London 1955.

DEVEREUX, W. C., *A Cruise in the Gorgon*, London 1869.

DICK, T., *The Christian Philosopher or The Connexion of Science and Philosophy with Religion*, London 1842.

DOLMAN, A., *In the Footsteps of Livingstone*, London 1924.

FLETCHER, R. S., *A History of Oberlin College*, Oberlin 1943.

FOSKETT, R. (ed.), *The Zambesi Journal and Letters of Dr John Kirk 1858–1863*, London 1965, 2 vols.

FRAZER, A. Z., *Livingstone and Newstead*, London 1913.

FREEMAN, J. J., *A Tour in South Africa*, London 1851.

GELFAND, M., *Livingstone the Doctor*, Oxford 1957.

GOODWIN, H., *Memoir of Bishop Mackenzie*, Cambridge 1865.

HEWART, G., *Curiosities of Glasgow Citizenship*, Glasgow 1881.

JOHNSTON, H. H., *Livingstone and the Exploration of Central Africa*, London 1891.

JOHNSTON, H. H., *The Story of My Life*, London 1923.

LEWIS, E., *Trader Horn*, New York 1927.

LEYLAND, J., *Adventures in the Far Interior of South Africa*, London 1866.

MACKENZIE, J., *Ten Years North of the Orange River*, Edinburgh 1871.

MACNAIR, J. I., *Livingstone the Liberator*, London 1940.

MARTELLI, G., *Livingstone's River*, London 1970.

METHUEN, H. H., *Life in the Wilderness: or, Wanderings in South Africa*, London 1846.

NORTHCOTT, C., *Robert Moffat: Pioneer in Africa 1817–1870*, London 1961.

OSWELL, W. E., *William Cotton Oswell*, London 1900, 2 vols.

RANSFORD, O. N., *Livingstone's Lake*, London 1966.

ROWLEY, H., *The Story of the Universities' Mission to Central Africa*, London 1866.

SCHAPERA, I. (ed.), *Apprenticeship at Kuruman: being the journals and letters of Robert and Mary Moffat, 1820–1828*, London 1951.

SEAVER, G., *David Livingstone: his life and letters*, London 1957.

SHEPPERSON, G., *David Livingstone and the Rovuma*, Edinburgh 1965.

SILLERY, A., *Sechele: the Story of an African Chief*, Oxford 1954.

SIMMONS, J., *Livingstone and Africa*, London 1955.

SLATER, M. I., *Isabella Price, Pioneer*, London 1931.

SMITH, E. W., *Great Lion of Bechuanaland*, London 1951.

STANLEY, D. (ed.), *The Autobiography of Sir Henry Morton Stanley*, London 1909.

STANLEY, H. M., *How I Found Livingstone*, London 1872.

TABLER, E. C. (ed.), *The Zambesi Papers of Richard Thornton*, London 1963, 2 vols.

WADDINGTON, J., *Congregational History*, London 1869–80, 5 vols.

WALLIS, J. P. R. (ed.), *The Matabele Journals of Robert Moffat 1829–1860*, London 1945, 2 vols.

WALLIS, J. P. R. (ed.), *The Zambesi Journal of James Stewart 1862–1863*, London 1952.

WALLIS, J. P. R., *Thomas Baines of King's Lynn*, London 1941.

WRIGHT, S., *Annals of Blantyre*, Glasgow 1885.

YOUNG, E. D., *The Search After Livingstone*, London 1868.

3. GENERAL BACKGROUND

AGAR-HAMILTON, J. A. I., *The Native Policy of the Voortrekkers*, Cape Town 1928.

CAIRNS, H. A. C., *Prelude to Imperialism*, London 1965.

COUPLAND, R., *The British Anti-Slavery Movement*, London 1933.

COUPLAND, R., *East Africa and its Invaders*, Oxford 1956.

COUPLAND, R., *The Exploitation of East Africa 1856–90*, London 1939.

CUST, R. N., *Notes on Missionary Subjects*, London 1889.

DUFFY, J., *Portuguese Africa*, Harvard 1959.

ESCOTT, H., *A History of Scottish Congregationalism*, London 1960.

FAULKNER, H. U., *Chartism and the Churches*, Columbia 1916.

GANN, L. H. and DUIGNAN, P., *Burden of Empire*, London 1968.

GLUCKMAN, H. M., 'As Men are Everywhere Else', *The Listener* 22 Sept. 1955.

GLUCKMAN, H. M., *Politics, Law and Ritual in Tribal Society*, Oxford 1965.

GLUCKMAN, H. M., and COLSON, E., *Seven Tribes of British Central Africa*, London 1951.

GROVES, C. P., *The Planting of Christianity in Africa*, London 1948–58, 4 vols.

HAIGHT, M. V. J., *European Powers and South East Africa*, London 1967.

HARRIES, L. P., *Islam in East Africa*, London 1954.

KOEBNER, R. and SCHMIDT, H. D., *Imperialism: The Story and Significance of a Political Word, 1840–1960*, Cambridge 1964.

LOVETT, R., *The History of the London Missionary Society*, London 1899, 2 vols.

LUCAS, W. V. and JAMES, E. O., *Christianity and Native Rites*, London 1950.

OLIVER, R., *The Missionary Factor in East Africa*, London 1952.

OLIVER, R. and MATHEW, G. (eds), *History of East Africa*, Oxford 1963.

PERHAM, M., *Lugard: The Years of Adventure, 1858–1898*, London 1956.

ROBINSON, R., GALLAGHER, J. and DENNY, A., *Africa and the Victorians*, London 1961.

ROSS, J., *A History of Congregational Independency in Scotland*, London 1900.

SCHAPERA, I., *The Tswana*, London 1953.

THEAL, G. MC C., *History of South Africa*, London 1926–7, vols v–vii (new edn).

WALKER, E. A., *A History of Southern Africa*, London 1957 (3rd edn).

NOTES

Abbrevations Used in the Notes

A.J.(1) & (2)	*Livingstone's African Journal 1853–1856*, ed. I. Schapera, London 1963, 2 vols.
Blaikie	*The Personal Life of David Livingstone*, W. G. Blaikie, London 1880.
Blantyre	The Livingstone Memorial, Blantyre, Scotland.
B.M. Ad. MS	British Museum Additional Manuscript
Chamberlin	*Some Letters from Livingstone 1840–1872*, ed. D. Chamberlin, London 1940.
D.L.	David Livingstone. I have similarly abbreviated all members of the Livingstone family: e.g. Charles L., Agnes L., etc.
F.L. (1) & (2)	*David Livingstone: Family Letters 1841–1856*, ed. I. Schapera, London 1959, 2 vols.
F.O.	Foreign Office. Livingstone's official Government correspondence in the Public Record Office F.O. series.
H.I.F.L.	*How I Found Livingstone*, H. M. Stanley, London 1872.
Kirk	*The Zambesi Journal and Letters of Dr John Kirk 1858–1863*, ed. R. Foskett, London 1965, 2 vols.
L.J. (1) & (2)	*The Last Journals of David Livingstone in Central Africa*, ed. H. Waller, London 1874, 2 vols.
L.M.S.	The London Missionary Society.
L.M. Zambia	Livingstone Museum, Zambia.
M.M.	*The Matabele Mission: A Selection from the Correspondence of John and Emily Moffat, David Livingstone, and others 1858–1878*, ed. J. P. R. Wallis, London 1945.
M.C.	*Livingstone's Missionary Correspondence 1841–1856*, ed. I. Schapera, London 1961.
M.T.	*Missionary Travels and Researches in South Africa*, D. Livingstone, London 1857.
Narrative	*Narrative of an Expedition to the Zambesi and its Tributaries*, D. and C. Livingstone, London 1865.

N.A.R.	National Archives of Rhodesia.
N.L.S.	National Library of Scotland.
P.J.	*Livingstone's Private Journals 1851–1853*, ed. I. Schapera, London 1960.
P.R.G.S.	Proceedings of the Royal Geographical Society.
Seaver	*David Livingstone: his life and letters*, G. Seaver, London 1957.
S.J.	*The Zambesi Journal of James Stewart 1862–1863*, ed. J. P. R. Wallis, London 1952.
U.S.J.	Unpublished sections of James Stewart's Journal in the National Archives of Rhodesia.
U.P.J.	Unpublished Private Journal of David Livingstone 1861–1863 in National Library of Scotland.
Z.J. (1) & (2)	*The Zambesi Expedition of David Livingstone 1858–1863*, ed. J. P. R. Wallis, London 1956, 2 vols.

Introduction

1. Blaikie 386

Part One: Aspiration

1. FACTORY BOY, 1813–1836

1. Notes written by Janet Livingstone *c.* 1880 for Dr. Blaikie, N.L.S.
2. *Curiosities of Glasgow Citizenship*, G. Hewart (Glasgow 1881), 112–13
3. *Parliamentary Papers*. Report of the Minutes of Evidence on the state of Children employed in Manufactories of the United Kingdom. 1816 (397) vol. 3
4. Neil Livingstone's letters, L.M.S. Archives. Janet Livingstone's notes for Dr Blaikie, N.L.S.
5. *Livingstone and the Exploration of Central Africa*, H. H. Johnston (London 1891), 57
6. M.M. 42
7. D.L. to L.M.S. 5.9.37, L.M.S. Archives
8. 'Dr Thomas Dick and Dr Livingstone', A. W. Ferguson, *Broughty Ferry Guide*, Feb. 1913; *People's Journal* (Dundee) 7.6.1952
9. D.L.'s *Essay on the Holy Spirit*, L.M.S. Archives

2. MEDICAL STUDIES AND MISSIONARY TRAINING, 1836–1840

1. Neil L. to L.M.S. 26.4.38, L.M.S. Archives
2. *Livingstone the Doctor*, M. Gelfand (Oxford 1957), Intro.
3. Answers to Questions, L.M.S. Archives

4. Neil L. to L.M.S. 26.4.38, L.M.S. Archives
5. R. Cecil to L.M.S. 26.1.39, L.M.S. Archives
6. R. Cecil to L.M.S. 23.2.39, L.M.S. Archives
7. Blaikie 22
8. Seaver 27
9. Blaikie 21
10. Chamberlin 12
11. D.L. to Janet L., 5.5.39, N.L.S.
12. D.L. to Janet L. 8.12.41, N.L.S.
13. D.L. to Thomas L. 24.9.69, N.L.S.
14. D.L. to L.M.S. 2.7.39, L.M.S. Archives
15. Mrs Moffat to R. Moffat 27.6.40, N.A.R.
16. Chamberlin 8
17. D.L. to G. Drummond 25.7.40, N.L.S.
18. Precise definition given by Miss I. Fletcher, Archivist L.M.S.
19. D.L. to Mrs. Neil L. (undated), N.L.S.
20. D.L. to Mrs. Neil L. 31.10.54, N.L.S.
21. 'The Niger Expedition', Charles Dickens, *Household Words* 19.8.48
22. D.L. to T. Prentice 5.3.41, L.M.S. Archives
23. A.J.(2).356

3. AFRICA AND SOUTH AFRICA IN 1841

This general chapter was based on material from:

A History of Southern Africa, E. A. Walker (London 1957), 3rd edn

Portuguese Africa, J. Duffy, Harvard University Press 1959

The Planting of Christianity in Africa, C. P. Groves (London 1948–58), 4 vols

The History of the London Missionary Society, R. Lovett (1899), 2 vols

History of South Africa, G. Mc C. Theal (London 1926–7), vols V–VII, new edn

Cambridge History of the British Empire vol. II (1940)

4. EARLY DISAPPOINTMENT: KURUMAN, 1841–1843

1. D.L. to D. G. Watt 7.7.41, L.M.S. Archives
2. D.L. to R. Cecil 13.5.41, *The Congregationalist* Oct. 1925
3. Ibid.
4. D.L. to D. G. Watt 14.4.42, L.M.S. Archives
5. D.L. to L.M.S. 23.9.41, M.C. 2
6. D.L. to Mrs McRobert 2.12.41, L.M.S. Archives
7. D.L. to D. G. Watt 14.4.42, L.M.S. Archives
8. D.L. to Janet and Agnes L., 30.3.41, F.L.(1).31
9. D.L. to D. G. Watt 7.2.41, L.M.S. Archives
10. D.L. to Janet L. 8.12.41, F.L.(1).44
11. D.L. to B. Pyne 22.12.41, Rhodes House
12. D.L. to Janet L. 8.12.41, F.L.(1).46

13. D.L. to B. Pyne 22.12.41, Rhodes House
14. Ibid.
15. D.L. to M. Prentice 8.4.42, L.M.S. Archives
16. D.L. to D. G. Watt 14.4.42, L.M.S. Archives
17. D.L. to Mr and Mrs Neil L., 29.9.41, F.L.(1).40
18. Blaikie 39
19. D.L. to L.M.S. 24.6.43, M.C. 36
20. Ibid.
21. D.L. to D. G. Watt 14.4.42, L.M.S. Archives
22. Ibid.
23. D.L. to G. Drummond 20.6.43, N.L.S.
24. D.L. to Janet L. 21.8.43, F.L.(1).80
25. D.L. to L.M.S. 30.10.43, M.C. 49
26. D.L. to D. G. Watt 14.4.42, L.M.S. Archives

5. A FALSE START: MABOTSA, 1844–1845

1. *A Tour in South Africa*, J. J. Freeman (London 1851),
   279–80. D.L. to L.M.S. 24.6.43, M.C. 42–3
2. *The Matabele Journals of Robert Moffat 1829–60*, ed.
   J. P. R. Wallis (London 1945), 2 vols: (1).29–30
3. D.L. to L.M.S. 3.7.42, M.C. 18
4. D.L. to Mr and Mrs Neil L. 14.5.45, F.L.(1).122
5. D.L. to G. Drummond 21.11.44, N.L.S.
6. D.L. to J. H. Parker 11.5.44, Wellcome Medical Library
7. Ibid.
8. D.L. to Janet L. 21.5.44, F.L.(1).101
9. D.L. to F. Ferguson 23.7.43, N.L.S.
10. D.L. to J. McRobert 24.7.43, L.M.S. Archives
11. M.T. 158–9
12. M.T. 20
13. P.J. 244
14. D.L. to Agnes L. 4.4.42, F.L.(1).56–7
15. D.L. to H. Dickson 8.5.40, N.L.S.
16. D.L. to G. Drummond 20.6.43, N.L.S.
17. A. B. Pyne Private Collection
18. D.L. to D. G. Watt 27.9.43, L.M.S. Archives
19. D.L. to B. Pyne 22.12.41, Rhodes House
20. D.L. to B. Pyne 22.6.43, Rhodes House
21. *Congregational History*, J. Waddington, 4 (London 1880),
    89–90
22. R. Moffat to L.M.S. 24.2.44, L.M.S. Archives
23. D.L. to B. Pyne 22.6.43, Rhodes House
24. D.L. to R. Moffat 15.2.44, F.L.(1).90
25. D.L. to L.M.S. 2.12.44, M.C. 59
26. D.L. to D. G. Watt 2.4.45, L.M.S. Archives
27. A. B. Pyne Private Collection.
28. D.L. to Mrs Neil L. 14.5.45, F.L.(1).121
29. D.L. to J. S. Moffat 2.10.58, M.M. 44
30. D.L. to M. L. Dyke 20.5.47, N.L.S.

31. *Trader Horn*, Ethelreda Lewis (New York 1927), 150
32. D.L. to D. G. Watt 15.8.45, L.M.S. Archives
33. D.L. to D. G. Watt 8.6.46, L.M.S. Archives
34. D.L. to D. G. Watt 18.6.43, L.M.S. Archives
35. *The Missionary Magazine and Chronicle* vii 50
36. D.L. to B. Pyne 28.1.45, N.L.S.
37. D.L. to D. G. Watt 15.8.45, L.M.S. Archives
38. D.L. to J. Moore 9.8.47, F.L.(1).198n
39. L.M.S. to D.L. 14.7.52, M.C. 208
40. D.L. to Miss M. Moffat 12.9.44, F.L.(1).105
41. D.L. to R. Moffat 1.7.46, F.L.(1).176
42. D.L. to D. G. Watt 23.5.45, L.M.S. Archives
43. Blaikie 62, Macnair 91–2

6. LIVINGSTONE AND THE BOERS: CHONUANE, 1845–1847

1. Blaikie 64
2. D.L. to A. Murray 10.6.47, Union Archives, Pretoria (copy L.M.S. Archives)
3. *Life in the Wilderness: or, Wanderings in South Africa*, H. H. Methuen (London 1846), 198
4. *Travels in the Interior of South Africa*, J. Chapman (London 1868), 2 vols: (1).113
5. *Ten Years North of the Orange River*, J. Mackenzie, Edinburgh 1871, 105
6. D.L. to Mrs McRobert 18.1.46, Wellcome Medical Library
7. D.L. to R. Moffat 5.9.45, F.L.(1).143
8. D.L. to R. Moffat 29.9.47, F.L.(1).219
9. D.L. to Agnes L. 11.11.45, F.L.(1).157
10. M.T. 9
11. D.L. to R. Moffat 12.5.45, F.L.(1).118
12. D.L. to L.M.S. 10.4.46, M.C. 91
13. D.L. to Neil L. 17.1.46, F.L.(1).161
14. Ibid.
15. L.M.S. to D.L. 30.12.45, M.C. 85
16. D.L. to R. Moffat 11.2.46, F.L.(1).165
17. M.T. 37
18. *The Native Policy of the Voortrekkers*, J. A. I. Agar-Hamilton (Cape Town 1928), 181
19. *Cape Town Mail* 26.4.53 (quoted F.L.(1).12)
20. D.L. to R. Moffat 11.2.46, F.L.(1).170
21. D.L. to R. Moffat 11.3.46, F.L.(1).171
22. D.L. to R. Moffat Nov. 1848, F.L.(1).261
23. Chamberlin 268
24. D.L. to L.M.S. 17.3.47, M.C. 108
25. L.M.S. to D.L. 23.12.48, M.C. 124

7. THE ONLY CONVERT: KOLOBENG, 1847–1849

1. *William Cotton Oswell*, W. E. Oswell (London 1900)
2. D.L. to J. J. Freeman 24.8.50, M.C. 152

3. Blaikie 71
4. D.L. to Mr and Mrs Neil L. 5.7.48, F.L.(1).160
5. D.L. to Neil L. 17.1.46, F.L.(1).160
6. D.L. to Mrs Neil L. 4.5.47, F.L.(1).199
7. D.L. to Janet L. 31.1.49, F.L.(2).18
8. D.L. to Mr and Mrs Neil L. 9.2.51, F.L.(2).122
9. D.L. to Janet L. 20.4.49, F.L.(2).32
10. D.L. to L.M.S. 24.6.43, M.C. 38
11. *Robert Moffat: A Pioneer in Africa 1817–1870*, C. North-
    cott (Lutterworth 1961), 83
12. D.L. to Mr and Mrs Neil L. 5.7.48, F.L.(1).246
13. D.L. to R. Moffat 1.7.46, F.L.(1).177
14. Chamberlin 25
15. M.T. 21
16. A.J.(1).57–8
17. D.L. to R. Moffat 29.9.47, F.L.(1).219
18. D.L. to D. G. Watt 13.2.48, L.M.S. Archives
19. M.T. 18
20. Fragments of Kolobeng Journal, P.J. 298
21. Ibid. 299
22. D.L. to H. Drummond 21.11.48, L.M.S. Archives
23. D.L. to R. Moffat Nov. 1848, F.L.(1).261
24. D.L. to Janet L. 31.1.49, F.L.(2).19
25. P.J. 304
26. D.L. to R. Moffat 11.4.49, F.L.(2).30
27. D.L. to R. Moffat 4.5.49, F.L.(2).43
28. D.L. to L.M.S. 26.5.49, M.C. 130
29. M.T. 5
30. A.J.(1).61
31. Ibid. 157
32. Ibid.
33. D.L. to L.M.S. 17.3.47, M. C. 108

Part Two: Achievement

8. NORTH TO THE ZAMBESI, 1849–1851

1. D.L. to L.M.S. 3.9.49, M.C. 134
2. Ibid. 133
3. D.L. to R. Moffat 8.7.50, F.L.(2).83–5
4. Ibid.
5. Ibid.
6. Ibid.
7. Seaver 129
8. D.L. to R. Moffat 24.8.50, F.L.(2).101–2
9. P.J. 70–71
10. D.L. to L.M.S. 3.6.51, M.C. 151
11. M.T. 79
12. P.J. 13

13. Ibid. 16
14. D.L. to Charles L. 8.10.51, *Atlantic Monthly* 1922 (July)
15. A.J.(2).320–21
16. P.J. 210
17. A.J.(1).157
18. A.J.(2).243
19. P.J. 167–8
20. A.J.(1).234
21. P.J. 282
22. D.L. to L.M.S. 17.10.51, M.C. 190
23. D.L. to Charles L. 8.10.51, *Atlantic Monthly* 1922 (July)
24. D.L. to W. Thompson 27.9.55, M.C. 286
25. D.L. to L.M.S. 17.10.51, M.C. 190
26. D.L. to R. Moffat 8.7.50, F.L.(2).85
27. D.L. to J. J. Freeman 9.1.50, M.C. 42
28. D.L. to L.M.S. 17.10.51, M.C. 189
29. D.L. to Mr and Mrs Neil L. 30.9.53, F.L.(2).228
30. M.C. xxii

9. RETURN TO LINYANTI, 1852–1853

1. D.L. to W. Thompson 6.9.52, M.C. 215
2. D.L. to Children Feb. 1853, F.L.(2).206
3. D.L. to R. Moffat 2.4.52, F.L.(2).172
4. Neil L. to L.M.S. 25.6.53, L.M.S. Archives
5. Mary L. to L.M.S. 19.10.53, L.M.S. Archives
6. D.L. to Mary L. 14.1.53, F.L.(2).202
7. D.L. to Mary L. 27.11.56, F.L.(2).294
8. D.L. to Children 2.10.53, F.L.(2).230
9. D.L. to Children Feb. 1853, F.L.(2).206
10. D.L. to Charles L. 29.5.52, *Atlantic Monthly* 1922 (July)
11. Ibid.
12. D.L. to L.M.S. 26.5.52, M.C. 203
13. P.J 90–91
14. D.L. to Mrs Moffat 26.9.55, F.L.(2).271
15. M.T. 121; & D.L. to Charles L. 6.2.53, F.L.(2).211
16. *Matabele Journals of Robert Moffat* i, 378–9
17. P.J. 104
18. Ibid.
19. D.L. to Charles L. 2.6.53, F.L.(2).213
20. M.T. 10
21. P.J. 108
22. Kolobeng Notebook 1850–3, Blantyre
23. P.J. 119
24. D.L. to W. Thompson 17.9.53, M.C. 241

10. FROM COAST TO COAST, 1853–1856

1. D.L. to R. Gray 28.11.60, Wellcome Medical Library
2. M.C. 194, 247, 281

3. *Travels in the Interior of South Africa*, J. Chapman (London 1868), i, 171, 289
4. P.J. 169
5. Ibid.
6. Ibid. 146
7. Ibid. 206
8. Ibid. 223
9. D.L. to Thompson 17.9.53, M.C. 243
10. P.J. 228
11. Ibid. 163
12. Ibid. 176
13. D.L. to L.M.S. 24.9.53, M.C. 250
14. Ibid. 252
15. P.J. 220
16. D.L. to L.M.S. 24.9.53, M.C. 250
17. Ibid. 250–51
18. *Dr Livingstone and the Royal Geographical Society*, W. D. Cooley (London 1874), 7–8
19. M.T. 229
20. Ibid. 230
21. A.J.(1).4
22. M.T. 243–4
23. Ibid. 250–51
24. A.J.(1).7
25. M.T. 212
26. A.J.(1).5
27. Ibid. 51
28. M.T. 279
29. Ibid. 281–2
30. A.J.(1).51–2
31. Ibid. 52
32. M.T. 301
33. A.J.(1).56
34. M.T. 298
35. A.J.(1).81
36. M.T. 239–42
37. A.J.(1).114
38. D.L. to L.M.S. 14.1.55, M.C. 270
39. D.L. to Thompson 13.9.55, M.C. 279, 281
40. M.T. 392
41. D.L. to Charles L. 8.11.54, F.L.(2).256
42. A.J.(1).151
43. A.J.(1).225–6
44. M.T. 357
45. A.J.(2).304
46. M.T. 441
47. Ibid.
48. A.J.(2).243
49. See note 3 above

50. M.T. 492
51. A.J.(2).331
52. D.L. to L.M.S. 12.10.55; M.C. 294
53. A.J.(2).326
54. Ibid. 346
55. M.T. 551–2
56. A.J.(2).373
57. Ibid.
58. Ibid. 374
59. D.L. to Mr and Mrs Neil L. 30.9.53, F.L.(2).228
60. M.T. 604
61. *The Way to Ilala: David Livingstone's Pilgrimage*, F. Debenham (London 1957), 120–1
62. D.L. to L.M.S. 2.3.56, M.C. 302–3
63. L.M.S. to D.L. 24.8.55, M.C. 277
64. *The Times* 8.8.54

Part Three: Fame

11. NATIONAL HERO: THE FIRST VISIT HOME, 1856–1858

1. Blaikie 178–9
2. *London Journal* Dec. 1856
3. Ibid.
4. Blaikie 189
5. D.L. to G. Adderley 19.5.65, N.L.S.
6. Charles L: Letters to his wife, L.M. Zambia
7. Ibid.
8. D.L. to Mary L. 28.8.57, B.M. Ad. MS. 50184
9. D.L. to Robert L. 31.5.59, L.M.S.
10. D.L. to E. Gabriel 4.4.56, Lane Papers L.M.S. Archives
11. D.L. to Mr and Mrs Neil L., 30.9.53, F.L.(2).228
12. D.L. to R. Murchison 5.8.56, Z.J.(1).xviii
13. R. Murchison to Lord Clarendon 5.1.57, Clarendon Papers Bodleian Dep C 80
14. Charles L.: Letters to his wife, L.M. Zambia
15. D.L. to J. S. Moffat 15.10.59, M.M. 85
16. L.M.S. Board Minutes
17. Ibid.
18. *Great Lion of Bechuanaland*, E. Smith (London 1957), 24, 28
19. L.M.S. Board Minutes (quoted Schapera M.C. xxiii)
20. D.L. to R. Murchison 22.12.56, Z.J.(1).xxii
21. D.L. to R. Murchison 15.4.57, Z.J.(1).xxiii–iv
22. D.L. to R. Murchison 26.1.57, Clarendon Papers Bodleian Dep C 80 224ff
23. D.L. to T. Maclear 13.5.57, Z.J.(1).xxiv
24. Charles L. to wife 5.5.57, L.M. Zambia
25. D.L. to Lord Clarendon 14.3.57, Clarendon Papers Bodleian Dep C 80

26. L.M.S. to R. Moffat 4.4.57, L.M.S. Archives
27. Board Minutes L.M.S. (quoted Schapera M.C. xxv)
28. D.L. to L.M.S. 22.2.58, L.M.S. Archives
29. D.L. to L.M.S. 6.3.58, L.M.S. Archives

12. THE PRICE OF OPTIMISM: THE MAKOLOLO
MISSION, 1857–1860

1. D.L. to L.M.S. 12.10.55, M.C. 293–4
2. D.L. to L.M.S. 24.9.53, M.C. 253
3. D.L. to L.M.S. 12.10.55, M.C. 302
4. R. Moffat to L.M.S. 19.4.58, L.M.S. Archives
5. Ibid.
6. *Ten Years North of the Orange River*, J. Mackenzie (Edinburgh 1871), 39
7. D.L. to L.M.S. 6.3.58, L.M.S. Archives
8. Mrs Helmore to O. Helmore 24.11.59, Helmore Papers L.M.S. Archives
9. D.L. to L.M.S. 10.11.60, L.M.S. Archives
10. D.L. to L.M.S. 25.2.62, L.M.S. Archives
11. D.L. to J. S. Moffat 24.11.61, M.M. 160
12. D.L. to Janet L. 1.1.62, N.L.S.
13. *Narrative* 300
14. D.L. to Agnes L. 30.11.60, N.L.S.
15. J. Mackenzie to L.M.S. 3.10.59, L.M.S. Archives
16. Charles L. to F. Fitch 8.8.62, N.A.R.

13. HER MAJESTY'S CONSUL

1. R. Murchison to Lord Clarendon 15.5.57, Clarendon Papers Bodleian Dep C 80
2. *The Way to Ilala: David Livingstone's Pilgrimage*, F. Debenham (London 1957), 129–30
3. Z.J.(2).416
4. *Narrative* 8
5. M.T. 679
6. D.L. to Lord Clarendon 19.3.57, Clarendon Papers Bodleian Dep C 80
7. D.L. to Lord Clarendon 1.12.57, F.O. 63/842
8. See note 2 above
9. *Livingstone's River*, G. Martelli (London 1970), 37
10. *Kirk on the Zambesi*, R. Coupland (London 1928), 92–3
11. Ibid. 90–91

Part Four: Reversal

14. THE ZAMBESI EXPEDITION SETS SAIL

1. Copy of Indenture dated 19.12.57, N.A.R.
2. Z.J.(1).3
3. Seaver 303

4. Charles L.: Letters to his wife. L.M. Zambia
5. *Kirk on the Zambesi* 105
6. Ibid. 106
7. D.L. to M. Elwin 22.3.58, Wellcome Medical Library

15. THE ROCKS IN GOD'S HIGHWAY, 1858

1. Z.J.(1).6
2. Z.J.(1).12
3. N. Bedingfeld to D.L. 11.6.58, Z.J.(1).13
4. D.L. to N. Bedingfeld 28.6.58, Z.J.(1).18
5. N. Bedingfeld to D.L. 30.6.58, Z.J.(1).22–4
6. D.L. to F. Fitch 28.10.59, N.A.R.
7. Z.J.(1).37
8. D.L. to T. Maclear 31.7.59, N.A.R.
9. Kirk 47
10. Ibid. 111
11. Ibid. 115
12. Ibid. 121
13. Z.J.(1).61
14. Ibid. 63
15. Ibid.
16. D.L. to J. S. Moffat 2.10.58, M.M. 43
17. Kirk 128–32
18. Z.J.(1).68
19. Kirk 133
20. *Kirk on the Zambesi* 136
21. D.L. to T. Maclear 19.12.58, N.A.R.
22. A.J.(2).409

16. COLONIAL DREAMS: THE SHIRE AND LAKE NYASSA, 1859–1860

1. Z.J.(1).88
2. D.L. to Agnes L. 1.6.59, B.M. Ad. MS. 50184
3. Z.J.(1).125
4. A.J.(2).409
5. O. N. Ransford supported Candido's claim in his book *Livingstone's Lake* (London 1966), 52–6
6. Kirk 153
7. U.P.J. 87, N.L.S.
8. D.L. to E. Gabriel, Lane Papers L.M.S. Archives
9. D.L. to W. C. Oswell 1.11.59, Rhodes House
10. Kirk 209
11. Ibid. 408
12. D.L. to F.O. 15.10.59, Z.J.(2).332–7
13. F.O.63/871
14. Lord John Russell to D.L. 17.4.60, N.A.R.
15. D.L. to R. Murchison 15.2.59, N.A.R.
16. D.L. to R. Murchison 8.8.59, N.A.R.
17. D.L. to Thomas L. 7.1.62, N.L.S.

18. A.J.(2).446
19. D.L. to R. Murchison 6.11.54, N.A.R.
20. Seaver 444
21. R. Gray to D.L. 31.3.59, N.A.R.
22. D.L. to R. Gray 31.10.59, N.A.R.
23. Kirk 156
24. *Narrative* 74
25. Kirk 156
26. Z.J.(1).84
27. D.L. to Robert L. 31.5.59, N.L.S.
28. Z.J.(1).85
29. Z.J.(1).136
30. Kirk 115, 128
31. Charles L. to his wife 15.11.58, L.M. Zambia
32. *Thomas Baines of King's Lynn*, J. P. R. Wallis (London 1941), 161–2
33. Charles L. to his wife 5.2.59, L.M. Zambia
34. Z.J.(1).xi
35. Kirk 210
36. Z.J.(1).59
37. Charles L. to his wife 30.7.59, L.M. Zambia
38. D.L. to T. Maclear 31.7.59, N.A.R.
39. O. Thornton to R. Thornton 1.12.59, N.A.R.; H. Thornton to R. Thornton 1.12.59, N.A.R.
40. Charles L. to his wife 28.11.59, L.M. Zambia
41. Kirk 264
42. Seaver 355–6
43. D.L. to W.C. Oswell 1.11.59, Rhodes House
44. Z.J.(1).134
45. Kirk 220
46. Charles L. to F. Fitch 4.12.60, N.A.R.
47. Z.J.(1).163–4
48. Z.J.(1).169
49. Kirk 307
50. Ibid.
51. Ibid. 310
52. Z.J.(2).252
53. D.L. to Secretaries of U.M.C.A. 29.11.60, N.A.R.
54. D.L. to Bishop of Oxford Nov. 1860, *Congregational History*, J. Waddington, vol. 4, 449
55. *Mackenzie's Grave*, O. Chadwick (London 1959), 20

17. DEATH OF A FIGHTING BISHOP

1. *The Universities' Mission to Central Africa*, H. Rowley (London 1866), 5
2. F.O. 63/894
3. *Congregational History*, J. Waddington, vol. 4, 451
4. F.O. 63/871
5. *U.M.C.A.*, H. Rowley, 42

6. *Kirk on the Zambesi* 191
7. Charles L. to his wife 11.2.61, L.M. Zambia
8. *Congregational History*, J. Waddington, vol. 4, 451
9. *Mackenzie's Grave* 48
10. Ibid. 49; *Narrative* 36; Z.J.(1).184; Kirk 358
11. *Mackenzie's Grave* 51
12. D.L. to Agnes L. 25.11.61, B.M. Ad. MS. 50184
13. U.P.J. 6, N.L.S.
14. Ibid.
15. N. R. Bennett and M. Yevisaker (eds.), *The Central African Journal of Lovell J. Procter 1860–64* (Boston 1971)
16. D.L. to J. S. Moffat 23.2.62, M.M. 164
17. *U.M.C.A.*, H. Rowley, 193
18. *Kirk on the Zambesi* 217
19. *Congregational History*, J. Waddington, vol. 4, 460
20. *Mackenzie's Grave* 104
21. *U.M.C.A.*, H. Rowley, 316
22. U.P.J. 23, N.L.S.
23. Kirk 419
24. Mary L. to Mrs F. Fitch 13.7.61, N.A.R.
25. *U.M.C.A.*, H. Rowley, 322
26. *A Cruise in the Gorgon*, W. C. Devereux (London 1869), 166–7
27. Ibid. 164–5
28. Ibid. 219
29. Kirk 415
30. J. Kirk to A. Kirk 25.7.62
31. U.S.J. 1.12.61, N.A.R.
32. Ibid. Jan. 1861
33. Charles L. to F. Fitch 16.3.62, N.A.R.
34. Charles L. Mrs Fitch 9.1.62, N.A.R.
35. Charles L. to his wife 28.2.62, L.M. Zambia
36. U.P.J. 41, N.L.S.
37. *Mackenzie's Grave* 123
38. S.J. 12
39. Kirk 419
40. Blaikie 248
41. D.L. to J. S. Moffat 3.3.62, M.M. 170
42. S.J. 208
43. *Congregational History*, J. Waddington, vol. 4, 459
44. D.L. to Rowley 15.3.62, *Christian World* 2.2.1933
45. D.L. to H. Waller 12.2.63, Blantyre

18. DISASTER AND COLLAPSE:
THE END OF THE ZAMBESI EXPEDITION, 1862–1864

1. D.L. to Agnes L. 28.4.62, Harryhausen Private Collection
2. Kirk 439
3. Blaikie 251–2

4. D.L. to Mrs Neil L. 29.4.62, Harryhausen Private Collection
5. U.P.J. 42, N.L.S.
6. Ibid. 45
7. D.L. to Mrs Neil L. 29.4.62, Harryhausen Private Collection
8. U.P.J. 45, N.L.S.
9. D.L. to Oswell L. 28.4.62, L.M.S.
10. U.P.J. 43
11. S.J. 62
12. D.L. to Mrs Neil L. 29.4.62, Harryhausen Private Collection
13. S.J. 59
14. U.P.J. 48, N.L.S.
15. L.M.S. to D.L. 9.10.62, L.M.S. Archives
16. Kirk 463
17. Ibid. 475
18. D.L. to R. Moffat 25.10.62, B.M. Ad. MS. 50184
19. *Scottish Historical Review* xxxix (1960), 121
20. Kirk 482
21. U.P.I. 10.1.63, N.L.S.
22. Ibid. 2.11.62
23. Charles L. to F. Fitch 27.1.63, N.A.R.
24. S.J. 321
25. Ibid. 220
26. U.P.J. 172, N.L.S.
27. *U.M.C.A.*, H. Rowley, 286
28. D.L. to Agnes L. Sept. 1869, B.M. Ad. MS. 50184
29. Kirk 482
30. U.P.J. 168, N.L.S.
31. S.J. 228
32. U.P.J. 178, N.L.S.
33. D.L. to Lord John Russell 28.4.63, U.P.J. 189 N.L.S.
34. D.L. to H. Waller 24.4.63, Rhodes House
35. D.L. to Agnes L. 8.7.63, B.M. Ad. MS. 50184
36. D.L. to T. Maclear 5.11.63, N.A.R.
37. D.L. to R. Moffat 10.8.63, B.M. Ad. MS. 50184
38. *Dr Livingstone's Cambridge Lectures*, W. Monk (Cambridge 1860), 352
39. D.L. to J. S. Moffat 12.12.63, M.M. 225–6
40. *Mackenzie's Grave* 221
41. D.L. to Bishop Tozer 19.12.63, N.A.R.
42. D.L. to J. S. Moffat 12.12.63, M.M. 226
43. *Narrative* 579
44. D.L. to F.O. 12.12.63, U.P.J. 231 N.L.S.
45. D.L. to Agnes L. 10.8.63, B.M. Ad. MS 50184
46. S.J. 227
47. D.L. to F.O. 22.2.62, N.A.R.
48. Blaikie 279

49. D.L. to Maclear 26.2.64, N.A.R.
50. Seaver 442
51. Blaikie 264
52. Charles L. to his wife 2.11.63, L.M. Zambia

Part Five: Rejection

19. LAST VISIT HOME, 1864–1865

 1. F.O. 97/322
 2. D.L. to Agnes L. 25.7.64, B.M. Ad. MS. 50184
 3. S.J. 231
 4. D.L. to Agnes L. 25.7.64, B.M. Ad. MS. 50184
 5. D.L. to J. Kirk 8.8.63 (copy of letter supplied by G. L. Guy Esq., Dullstroom, South Africa)
 6. D.L. to Thomas L. June 1864, Moir Papers L.M.S. Archives
 7. D.L. to T. Maclear 5.11.63, N.A.R.
 8. Robert L. to D.L. undated, N.A.R. (quoted Seaver 454)
 9. D.L. to Thomas L. June 1864, Moir Papers L.M.S. Archives
10. *Livingstone the Liberator*, J. I. Macnair (London 1940), 282
11. D.L. to Agnes L. Sept. 1869, B.M. Ad. MS. 50184
12. Ibid.
13. *City Island and Coast*, R. Burton (London 1872), ii, 101–3
14. *Prelude to Imperialism*, H. A. C. Cairns (London 1965), 206
15. D.L. to L.M.S. 25.5.65, L.M.S. Archives
16. D.L. to R. Murchison 29.11.65, N.A.R.
17. *The Way to Ilala*, F. Debenham, 293–4
18. D.L. to Agnes L. Sept. 1869, B.M. Ad. MS. 50184
19. D.L. to B. Braithwaite Nov. 1870, L.M.S. Archives
20. Lord John Russell to D.L. 28.3.65, F.O. 84/1249
21. Omitted by H. Waller from L.J.(2).72
22. D.L. to B. Braithwaite Nov. 1870, L.M.S. Archives
23. Lord John Russell to A. Layard 25.3.65, B.M. Ad. MS. 38991
24. Lord John Russell to Murray 26.4.65, F.O. 84/1249
25. D.L. to Lord John Russell 23.5.65, F.O. 84/1249
26. D.L. to B. Braithwaite Nov. 1870, L.M.S. Archives

Part Six: Atonement

20. NYASSA TO TANGANYIKA, 1866–1869

 1. *Livingstone's Last Journey*, R. Coupland (London 1947), 15
 2. Seaver 470

3. *The Zambesi Doctors*, R. Foskett (Edinburgh 1964), 109
4. L.J.(1).13–14
5. This information about Susi supplied by D. H. Simpson Esq., Librarian, Royal Commonwealth Society.
6. *East Africa and its Invaders*, R. Coupland (Oxford 1956), 325
7. D.L. to Agnes L. 29.1.66, Harryhausen Private Collection
8. L.J.(1).7
9. D.L. to R. Murchison 27.11.65, N.A.R.
10. L.J.(1).23
11. Ibid. 29
12. D.L. to Agnes L. 18.5.66, B.M. Ad. MS. 50184
13. L.J.(1).70
14. Ibid. 58
15. Ibid. 56
16. Ibid. 62–3
17. D.L. to Lord Clarendon 20.8.66, F.O. 84/1265
18. D.L. to Lord Clarendon 11.6.66, F.O. 84/1265
19. D.L. to Thomas L. 28.8.66, N.L.S.
20. D.L. to R. Murchison 18.12.67, N.A.R.
21. D.L. to Thomas L. 28.8.66, N.L.S.
22. Seaver 493
23. L.J.(1).115
24. Ibid. 141
25. Ibid. 168
26. Ibid. 170
27. *The Way to Ilala* 235
28. L.J.(1).173–6
29. *Livingstone's Last Journey* 55
30. D.L. to Seward 1.2.67, P.R.G.S. xii 180
31. L.J.(1).205
32. *The Way to Ilala* 243
33. D.L. to R. Murchison 18.12.67, N.A.R.
34. L.J.(1).287
35. D.L. to R. Murchison 18.12.67, N.A.R.
36. L.J.(1).288
37. D.L. to Lord Clarendon 8.7.68, P.R.G.S. xiv 8–9
38. D.L. to J. Kirk 8.7.68, P.R.G.S. xiv 8
39. L.J.(1).309
40. *The Way to Ilala* 256
41. L.J.(1).346
42. L.J.(2).2
43. D.L. to Agnes L. 4.7.68, B.M. Ad. MS. 50184
44. D.L. to A. Sedgwick 24.8.66, Rhodes House

21. FANTASY IN MANYUEMA, 1869–1871

1. L.J.(2).11
2. Ibid. 14
3. *Zambesi Doctors* 138

4. L.J.(2).47–8
5. D.L. to Agnes L. 5.2.71, B.M. Ad. MS. 50184
6. D.L. to Thomas L. 24.9.69, N.L.S.
7. D.L. to Agnes L. 5.2.71, B.M. Ad. MS. 50184
8. L.J.(2).93
9. Ibid. 59
10. Ibid. 72
11. U.P.J. 11,N.L.S.
12. D.L. to Agnes L., 5.2.71, B.M. Ad. MS. 50184
13. Herodotus *History* Book ii
14. L.J.(2).49–50
15. D.L. to T. Maclear Nov. 1870, P.R.G.S. xvii 68
16. D.L. to B. Frere 27.11.70, P.R.G.S. xviii 265–6
17. D.L. to Agnes L. Sept. 1869, B.M. Ad. MS. 50184
18. L.J.(2).135
19. Ibid. 154
20. H.I.F.L. 405–12. L.J.(2).156

22. STANLEY AND THE LIVINGSTONE MYTH
1. H.I.F.L. xvii–xviii (intro)
2. Ibid. 15
3. *The Autobiography of Sir Henry Horton Stanley*, ed. D. Stanley (London 1909), 295
4. H.I.F.L. 398–9
5. *The Other Side of the Emin Pasha Relief Expedition*, H. R. Fox Bourne (London 1891), 19
6. H.I.F.L. 411
7. Stanley *Autobiography* 264
8. H.I.F.L. 411
9. *I Presume: Stanley's Triumph and Disaster*, I. Anstruther (London 1956), 146
10. H.I.F.L. 416
11. L.J.(2).156
12. D.L. to W. Thompson Nov. 1872, L.M.S. Archives
13. D.L. to Agnes L. 18.11.71, B.M. Ad. MS. 50184
14. H.I.F.L. 416
15. *Livingstone's Last Journey* 213n
16. Ibid. 171
17. Stanley *Autobiography* (extract from diary 3.3.72) 274
18. D.L. to B. Braithwaite 8.1.72, L.M.S. Archives
19. D.L. to Dr Wilson 24.1.72, N.L.S.
20. D.L. to Agnes L. Feb. 1872, B.M. Ad. MS. 50184
21. D.L. to Agnes L. 18 Nov. 1871, B.M. Ad. MS. 50184
22. D.L. to Agnes L. 12.12.71, B.M. Ad. MS. 50184
23. R. Murchison to Lord Clarendon 1.4.70, F.O. 2/42 B
24. D.L. to Agnes L. 1.7.72, B.M. Ad. MS. 50184
25. D.L. to Bates 20.2.72, N.L.S.
26. Ibid.

27. Stanley *Autobiography* 279
28. Ibid. 279–80
29. *Standard* 6.8.72
30. *Morning Post* 7.8.72
31. Blaikie 384–5

23. THE LAST JOURNEY, 1872–1873

1. D.L. to Agnes L. 1.7.72, B.M. Ad. MS. 50184
2. D.L. to John Livingstone Dec. 1872, Private Collection of Mr Quentin Keynes
3. D.L. to Agnes L. 2.6.72, B.M. Ad. MS. 50184
4. L.J.(2).211–12
5. D.L. to B. Braithwaite 8.1.72, L.M.S. Archives
6. D.L. to Dr Wilson 24.1.72, N.L.S.
7. L.J.(2).182
8. Ibid. 174
9. D.L. to H. Waller 19.2.72, Rhodes House
10. D.L. to H. Waller 2.9.72, Rhodes House
11. Seaver 620
12. D.L. to Earl Granville 1872 (otherwise undated), B.M. Ad. MS. 50184
13. L.J.(2).188, 193–4
14. D.L. to B. Braithwaite Dec. 1870, P.R.G.S. xviii 278
15. L.J.(2).229
16. H.M. Stanley to D.L. 23.5.72, N.L.S.
17. H. M. Stanley to D.L. 27.5.72, N.L.S.
18. D.L. to Agnes L. 23.8.72, B.M. Ad. MS. 50184
19. *The Way to Ilala* 297–317
20. L.J.(2).269
21. Ibid. 277
22. Ibid. 42
23. *The Way to Ilala* 272
24. L.J.(2).288
25. Ibid. 294
26. Ibid. 298
27. D.L. to Earl Granville 20.2.72, B.M. Ad. MS. 50184
28. L.J.(2).303
29. Ibid. 299–308
30. J. Wainwright to O.L. Oct. 1873, L.M.S. Archives

24. LIVINGSTONE AND THE BRITISH EMPIRE

1. *Glasgow Herald* 20.4.74
2. D.L. to T. Maclear 26.2.64, N.A.R.
3. Quoted H.I.F.L. Intro. lxxviii, 2nd edn
4. S.J. 190
5. *Africa and the Victorians*, R. Robinson, J. Gallagher and A. Denny (London 1961)
6. Hansard 2nd series ccxcv, col. 979

7. *The Story of My Life*, H. H. Johnston (London 1923), 221; *Lugard—The Years of Adventure 1858–1898*, M. Perham (London 1956), 133
8. *The Missionary Factor in East Africa*, R. Oliver (London 1952), 157
9. *Lugard*, M. Perham 461
10. Z.J.(2).416
11. M.T. 679
12. Seaver 444
13. M.T. 29–30
14. Kolobeng Notebook 1850–3, Blantyre

Apart from the words listed above, I also found the following books and articles useful in writing this final chapter:

Prelude to Imperialism, H. A. C. Cairns (London 1965)
The Exploitation of East Africa 1856–90, R. Coupland (London 1939)
Burden of Empire, L. H. Gann and P. Duignan (London 1968)
The Planting of Christianity in Africa, C. P. Groves (London 1948–58)), 4 vols.
'Partition: A General View', R. Hyam, in *Historical Journal* no. 2 (Cambridge University Press)
Imperialism: The Story and Significance of a Political Word, 1840–1960, R. Koebner and H. D. Schmidt (Cambridge 1964)
'Nationalism and Imperialism', J. Stengers, in *Journal of African History*, vol. 3 no. 3 (Cambridge University Press 1962)
Nineteenth Century Africa (Oxford 1968)
History of East Africa (Oxford 1963)

INDEX

INDEX

In this index D.L. = David Livingstone

Aberdeen, 43

Adams, 291, 328

Admiralty, 238, 246, 257, 340, 373

African Association, 47

African Lakes Company, 457–458, 462

Ajawa, 267, 269, 271, 273, 292, 296, 297, 298, 299, 300, 301, 311, 313, 314, 323, 324, 327, 332, 376

Albert, Lake, 345–46, 348, 367–368, 383, 388, 394, 396, 397, 404, 425, 433

Albert, Prince Consort, 41, 339–340, 385

Alexandria, 403

Algoa Bay, 56

Ambaca, 176–77

Ambriz, 174

America, 30, 32, 36, 47, 48, 133, 175, 233, 247, 275, 342–43, 365, 420, 465

American Civil War, 412

Amoda, 362, 377, 435

Anderson's College, Glasgow, 33, 34, 35

Angola, 47, 117–18, 144, 152, 157–58, 162, 174–76, 181, 182, 190, 193–94, 270, 271

Anthropological Society of London, 420

Argyll, Duke of, 233

Arrowsmith, J., 385

Ashton, W., 146

Australia, 48, 233, 234, 246

Bagamoyo, 381, 434, 448

Baines, Thomas, 246, 257, 259, 261, 278–82, 322, 329

Baker, Samuel White, 16, 345–346, 348, 351, 367, 397, 404, 413, 428

Bakhatla, 65, 68, 69–70, 78, 88, 89, 91, 92, 98, 99, 147

Bakwains, 65, 67, 71, 91, 92, 95, 96, 99, 100, 147; attacked by Boers, 147–48; their indifference and opposition to Christianity, 96, 100, 101, 106, 114, 140, 235

Balobale, 166

Balonda, 165–66, 168, 169–70

Bamangwato, 65, 66, 71, 98

Bambarre, 398–99, 401, 403–404

Bangweolo, Lake, 368, 376, 378, 379, 380, 381, 383, 384, 385, 386–90, 394, 396, 397, 401, 403, 434, 435, 436–43, 444n

Barotse, 187, 189, 230

Barotseland, 157, 158, 159, 160, 185, 186, 229–30, 231, 455

Barotse Valley, 117, 130, 152, 157–59, 164–65, 185

Bates, H. W., 426

Bath, 344–48

Batoka Plateau, 130, 189, 190, 193, 199, 211, 220, 221, 226, 228, 232, 236, 241, 251, 258–259, 264, 265, 267, 269, 331

Bechuanaland (Botswana), 52, 54, 56, 57, 59, 61, 65–66, 70, 71–72, 80, 91, 98, 101, 111, 117, 130, 138–40, 145, 150, 156, 160, 341, 344, 431

Bedingfeld, Commander N.B., R.N., 180, 246, 254–58, 261, 277, 280, 293, 322, 329, 369, 456

Belgian Congo, 458

Belgium, King of, Leopold II, 458

Benguela, 160, 161, 174, 200–201

Bennett, James Gordon, 410–13, 418, 420, 427, 429

Birmingham, 109

Blantyre (Malawi), 457, 463

Blantyre (Scotland), 23–24, 25, 30, 34, 247

Boers, 49, 50, 51–52, 70, 111, 130, 139–40, 233, 466; attitude to Africans, 50–52, 97–100, 113, 466; attitude to missionaries, 50–51, 52, 97–100, 139; attack on Kolobeng, 147–48

Bombay, 331, 334, 362–63, 413, 425

Brazil, 44, 46, 133, 174, 193

British Association, 236–37, 344

British East Africa Association, 461

British Empire, 16, 18, 19, 233–234, 333, 464–65

Brougham, Lord, 292

Broughty Ferry, 29

Bruce, James, 47

Bubi, 95

Bulawayo, 130

Burrup, H. de W., 291, 301, 303, 304, 305–307, 314

Burrup, Mrs, 301, 303, 306, 310, 311

Burton, Richard Francis, 16, 238, 272, 345–51, 363, 367, 413–14, 415

Buxton, Sir Thomas Fowell, 41–42, 47, 51, 133–34

Cairo, 197

Cambridge University, 276, 290, 305

Cameron, Verney Lovett, 447–448

Canada, 233, 234, 464

Candido, José da Costa Cardosa, 264, 268–69, 332

Canton, 32

Cape, The, 45–49, 50, 51, 54, 79, 83, 97, 121, 137, 138–39, 145, 150, 154, 155, 177, 210, 245, 330, 455

Cape Colony, 48–51, 53, 55, 97, 142–43, 148, 175, 233

Cape Town, 45, 48, 49, 50, 54–55, 99, 104, 142–43, 147, 149, 230, 246, 250, 276, 290

Caribbean, 46, 47

Carpo, Arsenio de, 176–77

Casembe, Chief, 384, 386

Cassange, 175–76, 178, 182

Cecil, Richard, 37–38, 248

Chamberlain, Joseph, 463, 464

Chambesi, river, 380, 390

Chapman, James, 155, 185–86

Charles et Georges, 241, 271

Cheshunt College, 37

Chiboque, 171–73, 184

Chicova, 192

China, 32–33, 36, 40

Chitambo, Chief, 443–44, 446–47

Chitane, 380

Chobe, river, 129–31, 132, 137, 151–52, 187, 223

Chonuane, 91, 92, 95, 96, 98, 101–102, 105

Chuma, 362, 377, 427, 435, 442, 443, 445, 446, 447–49; devotion to D.L., 381, 398, 445–446

Church Missionary Society, 449, 459

Clapperton, Hugh, 47, 62, 146

Clarendon, Lord, 182, 196, 211–217, 232, 235–41, 354, 388, 418, 424

Cockin, Mr, 179–80

Collier, Miss, 40–41

Colonial Office, 245, 252, 463

Columbus, Christopher, 46

Congo, river (see also Lualaba, river), 16, 45, 146, 387–88, 394, 396, 397, 403, 428, 434, 440, 458

Congregational Union, 30, 42

Copernicus, 403

Coupland, Sir Reginald, 423

Crauford, Captain, R.N., 292

Crimea, 246

Cuba, 47, 133, 412

Cumming, Gordon, 99

da Cruz, Antonio Vincente, 194

da Gama, Vasco, 46

Daily Telegraph, 456–57, 458, 459

Darwin, Charles, 400

Decken, Baron von der, 324
Devereux, W. C., 308
Dick, Thomas, 28–29, 32, 400
Dickens, Charles, 44
Dickinson, John, 291, 324
Dillon, W. E., 447
Disraeli, Benjamin, 234, 464
Drummond, Henry, 30
Dublin, 208, 236, 238, 345
Dublin University, 276
Dugumbe, 405–407
Duncan, Captain, 254–55
Dundee, 29
Durham University, 276
Dutch, The, 47–50, 233
Dutch East India Conpany, 48, 49

East India Company (British), 49, 233
East Luabo, 306
Edwards, Rogers, 64–65, 79, 80, 87–91, 92, 248, 452
Edwards, Mrs. R., 90–91
Edwards, Sam, 129
Egypt, 402, 460, 461, 462, 464; Khedive of, 459, 460
Ethiopia, 413, 417; Theodore, King of, 413
Evangelical Magazine, 62, 80
Exeter Hall, 41, 133

Farebrother, Mr, 227
Farquhar, W. L., 415
Ferguson, Fergus, 30, 34, 36–37
Fernando Po, 456
Ferra, Caetano, 178, 180
Finney, C. G., 30–31
Fleming, George, 149
Foreign Office, 235, 241, 247, 263, 272–73, 274, 278, 280, 282–83, 293, 307, 315, 335, 345, 349, 352–54, 361, 373–374, 375, 385, 394, 423–24, 427, 429, 448
France, 49, 133, 459, 460, 463
Francis, James, 412
Franco-Prussian War, 418
Free Church of Scotland, 300–301, 309, 362, 456, 457

Freeman, J. J., 123*n*, 146–47
Frere, Sir Bartle, 363, 402, 429–430
Frolic, H.M.S., 196–97

Gabon, 230
Gabriel, Edmund, 177, 181–82, 196, 210
Galton, Francis, 385
Gambia, river, 47
Gamble, Mr, 291
Gardner, 398, 435, 446, 448
George, The, 44, 45, 56
Germany, 460–61, 465
Gladstone, W. E., 292, 339, 430, 460–63
Glasgow, 23, 24, 29, 33, 34, 36, 41, 43, 53, 205
Glasgow University, 35, 391
Gorgon, H.M.S., 306, 307, 308, 310, 316, 326
Gráça, Rodrigues, 118, 121
Grant, James Augustus, 345, 403, 413–14
Granville, Lord, 434, 442–43
Gray, Robert, Bishop of Cape Town, 276, 329, 330
Great Fish, river, 49
Grey, Sir Edward, 463
Griqua Town, 52, 55, 60
Gutzlaff, Karl, 32

Haileybury, 119
Hamilton, 30–32, 34, 43, 78, 143–144, 341
Hardesty, Mr, 316, 319
Havana, 412
Hay, General, 312
Hayward, Lionel, 352
Helmore, Elizabeth, 223
Helmore, Holloway, 218*n*, 222–230
Helmore, Mrs, 222–23
Helmore, Olive, 223–24
Herodotus, 402, 405, 407, 426, 433, 434, 440
Hetty Ellen, The, 304, 307
Hong Kong, 40
Horn, Aloysius, 86
Hottentots, 48, 50, 51, 54

House of Commons, 237, 349, 429–30, 461–62
Hunter, Mary, 23

Imperial British East Africa Company, 459
India, 36, 49, 69, 110, 234, 362–363, 461, 464
Indian Mutiny, 234, 237
Indian Ocean, 241, 271, 291, 331, 413, 461
Inglis, Walter, 38, 87–88

Johanna, island, 315, 320, 363, 377
Johanna men, 363, 371, 377, 410
Josut, 401

Kabompo, river, 165
Kafue, river, 401
Kalahari Desert, 98, 117, 119–120, 124–26, 221, 318
Katanga, 118, 269, 384, 401, 404, 435, 437
Katema, 170
Kebrabasa Rapids, 192–93, 199, 224, 226, 239, 251, 258–65, 277, 278, 284, 287, 325, 331–332
Kenya, 18, 459, 461
Kepler, 403
Khake, 95, 96
Kilimanjaro, Mount, 324
Kilwa, 269, 272, 374–75, 379, 387
Kirk, Dr. John, 246–47, 250, 257, 258, 259–60, 261, 262–63, 266, 267, 271, 277, 278, 281–82, 283, 284, 285, 286, 287, 289–290, 291–92, 293, 306, 309, 311, 316–17, 319, 320–21, 322, 325–26, 333, 342, 360, 366, 388, 393, 394, 403, 407, 408, 413–14, 417, 419–20, 421, 422–24, 425, 429, 448
Kitchener, Lord, 464
Kolobeng, 101, 102, 110–11, 117, 119, 120, 121–22, 123–24, 126, 129, 137, 139–40, 142, 309, 344; sacked by Boers, 147–48

Kongone, 251, 270, 283, 289, 304, 316, 328
Kuruman, 52–53, 56–57, 59–61, 62–63, 64–65, 66, 68–69, 70, 83, 84, 87, 89, 91, 92, 96, 99, 100, 126–27, 128, 142, 146, 147–49, 245, 251, 319, 341, 362

Lacerda, Francisco José de, 118, 382
Lady Nyassa, The, 308, 310, 311, 315–16, 319–20, 322–27, 330, 335, 340, 362, 377, 411, 425, 457
Laing, A. G., 47
Lancet, The, 35
Lander, Richard Lemon, 47, 62, 125, 146
Laurel Hill, Virginia, 343
Layard, Austen, 352–53, 354
Lennox, Jessie, 306
Leyland, J., 129
Liberia, 47
Lincoln, Lake, 402, 405
Lincoln, President, 402n
Liverpool, 245, 249, 412
Livingstone, Agnes (sister), 229
Livingstone, Agnes (daughter), 101–102, 103, 124–25, 316, 327, 341, 343–44, 370, 398–399, 419, 424, 425, 426, 430–431
Livingstone, Anna Mary (daughter), 309, 341, 344
Livingstone, Charles (brother), 27, 122, 145, 208, 215, 230, 247, 259, 261, 278–82, 284–287, 289–90, 293, 294, 310, 313, 320, 321, 323, 325–26, 456

Livingstone, David
SCOTLAND AND LONDON
parentage and birth, 23–24; child factory worker, 24–25, 31–32; desire to learn and early interests, 25–28; early religious fears and beliefs, 28–31; decision to become medical missionary, 32; medical studies, 33–35, 41; applies to

Livingstone, David (*cont'd*)
London Missionary Society, 35–36; missionary training, 37–40

AFRICA, FIRST PHASE

sails for the Cape, 44; initial disillusionment, 55–67; new mission station at Mabotsa, 69–70; friendship with Robert Moffat, 80–81; attacked by lion, 82–83; meets and marries Mary Moffat, 82–84, 85–86; quarrels with Rogers Edwards, 88–91; moves to Chonuane, 92; relations with Boers, 97–100; life at Kolobeng, 101–107; births of children, 101–102; conversion and lapse of Sechele, 108–10; decision to leave Bechuanaland, 110–12, 138–140, 145–47; first major journeys, 117–39; first journey to Lake Ngami, 119–21; acclaim in Britain, 122–23; second journey to Lake Ngami, 123–26; quarrels with Moffats, 126–28; first journey to Zambesi, 129–39; finds slave-trade in S. Central Africa, 132–35; plans mission with Makololo, 133–34; sends family home, 138–39, 143–48; at Cape Town, 142–43, 145–47; sets out for Linyanti, 147; aims of journey, 148–49; begins detailed geographical and botanical observations, 150–51; abortive search for mission site in Barotseland, 155–57; journey to Loanda, 161–77; severe illness, 177; discouraging results of journey, 178–79; journey from Loanda to Linyanti, 180–186; no conversions among Makololo, 185–86; his betrayal of them, 186–87; journey to Quilimane, 187–96; 'discovers' Victoria Falls, 188–89; the Batoka Plateau and its prospects, 189–90; misses Kebrabasa Rapids, 192–93; arrival at Tete, 192; reaches Quilimane and coast, 196; appraisal of trans-continental journey, 198–201

FIRST VISIT HOME

arrival in England, 198; a national hero, 205–208; leaves London Missionary Society and negotiates for government service, 208–19; his part in Makololo Mission disaster, 219–31; becomes H.M. Consul, 231–36; prepares for Zambesi Expedition, 236–42

ZAMBESI EXPEDITION

voyage out, 245–50; early difficulties, 251–59; quarrel with Bedingfeld, 254–57; 'discovers' Kebrabasa Rapids, 259–65; pins hopes on river Shire, 264–265; explores river Shire, 265–266; plans for Shire Highlands, 267–70, 272–76, 283–84; recommends Universities Mission to go there, 276; dismisses Baines and Thornton, 278–82; quarrels with brother Charles, 284–87; importance of Universities Mission to D.L., 289; arrival of Universities Mission, 289–90; early tensions with Mission, 291–93; frees slaves with Bishop Mackenzie, 295–296; fights Ajawa, 296–98; dissociates himself from Mission, 299–300; arrival of Mrs Livingstone, 306; learns of Bishop Mackenzie's death, 311–13; death of Mrs Livingstone, 316–21; recall of Zambesi Expedition, 326–28

LAST VISIT HOME

returns to England, 331; uncertain personal position after Zambesi Expedition, 333–36; Government cool towards, 339–40, 352–55; interest in Nile source debate, 345–47; dislike of Speke and Burton, 347–50; beginning of new role, 347, 350–51

LAST JOURNEYS

ambiguity of aims on Last Journeys, 359–61; lands on East African coast, 367; initial difficulties, 368–71; sees extent of Arab slave-trade, 372–375; reaches Lake Tanganyika, 380; at Lake Moero, 382; 'dis-

Last Journeys (*cont'd*)
covers' Lualaba, 383; reaches
Lake Bangweolo, 389; at Ujiji,
392–96; sets out for Manyuema, 397; at Bambarre, 398–
403; reaches Lualaba at Nyangwe, 404; massacre at Nyangwe, 406–407; returns to
Ujiji, 407–408; meeting and relations with Stanley, 409, 416–
421, 426, 435; reaches Lusizé
river, 425; against returning
home, 423–25; parting with
Stanley, 426; at Unyanyembe,
430–34; sets out for Lake
Bangweolo and Katanga, 435;
reaches Lake Bangweolo, 437;
attempts to skirt Lake Bangweolo, 437–43; death, 445;
body preserved and carried to
coast by followers, 447–48

EPILOGUE:
funeral in Westminster Abbey,
450; public acclaim, 450; retrospective analysis of character, ideas and exploration,
451–55; posthumous influence,
456–66

LIVINGSTONE'S CHARACTER

Ambitiousness: 61, 63–64, 89,
100, 122, 123–24, 129, 138–39,
140–42, 146, 181, 264–65, 347,
393–94, 420

Bravery: 171–72, 190–91, 200,
434, 440, 441–45, 447, 450

Character (general): 18–19, 25–
26, 27, 43, 44–45, 86–91, 149–
150, 162, 207–31, 247–49, 260–
261, 264–65, 276–78, 280, 281–
284, 286–87, 299–300, 307–
308, 311–14, 317–23, 325–26,
329–30, 335–36, 368–71, 384–
386, 390, 416, 422, 423–24,
426, 434, 439, 441–42, 450–56

Descriptive ability: 150–51, 164,
184, 378, 439–40

Endurance, powers of: 83, 149–
150, 151–52, 165, 173, 200,
248, 262–63, 325, 330, 333,
379–80, 385–86, 397–98, 439,
441–42, 450

Optimism: 136–37, 138, 150, 187,
190, 199, 219, 265–66, 267,
333–34, 360, 361–62, 368, 393–
394, 431–32, 433, 436, 450–52,
456

LIVINGSTONE'S ATTITUDES AND
IDEAS

Africans: his affection for, 182–
184, 191, 369–70, 371, 373,
386, 390, 399, 405–407, 420–
421, 432, 446, 452; their affection for him, 82, 171, 259, 286,
381, 398, 438, 442–48; he con-
siders them degraded, 77, 78,
156–57, 165, 183–85, 189–90

Arabs: his friendly relations with,
365–66, 374–75, 382, 384, 386–
387, 392, 394, 407; his hostility
towards, 372, 375, 394, 407–
408

British Government: his relations
with, 16, 211, 213–15, 231–32,
236–41, 263, 272–74, 282–84,
287–88, 327–28, 332–33, 339–
340, 351–55, 360–61, 373–74,
411, 418, 423–24, 428–30

British superiority: his belief in,
19, 136, 184–85, 234–35, 249,
275, 333, 464–65

Children, his: attitude to and
treatment of, 102–103, 124–26,
129–39, 142–45, 208, 278, 341–
344, 391–92, 398–99, 430–31,
452

*Colonies, colonial advances, col-
onization:* his views on, 16, 18,
135–37, 232–36, 238, 258–59,
265, 267, 272–76, 288–89, 333–
335, 350, 359–61, 454–55, 464–
466

Commerce and Christianity: his
theories on, 16–17, 41–42, 133–
142, 171, 181, 184–85, 190,
207–08, 231, 235–36, 350, 453

Conventional missionary aims:
his rejection of, 67–68, 77–78,
100–101, 111–12, 133–42, 453

Fellow missionaries: his differences with, 55–56, 68–69, 87–
91, 141–42, 145–46, 197–98,
451–52

Livingstone's Attitudes and Ideas
(*cont'd*)

Imperialism: his attitude to, 234–
235, 464–65

Marriage: his views on, 36, 79–
80, 84–86

Missionary ideas: 16–17, 41–42,
60–61, 77–78, 100–101, 106–
107, 111–14, 133–42, 181, 235,
276, 313–14, 348–49, 431–32,
453, 465

Missionary work and exploration:
conflict between, 100–101,
140–42, 197–98, 334–36, 350–
351, 359–60

Paradoxical thinking: 16–17, 77,
100–101, 111–13, 135–38, 140–
142, 182–85, 249–50, 264–65,
272–73, 275–76, 313–14, 333–
336, 360–61, 365–66, 431–32,
453–55, 464–65

Portuguese: his scorn for and
hatred of, 194–95, 240–41, 270,
282, 327, 333, 340, 344

Rivers as 'highways': his view of,
122, 132, 134, 138, 140, 181–
182, 187–88, 192–93, 199, 272,
291, 359, 453

Slave-trade: his views on, 132–
135, 157, 231–33, 268, 271–74,
295–98, 307, 321, 327, 350–
351, 359–61, 365–66, 372–73,
399, 407, 432–33, 453; effects
of his anti-slavery despatches,
420, 429–30

Tribal society: his understanding
of, 77–78, 112–14, 182–84,
420–21, 455; intends destruction of, 17, 135–36, 184–85,
249, 275–76, 313, 334, 359,
453–55

Livingstone myth, making of the,
17, 179, 199–201, 206–208,
359–60, 410–11, 416, 421–22,
427–28, 449–51

Livingstone Search and Relief
Expeditions: (1867) 411;
(1871–2) 428–29, 430, 434–35;
(1874) 447–48

Livingstone, Elizabeth (daughter),
102, 126

Livingstone, Janet (sister), 26,
27, 34, 103, 227, 229

Livingstone, Mary (wife), (née
Mary Moffat): 82, 83, 84, 101–
102, 103, 104–105, 186, 210,
212, 213, 220, 228, 229, 251–
252, 301, 304, 306, 315, 318–
319, 320, 321, 335, 376, 431;
marriage to D.L., 84; D.L.'s
view of her, 84–86; travels to
Lake Ngami with D.L., 124–
126; loses child and is partially
paralysed, 126; with D.L. on
journey to the Zambesi, 126–
138; hardships suffered in
Britain, 143–45; her drinking,
144, 309; sees little of D.L. on
his first visit home, 208; drops
out of Zambesi Expedition,
245; rejoins D.L. on Zambesi,
309–10; loss of faith, 309, 317;
death, 316–17

Livingstone, Neil (father), 23–
24, 28, 30, 32, 36, 78, 103, 144,
197

Livingstone, Mrs Neil (mother),
27, 42–43, 341, 355

Livingstone, Robert (son), 101,
103, 124, 208, 252, 278, 297,
309, 316, 341–43

Livingstone, Thomas (son), 39,
102, 124, 275, 343

Livingstone, William Oswell
(son), 102, 138, 245, 318–19,
343, 430–31

Livingstonia, 457

Loanda, 152–53, 158, 160–62,
167, 174–77, 178–79, 181, 182,
186, 209, 226, 246, 455

Loango, river, 190

Loangwa, river, 378

Lomani, river, 396, 404–405, 407,
425, 426, 433

London, 37, 40–41, 44, 53, 55,
61, 79, 169, 195, 205, 276,
339, 342, 343, 353

London Missionary Society, 32,
35–36, 37, 40, 42, 50–51, 52–
53, 55, 56, 101, 111, 121–22,
123, 137, 142, 143–44, 146,
180, 206–207, 456, 458; differences with D.L., 90, 197–
198, 208–31, 235, 250

Lualaba, river (upper Congo), 383–84, 385, 387–90, 394, 396–98, 401, 403–405, 424–425, 426, 428, 432, 433–34, 450, 458
Luapula, river, 383–84, 390, 444
Ludha Damji, 365
Lukuga, river, 397
Lulimala, river, 445
Lusizé, river, 425
Lyra, H.M.S., 289

Mabotsa, 70, 71, 77, 78, 80, 82, 86, 87, 88–90, 91, 96, 98, 248
Mabruki, 435
Macgregor Laird, 240
Mackenzie, Bishop, 289–306, 311–13, 315, 316, 324, 325, 328, 376–77
Mackenzie, John, 222, 223, 229
Mackenzie, Miss, 301, 303, 306, 310–11
Mackinnon, Sir William, 457–62
Maclear, Thomas, 145, 150, 215, 261, 263, 274
Madagascar, 45
Magomero, 295, 296, 298, 301–302, 303, 305, 306–307, 311, 312, 324, 431–32
Majwara, 445
Makhari, 108
Makololo, 121, 132, 135–36, 140, 148–49, 152, 161, 166, 168, 178, 179, 180, 195–96, 198, 213, 214–15, 216, 218, 220–31, 235, 258–59, 261–62, 283–84, 285, 286, 290, 295, 296, 331, 364, 373, 454, 455; history of, 129–31; reasons for helping D.L., 131, 154, 186, 211–12; bloodthirstiness, 131, 156–57, 170, 223; participation in slave-trade, 134, 155–56, 373; indifference to Christianity, 185; let down by D.L., 186–87, 265; annihilation of, 187
Makololo Mission, 212–20, 221–231, 250, 283–84
Malmesbury, Lord, 263
Mambari, 132, 134, 155, 156–57, 159, 167, 169, 172, 173, 176, 198, 373
Manchester, 144, 238

Manchester Chamber of Commerce, 237
Manenko, 166–67
Manganja, 267, 269, 273, 288, 296–99, 313, 332
Manyuema (area), 390–91, 394, 397–99, 403, 405, 414, 434
Manyuema (tribe), 399, 407, 420–21
Ma-Robert, The, 239–40, 251–252, 254, 255, 258, 260, 263, 265, 280–81, 287; deficiencies of, 256, 259–60, 277, 278, 282–283, 289–90
Matabele, 70, 128, 130, 131, 137, 152, 154, 180, 186, 187, 189, 211–13, 216, 217, 220, 221, 223
Matabele Mission, 213, 216, 217, 221, 228–29
Mauritius, 197
May, Mr, 293
Mazitu, 269, 376, 377
Mebalwe, 82, 96, 98, 110, 140
Meller, Dr, 293
Methuen, Henry, 93
Mexico, 46
Mikidani, 367
Missionaries: difficulties faced by, 62–63, 65–66, 71–76, 78, 112–13, 169–70; quarrels among (*see also* Livingstone, David: fellow missionaries differences with), 55–56; first missionaries in South Africa, 50–54; polygamy, attitude to, 73–74, 77; view of Africans, 73–79
Missionary Chronicle, 69, 88–89
Missionary Magazine, 62
Missionary Travels and Researches in South Africa (by D.L.), 205, 217, 224, 237, 245, 252, 270, 283, 311, 335, 457
Mississippi, 412
Moçambique, 46, 117–18, 132, 144, 152–53, 157, 188, 190, 193, 194, 199, 201, 231, 236, 239, 240, 241, 270–71, 290, 291, 316, 335
Moenepembé, 401
Moero, Lake, 118, 381–84, 387–390, 394, 396, 401, 405, 444n
Moffat, Ann, 82
Moffat, Elizabeth, 228

Moffat, John Smith, 85, 86, 218, 227, 250, 261, 312

Moffat, Robert, 40, 53, 54, 59–60, 61, 62–63, 64–65, 76–78, 80–81, 87–88, 94, 99, 109–10, 122, 124, 125, 126, 131, 140, 143, 144, 148, 154, 212, 216–217, 218, 220–22, 223, 228–29, 250, 321, 447, 452

Moffat, Mrs Robert, 63, 93, 126–128, 143, 148, 321, 342, 452

Moir, F., 457

Moir, J., 457

Mokokon, 108, 109

Molese, 95

Mombasa, 46

Monteith, James, 25

Moore, Joseph, 38

Morambala, Mount, 329–30

Moravian Missionary Society, 53

Morning Post, The, 428

Moseealele, 68, 69

Mosega, 89

Mosilikatse, 81, 130–31, 154, 212, 216, 220, 229

Mpende, 192

Mpepe, 156, 157

Muhammad bin Salim, 384, 385–386, 390

Muhammad Bogharib, 386–87, 390, 392, 394, 397, 398, 405

Murchison Cataracts, 266, 267, 268, 273, 284, 293, 294, 299, 302, 307, 311, 315, 316, 320, 321, 322, 324, 326–28, 330, 457

Murchison Falls, 266*n*, 346

Murchison, Sir Roderick, 123, 206–207, 209, 210–15, 227, 232, 235–36, 241, 246, 274–75, 314, 346–47, 350, 351, 367, 385–86, 396, 411, 418, 423–24

Murray, John, 188, 217

Murray, Mr, 353–54, 355

Murray, Mungo, 110–11, 119, 122, 123

Musa, 377

Muscat and Oman, 269

Muscat, Sultan of, 269

Mutesa, Kabaka of Buganda, 458–59

Namaqualand, 52

Napier, Sir Robert, 413, 417

Napoleonic Wars, 49, 233

Narrative of an Expedition to the Zambesi and its Tributaries (by D.L. and C.L.), 227–28, 282, 329, 344

Nassick boys, 362–63, 370, 371, 376, 377, 398, 399, 434, 435, 447

Nassick School, 363, 449

Natal, 290, 342, 343

Netherlands Missionary Society, 32

New Orleans, 412

Newstead Abbey, 344, 352

New York Herald, The, 15, 410, 412–13, 414, 420, 421, 435, 458

New Zealand, 234, 464

Ngami, Lake, 111, 112, 117, 119–122, 125, 129–30, 180, 206–207

Ngoni, 269, 299, 370, 376, 456

Niger Expedition, 41, 146, 238

Niger, river, 47, 125

Nigeria, 463

Nightingale, Florence, 15

Nile, 355, 359, 375, 377, 425, 428, 450, 461, 462, 463; D.L.'s theories about, 348, 367–68, 383, 387–89, 393–97, 400–405, 424–25, 434, 440; importance of to D.L., 361–62, 400–403, 432, 440; D.L.'s initial interest in Nile source debate, 345–51

Nyamoana, 165–66, 168

Nyangwe, 404–408, 420, 425, 428, 432

Nyasaland, 18, 457, 458, 460, 461, 462

Nyassa Anti-Slavery and Defence Fund, 462

Nyassa, Lake, 16, 158, 188, 265, 268, 269, 273, 277, 283, 287, 291, 298, 299, 302, 307–308, 321, 327, 330, 332, 345, 350, 368, 374, 375–76, 378, 379, 410, 411, 457, 458, 461, 462

Oberlin College, 31, 247

Okavango, river, 120*n*

Omdurman, 464

Ongar (Chipping Ongar), 37–38, 39, 62, 79, 208

Opium War, 40

Orange Free State, 52, 130, 154

Orange, river, 52, 54, 56, 233

Orange Sovereignty, 97

Oswell, William Cotton, 110–11, 118–24, 129–30, 131–32, 245, 248, 344, 402

Owen, Commander, R.N., 292

Oxford University, 205, 276, 314

Palmerston, Lord, 15, 237, 274, 339, 352, 354, 402, 464

Pangura, 192, 193

Paris, 53, 343, 410, 411, 418

Park, Mungo, 47, 62, 125, 146

Paul, 96–97, 98, 110, 140

Pearl, The, 245, 250–52, 254

Penguin, H.M.S., 367

Persia, 47, 413

Persian Gulf, 47, 361, 365

Peru, 46

Philip, John, 51, 54, 55–56, 80–81, 87

Pioneer, H.M.S., 290, 292–93, 298, 299, 301, 302, 303–304, 305, 307–308, 310, 311, 312, 314, 315, 316, 319, 322–23, 324, 328, 330

Playfair, Colonel, 366

Pluto, H.M.S., 180

Polyphemus, H.M.S., 179

Porto, Silva, 118, 121, 132, 134, 157–58, 160, 178, 180

Portugal, 133, 193, 199, 232, 237, 240, 270, 339, 462

Portugal, King of, 339, 385

Portuguese (*see also under* Slave-trade, *and* Livingstone, David), 132, 134, 157, 159, 167, 169, 181, 190, 191–92 198–99, 200, 205, 221, 232, 236, 237–38, 271, 272, 274, 279–80, 281–82, 284, 291, 317–318, 327, 332–33, 335, 339, 340, 344, 345, 347, 352, 382, 462; earliest settlements in Africa, 46–48; discoveries in South Central Africa, 117–18; attitude to Zambesi Expedition, 240–41, 269–71

Prentice, Thomas, 39

Price, Roger, 222–31, 458

Price, Mrs Roger, 222, 223

Prideaux, W. F., 448

Procter, L. J., 291, 302, 328

Ptolemy, 388, 401, 402–403, 426

Punch, 419

Pungo Andongo, 182

Pusey, Dr, 314

Quango, river, 174, 175, 176

Quilimane, 152–54, 187, 196, 197, 199, 208–209, 232, 241, 257

Rae, George, 247, 251, 259, 265, 267, 278, 282–83, 287, 301, 304, 308, 309, 315, 317, 319, 320, 321, 322–23, 326, 327, 331

Read, J., 50

Réunion, island, 241

Rhenish Missionary Society, 53

Rhodes, Cecil, 460

Rhodesia, 81, 128, 130, 147, 187–188, 459–60

Ridley, Catherine, 39–40

Rio de Janeiro, 44

Ripon Falls, 345–46, 348

Rosebery, Lord, 463

Ross, William, 55–56, 57, 64, 87, 146

Ross, Mrs William, 55–56, 90

Rovuma, river, 291–93, 294, 298, 299, 315, 320–23, 367

Rowlands, John, 411

Rowley, Henry, 290, 293, 294, 300, 302, 324

Royal College of Mines, 246

Royal Geographical Society, 122–23, 162, 180, 199, 205, 206–207, 246, 345, 347, 351–352, 354–55, 385, 394, 399, 411, 423, 426, 428–29, 448, 449–50

Royal Navy, 47, 133, 174, 176, 179, 180, 196–97, 233, 271, 274, 289, 292, 306, 307, 310, 328, 373, 374, 430, 456

Royal Society, 236

Rufigi, river, 413

Rugby, 119

Ruo, river, 302–305, 311, 313, 314, 315, 323, 332

Russell, Lord John, 274, 275, 282, 287, 290, 300, 327–28, 339–40, 344, 352–53, 354–55, 385, 464

Russia, 465

Sabine, General, 236–37
Sahara, 45, 205
St Anna, José, 260
St Asaph, 412
Salisbury, Lord, 460–63
Salisbury, North Carolina, 343
Sand River Convention, 148
Saudi Arabia, 47, 361, 365
Schleswig-Holstein, 339
Schmidt, George, 50
Scotland, 16, 23, 42, 103, 105, 109, 143, 251, 340–41, 458, 461, 462
Scudamore, H. C., 291, 302–303, 324, 328
Sebitoane, 121, 130–31, 134, 154, 230
Sechele, 67, 91, 95–96, 105, 106–107, 119, 131, 139, 161; character and appearance, 92–94; literacy of, 94, 109; conversion of, 107–08; lapse of, 109–110; attacked by Boers, 147–148
Sekeletu, 154, 155, 156, 161, 167, 180, 181, 186–87, 196, 223–24, 225, 226, 228, 230, 259, 283, 284–85
Sekhomi, 66–67
Sekwebu, 196–97
Sena, 46, 241, 258
Seph Rubea, 374–75
Sepoys, 363, 368, 369, 375–76, 377
Sesheke, 131, 163, 188, 224
Seward, Mr, 381
Sewell, Mrs, 80
Sewji, Jairam, 365, 422
Shaftesbury, Lord, 207
Shaw, J. W., 415
Sherif Bosher, 408
Shinte, 166, 167–70
Shire Highlands, 267–74, 276–77, 278, 283–84, 287–89, 291, 295, 300, 301, 307, 309, 312–14, 315, 319, 324, 327, 328, 329, 332, 335, 350, 359–60, 371,
376, 452, 454, 455, 456, 457, 462
Shire, river, 264–65, 266–68, 271, 273, 278, 283, 291, 294, 302, 303, 304, 307, 313, 314, 315, 316, 321, ·322–24, 326, 327, 328, 332, 360, 376, 456
Shirwa, Lake, 267, 269
Shupanga, 258, 308, 311, 315–316, 320, 322–23, 362
Sicard, Major, 195–96, 279
Sidon, H.M.S., 289–90, 292
Sierra Leone, 36, 46, 47
Simon's Bay, 45
Slave-trade (*see also under* Livingstone, David): British Government's attitude to, 31, 47, 50–51, 133, 174, 271, 349, 360–61, 373, 420; Arab involvement in, 18, 45, 47, 158, 268, 269, 271–74, 288–89, 299, 307, 313, 332, 350–51, 360–63, 365–66, 371–75, 390, 392–93, 405–407, 420, 429–30; French involvement in, 241, 271; Portuguese involvement in, 47, 132, 134, 158, 169, 174, 193–195, 240, 271, 272, 273, 288, 289, 292, 295–96, 299, 313, 327, 344, 350; African involvement in, 132, 134, 155–156, 169, 170–71, 173, 267, 269, 271, 295–96, 298, 313, 366, 372, 373, 455
Sofala, 45
Sotho, 130
South Africa, 36, 40, 42, 51, 55, 56, 138, 308, 466
South West Africa, 117
Southampton, 449
Speke, John Hanning, 16, 238, 272, 345–47, 350, 363, 367, 397, 403, 415, 428, 458
Standard, The, 427
Stanley, H. M. 15, 162, 410–30, 434–35, 436, 447, 458–59; and Livingstone myth, 410–11, 416, 418–19, 421–22, 427–28
Steele, Thomas, 69
Steere, Bishop, 458
Stewart, James, 309–11, 312, 316, 317, 319, 456, 457
Sturge, Joseph, 99
Sudan, 464
Suez Canal, 418, 460, 461

Susi, 362–63, 377, 381, 408–409, 427, 435, 438, 442, 443–49

Tanganyika, Lake, 118, 238, 345–348, 351, 365, 367–68, 375, 379, 380–81, 382–83, 384, 388, 390–91, 392, 394, 396–97, 398, 404, 416, 425, 432, 435–36, 458
Tanzania, 461
Tennyson, Alfred, Lord, 391
Tete, 46, 118, 132, 179, 192, 193–96, 210, 231, 239, 241, 251, 254, 258–59, 260, 261, 264, 265, 268, 271, 272, 278–279, 280, 281, 282, 284–85, 287, 289, 290, 295, 325, 326, 332, 382
Thamalakane, river, 120*n*
Thornton, Helen, 281
Thornton, Octavia, 281
Thornton, Richard, 246–47, 259, 261, 278–81, 324–25, 329, 331–332*n*
Tidman, Arthur, 122, 147, 209–211, 216–18, 221, 223, 224–227, 229, 320, 349
Times, The, 182, 196, 199, 331, 427
Tippu Tip, 382, 384
Tozer, Bishop, 328–30, 342, 458
Transvaal, 52, 70, 97, 98, 99–100, 113*n*
Treasury, 235, 273, 274, 335, 418, 429
Turkey, 413

Uganda, 18, 459–64
Ujiji, 365, 381, 383, 384, 385–386, 390–91, 392, 393–97, 401, 403, 405, 407–409, 413, 414, 416–17, 423, 425, 434, 455
Ulva, 23
Universities Mission, 276, 283, 287–88, 289–314, 324, 327–334, 339–40, 433, 454, 456, 458, 462
Unyanyembe, 408, 415, 416, 418, 422, 425, 428, 430–31, 434, 435, 445, 447

Vaal, river, 52, 81, 148, 233
Vanderkemp, J., 50
Victoria Falls, 188–89, 199, 218–219, 222, 224, 331
Victoria Nyanza, 345–46, 388, 393, 403, 458–59
Victoria, Queen, 189, 205, 339–340, 464
Vulture, H.M.S., 448

Wainwright, Jacob, 447, 449
Waller, Horace, 291, 294, 295, 298, 314, 335, 433
Walweitch, Dr, 181–82
Wardlaw, Dr, 30, 35
Washington, Captain, R.N. (later Admiral), 238, 239–40, 246, 314
Webb, Ethel, 344
Webb, William, 344
Webb, Mrs William, 344
West Indies, 36, 40, 47, 233, 234
Westminster Abbey, 15, 433, 448–49, 450, 457
Wikatani, 362, 377
Wilberforce, Dr S., Bishop of Oxford, 288, 292
Wilberforce, William, 41, 47, 51
Wilkes, Henry, 29–30
Wilson, Captain, R.N., 310–11
Wilson, J. H., 65, 119, 129

Xhosa, 49–50, 51–52

Young, E. D., 326–27, 330, 457
Young, James, 35, 355, 402, 448

Zambesi Expedition, 209, 218, 245–336, 339, 340, 341, 342, 360, 362, 363, 370, 385, 411, 414, 422, 429, 446, 454, 456, 457; inauguration of, 235–42; initial aims of, 215, 232–33, 238–39; early setbacks to, 251–265; period of main achievements, 265–68; problems faced by in Shire Highlands, 269–273; affected by Universities

Zambesi Expedition (*cont'd*)
Mission, 276, 287–89, 291–94, 300–301, 306–308, 311–14, 328–29, 333; changing aims of, 263–65, 272–76, 283–84, 307–308; personnel, problems with, 254–57, 277–83, 284–87, 310–311, 322–23; final disintegration of, 322–36; results of, 331–35

Zambesi river, 46, 48, 53, 117, 118, 130–31, 134, 137, 138, 139, 152, 153, 155, 156, 157, 159, 160–61, 162, 163–67, 178, 186, 187–96, 199, 215, 218, 221, 223, 224, 226–27, 232, 236, 237, 239, 240, 241, 251, 252, 254, 257–60, 264, 265–266, 269–70, 282–83, 284, 287–288, 291, 292, 302, 306, 307, 315–16, 322, 328, 330, 331, 334–35, 339, 342, 352, 355, 359–60, 376, 401, 452, 453; difficulties of navigation, 251–252, 256–57, 258, 259–64, 277, 290, 332

Zambia, 117, 187–88, 459–60

Zanzibar, 158, 200–201, 238, 269, 272, 329–30, 334, 345, 360, 363, 365–67, 373–75, 376, 380–381, 383, 391, 392–94, 410, 411, 413–14, 422–23, 430, 432, 443, 448, 455–56

Zanzibar, Sultan of, 361, 365, 374–76, 394, 430, 460

Zouga, river, 120–21, 125, 129, 142, 149

Zulus, (*see also* Ngoni, Mazitu, Matabele), 130, 269, 290

Zumbo, 190, 191–92, 193, 240